S0-BRS-470

HANDBOOK
of
CITIZENSHIP STUDIES

HANDBOOK
of
Citizenship Studies

Edited by
ENGIN F. ISIN *and*
BRYAN S. TURNER

SAGE Publications
London • Thousand Oaks • New Delhi

First published 2002

SAGE Publications Ltd
6 Bonhill Street
London EC2A 4PU

SAGE Publications Inc
2455 Teller Road
Thousand Oaks, California 91320

SAGE Publications India Pvt Ltd
32, M-Block Market
Greater Kailash - I
New Delhi 110 048

British Library Cataloguing in Publication data

A catalogue record for this book is available from the British Library

ISBN 0 7619 6858 x

Library of Congress Control Number available

Typeset by SIVA Math Setters, Chennai, India
Printed in Great Britain by The Cromwell Press Ltd, Trowbridge, Wiltshire

Contents

Contributors

BROWN: Michael Brown is Associate Professor of Geography at the University of Washington in Seattle, USA. He has also taught at the University of Canterbury in Christchurch, New Zealand. He is an editorial board member of Gender, Place, and Culture: A Journal of Feminist Geography, and is a member of The People's Geography of the United States Project and the Sexuality and Space speciality group of the Association of American Geographers. He has authored several articles on urban political geography, political theory, queer theory, and health politics. His current interest is in political theory and the changing locations of terminal care. His books include: *RePlacing Citizenship: AIDS Activism and Radical Democracy* (Guilford, 1997), and *Closet Space: Geographies of Metaphor from the Body to the Globe* (Routledge, 2000).

BURCHELL: David Burchell teaches in Humanities at the Univerity of Western Sydney, Australia. He has a history as an editor of political journals, and is chair of the editorial board of Australian Universities Review. He has published widely on the histories of citizenship, personhood and ethics.

CAIRNS: Alan Cairns is a visiting professor emeritus of Political Science at the University of Waterloo. He taught at the University of British Columbia from 1960 until his retirement in 1995. He has had visiting appointments at Harvard, Edinburgh, Memorial, York, University of Toronto, and the University of Saskatchewan. He is a Fellow of the Royal Society of Canada and an officer of the Order of Canada. His recent teaching and research interests have concentrated on Canadian federalism, the Charter, the Constitution, and Aboriginal issues. Four recently published collections of his essays are: *Constitution, Government and Society in Canada* (1988); *Disruptions: Constitutional Struggles from the Charter to Meech Lake* (1991); *Reconfigurations: Canadian Citizenship and Constitutional Change* (1995) – all edited by Douglas E. Williams – and *Charter versus Federalism* (1992), which explores the tensions between these two pillars of the constitutional order. His latest book is *Citizens Plus: Aboriginal Peoples and the Canadian State* (2000).

CURTIN: Deane Curtin is Professor of Philosophy at Gustavus Adolphus College, where he has served as Raymond and Florence Sponberg Chair of Ethics. His research focuses on environmental ethics and the ethics of community development. He was a National Endowment for the Humanities Visiting Scholar at Villa I Tatti, the Harvard Center for Italian Renaissance Studies in Fiesole, Italy. He was also a visiting professor at Kansai Gaidai University in Japan and at the Centre for a New International Economic Order in Madras, India. Curtin's most recent books are *Chinnagounder's Challenge: The Question of Ecological Community* (Indiana University Press, 1999) and *Institutional Violence* (Rodopi, 1999).

DAGGER: Richard Dagger is Professor of Political Science and Director of the Philosophy, Politics, and Law Program in the Barrett Honors College, Arizona State University, USA. His publications include *Civic Virtues: Rights, Citizenship, and Republican Liberalism* (Oxford, 1997), *Political Ideologies and the Democratic Ideal* (co-authored with Terence Ball, Longman, 4th ed. 2002), and many book chapters and articles in philosophy and political science journals on republicanism, rights, political obligation, punishment, and other topics in political and legal philosophy.

DELANTY: Gerard Delanty is Professor of Sociology at the University of Liverpool, UK. He was Visiting Professor, York University, Toronto in 1998 and in 2000 Visiting Professor, Doshisha University, Kyoto, Japan and has taught at universities in Ireland, Germany and Italy. He the Chief Editor of the *European Journal of Social Theory* and author of many articles in journals and chapters in books in social theory, the philosophy of the social sciences and the historical and political sociology of European societies. He is also the Editor of a book series, Studies in Social and Political Thought, published by Liverpool University Press. His books include *Inventing Europe: Idea, Identity, Reality* (Macmillan, 1995) *Rethinking Irish History: Nationalism, Identity, Ideology* (co-authored with P.O'Mahony, Macmillan, 1998), *Social Science: Beyond Constructivism and Realism* (Open University Press, 1997), *Social Theory in a Changing World* (Polity Press, 1999), *Modernity and Postmodernity: Knowledge, Power, the Self* (Sage, 2000), *Citizenship in a Global Era* (Open University Press, 2000).

GRAN: Brian K. Gran is an Assistant Professor of Sociology and Faculty Associate of the Center for Health Services Management and Research and the Sanders-Brown Center on Aging, the University of Kentucky. He earned a law degree from Indiana University (Bloomington) and a doctorate in Sociology from Northwestern University. Gran was a Robert Wood Johnson Foundation Scholar in Health Polity Research at Yale University prior to joining the faculty of the University of Kentucky. His interests include comparative social policy, political sociology, sociology of law, and methodology. Gran's most recent work appears in *Sociological Quarterly, Social Science Quarterly, Journal of Aging Studies, and International Journal of Health Services*. Gran's current research focuses oncomparative social policy as it is formed in the intersection of the public and private sectors.

ISIN: Engin F. Isin is Associate Professor of Social Science at York University. He is the author of *Cities Without Citizens: Modernity of the City as a Corporation* (Montreal, 1992), with P.K. Wood, *Citizenship and Identity* (London: Sage, 1999),

Being Political: Genealogies of Citizenship (Minnesota: University of Minnesota Press, 2002) and, editor, *Democracy, Citizenship and the Global City* (London: Routledge, 2000). He is the Managing Editor of *Citizenship Studies*. He and Gerard Delanty are currently editing *Handbook of Historical Sociology* (London: Sage, 2003).

JANOSKI: Thomas Janoski is Associate Professor of Sociology at the University of Kentucky. He is the author of *Citizenship and Civil Society* (Cambridge 1998) and *The Political Economy of Unemployment* (California 1990), and has co-edited *The Comparative Political Economy of the Welfare State* with Alex Hicks (Cambridge 1994). He is currently finishing a book called *Strangers into Citizens*, which examines naturalization and integration in 20 OECD countries. He is also editing the first *Handbook of Political Sociology* with Robert Alford, Alexander Hicks, and Mildred Schwartz. His work has appeared in journals such as *Social Forces, Sociological Forum, Comparative Social Research*, and *the International Journal of Comparative Sociology*. It has also appeared in the following books: *Models of Political Economy, The New Citizenship, Citizenship and Ethno-national Identities in the European Union*, and *The International Handbook of Labor Market Evaluation*. Two of his books have been translated into Chinese and one into Spanish.

JOPPKE: Christian Joppke is Professor of Sociology at the European University Institute in Florence. He is the author or editor of numerous books and articles on the politics of social movements, immigration, and citizenship. He is currently writing a book on ethnic-priority immigration in liberal states.

LINKLATER: Andrew Linklater is Woodrow Wilson Professor of International Politics at the University of Wales, Aberystwyth. His main publications are *Men and Citizens in the Theory of International Relations* (Macmillan 1982/1990), *Beyond Realism and Marxism* (Macmillan 1990), *The Transformation of Political Community* (Polity 1998) and the edited multi-volume work, *Theories of International Relations* (Routledge 2001). He is currently working on the sociology of international states-systems.

LISTER: Ruth Lister is Professor of Social Policy at Loughborough University, UK. She has also taught at Bradford University and was previously the Director of the Child Poverty Action Group. She was a member of the Commission on Social Justice, established by the former Leader of the Labour Party, the late John Smith; the Opsahl Commission on the Future of Northern Ireland; and the Commission on Poverty, Participation and Power. She is author of many journal articles and book chapters and has spoken widely on citizenship, welfare, poverty, and gender issues. Her books include *The Exclusive Society: Citizenship and the Poor* (Child Poverty Action Group, 1990) and *Citizenship: Feminist Perspectives* (Macmillan/New York University Presss, 1997).

MILLER: Toby Miller is Professor of Cultural Studies and Cultural Policy Studies at New York University. He is the author of *The Well-Tempered Self: Citizenship, Culture, and the Postmodern Subject* (1993), *Contemporary Australian Television* (1994), *The Avengers* (1997), *Technologies of Truth: Cultural Citizenship and the Popular Media* (1998), *Popular Culture and Everyday Life* (1998), *Globalization and Sport* (2001), *Sportsex* (2001), and *Global Hollywood* (2001), and editor of *SportCult* (1999), *A Companion to Film Theory* (1999), *Film and Theory: An Anthology* (2000), and *A Companion to Cultural Studies* (2001). He edits *Television and New Media* and was previously editor of *Social Text* and the *Journal of Sport and Social Issues*.

RASMUSSEN: Claire Rasmussen is a doctoral student in the department of political science at The University of Washington, Seattle, USA. Her interests include continental theory, cultural and political geography and cultural and theoretical constructions of autonomy as a political category. Her work has appeared in the *Electronic Book Review*.

ROCHE: Maurice Roche is Reader in Sociology at the University of Sheffield. He has also held posts at the London School of Economics and at McMaster University. He is a Board member of the University's Political Economy Research Centre and is a member of the Department of Sociological Studies. His research is concerned with the political sociology and public policy aspects of social and cultrual citizenship in European societies and in modernity more generally. He is a member of the editorial board of the journal *Citizenship Studies*. Since 1994 he has been the Coordinator of the SEDEC European social research network which is concerned with 'Social Exclusion and the Development of European Citizenship'. In 1998–2000 he co-ordinated the network's European Commission-funded project on 'Comparative Social Inclusion Policies in Europe'. He is currently co-editing the results of this project in a book entitled *Renewing the European Social Model* (Berghahn Press, forthcoming). He is the author of *Rethinking Citizenship: Ideology, Welfare and Change in Modern Society* (1996, Polity Press) and *Mega-Events and Modernity: Olympics and Expos in the Growth of Global Culture* (Routledge, 2000). He is co-editor (with Rik van Berkel) of *European Citizenship and Social Exclusion* (Ashgate Press, 1997) and editor of *Sport, Identity and Popular Culture* (Meyer and Meyer Verlag, 1998).

SASSEN: Saskia Sassen is the Ralph Lewis Professor of Sociology at the University of Chicago, and Centennial Visiting Professor at the London School of Economics. Her most recent books are *Guests and Aliens* (New Press, 1999) and the edited volume *Global Networks/Linked Cities* (Routledge, 2002). *The Global City* is out in a fully updated edition in 2001 (Princeton University Press). Her books have been translated into twelve languages. She is co-director of the Economy Section of the Global Chicago Project, a member of the National Academy of Sciences Panel on Urban Data Sets, and Chair of the newly formed Information

Technology, International Cooperation and Global Security Committee of the Social Science Research Council (USA).

SCHUCK: Peter H. Schuck is the Simeon E. Baldwin Professor of Law at Yale. His major fields of teaching and research are torts, immigration, citizenship, and refugee law, and administrative law, and he has written on a broad range of public policy topics. His most recent books include *Diversity in America: Keeping Government at a Safe Distance* (2003); *The Limits of Law: Essays on Democratic Governance* (2000); *Citizens, Strangers, and In-Betweens: Essays on Immigration and Citizenship* (1998); and *Paths to Inclusion: The Integration of Migrants in the United States and Germany* (co-editor, 1998). Earlier books include *Suing Government: Citizen Remedies for Official Wrongs* (1983); *Citizenship Without Consent: Illegal Aliens in the American Policy* (with Rogers M. Smith, 1985); *Agent Orange on Trial: Mass Toxic Disasters in the Courts* (1987); *Tort Law and the Public Interest: Competition, Innovation, and Consumer Welfare* (editor, 1991); *Foundations of Administrative Law* (1994) (editor); and *The Judiciary Committees* (1974). His writing appears in a wide variety of scholarly, professional, and popular journals. Prior to joining the Yale faculty in 1979, he was principal Deputy Assistant Secretary for Planning and Evaluation in the U.S. Department of Health, Education, and Welfare (1977–79), Director of the Washington Office of Consumers' Union (1972–77), and consultant to the Center for Study of Responsive Law (1971–72). He also practised law in New York City (1965–68), where he now lives.

SMITH: Rogers M. Smith is the Christopher H. Browne Distinguished Professor of Political Science at the University of Pennsylvania. He teaches American constitutional law and American political thought, with special interests in issues of citizenship and racial, gender, and class inequalities. He has published over 70 articles in academic journals and edited volumes and is author or co-author of four books: *The Unsteady March: The Rise and Decline of Racial Equality in America* (with Philip A. Klinkner, 1999); *Civic Ideals: Conflicting Visions of Citizenship in U.S. History* (1997); *Citizenship without Consent: Illegal Aliens in the American Polity* (with Peter H. Schuck, 1985); and *Liberalism and American Constitutional Law* (1985, rev. ed. 1990). *Civic Ideals* received six 'best book' awards from four professional associations and was also a finalist for the 1998 Pulitzer Prize in History. Formerly the Alfred Cowles Professor of Government at Yale University, where he taught from 1980 to 2001, Smith also received a Yale College Prize for Distinguished Teaching in the Social Sciences in 1984.

TURNER: Bryan Turner is Professor of Sociology at the University of Cambridge. He has written widely on the sociology of citizenship in *Citizenship and Capitalism* (1986) and *Citizenship and Social Theory* (1993). He edited with Peter Hamilton *Citizenship: Critical Concepts* (1994), and has been editor of *Citizenship Studies* since 1997. His empirical research has been on voluntary associations, the market and civil society. With Kevin Brown and Sue Kenny, he published a study of voluntary associations in *Rhetorics of Welfare* (2001).

WOODIWISS: Anthony Woodiwiss is Professor of Sociology at City University, London. Before he joined his current department in 1999, he was Professor and head of the Department of Sociology at the University of Essex. His teaching and research interests range from social theory, through comparative sociology, to human rights, and he has been a visiting professor in many countries including Japan, Hong Kong, the United States and Mexico. He is the author of *Social Theory after Postmodernism, Postmodernity USA, The Visual in Social Theory*, as well as three books on the sociology of labour rights, the most recent of which is *Globalization, Human Rights and Labour Law in Pacific Asia*. His current research focuses on finding ways of enforcing human rights which take account of the world's social diversity.

1

Citizenship Studies: An Introduction

ENGIN F. ISIN and BRYAN S. TURNER

From aboriginal rights, women's rights, civil rights, and sexual rights for gays and lesbians to animal rights, language rights and disability rights, we have experienced in the past few decades a major trend in Western nation-states toward the formation of new claims for inclusion and belonging. More recently, this trend has echoed around the world from Zapatistas to Chechen and Kurdish nationalists, framing their struggles in the language of rights and recognition. While some, such as Michael Ignatieff, (2001) have dubbed these trends the 'rights revolution', the articulation of rights for various groups has been the most recurring theme of 'Western' political history: from ancient Greek and Roman peasants and plebeians to Italian artisans and French workers, articulating rights as claims to recognition has always invoked the ideal of citizenship. What has been happening in the past few decades then is neither revolutionary nor new but has been a recurrent, if not a fundamental, aspect of democratic or democratizing polities. What is new is the economic, social and cultural conditions that make possible the articulation of new claims and the content and form of these claims as citizenship rights. As such, these trends cannot be interpreted narrowly as 'minority rights' either as Will Kymlicka has (1995) argued. For these rights are articulated by distinct groups and cultures that belie the designation 'minority'. In the 1990s, citizenship studies emerged as an incipient field that took as its focus the conditions that make possible these new claims to citizenship rights and their dangers and promises not only in Western polities but across the world.

While citizenship studies is not yet an institutionalized field, it has established itself as a *de facto* field in the humanities and social sciences in the 1990s. The reasons behind the emergence of citizenship studies are no doubt associated with those broader conditions defined as 'postmodernization' and 'globalization' along with their concrete manifestations such as the reconfiguration of classes, the emergence of new international government regimes, new rationalities of government, new regimes of accumulation of different forms of capital, as well as new social movements and their struggles for recognition and redistribution. All these have forced upon academics, practitioners and activists alike an urgent need to rethink the political agent or subject under these transformations. Major social issues such as the status of immigrants, aboriginal peoples, refugees, diasporic groups, environmental injustices, and homelessness have increasingly been expressed through the language of rights and obligations, and hence of citizenship. Moreover, not only are the rights and obligations of citizens being redefined, but also what it means to be a citizen and which individuals and groups are enabled to possess such rights and obligations have become issues of concern. In other words, the three fundamental axes, *extent* (rules and norms of inclusion and exclusion), *content* (rights and responsibilities) and *depth* (thickness or thinness) of citizenship are being redefined and reconfigured.

The modern conception of citizenship as merely a status held under the authority of a state has been contested and broadened to include various political and social struggles of recognition and redistribution as instances of claim-making, and hence, by extension, of citizenship. As a result, various struggles based upon identity and difference (whether sexual, 'racial', 'ethnic', diasporic, ecological, technological, or cosmopolitan) have found new ways of articulating their claims as claims to citizenship understood not simply as a legal status but as political and social recognition and economic redistribution. Hence the increase in the number of scholars who work in feminist studies, queer studies, Aboriginal studies, African studies, diaspora studies, postcolonial studies, race and ethnic studies, urban studies, immigration studies, and environmental studies, who are exploring and addressing concepts of sexual citizenship, ecological citizenship, diasporic citizenship, differentiated citizenship, multicultural citizenship, cosmopolitan citizenship and Aboriginal citizenship. These studies, taken together, have already made an impact on social and political thought and practice in constitutional as well as governmental policies. Indeed, there has been a spectacular growth of the field of citizenship studies, evidenced in numerous books,[1] articles,[2] and theses[3] dedicated to it.

All of these studies and initiatives suggest that the field is likely to expand in this decade. The scope of the field now certainly goes well beyond the mastery of any scholar. It is also a lively field, contesting and debating fundamental propositions of humanities and social sciences in important ways. It is by no means simplistic or optimistic to assume that in the next few years we shall observe the beginnings of new degrees, programs and specialties, establishing citizenship as a field of interdisciplinary studies in universities across the world.

Admittedly, a quantitative growth of a field cannot be taken as a measure of its academic quality or theoretical and practical impact. There is, however, growing evidence that citizenship studies is also making a major impact on our thinking about and practices of citizenship. The importance of accommodating some form of differentiated citizenship and the inadequacy of modern liberal citizenship are now widely accepted. As a result, it has been increasingly possible for various groups across the world to enact their claims to recognition and citizenship. Whether from common-sex partnership laws in Ontario or the rights of Kurds in Turkey, the modern, universal idea of citizenship has faced a significant challenge. Similarly, across the world many states have begun rethinking and revising their citizenship laws to recognize these growing demands. A revised German law now recognizes the rights of minorities and French laws recognize the rights of refugees: there is certainly a significant change taking place. This is the first volume that names the field as citizenship studies.

But all this does not mean that all is well and on a progressive path in citizenship studies or practices. There are enormous injustices, oppression and marginalization in 'democratic' as well as 'democratizing' states and the recognition of these injustices and their enactments of citizenship is anything but a straightforward struggle. While the Zapatistas marched through Mexico City, Chechens and Kurds are facing extermination. Citizenship studies is ultimately not about books and articles but about addressing injustices suffered by many peoples around the world, making these injustices appear in the public sphere, enabling these groups to articulate these injustices as claims for recognition and enacting them in national as well as transnational laws and practices, and thus bringing about fundamental changes. Citizenship studies is about producing analytical and theoretical tools with which to address these injustices with the depth, sensibility, scope and commitment that they demand and deserve.

Emerging from these studies and trends is a new conception of citizenship that challenges its modern variant. Modern citizenship itself was born of the nation-state in which certain rights and obligations were allocated to individuals under its authority. Modern citizenship rights that draw from the nation-state typically include civil (free speech and movement, the rule of law), political (voting, seeking electoral office) and social (welfare, unemployment insurance and health care) rights. The precise combination and depth of such rights vary from one state to another but a modern democratic state is expected to uphold a combination of citizenship rights and obligations. That said, however, three points must be borne in mind to avoid assuming citizenship rights and obligations as 'universal'. First, while within some states civil rights such as bodily control rights (medical and sexual control over the body) are guaranteed, some states deny even basic civil rights to its citizens, such as rights of access to courts and counsel. Similarly, while some states guarantee political rights and go so far as to franchise prisoners, others deny even such basic rights as refugee or naturalization rights. Citizenship obligations vary too, ranging from states where military service is required to those states where jury duty and taxes are the only responsibilities. Second, while many nation-states have elaborate rules and criteria for 'naturalization', the granting of citizenship to those not born in its territory, such rules and criteria are often contested and debated and vary widely. Third, even some basic citizenship rights are remarkably recent. We should remember that the property qualifications for citizenship were abolished as recently as, for example, 1901 in Australia, 1918 in Britain and 1920 in Canada. Even this should be interpreted cautiously as citizenship did not include Aboriginals in settler societies. Similarly, the franchise was extended to women as recently as 1902 in Australia, 1918 in Canada, and 1920 in the United States, while British women over the age of 21 have been able to vote only since 1928 and French women since 1944.

Thus, while cast in the language of inclusion, belonging and universalism, modern citizenship has systemically made certain groups strangers and outsiders. What determines the composition of citizens, strangers, and outsiders and their respective rights and obligations in a given nation-state depends on its historical trajectory. The typologies developed in citizenship studies to classify citizenship rights according to these trajectories are useful. For example, liberal, corporatist, and social democratic states, each of which rest upon a different interpretation of citizenship, can be identified. In liberal democracies such as the United States, Switzerland, and Australia, the state relies on markets to allocate social rights and emphasizes civil and political rights. In corporatist states such as Austria, France, Germany, and Italy, social rights are accorded a greater role but are not available universally. By contrast, in social democratic states such as Sweden, Norway, Finland, Denmark, and the Netherlands, social rights are given the highest priority and the state provides universal benefits such as the right to free vocational or higher education. There are, of course, states that do not neatly fit into these types. Canada, for example, combines a liberal emphasis on individual rights with a social democratic tradition of social rights, especially health and education. Britain also combines liberal and social democratic traditions.

Modern political theories about citizenship – liberalism, communitarianism, and republicanism – have grown out of these trajectories and roughly correspond to these three types of states. Liberalism puts a strong emphasis on the individual, and most rights involve liberties that adhere to each and every person. Concomitantly, communitarianism emphasizes the community (or the society or the nation), whose primary concern is with the cohesive and just functioning of society. Republican theories in both their conservative and radical variants put emphasis on both individual and group rights and emphasize the role of conflict and contest in the expansion or construction of such rights. Not all theories or theorists, however, neatly fit into these types. At any rate, in many democracies in the postwar era the debate *and* struggles over citizenship rights and obligations have been waged over either the *expansion* or the *protection* of rights. Most prominent have been the *expansion* of civil rights such as medical and sexual control over the body; political rights such as rights to naturalize, to aboriginal self-government or social movement or protest rights; and social rights such as old age pensions, unemployment insurance, health and education, job placement programs, affirmative action for minorities, collective bargaining, and wage earner and union investment funds. The *protection* of civil rights such as the rights of aliens to immigrate, political rights such as minority rights to equal and fair treatment, and social rights such as welfare or participation rights such as job security and workers' compensation have occupied governmental agendas. These debates and struggles have been mostly waged via the nation-state as both the source and appeal of authority.

While useful in the understanding of various theories and practices of citizenship rights and obligations across various postwar democratic states, these typologies and theories no longer capture the changing nature of citizenship in the twenty-first century. In the last two decades of the twentieth century, postmodernization and globalization challenged the nation-state as the *sole* source of authority of citizenship and democracy. Under these twin pressures, the blurred boundaries of citizenship rights and obligations and the forms of democracy associated with them brought citizenship on to the political *and* intellectual agenda, broadening the way in which citizenship is understood and debated. Rather than merely focusing on citizenship as legal rights, there is now agreement that citizenship must also be defined as a social process through which individuals and social groups engage in claiming, expanding or losing rights. Being politically engaged means practicing substantive citizenship, which in turn implies that members of a polity always struggle to shape its fate. Such developments have led to a sociologically informed definition of citizenship in which the emphasis is less on legal rules and more on norms, practices, meanings, and identities. Over the past several decades, the sheer mass of the academic literature on citizenship each year attests not only to the breadth of scholarly interest in it, but also to the extent that citizenship issues have become interwoven across academic disciplines. Citizenship studies is therefore decisively interdisciplinary.

There is no doubt that citizenship has also emerged as a major theme connecting policy domains that range from welfare, education, and labor markets to international relations and migration. Citizenship connects these because it brings within its orbit three fundamental issues: how the boundaries of membership within a polity and between polities should be defined (*extent*); how the benefits and burdens of membership should be allocated (*content*); and how the 'thickness' of identities of members should be comprehended and accommodated (*depth*). As a simple matter of law, nationality is the primary axis by which peoples are classified and distributed in polities across the globe. However, the continuing rise of new forms of cultural politics has challenged modern understandings of belonging and has contributed to rethinking the meaning of citizenship. The reality of immigration and emigration, the formation of such supranational and transnational bodies as the European Union (EU), the formation of new successor states, the movement of refugee populations, and the codification of international human rights norms has prompted increasing recognition of citizenship as a transnational matter. The growing incidence of plural nationality exemplifies the transnational dimension of citizenship not only as an object of policy but also increasingly as a source and marker of social identity. The difficulty in this growing recognition is that it has arisen through the interaction of citizenship rules that states, acting as sovereign agents, have adopted, but whose effects reach into the domestic jurisdictions of other states and invest individuals with binding affiliations to two or more states. This difficulty is compounded for nations that have seen themselves as ethnically or racially homogenous. Moreover, the increasing importance of cities in organizing and shaping cultural, social, symbolics, and economic flows has also prompted a recognition of their role in fostering citizenship. Thus, the sovereign state is no longer the only locus of citizenship. Yet very few citizenship laws are enacted either above or below national levels (e.g. EU). So while negotiations for citizenship take place above and below the state, laws are still enacted at national levels. Hence national trajectories and practices still constitute important issues in citizenship studies despite the fact that citizenship is now negotiated at a variety of levels and sites.

This is one of the reasons why multinational and settler societies such as Canada and Australia are watched with increasing interest by other nations as regards citizenship laws. Yet, as multinational and settler societies themselves struggle with issues of cultural recognition and multicultural citizenship, whether concerning the rights of immigrants or Aboriginal peoples, or separatism, many academics and policy-makers are surprised to discover that nations such as Germany, France, Britain, and those in Eastern Europe are keen to understand how such multinational states struggle with these issues. This is more than a paradox. For the questions that face the multinational and settler societies have now become (due to globalization and postmodernization) the questions that face states that originally saw themselves as ethnically homogenous, such as France, Germany, and even Japan. It has become increasingly difficult to imagine these nations as ethnically homogenous and racially pure.

What then of the future of citizenship studies? To put it starkly, there is neither a singular way of engaging with citizenship studies nor a singular way of investigating its objects. In fact, it is this dispersed discursive aspect that provides its vitality and liveliness, rather than an orthodox set of rules that govern conduct. Citizenship studies also embodies a potential to channel energies in various disciplines that focus upon social justice into a renewed focus with a vigor and robustness that so far have eluded 'postmodernized' and 'globalized' social sciences and humanities. As this introductory chapter has shown, there are many dimensions to the contemporary debate about citizenship and otherness, and we can predict that the evolution of citizenship theory will be equally complex, but we conclude with three issues that strike us as urgent. We will structure this discussion around the problem of national citizenship in relation to human rights, the question of the obligations and virtues of the citizen, and finally the problem of globalization and territoriality.

The first is the obvious problem of the historical connection between citizenship, nationalism and the nation-state. It has been frequently recorded that 'citizenship' (*citeseyn, cite/sein/zein*) is historically and etymologically connected to the city and then to the state. The citizen was originally a person who, by living in the city, participated in a process of cultivation or civilization. While the pagans lived in the countryside, the man of the city acquired both rights and culture. Citizenship was thus an exclusionary category. This is a generic problem, since that which includes must by definition exclude. But the historical connection has always been made from the perspective of not the excluded (strangers, outsiders, aliens) but the included (citizens). Following the Treaty of Westphalia and the creation of an international system of states, urban citizenship further developed as a basic foundation of the emergence of powerful nation-states. With the development of advanced administrative structures of the system of national governance, the state was able to mobilize citizenship as an aspect of nationalism. The state and citizenship became necessarily combined to form effective technologies of government.

Classical political philosophy and political economy also recognized the connections between citizenship and civil society. Hegel, while employing 'citizen' to mean a member of the state, recognized the associations between citizenship and civil society. In twelfth-century Europe, a burgher was a town-dweller, and in France *bourgeois* came to designate a stratum that was separate from the clergy and the nobility, but was also connected with 'market town'. Thus with the development of 'civil society' (*bürgerliche Gesellschaft*), there was an intimate set of interconnections between the bourgeoisie as a class, the creation of an autonomous civil society and citizenship. These cultural and social connections with urban middle class life were the origin of Marx's criticisms of citizenship. Using the emancipation of the Jews as an example, Marx argued that bourgeois citizenship made an artificial separation between politics and society, condemned the continuity of class inequality in liberal capitalism, and claimed that citizenship was a smoke screen that masked economic exploitation. Radical thinkers have often remained suspicious about the democratic thrust of citizenship rights and argued theoretically that the task of democratic politics was to restore the vitality of civil society.

While there is much substance to this claim, it is partial. The liberal theory of citizenship that emphasizes individual rights is only one version of citizenship theory. Historically the working class has often mobilized behind the discourse of citizenship to claim collective social rights, and citizenship as a set of institutions does not necessarily separate social and economic rights. On the contrary, the thrust behind modern citizenship has been to create a welfare state to achieve equality between citizens. Thus, the task of rebuilding civil society (or a public sphere) cannot be achieved without dynamic forms of citizenship.

Nevertheless, there has been a strong connection between citizenship and nation-state formation, as sociologists such as Reinhard Bendix (1964) recognized. In the nineteenth century Citizenship became a platform for racial exclusion and a foundation for 'national manhood'. In the twentieth century, it has often been intimately connected with the construction and maintenance of a global labour market of 'guests and aliens' as Saskia Sassen has demonstrated. If Marx was concerned about the tensions between political and social rights, we should be exercised by the problem of citizen and human rights.

Precisely because citizenship rights have been historically tied to the nation-state, it is often thought that the rights of aboriginal and native groups, stateless people, refugees and children may be better served by human than by social (citizenship) rights. Aboriginal rights against postcolonial states are the typical example. In Australia, the doctrine of *terra nullius* meant that after 1788 the Aborigines became invisible and were treated as *de facto* migrants who could only claim rights as aliens. In the twentieth century, international legal institutions were often pitted against the state under the banner of human rights legislation to protect the rights of people who were not covered by a state. Similarly, people who were in conflict with a nation-state which they did not recognize as having legal jurisdiction would often appeal to human rights as a form of protection. For example, the British government has been frequently embarrassed by human rights criticism of its actions in Northern Ireland against the IRA and other nationalist groups.

Although human rights and social rights often appear to be in conflict from a legal standpoint, in practice people typically claim human rights from the basis of a pre-existing or articulable citizenship right. Northern Irish oppositional groups who question the legality of the actions of the British state in Northern Ireland are already citizens. The problem with human rights has been historically that they cannot be (easily) enforced, because there is no political community to which they can refer or which they can mobilize. In the absence of a global state with legitimate juridical powers around the world that can over-ride state legislation, it is difficult to see how human rights legislation can have authority over the legal rights of citizens of legitimate states. The problem is in short that human rights are often not enforceable or in more technical terminology are not 'justiciable'. In more specific terms still, while some jurists would accept the notion that political rights could be enforced, the whole arena of the social and cultural rights of the UN charters is not justiciable. So human rights are rarely conceptualized in terms of a set of corresponding obligations, and therefore there is some doubt about whether human rights are rights at all, as Giorgio Agamben (1998, 1999) suggested. Critics might conclude that citizenship rights are distinct and justiciable, but human rights are vague, unenforceable, quasi-rights. We do not accept this bleak conclusion and would argue that, for the foreseeable future, human and social rights are more likely to be compatible than mutually exclusive. Where citizenship rights fail to provide protection of individuals from the state, the individuals will appeal to international courts for protection of human rights. While we anticipate that the enforceable domain of human rights will increase with globalization, there are clearly tensions between national and international courts, and between citizenship and human rights.

Secondly, in modern times citizenship has often been an important component of social movements to expand social rights. The development of social rights through the women's movement, the peace movement and the Civil Rights movement in the United States are classic examples. Citizenship, rather than a strategy exclusive to the 'ruling class' as Michael Mann (1987) argued, has in contemporary politics emerged as fundamental to rights discourse and to oppositional movements. Recent debates about environmental citizenship and sexual citizenship have served to reinforce the assumption that citizenship is a collection of rights. The notion that citizenship might entail obligations has strategically been appropriated by right-wing governments who wish to use citizen charters as techniques for regulating public utilities. Thus in Britain various conservative governments became interested in the idea of citizenship both as obligations to the state and community, and as rights to adequate service from public utilities such as the railways. There is of course a much more radical notion of citizenship obligation associated with the idea of virtue.

While 'virtue' had become unfashionable in mainstream political science, it has been revived in contemporary political and sociological theory by writers like Alasdair MacIntyre (1981) and Martha Nussbaum (2001). In this respect there is an important division between liberal (Anglo-American) and cultural (continental) theories of citizenship. The liberal theory is minimalist. It purports that the role of the state is to protect the freedom of its citizens and that it can best achieve this aim by removing the obstacles to free exchange between individuals in the market place. The role of the state is utilitarian, namely to maximize the happiness of the majority, but this 'happiness' is most effectively and efficiently measured by their individual wealth. Because for writers like Jeremy Bentham and J.S. Mill, push-pin is as good as poetry (that is, they are equal because they both produce happiness), it is not sensible for states to take much interest in culture. With the dominance of neo-liberalism in state policy since the 1970s, the liberal view of citizenship has been triumphant. The alternative view is associated with the classical Greek *polis*, with Rousseau, and with the cultural legacy of the German *Bildungsroman*. This tradition says that the education of the citizen in the virtues is essential if that individual is to achieve personal autonomy. There is a fundamental difference between these two conceptions of autonomy. While neo-liberals have argued that the citizen needs training in order to secure a job in the labor market, virtue ethics argues that a person requires education in order to become an individual. The politics of virtue has a thick rather than thin view of the citizen of a nation, namely of the citizen as a complex, educated and vibrant member of a society. There is therefore an important connection between virtuous citizens and effective and living institutions; this connection is through the dual operation of virtue and obligation. An autonomous citizen will want to be an active and involved participant in a community.

We would argue that the neo-liberal view of citizenship is in crisis. Participation in the market is obviously important and the idea of the worker-citizen has been a foundational aspect of modern society. However, there are clearly problems with this foundation, especially where there is profound casualization of labor, under-employment, early retirement and flexible hours of work. As Richard Sennett (1998) has argued, the modern market creates casualized employment that leads to a 'corrosion' of character. There has also been a widespread devaluation of education and the university system by neo-liberal governments that have reduced funding and attempted to destroy the autonomy of universities in providing an education that is not merely training for a job. The marginalization of the worker and the degradation of education has resulted in an erosion of citizenship that we can see manifested in low participation rates in elections, distrust of politicians, lack of social capital investment in society, the decline of the public sphere, and the decline of the universities.

The third issue concerns the place of citizenship in the dynamic relationships between region, state, and global society in the modern world. The notion that there could be a 'citizen of the world' has long been part of the utopian imaginary of the citizenship tradition. It was implicit in Augustine's idea of the City of God within which the legacy of Roman global society would be perfected. It was part of Kant's vision of a 'perpetual peace' in which the Enlightenment dream of a world free from irrational prejudice could be realized. It was part of Goethe's idea of world society that would transcend the narrow limitations of emerging German militarism. Despite his criticisms of bourgeois citizenship, Marx dreamt of creating an international movement in which workers would unite to overcome capitalism, to transform human nature, and to establish a world polity. In recent years, this dream has re-emerged in the idea that globalization will demand or make possible world governance within which cosmopolitan democracy can flourish.

The revival of cosmopolitan idealism is in fact closely connected with the classical idea of virtue. There is a republican tradition that had its origins in the Stoical tradition of Rome that promoted the idea of cosmopolitan virtue. This tradition in the modern period has attempted to distinguish between love of country (patriotism) and respect for the state (nationalism). We have lost this tradition, failing typically to recognize any distinction between patriotic and nationalist commitments. Writers such as Giuseppe Mazzini (1906) argued that love of one's own country was perfectly compatible with commitment to a commonwealth that embraced a love of humanity. Indeed an education in the love of *patria* moved inevitably towards a commitment to the *republica*. This language of virtue and the commonwealth has been lost to us in a world that has become dominated by calculating rationalism and the neo-liberal faith that our private vices (greed) are public virtues (wealth).

Statecraft today is concerned with wealth creation not value creation, but the language of *patria* and *pietas* need not be archaic. Indeed, if we are to have global rights and cosmopolitan citizenship, we need to evolve a language of obligation and virtue. What commitments might a cosmopolitan citizen have? We suggest that one answer would be respect for other cultures and that this commitment to protect the cultural multiplicity of the global commonwealth would constitute a cosmopolitan virtue. We detect elements of this development in the theory of cosmopolitan democracy that has been promoted by writers such as David Held (1995).

Often the contemporary celebration of globalization neglects previous historical examples of globalism and cosmopolitanism such as Greek and Roman civilization, various world religions including Islam, the ecumenical aspects of Christianity, the Enlightenment, and socialism. Unless we have a clear view of how other cultures have experienced globalization prior to modernity we will fall deeply into the trap of previous forms of orientalism. Any discussion of cosmopolitan citizenship must overcome orientalism.

Various trends and dimensions of the current debate point in the direction of cosmopolitan or global citizenship. One such example might be Aihwa Ong's idea (1999) of flexible citizenship which she has developed in her work on the Chinese diasporic élite, but this perspective could in principle apply to all diasporas. As the globalization process produces multiple diasporas, we can expect very complex relationships between homeland and host societies that will make the traditional idea of national citizenship increasingly problematic. The increasing rates of labour migration and the growth of dual citizenship arrangements indicate that citizenship itself will become differentiated to accommodate these new status positions and identities. These labor and other migratory movements will produce a variety of interconnected social changes that are associated with multiculturalism in terms of marriage, family structures, pluralism, and multiplicity. The politics of difference and identity attempts to address these cultural transformations, and this transformation of societies places new demands on traditional or national patterns of citizenship. The European Union has been attempting to address these questions through changes to citizenship status that as a minimum give some recognition to resident workers, for example Turks in Germany, who do not have full citizenship membership but nevertheless have rights by virtue of their presence as social groups.

In short, as societies are forced to manage cultural difference and associated tensions and conflict, there will be necessarily significant changes in the processes by which states allocate citizenship and a differentiation of the category of citizen. At a deeper level, these patterns of cultural multiplicity and identity raise questions about the porosity of political boundaries and cultural borders. Does a modern democracy require a strong sense of territorial integrity or can democracies evolve with very open and porous boundaries? There are many different answers to this question, but in terms of the republican legacy of patriotism, love of country prepares the way to respect for strangers and outsiders. Cosmopolitan openness might be compatible with a strong sense of place and tradition, provided there is a recognition of difference and otherness. This vision may appear utopian, but it is an important normative position from which to challenge the negative and closed features of nationalism, racism and fundamentalism. Citizenship must be a central component to whatever answers and policies emerge towards global governance.

NOTES

1 While citizenship studies is a young and contested field, already there are literally hundreds of books and thousands of articles spanning all disciplines in humanities and social sciences. As of 2001, a search in Canada's largest research library, Robarts, yielded more than 2,600 books, manuscripts and reports mentioning citizenship. Of these, 976 included citizenship specifically in their subject keywords, a vast majority of which were published in the 1990s. Of these 2,600, more than 900 specifically included 'citizenship' in their titles, which is a much stronger measure of their affiliation with the field. Of these 900, 37 were published in 2000, 38 in 1999, 57 in 1998, 49 in 1997, 45 in 1996, 35 in 1995, 32 in 1994, 42 in 1993, 36 in 1992, 16 in 1991, and 14 in 1990. Clearly, the 1990s was a decade of significant growth in books published in citizenship studies, with an upward trend toward the end of the decade. That nearly 50% of all books in citizenship studies were published in only one decade is remarkable.

2 While since 1997 *Citizenship Studies* has been amongst the most visible journals in the field, almost all journals in social sciences and humanities have published a significant amount of work in the last decade on

citizenship. As of 2001, a research on the journal indexes available on WebSPIRS database yielded interesting results. A search on the Social Sciences Index alone yielded more than 1,100 articles citing citizenship, more than 500 of which directly addressed citizenship in their subject keywords. A similar search in the Humanities Index yielded more than 200 articles, more than 100 of which specifically addressed citizenship in their subject keywords. Historical Abstracts alone yielded 1,170 articles in major world languages specifically using citizenship in their subject keywords. Also in Historical Abstracts, a search on title using 'citizens' or 'citizenship' yielded 696 articles in major world languages. The same searches restricted to English-language articles yield 725 and 403 articles respectively. A search on citizenship in Social Science Citation Index, provided by Web of Science, yielded 2,723 articles published since 1970 in English alone focusing on citizenship. Of these, 2,409 used a variant of 'citizenship' in their titles. The Index also listed 863 reviews of books on citizenship.

3 The Dissertation Abstracts Index, which covers the majority of North American theses, lists more than 1,000 theses in the 1990s with relevance to some aspect of citizenship studies, nearly 300 of which were specifically about citizenship. More than 150 of these theses included 'citizenship' in their titles. More specialized disciplines such as law also yield important results. The Index to Canadian Legal Literature for example yielded more than 1,100 articles specifically addressing the issue of citizenship in their subject keywords. More impressively, a search on the PAIS International Index yielded more than 500 items specifically containing citizenship in their subject keywords. The PAIS International database is a bibliographic index to the literature of public policy, social policy, and the social sciences in general and includes journal articles, books, government documents, statistical compilations, committee reports, directories, serials, reports of public, intergovernmental, and private organizations, and most other forms of printed literature from all over the world. PAIS therefore is a good index of 'discursive' interest in a topic ranging from academic to governmental and professional literatures.

REFERENCES

Agamben, G. (1998) *Homo Sacer: Sovereign Power and Bare Life, Meridian*. Stanford, CA: Stanford University Press.

Agamben, G. (1999) *The Man Without Content, Meridian, Crossing Aesthetics*. Stanford, CA: Stanford University Press.

Bendix, R. (1964) *Nation-Building and Citizenship: studies of our changing world*. New York: Wiley.

Held, D. (1995) *Democracy and the Global Order: from the modern state to cosmopolitan governance*. Cambridge: Polity Press.

Ignatieff, M. (2001) *Human Rights as Politics and Idolatry*. Princeton and Oxford: Princeton University Press.

Kymlicka, W. (1995) *Multicultural Citizenship: A Liberal Theory of Rights*. Oxford: Clarendon Press.

MacIntyre, A. (1981) *After Virtue*. South Bend: University of Notre Dame Press.

Mann, M. (1987) 'Ruling class strategies and citizenship' *Sociology*, 21(3): 339–54.

Mazzini, G. (1906) *Dell'amor patrio di Dante* in *Scritti editi e inediti ai Giuseppe Mazzini*. Imola.

Nussbaum, M.C. (2001) *The Fragility of Goodness: Luck and Ethics in Greek Tragedy and Philosophy*. Cambridge: Cambridge University Press.

Ong, A. (1999) *Flexible Citizenship: The Cultural Logics of Transnationality*. Durham and London: Duke University.

Sassen, S. (1999) *Guests and Aliens*. New York: The New Press.

Sennett, R. (1998) *The Corrosion of Character: The Personal Consequences of Work in the New Capitalism*. New York: W.W. Norton.

Part One

FOUNDATIONS

2

Political Citizenship: Foundations of Rights

THOMAS JANOSKI AND BRIAN GRAN

Citizenship is grounded in the guarantee of legal and political protections from raw coercive power, whether that power comes in the form of the sword blade or gun barrel of soldiers, the fists of an abusing spouse or parent, or an employer's shout of 'you're fired' that leads to a loss of work, income, status and possibly nourishment. These protections involve 'the many' obtaining control of the legitimate means of violence, the state, in order to enforce protections or rights against élites who wield public and private power. Equally important, citizenship involves protecting 'the few' who have little power (e.g. minorities of race, class, gender, and religious affiliations) who need shelter from the tyranny of the 'the many' and/or élites. These rights and protections also involve obligations or duties to interact within and promote the commonweal and political system in as much as they are needed. At a foundational level, all citizenship rights are legal and political because citizenship rights are legislated by governmental decision-making bodies, promulgated by executive orders, or enacted and later enforced by legal decisions. And what these legal and political bodies primarily make is 'law'. Thus, legal and political rights undergird many other citizenship rights.

Citizenship may be defined as passive and active membership of individuals in a nation-state with universalistic rights and obligations at a specified level of equality (Janoski 1998: 8–11, Bottomore 1993).[1] There are four main points of this definition. First, citizenship begins with determining *membership* in a nation-state, which means establishing 'personhood' or who out of the totality of denizens, natives, and subjects of a territory are recognized as being citizens with specific rights. Personhood began with a restricted group of élite citizens (e.g. the élites of Athens or the aristocrats of England) and then developed to encompass more people (e.g. 80–90% of residents in advanced industrialized countries).[2] Non-citizens within a state (e.g. stigmatized ethnic, racial, gender, class, or disabled groups) have slowly gained rights and achieved membership. External membership concerns how aliens obtain entry and then become accepted or naturalized as citizens.

Second, citizenship involves *active* capacities to influence politics and *passive* rights of existence under a legal system (Janoski, 1998; Thompson, 1970). With passive rights alone, a beneficent dictator could rule with limited legal rights and extensive social rights in a redistributive system. Active rights bring citizens in a democracy to the foreground in politics and even the economy. When citizens become active in citizenship rights, social scientists will be concerned with measuring the levels, causes, and consequences of their participation.

Third, citizenship rights are *universalistic rights enacted into law and implemented for all citizens*, and not informal, unenacted or special rights.[3] Private organizations or groups can advance claims or proposals for citizenship rights, but claims often derive from norms within subcultures and are enforced by social pressures or group rules, and they often conflict with norms in other subcultures.[4] The process of enacting citizenship rights is an attempt to make these rights as complementary as possible.[5]

Fourth, citizenship is a statement of *equality*, with rights and obligations being balanced within certain limits. The equality is not complete, but it most often entails an increase in subordinate rights vis-à-vis social élites. This equality is mainly procedural – the ability to enter the public courts, legislatures and bureaucracies – but it may also include guaranteed payments and services that have a direct impact upon substantive equality. The extent of rights actually used by citizens may also vary considerably with class and status group power (Turner 1990; Somers 1993: 602–6).

Citizenship rights and obligations exist at the individual, organizational or societal levels. At the societal level, they refer to the development of citizenship rights and obligations in countries, and the focus is on the existence, breadth, and extent of rights and obligations. At the organizational level, they concern the rights and obligations of groups to form and act in public arenas. At the micro-level, the individual definition of citizenship focuses on how each person sees the relationship of rights and obligations within a framework of balance or exchange. It traces the development of the 'self' in relation to various political groups and the state as a critical part of citizenship, especially the development of social movement or community-oriented attitudes and behaviors.

Citizenship rights exist to the extent that a claim is advanced by a particular group, and they are confirmed when the state enacts and enforces the rights to some degree. Innate or natural rights may exist as informal legal norms, rather than enacted rights (Martin, 1982). As such, they do not enter the realm of citizenship rights until they are at least politically asserted as a universal right in the public domain.[6]

As defined, this chapter delineates the legal and political foundations of citizenship, and then examines the distinctive nature of legal and political rights, and some of the debates surrounding them. We proceed in four steps. In the first section, we analyze the scope, meanings, and theories involved in the foundations of citizenship rights, ending with the debate about universalistic and group rights. Secondly, we examine the nature and range of political and legal rights at the national level in over thirty countries according to various regime types, and then look inside countries at the variation of rights at the regional and local levels of government. In the third part of the chapter, we focus on the emergence and transformation of rights based on the personhood of new groups in social movements, and the creation and formation of rights over decades and centuries at the level of countries and nation-states. And finally, we probe the political identity of citizens including the Marshallian 'social action' and more recent 'identity' approaches.

THE FOUNDATIONS OF POLITICAL AND LEGAL RIGHTS

In this section, we examine (1) the range of citizenship rights – legal, political, social and participation rights, (2) the theoretical variety of rights using Hohfeld's categories of rights, (3) four basic approaches to citizenship – liberal, consensual, participatory, and radical-pluralist theories, and (4) individually-based 'universalistic' and group-based 'particularistic' approaches to rights.

Table 2.1 *The Theoretical Range of Citizenship Rights*

Legal Rights	Political Rights	Social Rights	Participation Rights
1 *Personal Security* Illegal disappearances Torture protection Capital punishment Abortion Invasion of privacy	1 *Personal Political* Vote Stand for office Freedom of information Right to protest	1 *Enabling Rights* Health care Old-age pensions Rehabilitation Family counselling	1 *Labour market rights:* Labour market information Job placement Job creation Discrimination protection Job security
2 *Justice-Access and Process* Legal representation Free legal aid Waive legal fees Confront witnesses Jury trial Right to contract	2 *Organizational* Form political party Form trade/economic unions Social movement/ opposition Group right to assemble and protest Cultural/minority rights	2 *Opportunity Rights* Pre-primary education Primary and secondary education Higher education Educational counselling	2 *Advisory/ Determinative rights* Works councils/grievances Collective bargaining Co-determination (human resources decisions) Ethnic/Indigenous Councils
3 *Conscience and Choice* Free speech Free press Freedom of religion Martial choice Occupational choice Gender/ethnic choice	3 *Membership Rights* Immigration and denizen rights Naturalization rights Asylum rights Cultural rights	3 *Re-distributive and Compensatory Rights* War injury benefits Work injury benefits Low income rights Unemployment compensation Rights violation compensation	3 *Capital Control Rights* Wage earner funds Central bank controls Regional investment decisions Anti-trust and capital escape laws Co-determination (strategy decisions)

The Range of Citizenship Rights

In a comprehensive approach to citizenship, four rights can be identified (see Table 2.1).

Legal or civil rights are mainly procedural rights (Rawls, 1982; Raz, 1984; Blackburn, 1993).[7] In this sense, legal (and political) rights that create law are foundational and underlie other citizenship rights. Social rights of public assistance and medical care are not legal rights, but legal rights to access the court system may be necessary in protecting these social rights. Legal rights include personal security rights that protect citizens against illegal imprisonment, torture and death. They are also protections against invasions of privacy and aids for controlling one's body such as abortion rights. Legal rights include important procedural and access rights of legal representation: the ability to confront witnesses, the right to a trial by a jury of one's peers, and the waiver of legal fees when citizens cannot pay for court costs. In a less procedural vein, legal rights also include rights to freedom of conscience (e.g. rights to free speech at the personal level, freedom of the press, free expression of religion) and choice (e.g. unencumbered selection of one's occupation or profession, free choice of ethnic or multiracial identities, and freedoms of sexual expression including marriage).

Political rights refer to participation in the public arena and are also largely procedural because the process of enacting legislation is not synonymous with the substance of any particular right. Legislation may also deal with many laws that have no direct effect on citizenship. Political rights include citizens' rights to vote and participate in the political process. They also involve the procedures for electing political representatives, creating new laws, and running for and holding political office. Political rights for organizations may include legal ways of raising campaign funds, consulting with legislators on proposals, nominating political candidates, and lobbying for particular policies. Finally, political rights include oppositional rights, minority protections, protest and demonstration rights, free access to government information (e.g. Freedom of Information Act in the USA), and the ability to conduct political inquiries.

Social rights and participation rights are not the direct subject of this chapter, but to complete our foundational purposes, we briefly include them. Social rights support citizens' claims to social status and economic subsistence. Social rights are largely individual and consist of four parts. Enabling rights consist of health care, old age pensions, rehabilitation and family or individual counseling. Opportunity rights consist of the various forms of education from pre-primary programs to postgraduate university education. Redistributive and compensatory rights involve payments for rights deprivations and they can include war injury benefits, work injury benefits, programs for the disadvantaged, unemployment compensation, and other programs involving rights violations (e.g. payments to interned Japanese-Americans and enslaved German Jews during World War II). Through participation rights, states create rights in civil society and private arenas, whether in market, public organizations, or more private venues. They refer to the individual and group rights to participate in private decision-making through some measure of control over markets, organizations, and capital. Labor market intervention rights involve public participation in job placement, retraining, and job creation programs. Organizational participation rights can range from individual rights to participate in decisions at work in codetermination and works councils, to community rights to participate in health care and environmental impact decisions (Nagel, 1997).

Each right is often pursued in specific institutional forums: legal or civil rights are mainly exercised in the courts; political rights are used in voting booths, legislatures and street protests; social rights are often activated or disputed in government buildings; and participation rights take place in corporate works councils or participatory commissions. In sum, the essence of political democracy resides in civil and political rights, and the heart of economic democracy exists in social and participation rights.

Clarifying Citizenship Rights as Rights

Because citizenship rights are multidimensional, clarification of their diverse status is necessary. By using Hohfeld's (1978) theory of rights involving liberties, claims, powers and immunities, we can unravel much of this complexity.[8] One exercises a liberty without obliging others to help. A claim imposes a corresponding duty on others to help respect and protect the right. Thus, a claim requires cooperation and is bounded, whereas liberties are relatively open.[9] Powers are cooperative controls that may be imposed on others. Powers are the opposite of immunities that allow escape from controls and deliver us back to a particularistic version of personal liberties. Hohfeld's typology of rights meshes with Marshall's division of citizenship rights (see Table 2.2).

Civil or legal rights as *liberties* are open-ended. A citizen has the liberty to choose a religion and express any opinion, but liberties also require tolerance of each other's choices and state-implemented protections of those choices. Political and participation rights are *powers* that represent cooperative rights where persons and groups must work together to activate these rights. Social rights are *claims* that directly depend on taxes paid by others to fund unemployment and public assistance benefits. *Immunities* are compensation for rights violations that occurred in the past and at least partially make up for past injustices or uneven burdens. As a result, they are particularistic.

Table 2.2 *The Relationship of Citizenship Rights to Hohfeld's Categories of Rights*

Hohfelds's Categories	Citizenship Rights
1 *Liberties:* Unilateral protections or actions; refer to individual's ability to act as they please as long as others are not hurt.	1 *Legal rights:* Freedoms of religion, speech, due process, and general rights to use the legal system to protect other rights.
2 *Claims:* The right to goods or services that require correlative duties from others. Unlike liberties, claims require the positive and supportive action of other persons.	2 *Social rights:* Education, medical services, and cash payment for welfare and social security. Social rights depend upon claims that others pay taxes for services and payments.
3 *Powers:* The right to control cooperatively other persons or properties.	3 *Political rights:* By voting, citizens cooperatively control the agenda for political action in the future. By holding office, citizens control other citizens in a direct way. *Participation rights:* By participating in workers' councils, members of organizations help set the course and policy for their firms.
4 *Immunities:* The right to escape powers or claims.	4 *Legal rights:* As an exception to universalistic principles because of past deprivations of rights, legal rights can also refer to compensation for aggrieved groups.

For instance, citizens who were drafted into the military during wartime are given preference over other citizens in being hired or re-employed. This is an immunity from labor laws and personnel rules that require equal treatment. Because immunities violate the universalistic requirement of citizenship rights, they can only be considered citizenship rights when they are used to achieve larger universalistic goals. Similar arguments can be applied to affirmative action policies.

Thus, Hohfeld's classification shows that citizenship rights are varied and not the unilateral liberties that some critics see as foundational (Giddens, 1982, 1987, 1989; Held, 1989; Mishra, 1981; Nozick, 1974; Dworkin, 1977).

Theories of Citizenship Rights

With considerable generalization, we present four major theories of citizenship rights. To reconstruct any of these theories is a task far beyond the goals of this chapter, so we outline in Table 2.3 the basic themes of each approach (Gunsteren, 1978, 1994, 1998; Heater, 1999; Isin and Wood, 1999).

Of the four theories, liberalism is by far the dominant theory in philosophy and political theory in the Anglo-Saxon democracies, but less so in social science literatures and in other advanced industrialized countries (Locke, 1967; Kymlicka, 1990; Waldron, 1984, 1993). Liberalism puts strong emphasis on the individual, and most rights are based on liberties that adhere to each and every person (i.e. negative rights or freedoms from state or social interference). There are several theories of liberalism, but our main concern here is the position of rights and obligations in this theory.[10] Although there are a few basic obligations to obey the laws (generally to pay taxes, refrain from assault and rebellion, and to serve in the nation's armed forces), liberalism places the clear weight of its ethical and moral theory behind individual and negative rights. Legal and political rights come first, especially civil liberties and property rights, and are balanced by only a few obligations.

Table 2.3 *Four Basic Theories of Citizenship*

	Individual and Consensus	Groups	Rights and Obligations	Political Institutions	Ideational Impetus
1 *Liberal Theory:* John Locke, Adam Smith, T.H. Marshall, early R. Dahl, J. Rawls a Traditional liberalism, b Modern liberalism/pluralism	Citizens are self-interested, but this is good. Consensus is not likely but also not ruled out.	The individual is supreme and their voluntary participation in pluralistic groups is representative of them.	Universalistic individual rights have precedence over obligations and the state. Group rights do not exist for ascriptive categories. Groups have rights secondary to individuals.	Political parties aggregate categorical interests expressed by interest groups. Most action takes place in representative legislatures.	Citizens follow self-interests and rules in the pursuit of happiness while being tolerant.
2 *Consensual Order:* Aristotle, J.J. Rousseau, A. Etzioni, W. Galston, A. Oldfield, P. Pettit a Communitarianism b Civic Republicanism	Citizens can be molded into good or virtuous citizens. Consensus is highly desirable and the main goal.	The 'general will' in society as a whole and in its constitutive groups are more important than self-interest.	Obligations representing the 'general will' are more important than individual rights. But obligations help enforce and buttress universalistic rights.	The state as a moral entity has the duty to enforce the obligations of the populace. To some degree, civil society also enforces obligations.	Citizens obey duties and work together in order to share in the good society.
3 *Participatory Republicanism:* J. Habermas, J. Bohman, H. van Gunsteren, Benjamin Barber, M. Warren a Neo-republicanism b Expansive democracy	The human nature of citizenship is complex, but this is not a barrier to participation. Consensus gives way to participation and procedure.	Individuals are under-represented. Their participation in groups should be encouraged following certain communicative procedures. Groups must respect individual rights.	Universalistic rights and obligations are in a complex balance. One must be careful of enforcing state obligations, but some obligations are necessary. One must similarly be careful about groups.	The state and civil society formally create deliberative institutions like deliberative polling, town meetings, works, councils, co-determination, citizen-police councils, etc.	Citizens participate in a tolerant and fair way in community councils and forums in order to establish a just society.
4 *Moderate Post-modern Pluralism* E. Laclau, C. Mouffe, E. Isin, J. Torfing, W. Kymlicka a Radical pluralism b Multi-culturalism	The identities of citizens are complex. This fundamentally rules out substantive consensus.	Large-scale societal groups are a bad fit to the interests of most post-modern individuals, who tend to find their expression in social movements.	Cultural and ascriptive groups have cultural and procedural rights. Universal rights do not exist or exist to a limited degree. Group rights particular to cultural and ascriptive groups are important.	Social movements and the media are the motive force for institutional change. Both involve elites of various groups presenting particularistic rights while ignoring obligations.	Citizens pursue group identities through group or cultural rights, or resist and attain such rights in social movements.

Thus, individual rights are primary and represent massive residual areas of wide-ranging freedoms of action. Obligations, except for obeying laws, are not emphasized, and social and participation rights are often difficult to incorporate in liberal theory mainly because they require more extensive obligations to work well. The relationship between rights and obligations is contractual or one of immediate reciprocity; that is, for each right there generally is an equal obligation (Waldron, 1984, 1993; Putnam, 1993: 87; Kymlicka, 1990; Tyler, 1990).

While social and group rights tend to violate liberal principles based on the individual, liberal theory often engages pluralistic theory by which individual positions on political issues are aggregated so they can be represented in democratic legislatures. John Rawls in *Political Liberalism* (1993) formally marries liberal and plural approaches. However, interest group liberalism does not involve group rights, but simply aggregates the rights of similar individuals in a procedural democracy. As a result, pluralist principles generally parallel liberal theory.

The second group of theories focus on consensual order, and include communitarianism and civic republicanism. Communitarianism generally opposes liberalism by putting strong emphasis on community goals. The primary concern of many communitarian theories is the effective and just functioning of society. The good society is built through mutual support and group action, not atomistic choice and individual liberty. Obligations to society may often predominate over rights because their goal is to build a strong community based on *common* identity, mutuality, participation, integration and some autonomy (Selznick, 1992: 362–3). In their view, liberalism is far too rights-centered (Selznick, 1992: 376–80), but while communitarianism seeks to re-establish the importance of obligations, it still tried to guarantee rights. Rights and obligations are related in a less immediate way than in liberal theory, and citizens may be expected to fulfill obligations without expecting immediate returns. Thus, there is a clear emphasis on obligations in communitarianism (Etzioni, 1991, 1993; Galston, 1991; MacIntyre, 1981, 1983; Putnam, 1993: 87; Sandel, 1982, 1984, 1996; Sullivan, 1982; Walzer, 1983, 1989, 1990).

With a long history dating back to Aristotle, Machiavelli and Rousseau (Oldfield, 1990; Heater, 1999), civic republicanism is sometimes difficult to separate from a motivational ethic in liberalism, but in many ways it is similar to communitarianism in that it emphasizes citizen obligations. However, this emphasis comes through the concept of civic virtue rather than state obligations. Pettit separates himself from liberalism by emphasizing non-domination from the liberal's non-interferences (2000: 10). Yet he also separates his views from communitarianism, which relies too much on the state (120–21). The emphasis of civic republicanism is clearly on civil society and how to foster the virtues of good citizens who act on behalf of others.

The third group, theories of participatory democracy, consists of expansive democratic and neo-republican theories. Expansive democracy theory emphasizes the rights and increased participation of the lower classes, women, and other excluded groups more than previous theories do. It often takes an intermediate position between liberalism and communitarianism (Singer, 1993: xiii). This position can be built on Mark Warren's notion of expansive democracy in emphasizing both rights and obligations.[11] Its emphasis is on balancing group and individual rights and obligations in both cooperative and competitive relationships. The result is a self-identity that fuses individual interests through participation in community activities, whether they are work, neighborhood, or welfare-related needs, but at the same time it protects individual civil rights. Some might refer to this as social democratic theory but this 'political party' rubric is a bit too large and unwieldy to delineate the theory presented here.

Although both communitarian and expansionary democracy theories are conceived to combat alienation and aid self-transformation, expansive democracy theory emphasizes rights to empowerment and participation (Habermas, 1989; Warren, 1992; Janoski, 1998). Deliberation in democratic processes rather than merely following democratic procedures is important. Again, balancing the influence of the state with that of groups in civil society is critical to maintaining participatory communication through many different venues from town meetings to works councils. Deliberative polls as proposed and implemented by Fishkin (1993) are important additions to the élite dominated process of public opinion formation. Work on deliberation has become highly complex (Habermas, 1996; Bohman, 1996; Fishkin, 1994), yet the principle is still simple – allow citizens to participate and communicate freely in the making of their political decisions.

Neo-republicanism describes a position taken out of civic republicanism. It emphasizes three points: that citizens (1) act publicly with other citizens in civil society (i.e. not as individuals), (2) enact an office with formal rights and duties, and (3) organize a plurality (not a majority) to guide their community of fate (van Gunsteren, 1998: 24–30). However, duty requires a certain amount of competence and operates through deliberation, debate, and tolerance. It consists of a strong and deep democracy that no longer emphasizes nationalism but rather acknowledges deep differences and loyalties between citizens (Gunsteren, 1998: 26; Barber, 1984).

In the fourth group, moderate postmodern theories of citizenship are the newest and most controversial addition to citizenship theories. While some postmodern theories claim that citizenship is dead (Wexler, 1990), others accept citizenship and politics, but modify them toward group or particularistic rights (Isin and Wood, 1999). Of these theories, we focus on two: the radical pluralist theories of citizenship and explicit theories of multicultural citizenship. Radical pluralism rejects both liberal pluralism and consensual communitarianism (LaClau and Mouffe, 1985). It envisages a constant conflict of what Mouffe refers to as 'agonistic pluralism' where antagonism is turned into consensus on basic democratic procedures and values while a certain amount of dissent is allowed over interpretation and implementation of these positions (Laclau and Mouffe, 1985; Mouffe, 1993a, 1993b, 1993c, 1995, 1996; Torfing, 1999: 255). Mouffe separates her position from 'deliberative democracy' that 'aims to establish a consensus through free and unconstrained public discussion' (Torfing, 1999: 261). She postulates an agonistic democracy that envisages 'confrontation between adversaries who agree on the ... rules of the game while disagreeing not only about substantial, political and moral issues but also about the precise interpretation of the rules of the game' (Mouffe, 1995: 502; Torfing, 1999: 261). The citizen is active and protesting. Within this multicultural and non-essentialistic theory, a modified socialist project emerges as a goal for one competing group of progressive citizens. This progressive group includes many different people, some closer to socialism but also others closer to postmodern fragmentation. Nonetheless, their major contention is that a cultural turn has taken place and that various race/ethnic/gender and other groups have a claim to some type of group or cultural rights. This is the topic of the next section.

Universalistic Versus Particularistic Rights

Liberal theory has largely been hostile to the idea of group rights because liberalism is thoroughly based on the individual. Theories influenced by the 'cultural turn' and postmodern influences find group or particularistic rights quite amenable to their purposes. While liberal and multicultural positions on group rights may claim fundamental differences, a closer look suggests a great deal of overlap in theory and practice. Much of what is referred to as women's 'group rights' falls under contingent (e.g. abortion rights), compensatory (e.g. affirmative action rights), and organizational rights (e.g. the National Organization of Women fighting for positive media coverage and legislative action). In some ways, whether contingent, compensatory or organizational rights are associated with multicultural or liberal theory probably is a moot point; they are related to both theoretical perspectives. If we look beyond these three types of rights that are shared by each theory, a small amount of conflict between universalistic and groups rights is left. We will discuss these three different forms of rights below and then answer the question we have just posed.

First, universalistic rights nominally apply to everyone who is a citizen and who fits the situation for which the rights were intended. In other words, universalistic rights can be contingent without losing their universality. For instance, in some countries, all citizens have a right to public assistance, but that right is contingent on being poor and without resources (i.e. billionaires do not have a right to receive public assistance payments). Similarly, healthy citizens in their thirties who work for good wages do not qualify for old age pensions (i.e. one must be old to receive a retirement pension). The contingencies of these rights are based on clear and sensible conditions. Moving on to gender issues, the right to any kind of medical procedure or treatment including the right to an abortion is contingent on having a medical condition that requires such treatment (i.e. being pregnant). These rights are universal in that they fall under general welfare and medical care rights that are activated when citizens need them and fit the criteria for which they are intended. Saying that only men have a right to prostate operations because only they have prostates or only women have rights to abortions because only they can give birth does not erase the fact that these rights in many countries may be universal but simultaneously contingent.[12]

Second, some citizens have suffered rights deprivations in the past, and as a result, they are entitled to some form of special treatment. Affirmative action programs in the USA have provided special rights for veterans, women, African-Americans, Hispanics and others (Burstein, 1998; Pencak, 1984; Skocpol, 1992; Ross, 1969). Considering Hohfeld's theory, these compensatory rights are temporary 'immunities' to equal treatment requirements of law because equal treatment for these groups has been violated in the past. If affirmative action programs and procedures become permanent rather than temporary, they are no longer compensatory rights but categorical rights, which are discussed below. Compensatory rights may also involve cash payments (e.g. the federal government in the USA paid Japanese Americans interned during World War II, and there were German payments to Jewish emigrants and victims whose property was stolen).

Third, universalistic citizenship rights also encompass organizational rights, which at the political level include the rights to form political parties and interest groups; trade unions and employer federations; and ethnic, racial or gendered associations and social movements. These are not particularistic group rights as the term is typically used. Rather, they are organizational rights whereby groups of people have rights to collectively organize and act. For example, trade unions have rights to recruit members, negotiate grievances, bargain over wages with management, and conduct strikes with protests and picketing. These active rights are specific to groups of workers who have formed trade unions, and if workers choose not to have a union, they do not have these rights. This does not make them particularistic or group rights. These rights are also contingent on having formed the organization in question. Similar organizational contingencies apply to interest groups formed by women, gays, and citizens of color. These rights are universalistic given the fact that all citizens may follow the legal procedures to establish their own organizations or voluntary associations.

Two common mistakes often occur with political and organizational rights. One concerns labeling all political gains or policies as rights, even though they are neither guaranteed nor universal. For instance, with organizational rights, trade unions and women's groups bargain for certain life-sustaining wages and limitation on hours. However, these bargained solutions exist for a union or interest group at one particular time and are not citizenship rights. Similarly, many different types of legislation are not citizenship rights: providing a building and budget for a new social program, designating Children's Protection Week, and giving special tax shelters or oil depletion allowances. These are not citizenship rights guaranteed by the state. It is important to recognize that all political action by legislatures and courts does not create citizenship rights. The other mistake was discussed above, but it is worth reiterating that rights of action or benefit within an organization are not citizenship rights (e.g. 'an employee of my stature has a right to a desk or a company pension'). These may be recognized within organizations as rights, but they are not citizenship rights available to all citizens.

Finally, categorical rights (i.e. often referred to as cultural or group rights) involve an exclusive entitlement to a particular activity or status, which others could use but cannot receive. In other words, these are not contingent, compensatory, or organizational rights. They form the core of what many theorists refer to as group or cultural rights, but we will call them 'categorical rights.'[13] These kinds of rights can exist to different degrees and are laid out in Table 2.4.

In 'part a' of the section on indigenous and aboriginal rights, we list a rather wide range of rights that may not be available to the general citizenry. Self-government and sovereignty give categorical rights their own flavor. But in 'part b' of this same section, the rights do not consist of a separate system but rather particular exceptions to universalistic rights: for example, American Indians' rights to catch salmon with gill nets or to establish casinos on reservations in the USA which are denied to most other American citizens, or the existence of separate legal systems in Canada that allow alternative punishments to prison (e.g. sweat houses or banishment) (Havemann, 1999, Isin and Wood, 1999). A more formal example concerns categorical rights that are allowed by the Spanish constitution and further negotiated between political parties and grants autonomy to the many language-based regions of the country (e.g. Basque provinces collect their own taxes and then pass on some monies to the central government) (Colomer, 1999; Rothschild, 1981; Newton, 1997).

Unlike the theoretical agreement on the three types of group rights discussed above, further positions on categorical rights in liberal and postmodern pluralist theory differ: liberal theory is strongly against categorical rights and multicultural or postmodern theory favors them. We discuss the pros and cons of each theory below concerning issues of universality, discrimination, representation, and domination. First, the use of group rights involves a specific targeting of benefits to various groups, but this entails an obvious loss of universality. Kymlicka's (1995, Gray, 1989) multicultural position is extremely critical of states viewing citizens as de-culturized and non-ethnic persons. He states that: 'The common rights of citizenship, originally defined by and for white, able-bodied, Christian men, cannot accommodate the special needs of these groups. Instead, a fully integrative citizenship must take these differences into account.' (1995: 181). Kymlicka mentions that 'there is ample evidence that these social rights have indeed served to promote the integration of the working class in various countries ...' (1995: 180). On the other hand, there also is ample evidence that universalistic laws have served social movements representing women and African-Americans quite well.[14] More to the point, Kymlicka does not see the need to include African-Americans under the category of group rights (2000: 233). According to him, American law has served them well enough to pursue their rights claims through the courts (Smith, 1997; Shklar, 1991; Morris, 1984). Our main point is that universalistic rights provide a powerful tool to social movements in achieving their claims and that these tools may be

Table 2.4 *Group Rights as Categorical Rights in a Number of Countries*

	Legal Rights	Political Rights	Social Rights
1 Indigenous or Aboriginal rights	*a National sovereignty rights* Indigenous law supplants universalistic law	*a National sovereignty rights* Self-government by tribe or nation on or off reservations, semi-autonomous substate.	*a National sovereignty rights* Independent expenditures, taxes and budget for welfare, cultural and medical programs.
	b Particularistic rights Fishing monopolies, public schooling exemptions, gambling on reservations Legal, schooling and public signage rights in native language Special land and water rights Ethnic dress exemptions Festival and holiday rights with subsidies (These rights would be universalistic if offered to all ethnic groups)	*b Particularistic rights* Special status or vetoes in legislature Guaranteed number of seats in legislature Gerrymandering districts to create minority 'majorities' Ethnic advisory councils in general and for especially for police (Election ballots translated into ethnic language)	*b Particularistic rights* Special welfare benefits Business start-up programs Preferential government business Language rights in schools Cultural awareness programs only for groups Multicultural rights in schools like special holidays for indigenous persons only
2 Ethnic and immigrant rights	Rights of return to originating country (Civil rights for immigrants) (Translation rights in police actions) (Naturalization and dual nationality rights)	Immigrant advisory councils (Election ballots translated into immigrant or ethnic citizen's primary language)	Special welfare benefits Business start-up programs Language rights in schools Multicultural rights in school like special ethnic holidays for group members only
3 Women's rights	(Abortion as bodily control rights) (Abuse rights for wives and children) (Child support rights) (Affirmative action rights)	[None, but special seats reserved for women are possible.]	(Multigender rights in curriculum) (Special welfare benefits) (Women's protection centers) (Women's studies programs)

Continued

Table 2.4 *Continued*

	Legal Rights	Political Rights	Social Rights
4 Gendered rights	(Civil rights at work) (Benefits for gay partners at work) (Gay marriage rights)	[None, but special seats reserved for gays are possible.]	(Multigender rights in schooling) (Adoption rights) (AIDS treatment rights) (Social security rights for gay partners)
5 Regional rural and urban rights	Internal travel privileges for urban citizens/restrictions on rural people to urban areas, or vice versa External passport privileges for certain groups	Regional self-government	Rural development or assistance programs

Sources: Partially based on Levy 1997, Isin and Wood 1999, Kymlicka (1995: 29–35), UN (1993)

Parentheses indicate right considered to be contingent or compensatory citizenship rights. Brackets indicate rights that do not exist but could exist.

exchanged for the more uncertain tools of group rights, which may have less legitimacy to non-group members. Thus, there are gains and losses for each approach: group rights attain greater specificity and targeting to culturally sensitive groups, while universal rights enable greater legitimacy and discursive leverage in legislatures and the courts to these same groups.[15]

Second, particular groups may pursue and obtain categorical rights, but these rights are inherently particularistic and may become discriminatory. When achieved by specific minority groups who want full expression of their culture through rituals and social structures, these rights become discriminatory toward other citizens living in the same area who become strangers without the same cultural rights.[16] The complete achievement of group rights for ethnic and other groups might lead to a decentralized system of 'feudal' societies each with particularistic rights and different legal orders, which Dahrendorf refers to as 'sectoral citizenship' (1974: 693). Rights to free movement (geographical mobility) and employment (occupational mobility) would become strained because a system of group rights encourages separatism into substates and subsocieties.

Categorical or group rights may work better than individual rights for ethnic or racial groups who are primarily of one group; however, they may also abandon citizens with complex ethnic heritage. Multiracial or multiethnic citizens with less than a tenth of any particular group are left without categorical rights. Are they not 'different' and are not all citizens entitled to be racially, ethnically, and sexually recognized? Further, some ethnic groups may not feel as strong a sense of culture and may indeed see themselves as relatively non-ethnic even though everyone has an ethnic heritage (Howard, 1992: 97–9; Dan-Cohen, 1986; Nickel, 1997; Wal, 1990).

Ethnic groups may argue that the nation-state already advocates a dominant ethnic culture, which is often true. The very name 'nation-state' implies this. However, much of this is not formalized into a system of rights in law, and what has been formalized is in the process of being removed (e.g. in the USA the transfer of social security benefits to spouses has been largely completed, and 'In God we Trust' on coins can easily be replaced by multicultural symbols). Feminist groups make the argument that citizenship is gendered and this is also true. Citizenship rights reflect the societies in which they are created. However, many current 'gendered rights' are clearly preferable to past 'gendered rights,' and considerable change has occurred in this area. Where group rights have the strongest case concerns indigenous peoples whose 'racialized rights' cannot be easily accommodated by simply extending the availability of rights. Indigenous cultures based on collective or unowned property are clearly distinct from most Western and many non-Western cultures.

Third, categorical rights require representation but often these representatives are not elected or otherwise legitimated. This issue does not reflect representation *per se*, but rather the tendency of dominant political élites to appoint ethnic or racial élites to represent 'their' people. As a result, these appointed leaders, who may be charismatic to dominant élites and legitimate to mainstream politicians, may sponsor positions that their constituents or group members do not want. In fact, the very lack of group support for cultural policies or positions may serve as evidence for the necessity of categorical rights (i.e. their group has underdeveloped or false consciousness). Categorical rights concerning citizenship need some assurances that democratic processes operate within these groups (e.g. the Landrum-Griffin Act assuring democracy within trade unions in the USA).

Representation may also affect tolerance within groups. If a group culture devalues women, the old, the young, or some other segment of their society (e.g. the American South with lynching, present-day USA with the death penalty, some African Muslim societies with clitoridectomy, the Amish with shunning, etc.), should a democratic society accept that devaluation as being legitimate because of its embeddedness in that culture?

Kymlicka (1995: 172) recognizes the problem but concludes that 'dismissing the idea of self-government' will not make it go away, but we note that neither will accepting self-government. Vyver (1996: xli–lxii) discusses the doctrine of 'sphere sovereignty' that allows religious groups sovereignty over such actions, but the cultural relativism implied here is often difficult to accept. In actuality, USA and Canadian courts have allowed many exceptions with religious sects such as the Amish, Hutterites, Mennonites and Doukhobors (Janzen, 1990; Durham, 1996; Vyver, 1996). Kymlicka sees external protections of ethnic and racial groups as valid, but internal restrictions on group members as invalid. This leads to some difficult distinctions on controlling the internal affairs of groups to which he would like to give self-governing rights (e.g. accepting most of French culture but being less tolerant of certain aspects of Muslim culture (Kymlicka, 1995: 42, 164–172; Mayer, 1999). This is not an easy issue for any of the theories considered here.

Fourth, the power of dominant groups may give them undue influence over group rights in a number of ways. For instance, having legal status and the many corresponding rights accorded to them, corporations can acquire large resources and considerable power. Individuals and communities cannot match this organizational power. Consequently, countervailing power resources – labor organizing, codetermination, works councils, and environmental monitoring laws – are often necessary to balance the bargaining. But what are corporate rights? In essence, they are group rights for investors who have their private assets sheltered from liability claims, and this 'limited liability' has amassed considerable power and profit. Corporate rights also enable chief executive officers and other corporate officials to wield significant power in our society. Changing this form of group right, while not impossible and not without supporters, is unlikely. Once a group right becomes ensconced, it can be very difficult to dislodge.

While group rights have been intended for minority groups, majority groups and dominant élites can take advantage of group rights in other ways. Trade unions in the USA wanted to place their Committee on Political Education (COPE) on more solid legal footing by making it a political action committee (PAC) (Corrado et al., 1997). They were successful but corporations with deeper pockets were able to use PACs to overwhelm the contributions made by trade unions. Majorities or élites may also be able to use other group rights much more effectively than minorities. In the USA, powerful Christian churches are having success in putting forth a proposal about group rights to use 'faith-based organizations' (e.g. churches) to implement state social policies (Durham, 1996, Vyver, 1996). Can these organizations then discriminate against racial, gender, or religious groups? In the end, dominant religious groups may be much more successful than minority groups in attaining group rights despite the intent of social theorists.

Thus, there are some difficult trade-offs and thorny issues concerning these four issues of (1) the different strategic advantages of operating under a system of universal or categorical rights, the implications of (2) discrimination and (3) representation in categorical rights, and (4) the question of dominant élites co-opting categorical rights for their own benefit and domination of minority groups.

We have kept the right to self-determination separate because it involves the liberation of nations, the creation of additional states with sovereignty, and the institutionalization of new legal systems. Nonetheless, it is a very important aspect of categorical rights. In a claim to secede, we see two issues that present great difficulties but are not necessarily insurmountable (Bartkus, 1999; Buchanan, 1991; Buchheit, 1978; Cobban, 1969; Eagleton 1953; Wood, 1981).

First, an independence movement is a clear threat to the existing state and larger society advocating universal citizenship. It can result in brutal civil wars and make the state vulnerable to external threats because of destabilized international relations. According to Weber, the state has the legitimate right to use of force, which means that secession creates a dispute between two groups that claim coercion as a means to obtain their goals. While secession may be peaceful (e.g. the separation of the Slovak and Czech Republics, Norway and Sweden, and Scotland and Wales in the UK), more often it involves considerable violence. For instance, the Iraqi government killed over 5,000 Kurds and forced over 1,700,000 Kurds to seek asylum in Iran and Turkey (Bartkus, 1999: 65). Other recent examples involve Bengalis in Pakistan; Biafrans in Nigeria; Eritreans in Ethiopia; Nagas and Kashmiris in India; Karen in Burma; Katangans in the Congo; Chechens in Russia; Basques and Catalonians in Spain; Tamils in Sri Lanka; and Tibetans in China. The violence in these attempted secessions has been highly destructive and caused great loss of rights and life. On the other hand, the vast majority of violence has often been committed by states who oppose secession, and if these states were to forego their claims, less violence would result.

Second, the self-determination of a people assumes a fixed and somewhat pure ethnic or racial group that has closure over culture and other norms. This very group must not have subcultures or subgroups that may themselves seek independence. Claims for the presumably closed and homogenous groups are very difficult to make clearly in multicultural societies with substantial but variable rates of intermarriage (Packer, 1999; Little, 1996). More often than not, such closed societies do not exist, especially because of international migration and globalization, which are at odds with closure. Even worse, this strong need for ethnic or racial community has a tendency toward ethnic cleansing, which ranges from encouraging emigration to plain murder (e.g. the Christian cleansing of Muslims in the former Yugoslavia in the 1990s, and the newly formed Hungarian state pushing an ethnic purification policy after it gained independence from the Austrians in the second half of the nineteenth century). Thus, ethnic repression against these smaller minorities within the new state may actually be greater than before secession.

Arguing against this point of 'minority nationalism,' Kymlicka uses the term 'post-ethnic multi-culturalism' (2000: 229–32), which appears to mean a form of tolerance that can exist within nation-state and/or within semi-autonomous regions or groups within the nation-state (e.g. the wide-ranging acceptance of immigrants from all over the world in Quebec). While groups such as the Québécois may have a sense of group culture and the boundaries of that culture, that does not mean that they cannot at the same time be open to multiculturalism. How far many countries are past 'minority nationalism', however, is a telling question on whether this concept works or not.

There may very well be legitimate claims to secession, but the point we are making is that to exercise this controversial right may be more complicated and involved than nationalist groups think. Secession's provocation of violence should clearly make one extremely careful in using it (as one would be careful calling for revolution). Many of these ethnic and racial problems can be solved through participatory structures (rather than complete sovereignty) that allow greater democratic control over local and regional resources.[17] However, these processes do not always work (e.g. despite considerable autonomy, the Basque claims to secession are still backed by terrorism) (Gibbons, 1999: 13–38). Or they can be solved by independence in successful secession, but this process may be hard to control and ungovernability may be lurking for many years.

In sum, the nearly opposite theoretical positions of liberalism and multicultural theory have more in common than most recognize. Contingent, compensatory, and organizational rights supply an overlap between the two theories. For the most part, liberal theories fail to recognize the frequent existence and value of group rights in many democratic societies, and multicultural theories fail to perceive the usefulness of universalistic rights in advancing many ethnic, racial and gender groups.

The strongest cases for group rights are advanced by indigenous peoples since they often form fundamentally different countercultures with at least some geographical closure – American Indians, New Zealand Maori, Canadian Inuit, Nordic Sami, and Australian Aborigines (Havemann, 1999; Isin and Wood, 1999: 47–70). They can also claim some initial citizenship (i.e. *jus soli* as first citizens rather than *terra nullis* as non-inhabitants). Since special rights for cultural categories work best for groups who have clear cultural and geographical boundaries, indigenous populations can effectively make claims because they have these boundaries. Also their conceptions of property and social organization are often inherently collective, making their law quite different (as are the Amish and other religious sects who live collectively and have received exemptions). If a nation lives more or less separately, then rights and obligations can be relatively clear and cultures can be celebrated with state support. For categories of people who intend to live together with other peoples, contingent, compensatory, and organizational rights may very well be enough (e.g. women, gays, racial minorities, and various immigrant groups). But for the most part, special and universalistic rights will continue to live together in an uneasy relationship, and we must avoid a politically naïve position that powerful groups will not use categorical rights to increase rather than lessen domination.

THE EXTENT OF LEGAL AND POLITICAL RIGHTS

The range and nature of legal and political rights differs considerably around the world and we now look at these differences in thirty countries.

Legal Rights

We group legal rights and duties into three categories: reasonable security of person, access to justice, and freedom of conscience. Rights to personal security include freedoms from government torture, the imposition of the death penalty, and freedom to control your own body through contraception. The right to personal security 'consists in a person's legal and uninterrupted enjoyment of his life, his limbs, his body, his health, and his reputation' (Kriegel, 1995: 40). It allows individuals to conduct their lives without interference from the state, other groups, and individuals. It obligates the state to protect the individual's right to personal security. An example of the right to personal security is the right to be secure from marital rape. Although the right to be secure from marital rape may belong to the right to control one's body, the notion here is the right to be personally secure and safe. Another example is a child's right not to be subject to harm or abuse.

The right to control one's body is the ability to decide how one takes care of one's body and mind and one's health. This right may be active compared to the right to personal security, but in the same way protects the individual from interference from the state, other groups, and individuals. This right also obligates the state to protect individuals' right to control their body and mind. An important contemporary example is the freedom to choose or reject an abortion. Although abortion is sometimes based in the right to privacy, the decision to abort frequently involves the mother's right to control her own body. The decision whether to receive medical and psychiatric treatment is also based on the right to control the body and mind.

In some countries, the right to privacy is the basis of the right to personal security and the right to control one's body. We differentiate the right to privacy because in some countries it does not provide the legal foundation of these other rights and because it is apparently becoming important in other areas of life, most notably use of electronic devices and the Internet.

Like the rights to conscience and choice, the right to personal security necessitates the willingness to obey laws and tolerate other people's choices. The effective use of the right to personal security also obligates individuals to report violations of those rights and to help others.

Second, rights that support or facilitate access to justice are rights that provide access to court and, once in court, support efforts to gain justice. Rights that support access to justice typically are legal rights and include the rights to legal representation, free legal assistance, waiver of court fees, confrontation with your accuser, and a jury trial. The right to legal representation means an individual has the right to have legal counsel in court, whether criminal or civil. This right is important when confronting the complexity of some kinds of legal proceedings and the difficulty of representing one's own interests. States must ensure this right is fulfilled by providing legal representation without direct charge to the represented. Many governments fulfill this right for criminal cases, but not all states fulfill this right for civil cases. The right to free legal representation is similar to the right to legal representation, but it is typically available to indigents to ensure that they receive legal representation and advice in court.

The right to confront your accuser is based in the notion of procedural and substantive due process. A person has the right to confront the party who may affect their liberty and property. The notion of 'due process of law' implies the right of an individual to be present before the tribunal that pronounces judgment upon her or him. To enforce this right to the fullest means the individual has the opportunity to be heard, by testimony or otherwise, and to challenge every material fact that bears on the question. It allows one to be heard in court while prohibiting the state and others from damaging one's liberty or property without notice.

Obligations supporting rights that provide access to justice include the obligation to testify, appear in court as a party to a lawsuit, and to serve on a jury. The duty of testifying in court obligates an individual to appear so that another citizen who is subject to legal action is not deprived of their rights. It gives substantive meaning to the right to confront and be judged by your peers. The right to a jury trial, of course, is meaningless if juries cannot be formed from a pool of responsible citizens, which means those citizens must be willing to serve.

Third, rights to conscience and choice allow individuals to maintain their values and beliefs in and live according to religious, philosophical, or even amoral principles. Rights to conscience and choice usually are legal rights and include the freedom of speech and the press, the freedom to practice religion, the right to choose a marriage partner, the right to choose an occupation, and other rights. The freedom of speech and the press is the ability to speak, write, and communicate whether speaking, advertising, telephoning or e-mailing. These rights are universalistic rights that allow individuals and groups to challenge and criticize the state, to comment on other individuals and groups, and to do so without interference from the state or others in civil society. The freedom to practice or not to practice religion and to maintain one's conscience is the ability to believe in and live according to religious, philosophical or other principles. The freedom to marry allows an individual to choose a partner freely and without interference from the state. The rights to conscience and choice include other rights such as the right to choose a gender and the right to choose membership in an ethnic group.

Obligations supporting the rights to conscience and choice include tolerance and obeying the law. The obligation to tolerate the practice of others' rights, opinions, and lifestyles is a universal obligation. An example is allowing others' religious opinions and modes of worship that are contrary to, or different from, those of the established religion or dominant beliefs. Laws are frequently implemented to safeguard the rights to conscience and choice, and obeying these laws is important for allowing individuals to exercise these rights and freedoms.

These various laws may often conflict (e.g. unconditional freedom of speech versus freedom from racial or sexual discrimination in banning hateful and public actions) so that ironing out conflicting rights may be quite complex (Rowan, 1999; Anderson, 1987).

Political Rights

This discussion of political rights focuses on four types of rights: personal political rights, organizational rights, membership rights, and group self-determination rights. First, personal political rights consist of voting in elections for a multiplicity of competing candidates chosen through a democratic political process. Assuring the legitimacy of elections has proven more difficult than previously assumed in the USA with the very close 2000 presidential elections. Countries differ according to how difficult it is to vote (e.g. registration procedures, secrecy of the ballots, disqualifications for past crimes, poll taxes, literacy tests, and outright discrimination) (Piven and Cloward, 1988). Voting methods may allow for serious undercounts by spoiled ballots or outright corruption (e.g. the confusing 'butterfly ballot' in the 2000 Florida presidential election). Standing for office is restricted to certified citizens and particular offices may have various ascriptive requirements. For instance, there are age and birth requirements for the USA presidency (candidates must be at least 35 years old and born in the country).

Second, organizational political rights refer to the rights of political parties, interest groups, and social movements to form and take action in legislative forums, the courts, and in the media. As with voting and legislating, these rights are not substantive but procedural. Political parties can freely form to participate in selecting candidates to run for office, and if they win, political parties may play a prominent role in the ruling of the country. Interest groups may form, collect money through contributions, give money to candidates in many countries, and influence politicians to enact their policy preferences. In the USA, corporations and trade unions cannot give candidates money directly, but there are ruses (soft money and separate organizational principles) that allow them to subvert these rules (Corrado et al., 1997). Social movements and trade unions may take part in specific oppositional activities such as protesting, demonstrating, and striking. These rights are considerably different between countries.

Third, countries differ according to their propensity to grant membership to citizens within and outside of their borders. Immigration quotas for certain sending countries were quite popular before the 1960s, especially concerning Asian immigrants (e.g. the USA and Australia had very small quotas for Chinese immigrants). More recently, immigrants have been controlled through occupational and family reunification procedures. Some countries deny being countries of immigration (e.g. Germany and Switzerland) and as a result restrict many immigrants to guest-worker status with the expectation that they will return to their home countries. By and large, only Switzerland has been successful in sending immigrants back. Other countries ban certain types of immigration within their country and emigration to other countries (e.g. the USSR and other communist governments).

Naturalization rights refer to the procedures that an immigrant must go through in order to become a citizen. In the most general cases, immigrants must be in the country for a specified period of time (three years in Australia to twelve in Switzerland), demonstrate knowledge of the language (rudimentary in the USA or more advanced in Germany), have good character (not having a traffic ticket in Japan or being a felon in the USA), and so on (Janoski and Glennie, 1995; Hammar, 1985; 1990; Soysal 1994). In two specific cases, naturalization may be short-term or even immediate. Spouses of citizens and adopted young children from other countries are afforded courtesy naturalization, and children born in the country are allowed to become a citizen in many Anglo-Saxon countries under *jus soli* principles.

Fourth, the right of a group of people to self-determination is not an individual right since one person cannot form a government. This is a group right afforded to regional, ethnic, or racial groups who claim that they are a nation and should stand independently with some form of sovereignty. Countries can emerge out of other larger countries or empires in one of two ways: decolonization and secession. Decolonization takes place when a country existed and then was taken over by a colonizing country. The usually distinct peoples of the colony develop nationalistic consciousness often through discrimination and illegitimacy claims, with social movements and political parties, and through force or sometimes non-violent resistance pressure the colonizer to grant them freedom and sovereignty. The major European colonizers have largely gone through the decolonization process and former colonies are now independent states (e.g. Algeria and Vietnam decolonized from France; Nigeria and India separated from the UK; and Indonesia and Surinam gained independence from the Netherlands).

Countries can also emerge out of non-colonial secession processes but this is more difficult (Bartkus, 1999: 10–12). To succeed, secession movements need discontent, leaders, a distinct community and a geographical base (e.g. secession from within occurred with Singapore from Malaysia and by invasion from a neighboring country with Texas from Mexico). Nations such as the Kurds have had a great deal of difficulty because their peoples span four countries (Turkey, Iran, Iraq and Pakistan), which makes the secession process difficult. Unsuccessful secession attempts are numerous, but the Southern states attempt during the USA Civil War is one example. Indigenous peoples often make secessionist claims for national status, but more often than not, these are more limited separations that may evolve into limited sovereignty (e.g. Nunavit in Canada) or consociationalism (e.g. the Flemish and Walloons in Belgium).

In Table 2.5, we examine some measures of political and legal rights in 31 countries. We summarize the level of legal and political rights for these countries across democracies, democratizing countries, and countries governed by dictatorships. Democracies are characterized by their political-economic orientation: social democratic, traditional and liberal.[18]

Among the social democratic countries, all countries have Humana (1983, 1992) rights scores above 83. Based on group summary scores, the social democratic countries have the highest level of legal and political rights, which is also indicated on the Freedom House ranking (1999). Traditional countries have Humana rights scores ranging from 66 to 100, but Italy scores lowest among the traditional democracies with a summary score of 90. The liberal democracies range from 44 to 100, although Freedom House summary scores rank them in the 1 category. Japan receives the lowest Humana score among the liberal democracies at an average of 82. On the whole, these democracies score high on measures of legal and political rights, but across categories differences exist with social democracies scoring highest and liberal democracies tending to score lowest.

The democratizing countries score two to four on the Freedom House measure with the Humana scores for specific legal and political rights range from 33 to 92. Within this group, Poland and Argentina score highest while Nigeria, South Africa, and India score much lower. Governments characterized as dictatorships receive the lowest scores on legal and political rights. China, North Korea and Iraq earn Freedom House's lowest score of six and seven, and on certain rights they sometimes drop to Humana's lowest score of zero.

Levels of Government Organization and Citizenship

Citizenship varies most across different levels of government in federal systems but much less so in more centralized countries (Norton 1994). In the USA, states have their

Table 2.5 *Measures of Legal and Political Rights in 31 Countries*

	Legal Rights								Political Rights						
	(1) *Summary*		(2) *Security-person*		(3) *Access to Justice*		(4) *Conscience*		(5) *Summary*	(6) *Personal*		(7) *Organization*		(8) *Membership*	
	FH/ Humana		Torture/death/ contra		Detention/ lawyer		Relig/speech/ gender		FH	Vote/info		Assmb/opp/ union		Emgr/natz/dual	
Democracies															
Social Democratic															
Denmark	1	98	100	YYY	83	Yy	97	YYY(92)	1	100	YY	100	YYY	100	YYY
Finland	1	99	100	YYY	100	YY	100	YYY	1	100	YY	100	YYY	100	YYY
Netherlands	1	98	100	YYY	100	YY	97	YYY(92)	1	100	YY	100	YYY	100	YYY
Sweden	1	98	100	YYY	83	Yy	100	YYY	1	100	YY	100	YYY	100	YYY
Traditional															
Austria	1	95	89	yYY	83	Yy	97	YYY(92)	1	100	YY	100	YYY	100	YYN
France	2	94	89	yYY	100	YY	97	YY(88) Y(92)	1	100	YY	100	YYY	100	YYY
Germany	2	98	100	YYY	83	Yy	97	YYY(92)	1	100	YY	100	YYY	67	YYN
Italy	2	90	89	yYY	66	yy	97	YY(88) Y(92)	1	100	YY	100	YYY	67	YYN
Switzerland	2	96	100	YYY	100	Yy	90	YY(87) Y(83)	1	100	YY	100	YYY	67	YYN
Liberal															
Australia	1	91	87	yYY	83	Yy	90	YY(92) y(77)	1	100	YY	100	YYY	87	Yyy
Canada	1	94	87	yYY	83	Yy	100	YYY	1	100	YY	100	YYY	100	YYY
Ireland	1	94	87	Yyy	83	Yy	92	YYY(75)	1	83	Yy	100	YYY	87	YyY
UK	2	93	87	yYY	100	YY	97	YY(88) Y(92)	1	83	Yy	100	YYY	100	YYY
USA	1	90	66	ynY	83	Yy	90	YY(87) Y(83)	1	83	Yy	100	YYY	87	Yyy
Japan	2	82	44	yNy	50	yn	87	Yy(77) Y(83)	1	83	Yy	100	YYY	33	YNN
Democratizing															
S. Korea	2	59	44	nNY	50	ny	73	Yn(44) Y(75)	2	50	ny	33	nnn	55	YyN
South Africa	2	50	44	nNY	33	nn	74	Yy(55) Y(66)	1	50	NY	44	nny	100	YYY
Poland	2	83	55	yny	83	Yy	92	YYy(75)	1	100	YY	87	Yyy	33	NYN
Argentina	3	84	78	nYY	83	Yy	81	Yy(78) Y(66)	3	100	YY	100	YYY	67	NYY

(Continued)

Table 5 *(Continued)*

	Legal Rights								Political Rights						
	(1) *Summary*		(2) *Security-person*		(3) *Access to Justice*		(4) *Conscience*		(5) *Summary*	(6) *Personal*		(7) *Organization*		(8) *Membership*	
	FH/ Humana		Torture/death/ contra		Detention/ lawyer		Relig/speech/ gender		FH	Vote/info		Assmb/opp/ union		Emgr/natz/dual	
India	3	54	33	NNY	50	ny	53	yy(44) y(50)	2	83	yY	66	yyy	100	YYY
Brazil	4	69	44	NnY	83	yY	87	YY(87) Y(75)	3	83	Yy	87	Yyy	67	NYY
Mexico	4	64	44	NnY	33	Ny	81	Yy(77) y(66)	3	66	yy	66	yyy	67	NYY
Russia†/USSR*	4†	54*	33*	nNY	50*	ny	76*	yy(66) y(83)	4†	66*	yy	66*	yyy	55*	nYn
Nigeria	4	49	55	yNY	33	Ny	79	yy(87)Y(83)	6	33	Ny	66	yyy	100	YYY
Dictatorships															
Algeria	5	66	44	nNY	83	yY	68	Yy(55) y(50)	6	50	ny	66	yyy	33	NYN
Pakistan	5	42	33	NNY	50	ny	31	ny(44)N(17)	4	66	yy	44	nyn	33	NNY
Egypt	6	59	44	nNY	17	Nn	39	nn(33)y(50)	6	50	yn	55	nyy	33	NYN
Iran	6	22	22	Nny	0	NN	18	nN(11)N(8)	6	17	Nn	0	NNN	33	NYN
China	6	21	66	NNY	17	Nn	43	yn(22)n(41)	7	0	NN	0	NNN	0	NNN
Iraq	7	17	22	Nny	33	NY	49	yn(22)y(58)	7	0	NN	0	NNN	33	NYN
N. Korea	7	20	66	NNY	17	Nn	30	nN(0)y(58)	7	0	NN	0	NNN	0	NNN

Sources: Freedom House/FH (1999); Humana (1992).

Variables: (1) Summary of legal rights comes from both Freedom House (ranked 1 = high in rights to 7 = low in rights) and Humana (100 = high in rights, 0 = low; averages taken of following scores: Y = 100, y = 66, n = 33, N = 0); (2) The security of person: freedom from torture, absence of the death penalty, and freedom to contracept (Humana); (3) Access to justice: freedom from unlawful detention and ability to be represented by a defense attorney (Humana); (4) Freedom of conscience: freedom of religion, freedom of speech (average of three variables – censorship of art, the press, and mail/phone – reported in parentheses), and freedom of gender choice (average of four variables – female equality, marriage, divorce, and privacy – reported in parentheses) (Humana); (5) Summary of political rights comes from Freedom House (Humana); (6) Personal political rights: voting and ability to hold office (Humana); (7) Organizational rights: assembly, opposition, and trade unions organization (Humana); (8) Membership rights are an index of emigration, naturalization, and dual nationality rights (Humana on first, and Janoski and Glennie on next two).

own constitutions and statements of rights. Federal law takes precedence on issues and claims over which it has jurisdiction, but otherwise, state law controls. On the whole, there are three levels of citizenship rights. First, national-level rights are found in constitutions and national legislation that maintain basic principles of legal and political rights, including due process rights and voting rights. Second, regional rights exist at the state, provincial, departmental, and Land level. These regions may have constitutions and bills of rights, but they generally are subject to the sovereignty of national rights. For instance, in Canada many strong rights are unique in Quebec, but in France much weaker rights are provided at the *département* level.

One example of the regional division of rights concerns the financing of political elections in the USA. Under federal election law, expenditures are limited for federal candidates, but states have entirely different laws for state and local elections (Corrado et al., 1997). Difficulties often arise when political parties merge campaign funds for election campaigns that are inherently mixed (e.g. state and federal candidates often share the same podium endorsing each other as a matter of course). Further, some states are lax and allow large campaign contributions to be made to state candidates and parties, while federal campaign contributions tend to be more restrictive and require extensive reporting. Although laws regulating campaign finance are in flux with reform movements, federal and regional rights are divided between these two levels of government on who can contribute and how much they can give.

A second example of divisions between components of the state concerns restrictions on the right to vote for inmates and former prisoners. In *Losing the Vote*, the Sentencing Project and Human Rights Watch (SPHRW) estimate that 3,900,000 Americans, 2% of all adults, have currently or permanently lost the ability to vote because of a felony conviction. Nearly all states prevent inmates from voting with only Maine and Vermont allowing them the franchise (SPHRW, 1998). After citizens serve their sentences, 32 states prohibit them from voting while on parole and 29 prohibit voting while on probation. Nine states categorically prohibit the right to vote to ex-convicts, while five states prohibit the right to vote for some ex-convicts. Thirteen percent of African-American men have lost the right to vote, which means that 36% of the disenfranchised population are black men (SPHRW, 1998). The ability of states in the USA to decide whether to restrict the right to vote for individuals convicted of a crime is an important example of states exerting considerable influence over and perhaps subverting rights found in the federal constitution.[19]

Rights based at the local or municipal level tend to affect local or municipal concerns, such as rights to zoning property and eminent domain. Although some rights are enumerated in national constitutions, they are effectively provided at the local level. An example is the right to free legal representation. While the right to free legal representation is founded at the national level and applies to both criminal and civil cases, this right is more strongly protected by some states and local governments than others. In Sweden the right to free legal representation is found in the Swedish Constitution, but the responsibility to provide free legal representation is based at the county level.

At the international level, transnational or multinational rights exist in a number of areas. The European Union protects the right to move across national borders for workers and their families. International legal conventions exist for rights and obligations arising from war crimes. According to Article 1 of the Declaration on Territorial Asylum of December 1967, national governments are precluded from granting asylum to an individual who is reasonably suspected of committing a 'crime against peace, a war crime or a crime against humanity'. In the situation of detecting, capturing, and extraditing a person who may have committed a war crime or crime against humanity, national governments are expected to conform with the provisions of the 'Charter of the United Nations' and the 'Declaration on Principles of International Law concerning Friendly Relations and Co-operation among States.' These documents require national governments to protect human rights and fundamental freedoms as defined by the UN. Other provisions exist in the World Court, the European Parliament, and in the court of public opinion (Meehan, 1993). Claims for rights are supported by organizations in international civil society (e.g. Human Rights Watch, Amnesty International, Witness for Peace).

EMERGENCE AND TRANSFORMATION OF CITIZENSHIP

Two points about how citizenship rights and obligations are created and changed are important: personhood or the recognition of various groups and identities of citizens, and the long-term political, economic, and cultural battles that move citizenship rights to and fro over decades and centuries.

Personhood and the Right to be Recognized as a Citizen

Identity has always been an important aspect of citizenship that enables those excluded persons knocking at the door of citizenship to organize into social movements and interest groups so that they can participate as citizens with legal, political, and social rights. Turner emphasizes that citizenship rights are 'the outcome of social movements that either aim to expand or defend the definition of social membership' (1986a: 92). He finds that the long-term consequences of these social movements have been to push and universalize citizenship rights for an ever widening and diverse array of 'persons' (1986b). Yet at the same time, citizenship is an act of closure about a group of people it calls citizens and some people are left out (Murphy, 1988; Brubaker, 1992).

Building on Hoffman (1986: 83), there are at least four categories of excluded persons who may claim citizenship: stigmatized, impaired, potential, and quasi-humans.[20] Stigmatized humans are the most common category of candidates for citizenship, whether class-denigrated poor, gender-disqualified women, status-degraded racial or ethnic groups, or gender-despised homosexual groups. Each group tends to be thought unable to perform the duties and accept the rights of citizenship because of short-sighted or impaired interests that will not benefit the community (e.g. selling their votes, being swayed by their husbands or caretakers, or not having enough education or mental capacity to make a decision). Religious and gendered minorities are perhaps the exception to this rule because objections to their citizenship are often based on cultural or value dissensus. They are not stigmatized by incompetence but rather by opponents' claims that foreign religions, domestic cults, or gay behavior will destroy the basic values of society and hence the survival of the dominant group (e.g. Muslims may destroy Christian culture or gays may threaten straight culture). But these groups may form social movements to promote their acceptance and access to rights and obligations.

Second, the group of impaired humans may come from established citizen groups, but their competence to fulfill rights and obligations is questioned because of physical or mental disabilities that preclude action and judgment, and establish dependence. Physically disabled groups have mounted a strong campaign for rights (Shapiro, 1993; Driedger, 1989) and with relatively small and usually material adjustments (e.g. wheelchair access or orally operated typing mechanisms) they can operate in society as full citizens. Mentally disabled groups have had more problems because self-advocacy has proved to be more difficult (Rothman, 1982). Nonetheless, the inclusion movement in schools, employment, and leisure has brought about changes in many

American schools in order to integrate students who fall into this category. Employment is following close behind with the support of a number of important employers (Sailor et al., 1989).[21]

Third, potential humans include the fetus in the womb, accident victims in a permanent coma, unconscious patients, or aged citizens who have lost all thought and activity processes other than involuntary life sustenance. The rights and status of the fetus have been and will likely be debated for some time. The fetus cannot effectively communicate, but the permanently impaired and non-communicative citizen is also in a difficult position. While many speak of the rights of these citizens, few speak of their obligations.

Finally, there exists a category of fictional- or quasi-humans, such as corporations, nations (ethnic groups, races, and even religions), and offices. Corporations have been accorded rights; however, these rights really represent groups of people (e.g. shareholders and to a lesser extent employees). These groups and the corporation are different in some ways, including separability, but corporate rights are a form of group rights. In fact, the connection of the group to the corporation for collecting profits through dividends, but separation of the corporation from the group for the purposes of limited liability, are the major advantage of corporate existence with rights (i.e. when the corporation loses money the stockholders cannot be sued for debts).

Group political and legal rights also exist (e.g. the French in Canada, the Flemish and Walloons in Belgium, the Danish in Northern Germany, and the Maori in New Zealand). These rights exist to protect the special status of these cultural and language groups. Although some group and organizational rights legitimately exist, many rights theorists accord them a status that is less forceful than individual rights whenever the two types of rights are in conflict because organizational rights derive are derivative from individual rights (Dan-Cohen, 1986: 102–13; Fleras, 1999; Pogge, 1997).[22]

The Development of Legal and Political Citizenship

There is an immense amount of material written about the rise of democracy, which cannot possibly be reviewed here, and a massive literature on the rise or fall of authoritarianism (e.g. the literature on the causes of fascism). In this sketch, we will outline four main currents in this literature.

Using a focus of long-term development over centuries, Barrington Moore follows four paths of development: the capitalist/parliamentary approach of France, the UK, and the USA, the capitalist/fascist reactionary approach of Germany and Japan, the communist revolutionary development of Russia and China, and the mixed pattern of India and other countries. Moore's *The Social Origins of Dictatorship and Democracy* (1965) lays out each of these paths based on social movements of labor struggling with capital, élite strategies involving war and conquest, and changes in the mode of production that allow peasants greater resources, mobility, and organizational capabilities (Turner, 1986a). Michael Mann emphasizes élite strategies of liberal, reformist, fascist, authoritarian monarchist and authoritarian socialist regimes (1988: 190). Charles Tilly and Brian Downing provide a greater focus on war and international development on citizenship. Tilly (1991) focuses on two paths. One is the coercion path with emphasis on the means of coercion (i.e. soldiers, technology and strategy) leading to the growth of states and much less in terms of citizen freedoms. The other is the capitalist path that focuses on the accumulation and concentration of capital leading to the growth of economies and cities, which then lead to toleration and liberal democracy. Downing (1992) makes similar Weberian arguments that medieval constitutionalism was embedded at an early point in many European cultures, and by implication, not part of Asian or African cultures. Mann (1986) probably provides the greatest integration to this approach with his IEMP (ideology, economy, military and state power) approach to state development.

Largely within these traditions, T.H. Marshall (1964) contends that citizenship rights tend to progress from legal to political, and then on to social rights. Countries that do not follow this order will have difficulties (e.g. Russia, Germany, Austria, etc.). While Marshall was heavily criticized for this theory, there does seem to be considerable evidence that when a country leaps over political rights to social or participation rights, there will be problems protecting legal and developing political rights (see Janoski, 1998: 199–216).

Second, there are a number of political economy approaches more or less connected to Marx but not unrelated to the theories discussed above. Many class-based theories have discussed the power of the middle classes and bourgeoisie over landed aristocrats and nobility, with the bourgeoisie triumphing in different ways in England, the USA, and France, and the landed *Junker* in Germany (Gerschenkron, 1966; Luebbert, 1991; Rokkan, 1970, 1974a,b). Seymour Martin Lipset (1977, 1981, 1994) furthers this 'social requisites of democracy' argument in stating that successful free market capitalism is necessary for a strong middle class that fosters democracy. Strong or at least sufficient political institutions are next (1994: 16–17). These can be interpreted in a radical or conservative way as a mode of production argument for the social bases of politics. For instance, Paige (1975) explains a wide variety of revolts based on five types of agricultural production and Stinchcombe (1983) generalizes these arguments even further. Wallerstein's work (1974) on the core countries in the modern world system developing and requiring tolerance and the free flow of ideas is another angle on this perspective, with the peripheral and semiperipheral countries lacking capital and state power's interests in tolerance.

These class-based arguments tended to focus on the middle or bourgeois classes, but the next step is to look at the development of the working classes in extending democracy. Walter Korpi (1985, 1989) and Michael Shalev (1983) have developed this idea into what is called power resources theory, which explains much of citizenship policies that get passed in democracies by the power of labor parties and trade unions. Reuschemeyer, Stephens and Stephens (1992), Baldwin (1990) and Luebbert (1991) have extended this with working class and other coalitions. This approach, while tending toward working class issues, can be easily extended to the 'power-resources' of gender, race, and ethnic groups of many different kinds. Finally, Esping-Andersen (1990) has extended this class-based approach to one more sensitive to institutional or regime differences between countries (as used for the democracies in Table 2.5), and this provides a transition to the next theoretical approach.

Third, state-centric or polity-centered accounts of rights look at the state as an institution with complex features of its own. Skocpol's *States and Social Revolutions* (1979) presented state-centralized strength and peasant revolts as a critical element in social revolutions that created new rights, some political (such as France) and others more social (such as the USSR). State mobilization for war and economic development can occur in many different ways, but into the twentieth century greater reliance has been placed on populations at home and abroad. The result is greater emphasis on education, schooling, and tolerance. This builds pressure for legal and political equality and citizenship rights. The state-centric approach to citizenship is especially useful in delineating differences between countries over long periods of time. Constitutions, legal traditions, political institutions, and political culture can play a strong role here (Skocpol, 1992; Amenta, 1993; Amenta and Carruthers, 1988).

Fourth, cultural values and identity have a strong impact on citizenship. There has been a strong tradition of referring to cultural differences in basic political values between countries (Almond and Verba, 1965, 1980; Dahl, 1986; Lipset, 1994: 3–4). When not referring to constants, cultural affinities to modernity were stressed. However, this approach has tended to refer to cultural constants rather than to a more dynamic analysis of citizenship discourse in particular cultures. Since the 1980s and postmodernity, cultural approaches have exploded within the social sciences with an intense interest in Foucault and other French theorists. Cultural explanations have a wide range of work: the rise of the 'gaze', surveillance, discipline, and punishment in Foucault (1979), the figural action, discursive fields, and social horizons in the rise of reformation, reason, and socialism in Wuthnow (1989), the cultural idioms of *jus soli* and *jus sanguinis* in Brubaker (1992), the civic identity theory to explaining citizenship rights of Smith (1997), and the five different paths to the transvaluation of values in Greenfeld (1992). Somers (1993, 1995a, 1995b) formulates much of this approach in terms of civil society and relational theory. Yet, while the implied Weberian rationalization or modernization theses have been severely questioned (e.g. Marsh, 2000; Weber, 1978), they are not yet replaced. For example, despite the democratization of Taiwan, citizenship is still awaiting development in China and the Islamic world. However, much of this analysis is taking place in new social movements and international civil society rather than in the legislation of citizenship rights (Nash, 2000), and other advances are taking place in terms of normative rather than explanatory work (Mouffe, 1992, 1993a, 1993b).[23]

POLITICAL IDENTITY AND CITIZENSHIP

The process of gaining citizenship rights and assuming citizenship obligations and then losing them is gradual and curvilinear over the life course. Gaining rights and obligations generally takes place within a family and becomes more conscious during adolescence (Demo, 1992: 310–6; Jones and Wallace, 1992: 18–23, 146–51; Morgan, 1984). During adolescence teenagers learn many citizenship processes through civic education in the schools and participation in the neighborhood and community. Children and adolescents to some degree are provided with rights they have not earned and in a sense they are born with an obligational deficit.

Consequently, young citizens emerge out of this dependent position to engage in various types of exchange being already indebted with emotional and sometimes rational obligations toward family and community. The rational being, making calculations independent of all persons and institutions, is perhaps the furthest from the actual development of citizenship that one might imagine. And to a large degree, adolescents and young adults are doing their utmost to construct a viable self at this time that will take rights and obligations into account. They realize that they must develop some independence from parents and the state (as experienced in the school) before they can fulfill obligations. In the family, parents give to their children and those children end up giving to their offspring, and sometimes the children give back to their parents. Thus, much of one's self-construction arises around exchanges with family, social networks, and community.

Independence and hence citizenship diminishes during old age (Demo, 1992: 317–38). Participation in work tends to cease with retirement, while political and other forms of participation, especially voluntarism, frequently increase for a number of years (Chambré, 1987). Nonetheless, when failing health and deteriorating mental condition occur, many older citizens often give up their freedom to guardianship under the care of relatives or nursing homes. When older citizens are hospitalized and unconscious, many serious decisions are made by doctors and immediate family with informed consent (Barber, 1983: 141–9). Family and medical personnel may even decide to avoid extraordinary measures to save the older citizen's life. Thus, the extent of citizenship rights and obligations is directly connected to independence, and when a person is at the beginning and

Table 2.6 *The Citizen Identity by Action Position and Value Involvement*

Action Position – Behavior	Value Involvement – Belief		
	Allegiance	*Apathy/Self-interest*	*Alienation*
Active – Citizen Participant	1 Incorporated Citizen	2a Opportunistic Citizen	3 Active Citizen
Passive – Citizen Subject	4 Deferential Citizen	2b Opportunistic Citizen	5 Cynical Citizen
Inactive – Aliens and Neglected Citizens	7a Fatalistic Loyalist	6a Marginal Citizen 6b Marginal Citizen	7b Fatalistic Opposition

end of life, their condition of dependence lessens their full use of rights and exercise of obligations.

Citizens form a self-concept in relation to the state with its rights and obligations, which they express to others (Portis, 1985: 461–72; Roche, 1992: 375–81). Modern theories describe the self as not only dynamic but also multifaceted. Markus and Wurf refer to the self as a confederation of 'actual-, ideal-, ought-, and even counter-selves' (Markus and Wurf, 1987: 301–3; Demo, 1992; Oosterwegel and Oppenheimer, 1993). This helps explain why attitudes are not always consistent and may not predict behavior. People reflexively interpret and reinterpret their reasons for engaging in citizenship behavior. Markus and Wurf indicate that 'individuals often rewrite their personal histories to support a current self-view' (1987: 316). After the self develops in childhood and adolescence, it becomes a complex coherent structure on its own and is not a simple reflective mechanism of significant others.

Social Action Approach toward Citizenship Identity

The construction of the citizen-self is largely symbolic and often indirect. Much of the interaction ritual chains of rights and obligations involve few goods being directly exchanged with the state. Many citizens are not directly conscious of sales taxes, interstate highway systems, and who is receiving what from the state. Instead, most citizens read about the state in the newspapers, watch the TV news, and then engage in discussions with other citizens. The state is brought down to the personal level with announcers, newscasters, friends and acquaintances involved in interaction rituals.

A typology of six different types of citizen-selves motivated by value involvement and behavioral activity can be constructed.[24] This typology – incorporated, active, deferential, cynical, opportunistic, marginal and fatalistic citizen-selves – operates within a context of active or passive social motivation and allegiant or oppositional positions (see Table 2.6).[25]

First, there are two types of participant citizens: the incorporated and the active citizen. The incorporated citizens are generally part of the élite, or feel that they are. They identify with party and governmental interests, and actively participate and support party goals. Self-interest may be involved if they have political jobs or appointed positions, but it is usually not dominant because most will never be compensated for the large amounts of time and money they volunteer for their beliefs. The incorporated citizen is part of the regime, not the grassroots opposition, and is in the middle spectrum of pragmatic politics. Incorporated citizens tend to trust their leaders and operate somewhat altruistically because they benefit from the political system.

Active citizens participate in the many political activities and have concern for the people in their group. However, the active citizen is often engaged in conflict with established élites and most often approaches problems from the grassroots level. The active citizen may belong to a political party, social movement, or some other active association involved in proselytizing an ideology of change. The active citizen is not necessarily left or right, but tends to be in the opposition and the more radical of each political persuasion. This type can include social reformers of an established party, grassroots organizers of any political position, or radical revolutionaries with an activist orientation. Active citizens believe that much can be done altruistically (i.e. for 'the people' or 'the country'); however, in dealing with the opposition, they can be somewhat ruthless.

Second, there are three types of non-participant citizens: the deferential, the cynical, and the marginal citizens. The deferential citizen accepts authority and the leadership of élites but does not strongly internalize the goals of the party or state. The deferential citizen follows tradition and socialization from family experience, but avoids most political activities. Deferential citizens are neither conservative nor radical, although the leadership of élites may come from either direction. Deferential citizens tend to trust political élites because they feel that they clearly benefit from their leadership, but often these behaviors are ritualized and based on tradition. The deferential citizen will leave political participation to élites but will vote and contact politicians for help when in trouble.

Cynical citizens are similar to active citizens, but they do not participate in politics because it is impossible to really do anything about most situations. Cynical citizens may talk about the necessity of political action, but since success is doubtful, they look to improving their own interests. They are passive but often bitter critics of politics and the state.

Marginal citizens are extremely detached and alienated from the system often because of having few resources and little power. Often being in poverty and under extreme emotional distress, they rarely vote or volunteer. Many are targets of policymakers due to fears of deviance or crime. Outside forces or fate appear to control the behavior of marginal citizens, which causes their behavior to appear irrational in the long term or survival-oriented (e.g. short-term 'street skills'). Immigrants as marginal citizens may simply owe allegiance to another country, and they orient themselves toward family and friends in that society. And in terms of inactivity, both fatalistic loyalist and opposition citizens are closely related to the marginal citizen.

And third, there is the special category of the opportunistic citizens, who are highly motivated to make rational decisions about material interests that affect their short-term and immediate interests. Opportunistic citizens do not participate in political activities unless these activities directly affect their interests, involve substantial income or major services, *and* can actually achieve the desired outcomes. Otherwise the opportunistic citizen lapses into his or her own private world of interests. In general, politics and ideology are uninteresting to the opportunistic citizen. This citizen represents the self-interest concept with a free rider approach and believes that nothing is being done for free or altruistically. The opportunistic citizen is guided by restricted exchange with time horizons focusing on short-term paybacks. With the rise of individualism in the USA and Europe, this type of citizen-self has been identified as the 'demanding citizen' responsible for the breakdown of community and other social institutions.[26]

This typology of citizen-selves can be seen as a cross-classification of value involvement and action position (Almond and Verba, 1965: 21; Thompson, Ellis and Wildavsky, 1990: 219, 247–8).[27] Value involvement concerns accepting the value position of the dominant political regime, which ranges from allegiance to apathy and alienation. The citizen's affectual relationship to the regime is consequently an important and defining dimension of the typology (e.g. incorporated and deferential citizens identify with the regime, whereas activist and cynical citizens oppose it). The regime may benefit or repress the marginal and opportunistic citizens, but they have little value involvement and more apathy toward the regime. Action position refers to behavior including active participation, deferential subjection, and inactive domination or disability. Citizenship activity ranges from little to extensive participation (Verba, Schlozman and Brady, 1996; Verba and Nie, 1972; Janoski, Wilson and Musick, 1997).

Multilayered Citizenship Identities in Politics

Another approach to citizen identity views individuals constructing identities from social interaction in groups and new social movements, which are themselves fundamentally centered upon identity. In this sense, identity explains political action rather than identity being a consequence of economic or other social positions. Primordial loyalties or ascriptive categories – gender, ethnicity, race, idigeneity, and physical or mental challenges – become fundamental political identifiers. This does not mean the identity processes are automatic, but it does imply that they are strongly felt and can be relatively easily mobilized. There are some positions that are not necessarily ascriptive – world, cosmopolitan, religious and environmental identities – but these tend not to be the main examples of this approach and could be more easily incorporated into the prior approach.[28] And finally, there are different layers of supranational (e.g. European Union), national, state/province, and local identities that offer formal governmental and/or regional loyalties of citizens (Heater, 1999: Chapter 5). The cultural approach is strongly connected to the new social movement literature which came out of Europe and avoided the class basis of earlier social movement theories. New social movements are predicated on the centrality of identity rather than a class position in the mode of production (Herb and Kaplan, 1999; Teske, 1997).

The cultural approach is not essentialist but rather sees each self as nested, multiple, or multilayered from the individual's perspective (Heater, 1999: 115–54; Deveaux, 2000: 155–57), and that citizenship rights should be differentiated to match this complexity. The concept of multiple selves or the 'dynamic self' has developed within the social psychological literature since the mid-1980s as a healthy description of identity (Markus and Wurf, 1987; Oosterwegel and Oppenheimer, 1993) but it is relatively new to the aggregate level, especially concerning citizenship (Janoski, 1998, Chapter 4).[29] Using geologic metaphors, one might look at this self as a multilayered stratum or a conglomerate rock formed from igneous processes fusing many different minerals. The point of this complexity of the self or identity is that it leads to cultural politics where certain group loyalties (i.e. especially class) are not privileged, but negotiated in a complex way.

One major position in this approach to citizenship is the discriminatory nature of universalistic rights, which are seen to be centered upon Western, white, male, straight and class-based cultures (Young, 1990; 1997; Lister, 1990; 1991 and in this volume; Dietz, 1985, 1992; England, 1993; Fraser, 1987; Hernes, 1987; Minow, 1990, Vogel, 1991). These previously dominant cultures are seen as being largely incompatible with the emerging identity approaches of various ethnic, gender, cultural, and multiracial minorities. As a result, these identities can never be subsumed under universalistic rights and require special or particularistic rights to secure their group's central identities. As mentioned in the earlier section on categorical rights, the strongest claim for the existential priority of identity in this approach is best seen with indigenous peoples whose very acceptance of a Western concept of property rights violates their sense of shared or unowned space (Isin and Wood, 1999; Kymlicka, 1995; Anaya, 1997).

This approach to identity challenges the universalistic foundations of citizenship, not with a complete frontal assault on universality, but with a compromise position of differentiated universalistic and particularistic rights to match the highly differentiated and complex identities of multiethnic and multicultural societies. Globalization and increased immigration have helped create this cultural complexity. Marshallian approaches to citizenship use universalistic rights to combat obvious and direct injustices, and then employ immunities and compensation to deal with past residues of unequal results. The cultural approach redefines immunities and compensation into categorical (i.e. cultural rights) that they believe will more strongly defend and promote these threatened identities. Much of this approach needs to be worked out further in terms of avoiding a theory that assumes strongly bounded groups that would then claim these special rights in a pluralistic society (Deveaux, 2000: 154–65).

CONCLUSION

In the twenty-first century, the political foundations of citizenship are and will be more contested than during the last century. As politics in Foucaultian and postmodern theory has come to see power everywhere (Torfing, 1999; Dyrberg, 1997), theories of citizenship have expanded from the state-citizen relationship to everything citizens might do to change their circumstances whether or not the state is involved (Isin and Wood, 1999: 4). Politics in a Marshallian lens may restrict the term to activities more directly related to the states' monopoly on legitimate violence, and in so doing, nests citizenship within a social system as a protection against markets/capitalism and various culturally dominant groups.

While some may see this as the cyclical generation of new social theories, what is at stake is more important. Ideas form the foundations of political regimes who use the state to implement policies to promote and protect the wide diversity of peoples. The Marshallian approach with its universalistic rights made more sensitive to differences with contingent and compensatory rights has provided a useful approach to advance the rights and protect many citizens from abuses from civil society (e.g. the Klu Klux Klan or neo-Nazi groups) and the state (e.g. the police). And to a certain degree, cultural rights can be successfully applied to separable national groups such as the Nunavit nation in Canada and Maori in New Zealand. But when and if the cultural approach of differentiated rights is applied through law and state bureaucracies, it may very well achieve some greater protections for non-separable minorities, but will it create a governable system of rights that will also satisfy majorities and the 'non-grouped'? What applies to the Inuit in the Arctic may not work with women and other ethnic minorities who do not want a separate legal system. The challenge to citizenship theories in the future is not an all-or-nothing choice of group or individual rights, but rather the complex *bricolage* of both approaches that will work in a system of legitimate rights (Martin, 1993; Gewirth, 1996).

On the other hand, there is a certain complementarity between the two approaches. Marshallian citizenship theory focuses on interest groups and the state's creation of citizenship rights. Cultural approaches focusing on identity are much more concerned with the formation and operation of social movements, and skipping a level, globalization and international civil society. The strengths of each approach tend to the weaknesses of the other, and with further development both can be fruitfully combined to provide a comprehensive explanation of citizenship. Along with citizenship rights as being connected to the state, theories of civil society also need to be developed to provide the informal aspects of citizenship integrating both the public and private spheres. The end result would be a stronger foundation of the rights and obligations of citizenship.

NOTES

1 Many feminist and other multicultural authors question 'universality' as an operative aspect of citizenship (Isin and Wood 1999: 3, 36–45; Singer, 1999: 170–1; Lister 1997: 3–9, 66–90; Young 1990: 156–83). They speak of differentiated citizenship, group-differentiated citizenship, multilayered citizenship, cosmopolitian citizenship, and so forth. Universality may be present to varying degrees for a citizenship theory to work. Removing universality from the definition results in what Wexler (1990) calls 'the death of citizenship' (i.e. one is no longer talking about 'citizenship'). While using 'universality' in this definition, our chapter will be sensitive to the interrogation of 'universality' by many authors. This is mainly because we do not see universal and group rights in an inherently mutually exclusive relationship. Singer sees support for this: 'Despite the severity of the critiques of universalism, many are still wedded to a reformulation of citizenship ... [and] reluctant to forgo the political and moral power of appeal to the ideas of equality and universality...' (1999: 171).

2 The Romans extended citizenship first to the plebeians of Rome, then to conquered peoples, and finally to the vast majority of male imperial subjects with the edict of Caracalla. Only women and the underclass were excluded (Nicolet, 1988, 1993; Sherwin-White, 1939; Reisenberg, 1992). From a different direction, group rights were developed quite extensively under the Ottoman Empire, but this was not generally considered to be a political system of citizenship (Kymlicka, 1995: 183, 156–8; Davison, 1982; Findley, 1982).

3 One exception to this statement to be discussed in the next few pages are immunities to specific laws as compensation for systematic violations of citizenship rights in the past. Another rather systemic exception occurs in cultural approaches to citizenship, which will be discussed shortly.

4 Writers on citizenship have to be careful about this type of right when referring to group rights. Any organization can create group rights for their own internal norms and these can even be enforced by the state as a contract. However, when the state creates rights for specific groups, this is an entirely different matter. The section on universalistic and group rights will discuss these distinctions further.

5 Some claims can never be citizenship rights. Peoples may have personal or group 'customs' or 'moral imperatives' but they lack universal application and legitimation (Giddens, 1987: 320). Many enacted policies or programs may entail rights, but they may not be universalistic or guaranteed in any way. Hence, they also are not citizenship rights.

6 Our position toward citizenship takes a social science perspective embracing an empirical position, which leaves it closer to the legal realist or positive law perspective. Nonetheless, any group in claiming rights can invoke natural rights claims or rhetoric, and this would be part of an appropriate ideological analysis.

7 This chapter uses civil rights as synonymous with legal rights; consequently, political rights are excluded from this category. Some authors use civil rights to refer to both.

8 Hohfeld is used in sophisticated discussions of rights, and Sumner states that 'the beginning of wisdom ... [on rights]... lies in Wesley Hohfeld's celebrated classification of "fundamental legal conceptions"' (1987: 18). John Commons used Hohfeld in his book *The Legal Foundations of Capitalism* as have more recent rights theorists such as John Rowan (1999).

9 A number of noted theorists cannot seem to conceptualize rights beyond liberties (Rawls, 1971, Benn and Peters, 1959: 72, 93; Dworkin, 1977; Nozick, 1974). They largely ignore Hohfeld's clarification of rights. Liberties are assumed to be open to the extent that they can be achieved unilaterally, while Hohfeld's claims, powers, and immunities cannot. However, no right is totally unilateral because even liberties are limited when they conflict with other people's liberties *and* where they require societal enforcement and group support mechanisms. Liberal legal theorists like Nozick (1974), Dworkin (1977), and Mead (1986) often ignore, downplay, or subordinate Hohfeld's multilateral rights. Hart (1983: 217) summarizes two of these positions: 'For Nozick the supreme value is freedom – the unimpeded individual will; for Dworkin it is equality of concern and respect ...' Though their theories may differ on many counts, their focus is on atomistic individual rights (Wolgast, 1987: 12–18), which biases their analysis of rights in the direction of liberties away from claims and powers.

10 See Shapiro (1986) and Wellman (1985, 1995, 1997) for an extended discussion on rights in liberal theory.

11 Warren defines social democratic or expansive democratic theory to include: '...participatory democracy, democratic socialism, and the more radical strains of liberal democracy that stem from Rousseau, John Stuart Mill, T.H. Green, and John Dewey (1992: 9). These theories want increased participation in democratic decision-making in small scale and mass settings.

12 Of course, rights to an abortion may be and are universalistically denied in some countries.

13 We call them categorical rights because group-rights fit into too many different conceptions of rights (e.g., contingent and organizational rights). Also categorical rights apply to citizens who often (but not always) have a common sense of culture but do not always belong to an interest group or organization (i.e. there is no actual 'group' to which they are connected). Similarly, cultural rights could be perceived as the symbolic expression of culture in parades, dress, and so forth, and miss the collective aspect of categorical rights.

14 On achieving various forms of women's rights, see Cook (1994), Flanz (1983), Frevert (1988), Hernes (1987), Hoff-Wilson (1991), Lawson (1992), Smith (1997), Minow (1990), Mouffe (1993c), Skocpol (1992), Stetson (1987), Wenig (1995), Young (1990). On disability

groups, see Morgan (1984), Driedger (1989), Rothman (1982), Sailor et al. (1989), and Shapiro (1993). For ethnicity and race, see Feagin and Feagin (1996), Freeman (1979), Green (1995), Hammar (1985, 1990), Horowitz (1997), Morris (1984), Shklar (1991), Smith (1997), Waters (1990, 2000), and Wilson (1978).

15 Kymlicka is clearly an exceptional liberal. In some ways, many would dispute whether that term applies, but he himself uses it. Isin and Wood (1999: 56–62) agree with his embedding of citizens in a culture, but disagree with his reliance on Quebec in Canada as his major example. This is because it leads to a binary relationship between only two cultures that are clearly geographically defined, and because in many ways French-Canadians in Quebec are hardly the powerless minorities that many other ethnic and sexual groups might be. For instance, his position is clearly more generous to large and bounded groups than to intermixed sexual groups, and much more friendly to French than Muslim cultures and communities. Within liberal theory, Deveaux (2000: 127–37) criticizes what she calls Kymlicka's perfectionist reasoning that leads him to base the primary good of cultural embeddedness under the highly liberal (and somewhat surprising) value of increasing autonomy. She would rather see cultural rights upheld by community deliberation and democracy rather than autonomy (2000, 138–79). There are many other critiques of his positions, but they lead further into the intricacies of liberal theory.

16 See the conflicts between English-speaking groups in French-speaking Quebec over the use of English signs, and native language signs (e.g. Bengali) versus the use of English or Hindi in India (Maxitzen, 1987).

17 The exception to this is an ethnic group that is dispersed throughout a nation, which would be swamped in any one regional or local council.

18 Most of the legal and political rights data come from Humana (1992) and are for 1991, but the summary measures in columns 1 and 5 come from Freedom House (1999) and are for the year 1998.

19 This variation concerning the voting of felons may have some connections to the recent high level of incarcerations in the USA and to the earlier problem concerning African-Americans' right to vote in the Southern states, which was purportedly corrected by the federal Voting Rights Act of 1964.

20 This chapter does not consider the personhood of nature or the environment because these concepts have no direct connection to human beings (Etzioni, 1993: 8–9; Turner, 1986b: 9). For such objects to have citizenship, they would have to have a self and the capacity to carry out rights and responsibilities. Inanimate objects simply do not act, and botanical organisms require total human representation. The citizenship of rocks and sky are derivative of human citizenship issues of health, safety, and a spiritual environment.

21 Within this category, however, there is a complication, which is somewhat analogous to the deserving and non-deserving poor. This is between the people with natural, accidental, and self-inflicted impairments. In societies that grant the disabled rights, persons born with naturally occurring or accidental disabilities are afforded the full range of rights and benefits with little question. Persons born of conditions that appear to be volitional on their parents' part – drug-induced or careless action – have a more difficult time. Some citizens will fault the parent, but not the offspring. However, persons who are the cause of their own impairments, whether it be through chronic drug use or extraordinarily reckless behavior, have the least successful claims for benefits. Or if they are successful, backlash results. The question is not new, and Tocqueville comments that '(n)othing is so difficult to distinguish as the nuances which separate unmerited misfortune from an adversity produced by vice' ([1845–40] 1969: x). Many citizens will see the reckless person as violating obligations to prudent behavior, and although these impaired persons may be afforded rights, they will be given at a minimum and grudgingly.

22 This statement clearly relies on liberal theory. Communitarian theory would reject this statement, and would probably reverse it. Nonetheless, it is a more defensible position to build from individual civil rights than from group rights (see Martin, 1993; Wellman, 1985).

23 Explanations of citizenship have been promised by theories and studies of civil society. For the most part, they are still in the development stage. Alexander (1998), Curtis et al. 1992, and Janoski (1998) have done the most to operationalize many of these concepts. On the more theoretical approach, see Cohen and Arato (1992), Habermas (1989, 1996), Hall (1995), Keane (1987a, b; 1988a, b), Kumar (1993) Pateman (1979, 1983), Rawls (1999), Sales (199), Seligman (1992), Taylor (1990, 1989), and Welch (2000).

24 This typology comes from expanding 'working class images of society' (Bulmer, 1975; Lockwood, 1975; Goldthorpe et al., 1969) and Almond and Verba's (1965) classification of citizens. It can be seen in more detail in Janoski (1998, Chapter 4).

25 This typology is based on Almond and Verba (1965), Bulmer (1975), Devine (1992), Dufty et al. (1969), Lane and O'Dell (1978), and Lockwood (1975). There are other typologies. Leca (1990: 159–61) develops a different typology consisting of activist (military), civil, participative and private citizenship. Verba and Nie's (1972) typology includes inactives, voting specialists, parochial participants, communalists, campaigners, and complete activists. However, their typology focuses only on political rights, and mixes dimensions (i.e. political activity in voting, containing and campaigning with level of activity of cosmopolitans and locals. Parry, Moyser and Day's typology is based on almost inactives, just voters, collective activists, contacting activists, direct activists, party campaign activists, and complete activists (1990: 227–37). Verba, Schlozman and Brady (1993: 307) are somewhat similar, but include social participation as well in their typology: voters, canvassers, protestors, community activists, board members, campaign workers, and campaign givers.

26 The 'discovery' of the opportunistic citizen as the 'privatized worker' was based on upwardly mobile

workers moving as individuals to suburban homes and leaving their closely knit, working class communities behind (Goldthorpe et al., 1969).

27 This approach has a number of important differences from Almond and Verba (1965), who carry baggage from functionalist and modernization theory. They use 'parochial' in a way that looks more like apathy, and construct a mixed typology – parochial-subject, subject-participant, and participant-parochial (1965: 16–26). In a related work, Thompson, Ellis and Wildavsky (1990) range from full activity to inactive fatalism.

28 When religion becomes fundamentally intertwined with race, ethnicity or culture, then it is difficult to choose a religion and it falls within the ascriptive category. But inasmuch as individuals are free to choose a religion, then this is not ascriptive.

29 Of course, multiple selves have always been part of the pathological literature in terms of bipolar disorders and schizophrenia. The dynamic self is seen as a 'normal' and desirable psychological development.

We would like to thank Engin Isin for helpful comments concerning the direction and content of this chapter, and Matthew Renfro-Sargent for critical readings of a latter draft. Errors and omissions, however, remain our own responsibility.

REFERENCES

Alexander, Jeffrey (1998) *Real Civil Societies: Dilemmas of Institutionalization*. Thousand Oaks: Sage.

Almond, Gabriel and Verba, Sidney (1965) *The Civic Culture*. Boston: Little Brown.

Almond, Gabriel and Verba, Sidney (1980) *The Civic Culture Revisited*. Boston: Little Brown.

Amenta, Edwin (1993) 'The State of the Art in Welfare State Reseasrch on Social Spending Efforts in Capitalist Democracies Since 1960', *American Journal of Sociology*, 99 (3): 750–63.

Amenta, Edwin and Carruthers, Bruce (1988) 'The Formative Years of US Social Spending Policies', American Sociological Review 53 (5): 661–78.

Anaya, S. James (1997) 'On Justifying Special Ethnic Group Rights', in Ian Shapiro and Will Kymlicka (eds) *Ethnicity and Group Rights: Nomos XXXIX*. New York: New York University Press, pp. 222–31.

Andersen, Bent Rold (1987) 'The Quest for Ties between Rights and Duties,' in Adalbert Evers and Helga Nowotny, *The Changing Face of Welfare*. Aldershot, UK: Gower, pp. 166–83.

Aron, Raymond (1974) 'Is Multinational Citizenship Possible?' *Social Research*, 41: 638–56.

Bader, Veit (1995) 'Citizenship and Exclusion: Radical Democracy, Community, and Justice,' *Political Theory* 23 (2): 211–46.

Baldwin, Peter (1990) *The Politics of Social Solidarity*. Cambridge: Cambridge University Press.

Barbelet, J.M. (1988) *Citizenship*. Minneapolis: University of Minnesota Press.

Barbelet, J.M. (1993) 'Citizenship, Class Inequality and Resentment', in Bryan Turner (ed.) *Citizenship and Social Theory*. Newbury Park, CA: Sage, pp. 36–56.

Barber, Bernard (1983) *The Logic and Limits of Trust*. New Burnswick, NJ: Rutgers University Press.

Barber, Benjamin (1984) *Strong Democracy*. Berkeley: University of California Press.

Barber, Benjamin (1990) 'Service, Citizenship, and Democracy. Civil Duty as an Entailment of Civil Rights', in Williamson Evers (ed.) *National Service: Pro and Con*. Stanford: Hoover Institution Press, pp. 27–43.

Bartkus, Viva Ona (1999) *The Dynamic of Secession*. Cambridge: Cambridge University Press.

Bendix, Reinhard (1964) *Nation-Building and Citizenship*. New York: John Wiley and Sons.

Benn S. and Peters R.S. (1959) *Social Principles and the Democratic State*. London: Allen-Unwin.

Berry, Jeffrey, Portney, Kent and Thomson, Ken (1993) *The Rebirth of Urban Democracy*. Washington, D.C.: Brookings Institution.

Blackburn, Robert (1993) *Rights of Citizenship*. London: Mansell.

Bohman, James (1996) *Public Deliberation*. Cambridge, MA: MIT Press.

Bottomore, Tom (1992) 'Citizenship and Social Class, Forty Years On,' in T.H. Marshall and Tom Bottomore, *Citizenship and Social Class*. London: Pluto Press, pp. 55–93.

Bottomore, Tom (1993) 'Citizenship'. p. 75 in William Outhwaite and Tom Bottomore, *The Blackwell Dictionary of Twentieth Century Social Thought*. Oxford: Blackwell.

Bowring, Bill (1999) 'Multicultural Citizenship: A More Viable Framework for Minority Rights?' in Deirdre Fottrell and Bill Bowring *Minority and Group Rights in the New Millennium*. The Hague: Martinus Nijhoff, pp. 1–24.

Bridges, Thomas (1994) *The Culture of Citizenship*. Albany: State University of New York Press.

Brubaker, William Rogers (1992) *Citizenship and Nationhood in France and Germany*. Cambridge, MA: Harvard University Press.

Buchanan, Allen (1991) *Secession: The Morality of Political Divorce from Fort Sumter to Lithuania and Quebec*. Boulder, CO: Westview.

Buchheit, Lee (1978) *Secession: The Legitimacy of Self-Determination*. New Haven, CT: Yale University Press.

Bulmer, Martin (1975) *Working Class Images of Society*. London: Routledge and Kegan Paul.

Burstein, Paul (1998) *Discrimination, Jobs and Politics*. Chicago: University of Chicago Press.

Chambre, Susan (1998) *Good Deeds in Old Age*. Lexington, CN: D.C. Heath.

Clarke, Paul B. (1996) *Deep Citizenship*. London: Pluto Press.

Cobban, Alfred (1944) *National Self-Determination*. London: Oxford University Press.

Cobban, Alfred (1969) *The Nation State and National Self-Determination*. London: Collins.

Cohen, Jean and Arato, Andrew (1992) *Civil Society and Social Theory*. Cambridge, MA: MIT Press.

Colomer, Josep (1999) 'The Spanish 'State of Autonomies': Non-Institutional Federalism" in Paul Heywood (ed.) *Politics and Policy in Democratic Spain* London: Frank Cass, pp. 40–52.

Cook, Rebecca (1994) *The Human Rights of Women*. Philadelphia: University of Pennsylvania Press.

Corrado, Anthony, Mann, Thomas, Ortiz, Daniel, Potter, Trevor, and Sorauf, Frank (ed.) (1997) *Campaign Finance Reform: A Sourcebook*. Washington, D.C.: Brookings Institution.

Curtis, James, Grabb, Edwin, and Baer, Douglas (1992) 'Voluntary Association Membership in Fifteen Countries,' *American Sociological Review*, 52 (2): 139–52.

Dagger, Richard (1985) 'Rights, Boundaries and the Bonds of Community,' *American Political Science Review*, 79 (2): 436–47.

Dahl, Robert (1986) *Democracy, Liberty, and Equality*. Oslo: Norwegian University Press.

Dahrendorf, Ralf (1974) 'Citizenship and Beyond: The Social Dynamics of an Idea', *Social Research* 41: 673–701.

Dahrendorf, Ralf (1994) 'The Changing Quality of Citizenship', in Bart van Steenbergen, *The Condition of Citizenship*. Newbury Park, CA: Sage, pp. 10–19.

Dan-Cohen, Meir (1986) *Rights, Persons and Organizations*. Berkeley: University of California Press.

Davison, Roderic (1996) 'The *Millets* as Agents of Change in the Nineteenth-Century Ottoman Empire', in Benjamin Braude and Bernard Lewis *Christians and Jews in the Ottoman Empire: The Functioning of a Plural Society*. New York: Holmes and Meier, pp. 319–337.

Demo, David (1992) 'The Self-Concept over Time', *Annual Review of Sociology* 18: 303–26.

Deveaux, Monique (2000) *Cultural Pluralism and Dilemmas of Justice*. Ithaca: Cornell University Press.

Devine, Fiona (1992) 'Social Identities, Class Identity and Political Perspectives', *Sociological Review* 40 (2): 229–52.

Dietz, Mary (1985) 'Citizenship with a Feminist Face', *Political Theory* 13 (1):19–37.

Dietz, Mary (1992) 'Context Is All: Feminism and Theories of Citizenship', in Chantal Mouffe, *Dimensions of Radical Democracy*. London: Verso, pp. 63–85.

Donati, Pierpaolo (1995) 'Identity and Solidarity in the Complex of Citizenship', *International Sociology* 10 (3): 299–314.

Dore, Ronald (1987) 'Citizenship and Employment in an Age of High Technology', *British Journal of Industrial Relations*, 25: 202–25.

Downing, Brian (1992) *The Military Revolution and Political Change*. Princeton: Princeton University Press.

Driedger, Diane (1989) *The Last Civil Rights Movement*. New York: St. Martin's.

Dufty, N.F. (ed.) (1969) *The Sociology of the Blue Collar Worker*. Leiden: E.J. Brill.

Durham, W. Cole. (1996) 'Perspectives on Religious Liberty: A Comparative Perspective', in Johan van der Vyver and John Witte *Religious Human Rights in Global Perspective*. The Hague: Martinus Nijhoff, pp. 1–44.

Dworkin, Ronald (1977) *Taking Rights Seriously*. Cambridge, MA: Harvard University Press.

Dyrberg, Torben (1997) *The Circular Structure of Power*. London: Verso.

Eagleton, Clyde (1953) 'The Excesses of Self-Determination', *Foreign Affairs* 31 (4): 594–604.

Eliasoph, Nina (1990) 'Political Culture and the Presentation of a Political Self', *Theory and Society* 19 (4): 465–94.

England, Paula (1993) 'The Separative Self: Androcentric Bias in Neoclassical Assumptions', in Marianne Ferber and Julie Nelson (eds), *Beyond Economic Man*. Chicago: University of Chicago Press, pp. 37–53.

Esping-Andersen, Gøsta (1990) *The Three Worlds of Welfare Capitalism*. Princeton, NJ: Princeton University Press.

Etzioni, Amitai (1991) *A Responsive Society*. San Francisco: Jossey-Bass.

Etzioni, Amitai (1993) *The Spirit of Community*. New York: Crown Publishers.

Feagin, Joe and Feagin, Clairece (1996) *Racial and Ethnic Relations, Fifth Edition*, Upper Saddle River, NJ: Prentice-Hall.

Findley, Carter V. (1996) 'The Acid Test of Ottomanism: The Acceptance of Non-Muslims in the Late Ottoman Bureaucracy', in Benjamin Braude and Bernard Lewis (eds) *Christians and Jews in the Ottoman Empire: The Functioning of a Plural Society* New York: Holmes and Meier, pp. 339–368.

Fishkin, James (1993) *Democracy and Deliberation*. New Haven, CN: Yale University Press.

Fishkin, James (1994) 'The Televised Deliberative Poll: The British Experiment', Paper presented at the American Sociological Association Convention, Los Angeles.

Flanz, Gisbert (1983) *Comparative Women's Rights and Political Participation in Europe*. Dobb's Ferry, New York: Transnational.

Fleras, Augie, (1999) 'Politicising Indigeneity', in Paul Havemann (ed.) *Indigenous Peoples' Rights in Australia, Canada, and New Zealand*. Auckland: Oxford University Press, pp. 187–234.

Foucault, Michel (1979) *Discipline and Punish*. Harmondsworth, UK: Penguin.

Fraser, Nancy (1987) 'Women, Welfare and the Politics of Need Interpretation', *Hypatia* 2 (1): 103–21.

Freeden, Michael (1991) *Rights*. Minneapolis, MN: University of Minnesota Press.

Freedom House (Adrian Karatnycky et al.) (1999) *Freedom in the World: The Annual Survey of Political Rights and Civil Liberties 1998–1999*. New York: Freedom House.

Freeman, Gary (1979) *Immigrant Labor and Racial Conflict in Industrialized Societies*. Princeton, NJ: Princeton University Press.

Frevert, Ute (1988) *Women in German History*. Oxford: Berg.

Fullinwider, Robert (1988) 'Citizenship and Welfare,' in Amy Gutmann (ed.) *Democracy and the Welfare State* Princeton: Princeton University Press, pp. 261–78.

Galie, Peter (1988) 'State Courts and Economic Rights', *Annals of the American Academy of Political and Social Science* 496: 76–87.

Galston, William (1991) *Liberal Purposes*. Cambridge: Cambridge University Press.

Gerschenkron, Alexander (1966) *Bread and Democracy in Germany*. New York: Fertig.

Gewirth, Alan (1978) *Reason and Morality*. Chicago: University of Chicago Press.

Gewirth, Alan (1982) *Human Rights*. Chicago: University of Chicago Press.

Gewirth, Alan (1996) *The Community of Rights*. Chicago: University of Chicago Press.

Gibbons, John. (1999) *Spanish Politics Today*. Manchester: University of Manchester Press.

Giddens, Anthony (1982) 'Class Division, Class Conflict and Citizenship Rights,' in Anthony Giddens (ed.), *Profiles and Critiques in Social Theory*. Berkeley: University of California Press, pp. 164–80.

Giddens, Anthony (1987) *The Nation-State and Violence*. Berkeley: University of California Press.

Giddens, Anthony (1989) 'A Reply to My Critics,' in David Held and John B. Thompson (eds), *Social Theory of Modern Societies*. Cambridge: Cambridge University Press, pp. 249–301.

Glazer, Nathan (1995) 'Individual Rights Against Group Rights', in Will Kymlicka (ed.), *The Rights of Minority Cultures*. Oxford: Oxford University Press, pp. 123–138.

Glendon, Mary Ann (1991) *Rights Talk*. New York: Free Press.

Goldthorpe, John, Lockwood, David Bechhofer, Frank, and Platt, Jennifer (1969) *The Affluent Worker*. Cambridge: Cambridge University Press.

Gorham, Eric (1992) *National Service, Citizenship and Political Education*. Albany: SUNY Press.

Gostin, Larry (1995) 'Towards Resolving the Conflict,' in Larry Gostin, *Civil Liberties in Conflict*. London: Routledge, pp. 7–20.

Gray, John (1989) *Liberalisms*. London: Routledge.

Green, Leslie (1995) 'Internal Minorities and their Rights' in Will Kymlicka (ed.), *The Rights of Minority Cultures*. Oxford: Oxford University Press, pp. 257–.

Greenfeld, Liah (1992) *Nationalism: Five Roads to Modernity.* Cambridge: Harvard University Press.

Gunsteren, Herman van (1978) 'Notes on a Theory of Citizenship,' in P. Birnbaum, J. Lively, and G. Parry, (eds), *Democracy, Consensus and Social Contract*. London: Sage, pp. 9–35.

Gunsteren, Herman van (1994) 'Four Conceptions of Citizenship,' in Bart van Steenbergen (ed.), *The Condition of Citizenship*. Newbury Park, CA: Sage, pp. 36–48.

Gunsteren, Herman van (1998) *A Theory of Citizenship*. Boulder, CO: Westview.

Gutmann, Amy (1988) *Democracy and the Welfare State*. Princeton: Princeton University Press.

Habermas, Jürgen (1989) *The Structural Transformation of the Public Sphere*. Cambridge, MA: MIT Press.

Habermas, Jürgen (1994) 'Citizenship and National Identity,' in Bart van Steenbergen, *The Condition of Citizenship*. Newbury Park, CA: Sage, pp. 20–35.

Habermas, Jürgen (1996) *Between Facts and Norms*. Cambridge: Polity Press.

Hall, John H. (1995) *Civil Society: Theory, History, Comparisons*. Cambridge: Polity Press.

Halsey, A.H. (1984) 'T.H. Marshall: Past and Present 1893–1981', *Sociology* 18: 1–18.

Hammar, Tomas (1990) *Democracy and the Nation-State*. Aldershot, UK: Avebury.

Hammar, Tomas (1985) *European Immigration Policy*. Cambridge: Cambridge University Press.

Hannam, June, Auchterlonie, Mitzi and Holden, Katherine (2000) *International Encyclopedia of Women's Suffrage*. Santa Barbara, CA: ABC–CLIO.

Hart, H.L. (1983) 'Between Utility and Rights', in Marshall Cohen *Ronald Dworkin and Contemporary Jurisprudence*. Totowa, NJ: Rowman and Allanheld, pp. 214–26.

Havemann, Paul (1999) *Indigenous Peoples' Rights in Australia, Canada, and New Zealand*. Auckland: Oxford University Press.

Heater, Derek (1999) *What is Citizenship?* Cambridge: Polity Press.

Held, David (1989) 'Citizenship and Autonomy,' in David Held and John Thompson, *Social Theory of Modern Societies*. Cambridge: Cambridge University Press, pp. 162–84.

Herb, Guntrum H. and Kaplan, David (eds) (1999) *Nested Identities*. London: Rowman and Littlefield.

Hermet, Guy (1990) 'The Citizen-Individual in Western Christianity', in Pierre Birnbaum and Jean Leca, *Individualism*. Oxford: Oxford University Press, pp. 116–40.

Hernes, Helga Maria (1987) *Welfare State and Woman Power*. Oslo: Norweigian University Press.

Heywood, Paul (ed.) (1999) *Politics and Policy in Democratic Spain*. London: Frank Cass.

Hirschmann, Nancy (1992) *Rethinking Obligation*. Ithaca, NY: Cornell University Press.

Hoff-Wilson, Joan (1991) *Law, Gender, and Justice*. New York: New York University Press.

Hoffman, Daniel (1986) 'Personhood and Rights', *Polity* 19: 74–96.

Hohfeld, Wesley (1978) *Fundamental Legal Conceptions*. Westport, CN: Greenwood Press.

Horowitz, Donald (1997) 'Self-Determination: Politics, Philosophy and Law', in Ian Shapiro and Will Kymlicka (eds) *Ethnicity and Group Rights: Nomos*

XXXIX. New York: New York University Press, pp. 421–63.

Howard, Rhoda (1992) 'Dignity, Community, and Human Rights'. in A. An-Na'im *Human Rights in Cross-Cultural Perspective*. Philadelphia: University of Pennsylvania Press, pp. 81–102.

Humana, Charles (1992) *World Human Rights Guide, 3rd Edition*. New York: Oxford University Press.

Humana, Charles (1983) *World Human Rights Guide*. New York: PICA Press.

Isin, Engin and Wood, Patricia (1999) *Citizenship and Identity*. Thousand Oaks, CA: Sage.

Janoski, Thomas (1998) *Citizenship and Civil Society*. Cambridge: Cambridge University Press.

Janoski, Thomas and Glennie, Elizabeth (1995) 'The Roots of Citizenship: Explaining Naturalization in Advanced Industrialized Nations,' in Marco Martinello, (ed.), *Citizenship in the Economic Community*. Aldershot: Avebury, pp. 11–39.

Janoski, Thomas, Wilson, John and Musick, Mark (1997) 'Being Volunteered: A LISREL Analysis of Citizenship Attitudes and Behaviors as Causes of Volunteering', *Sociological Forum*.

Janzen, William (1990) *Limits on Liberty: The Experience of Mennonite, Hutterite, and Doukhobor Communities in Canada*. Toronto: University of Toronto Press.

Jones, Gill and Wallace, Claire (1992) *Youth, Family and Citizenship*. Milton Keynes, UK: Open University Press.

Kalberg, Stephen (1993) 'Cultural Foundations of Modern Citizenship,' in Bryan Turner (ed.) *Citizenship and Social Theory*. Newbury Park, CA: Sage, pp. 91–114.

Keane, John (ed.) (1987a) *Re-discovering Civil Society*. London: Verso.

Keane, John (1987b) *Socialism and Civil Society*. London: Verso.

Keane, John (1988a) *Democracy and Civil Society*. London: Verso.

Keane, John (ed.) (1988b) *Civil Society and the State*. London: Verso.

Kettner, James H. (1978) *The Development of American Citizenship, 1608–1870*. Chapel Hill: University of North Carolina Press.

Korpi, Walter (1985) 'Power Resources Approach vs. Action and Conflict', *Sociological Theory* 3: 31–55.

Korpi, Walter (1989) 'Power, Politics, and State Autonomy in the Development of Social Citizenship' *American Sociological Review* 54: 309–28.

Kriegel, Blandine (1995) *The State and the Rule of Law*. Princeton, NJ: Princeton University Press.

Kukathas, Chandran (1992) 'Are There Any Cultural Rights?' *Political Theory* 20 (1): 105–39.

Kumar, Krishnan (1993) 'Civil Society: An Inquiry into the Usefulness of an Historical Term', *British Journal of Sociology* 44 (3): 375–95.

Kymlicka, Will (1990) *Contemporary Political Philosophy*. Oxford: Clarendon Press.

Kymlicka, Will (1992) 'The Rights of Minority Cultures', *Political Theory* 20 (1): 140–46.

Kymlicka, Will (1995) *Multicultural Citizenship: A Liberal Theory of Minority Rights*. Oxford: Clarendon Press.

Kymlicka, Will (1998) *Finding Our Way*. Toronto: Oxford University Press.

Kymlicka, Will (2000) 'American Multiculturalism and the "Nations Within"', in Duncan Ivison, Paul Patton and Will Sanders (eds), *Political Theory and the Rights of Indigenous Peoples*. Cambridge: Cambridge University Press, pp. 216–36.

LaClau, Ernesto and Mouffe, Chantal (1985) *Hegemony and Socialist Strategy*. London: Verso.

Lane, David and O'Dell, Felicity (1978) *The Soviet Industrial Worker* New York: St. Martin's Press.

Lawson, Edward (1992) *Encyclopedia of Human Rights*. New York: Taylor and Francis.

Lapidoth, Ruth (1997) *Autonomy: Flexible Solutions to Ethnic Conflicts*. Washington, DC: United States Peace Institute.

Leca, Jean (1990) 'Individualism and Citizenship', in Pierre Birnbaum and Jean Leca (eds), *Individualism*. Oxford: Oxford University Press, pp. 141–89.

Levy, Jacob. (1997) 'Classifying Cultural Rights', in Ian Shapiro and Will Kymlicka (eds) *Ethnicity and Group Rights: Nomos XXXIX*. New York: New York University Press, pp. 22–66.

Lipset, Seymour Martin (1977) 'Why No Socialism in the United States?' in S. Bialer and S. Sluzar, *Radicalism in the Contemporary Age*. Boulder, CO: Westview Press, pp. 31–149.

Lipset, Seymour Martin (1981) *Political Man*. Expanded edition. Baltimore, MD: Johns Hopkins University Press.

Lipset, Seymour Martin (1994) 'The Social Requisites of Democracy Revisited' *American Sociological Review*. 59 (1): 1–22.

Lister, Ruth (1990) 'Women, Economic Dependency and Citizenship', *Journal of Social Policy* 19 (4): 445–67.

Lister, Ruth (1991) 'Citizenship Engendered', *Critical Social Policy* 32: 65–71.

Lister, Ruth (1997) *Citizenship: Feminist Perspectives*. New York: New York University Press.

Little, David (1996) 'Studying "Religious Human Rights": Methodological Foundations' in Johan van der Vyver and John Witte (eds), *Religious Human Rights in Global Perspective*. The Hague: Martinus Nijhoff, pp. 45–77.

Locke, John (1967) *Two Treatises of Government*. New York: Mentor Books.

Lockwood, David (1975) 'Sources of Variation in Working Class Images of Society,' in Martin Bulmer, (ed.), *Working Class Images of Society*. London: Routledge and Kegan Paul.

Luebbert, Gregory (1991) *Liberalism, Fascism, or Social Democracy*. Oxford: Oxford University Press.

MacIntyre, Alasdair (1981) *After Virtue*. Notre Dame, Ind: University of Notre Dame Press.

MacIntyre, Alasdair (1983) 'Moral Philosophy: What Next?', in Stanley Hauerwas and Alasdair MacIntyre, *Revisions*. Notre Dame, Ind: University of Notre Dame Press, pp. 1–15.

Mann, Michael (1986) *The Sources of Social Power*. vol. 1, Cambridge: Cambridge University Press.

Mann, Michael (1988) 'Ruling Class Strategies and Citizenship,' in Michael Mann, *States, War and Capitalism*. London: Basil Blackwell, pp. 188–209.

Mann, Michael (1994) *The Sources of Social Power*. vol. 2, Cambridge: Cambridge University Press.

Markus, Hazel and Wurf, Elissa (1987) 'The Dynamic Self-Concept: A Social-Psychological Perspective,' *Annual Review of Psychology* 38: 299–337.

Marsh, Robert (2000) 'Weber's Misunderstanding of Traditional Chinese Law', *American Journal of Sociology* 106 (2): 281–302.

Marshall, T.H. (1964) *Class, Citizenship and Social Development*. Chicago: University of Chicago Press.

Martin, Rex (1982) 'On the Justification of Rights', in G. Fløstad (ed.) *Contemporary Philosophy*. The Hague: Martinus Nijhoff, pp. 153–86.

Martin, Rex (1993) *A System of Rights*. Oxford: Clarendon Press.

Mayer, Ann Elizabeth (1999) *Islam and Human Rights: Tradition and Politics*. Boulder, CO: Westview Press.

Mead, Lawrence (1986) *Beyond Entitlement*. New York: Free Press.

Meehan, Elizabeth (1993) *Citizenship and the European Community*. Newbury Park, CA: Sage.

Melden, Abraham I. (1985) *A Theory of Rights*. Totowa, NJ: Rowman and Allanheld.

Minow, Martha (1990) *Making all the Difference*. Ithaca: Cornell University Press.

Mishra, Ramesh (1981) *Society and Social Policy*. Atlantic Highlands, NJ: Humanities Press.

Moore, Barrington (1965) *The Social Origins of Dictatorship and Democracy.* Boston: Beacon.

Morgan, Robert (1984) *Disabling America*. New York: Basic Books.

Morris, Aldon (1984) *The Origins of the Civil Rights Movement.* New York: Free Press.

Moskos, Charles C. (1988) *A Call to Civic Service.* New York: Free Press.

Moskos, Charles C. (1990) 'National Service and Its Enemies,' in Williamson Evers, *National Service*. Stanford: Hoover Institution Press, pp. 191–208.

Mouffe, Chantal (ed.) (1992) *Dimensions of Radical Democracy*. London: Verso.

Mouffe, Chantal (1993a) 'Citizenship', in Joel Krieger et al. *The Oxford Companion to Politics of the World*. New York: Oxford University Press, pp. 138–9.

Mouffe, Chantal (1993b) 'Feminism, Citizenship and Radical Democratic Politics', in Judith Butler and Joan Scott, *Feminists Theorize the Political*. New York: Routledge, pp. 367–84.

Mouffe, Chantal (ed.) (1993c) 'Introduction: For an Agonistic Pluralism', in Chantal Mouffe (ed.), *The Return of the Political*. London: Verso, pp. 1–8.

Mouffe, Chantal (1995) 'The End of Politics and the Rise of the Radical Right', *Dissent*. Fall: 498–502.

Mouffe, Chantal (1996) 'Deconstruction, Pragmatism and the Politics of Democracy', in Chantal Mouffe (ed.), *Deconstruction and Pragmatism*. New York: Routledge, pp. 1–11.

Mouritzen, Poul (1987) 'The Demanding Citizen: Driven by Policy, Self-Interest, or Ideology?', *European Journal of Political Research* 15 (4): 417–35.

Murphy, Raymond (1988) *Social Closure*. Oxford: Clarendon Press.

Nagel, Jack (1987) *Participation*. Englewood Cliffs, N.J: Prentice–Hall.

Nash, Kate (2000) *Contemporary Political Sociology*. London: Blackwell.

Newton, Michael (1997) *Institutions of Modern Spain*. Cambridge: Cambridge University Press.

Nickel, James (1987) *Making Sense of Human Rights*, Berkeley: University of California Press.

Nickel, James (1997) 'Group Agency and Group Rights' in Ian Shapiro and Will Kymlicka (eds.) *Ethnicity and Group Rights: Nomos XXXIX.* New York: New York University Press, pp. 235–56.

Nicolet, Claude (1988) *The World of the Citizen in Republican Rome.* Berkeley: University of California Press.

Norton, Alan (1994) *International Handbook of Local and Regional Government: A Comparative Analysis of Advanced Democracies*. Brookfield, VT: Edward Elgar.

Nozick, Robert (1974) *Anarchy, State, and Utopia*. New York: Basic Books.

Oakeshott, M. (1975) *On Human Conduct*. Oxford: Oxford University Press.

Oldfield, Adrian (1990) *Citizenship and Community*. London: Routledge.

Oommen, T.K. (1997) *Citizenship, Nationality and Ethnicity*. London: Polity Press.

Oosterwegel, Annerieke and Oppenheimer, Louis (1993) *The Self-System.* Hillsdale, N.J: Lawrence Erlbaum Associates.

Packer, John (1999) 'Problems in Defining Minorities', in Deirdre Fottrell and Bill Bowring (eds), *Minority and Group Rights in the New Millennium*. The Hague: Martinus Nijhoff, pp. 223–73.

Paige, Jeffrey (1975) *Agrarian Revolution*. New York: Free Press.

Parry, Geraint (1991) 'Conclusion: Paths to Citizenship,' in Ursula Vogel and Michael Moran, (eds), *The Frontiers of Citizenship*. New York: St. Martin's, pp. 166–201.

Parry, Geraint, Moyser, George and Day, Neil (1992) *Political Participation and Democracy in Britain*. Cambridge: Cambridge University Press.

Pateman, Carole (1979) *Participation and Democratic Theory*. Cambridge: Cambridge University Press.

Pateman, Carole (1983) 'Feminist Critiques of the Public/Private Dichotomy', in S. Benn and G. Gaus. (eds). *Public and Private in Social Life*. London: Croom Helm.

Pencak, William (1984) 'Veterans' Movements', in *The Encyclopedia of American Political History*. Vol. 3, New York: Scribners, pp. 1332–47.

Pettit, Philip (1997) *Republicanism: A Theory of Freedom and Government*. Oxford: Clarendon.

Pettit, Philip (2000) 'Minority Claims under Two Conceptions of Democracy', in Duncan Ivison, Paul Patton and Will Sanders (eds), *Political Theory and the Rights of Indigenous Peoples*. Cambridge: Cambridge University Press, pp. 199–215.

Piven, Frances Fox and Cloward, Richard (1988) *Why Americans Don't Vote*. New York: Pantheon.

Pogge, Thomas W. (1997) 'Group Rights and Ethnicity', in Ian Shapiro and Will Kymlicka (eds.) *Ethnicity and Group Rights: Nomos XXXIX*. New York: New York University Press, pp. 187–221.

Portis, Edward (1985) 'Citizenship and Personal Identity', *Polity* 18: 457–72.

Putnam, Robert D. (1993) *Making Democracy Work*. Princeton, NJ: Princeton University Press.

Rawls, John (1971) *A Theory of Justice*. Cambridge, MA: Harvard University Press.

Rawls, John (1982) 'The Basic Liberties and their Priority,' pp. 1–87 in Sterling McMurrin, *The Tanner Lectures on Human Values*. Salt Lake City, UT: University of Utah Press.

Rawls, John (1993) *Political Liberalism*. New York: Columbia University Press.

Rawls, John (1999) *The Law of Peoples*. Cambridge, MA: Harvard University Press.

Raz, Joseph (1984) 'Legal Rights', *Oxford Journal of Legal Studies*. 4:1–21.

Raz, Joseph (1986) *The Morality of Freedom*. Oxford: Clarendon.

Reisenberg, Peter (1992) *Citizenship in the Western Tradition*. Chapel Hill: University of North Carolina Press.

Roche, Maurice (1992) *Rethinking Citizenship*. London: Polity Press.

Rokkan, Stein (1970) 'Nation-Building: A Review of Models and Approaches', *Current Sociology* 19 (3): 7–38.

Rokkan, Stein (1974a) 'Cities, States and Nations', pp. 73–97 in Shmuel Eisenstadt and Stein Rokkan, *Building States and Nations*. Beverly Hills, CA: Sage.

Rokkan, Stein (1974b) 'Dimensions of State Formation and Nation-Building,' pp. 562–600 in Charles Tilly, *The Formation of Nation States in Western Europe*. Princeton, NJ: Princeton University Press.

Ross, Davis (1969) *Preparing for Ulysses*. New York: Columbia University Press.

Rothman, David (1982) 'Who Speaks for the Retarded? The Rights and Needs of Devalued Persons,' pp. 8–27 in Stanley Hauerwas (ed.) *Responsibility for Devalued Persons*. Springfield, Ill.: Charles C. Thomas.

Rothschild, Joseph (1981) *Ethnopolitics, A Conceptual Framework*. New York: Columbia University Press.

Rowan, John R. (1999) *Conflicts of Rights: Moral Theory and Social Policy Implications*. Boulder, CO: Westview Press.

Rueschemeyer, Dietrich, Evelyne Huber Stephens and John D. Stephens (1992) *Capitalist Development and Democracy*. Chicago: University of Chicago Press.

Sailor, Wayne, Anderson, Jacki Halvorsen, Ann Doering, Kathy Fuller, John and Goetz, Lori (1989) *The Comprehensive Local School*. Baltimore: Paul H. Brookes.

Sales, Arnaud (1991) 'The Private, the Public and Civil Society' *International Political Science Review* 12 (4): 295–312.

Sandel, Michael (1982) *Liberalism and the Limits of Justice*. Cambridge: Cambridge University Press.

Sandel, Michael (1984) 'The Procedural Republic and the Unencumbered Self', *Political Theory* 12: 85–93.

Sandel, Michael (1996) *Democracy's Discontent*. Cambridge, MA: Harvard University Press.

Saunders Peter (1993) 'Citizenship in a Liberal Society', pp. 57–90 in Bryan Turner *Citizenship and Social Theory*. Newbury Park, CA: Sage.

Seligman, Adam (1992) *The Idea of a Civil Society*. New York: Free Press.

Selznick, Philip (1992) *The Moral Commonwealth*. Berkeley: University of California Press.

The Sentencing Project and Human Rights Watch (1998) *Losing the Vote: The Impact of Felony Disenfranchisement Laws in the United States*. New York: Human Rights Watch.

Sewell, William (1985) 'Ideologies and Social Revolutions: Reflections on the French Case', *Journal of Modern History* 57: 57–85.

Shalev, Michael (1983) 'The Social Democratic Model and Beyond', *Comparative Social Research* 6: 315–52.

Shapiro, Ian (1986) *The Evolution of Rights in Liberal Theory*. Cambridge: Cambridge University Press.

Shapiro, Joseph P. (1993) *No Pity*. New York: Random House.

Shelton, Dinah (1992) 'Subsidarity, Democracy and Human Rights,' pp. 43–54 in D. Gomian, *Broadening the Frontiers of Human Rights*. Stockholm: Scandinavian University Press.

Sherwin-White, A.N. (1939) *Roman Citizenship*. Oxford: Clarendon Press.

Shklar, Judith (1991) *American Citizenship*. Cambridge, MA: Harvard University Press.

Shotter, John (1993) 'Psychology and Citizenship: Identity and Belonging,' pp. 115–38 in Bryan Turner, *Citizenship and Social Theory* Newbury Park, CA: Sage.

Singer, Beth (1993) *Operative Rights*. Albany, NY: SUNY University Press.

Skocpol, Theda (1979) *States and Social Revolutions*. Cambridge: Cambridge University Press.

Skocpol, Theda (1992) *Protecting Soldiers and Mothers*. Cambridge, MA: Harvard University Press.

Smith, Anthony (1991) *National Identity*. Reno: University of Nevada Press.

Smith, Rogers M. (1997) *Civic Ideals: Conflicting Visions of Citizenship in US History.* New Haven: Yale University Press.

Smith-Lovin, Lynn (1993) 'Can Emotionality and Rationality be Reconciled?' *Rationality and Society* 5 (2): 283–93.

Somers, Margaret (1993) 'Citizenship and the Place of the Public Sphere', *American Sociological Review* 58: 587–620.

Somers, Margaret (1995a) 'What's Political or Cultural about Political Culture and the Public Sphere?', *Sociological Theory* 13 (2): 113–44.

Somers, Margaret (1995b) 'Narrating and Naturalizing Civil Society and Citizenship Theory', *Sociological Theory* 13 (3): 229–74.

Soysal, Yasemin (1994) *The Limits of Citizenship*. Chicago: University of Chicago Press.

Spinner, Jeff (1994) *The Boundaries of Citizenship*. Baltimore, MD: Johns Hopkins University Press.

Steenbergen, Bart van (1994) *The Condition of Citizenship*. Thousand Oaks, CA: Sage.

Stephens, John D. (1989) 'Democratic Transition and Breakdown in Europe, 1870–1939', *American Journal of Sociology* 94 (5): 1019–77.

Stephens Huber, Evelyn and Stephens John D. (1982) 'The Labor Movement, Political Power and Workers'. Participation in Western Europe', *Political Power and Social Theory* 3: 215–49.

Stern, Frederick (1957) *The Citizen Army*. New York: St. Martins.

Stetson, D. (1987) *Womens' Rights in France*. New York: Greenwood.

Stinchcombe, Arthur. (1983) *Economic Sociology*. New York: Free Press.

Stråth, Bo and Torstendahl, Ralf (1992) 'State Theory and State Development,' pp. 12–37 in Ralf Torstendahl, *State Theory and State Development*. London: Sage.

Sullivan, William (1982) *Reconstructing Public Philosophy*. Berkeley: University of California Press.

Sumner, L.W. (1987) *The Moral Foundation of Rights* Oxford: Clarendon Press.

Taylor, Charles (1990) 'Modes of Civil Society', *Public Culture*. 3 (1): 95–118.

Taylor, Charles (1986) 'Human Rights: The Legal Culture,' In UNESCO *Philosophical Foundations of Human Rights*. Paris: UNESCO.

Taylor, Charles (1989) *Sources of the Self.* Cambridge: Cambridge University Press.

Teske, Nathan (1997) *Political Activists in America*. Cambridge: Cambridge University Press.

Therborn, Göran(1977) 'The Rule of Capital and the Rise of Democracy', *New Left Review* 103: 3–41.

Therborn, Göran (1992a) 'The Right to Vote and the Four World Routes to/through Modernity,' pp. 62–91 in Rolf Torstendahl, *State Theory and State History*. Thousand Oaks, CA: Sage.

Therborn, Göran (1992b) 'Lessons from 'Corporatist' Theorizations,' pp. 24–43 in Jukka Pekkarinen, Matti Pohjola, and Bob Rowthorn, *Social Corporatism*. Oxford: Clarendon.

Thompson, Dennis (1970) *The Democratic Citizen*. Cambridge: Cambridge University Press.

Thompson, Michael, Ellis, Richard and Wildavsky, Aaron (1990) *Cultural Theory*. Boulder, CO: Westview Press.

Tilly, Charles (1990) 'Where do Rights Come From?' Center for Studies of Social Change, New School for Social Research, Working Paper Series no. 98. July.

Tilly, Charles (1991) *Coercion, Capital, and European States, AD 990–1990*. London: Blackwell.

Tocqueville, Alexis de (1968) *Democracy in America*. New York: Doubleday.

Torfing, Jacob (1999) *New Theories of Discourse*. London: Blackwell.

Turner, Bryan (1986a) *Citizenship and Capitalism*. London: Allen Unwin.

Turner, Bryan (1986b) 'Personhood and Citizenship', *Theory, Culture and Society* 3 (1): 1–16.

Turner, Bryan (1988) *Status*. Minneapolis: University of Minnesota Press.

Turner, Bryan (1990) 'Outline of a Theory of Citizenship' *Sociology* 24: 189–217.

Turner, Bryan (1993a) 'Contemporary Problems in the Theory of Citizenship,' pp. 1–18 in Bryan Turner, *Citizenship and Social Theory*. Newbury Park, CA: Sage.

Turner, Bryan (1993b) *Citizenship and Social Theory*. Newbury Park, CA: Sage.

Turner, Bryan (1994) 'Postmodern Culture/Modern Citizens,' pp. 155–68 in Bart van Steenbergen, *The Condition of Citizenship* Newbury Park, CA: Sage.

Tyler, Tom R. (1990) *Why People Obey the Law*. New Haven: Yale University Press.

United Nations (1993) *Human Development Report 1993*. New York: United Nations.

Verba, Sidney and Nie, Norman (1972) *Participation in America*. New York: Harper and Row.

Verba, Sidney, Kay Lehman Schlozman and Henry Brady (1996) *Voice and Equality*. Cambridge, MA: Harvard University Press.

Vogel, Ursula (1991) 'Is Citizenship Gender-Specific?' pp. 58–85 in Ursual Vogel and Michael Moran, *The Frontiers of Citizenship*. New York: St. Martin's.

Vyver, Johan van der (1996) "Introduction: Legal Dimensions of Religious Human Rights" pp. xi–xlvii in Johan van der Vyver and John Witte *Religious Human Rights in Global Perspective*. The Hague: Martinus Nijhoff.

Wal, Koo van der (1990) 'Collective Human Rights,' pp. 83–98 in Jan Berting et al., *Human Rights in a Pluralist World*. Westport, CN: Meckler.

Waldron, Jeremy (1984) *Theories of Rights*. Oxford: Oxford University Press.

Waldron, Jeremy (1993) *Liberal Rights*. Cambridge: Cambridge University Press.

Wallerstein, Immanuel (1974) *The Modern World System*. New York: Academic Press.

Walzer, Michael (1983) *Spheres of Justice*. New York: Basic Books.

Walzer, Michael (1989) 'Citizenship', pp. 211–19 in Terence Ball, James Farrand and Russell Hanson, *Political Innovation and Conceptual Change*. Cambridge: Cambridge University Press.

Walzer, Michael (1990) 'The Communitarian Critique of Liberalism', *Political Theory* 18 (1): 6–23.

Warren, Mark (1992) 'Democratic Theory and Self-Transformation' *American Political Science Review* 86 (1): 8–23.

Waters, Mary (2000) *Black Identities: West Indian Immigrant Dreams and American Realities*. Cambridge: Harvard University Press.

Waters, Mary (1990) *Ethnic Options: Choosing Ethnic Identities in America*. Berkeley: University of California Press.

Weale, Albert (1991) 'Citizenship Beyond Borders,' pp. 155–64 in Ursula Vogel and Michael Moran *The Frontiers of Citizenship*. New York: St. Martin's.

Weber, Max (1978) *Economy and Society*. Berkeley: University of California Press.

Welch, Claude (2000) *NGOs and Human Rights*. Philadelphia: University of Pennsylvania Press.

Wellman, Carl (1985) *A Theory of Rights*. Totowa, N.J.: Rowman and Allanheld.

Wellman, Carl (1995) *Real Rights*. New York: Oxford University Press.

Wellman, Carl (1997) *An Approach to Rights*. Dordrecht: Kluwer Academic.

Wenig, Mary M. (1995) 'Marital Property and Community Property,' pp. 442–48 in David Levinson, *Encyclopedia of Marriage and the Family*. New York: Macmillan/ Simon and Schuster.

Wexler, Philip (1990) 'Citizenship in the Semiotic Society,' pp. 164–75 in Bryan Turner, *Theories of Modernity and Post-Modernity*. Newbury Park, CA: Sage.

Wilson, William Julius (1978) *The Declining Significance of Race*. Chicago, IL: University of Chicago Press.

Wolgast, Elizabeth (1987) *The Grammar of Justice*. Ithaca, NY: Cornell University Press.

Wood, John (1981) 'Secession: A Comparative Analytical Framework' *Canadian Journal of Political Science* 14: 107–34.

Wuthnow, Robert (1989) *Communities of Discourse*. Cambridge, MA: Harvard University Press.

Young, Iris (1990) *Justice and the Politics of Difference*. Princeton: Princeton University Press.

Young, Iris (1997) 'Deferring Group Representation' pp. 349–76 in Ian Shapiro and Will Kymlicka (eds.) *Ethnicity and Group Rights: Nomos XXXIX*. New York: New York University Press.

3

Economic Citizenship: Variations and the Threat of Globalisation

ANTHONY WOODIWISS

By the middle of the nineteenth century the liberal economic rights to own property, make contracts and to work – in the sense of choose one's occupation – were regarded as basic civil rights throughout much of Western Europe and North America. By the end of the same century the gradual enfranchisement of the propertyless allowed these civil rights to be augmented and indeed qualified by variously configured rights to collective organisation and bargaining. The latter rights 'created … secondary system[s] of industrial citizenship' (Marshall, [1949] 1994; see also: Black, 1984; Katznelson and Zolberg, 1986; van der Linden and Price, 2000) which were then used in conjunction with political rights to establish equally variously configured sets of social and other economic rights during the twentieth century (Esping-Andersen, 1990; Mann, 1993; Stephens, 1979). In other words, economic rights have been both basic and central to the development of citizenship. It is therefore both unsurprising and particularly disturbing that they are the rights that are most directly threatened by the neo-liberalism that purports to guide the current moves in the direction of globalisation.

Given the space available, it is not possible to discuss the full range of economic rights, especially because I wish to argue comparatively. For this reason, and also because, up to now at least, they have been the major point of articulation within the overall system of economic rights, I will focus on the 'secondary system[s] of industrial citizenship' and the variable nature of the collective labour rights that underpin them.[1] This said and precisely because of their articulatory function, I will relate collective labour rights back, so to speak, to property and contractual rights and forward to social rights, at least in a schematic fashion. More specifically, I will relate the development of labour rights both back to the changing nature of the relations of possession, control and title that define the internal structure of property ownership, and forward to the social rights that have in some ways compensated labour for the limited nature of the constraints on property owners in capitalist societies.[2]

The point I wish to emphasise is that contemporary labour rights and therefore the forms of economic citizenship vary greatly. Thus, without explaining the origins of this typology (but see Woodiwiss, 1998: 48), they may take the form, primarily but never exclusively, of liberties (as in the American case), immunities (as in the British case), powers, for example, to take issues to various adjudicatory or policy-making bodies (as in the

Australian, French and many Western European cases), or claims to, for example, certain labour standards, job security and social entitlements (as in the Japanese, Singaporean and, again, many Western European cases).

These different forms of labour rights relate to the three dimensions of property rights in the following ways:

(a) They may alter the balance with respect to the economic possession of the means of production to labour's advantage by granting certain liberties to bargain over the terms of employment, and/or by inscribing certain claims within the conditions governing the hiring of labour and therefore the validity of the employment contract. The latter are generally referred to as 'labour standards' and include rules governing the payment of wages, rest periods, and holidays. Such aspects of collective labour law may also affect possessory power pertaining to the permissibility or otherwise of the closed shop. Finally, the promulgation or inscription of such liberties and/or claims may or may not also be accompanied by the granting to labour of participative powers of one kind or another with respect to the setting of such standards.

(b) They may alter the balance with respect to political or disciplinary control of the means of production to labour's advantage in three ways: first, by granting certain liberties to bargain over the conditions of employment and/or by inscribing certain claims within the employment contract in the form of those aspects of 'labour standards' that refer to workplace rules; second, by limiting the contract's purview through specifying certain additional liberties which may allow its temporary suspension for bargaining purposes; third, by specifying in workplace rules and/or the employment contract certain claims that allow for the exercise of powers of one kind or another which afford varying degrees of co-determination as well as the adjudication of disputes by tripartite tribunals or mutually agreed third parties.

(c) They may alter the balance with respect to title to the means of production to labour's advantage by granting certain liberties to bargain over ownership and/or by inscribing various claims within property, company and taxation law in order to achieve such as profit-sharing, employee share-ownership, nationalisation, and/or distribute social benefits of one kind or another. Again, the granting of such liberties and/or the inscription of such claims may or may not be accompanied by the granting of certain participative powers to labour at the enterprise and/or national levels.

Perhaps the best-known attempt to give a narrative form to or periodise the development of labour's economic rights and their relationship to the wider society is that produced by Franz Neumann in the 1920s and introduced to an English-speaking audience by Otto Kahn-Freund in the 1940s. According to Neumann and to Kahn-Freund (1944; see also Jacobs, 1986), labour law systems typically pass through three phases – repression, toleration and recognition – reflecting the developing but never complete equalisation of class balances.[3] As all who have used this periodisation have pointed out, if applied too mechanically it is an excessively evolutionistic as well as optimistic and even Anglo-centric narrativisation. Nevertheless, when shorn of its teleological associations and as I will show below, it remains useful as a means of summarising the nature of and the differences between particular conjunctures.

In order to reduce the likelihood of repetition as well as to provide at least a tacit acknowledgement of certain critical differences with respect to levels of development, social structures and transnational conditions of existence, I will divide my highly schematic discussion of histories and systems into three groups: first, the early industrialisers (Britain, the United States and France); second, the first wave of 'late' industrialisers (Sweden, Canada, Australia, and Japan); and third, the post-1945 industrialisers (Argentina and Brazil).

LIBERAL DEMOCRACY, SOCIALISM AND LABOUR RIGHTS

The first laws specifically applied to capitalist wage labour in Britain and its former colony the United States were the British Combination Acts of 1799 and 1800. Far from altering any of the employment balances to labour's advantage, and despite their provisions relating to compulsory arbitration (labour had no say in the choice of arbitrators), these Acts generalised some earlier, more narrowly targeted punitive statutes. Thus their desired effect was the prevention of combinations of labourers from organising and acting to enhance their positions with respect to possession and control and therefore undermining the prerogatives of title with respect to the disposition of any surplus arising from production. The partial repeal of the Combination Acts thanks to an 1825 Act in Britain and an 1842 decision by Massachusetts Justice Lemuel Shaw (*Commonwealth* v. *Hunt*) in the United States meant that what unions there were (there were far fewer in both countries in the second quarter of the nineteenth century than there had been in the first) no longer committed a criminal offence by their simple existence. However, not only did the increased tempo of industrialisation and recurrent recessions make it difficult for them to survive, but they also found that their freedom to bargain over wages and conditions made little difference to their possessory or control positions. This was because they lacked any legal means of exerting pressure on employers since picketing and striking, for example, were most often found by judges to instance the 'violence', 'threats', 'molestation', 'intimidation', or 'obstruction' still forbidden by the 1825 Act and the Massachusetts decision. Moreover, when unions did begin to reappear in the 1850s in Britain, individual strikers knew that they could easily be prosecuted for breach of contract. Interestingly, this was not quite the case when unions reappeared in the 1870s in the United States where a rather different, newer and more obviously ideological fault, which I have termed 'breach of freedom of contract', had first to be invented (Woodiwiss, 1990b: 42ff., 89ff.) Contra Karen Orren (1991), this seems to have been necessary because of the more expansive meaning given to contractual freedom during the first three quarters of the nineteenth century in that much less feudal society.

However, the brief juridical hiatus that waiting on this development produced provided only some short-lived and cold relative comfort to American trade unionists. Their British counterparts were by then enjoying the new freedoms granted by the Trade Union Act (1871) and the Conspiracy and Protection of Property Act (1875), whilst they themselves were about to become the victims of 'government by injunction'. The British Acts for the first time gave unions some financial security, positively sanctioned their non-violent resort to strikes and picketing, and therefore allowed them certain liberties to contest capital's possessory and control positions. Thus British labour law entered the phase that Kahn-Freund termed 'toleration' in that labour was allowed to seek such alterations to the balances between itself and capital as its industrial muscle allowed. In the event such alterations were minimal because of a whole host of wider social-structural conditions that prevented labour from taking immediate advantage of its liberties. What is more, the liberties themselves soon lost much of their allure since under certain, far from rare conditions they could result in the bankrupting of a union. This was because of the judicial development of civil liability in tort with respect to trade disputes, as a result of which unions could be sued for damages by companies that suffered as a result of their actions.

However, by the time of the House of Lords' Taff Vale judgment of 1901, which confirmed the legality of such suits, the wider social-structural conditions had changed still more but this time to labour's advantage. Unions had spread beyond their traditional constituency of skilled workers to organise many of the unskilled as well as the new category of the semi-skilled. But perhaps most importantly labour had become a political force that warranted respect. Hence the passage of the 1906 Trade Disputes Act, which initiated the phase of recognition not by the grant of any more explicitly or rigorously defined liberties but rather by the grant of immunities with respect to what would otherwise be regarded as actionable wrongs. Up to the present the alterations to local workplace balances between labour and capital produced by the resulting system of 'collective laissez-faire' have varied according to the scope subsequently allowed to the immunities. These variations have occurred according to a rhythm determined by labour's variable access to political power. They have also been accompanied by a similarly determined ebb and flow of statutory claims inscribed within individual employment contracts and government social policies as well as participative powers in national tripartite bodies. The latter, like the economically determined alterations, were largely restricted to possessory relations but did sometimes relate to proprietary relations when questions of taxation, nationalisation and privatisation were at issue.

By contrast, American labour law slipped back from a phase that has been characterised as one of 'reluctant tolerance' (Lieberman, 1950) to one of repression, thanks to the rise of the labour injunction in the last quarter of the nineteenth century. Although this device was made possible by very similar juridical developments to those which made a trade dispute a possible occasion of civil injury in Britain, it was more directly repressive in that to disobey such an injunction carried the threat of imprisonment for contempt of court, and it could be invoked during or even before a dispute took place rather than afterwards as in the case of the British tort action. Thus when invoked it instantly negated all liberties, since as a judicial order to 'cease and desist' it had its effect at the level of control relations. This negation had particularly inequitable consequences because the constitutional backing that the American courts gave to their own law-making meant that they had been able to strike down any legislative efforts to inscribe any possessory claims in contracts of employment. Moreover, because of the wider social-structural differences between the United States and Britain – a narrowly based labour movement, an ethnically and racially divided labour force, and a minimal labour presence in politics – which also contribute something to the explanation for judicial supremacy, this assault on labour's liberties did not initiate the successful counter movement that it did in Britain.

In the absence of such a response, labour was left to make what use it could of its fragile liberties, which was not much. In contrast to Britain, these liberties were eventually explicitly defined but not because labour demanded this. Rather, they were a grudgingly accepted gift from a politically needy but neither socialist nor even labourist Democratic Party. Unsurprisingly, the courts rapidly restricted the ambit of the liberties that the Wagner Act (1935) had granted to the sphere of possessory relations. A rapidly produced doctrine of the 'managerial prerogative' meant that most control issues were non-negotiable, whilst labour's lack of political clout meant that few claims were statutorily inscribed within employment contracts. In addition, labour's non-socialist character meant that it sought few if any participative powers and title has seldom been a public issue even under the heading of taxation, since there was no demand for the state to distribute any more than a minimum of social benefits that is now fast approaching vanishing point. This said, title has proved to be a local or private issue in an increasing and now significant number of companies as they seek either increased capitalisation or escape from bankruptcy during recessions through the establishment of Employee Share Ownership Plans (ESOPS). However, the legal enforceability of collective contracts, the fact that they include as bargained claims on the company many of the items that are statutorily defined social claims on the state in Britain, as well as no-strike and arbitration clauses, mean that the conditions under which even possessory liberties can be asserted through industrial action of any kind have become very limited – too much is at risk.

Startlingly, as Katherine Stone (1999) has made clear, the availability of union-negotiated claims on companies now excludes their recipients from access to the now apparently increasing quantum of statutorily established possessory claims. The latter are therefore not an automatically inscribed set of minima in all employment contracts to be improved upon through collective negotiation as is the case in Western Europe. Instead, they function as an incentive to de-unionisation and therefore to the sacrificing of any remaining collectively exercisable liberties to challenge even capital's possessory power.

Turning to France, one encounters a history where the central state plays a far more important role in societal governance than in either the United States or Britain. As a consequence the critical modality of employment relations is that of politics or control, whilst the critical modality of legal regulation is that of powers or what the French call 'police' rather than liberties or immunities either in themselves or as the source of claims in individual or collective contracts. What is significant in the present context is not so much that, as it happens, this has been to the benefit of labour as that morphologically the history of labour rights in France is more or less the mirror image of that of the United States. One sign and indeed a major facilitator of the greater role of the state in France is the codified and rational nature of the legal system. This, however, does not mean that a phase of toleration or indeed ambiguity is absent from the history of French collective labour law any more than it is absent from the history of French industrial relations. Indeed the willingness and indeed inability or unwillingness of the state to exercise its power has meant that the history of French labour rights is a history of ambiguity.

Thus, although the period 1791 to 1864 may be clearly defined as one of repression, this does not mean that liberty of contract was sacrosanct. As Bernard Edelman (1979) has made particularly clear, private property is the core assumption of the Civil Code, and as Norbert Olszak (1999) has explained, this meant that for a long time there was no way in which collective action could be recognised as legal. This said, from the beginning the state allowed the possibility that if it so wished it could continue to exercise its power to inscribe certain claims in some individual contracts of employment where safety or some national interest might be at stake. It was also willing to delegate some of its powers to 'boards of masters and men' in order to regulate wages, which it did with widely varying degrees of success. However, even the state was not entirely free to decide on either the disposition or range of its power. And even after the commencement of the recognition phase in 1884, the courts refused to accept that terms agreed in the course of collective bargaining automatically applied to the individual contracts of those covered by the negotiations.

Because of labour's political weight, as in Britain and in contrast to the United States, and in the absence of a juridical solution, a legislative solution to this problem was provided by laws passed in 1906, 1919 and 1920 which in the end extended any benefits won in negotiations to the entire labour force of the enterprises concerned. As a result of the Matignon Accords negotiated under the Popular Front Government in 1936, the scope of negotiations and their applicability were both hugely extended so that they became sectorally and/or geographically binding. However, in 1938 the state reasserted its interest in the outcomes of such otherwise private negotiations in a way which paved the way for the establishment of the Vichy government's corporatism.

In 1950, the 1936 system was restored and in 1971 it was given an even more robust foundation by the declaration that collective labour rights were at base individual rights. The latter change has given a new emphasis to local bargaining as the regional and sectoral institutions created by the delegation of state power have apparently atrophied or become moribund. In sum, looking backwards from the present, the French trajectory has been the reverse of that in the US; that is, it has been a movement from a public-powers-based system to a private-liberties-based one. This said, it is important to emphasise that the result is far short of convergence. The state-inscribed claims in American employment contracts and at the level of social policy remain far, far fewer and less significant than is the case in France or even Britain. And not the least of the reasons for this is that political or control relations have nowhere near the salience for employment relations in the United States that they continue to have in Western Europe despite all the neo-liberal-inspired efforts to re-privatise not just nationalised industries but economic life as a whole.

LATE DEVELOPMENT AND LABOUR RIGHTS IN THE 'WEST'

There has even been talk of such a re-privatisation in that most social democratic of countries, Sweden. Thus far, however, there is little sign of a significant re-structuring of Swedish labour law. The history of this labour law if not the wider history of Swedish industrial relations does not include clear periods of either repression or toleration since trade unions only appeared after the promulgation of the 1866 Constitutions, which contained a general right to freedom of association. Thus Swedish unions were at no time regarded as either intrinsically criminal or, as in France, a legal impossibility, even though incitement to strike was an offence. However, despite its absolutist past, its monarchical form and its codified legal system, the Swedish state was at first very reticent about both the exercise and the delegation of its power. Thus the state acted neither to legalise nor prohibit the industrial actions that can make freedom of association into a potent industrial weapon. Nor indeed did it pass much legislation to protect vulnerable workers. Consequently, employment relations revolved around the possessory dimension and legally labour's liberties were pitted against those of capital.

Even when the state did intervene in a significant way following the December Compromise of 1906 between the unions and the employers' association, it did so in the same reticent manner; that is, by passing the Mediation Act in which the state offered but did not require the acceptance of its good offices to aid the conflicting parties in coming to an agreement. Similarly, when the Arbitration Act was passed in 1920 it too provided for a voluntary process. State compulsion entered Swedish industrial relations in 1928 when a conservative government removed contract disputes from the private to the juridical domain through the Collective Contracts Act and the Labour Court Act. In 1932 the Social Democrats began their four uninterrupted decades in power. Not only did they refuse to repeal these two Acts but also in 1936 they passed the Collective Bargaining Act, which required new unions to register with the Social Welfare Board if they were to be granted negotiating rights. The *quid pro quo* for the unions' acceptance of the diminution of their liberties represented by the juridification of most aspects of industrial relations was twofold. First, the state established a comprehensive social welfare programme, and second, it sanctioned the negotiation in 1938 of the core text within the Swedish industrial relations system, the Basic Agreement. The net result was and remains a system of labour rights still focused on possessory relations wherein the state uses its power to inscribe certain minimal claims in individual contracts and establish and maintain some rather substantial claims to social benefits, and enforces contractual agreements, whilst the parties are left free to use their liberties to bargain over the initial terms and conditions of the agreements.

In the postwar period these arrangements were augmented and indeed maintained by the state's further use of its power in a number of ways. First, in accordance with the Rehn Model of 1960, it pursued an 'active labour market policy' and so added certain claims to training and other support to the possessory equation. Second, through the Co-determination Act of 1976, it acted to allow some moves in the direction of the equalisation of control relations. And finally, through the establishment of union-administered, regional Wage Earner Funds it even allowed labour to encroach upon title (Abrahamson and Brostrom, 1980). Despite the minimal results of the last measure, much talk of economic crisis, an end to Social Democratic hegemony, and accession to the European Community, there has as yet been little movement in the direction of negotiations outside of the centralised structure established by the Basic Agreement. At present therefore, the Swedish labour law system remains uniquely favourable to the equalisation if not the dissolution of capitalist employment relations.

The evolution of Canadian labour rights provides an interesting contrast to that of Sweden in that, as in France, an initially similar post-recognition system based on powers and focused on possessory relations eventually gave way to one based on liberties. Canada remained a political colony until 1931, a legal colony for much longer, and shares a very long border and many economic links with the United States. It is therefore not surprising that the development of Canadian labour law shows many signs of British and American influence. Thus the same variably enforced repressive laws initially governed industrial relations in Canada as governed them in Britain and the United States. However, the transition to a regime of toleration occurred rather differently. Initially, the British model was followed through the passage of legislation in 1872 and 1876, but the protection offered by the Canadian legislation was even more uncertain and its range more restricted. It was more uncertain because it was only available to registered unions and many refused to register, and its range was more restricted because it did not apply to 'public works' of many kinds. Moreover, no equivalent to the 1906 Trades Disputes Act was passed to nullify the legal reasoning that resulted in the British Taff Vale judgment of 1901. Instead, an element of recognition was added to an already hybrid regime of repression and toleration through the passage of a Conciliation Act (1900) and, more important, an Industrial Disputes Investigation Act (IDIA) (1907). These were intended to and indeed often did prevent any disruption that might lead to suits for damages by making an appeal to a tripartite tribunal available to any group (that is, not necessarily a unionised one) of ten or more employees. However, in contrast to the Swedish and French cases no negotiation, let alone industrial action, was allowed prior to the commencement of conciliatory hearings. Moreover, following the 1919 General Strike in Winnipeg, the limits of legal strike action were still further restricted and therefore the attractiveness of even such a disadvantageous conciliation system was increased by changes to the provisions relating to 'sedition' in the Criminal Code. Despite a 1925 British Privy Council decision that the IDIA was unconstitutional, which meant that somewhat varying versions of it had to be re-enacted in the individual states, this system remained in place until World War II.

The first significant American contribution to the development of Canadian labour thinking came as a result of the triumph at the 1902 Trades and Labor Congress of policies inspired by the American Federation of Labor concerning the preferability of sole bargaining rights over dual unionism and voluntary over compulsory arbitration. Eventually, legislation incorporating these preferences and modelled on the Wagner

Act, the Industrial Relations and Disputes Investigation Act (1948) in its federal and state forms, replaced the IDIA and instituted a regime premised on recognition. The liberties central to this regime, now somewhat more developed as the Labor Code (1970), were later both further entrenched by the presence of indirectly supportive articles in the Charter of Rights and Freedoms (1982) and, more importantly, augmented by the establishment of a far more elaborate array of social claims than in the United States. This said, many of the latter claims are currently threatened, and far more grievously than in Sweden or France, by an ongoing process of 'privatisation'. The Canadian labour movement remains far healthier than that of the United States (Weiler, 1983). However, it is interesting to speculate that it might have been still healthier if, contrary to American-inspired trade-union verities, the conciliation system had been underpinned by strengthened liberties, which would have allowed, for example, Swedish-style prior bargaining, instead of being replaced by such liberties. Under such circumstances, 'Big Labor' (that is, in the popular mind, sectionalist and striking labour) might not have become such a bugbear, control relations might have displaced possessory ones as the critical dimension of class relations because of the political sources and institutional density of a regime based on powers, and there might therefore have been less likelihood of the disestablishment of so many social claims.

Finally, Australian developments have been in very general terms structurally similar to those in Canada except that they exhibit a very different content and temporality. As another former British settler colony, the early history of Australian labour law reflected British developments very closely in all but two major respects. First, the pace at which British statutes were received varied greatly between the different colonies into which the continent had been divided. Second, because of the exigencies created by a generalised labour shortage, the individual labour law represented by Master Servant Law appears to have been far more salient to the disciplining of labour than collective labour law for most of the nineteenth century. Thus, although collective labour law followed the same trajectory from repression to toleration as in Britain and Canada, individual employees seldom experienced this as a benefit since they continued to suffer the repressiveness of Master Servant Laws that remained effective and rather widely used until the 1890s. However, despite this unsupportive legal environment and the ravages of the Depression of the 1890s but largely because of the democratic political environment, unions not only established themselves as significant social institutions but also gained a very significant ally in the form of the Labor Party. With the sometimes ambivalent support of the unions, the Labor Party put its very considerable political weight behind the proposals for a compulsory arbitration system which were enacted from 1900 onwards. Thus recognition came to unions in Australia far earlier than in Sweden and in a far more effective form than in Canada. It took the form of the establishment of a 'powers-based' system at the Commonwealth (later Federal) and state levels which entitled unions, and only unions, to take or respond to a gradually broadened array of grievances over pay and conditions to conciliation and arbitration courts presided over by senior judges. This system only began to change in the 1990s when the Labor Party led by Paul Keating began to dismantle it in the name of a *rapprochement* with neo-liberalism supposedly made necessary by the competitive pressures attendant on globalisation.

LATE INDUSTRIALISATION, PATRIARCHALISM AND LABOUR RIGHTS

Since the concept of patriarchalism plays an important role in the remainder of the present argument, it is important that I explain what I mean by it. For Max Weber, patriarchalism was one of the elementary forms of traditional authority:

> [It] is the situation where, within a group (household) which is usually organised on both an economic and kinship basis, a particular individual governs who is designated by a definite rule of inheritance. *The decisive characteristic ... is the belief of the members that domination, even though it is an inherent traditional right of the master, must definitely be exercized as a joint right in the interests of all members and is thus not freely appropriated by the incumbent.* In order that this shall be maintained, it is crucial that in both cases there is a complete absence of a personal (patrimonial) staff. Hence the master is still largely dependent upon the willingness of the members to comply with his orders since he has no machinery to enforce them. Therefore the members are not yet really subjects. (Weber, 1978: 231, emphasis added).

For Weber, then, patriarchalism was a strictly hierarchical political structure justified by a familialist discourse and resting on an economy structured in part by kinship relations. Clearly, given the nature of contemporary state and economic formations, patriarchalism no longer has a political or economic referent. However, it seems to me that the discursive 'decisive characteristic' does have a referent. Thus I will use patriarchalism to signify a familialist discourse that, regardless of institutional context, both assumes the naturalness of inequalities in the social relations between people and justifies these by reference to the respect due to a benevolent father or father-figure.

As Sheldon Garon (1987) has pointed out, the law which initiated the postwar recognition phase and represents the core of the present Japanese labour law system, the Trade Union Law of 1949, owed as much if not more to a draft prepared by the Japanese Home Ministry's Social Bureau in 1925 than to the American Wagner Act as most previous writers on the topic have argued. In my view, the most striking consequence of this continuity which extends to the other labour laws that have defined the postwar system, notably the Labour Standards Law and Labour Relations Adjustment Law, is the significance retained by conciliatory institutions within the Japanese system of industrial relations. Thus, as in Sweden and although the system also rests on the grant of certain unambiguously specified liberties, it has become one based on powers and claims in its operation: above all, powers to require representation on the panels of the Labour Commissions that are the instruments of conciliation, as well as to refer disputes to such commissions. When combined with the broader social continuities between pre- and postwar Japan as well as the court system's preference for conciliation over adjudication, the net result has been the restoration of a transformed and very un-Swedish patriarchalism to Japanese labour law in the form of what I and others have termed *kigyoshugi* (enterprisism) (Woodiwiss, 1992: Ch. 5).

The entry of *kigyoshugi* into labour law has transformed the conception of the employment relationship in the private sector that was basic to both the New Constitution of 1946 and the 1949 Trade Union Law. That is, the American-inspired recognition of the different interests of capital and labour that was fundamental to the postwar legislation has been ever more confidently denied as the social and judicial commitment to the limited and hierarchical communitarianism of the company has grown. In a surprising and fascinating instance of transnationally inspired hybridity, it seems that, alongside *kigyoshugi*, arguments drawn from the Weimar Republic's social democratic labour law by lawyers acting for the unions played a significant role in helping the judiciary arrive at this commitment (Kettler and Tackney, 1996). In my terms, then, the period since 1949 has seen a striking reduction in the liberties of Japanese employees and unions as the control dimension of the property relation has become ever more salient within large companies, and as an anyway very prescriptive legal framework has become more and more proscriptive. The same period has also seen these reductions compensated for not only by a small increase in powers (to participate in joint consultation fora, for example) but also by very substantial increases in claims to company welfare benefits, for instance, and, most important, to an apparently irreversible claim to 'lifetime employment'.

Restricted though the numbers concretely as opposed to nominally benefiting from these claims may be, it is nevertheless important to acknowledge that, thanks to the demand for consistency inherent in legal discourse under conditions of judicial independence, successful but as yet not fully tested efforts have been made to extend the legal entitlement to 'lifetime employment' beyond the confines of the large-scale corporate sector (Schregle, 1993; Sugeno, 1992: 65, 156). Thus, in the absence of a written contract to the contrary (still a very common state of affairs in Japan), the courts will generally find an implied promise to provide lifetime employment no matter what the size of the company. Moreover, the wider legal, social-structural and cultural supports that this doctrine possesses have thus far proved robust enough to sustain it through a prolonged recession and the continuing 'hollowing out' of the economy as production has been relocated to other and sometimes lower-waged countries. Of course, many companies have sought either to reduce their exposure to the doctrine's consequences by taking on far fewer 'regular' employees, or to avoid its consequences by offering inducements (not all of them pleasant; see Salgardo, 1999) to those whom they would like to see take early retirement. However, the very fact that such measures have had to be adopted suggests both the legal strength of the position of young and mid-career regular employees and the wider ideological value of 'lifetime employment'.

However, if it is to be successful any attempt to maintain a meaningful form of economic citizenship in a patriarchalist context has to be rigorously enforced, preferably by unions as well as by the state, and therefore to involve the maintenance of certain irreducible liberties as well as labour access to political power. Here again the Japanese case is instructive and indeed South Korea has recently followed Japan in this regard (Lee, 1998). In my view the most critical of these liberties and immunities are those that protect the freedom of ordinary employees to withhold their consent without having to choose 'exit' over 'voice' (Hirschman, 1970). In other words, where one has enterprise or 'in-house' unions, as in Japan, it is essential not simply that labour rights are fundamentally employee rather than union rights, but also that, again as in Japan (Woodiwiss, 1992: 142–4), they are continuously exercisable not only vis-à-vis employers but also vis-à-vis incumbent unions through employees exercising a 'liberty' to create a second or sustain a 'minority' union. So, from labour's standpoint and contrary to 'Western' labour's experience, the possibility of dual unionism should be seen in a positive rather than in a negative light – that is, where the efficacy of the negative labour rights represented by American-style employer 'unfair labour practice' provisions are reduced, as they invariably are where there are participative structures and/or enterprise unions, it is important that this be balanced by a strengthening or a broadening of a positive right to self-organisation on the part of all employees in order to prevent the suborning of unions (see also, Leader, 1992: Ch. 10).

POST-COLONIAL DEVELOPMENT, PATRIARCHALISM AND LABOUR RIGHTS

Brazil and Argentina may both be characterised as patriarchalist, albeit of a Roman Catholic rather than Confucian variety. Thus it is not surprising that there are some striking similarities with Japan in the ways in which their labour law systems have evolved. However, there are also some equally striking differences because of their greater openness to 'Western' influences.

In Brazil during the first third of the twentieth century elements of repression and toleration co-existed within the labour law system. A sometimes unused repressive police power was combined with seldom enforced protective claims with respect to vulnerable workers. Under the Vargas regime unions with sole bargaining rights were legally recognised provided they fulfilled certain rigorous registration criteria. In return, they gained the powers associated with the right of representation on the benches of the tripartite Labor Court whilst their members gained the right to certain claims with respect to holidays and pensions as well as access to the Labor Courts. When the Vargas regime reconstructed itself on Italian fascist principles in 1937, the Labor Courts remained but strikes were totally forbidden. The unions were 'compensated' by the powers that followed from them becoming agents of political representation. The most significant of the compensations were a substantial share of the receipts of a state-imposed 'union tax' out of which unions were expected to meet various welfare claims from their members and, in 1939, a minimum wage law.

Despite Vargas' fall in 1945, little has changed formally since, although there have been significant changes in the way in which the system has been applied depending on the political complexion of the government. Many of the strikes that eventually forced a very marked liberalisation of the system's application in the 1980s, especially with respect to union autonomy, were organised outside of the 'official' unions because employees were dissatisfied with the latter's use of their powers and perhaps especially their use of the union tax with respect to the enhancement and enforcement of their claims.

Argentina's labour law system has also been indelibly marked by the patriarchalist context within which it emerged. This context meant that political or control relations rapidly gained pre-eminence amongst the ensemble of class relations as the society developed, with the result that the executive apparatuses of the state quickly became the principal location of state power and therefore object of political interest. In contrast to the Japanese and Brazilian cases but because of the relatively greater strength of the labour movement, by 1920 labour's private bargaining had gained the surprisingly positive support of a state executive which refused to deploy its repressive powers and instead provided sympathetic mediation and issued decrees favouring the labour interest. However, these gains were not juridified and institutionalised as powers or claims and proved to be very short-lived, with the result that a brief period of toleration rapidly gave way to a prolonged one of repression.

Recognition occurred only after a revived trade union movement had again succeeded in forging an alliance arising out of mutual need with elements of the executive. In 1946, the incoming Peronist government granted registered and therefore state-approved unions a combination of benefits (American-style sole bargaining rights and conditional support from the Labor Secretariat), specific liberties (organising and bargaining rights) and some vaguer participative powers. This system was legally formalised in 1953 but by then its dependence on state sponsorship had become clear, with the result that it became increasingly difficult for unions to exercise their liberties and their powers disappeared once they refused to become unquestioning clients of the executive. Succeeding periods of Peronist dictatorship, military repression, liberalisation, military repression, the restoration of Peronism, military repression, and beginning in 1983 liberalisation again have left the system remarkably unchanged formally. Instead, it has simply been in varying states and degrees of suspension. Ironically and tragically, in institutional if not industrial terms the unions have tended to do best during periods of repression, when they have become the repositories of oppositional sentiment. The result is that their leaders have tended to become self-interested political brokers rather than effective economic negotiators, able to block the construction of a new system but unable to restore the old one.

CONCLUSION

The preceding discussion makes it clear that, of the cases discussed, only the United States has a form of economic citizenship whose critical premise is a 'liberty', whilst other systems that are not only wholly justiciable but also far more effective in their contexts have been democratically approved and have as their critical premises either powers (Australia and France) or claims (Japan and Sweden). It also makes clear therefore that whilst the major failings of the less effective or otherwise flawed systems (Argentina and Brazil) relate to limitations on freedom of association, this does not necessarily mean that they should be reconstructed on American lines but most likely that the existing claims and powers – that is, what are referred to as social and economic rights in international human rights discourse – should be more effectively articulated with this 'liberty'.

The latter point seems to me to become all the more compelling once one recognises that the context within which we now have to think about labour rights is marked by two significant changes: first, a shift from possession to control as the critical dimension of employment relations; and second, the onset of a process of economic globalisation that has thus far been guided by a neoliberalism that is intrinsically hostile to labour rights in general and to those configured in terms of powers and claims in particular. In order to bring out the significance of these changes, I would like to approach my conclusion by specifying the national and transnational context-dependency of the effectiveness of the various modalities of legal intervention in the capital/labour relation by comparing two polar cases. In a 'Northern' economy (like that of the United States in the 1950s) composed primarily of medium-sized and/or first-generation corporate capitals, operating at the heads of commodity chains, within a protected market, and producing goods for which there is strong domestic demand, a traditional labour law system configured in terms of liberties and focused on possessory relations may often be sufficient to allow labour to secure some redress of the inequalities that are intrinsic to capitalist relations of production. Under such circumstances an employer possesses some autonomy and labour is free to attempt to take advantage of this. However, in a strongly dualistic 'Southern' economy (like that of Brazil and the South more generally today), wherein a large number of petty commodity producers and small capitals are organised by a small number of large capitals (many of which are transnationals), operating within an 'open' global market at the lowest level of the commodity chain, a traditional labour law system configured in terms of liberties is most unlikely to be adequate to secure labour's ability to seek a redressing of the imbalances in the employment relation. Although possessory relations may continue to be the most salient of the elements within the property relation to local capitals as such, the wider economic context and especially local capital's subordination to transnational capital means that the control relations that are most salient to transnational capital take effective precedence in the governance of the small enterprises and so render moot the effects of a labour law system based on liberties.

In sum, under the latter circumstances the local employer often possesses very little autonomy and so it is often beside the point that one has the liberty to attempt to force him or her to exercise it to labour's benefit. As in the case of many Northern main contractor/subcontractor relations too, if the exercise of such a liberty interrupts production, the corporation at the head of the commodity chain can readily reduce its orders or seek new suppliers and in this way render labour's local liberties and therefore the idea of economic citizenship largely meaningless. The obvious solution from labour's point of view is that economic citizenship too should be globalised. At first sight this may seem to be a far less daunting task than the non-specialist might suppose, since not only have most labour rights already been globalised in the form of the conventions promulgated by one of the oldest global organisations, the International Labour Organisation (ILO), but also these conventions privilege no particular variety or configuration of labour rights. Thus the preamble to the ILO's constitution, which was written in 1918 and remains unchanged, reads as follows:

> Whereas universal and lasting peace can be established only if it is based upon social justice;
>
> And whereas conditions of labour exist involving such injustice, hardship and privation to large numbers of people as to produce unrest so great that the peace and harmony of the world are imperilled; and an improvement in those conditions is urgently required; as, for example, by the regulation of the hours of work, including the establishment of the maximum working day and week, the regulation of the labour supply, the prevention of unemployment, the provision of an adequate living wage, the protection of the worker against sickness, disease and injury arising out of his employment, the protection of children, young persons and women, provision for old age and injury, protection of the interests of workers when employed in countries other than their own, recognition of the principle of equal remuneration for work of equal value, recognition of the principle of freedom of association, the organisation of vocational and technical education and other measures;
>
> Whereas also the failure of any nation to adopt humane conditions of labour is an obstacle in the way of other nations which desire to improve the conditions in their own countries …

The problem with the conventions which now embody the rights prefigured in the preamble is that, whilst member states are undeniably under pressure to ratify them, there is no compulsion. Moreover, although they may be subject to criticism if they violate any conventions they have ratified, no significant sanctions can be imposed upon them. Thus it is profoundly ironic that the most serious effort thus far to address these weaknesses, namely the ongoing efforts to add what is known as the 'social clause' to the protocols of the World Trade Organisation (WTO), should also represent a perhaps even more serious assault on their potential global pertinence.

The proposed 'social clause', whose violation could result in the imposition of trade sanctions on offending states, consists of seven already existing ILO conventions that have been selected from a total of more than 180 such conventions and defined as 'core'. These seven conventions are those pertaining to: freedom of association and protection of the right to organise; the right to organisation and collective bargaining; forced labour; abolition of forced labour; discrimination in employment; equal remuneration; and the establishment of a minimum age for employment. Thus the problem is, as I have explained at length elsewhere (Woodiwiss, 2000), not so much that the efforts to introduce a 'social clause' have failed so far as that the proposed set of 'core labour standards' is inadequate to the task of securing economic citizenship within a global environment. This is because, reflecting the American origin of the proposed 'social clause', it emphasises the very liberties whose effectiveness globalisation has so dramatically reduced. Moreover, it is much easier for Western governments to ratify and locally enact the core standards than it is for Southern ones. This automatically and I am sure unintentionally presents many Southern societies in a bad light, which is not warranted if one takes into account their achievements across the full range of labour standards. Most Western societies have little trouble agreeing that, for example, child labour, gender or racial discrimination in employment, and limitations on freedom of association are bad things that something can be done about, because of the existence of powerful or at least well organised pressure groups within them. By contrast, in many Southern societies not simply the absence of such groups but also sometimes the presence of antithetical but nevertheless valued cultural preferences makes it very difficult to agree that such practices are bad, let alone that something should be done about them.

In other words, what may make it especially galling for some developed Asian as well as Southern nations and indeed employers to see themselves rhetorically disadvantaged in this way is the fact that the current core standards exclude the possibility of any reference to their achievements with respect to standards outside of the proposed core standards. These latter, as I have suggested above in my account of developments in Japan and elsewhere in my accounts of developments in Hong Kong and Singapore (Woodiwiss, 1998), are standards that are consistent with their values, and supported by their social-structural arrangements and generally mitigate the consequences of any derelictions with respect to the proposed core standards.

All that said, the securing of the liberties included in the proposed core should, of course, be part of any future effort to globalise economic citizenship, since they provide employees with the means to take part in the enforcement of their entitlements. However, as is re-emphasised by the fact that it is only in the inter-*governmental* context represented by the WTO that talk of labour rights carries any weight in global economic circles, the currently proposed set of core labour standards ought to be augmented by those that grant labour powers to participate in economic decision-making and/or recognise its compensatory claims. As the histories I have outlined above demonstrate, such powers and claims represent the means through which economic citizenship has actually been secured in many societies. Moreover, the far greater economic security today of working people in those more developed societies where labour rights have been configured as powers and claims rather than as liberties alone suggests that the former are likely to be ever more widely recognised even in countries like Argentina and Brazil as the most effective means through which economic citizenship may be secured in a globalising economy. At the moment and ironically this effectiveness is most often recognised by those who are least supportive of the values underlying the idea of economic citizenship and who describe its consequences as 'labour market rigidities'. My point being that 'rigidity' and indeed 'inflexibility' do not simply suggest obstacles but also connote strength, resistance and the necessity of negotiation and/or democratic resolution if obstacles to competitiveness or whatever are to be overcome. In other words, they connote that demand for respect which has always motivated those who believe in economic citizenship (for a contemporary, sociological version of this demand see Twine, 1994).

NOTES

1. The present chapter is an abridged and reworked version of a piece that was first written as a comparative sociological commentary on a series of studies commissioned by the International Institute of Social History (Amsterdam) and selected by Marcel van der Linden of the Institute and Richard Price of the Department of History, University of Maryland (van der Linden and Price, 2000). The other participants and their areas of expertise were as follows:

James Adelman (Argentina), Suzanne Fransson (Sweden), Sheldon Garon (Japan), Dale Gibson (Canada), Michel Hall (Brazil), Norbert Olszak (France), Raymond Markey (Australia), Gerry Rubin (United Kingdom), G.S. Shieh (Taiwan), and Katherine Stone (United States).

2. I owe this tripartite 'sociological' conception of the property relation to the work of Kelvin Jones (1982, pp. 76ff). I have defined the critical terms elsewhere (Woodiwiss, 1990a: 130–1) in the following way:

> As I read Jones, by 'possession' he means the narrowly economic ability to determine the use or operation, as such, of the production process. By

'control', he means the ability or power to determine the actual deployment of means of production in the production process. Finally, what he means by 'title' refers to the significatory basis upon which claims to any surplus may be made, and so it is not restricted to: 'the formal legal right to a claim upon a company or an estate but depends upon the sorts of calculations which govern the circulation of legal titles ... title involves the sort of calculations and conditions that govern the more general provision of finance, the socialisation of debt, the exchange of guarantees and the constitutional position of shareholders' (Jones, 1982: 77–8).

In addition, and critically, Jones also points out that whereas within small and medium-size enterprises the possessory relation is critical, within large corporate enterprises the control relation is critical. Thus, as I have explained elsewhere (Woodiwiss, 1990b: 272), where labour law systems do not include provisions relating to codetermination and/or title-sharing (e.g. the Swedish Wage Earner Funds), which means in most of the world outside of Western Europe, their pertinence is largely confined to a set of relations (possessory) that are of decreasing significance as loci of power within contemporary economies. Consequently, one may argue that the legal position of trade unions has been weakened throughout much of the world as much by the increasing irrelevance of extant labour law as by restrictive 'reforms'.

3. Both Neumann and Kahn-Freund also refer to a fourth phase of 'incorporation' or 'integration' (Kahn-Freund, 1981: 30 108–61; and see also Ramm, 1986) where the central institutions in the sphere of industrial relations are participative and include a central role for special labour courts. Although it would be inappropriate to fully justify this conclusion here, I have not sought to discern such a phase in the histories I am considering because I am not convinced that it can be clearly distinguished from that of recognition. Suffice it to say that I do not regard the presence of participative and judicial institutions as necessarily incorporative, let alone fascistic, in their effects since the wider social significance of the legal powers upon which they rest can vary greatly depending upon liberties and/or claims with which they are articulated as well as on the nature of the social context within which they are embedded – *vide* Sweden.

REFERENCES

Abrahamson, B. and Brostrom, A. (1980) *The Rights of Labor*. Beverley Hills: Sage.

Black, A. (1984) *Guilds and Civil Society in European Political Thought from the Twelfth Century to the Present*. Ithaca: Cornell University Press.

Edelman, B. (1980) 'The Legalisation of the Working Class', *Economy and Society*. 9 (1): 50.

Edelman, R. (1979) *Ownership of the Image*. London: Routledge.

Esping-Andersen, G. (1990) *The Three Worlds of Welfare Capitalism*. Princeton, NJ: Princeton University Press.

Frenkel, S. and Harrod, J. (eds) (1995) *Industrialization and Labor Relations: Contemporary Research in Seven Countries*. Ithaca: ILR Press.

Hepple, B. (ed.) (1986) *The Making of Labour Law in Europe*. London: Mansell Publishing Ltd.

Hirschman, A.O. (1970) *Exit, Voice and Loyalty: Responses to Decline in Organizations, Firms and States*. Cambridge, MA: Harvard University Press.

Hirst, P. (1979) *On Law and Ideology*. London: Macmillan.

Hohfeld, W. (1919) *Fundamental Legal Conceptions as Applied to Judicial Reasoning, and Other Legal Essays*. New Haven, Conn.: Yale University Press.

Jacobs, A. (1986) 'Collective Self-Regulation', in B. Hepple (ed.), *The Making of Labour Law in Europe*. London: Mansell Publishing Ltd.

Jones, K. (1982) *Law and Economy*. Canada: Academic Press.

Kahn-Freund, O. (1944) 'The Illegality of a Trade Union', *Modern Law Review*, 7: 192.

Kahn-Freund, O. (1981) *Labour Law and Politics in the Weimar Republic*. Oxford: Blackwell.

Katznelson, I. and Zolberg, A. (eds) (1986) *Working Class Formation: Nineteenth-Century Patterns in Western Europe and the United States*. Princeton: Princeton University Press.

Kettler, D. and Tackney, C. (1996) 'Light from a Dead Sun: The Japanese Lifetime Employment System and Weimar Labor Law', mimeo, New York: Bard Centre.

Koh, T. and van der Linden, M. (eds) (2000) *Labour Relations in Asia and Europe*. Singapore: Asia-Europe Foundation.

Leader, S. (1992) *Freedom of Association: A Study of Labor Law and Political Theory*. Newhaven, Conn: Yale University Press.

Lieberman, E. (1950) *Unions Before the Bar*. New York: Harper.

Liou, C. (1993) 'The Influences of Foreign Laws on the Contemporary Union Rights Policies in Taiwan', mimeo, Tokyo: Japan Institute of Labor.

Mann, M. (1993) *The Sources of Social Power*, vol. 2, Cambridge: Cambridge University Press.

Marshall, T.H. (1994 [1949]) 'Citizenship and Social Class' in B. Turner and P. Hamilton (eds), *Citizenship and Social Rights*. London: Sage.

Olszak, N. (2000) 'The Historical Development of Collective Labour Law in France', in M. van der Linden and R. Price (eds), *The Rise and Development of Collective Labour Law*. Berne: Peter Lang.

Orren, K. (1991) *Belated Feudalism: Labor, the Law, and Liberal Development*. Cambridge: Cambridge University Press.

Pritt, D.N. (1970) *Law, Class and Society*. 2 vols, London: Lawrence and Wishart.

Ramm, T. (1986) 'Workers' Participation, the Representation of Labour and Special Labour Courts', in (ed.), *The Making of Labour Law in Europe*. London: Mansell Publishing Ltd.

Renner, K. (1949) *The Institutions of the Private Law and their Social Functions*. London: Routledge.

Salgardo, G. (1999) 'Early Retirement in Japan: the Loss of a Privileged Citizenship?', unpublished PhD thesis, Department of Sociology, University of Essex.

Schregle, J. (1993) 'Dismissal Protection in Japan', *International Labour Review*, 132(4).

Selznick, P. (1980) *Law, Society and Industrial Justice*. New York: Transaction Books.

Stephens, J. (1979) *The Transition from Capitalism to Socialism*. London: Macmillan.

Stone, K. (2000) 'Labor and the American State: The Evolution of Labor Law in the United States', in M. van der Linden and R. Price (eds), *The Rise and Development of Collective Labour Law*. Berne: Peter Lang.

Strinati, D. (1982) *Capitalism, the State and Industrial Relations*. London: Croom Helm.

Sugeno, K. (1992) *Japanese Labor Law*. Seattle: University of Washington Press.

Turner, B. and Hamilton, P. (eds) (1994) *Citizenship: Critical Concepts*. London: Routledge.

Twine, F. (1994) *Citizenship and Social Rights*. London; Sage.

van der Linden, M. and Price, R. (eds) (2000) *The Rise and Development of Collective Labour Law*. Berne: Peter Lang.

Weber, M. (1978) *Economy and Society*, 2 vols, Berkeley: University of California Press.

Wellman, C. (1989) 'A New Conception of Human Rights', in M. Winston (ed.), *The Philosophy of Human Rights*. Belmont: Wadsworth Publishing Co.

Winston, M. (ed.) (1989) *The Philosophy of Human Rights*. Belmont: Wadsworth Publishing Company.

Woodiwiss, A. (1990b) *Rights v. Conspiracy: A Sociological Essay on the Development of Labour Law in the United States*. Oxford: Berg.

Woodiwiss, A. (1992) *Law, Labour and Society in Japan: From Repression to Reluctant Recognition*. London: Routledge.

Woodiwiss, A. (1998) *Globalisation, Human Rights and Labour Law in Pacific Asia*. Cambridge: Cambridge University Press.

Woodiwiss, A. (2000) 'Towards a "Level Playing Field" in Labour Standards: Taking Cultural Difference Seriously', in T. Koh and M. van der Linden, (eds), *Labour Relations in Asia and Europe*. Singapore: Asia-Europe Foundation.

4

Social Citizenship: Grounds of Social Change

MAURICE ROCHE

This chapter is concerned with understanding 'social citizenship', or more accurately the social dimension of citizenship, against the background of the citizenship discourses and regimes which have been established in modern nation-states and in their postwar 'welfare states'. Subsequent social change and the emergence of challenges to these discourses and regimes in the contemporary period imply that social citizenship is recurrently being rethought in theory and either has been, or needs to be, renewed in practice (see also Roche 1987, 1992, 1995a, 1995b) The general aim of the chapter is to explore these issues particularly in relation to national-level versions of social citizenship. The contemporary challenges include on the one hand ideological critiques from across the political spectrum, and, on the other hand, the structural imperatives and institution-building responses generated by globalisation. The chapter is divided into two main sections addressing these two types of challenge.

The first section aims to review the analysis of national-level social citizenship and also to discuss some of the ideological critiques. The focus is on the key themes of 'complexity' and 'context' in the mainstream analysis of social citizenship, and on the need to rethink the analysis in theory and renew it in practice. It is suggested that, in spite of their apparent differences, these challenges have connections and lead to comparable policy responses. Thus the section discusses what can generally be called new 'social contractualist' approaches to social policy and social citizenship in the contemporary period, in which various attempts have been made to review and renew the postwar 'social contracts' prevailing between nation-states and their citizens.

The second section is concerned with differences and commonalities in national versions of social citizenship in comparative and international perspective. On the one hand it aims to review analyses and assessments of the internationally diverse range of models of national social citizenship and national 'welfare capitalism' that have emerged in the developed societies in modernity and their capacity for adaptation and renewal in contemporary conditions. On the other hand it reviews analyses and arguments relating to 'the new convergence thesis', namely commonalities in approaches to social policy and social citizenship deriving particularly from the impacts of globalisation.

In conclusion it is suggested that the contexts in which national-level forms of social citizenship are theorised and practised are changing. These changes require us to attempt to understand new transnational levels of theory and practice in the fields of citizenship in general and social citizenship in particular, both the global level and also the level of world-regional formations of the kind currently being pioneered by the European Union (Roche 1992: Ch. 8; 1997; 2000).

SOCIAL CITIZENSHIP: RE-THINKING CONTEMPORARY DEBATES

This section critically reviews contemporary debates in the analysis of citizenship in general and social citizenship in particular. After an outline of the main positions and developments, the focus is on the key themes of complexity and context, and on the challenges of additional complexities and contexts evident in the contemporary period. The strategy of 'social contractualism' is considered as a common societal and policy response to these challenges.

The Study of Social Citizenship: T.H. Marshall and Subsequent Developments

There is a good case for regarding the British sociologist T.H. Marshall as the writer who put citizenship 'on the map' for sociology and the social sciences more generally, in his early seminal lectures on 'Citizenship and Social Class' in 1949 (Marshall, 1973). He argued that there are three main dimensions to citizenship – civil, political and social. These dimensions involve distinct rights and three sets of institutions in modern societies (namely legal systems, democratic government systems and welfare systems respectively) have developed to address and service them. These dimensions of citizenship rights and systems developed as part of modernisation processes in Western societies involving the development of industrial, capitalist and nation-state-based societies from the eighteenth century onwards. Citizenship status extended throughout modern societies and it intensified and accumulated first the civil dimension, subsequently the political dimension, and finally the social dimension. Marshall illustrated the analysis particularly in relation to Britain and its modernisation process, and argued that in the British case this sequence occurred over the eighteenth, nineteenth and twentieth centuries respectively. Generally Marshall saw the principles of citizenship and the principles of capitalism as being 'at war' in the course of which the former operated to 'civilize' the latter (ref). Relatedly Marshall also saw modern society as a complex (or 'hyphenated') structure, consisting of varying combinations of the three systems of political democracy, welfare state and capitalist economy.

Marshall's analysis initially found a resonance in historical and comparative postwar American sociology, particularly that concerned with understanding the modernisation process (Bendix, 1964; Rimlinger, 1971). The impetus he gave to the sociology of citizenship in general and of its social dimension in particular seemed to be lost for a period in the late 1970s and early 1980s. However, it revived substantially in the early to mid-1980s and early 1990s (Giddens, 1983; Turner, 1986, 1993; Roche, 1987, 1992; Barbalet, 1988; Culpitt, 1992; Twine, 1994; van Steenbergen, 1994) and it is currently used as an important reference in the development of the comparative study of welfare regimes and social rights systems (Esping-Andersen, 1990, 1999; also Janoski, 1998; Mishra, 1990, 1999).

Marshall's analysis has generally helped to inspire the study of social rights and of the ways in which they were or were not served by welfare systems and social policy. However, it is important to note that this study was sociologically and normatively contextualised. It was sociologically based in an analysis of the changing societal context involved in modernisation processes. And it assumed, as matters of both sociological and normative significance, the preexistence of developed forms of modern citizenship, in particular the civil and political rights, as the context in terms of which the social dimension of citizenship was developed. This contextualising concern also animates the interests of this chapter.

In spite of the changing social context in recent years and the increasing salience and impact of globalisation Marshall's analysis has continued to be a notable point of reference, whether positive or negative, for studies of the contemporary social and political significance and role of citizenship. This is both in general and also in relation to such particular issues as its relevance for the politics of social obligation (Roche, 1995b; Janoski, 1998; Dwyer, 2000), feminism (Lister, 1997), culture (Isin and Wood, 1999; Stevenson, 2000) and environmentalism (van Steenbergen, 1994). In recent years the sociology and politics of citizenship have also increasingly begun to explore areas which Marshall did not map out, particularly the new normative and structural social contexts and implications of transnational social developments. In relation to the global level this has generated new interest in such topics as universal social rights, global citizenship and cosmopolitan citizenship (Doyal and Gough, 1991; Held, 1995; Deacon, 1997; Mishra, 1999; Delanty, 2000; Falk, 2000). At the 'world regional' level it has generated new interest in the topic of European Union citizenship (Meehan, 1993; Roche, 1992, 1995, 1997, 2000; Roche and van Berkel, 1997; Wiener, 1997).

The Importance of Complexity and Context in Citizenship Analysis

The mainstream analysis focuses on national citizenship and provides some key elements of a *complex* and *contextual* understanding of citizenship in general and of social citizenship in particular. This analysis stresses (i) the (internally, structurally) complex character of fully developed status of modern citizenship, and (ii) its contextualised character, its dependence on particular socio-historical conditions in modernity. We can take each of these elements in turn, and then consider some of the main contemporary challenges to them.

Complexity

In the mainstream theory and practice citizenship is pictured as a multidimensional complex consisting at least of the three familiar dimensions of civil, political and social citizenship, together with their related institutions. To characterise them negatively, modern social rights have been developed to address and minimise individuals' risks of suffering such problems as poverty and gross inequality and related problems of health and social exclusion in modern capitalist societies. More positively, they refer to such things as individuals' lifelong rights to income maintenance, and to access to employment, to health services, and to accommodation on the basis of need. Such rights are often rationalised, both in analytic and constitutional terms, as national embodiments of universal human rights (Doyal and Gough, 1991; Held, 1995). Systems of income distribution and maintenance to counterbalance the distributional and cyclical effects of capitalist labour markets and of progression through the lifecycle on individuals' incomes are traditionally regarded as being at the heart of a state's commitment to the social rights of its citizens. The extent of this commitment and of these rights can be assessed by the degree to which, and the level at which, they provide need-satisfying consumption resources at all stages of the life cycle and across all of life's vulnerabilities and risks (in infancy and childhood, through working age, when unemployed, when in and out of married relationships, when in temporary ill health, if permanently disabled, in retirement etc.). Access to state-financed education may also be included as a social right of citizenship, particularly insofar as it develops employable skills and human capital, and life skills more generally (although alternatively it might be seen as central to another dimension of rights, namely the cultural rights of citizenship, see later).

Context

The theory and practice of citizenship require that social rights are seen as being contextualised in both socio-historical and normative terms. From a socio-historical perspective in the modern period the capacity of the modern state to directly provide, or indirectly guarantee the provision of, at least needs-adequate minima of incomes and services has always been, and remains, contextualised by (or more strongly, dependent on) the effective organisation of a modern national capitalist economy. In addition, to generate, to continuously replenish and to increase the tax base and the stock of human resources from which rights-oriented distributions can be drawn it has been necessary for the state to embed and regulate the capitalist economy and institutionalise its capacity for innovation and growth. Marshall's mainstream analysis of citizenship assumes the existence of such systems, which can usefully be refered to as 'national functionalist' systems (Roche, 1992).

From a more normative perspective, Marshall and citizenship analysis in general understand social rights as being contextualised by and connected with the prior history and institutionalisation, and the contemporary concurrent operation, of fundamental civil and political rights. Technically it might be possible to develop and deliver social rights in isolation and for their own sake, disconnected from civil and political rights. Indeed, the ruling groups in fascist and communist societies in the early twentieth century arguably developed such de-contextualised social rights precisely in order to 'buy off' demands for civil and political rights, and thus for full citizenship which they otherwise suppressed. However, by comparison, most citizenship analysis addresses citizenship as a complex and contextualised status giving expression to ideals of personal autonomy, social justice, equality and inclusiveness in modern societies, societies which Marshall understands as complex 'democratic-welfare-capitalist' formations. In these contexts social rights are best interpreted as serving and giving substance to, rather than helping to repress, the personal autonomy assumed and expressed in the exercise of civil and political rights. In turn, in Marshall's analysis, the full complex citizenship status, together with the nation-state ('national functional') system which supports it, helps to 'civilise' the otherwise 'uncivilised' and conflictual dynamics of capitalism and capitalist societies.

Much of conventional citizenship analysis, then, is reasonably complex and contextually sensitive. However, this paper argues that if it is to remain relevant to contemporary conditions and to social change citizenship analysis needs to be developed further in at least two main respects relating to the two themes of complexity and context.

Rethinking Citizenship Analysis: Additional Complexities and Contexts

There is now a need to rethink the citizenship analysis and recognise on the one hand underlying and additional dimensions, *additional complexities*, of the citizenship status, and on the other the *additional contexts* of social formations beyond the level of the nation state within which we all increasingly find ourselves living and operating, particularly in Europe.

Additional Complexities

Firstly, over the last decade or more there have been various ideologically-based challenges to the mainstream theory and practice of national citizenship from across the political spectrum, from the New Right to the New Left, and from new social movements such as feminism, environmentalism and multiculturalism. These challenges have concerned aspects not adequately recognised or addressed within mainstream analysis. The relevant aspects include the nature and role of *citizens' responsibilities* (e.g. Roche, 1992, 1995b; Janoski, 1998). On the one hand this theme has been taken up in political debate from a New Right perspective in relation to the 'traditional responsibilities' involved in the longstanding commitment of societies and their members to national versions of the work ethic and the family ethic. On the other hand arguably a 'new responsibilities' discourse has been developed in the social movements of feminism (e.g. relating to males' responsibilities of non-violence and care towards women and children), and environmentalism (e.g. our responsibilities towards other life forms, future generations etc.).

In recent years new social and cultural movements, sometimes arguably labelled 'postmodern', have developed to promote interests and agendas in the fields of the politics of identity and recognition, of multiculturalism and anti-racism, of sexuality and lifestyle, of consumption and communication. These movements have renewed interest in the politics of citizenship in general and also in the theoretical proposition that citizenship has a distinct and analysable *cultural dimension* of rights and related cultural institutions and responsibilities (e.g. Isin and Wood, 1999; Stevenson, 2000). Arguably a cultural dimension has always been present in the politics of and development of modern citizenship in general since the 19th century, albeit in contestable national monocultural versions. This is evident in the development of such cultural institutions as national education and media systems and citizens' rights in relation to them. However the cultural dimension, whether envisaged in national monocultural terms or in contemporary multicultural and pluralistic terms has never been adequately represented in the mainstream citizenship analysis. At the very least the new social and cultural movements and their politics can be said to reveal and address new levels of complexity in the status and implications of national citizenship. Thus additional contextualisation is required in the mainstream analysis of citizenship if the nature and prospects of social citizenship in the contemporary period are to be adequately grasped.

Additional Contexts

The nation-state and the national level of citizenship may no longer be adequate units of analysis in the contemporary world, in which globalisation, particularly the creation of a global capitalist economy, is such a powerful long-term dynamic. Taking the transnational level seriously means adding further to the complexity of our understanding of the structures of contemporary citizenship and also adding further to the societal contexts we need to take into account when analysing social rights. These issues are taken up in the second section of this chapter, which provides a link between national-level and transnational contexts by looking at the international context in which different national systems of citizenship and social rights coexist, in which they could be said to compete with each other. Globalisation can be said to be creating a new common context for all countries as welfare states, a context in which, arguably, new ideals and standards of global citizenship and social rights will increasingly need to be envisaged and debated.

Before addressing these issues I shall consider the general nature of the main political responses to the ideological and political challenges outlined in relation to the new complexity theme above. These can be said to have taken the form of versions of 'social contractualism'.

Renewing the Practice of Social Citizenship: The Development of Forms of 'Social Contractualism'

The Postwar Social Contract

In effect the social order of modern postwar societies was formed around quasi-constitutional and/or tacit and traditional general 'social contracts' (relating to identities, rights and responsibilities) which can be said to exist both between citizens themselves and between citizens and the state (Roche 1992: Chs 1 and 9). These foundational postwar social contracts were mediated through the domains of civil society, the market and the family, all of which involve more particular forms of contractual relationship (e.g. those involved in association membership, employment, marriage etc.). All of these dimensions of the postwar social contract are now the subjects of reflective political activity, are being made explicit, and in many cases are being redefined and renegotiated even where the original arrangements are only being reaffirmed and updated. However, particularly in many European countries at present, they are being changed and a new priority is being given to 'active' and new contractualist forms of work and welfare policy development and implementation (Heikkila, 1999).

The Influence of the New Right

Social contractualist political strategies and social policy developments have evidently been influenced by New Right and pro-market political economic ideologies and forces, particularly in the USA and the UK in the 1980s (Roche, 1992; Jordan, 1998). These have included general governmental strategies such as privatisation of state agencies and functions, deregulation of labour markets, 'cuts' in public expenditure particularly on the welfare state, and reduction in the power of organised labours particularly public sector workers and professionals. Particularly in the UK, but even in the more pro-market USA, these strategies have been strong on rhetoric, but have had less effect in practice than has often been claimed. The most successful was the reduction in the power of public sector workers and some public sector professionals. The effects on the governance system as a whole have been much less clear. In the UK in particular 'cuts' policies have tended merely to exercise a braking effect on the rate of the long-term growth of public expenditure as a proportion of GDP, rather than producing real reductions. Similarly, labour market deregulation cannot be pursued indefinitely: limits are ultimately reached in relation to the basic need of markets for a supportive institutional and legal framework, not to mention workers' and consumers' basic constitutional rights and electoral power in modern democratic societies. Finally, in the UK privatisation generated a new wave of 'regulationist' activity by the state in order to retain elements of public sector governance and accountability in relation to the services affected on behalf of service user-citizens. This development of a new citizen-oriented 'regulationist' approach by the state, although initiated by New Right Conservative governments, has been continued and taken further by the New Labour government since 1997.

The Influence of Changing Structural Contexts

The conditions and stimuli for this 'social contractualism' in the reconstruction of the welfare state are emerging in various sectors of contemporary society, notably the labour market and the family. In these two areas contractualism of various kinds is becoming more important, particularly in the labour market, as part of the general 'flexibilisation' dynamic in contemporary capitalism and structural socio-economic change (Standing, 1999). The experience and role of employment are being significantly and irreversibly changed by the increased bargaining power of employers and their pursuit of time-limited and highly conditional 'economic contractualism' in the use of their labour. Economic contractualism and the complex and changing environment of economic networks it creates seems to be an adaptive response to the new global–local (transnational–subnational) market dynamics operating within and beyond the sphere of the nation-state and the national economy. As such it is consistent with the emergence of network formations at and between all of these levels as a result of contemporary processes of globalisation and informationalisation (Castells, 1996; Held et al., 1999).

The family is changing profoundly as a result of the contribution of feminism and the movement of women into the labour market in advancing women's civil, political and social citizenship rights (Lister, 1997; Esping-Andersen, 1999). Particularly in relation to child-rearing, the welfare state (through its childcare services, educational services and juvenile justice services) is pursuing new contractualist and/or quasi-contractualist relationships with parents to ensure that the (citizen) obligations of parenting are carried out, the (citizen) rights of children are protected and the (citizen) rights of parents to state (i.e. tax-payers') support for the costs of parenting is being promoted. The emergence in contemporary society of newly contractualised labour relations and newly contractualised parenting relations add to the climate in which 'social contractualist' processes and politics are likely to develop and take root.

Changing Policy Discourses

The new 'politics of social contract' being witnessed in contemporary societies in many different forms is fuelled in part by by the influence of New Right individualistic liberal market ideologies, as already observed. But it is also influenced by the demands of a range of new (and/or renewed) social movements (such as feminism, ecology, and communitarianism, and also consumerism) and also by the evident need to adapt outdated governance and welfare systems to new historical and political-economic conditions and to legitimate these adaptations through the democratic process. The contemporary restructuring of socio-economic policies under way in European states often manifests itself in the greater prioritisation of 'citizenship' and 'civil society' concepts and criteria in the genesis, construction, delivery and assessment of social policy in particular. These processes can be understood as involving the development of a new order of 'social contractualism' in contemporary societies.

Some examples of 'social contractualist' politics in contemporary European societies at various levels from the transnational to the local include: (i) the recurrent constitutional (Europeanist, nationalist, federalist, regionalist) politics involved in the process of European Union (EU) legal and economic integration; (ii) the central and local state 'contracting out' public sector social services to either private sector or voluntary sector organisations, while maintaining the state's regulatory role; (iii) the development of 'individualised client contract' and 'client charter' approaches in the public and social services in which the rights and responsibilities of both particular citizens (in the former case) and public sector-based agencies (in the latter case) are explicitly recorded as a reference for assessing both citizen and agency actions in a 'contract-conditional' way; and (iv) the development of the role of key forms of civil society (i.e. voluntary and community organisations) in work and welfare policy, necessarily involving principles and practices of 'associationalism' between citizens and 'contractualism' between citizen organisations and the state (also see Culpitt, 1992).

Policies of the British New Labour government elected in 1997 can be said to have this 'social contractarian' character. New Labour claims to be pursuing a political agenda influenced by social principles connected with 'left-centrist' political approaches such as 'communitarianism', 'stakeholding' and a 'third way' view of social democracy, rather than the preceding Conservative mixture of New Right neo-liberalism and neo-conservativism (Etzioni, 1993, 2000; Giddens, 1998, 2000). However, with the possible exception of their approach to organised worker/professional interest groups, it is arguable whether they have radically reversed the Conservative policies they inherited. New Labour's approach is that social goals can be achieved pragmatically by a variety of means in addition to and other than direct state provision. These other means include macro-economic prudence to create the conditions for economic growth, continued control of the growth of public expenditure, flexible re-regulation of the labour market on the basis of EU rules and principles, and the further development of the regulatory rather than direct provisory role of the central and local state in public and social services, (involving more privatisations, state–private sector 'partnerships' and 'contracting out').

It would be a mistake to exaggerate the achievements and sustainability of the radical New Right neo-liberal agenda which was pursued during the 1980s and 1990s. But it would also be a mistake to reduce the significance of the contemporary New Labour approach merely to a re-run of the New Right agenda and of the 'liberal market' type of welfare regime. What was emerging even under Conservative governments in the UK over the last decade using pro-market rhetoric, and what is being developed further by New Labour using communitarian rhetoric, could be described as a new kind of work and welfare regime, a new accommodation between state, market and civil society.

There has been a renewal of interest and reflection by citizen communities and taxpayers, in Britain and in many countries, about the terms and limits of the *de facto* 'social contract' which, in developed and democratic societies, can be argued to exist between them and the state. Citizen community as a whole can be said to contract with state, seen as a political mechanism, to deliver and/or organise a range of services and rights on their behalf, and agree to pay for this via taxes. From the 1980s and through the 1990s we have seen some important shifts in many countries in the nature of the traditional citizen–state 'social contracts' established earlier in the 20th century and particularly in the early postwar period. For good or ill as we move into the 21st century these common changes continue. Evidently this rethinking and renegotiating of the various social contracts embodied in the institutional designs of modern societies, particularly those between the citizenry and the state, is more politically visible in some countries than in others. Where it becomes a matter of political visibility and societal reflexivity we can understand it as the addition of a new 'social contractualist' policy dynamic, a new commonality increasing the comparability of different nations, their welfare states and their versions of social citizenship.

SOCIAL CITIZENSHIP IN COMPARATIVE AND GLOBAL CONTEXTS: PRESSURES FOR REFORM AND RENEWAL

This section is concerned with differences and commonalities in contemporary national versions of social citizenship in comparative and international perspective. Firstly it reviews 'welfare regimes' analysis and comparisons between 'worlds of welfare capitalism'. Secondly, it reviews 'the new convergence thesis', namely the argument that the emergence of commonalities in national approaches to social policy and social citizenship derives particularly from the impacts of globalisation and structural change.

'Welfare Capitalism' and Social Citizenship: Reviewing 'Welfare Regimes'

Marshall, as we have seen, analysed social citizenship rights as a dimension of the full and complex status of citizenship, and argued that this in turn had been achieved in the context of the social politics and historical development of modern 'democratic-welfare-capitalist' nation-states and social formations. However, this recognition of complexity and context provides an impetus rather than a terminus for social citizenship analysis. Evidently national citizenship in general and national social citizenship in particular has been established in very different ways during the different experiences of modernisation and nation-building processes in different societies, particularly

European societies. Nevertheless Marshall's conception has been influential in stimulating and informing subsequent comparative developmental, sociological and policy research into and assessment of the systemic differences between social models from early studies (e.g. Bendix, 1964; Rimlinger, 1971) to more recent ones (e.g. Esping-Andersen, 1990, 1996, 1999; Janoski, 1998).

In his notable comparative work Gösta Esping-Andersen in particular (e.g. Esping-Andersen, 1990) has argued for the need to recognise the systemic and traditional political and sociological differences between what he identifies as three main types of national social model or national 'worlds of welfare capitalism'. These are, firstly, the liberal market model exemplified particularly in the USA but also to some extent in the UK. In this model priority is given to civil rights and the pursuit of economic growth, and social rights and associated state welfare costs are minimised through means-tested social assistance 'safety net' policy approaches. Secondly there is the conservative corporatist model, exemplified particularly by Germany and other continental European societies such as Austria and France. This aims to promote high levels of employment and institutionalises a 'social dialogue' in the industrial relations and social policy-making systems between employers' and workers' organisations. It protects the social rights particularly of established full-time male employees and their families well, but it also involves rigidities and exclusionary social categorisation in relation to women and the operation of labour markets. Thirdly there is the social democratic model which is exempified in the Scandinavian countries (and also arguably in the Netherlands, Goodin et al., 1999). This aspires to apply egalitarian, universalistic and inclusive ideals and values and thus to address people as modern citizens with legitimate claims to well-resourced social rights. Like the corporatist model this model aims to promote high levels of employment and involves social dialogue approaches to policy-making. In addition it uses relatively high tax levels to fund extensive childcare and related services and public sector employment in order, in turn, to provide employment opportunities for women and generally a family-supportive social and labour market environment for all citizens.

The 'three worlds' analysis has been criticised on various fronts, including from feminist perspectives, which argue that it underplays the patriarchally structured second-class citizenship in all welfare regimes associated with the traditionally central role of women and their production of care work and welfare in the family (e.g. Orloff, 1993; Lewis, 1992; Esping-Andersen, 1999). Also, while the analysis could be said to capture reasonably well the main regime differences across much of Europe, nonetheless it is not comprehensive. It has been justly criticised for having little to say about what arguably amounts to an additional regime type, namely the traditionalistic approach to social policy and social citizenship based on the role of the family, civil society and obligations, which is characteristic of Spain, Italy and other southern European countries (Ferrara, 1996). It also needs to be supplemented to take account of the distinctive features presented by citizenship and social rights regimes, such as they are, in the 'transitional' post-Communist East European societies (Deacon, 1997).

Comparative social policy research has long argued that, compared with the other models, the social democratic model provides the fullest development and realisation of the social rights of citizenship (Ginsburg, 1992; Gould, 1993; Hill, 1996). In recent years the need to adapt to the forces of the relatively unregulated market of the emerging global capitalist economy has gained increased importance in the management of national economies and economic policy-making. Correlated with this has been a increase in the political influence of pro-market neo-conservative and neo-liberal political ideologies in most national polities in the developed world. Thus the phenomenon of globalisation could be said to create structural imperatives towards convergent national adaptations to, if not wholescale adoptions of, the liberal market model of 'welfare capitalism'. This has led to arguments that the societal and political economic conditions supporting the social democratic model have been fatally undermined, and that the model is in long-term and terminal decline. However, contemporary comparative research indicates that, in spite of these structural pressures towards policy convergence, differences between the main models of welfare capitalism and social citizenship remain marked, and also that the social democratic model is capable of adaptation and renewal. Indeed research findings notably indicate that the social democratic model continues to perform economically as well as the other models, and continues to outperform them in terms of the degree to which it enables social rights and the social dimension of citizenship to be realised in practice.

The most searching recent comparative analysis of social models is that of Goodin et al. (1999). This proposes that national welfare regimes or models of 'welfare capitalism' can be assessed, on the one hand in terms of economic efficiency and performance and on the other in terms of their performance in improving people's lives, by promoting individuals' (citizens') autonomy and the social conditions for this, namely minimising poverty, and promoting social equality, social integration and social stability. The study examined comparable longitudinal (over ten years) data sets (particularly household panel surveys) for indicators for each of six variables (efficiency, poverty, equality, integration, stability and autonomy) from the Netherlands, Germany and the USA as key national examples of the social democratic, conservative corporatist and liberal market models respectively. They discussed social citizenship particularly in relation to equality and the social democratic model. They found that:

> the social democratic welfare regime is 'the best of all possible worlds'. [It] turns out to be the best choice, regardless of what you want it to do. [It] is clearly best on its home ground of minimizing inequality. But it also turns out to be better at reducing poverty than liberal welfare regime, which targets its policy on that to the exclusion of all else. [It] is also at least as good at promoting stability [and ... social integration] as is the corporatist welfare regime which ostensibly attaches most importance to those goals. [It] is also best at promoting key elements of autonomy, something valued by all regimes if not necessarily prioritized by any. (Goodin et al., 1999: 260)
>
> [If one's] 'bottom-line' concern with efficiency is with the way in which welfare policy might undermine economic productivity, then the crucial fact is simply that the social democratic system on which we have focussed – the Netherlands – managed to sustain economic growth on a rate certainly on a par with (and in some ways higher than) the other countries under study. And both the social democratic and corporatist regimes passed on much more of the growth dividend to middle-income earners than did the liberal regime under study, at least over this period. (Goodin et al., 1999: 261).

This study argues that its findings call into question classical liberal economic assumptions about the social conditions necessary for growth in productivity, and suggest that 'there seem to be several different paths' to this goal (Goodin et al., 1999: 261).

The findings of the Goodin team study challenge the mainstream liberal economics-inspired assumption that countries necessarily always face a stark zero-sum choice, a necessary trade-off, in organising economic and social policy between economic objectives and social objectives. These findings about the continued socio-economic strength and adaptability of the social democratic model have also been confirmed in other recent studies of the Netherlands

(Hout, 1997), of Sweden (Esping-Andersen, 1999), of these two countries together with Denmark (Hirst and Thompson, 1999: Ch. 6) and of the 'Nordic Model' in general (Kautto et al., 1999).

Structural Change, Globalisation and Social Citizenship: Reviewing the 'Convergence Thesis'

The dominant postwar forms of the welfare state, whatever their apparent differences, can be argued to represent broadly common policy responses to the common needs for welfare and social cohesion deriving from the common causal conditions of capitalist industrialisation, conditions which had developed in comparable ways from from the late nineteenth century to the mid-twentieth century (e.g. Marshall, 1973; Rimlinger, 1971; Roche, 1992; Janoski, 1998). Late twentieth-century and now early twenty-first-century structural change, involving postindustrialism and globalisation (e.g. Castells, 1996; Held et al., 1999), is of a comparable scale. By analogy, then, these new common causal conditions influencing welfare states should produce relatively common social problem effects and social policy responses. As we have seen, Esping-Andersen is a leading proponent of national differences and 'path-dependent' logics of development. Nonetheless even he registers something of the force of this 'logic of common structural change' perspective when he concludes his collection of studies of the adaptations of national welfare states to globalisation and postindustrialism by observing that '[A] major overhaul of the existing welfare state edifice must occur if it is meant to produce a positive-sum kind of welfare for postindustrial society' (1996: 267).

The impact of globalisation on national social policies, welfare states, and indeed public policy more generally is evidently a major emergent contemporary problem for analysis and policy. However, in spite of this, this structural change paradigm has not yet attracted a sufficiently searching and substantive base of systematic comparative research (see for instance Rhodes, 1996; Castles and Pierson, 1996; OECD, 1996; Gough et al., 1997; and Mishra, 1999). The structural change paradigm has been christened 'the new convergence thesis' and the following sections consider some arguments and evidence for and against it.

Common Structural Changes and Social Problems: the Potential for Policy Convergence

According to many observers, structural changes in the labour markets (LMs) and employment regimes (ERs) of the advanced industrial societies in the late twentieth century involved the development of (structural) unemployment and/or underemployment and/or flexibilisation of employment (Standing, 1999). A general picture of these changes can be painted in growth trends in cross-national rates of (i) unemployment (particularly long-term, youth and two-household unemployment); and (ii) part-time and temporary employment. Their effects can be seen in trends in measures of poverty and social exclusion, and also in policy trends such as the development of targeted benefits systems to address these particular problems.

A recent cross-national survey of national social policy-makers confirms problems of rising unemployment and the need for employment-creation policies this perception is shared perception across European societies. 'The big issues are the cost of (welfare, MR) provision and the high levels of unemployment, in line with recent EU debate' (Taylor-Gooby, 1997: 8). In addition the growth of labour market flexibility, particularly in the form of part-time employment, has been a common feature across Europe, albeit to different extents and at different rates in different nations. Part-time employment, which has tended to be taken mainly by women, grew by 3% per year from 1987 to 1990 in the EU, and in core economies such as that of Germany this was virtually the only kind of employment growth. In the subsequent period 1990–1994 part-time employment grew by 13% in the EU against the background of a decline in the overall number of people in full-time employment. Another indicator of Labour Market flexibility, namely temporary employment, has been growing at a slower rate than part-time employment. Nonetheless it amounted to over 10% of all employment in the EU in 1994, and a much higher proportion of the labour market in particular countries (e.g. it amounted to 33% of total employment in Spain in 1994), (data from Huws, 1997).

These sorts of labour market changes can be argued to promote social exclusion (understood as an undermining of people's access to the social rights and social goods of recognition, income and work) in two ways at two different levels. Firstly unemployment and/or underemployment can be said to directly produce exclusionary experiences among individuals involuntarily affected by them through the loss of income and work they involve. Secondly, they can be said to indirectly produce the potential for individual exclusionary experiences, by their effects at the macro level generally on state taxation sources and spending constraints, and thus on social policy and the welfare state. Under the common structural change pressures indicated above, welfare regimes have commonly tended to respond by moving towards more targeted and selective patterns of welfare income distribution.

Policy Responses to Structural Change: For and Against the Convergence Thesis

In Favour of the Convergence Thesis

Cross-national commonality of policy response to structural change can be seen in a number of areas. These include the development of 'social contractualist' and 'active' approaches to labour market and employment policy noted earlier. They also include social assistance policy. Each of the main models of postwar welfare state, in spite of their differences, has typically consisted of two parts. The primary part has conventionally been regarded as the widespread or universal provision of welfare benefits for those not able to support themselves on income from the labour market because of unemployment, sickness or retirement. This was often organised by the state through funds created by contributory insurance schemes for employees and/or financed by the state through transfers from current taxation. The part conventionally regarded as of secondary importance in the characterisation and assessment of the postwar welfare state is often referred to as 'social assistance'. This part typically aims to provide 'a safety net' for those people not supported by market income or by the primary welfare system, and is characterised by various forms of targeting and conditionality (via income/means tests, work availability/work search tests etc.) rather than universality in the provision of benefits. It deals with the truly disadvantaged, those unemployed people who have never or rarely been employed, the long-term unemployed, those raising young children for long periods in households with low income and little or no employment, and so on, who effectively become significantly 'dependent' for their survival in society and their quality of life on this part of the welfare system.

A notable comparative study of social assistance policies in 24 countries was conducted for the OECD in 1996 (Eardley et al., 1996; Gough et al., 1997). The study focused on policy inputs rather than outcomes. The authors aimed 'to chart and classify the species of social assistance we observe in the world rather than to offer a comprehensive theory of their variety and different forms of evolution' (Gough et al., 1997: 18). The major groups of recipients of social assistance are (i) the unemployed, (ii) older people, (iii) lone parents and (iv) women (p. 28). The findings of the study indicate that 'means-testing, targeting and selectivity' need to be 'brought back into the comparative study of European and wider welfare systems' (p.17). They showed that 'All types of welfare regime exhibited a rising share of expenditure on means-tested schemes in the 1980s – a notable convergence of otherwise disparate national patterns' (Eardley et al., 1996: 3) These social assistance schemes tend to develop new combinations of incentives and sanctions intended to influence the attitudes and behaviour of benefit recipients, in particular to influence them to search for, gain and hold employment in the labour market. The incentives typically include such policies as: reducing the (pre-existing and usually disincentivising) rate of withdrawal of benefit as employment-based earnings rise; providing education, training and work experience programmes for the unemployed; and extending childcare and other benefits to enable claimants with caring responsibilities to combine these with paid work. The sanctions typically include such policies as: enhanced monitoring of able-bodied claimants; stricter tests of job-search activities, time-limited benefits, and reductions in benefit levels relative to income available from the labour market (Eardley et al., 1996: Ch. 8).

The study analysed the social conditions generating the common growth of social assistance and the new patterns of benefit provision observed into 'external' and 'internal' pressures on states. 'External pressures' are trends operating generally throughout the advanced societies. They include demographic trends (an ageing population, etc.), family structure changes (fragmentation of family types, the rise of lone parent families etc.), labour market changes, and housing and fuel costs increases. 'Internal pressures' are political factors operating within each nation. They include the perceived breakdown in the effectiveness of traditional social insurance and welfare systems, programmes of public expenditure limitation, conflicts between central and local government around these programmes, and pressure from public sector workers, trade unions, professions and clients.

Overall the OECD study argues that 'means-tested social assistance schemes have in recent years acquired an importance which has not been reflected in the comparative literature on welfare states' (ibid: 40/1). This is because such schemes are more relevant to the 'new poverty' and the new problems of social exclusion connected with contemporary social conditions than to the older problems which welfare states were originally developed to address. The authors argue that these schemes should now be seen as having a new strategic significance in the current operation and the future development of social policy and the welfare state in the advanced societies.

Against the Convergence Thesis

A notable comparative study which suggests limits to 'the convergence thesis' is that of Castles and Pierson (1996). They provide a cross-national assessment of the degree of impact of globalisation on social policy in the UK, Australia and New Zealand. As background to this study Castles and Pierson acknowledge some limited validity in the idea of commonality and convergence in the early development of modern welfare states in response to the developing needs of industrial capitalist societies. They also acknowledge that international economic crises and developments in the mid-1970s had a major impact on most developed countries, particularly the three under consideration in this study. The inflationary impact of the increased price of oil imports on all these countries affected their monetary and fiscal policies, were connected with changes in their labour markets, and led them to adopt similar neo-liberal solutions to their problems. These three countries were selected in part to maximise the possibility of finding significant commonalities in their contemporary social policies. They share a common language and an interconnected history and culture, and they face common challenges in the new global economic environment facing nation-states.

Castles and Pierson suggest that 'The big question for the new convergence thesis ... is whether the social policy reforms made under these circumstances (MR of common international pressures) have all been in the direction of the leaner, meaner welfare state supposedly implied by economic inter nationalisation.' Their study found that while the three countries did develop similar sorts of policy instruments there remained significant differences between them. In the UK throughout the decade of the 1980s there was a disjunction between, on the one hand, the governmental rhetorical threats to 'roll back' the welfare state associated with Prime Minister Margaret Thatcher and with the hegemony of the neo-libertarian 'New Right' in terms of political ideology and policy discourse, and on the other hand the failure of these forces actually to make any significant reductions in the absolute and relative level of state spending on the welfare system. By contrast in New Zealand substantial real reductions in welfare spending were achieved. Finally, in Australia an increase in the targeting of welfare spending, normally associated with an effort to reduce spending levels in general and benefit levels of those targeted in particular, in practice involved increases in benefit levels for those targeted.

Castles and Pierson argue that 'the new convergence thesis fails to capture the reality of these countries' social policy development in the 1980s'. While there may have been a similarity in the policy rhetoric of the need for reductions in state welfare spending, the effects of this in policy practice, particularly in the UK and Australia cases, were variable and characterised by caution. These effects were just as predictable from a knowledge of the traditional class-related power bases and coalitions connected with the postwar welfare state as they were from knowledge of the new international pressures affecting these countries. They argue that any single-factor explanation for contemporary social policy and welfare state developments and changes, such as that involved in a prioritisation of the globalisation factor, is inadequate. Any explanation requires at least three factors to be considered. Firstly there is globalisation. They acknowledge that 'Certainly global economic forces are likely to have some impact on domestic public policy' and that this is all the greater when those forces are actively embraced by governments and policy-makers. Secondly there are the interest groups involved in the operation of the welfare state and general popular support for relatively high levels of public spending on welfare systems. Thirdly there are the poor and the 'have nots' who have traditionally benefited from the welfare state's redistributive effects and whose interests can exercise a pressure on governments. In general Castles and Pierson conclude that in such comparative analyses 'politics still matters' and thus national differences still matter. In their view, although the convergence thesis contains some substance, it needs to be 'heavily qualified'. This picture is consistent with other recent comparative research and analysis (e.g. Hirst and Thompson, 1999; Alber and Standing, 2000).

In his review of the literature on the impact of globalisation on welfare states, Rhodes (1996) argues that the current crises of national welfare states in the West derive from two connected contradictions. Firstly globalisation tends to generate unemployment, and thus simultaneously raise the cost of welfare while undermining the tax base necessary to pay for it. Secondly, although globalisation depends to a significant extent on nationally and internationally based social compacts, arrangements and cohesion (particularly between classes associated with power in the realm of the state and the economy and their hegemonic influence over subordinate classes and groups), nonetheless it stimulates forces which are destabilizing and destructive of these national and international social orders. The future of welfare is bound up with the capacity of states individually and collectively, through such world regional organisations as the EU, to manage and balance these contradictions. One of Rhodes' main concerns is to assess whether it is credible to consider that there might be a 'third way' between globalist and nationalist approaches to economic growth and the provision of welfare. He recommends a 'progressive competition state' approach which aims to simultaneously develop the innovative capacity of nation-states (their capacity to innovate economically, socially, politically and institutionally), and build public coalitions of support for the welfare functions of compensating 'the victims of globalization', and suggests that the EU has a role to play in promoting this agenda (also see Deacon, 1997 and Mishra, 1999).

To summarise, many of the analyses of social citizenship considered here stress the role and diversity of response of the nations and their citizens' political debates and decisions. However, they also recognise the great and arguably increasing importance in such processes of the kind of common structural change factors I have outlined. As noted, Esping-Andersen characteristically endorses the relevance of the political dimension. Nevertheless he does concede the importance of structural change in his concern with 'national adaptions' to 'global economies' and to 'postindustrialism'. He suggests that 'The political problem today is how to forge coalitions for an alternative, postindustrial model of social citizenship and egalitarianism' (Esping-Andersen, 1996: 267). Comparably Rhodes, while he is sceptical about European nations' and the EU's capacity to contribute to the process of 'compensating the victims of globalization', nonetheless implies that this might be conceivable providing the member states committed themselves to the development of social citizenship at the transnational EU level (Rhodes, 1996, also see his contribution to Ferrara et al., 2000).

CONCLUSION

This chapter has recognised that there are important and enduring differences between national models of citizenship and social rights in the developed and democratic societies. Nevertheless these societies each inhabit new and changing international political-economic contexts in which alternative national models of 'welfare capitalism' coexist and compete, and in which pressures deriving from globalisation are increasing (Deacon, 1997; Mishra, 1999). This new international context and the new dynamics operating between, on the one hand, 'path-dependent' diversity and, on the other, pressures towards convergence need to be taken into account when attempting to understand the contemporary condition of and prospects for national-level social rights and social citizenship within any given nation-state. Some of the main commonalities are the increasing importance of the social assistance element within welfare systems, the growth of 'active' approaches to labour market and employment policy, and generally the growth of what can be called varieties of a new 'social contractualism' in the relation between citizens and the state in the contemporary period. These issues are not always adequately addressed within mainstream comparative social policy and social citizenship research.

The review of the topic of social citizenship undertaken in this chapter suggests that projects and processes of renewal will have to engage with the new complexities and new contexts of citizenship in general. It is suggested that, in future projects of renewal of social rights, the originary and fundamental connections of social rights, on the one hand, with social responsibilities and, on the other hand, with citizenship's civil, political, and cultural rights and responsibilities more generally, will need to be re-affirmed and re-institutionalised. In addition projects to renew national social rights will need to be undertaken in an awareness of the relevance of transnational levels of rights and responsibilities. At a global level this involves taking seriously the possibilities for developing the interest in and capacity of global policy institutions such as the United Nations, the International Labour Organisation, the World

Bank and the International Monetary Fund to recognise and promote social rights and the full complex of rights associated with citizenship (Held, 1995; Deacon, 1987; Mishra, 1999). In Europe, understood as a 'world region', this involves particularly an awareness of the increasing importance for individuals and nations of their participation in the European Union (EU) and thus of the possibilities for developing social citizenship at a transnational as well as at national levels.

What the development of the transnational EU project means for the national-level citizenship regimes of EU member states in general, and their social citizenship regimes in particular, is currently not at all clear. On the one hand, and in the short to medium term, there is the possibility that there may be few implications. This is because of the diversity in national social models around Europe noted in this chapter and also, within the EU system, because of the subsidiarity principle and the persistence of national control and veto power over taxation and welfare policies. On the other hand, and in the medium to longer term, arguably there is a political and social logic connected with the economic logic of the construction of the Single Market, the single currency and the Economic and Monetary Union project in general. This could generate policy 'spill overs' into the spheres of social and citizenship policy, comparable with 'spill over' processes in many policy areas which have long characterised the process of development of the EU. In addition the process to enlarge the EU to include postcommunist Eastern European states and the Economic and Monetary Union integrative process in general, if they are successful, are each likely to lead to increases in intra-EU labour mobility. These issues are likely to increase the pressure to develop more standardised and portable EU-level citizenship and social rights systems, and this in turn may require a reorganisation and relative standardisation of elements of national social policies and welfare systems. The adaptability of the well-resourced national social citizenship systems of the social democratic model to globalisation reviewed in this chapter will need to be matched by further adaptation to the related transnational process of Europeanisation. For the future of the citizens of the member states of the increasingly interconnected and interdependent European Union it is now time to begin to put some flesh on what are currently only the bones of EU citizenship and social rights (Roche, 1997; Roche and van Berkel, 1997). Processes of reform and renewal of social citizenship at the national level in European societies during the early 21st century will increasingly need to take this transnational EU level of social citizenship into account.

REFERENCES

Alber, J. and Standing, G. (2000) 'Social dumping, catch-up or convergence? Europe in a comparative global context', *Journal of European Social Policy*, 10 (2): 99–119.

Barbelet, J. (1988) *Citizenship: Rights, Struggle and Class Inequality*. Milton Keynes: Open University Press.

Bendix, R. (1964) *Nation-Building and Citizenship*. New York: John Wiley.

Castells, M. (1996) *The Rise of the Network Society (The Information Age*, vol. 1). Oxford: Blackwell.

Castles, F. and Pierson, C. (1996) 'A new convergence?', *Policy and Politics*, 24 (3): 233–45.

Cattacin, S. and Tattini, V. (1997) 'Reciprocity Schemes in Unemployment Regulation Policies: Towards a pluralistic citizenship of marginalisation?', *Citizenship Studies*, 1 (3): 351–64.

Culpitt, I. (1992) *Welfare and Citizenship: Beyond the Crisis of the Welfare State?* London: Sage

Deacon, Bob (1997) *Global Social Policy*. London: Sage.

Delanty, G. (2000) *Citizenship in a Global Age*. Milton Keynes: Open University Press.

Doyal, L. and Gough, I. (1991) *The Theory of Human Needs*. London: Macmillan.

Dwyer, P. (2000) *Welfare Rights and Responsibilities: Contesting Social Citizenship*. Bristol: The Policy Press.

Eardley, T., Bradshaw, J., Ditch, J., Gough, I. and Whiteford, P. (1996) *Social Assistance in OECD Countries*. London: HMSO.

Esping-Andersen, G. (1990) *The Three Worlds of Welfare Capitalism*. Cambridge: Polity Press.

Esping-Andersen, G. (ed.) (1996) *Welfare States in Transition: National Adaptations in Global Economies*. London: Sage.

Esping-Andersen, G. (1999) *The Social Foundations of Post-Industrial Economies*, Oxford: Oxford University Press.

Etzioni, A. (1993) *The Spirit of Community*. New York: Crown.

Etzioni, A. (2000) *The Third Way to a Good Society*. London: Demos.

Falk, R. (2000) 'The Decline of Citizenship in an Era of Globalization', *Citizenship Studies*, 4 (1): 5–17.

Ferrera, M. (1996) 'The "Southern Model" of Welfare in Social Europe', *Journal of European Social Policy*, 6 (1): 17–37.

Ferrera, M., Hemerijk, A. and Rhodes, M. (2000) *The Future of Social Europe: Recasting Work and Welfare in the New Economy*, Oeiras: Celta.

Flynn, R. (1997) 'Quasi-welfare, Associationalism and the Social Division of Citizenship', *Citizenship Studies*, 1 (3): 335–50.

Giddens, A. (1983) 'Class division, class conflict and citizenship rights', in A. Giddens, *Profiles and Critiques in Social Theory*. London: Macmillan.

Giddens, A. (1998) *The Third Way: The Renewal of Social Democracy*. Cambridge: Polity Press.

Giddens, A. (2000) *The Third Way and its Critics*. Cambridge: Polity Press.

Ginsburg, N. (1992) *Divisions of Welfare: A Critical Introduction to Comparative Social Policy*. London: Sage.

Goodin, R., Headey, B., Muffels, R. and Dirven, H.J. (1999) *The Real Worlds of Welfare Capitalism*. Cambridge University Press: Cambridge.

Gough, I., Eardley, T., Bradshaw, J., Ditch, J. and Whiteford, P. (1997) 'Social assistance in OECD countries', *Journal of European Social Policy*, 7 (1): 17–43.

Gould, A. (1993) *Capitalist Welfare Systems: A Comparison of Japan, Britain and Sweden*. London: Longman.

Heikkila, M. (ed.) (1999) *Linking Welfare and Work*. Dublin: European Foundation.

Held, D. (1995) *Democracy and the Global Order: From the Modern State to Cosmopolitan Governance*. Cambridge: Polity Press.

Held, D., McGrew, A., Goldblatt, D. and Perraton, J. (1999) *Global Transformations: Politics, Economics and Culture*. Cambridge: Polity Press.

Hill, M. (1996) *Social Policy: A Comparative Analysis*. London: Prentice Hall/Harvester Wheatsheaf.

Hirst, P. and Thompson, G. (1999) *Globalization in Question*. 2nd edition, Cambridge: Polity Press.

Hout, W. (1997) 'Globalisation and European Welfare States', unpublished paper, COST A7 Final conference, London.

Huws, U. (1997) 'Flexibility and Security: Towards a new European balance', *Citizens Income Trust Discussion Paper 3*, London: Citizens Income Trust.

Isin, E. and Wood, P. (1999) *Citizenship and Identity*. London: Sage

Janoski, T. (1998) *Citizenship and Civil Society*. Cambridge: Cambridge University Press.

Jordan, B. (1998) *The New Politics of Welfare*. London: Sage.

Kautto, M., Hekkila, M., Hvinden, B., and Marklund, S. Ploug, N. (1999) *Nordic Social Policy: Changing Welfare States*. Routledge: London.

Leibfried, S. and Pierson, C. (eds) (1995) *European Social Policy*. Washington DC: Brookings Institute.

Lewis, J. (1992) 'Gender and the development of welfare regimes', *Journal of European Social Policy*, 2 (3): 159–173.

Lister, R. (1997) *Citizenship: Feminist Perspectives*. London: Macmillan.

Marshall, T.H. (1973) 'Citizenship and Social Class', in T.H. Marshall *Class, Citizenship, and Social Development*. Westport, Conn.: Greenwood Press.

Meehan, E. (1993) *Citizenship and the European Community*. London: Sage.

Mishra, R. (1990) *The Welfare State in Capitalist Society*. Hemel Hempstead: Harvester Wheatsheaf.

Mishra, R. (1999) *Globalization and the Welfare State*. Cheltenham: Edward Elgar.

Orloff, A. (1993) 'Gender and the social rights of citizenship: the comparative analysis of gender relations and welfare states', *American Sociological Review*, 58 (June): 303–28.

Rhodes, M. (1996) 'Globalization and West European Welfare States: A critical review of recent debates', *Journal of European Social Policy*, 6 (4): 305–27.

Rimlinger, G. (1971) *Welfare Policy and Industrialization in Europe, America and Russia*. New York: John Wiley.

Roche, M. (1987) 'Citizenship, Social Theory and Social Change', *Theory and Society*, 16: 363–99.

Roche, M. (1992) *Rethinking Citizenship: Ideology, Welfare and Change in Modern Society*. (reprinted 1996) Polity Press: Cambridge.

Roche, M. (1995a) 'Citizenship and Modernity', *British Journal of Sociology*, 6 (4): 715–33.

Roche, M. (1995b) 'Citizenship, Obligation and Anomie; themes in the analysis of contemporary political ideologies and social movements' in S. Edgell, S. Walklate and G. Williams (eds), *Debating the Future of the Public Sphere*. Aldershot: Avebury, Ch. 30.

Roche, M. (1997) 'Citizenship and Exclusion in the European Union', in M. Roche and R. van Berkel (eds), European Citizenship and Social Exclusion. Aldershot: Ashgate, Ch. 3.

Roche, M. (2000) 'Citizenship and the cultural dimension in Europe', in N. Stevenson (ed.) Culture and Citizenship. London: Sage, Ch.

Roche, M. and van Berkel, R. (eds) (1997) *European Citizenship and Social Exclusion*. Aldershot: Ashgate.

Standing, G. (1999) *Global Labour Flexibility*. London: Macmillan.

Stevenson, N. (ed.) (2000) *Culture and Citizenship*. London: Sage.

Taylor-Gooby, P. (1997) 'European Welfare futures', *Social Policy and Administration*, 31 (1): 1–19.

Turner, B. (1986) *Citizenship and Capitalism*. London: Allen and Unwin.

Turner, B. (ed.) (1993) *Citizenship and Social Theory*. London: Sage.

Twine, F. (1994) *Citizenship and Social Rights*. London, Sage.

van Steenbergen, B. (ed) (1994) *The Condition of Citizenship*. London: Sage.

Wiener, A. (1998) *'European' Citizenship Practice: Building Institutions of a Non-State*. Oxford: Westview Press.

Part Two

HISTORIES

5

Ancient Citizenship and its Inheritors

DAVID BURCHELL

In the modern West the history of citizenship is most commonly presented in terms of a sharp contrast between its ancient and modern (meaning post-medieval) forms. In ancient citizenship, according to this view, the citizenry is its own political master: modern historians have made much of Aristotle's famous phrase that in democracies the citizen is both ruler and ruled in turn (Politics: 1283b). There is no locus of sovereignty outside the body of the citizens themselves. Rule may be exercised in practice by consuls, magistrates, assemblies or even kings – yet these are understood simply as custodians of the people's authority. And politics demands at least the potential participation of citizens in decision-making. Here citizenship is expressed as the activity of fulfilling one's obligations towards one's fellow-citizens. In modern citizenship, by contrast, citizens are aware that they owe a primal obligation of obedience to some supreme sovereign ruler, and that this subjection limits their personal political autonomy in a quite profound manner. Even where sovereignty is described as vested in the people themselves, they participate in their sovereign role only in the context of an elaborate system of political representation at a distance, carried out in the shadow of a permanent professional administrative apparatus. Hence citizenship is expressed only 'passively', as a form of constraint upon action, or delegation of action to others (cf. Burchell, 1995).

This received modern account of ancient citizenship is generally delivered in the register of political theory. And so it tends to present a picture of ancient civic life which is strong on political ideals and principles, and decidedly thin on political culture and routine civil life. It is not always easy, when reading modern accounts of ancient citizenship, to imagine how the figure of the active citizen dovetails into the mundane civil affairs of relatively peaceable societies – let alone what value, if any, was accorded to the unheroic practices of 'passive' citizenship. A further complication is that modern images of ancient citizenship do not come to us directly from the ancient texts themselves. Rather, in good measure they are a product of the highly charged political controversies of the early modern world, when ancient 'republicanism' was held up as an idealised alternative to everything which critics disliked about the contemporary world of territorial states and the claims of secular sovereign power. And so modern accounts of ancient 'republicanism', which are so influential in modern images of ancient citizenship, often bear a striking resemblance to the self-styled republican political theories of writers in the

Northern Italian Renaissance (c. 1400–1600), or the Dutch Revolt (c. 1570–1650), or the English Revolution of the 1640s and 1650s. Finally, it was inevitable that early modern revivals of ancient 'republicanism', and the images of 'active' citizenship which went along with them, were refracted through the violent religious controversies of the epoch. It is impossible to understand the republicanism of the Dutch Revolt, or of the English Revolution, for instance, without recognising that they were products of distinctive and specific Protestant religious cultures. And so, deliberately or otherwise, modern republicanism often owes more to Calvin than it does to Cicero.

Here I want to outline a relatively novel account of ancient citizenship and its broader legacy in the early modern and modern worlds, one which seems to me more in sympathy with the general approach of the present volumes. I will suggest that it is possible to find an ancient ancestry for both the 'passive' and 'active' citizens of the early-modern and modern worlds – and indeed, that the two concepts were often seen as integrally related. And I will argue that, contrary to modern accounts which present ancient citizenship as an antidote or alternative to the modern sovereign state, the ancient civic legacy and its significance were adopted and contested on both sides of the debate over the roles of sovereign power. In so doing I want to stress the genuine complexity and ambivalence of images of citizenship and civic life in the ancient world. For Cicero civic activism was dangerous as well as laudable, disruptive as well as potentially liberatory. Civic heroes needed to be treated with kid gloves. And so those writers in the early modern world who stressed the importance of what we moderns are bound to see as purely passive forms of citizenship – such as tolerance and respect for others, or simply minding one's own business – may not be so new-fangled as they are sometimes depicted. And this should not really surprise us, since some of them were among the greatest classicists of their era.

SOVEREIGN AND CITIZEN

The sense of a sharp break between ancient and modern conceptions of citizenship dates at least to the latter seventeenth century. In the Northern Italian Renaissance of the fifteenth century the classical 'political life' – as especially vividly depicted in the first-century BCE Roman statesman Cicero's speeches and letters – had served as a propaganda counterpoint to those models of political domination and subjection which had been inherited from the Carolingian empire and the feudal epoch, and which were associated with the political cultures of the Italians' threatened foreign rulers. This reconstructed neo-classical citizenship was sometimes described as republican, following the Latin term denoting the polities of the ancient city-states. And it may or may not have been associated with political theories of forms of rule and 'mixed constitutions'. The significance of this political language of republicanism in the secular political cultures of the Renaissance states has sometimes been overstated by modern historians. Few other scholars, for instance, have ever been entirely convinced by Hans Baron's account of a triumphant 'civic humanism' in the Italian city-states (Baron, 1966). Again, in the northern monarchies of the sixteenth century the neo-Roman civic ethos was often reconstructed quite pragmatically as an ethic of counsel to sovereign monarchs, in the form of manuals of 'advice to the prince'. Perhaps more significant for practical purposes was the fact that what were depicted as classical 'republican' doctrines were widely enlisted in the 'resistance' theories of various Christian confessional groupings, both Protestant and Catholic, during the long period of bitter religious struggle (c. 1570–1650) which followed the Reformations (Skinner, 1978).

It was in this latter, theological, incarnation as a theory of resistance by (Christian) subjects to unjust (secular) rulers that born-again versions of ancient citizenship became increasingly controversial and contested.

For while seventeenth-century theorists of sovereignty such as Hobbes and Pufendorf were consummate Latinists and admirers of Roman personal ethics, they were resolutely opposed to the role played by republican doctrines in the religious controversies of the day. Their reasoning was simple. From the Reformations onwards the old feudal kingdoms of western and central Europe had been drowned in successive waves of internal and international strife and bloodshed, all prompted in good measure by the claim that the call of religious authenticity, which was to be found within the individual Christian believer's breast, took moral primacy over the calls of order, reason and the rule of law. The only cure for the disease of intractable religious turmoil, according to the theorists of sovereignty, was a general agreement in the primacy of sovereignty over all other political values (Pufendorf, [1673] 1991: 139–41, 175–7).

Hobbes and Pufendorf explicitly associate the contemporary renovation of classical civic culture, as refracted through the concerns of humanistically trained Reformation theologians, with the religious and political chaos of their era. According to Pufendorf it is the 'absurd and erroneous' political 'dogmas' of Plato and Aristotle, as transmitted through the early modern university curriculum, which have brought tumult and convulsion to modern states (Pufendorf, 1955: 'Praefatio lectori benevolos').[1] Hobbes blames the ancient civic tradition for all the tumults of his time, and 'the effusion of so much blood': 'there was never anything so dearly bought, as these Western parts have bought the learning of the Greek and Latin tongues'. Just as the Reformation theologians' location of spiritual authority within the individual believer's breast led to interminable religious dispute, so the republicans' location of moral authority within the breast of the individual citizen would lead to endless religious conflict. Worse still, if primacy of the spiritual conscience in religious belief were allied to civic activism in political belief, neither established religion nor established political order would ever be left in peace. Everybody would be free all the time to engage in tumult and sedition in favour of the particular religious-political order dictated by their conscience.

In any case, for Hobbes the modern search for freedom, whether spiritual or political, was self-defeating – since (whether it is formally acknowledged or not) every stable form of government has a seat of sovereignty, and every one requires submission to the rightful sovereign. Here Hobbes was drawing also upon the ancient critics of democracy such as the historian Thucydides, who had observed that the direct democracy of the assembly, which seemed ostensibly the 'freest', was the form of government most likely to degenerate into simply personal tyranny, since the actual seats of authority were hidden behind the mask of popular rule (Hobbes, [1628] 1989: 571–3). The 'freedom of citizens' for Hobbes is determined not by the presence or absence of assemblies or seats of representation, but by the capacity of the sovereign to secure and protect those freedoms: 'whether a commonwealth be monarchical, or popular, the freedom is still the same' (Hobbes, [1651] 1991: 149–50; cf. Hobbes, [1647] 1998: 121).

Of course, Hobbes' contemporaries viewed these arguments with deep suspicion. The loudest and most numerous of Hobbes' opponents condemned his dismissal of religious authority as political atheism. Others, such as the republican James Harrington, criticised him for replacing an ancient 'art of government', based upon 'the foundation of common right or interest', with a modern art of government by means of which 'some man, or some few men, subject a city or a nation, and rule it according unto his or their private interest'. The one, according to Harrington, was a *de jure* government based on the rule of laws rather than men; the other a *de facto* government based on the rule of men rather than laws (Harrington, [1656] 1992: 8–9).

ANCIENTS AND MODERNS

Historically, of course, Western polities broadly followed the course advocated by Hobbes and Pufendorf (if not Hobbes' controversial theological prescriptions). They established civil peace on the basis of a universal subjection to political sovereignty, and they emphasised the figure of the dutiful 'passive' citizen ahead of the self-determining civic activist who, in Hobbes' and Pufendorf's minds, had provided the role-model for the self-directed religious zealot. And in important respects these political values became the linchpin of modern representative states. Modern historians of citizenship, on the other hand, have tended to take a much bleaker view of 'Hobbes' choice'. Following in Harrington's footsteps, modern scholars decry the passage in Hobbes and his fellow theorists of sovereignty from a classical 'language' of politics to an early modern lexicon of reason of state, in which the community based upon justice is replaced by rule based upon the fear of the sovereign (e.g. Viroli, 1992; Skinner, 1998). For these scholars a twice reborn republicanism appears to provide a way out of what might uncharitably be described as the self-created impasse of contemporary political thought, the supposed Scylla and Charybdis of individualism and collectivism, individual rights and social rights, the right and the good (e.g. Pettit, 1997: Chs 2–3; Skinner, 1998: Chs 1–2).[2]

Yet the modern view of Hobbes and the other theorists of sovereignty is paradoxical. On the one hand many contemporary political theorists side with Harrington in rejecting Hobbes' view of sovereignty as simply a legitimation of untrammelled personal rule, or else as a transference of sovereignty from the people to the blank visage of the impersonal state (e.g. Skinner, 1989). On the other hand, modern scholars are surprisingly willing to take Hobbes' own polemical depiction of the gulf between ancient and early modern political cultures as if it were a simple statement of fact. Following Hobbes, they characteristically equate the classical 'republics' with formal doctrines of popular sovereignty expressed through a unified 'popular will' (e.g. Skinner, 1998: 24–36). At the same time, they tend to take on trust the claims of Hobbes and others that classical political thought is defined by its exaltation of the figure of the active, independent citizen. Thus the classical 'art of politics' is depicted as founded on a universal figure of the 'political man', a creature in whom is vested the power of politics and rhetoric, and even the capacity to assume the city's 'point of view' (e.g. Viroli, 1992: 71–125, 289).[3] I want to suggest in what follows that these presumptions seriously underestimate the complexity of ancient civic thought, and of its various early modern uses and abuses.

GREEKS AND ROMANS

One source of the prevalent modern confusion over ancient citizenship is culture and language. Hobbes and Pufendorf were Grecians as much as Latinists, and the prime culprit of their accounts is Aristotle, the fourth-century Greek academic philosopher. This was convenient, since it allowed them to conflate 'republicanism' with the 'decrepit' Aristotelian philosophy of the late medieval 'schoolmen', who were their major polemical opponents.[4] Until recently modern accounts of early modern republicanism – drawing upon a tradition established by nineteenth-century German scholars – also fashioned their image of ancient civic thought mainly out of Greek sources such as Aristotle, Plato and Polybius (e.g. Pocock, 1975). Yet this is misleading, for Greek philosophy was far less influential in the early modern world than was the Latinate culture of Roman politics, rhetoric and law. (Hobbes and Pufendorf themselves were consummate Roman lawyers.) The key texts of ancient political thought for early modern writers were speeches and histories rather than the lecture notes of the philosophy academies, and their exemplar was the worldly Roman rhetorician Cicero rather than the schoolmaster Aristotle – a philosopher who in any case had been so completely absorbed into Western religious culture as to be thought of almost as a theologian, rather than a politician.

The phenomenon widely known as Ciceronianism waxed and waned in academic fashion, but it remained the cornerstone of early modern political culture for three centuries. The Northern Italian Renaissance humanists had mourned Cicero's 'martyrdom' in what they liked to call his 'last fight for the republic'. This cult of Cicero the republican martyr was still in rude health in mid-eighteenth-century England, when Conyers Middleton published a hagiographic biography of Cicero to great acclaim. For the eighteenth century it was Roman civil philosophy – and Cicero above all others – which incarnated a 'polite' form of political manners, allied with a gentlemanly ethos of civic life. This Ciceronian personal culture, based on an ethic of public service, continued to shape the demeanour of upper-middle-class British and American schoolboys into the twentieth century, long after it fell out of favour among scholars.

Not until the nineteenth-century Romantics produced a rival cult of the Great Man, who for many classicists was Cicero's populist opponent Julius Caesar, was the ghost of Cicero finally stilled. German classicists, spellbound by the Romantic cult of Homer and demanding from the ancients a totalising social theory on the nineteenth-century model, exalted the speculative philosophy of Plato and dismissed the Roman tradition of practical civil science as a 'mongrel compound of history and philosophy' (Schofield, 1995). The German Romantic historian Theodor Mommsen, whose heart lay on the barricades of 1848, exalted Caesar as the spirit of Action, and contemptuously dismissed Cicero as an orator of 'no conviction and no passion', 'a statesman without insight, idea or purpose' and a literary 'dabbler' (Mommsen, [1854–6] 1901: 504–5). He had no shortage of twentieth-century supporters (e.g. Syme, 1939; Stockton, 1975). Even today classical political thought is understood almost exclusively through Plato's utopias and Aristotle's digests, while Cicero's letters and tracts are consigned to the ranks of primary source material. This severely impedes our ability to understand the significance of ancient citizenship both for the ancients themselves, and for the 'new Romans' of the early modern world. For where they saw example and precept, we see doctrine and theory. And where they groped towards political stability, we restlessly seek after political liberation.

RES PUBLICA

Modern scholars, then, have staked a good deal on reclaiming what they see as the distinctively 'republican' political culture of the ancient city-states.[5] Yet 'republicanism', as a presumed doctrine about the nature of politics in the classical city, is a modern invention – albeit one of such long standing that for many scholars it has become second nature. *Res publica* in Ciceronian Latin has many meanings, but 'republic' and 'republicanism' are not among them (Schofield, 1995). In its most primal sense *res publica* simply denotes the 'public affairs' of the city, where these are understood to allow the capacity of at least some of the citizenry to intervene in those affairs with some effect. In a more extended sense it may suggest the affairs of the 'people' (*populus*), where this is understood not as a moral entity but as a specific political community founded under justice and the rule of law.[6] Or it may denote the political interests of one's own country (the *patria*) in its relations with others. None of these usages presumes a specific political constitution or order, beyond the presence of some kind of 'public' space in which political affairs can be debated. In principle, this space may be preserved under any of the primary forms of political constitution, or indeed under any mixture of these forms – and the 'deviant' versions of those forms (mob rule, oligarchy, despotism) represent situations where one part of the polity deprives the remainder of that capacity.

In his tract *De Re Publica* Cicero allows that *res publica* may flourish under any of the main forms of government (monarchy, aristocracy, democracy) prescribed by Polybius. Yet the liberty of each social group will necessarily vary: under an aristocracy the populace may see itself as enduring a kind of servitude, while the unrestrained domination of the multitude may likewise be experienced by their victims as a kind of mob rule (De Re Publica: I. 39, I. 43).[7] Hence in practice the political order must be balanced in such a fashion as to find a stable resting-point, according to the sociological composition of the particular city (*civitas*) in question. And the trick of politics is to find that balancing-point in public liberty which will allow 'the appropriate exercise of different capacities by the different elements of society' (Zetzel, 1995: 19). As Scipio explains in *De Re Publica* (I. 57–58), there must be an even balance in the city of rights, duties and offices, so that the magistrates possess sufficient power, the bodies of leading citizens sufficient authority, and the people sufficient liberty, that *res publica* can be saved from the threat of constant instability and change (cf. Schofield, 1999). In this sense the *res publica* of Cicero's letters is a specifically Roman manifestation of this wider rule of political balance. It is an historical accommodation, the role of which is to harmonise the traditional moral authority of the senatorial nobility with the hard-won political victories of the plebs.

By the same token, where the delicate balance of the political culture is upset, *res publica* can rapidly sicken and die. This sense of *res publica* as a kind of fragile hothouse plant, a precarious artefact of civic horticulture, resonates through the literature of the last decades of the Roman 'Republic'. In letters and tracts across two decades Cicero over and over decries what he sees as the present or imminent destruction of *res publica* at the hands of overweeningly powerful individuals. *Res publica* persists in name, though its reality has long since been lost; nothing but a semblance of the real *res publica* remains to us; *res publica* is no more (*nulla est res publica*); the commonwealth (*civitas*) has lost its very sap and blood. There are brief periods of optimism: he has visions of the pristine *res publica* of yore rising as if from the dead; he recovers his old spirit and character in its defence. Yet in the end it remains for him only to mourn *res publica*'s loss, and the lost liberty of the city (*De Re Publica* V.2; *Ad Atticum* IV.19, IV.18; *Ad Familiares* IV.4, X.28, XII.28, IX.16).

Historians have sometimes been inclined to explain the shrillness of these passages as a product of Cicero's overheated political imagination. Yet the anxiety shared by Cicero and his contemporaries towards the health and well-being of *res publica* was real enough. For as Cicero explains, it is a difficult art to rule over *res publica* rightly, as a statesman does, and much easier (like Caesar and Pompey) to rule like a king (Ad Atticum: VII.25, VIII.11). Even one man, if he is sufficiently powerful and charismatic, may suffice to overturn everything. At the outset of Rome's final ruinous bout of civil wars Cicero observes of his nemesis Caesar that 'even when he was very weak, he prevailed over the whole *res publica*. What do you think would happen now? (Ad Atticum: VII.9) And the last century of Roman *res publica* sees a lengthy parade of such men. The Gracchi, Marius, Sulla, Pompey, Crassus, Caesar, Antony, Octavian: each and every one of them strides over the civic garden with hobnail boots. Worse still, those who rise up to challenge overweening individuals will tend inevitably to acquire the same dangerous characteristics as their foes. When Pompey raises his standard in a last bid to defeat Caesar, Cicero is despairing. Now supporters of *res publica* have a choice between the horrors of war and the indignity of servitude, between the domination of Caesar and the violent instincts for revenge of his opponents. And this is really no choice at all, since in either course the outcome will be the loss of *res publica*.

DIGNITAS

The public space of *res publica* is a tangible, geographic zone of daily life. It corresponds to the free flow of persons traversing the city on their ordinary business, stopping to 'chew the cud' or solicit favours or attention. Demagoguery and political tyranny can be measured, physically, by the extent to which the demagogues restrict this free flow of persons with their bodyguards, private armies or thugs. Thus Cicero's greatest moment – the memory of which he never tires of recounting – comes where he rescues the Roman streets from the threat of the conspirator Cataline's goons. Given the pervasiveness of our post-Enlightenment political fantasies concerning an abstract 'public sphere' and the 'civil society' which supposedly dwells in it, it should be emphasised that there is nothing remotely democratic or even egalitarian about this kind of public liberty. The Roman streets are not public thoroughfares, nor is there a self-evident human right to equal space or an equal share of human dignity on their cobblestones. *Dignitas*, as the Romans called it, is an explicitly status- and gender-specific attribute.[8]

Nonetheless, *dignitas* is the crucial attribute of that special group of citizens who aspire to high political office. As a public citizen one needs to walk the streets in freedom in order to exhibit one's personal capacity 'in the round', as it were, through the daily drama of mutual friendship and complaisance towards clients and acquaintances. As Cicero explains in his most influential moral tract, *dignitas* is a form of political charisma: it manifests itself as a kind of beauty displayed on the person. And, like the beauty of the philosophers, it consists in order, balance and harmony. One assembles *dignitas* out of a compound of personal features: a good appearance (neither negligent nor affected); a careful gait (neither halting nor mincing, hurried nor listless); a finely calibrated mode of speech (neither loquacious nor curt, appropriate to the situation at hand); even one's choice of house (De Officiis: I. 126–39). In short, in one's *dignitas* one displays one's sense of civic poise and balance. Yet one can only achieve this through ceaseless small efforts of self-projection, self-assertion and self-display.

This civic drama of 'republicanism', then, is rather like the stage drama of Shakespeare – which, at several removes, is indeed derived from it. It is a tragedy of great personalities, bursting with potential and with contradiction: Rosencrantz and Guildenstern are doomed to be always bit players. Caesar's famous audacity, Octavian's cold ruthlessness, Antony's violent rages, Cicero's legendary self-praise, are all the attributes of the larger-than-life public citizen. And as in Shakespearian tragedy, the man of *dignitas* is a Janus-faced figure. In order to maintain and extend his *dignitas* he is bound to a restless pursuit of 'power and glory, position and prestige' (Earl, 1967: 16). Thus, like Machiavelli's 'virtuous' citizen, he is at once a dynamic force and a destructive one: he is the bulwark of *res publica* against threats from without, but also its greatest threat from within. By his heroism he secures and enlarges the majesty of *res publica*; by his overweening pride and lust for glory he is always threatening to plunge that selfsame *res publica* into chaos. The rest of the citizenry, the 'private citizens', are required to compensate for this turbulent, glory-seeking behaviour by seeking only stability and peace.

Hence Cicero's stark distinction between the ethical duties of public and private, 'active' and 'passive', citizens. For Cicero moral duties are specific to particular types of person and their public roles (Hellegouarc'h, 1963: 152–6). His major ethical treatise, revered by the early moderns as 'Tully's *Offices*', is explicitly directed towards the personal ethical demands of this public citizen. By developing the great Stoic attributes of *constantia* and *apathaeia* he is to be made capable at once of personal self-assertion and of civic self-control. And he is to understand that the quest to enlarge his own *dignitas* is secondary to his quest to maintain the *dignitas* of the city (Burchell, 1998). Cicero's political theory, when he resorts to that style of argument, also serves as a kind of leash for the man of *dignitas*, a method for domesticating the beast. In his *De Re Publica* he describes his ideal statesman. This individual should regard himself as a pilot (*gubernator*), ensuring the safety of the passengers, rather than as a military hero, ensuring their own immortality through glory: his reward will come in another life.[9] Yet Cicero is always disappointed by the incapacity of the 'great men' of his time to submit themselves to this form of self-constraint: instead, they always want to rule, 'like kings', by the force of their own personality.

For the remainder of the citizenry – the great mass of the free male population – Cicero's formula is much simpler. The private citizen (*privatus*) should seek only to live on fair and equal terms with his fellow citizens, neither submissively and abjectly nor inflating his own importance. And he should will that *res publica* be preserved in peace and honour. Such is the man we call a good citizen (De Officiis: I. (24); cf. Burchell, 1998). Hence the private citizen becomes the necessary foil to the more charismatic but unstable public one. And the unheroic virtues of civility – trying to be fair and reasonable with others, not raising one's voice above the throng – become an antidote to the sometimes uncivil civic-mindedness of the great.

At the same time, in Cicero's Rome the almost desperate need for the great citizens to shape and enhance their *dignitas*, and to secure a kind of immortality through their exploits, can pose a real threat to the lives and liberties of the great mass of the 'private' citizenry. As the classical historian Frank Adcock once put it, 'the political stage was too full of actors, all burning to play a leading role'. Hence, Roman public life is in good measure a tense tug-of-war between the '*dignitas* of the great man' and the '*libertas* of the small man', the former exercised through the quasi-monarchical authority of the great public offices, and the latter through the legal protections afforded private citizens in the courts (Adcock, 1959: 13, 62). Modern political theorists have debated at great length 'positive' and 'negative' characterisations of freedom, usually defined in relatively abstract terms. In Roman political culture 'positive' and 'negative' liberty were political facts, vested in specific life-situations. The *libertas* of the great was the exemplar of active freedom, since it subsisted in the independence of great citizens from ties of obligations to others, and the prestige afforded them by the quantity of others who owed obligations to them. The largely 'negative' *libertas* of the small, on the other hand, resided chiefly in their freedom from the extra-legal predations of the great. Until recently historians of Roman citizenship, eager to follow in the footsteps of Great Men, overwhelmingly stressed the political rights and duties of citizenship – usually monopolised by a small number of great citizens – to the exclusion of these 'private rights' (*iura privata*), rights which arguably formed the actual 'core and heart' of citizenship for ordinary Roman citizens and their legal dependents (cf. Gardner, 1989: 1–6, 155–78). The three great precepts of Roman law for its citizens were (in the words of Justinian's *Institutes*, the most influential summary of Roman legal doctrine) 'to live honourably, not to cause harm, and to give each their due (Institutiones: I.i). Like Cicero's formula for the 'private citizen', this could almost be taken as the script for early modern 'passive' citizenship.

MONARCHY AND IMPERIUM

Cicero died among the ruins of the old Senatorial order, before the birth of imperial rule. Yet the imperial Roman historians who followed him tended on the whole to endorse his pathology of the old Senatorial political culture, and the morbid symptoms afflicting the great 'public' citizens. The first of these post-Republican moralists, Sallust, describes in mordant tones the decline and fall of the traditional virtues of the great governing families. For Sallust the 'active citizens' of this ilk are genuinely tragic figures, laid low, in the best Shakespearian fashion, by their own fatal flaws. The great citizens of the early Republic, he explained, had been driven to success by personal rivalry and patriotic ardour. But above all they were driven by ambition and the desire for personal glory – passions which had roused them to great deeds. For ambition (Sallust explains), while perhaps a defect, is near to virtue. (The Roman word, *virtus*, is in fact ambiguous between moral honour and personal courage.) The good and the bad alike aspire to glory, honour and mastery over men – only by different paths. Yet time and success had turned good *mores* into bad: what had been a noble thirst for glory became base avarice, and wealth and success in turn undermined ambition and liberty (Bellum Catilinae: vii–xi).

The early church father St Augustine – an acute reader of Cicero and Sallust – adopted the latter's analysis of civic decline in his attack on the worldly morality of the pre-Christian Romans. Augustine agreed with Sallust that the love of glory had led the early Romans to great deeds – although as a Christian he of course censured the search for glory as an end in itself. And he added the distinctively Christian, but acute, observation that behind their desire for glory had lain a veritable lust for liberty. Since liberty of this ('active') kind lay in freedom from domination by and obligation to others, it was an essential prerequisite of glory. And so, since to serve was inglorious, their greatest goals were to die bravely or to live free. But once liberty was achieved, so far were they overcome by their desire for glory that wherever the zeal for liberty had been, the desire for domination soon followed (De Civitate Dei: V. 12). And domination in time turned to despotism. Thus the Roman lust for liberty caused first the enslavement of others, and ultimately that of themselves. Augustine's insights into the ambivalence of Roman liberty were perhaps more subtle than our modern panegyrics to 'liberty as non-domination' (Pettit, 1997).

Sallust's successor Tacitus extended his gloomy analysis into the period of the principate itself. By this time, he contends, the fatal flaws of the great citizens had played themselves out. Augustus assumed *imperium*, he tells us, over a citizenry exhausted by civil discord: he proceeded to unite within his own person the offices of the Senate, the magistrates and the law-makers. The greatest spirits among the old nobility were proscribed or dead. And among those who remained, the quest for *gloria* had been stilled: the very same individuals who had advanced their reputations by revolution and discord could now be seen embracing servility and the security of the new order ahead of the dangers of the old. While the magistrates still bore their old titles, nothing of the old, authentic Roman moral character remained. Equality under the law was cast off, and all were required to observe the decrees of the *princeps*. Consuls, Senators and the equestrian order alike all hastened into servitude (Annals: I.1–I.4, I.7). In this moral universe imperial rule resembles one long dark night of trial and test.

Modern scholarship has generally echoed Tacitus' stylish moral pessimism. Modern historians tend to view the Principate and the rule of the later emperors as involving the destruction not only of Cicero's empirical description of 'Republican' citizenship, but indeed of any conception of *res publica* worthy of the name. From an active political status, in Mommsen's formulation, citizenship under the empire became a set of 'passive' legal rights; 'the old privileges and duties of the *civis Romanus*' were 'effaced', to be replaced with an imperial citizenship expressed through passive legal rights (Sherwin-White, 1973: 222). According to this view, the development of imperial rule eroded the 'positive' and active character of republican citizenship from several directions simultaneously. Public office-holding gradually lost its significance as a marker of civic autonomy and glamour. Under the *princeps* public offices multiplied, yet public officials, as servants of the *princeps*, ceased to be sovereign over their own respective domains, and became simple 'functionaries' of an imperial administration (Boissier, 1899: 315–17). The most nearly universal of civic obligations – that of military service – dwindled and finally disappeared over the imperial period as armies were raised first on a regional, and then on a purely professional basis. Finally, the granting of citizenship to a vast collection of heterogenous non-Roman communities and individuals undermined its centrality to personal identity.

Yet the 'decline' of Roman citizenship is not nearly so simple a story as this account may suggest. In Cicero's day great public honours had effectively been restricted to a handful of leading families, and the ambitious son of a father from beyond the city walls had to struggle for respect his whole long life – as Cicero himself knew to his cost. While everyone was theoretically free to seek office, its actual attainment was 'a matter not of *libertas* but *dignitas*'. The Principate opened up public office first to other social groups, and later to non-Romans and non-Italians: 'office was open to a wider circle through the favour of the emperor … than ever in the free Republic' (Sherwin-White, [1939] 1973: 265–8). And while the Senatorial nobility continued to reproduce itself, the imperial civil service was increasingly staffed by members of the more modestly affluent equestrian class, with few cultural or emotional ties to the old Republican order. This was a disaster for the old noble families, but not necessarily for the citizenry as a whole.

The complaint that the extension of citizenship necessarily diminished its value is also a rather partial one. For many 'ethnic' Roman citizens (as for some modern historians) the extension of citizenship into new and sometimes remote communities of the empire doubtless seemed to entail an intolerable diminution of the value of their own civic rights. One modern authority perhaps speaks for many of them when he complains of the 'assimilation' of a 'vast accumulation of extraneous matter' in civic identity over the later imperial period: now one could be a Roman citizen, a Spaniard and a resident of a non-Roman jurisdiction at one and the same time (Sherwin-White [1939] 1973: 274). When rights are extended beyond the boundaries of the 'original' citizenry it is perhaps inevitable that they should be seen by those 'originals' as diminished. It is less clear that their new possessors regarded them as such. St Paul can hardly have been the only 'foreigner' to defend himself from summary justice with the declaration 'I am a Roman citizen'.

In any case, Tacitus' bleak account of the death of *res publica* and liberty is deceptive. In practice, as Ronald Syme observed, Tacitus' attitude towards the civic life of the empire is profoundly ambiguous. While he appears to mourn the loss of liberty, he also endorses the peace and security of the Principate against the license and chaos of liberty unravelled. And while he deplores (and lovingly retells) the monstrous excesses of bad emperors like Caligula and Nero, Tacitus still speaks of Rome's political life as *res publica*, and he describes in detail the *dignitas* and *libertas* of its most worthy and intrepid citizens. 'Monarchy or Republic, that was not the real antithesis.' Rather, bad government was that which denied its leading citizens the capacity to express their political personality (Syme, 1958: 547–50, 549). Yet in many circumstances the leading citizens might need to be protected from themselves, so to speak – and it was here that the role of the *princeps*, as 'first man' above the contending factions, was crucial.

In fact the early emperors went to great lengths to preserve the forms and institutions of traditional Roman *res publica*. Augustus in his testament carefully presented himself as a humble servant of the Roman people: he even drew his salary on the authority of the Senate. He was the 'first man' not in office but – as he himself put it – solely in *auctoritas*. As Adcock remarked, such a form was cunningly contrived to placate the leading 'active' citizens, since *auctoritas* denoted neither official position or legal power, but rather 'an admitted primacy towards which other men could yield without loss of self-respect', and without becoming mere 'courtiers of a monarch' (Adcock, 1959: 71–88; 79). In practice, of course, the *dignitas* of the leading citizens had to shrink – and shrink steadily – in order to make space for this overarching personal *auctoritas*. Yet for at least a century after the accession of Augustus principacy was presented as a burden to be borne, or as the ultimate form of service to the community, rather than as an expression of personal power (Adcock, 1959: 89–104).

Even under the supposed 'Oriental despotism' of the later emperors 'the emperor's vast notional power' was circumscribed by a range of compelling practical constraints: the sheer scale of imperial administration, the multiplication of jurisdictions across the provinces, the ever expanding army of expert public officials dispersed across multiple metropolises (Brown, 1992: 8–13). Thus a fourth-century commentator such as the historian Ammianus Marcellinus still finds it entirely reasonable to cite Cicero in explicating the office of emperor, and to explain the relationship of the emperor towards men of goodwill (the *boni*) as directly analogous to that of the great public citizen of the late Republic. For Ammanius 'the emperors had inherited the protection of law and settled life from the senatorial governments of the Republic'. And even if individual governors and magistrates succumbed to the lure of tyranny and cruelty, at least in principle Ammianus viewed himself as living under the protection of 'properly instituted courts of law and regular procedures', in what he termed a 'civil and lawful political order' (Matthews, 1989: 231–52).[10] Ammianus' invocation of *imperium* here is salutatory. For our conception of 'empire' as a specific mode of political rule is, like our notion of 'republicanism', a modern creation. For the Romans *imperium* was the domain within which the jurisdiction of a ruler operated, be that civil or military, metropolitan or provincial, 'republican' or 'imperial'. The 'emperor' (imperator) was so called simply because as a matter of historical fact Augustus had appropriated the conventional honorific adopted by individuals entrusted by the Senate with *imperium* over an army or province. In this sense 'imperial' rule was not inherently different in its relationship to the laws to any other kind of lawful authority. *Imperium* was exercised appropriately where it was limited to the proper tasks of sovereign rule under the laws, and where it was confined to the bounds of dominion as vested in its exerciser.[11]

This is the other side of the equation of Roman *imperium* as relayed to us by Tacitus. For it is possible to condemn the excesses of particular emperors only if there is some yardstick of good governorship, rather than simple domination, against which to measure them. Thus Tacitus writes of the emperor Nerva that he has combined two things too long treated as incompatible, the principate and liberty, and that under his principate you may think what you wish and say what you think (*Agricola*: 3; *History*: I.1). Again, it is possible to deplore the sycophancy and servitude of leading Roman citizens only if there is a model of civic activity under the rule of a *princeps* against which to find them wanting. Tacitus provides his readers with several role-models in this respect. One is the prominent senator and Stoic martyr Thrasea Paetus, a man whose forthright *libertas* in the Senate shattered the servitude of his fellow citizens, but called upon him the wrath of Nero. Yet Tacitus observes that Thrasea's constancy was vitiated on this occasion by a lack of prudence: he created danger for himself without instilling liberty in others (Annals: XIV.48–49; XVI.21–35; XIV.121). Another role-model is the minister of Nero turned Stoic philosopher, Seneca, who dictates to his pupils even as his veins ebb their lifeblood. A third is Tacitus' own father-in-law Julius Agricola, the subject of his first, laudatory history. Agricola was, we are told, in turn an astute general, an impartial magistrate, a hardworking and self-effacing governor, an impartial administrator and, last but not least, a skilled orator (*Agricola*: 9,

18–19, 22, 33–5). He was capable of prudence in the face of tyranny, as well as valour in defence of liberty. And he died with his *dignitas* unimpaired (*Agricola*: 6, 44). This was a citizen!

Tacitus' moral seems clear. The role of the *princeps* is to restrain the over-large political personalities of the leading citizens under his aegis. Under such a system of rule the good public citizen has of necessity to be prudent: ancient philosophy as well as common sense counselled against throwing away one's own life unnecessarily. Yet he has also to enable the expression of his political personality, and to stand up to efforts to suppress it, if necessary at the cost of his life. Hence for Tacitus the spectres of the old 'republican' martyrs retain their glamour. It is surely no coincidence that Tacitus' account of Seneca's death echoes so closely Cicero's estimation of the 'philosophical suicide' of Cato of Utica, the greatest 'republican' martyr of them all.

GOVERNANCE AND CITIZENSHIP

In practice it was this 'imperial' citizenship, rather than the 'republican' citizenship which preceded it, which attracted the attention of the political writers of the era of early modern state-building. In particular, during the period of the interconfessional religious wars (c. 1570–1650), political and moral writers alike delved into the histories of Tacitus and Sallust, and the moral essays and letters of Seneca, in order to create a model of civic demeanour appropriate to a world searching for political stability among religious tumult. Contemporary historians have overwhelmingly depicted the political theory of this period from the mid-sixteenth to the mid-seventeenth century as marking a conscious and decisive rejection of classical civic life (e.g. Skinner, 1978; Tuck, 1993; Viroli, 1992; Burke, 1991). There have been accounts of a movement from a Ciceronian 'art of politics' to a Tacitean 'reason of state', and of the seemingly inexorable rise of 'princely Tacitism'.[12] According to this view the modern Taciteans counselled a fatalistic sense of resignation on the part of citizens in the face of absolute monarchical authority (Tuck, 1993: 45–61; Burke, 1991: 484–90). And the chief Tacitean teaching was the necessity of submission 'to the existing order of things, never resisting the prevailing government but accepting and where necessary enduring it with fortitude' (Skinner, 1978: 279).

This view of early modern 'Tacitism', while convenient, is a highly selective and partial one. For the modern heirs of the Roman imperial moralists were never simply philosophers of princely subjection. The most famous and celebrated of them, the Flemist humanist Justus Lipsius, has been described as an 'anti-Ciceronian', and his writings presented as an attempt to supplant a Ciceronian republican politics with a Tacitean monarchical one. Yet Lipsius never renounced Cicero as a political or rhetorical influence, and he cites him liberally across his political writings.[13] The introductions to the various imprints of Lipsius' edition of Tacitus are studded with Ciceronian invocations of the statesman as pilot (*gubernator*) of the ship of state, as well as with conventional Tacitean laments about lost liberty and the misuse of power by tyrants ancient and modern (Morford, 1993: 136–40; 1991: 153–4). On the allegorical frontispiece of Lipsius' *Opera Omnia* the personification of Politics wears a crown depicting the city (*civitas*): in each hand she holds a rudder (*gubernaculum*), the symbol of civil governance, and the spear of military *imperium*, rather than the sword and sceptre of Hobbes' Leviathan.

In his *Politics* Lipsius defines 'civil life' (*vita civilis*) in orthodox Ciceronian terms as a social partnership under justice. He adopts Cicero's depiction in the *De Re Publica* of the statesman as a *gubernator* whose fixed purpose must be to bring happiness to the citizenry, and who should promote plenty, glory and honour.[14] And he distinguishes explicitly and repeatedly between government (*gubernatio*), which is rule over those who assent of their own free will, and the simple exercise of sovereign power through the threat of force (*vis*). Governance, it is true, requires the threat of physical force in order to secure obedience to the laws, but it requires prudence even more. In governance prudence is manifestly preferable to force, Lipsius tells us, 'because it alone provides the gentle bridle which brings men within the path of obedience by their own free will' (Lipsius, 1637b: 37; cf. Lipsius, [1594] 1970: 42).

For Lipsius Tacitean politics is not an alternative to Ciceronian civil science: rather, it is a supplement to and revision of it appropriate to the dark times of storm and stress in which citizens of the contemporary world find themselves (Oestreich, 1982). Like Tacitus, Cicero had understood the folly of the multitude, led astray by their passions into supporting demagogues and tyrants. And Lipsius assembles a montage of quotations – from Cicero and Tacitus alike – to this effect: the untutored multitude are slaves to their passions and inconstant in their enthusiasms; incapable of restraining themselves in their own speech, they are susceptible of being roused to rage by any hot-blooded orator (Lipsius, 1637b: 49–50; cf. Lipsius, [1594] 1970: 68–9). Yet while he instructed the great public citizens in the skills of Stoic self-constraint, Cicero had little to say about the civic instruction of the multitude. His chief response to the problem of civil dissension and tumult had been the rather idealistic notion of a *concordia ordinum* or 'compromise of the classes' against demagoguery and in favour of civil peace. Cicero's political thought hankered after stability, but for Lipsius and his successors it was blind to the springs of instability and civil war. Here Lipsius turned to classical ethics – and particularly the Stoicism of Seneca – as a source of moral guidance not just for the philosophical adept, but for the citizenry as a whole.

This 'neo-Stoic' ethics has been reduced to parody in some contemporary histories. One recent commentator contends that for Lipsius the rational life 'consists neither in political participation nor the elaboration of speculative disciplines, but in the cultivation of an *emotional state*, that of the unimpassioned and undespairing observer' (Tuck, 1993: 52). It is doubtful if Lipsius would recognise this depiction of the citizen as early modern *étranger*. The 'neo-Stoics' of the latter sixteenth century were certainly preoccupied with the ancient Stoic virtue of *constantia* (the cultivated indifference to the vicissitudes of fortune). Yet *constantia* was never intended primarily as a recipe for passivity: on the contrary, it was intended to steel the citizen against the bad times which would reduce other mortals to flight or despair, as well as against the passionate temptations which led other men into rebellion and civil chaos. For Lipsius, to resist the temptation to civil insurrection was a greater act of self-discipline than to give in to it. But this was not a license for passivity. Lipsius considered writing a study of Tacitus' Stoic hero Thrasea, and he was fond of repeating Thrasea's dying words at the very end of the extant text of Tacitus' *Annals*: 'You have been born into such a time that it is advisable to strengthen your spirit with examples of constancy.' It was imprudent to follow Thrasea in provoking authority without any tangible benefit to liberty. Yet only Thrasian constancy enabled the citizen to live up to the spirit of what Lipsius terms, generically, 'ancient morals' (Morford, 1991: 149–53).

Hobbes was familiar with, and indebted to, the modern Taciteans and their understanding of citizenship within the *imperium* of a modern monarchy. He was a careful reader of Lipsius' *Politics*, and adopted his doctrine of the formation of citizens out of public discipline. (Burchell, 1999). Yet his representation of this civic tradition is completely one-sided – as one might perhaps expect from such a single-minded polemicist. He stresses almost entirely the subjection of subjects to the sovereign power, and has very little to say about the means whereby they are to be brought to this subjection of their own free will – other, it seems, than by the sheer force of Hobbes' own arguments. And while he inveighs against the power of irresponsible demagogues over the citizenry, he has little to say about the character-traits which might enable the constant citizen to resist the lure of demagoguery. Modern historians, while deploring Hobbes' politics, have echoed these prejudices and preoccupations, and have tended to elide altogether the roles of governance and civic discipline in this 'neo-Roman' early modern political thought. As a result they have oversimplified the inheritance of ancient civic culture in the political life of the early modern states.

For in the final analysis the exemplary modern opposition between active and passive modes of citizenship is a creation of modern political theory more than ancient politics. The attributes of Cicero's 'active' citizen – his larger-than-life political personality, his hunger for space in the political limelight – had always been premised on a much larger number of 'passive' citizens whose self-control and forbearance made the stability of the city possible. This conception was supported by the precepts of ancient psychology, which likewise depicted a world in which the forces of the passions and elemental character-traits had to be tamed and constrained by the tutored attributes of self-discipline and self-abnegation. The 'active' and 'passive' citizenship of the ancients are in this sense specifically political manifestations of the vast drama of human nature and even nature itself. Perhaps the great innovation of the early moderns was not in separating out these characteristics of active and private citizenship, but on the contrary in imagining a figure of the universal citizen – a figure within whom both sets of characteristics might be deployed in an uneasy tension. The self-disciplined citizen of Hobbes and Pufendorf has, as it were, internalised the great dramas of ancient citizenship within his own breast, as the contrasting impulses towards sociality and subjection, community and civility. And it is perhaps out of this profound internal tension that our modern traumas of political identity and autonomy were born.

NOTES

I would like to thank Conal Condren, Engin Isin and Jeffrey Minson for their thoughtful and illuminating comments on an earlier draft of this chapter. The usual disclaimer applies.

1 All the Latin translations and paraphrases that follow are my own.

2 Ancient historians, it is true, have only rarely fallen victim to the enthusiasms of the early modern historians and political theorists. Thus classicist supporters of the ancient republican tradition such as Moses Finley and Peter Brunt have made far more modest claims for the sweep of classical citizenship than their modern-focussed counterparts. Finley argues for a limited but real capacity for participation in ancient political decision-making: 'beyond that, the principle of inequality, of hierarchy, operated' (Finley, 1983: 140). Brunt insists upon the limited and status-specific character of Roman *libertas*, which could just as well refer to the protection of the people from magistrates, or of the aristocracy from the people (Brunt, 1988).

3 In support of this last claim Viroli cites Cicero's tract *De Officiis* (I.124), but decidedly out of context. What Cicero actually says is that the *magistrate* assumes the 'persona of the city' when he takes up his post; he explicitly distinguishes this from the role of ordinary citizens.

4 The term 'decrepit' is Pufendorf's. The preface to his major political work (Pufendorf, [1672] 1955) again echoes Hobbes' sentiments almost precisely: see 'Praefatio lectori benevolos'. Mark Goldie has recently emphasised the central role of neo-Aristotelians in the hostile reception of Hobbes' thought (Goldie, 1991: 589–94).

5 It should be noted that Skinner avoids the term 'republican' as 'liable to confuse' (see Skinner, 1998: 22–3 and n. 67). Yet the substance of Skinner's and Pettit's claims about the supposed theoretical underpinnings of 'neo-Roman thought' are more or less indistinguishable.

6 Schofield (1995) makes a great deal out of Cicero's statement that '*res publica* is *res populi*'. (*De Re Publica*, I.39, I.43). Yet if *res publica* is understood in the terms I have just suggested, this is little more than a tautology.

7 The *De Re Publica* existed only in the form of isolated fragments from the early Middle Ages until the 1800s (Zetzel, 1995: 33–4). Yet it remains important as Cicero's major treatment of the subject.

8 Chiefly it is confined to the owners of landed property: those whom Cicero terms *liberales*, and who in early modern Britain would be termed 'gentlemen'. Money-lenders, tradesmen and wage-earners cannot possess *dignitas* (*De Officiis*: I.150–1); women can only possess charm or grace (*venustas*: see De Officiis: I.130).

9 Most of this discussion, in Book V of *De Re Publica*, has been lost: however, Cicero summarises it in *Ad Atticum* (VIII.11). The afterlife of the *moderator* is expounded in *De Re Publica* Book VI, the only section of

the work to survive more or less intact in Christian culture, as the so-called 'Dream of Scipio'. On the significance of the nautical imagery of the *gubernator*, see Bonjour, 1982.

10 A *civile iustumque imperium*. This is my translation of the phrase cited by Matthews, chosen to emphasise the point made immediately below. Matthews translates the same phrase as 'civil and rightful empire' (Matthews, 1989: 252).

11 On this topic Cicero's views are much closer to Ammianus' than might be assumed: see Mitchell (1991: 205–11).

12 Tuck tries to distinguish between two schools of modern Tacitism: a Ciceronian, republican one in northern Italy in the early sixteenth century, and an anti-Ciceronian, monarchical one in northern Europe later in the century (Tuck, 1993: 39–45). Like others, I find this contrast ingenious but unconvincing.

13 The American literary critic Morris Croll inaugurated the 'anti-Ciceronian' tag as a description of Lipsius' rhetorical views. Croll based his claim in good measure upon some highly creative translations of Lipsius' letters on literary style (Croll, 1966: 18–21). What Lipsius actually said was: 'I love Cicero. Once I used also to imitate him.' Now, he adds, he prefers to imitate the 'Attic' authors such as Tacitus (Lipsius, 1637a: 74–5).

14 Lipsius drew this crucial extract from the *De Re Publica* out of one of Cicero's letters (*Ad Atticum*: VIII.11): see n. 16 above.

REFERENCES

Adcock, F.E. (1959) *Roman Political Ideas and Practice*. Ann Arbor: University of Michigan Press.

Aristotle ([c. 322BCE] 1959) *The Politics and the Athenian Constitution*. tr. J. Warrington. London: Everyman.

Augustine ([c. 426] 1960) *The City of God Against the Pagans*. tr. W.C. Greene. Cambridge, Mass.: Harvard University Press.

Baron, Hans (1966) *The Crisis of the Early Italian Renaissance*. 2nd edition. Princeton, NJ: Princeton University Press.

Birks, Peter and McLeod, Grant (eds) (1987) *Justinian's Institutes*. Ithaca, New York: Cornell University Press.

Boissier, Gaston (1897) *Cicéron et Ses Amis*. tr. (1970) as *Cicero and His Friends*. New York: Cooper Square Publishers.

Bonjour, M. (1982) 'Cicero Nauticus', in R. Chevallier (ed.), *Présence de Cicéron*. Paris: Société d'édition Les belles lettres.

Brown, Peter (1992) *Power and Persuasion in Late Antiquity*. Madison, Wisconsin: University of Wisconsin Press.

Brunt, Peter (1988) *The Fall of the Roman Republic and Other Essays*. Oxford: Clarendon Press.

Burchell, David (1995) 'The Attributes of Citizens: Virtue, Manners and the Activity of Citizenship', *Economy and Society*, 24 (4): 540–58.

Burchell, David (1998) 'Civic Personae: MacIntyre, Cicero and Moral Personality', *History of Political Thought*, 19 (1): 101–18.

Burchell, David (1999) 'The Disciplined Citizen: Thomas Hobbes, Neostoicism and the Critique of Classical Citizenship', *Australian Journal of Politics and History*, 45 (4): 506–25.

Burke, Peter (1991) 'Tacitism, Scepticism and Reason of State', in J.H. Burns and Mark Goldie (eds), *The Cambridge History of Political Thought, 1450–1700*. Cambridge: Cambridge University Press.

Cicero, M. Tullius ([c. 51 BCE] 1928) *De Re Publica, De Legibus*, tr. C.W. Keyes. Cambridge, Mass.: Harvard University Press.

Cicero, M. Tullius ([44BCE] 1994) *De Officiis*, ed. M. Winterbottom. Oxford: Clarendon Press.

Croll, Morris W. (1966) *'Attic' and Baroque Prose Style: The Anti-Ciceronian Movement*. Princeton, NJ: Princeton University Press.

David, Jean-Michel (2000) *La République Romaine: Crise d'un Aristocracie*. Paris: Éditions du Seuil.

Earl, Donald (1967) *The Moral and Political Tradition of Rome*. Ithaca, NY: Cornell University Press.

Finley, M.I. (1983) *Politics in the Ancient World*. Cambridge: Cambridge University Press.

Gardner, Jane (1993) *Being a Roman Citizen*. London: Routledge.

Goldie, Mark (1991) 'The Reception of Hobbes', in J.H. Burns (ed.), *Cambridge History of Political Thought, 1450–1700*. Cambridge: Cambridge University Press.

Griffin, M.T. and Atkins, E.A. (eds) (1991) [44BCE] *Cicero: On Duties*. Cambridge: Cambridge University Press.

Harrington, James ([1656] 1992) *The Commonwealth of Oceana and A System of Politics*, ed. J.G.A. Pocock. Cambridge: Cambridge University Press.

Hellegouarc'h, J. (1963) *Le vocabulaire Latin des relations et des partis politiques sous la République*. Paris: Société d'édition Les belles lettres.

Hobbes, Thomas ([1628] 1989) *Thucydides: The Peloponnesian War: The Complete Hobbes Translation*, ed. David Grene, Chicago: University of Chicago Press.

Hobbes, Thomas ([1651] 1991) *Leviathan*, ed. Richard Tuck, Cambridge: Cambridge University Press.

Hobbes, Thomas ([1647] 1998) *On the Citizen [De Cive]*, ed. Richard Tuck and Michael Silverthorne, Cambridge: Cambridge University Press.

Kirk, Rudolph (ed.) ([1594] 1930) *Two Bookes of Constancie, Written in Latin by Justus Lipsius*, tr. J. Stradling, New Brunswick, NJ: Rutgers University Press.

Lipsius, Justus (1637a) *Opera Omnia. vol. 2, Epistolarum Selectarum*. Antwerp: Plantin.

Lipsius, Justus (1637b) *Opera Omnia. vol. 4, Proprie ad Prudentiam et Civilem Doctrinam*. Antwerp: Plantin.

Lipsius, Justus ([1594] 1970) *Sixe Bookes of Politickes or Civil Doctrine [Politicorum Libri Sex]*, tr. William Jones. Amsterdam: Da Capo Press.

Matthews, John (1989) *The Roman Empire of Ammianus*. London: Duckworth.

Mitchell, Thomas N. (1991) *Cicero: The Senior Statesman*. New Haven, CT: Yale University Press.

Mommsen, Theodor ([1854–6] 1901) *The History of Rome*. vol. 5, tr. W.P. Dickson, London: Macmillan.

Morford, Mark (1991) *Stoics and Neostoics: Rubens and the Circle of Lipsius*, Princeton, NJ: Princeton University Press.

Morford, Mark (1993) 'Tacitean *Prudentia* and the Doctrines of Justus Lipsius', in T.J. Luce and A.J. Woodman (eds), *Tacitus and the Tacitean Tradition*. Princeton, NJ: Princeton University Press.

Oestreich, Gerhard (1982) *Neostoicism and the Early Modern State*. Cambridge: Cambridge University Press.

Pettit, Philip (1997) *Republicanism: A Theory of Freedom and Government*. Oxford: Clarendon Press.

Pocock, J.G.A. (1975) *The Machiavellian Moment: Florentine Political Thought and the Atlantic Republican Tradition*. Princeton, NJ: Princeton University Press.

Pufendorf, Samuel von ([1672] 1955) *De Jure Naturae et Gentium Libri Octo*, 2 vols. Buffalo, NY: William S. Hein.

Pufendorf, Samuel von ([1673] 1991) *On the Duty of Man and Citizen According to Natural Law, [De Officio Hominis et Civis]*. ed. James Tully. Cambridge: Cambridge University Press.

Sallust [Gaius Sallustius Crispus] ([c. 40 BCE] 1921) *The War with Catiline*, tr. J.C. Rolfe, Cambridge, MA: Harvard University Press.

Schofield, Malcolm (1995) 'Cicero's Definition of *Res Publica*', in J.G.F. Powell (ed.), *Cicero the Philosopher*. Oxford: Clarendon Press.

Schofield, Malcolm (1999) *Saving The City: Philosopher Kings and other Classical Paradigms*. London: Routledge.

Sherwin-White, A.N. ([1939] 1973) *The Roman Citizenship*. Oxford: Clarendon Press.

Skinner, Quentin (1978) *Foundations of Modern Political Thought*. vol. 2. Cambridge: Cambridge University Press.

Skinner, Quentin (1989) 'The State', in Terence Ball, James Farr and Russell L. Hanson (eds), *Political Innovation and Conceptual Change*. Cambridge: Cambridge University Press.

Skinner, Quentin (1998) *Liberty Before Liberalism*. Cambridge: Cambridge University Press.

Syme, Ronald (1939) *The Roman Revolution*. Oxford: Clarendon Press.

Syme, Ronald (1958) *Tacitus*. vol. 2, Oxford: Clarendon Press.

Tacitus, Cornelius (1931) *Histories and Annals*, 5 vols, tr. C.H. Moore and J. Jackson, Cambridge, MA: Harvard University Press.

Tacitus, Cornelius (1970) *Agricola, Germania, Dialogus*. tr. various, Cambridge, MA: Harvard University Press.

Tuck, Richard (1993) *Philosophy and Government, 1572–1651*. Cambridge: Cambridge University Press.

Viroli, Maurizio (1992) *From Politics to Reason of State*. Cambridge: Cambridge University Press.

Zetzel, James E.G. (ed.) (1995) *Cicero: De Re Publica: Selections*. Cambridge: Cambridge University Press.

6

Modern Citizenship

ROGERS M. SMITH

What does citizenship mean today? How does this meaning or set of meanings differ from what it has meant in the past and what it may mean in the future? To the question of the distinctive modern meaning of citizenship, we scholars can give some reasonably concrete and widely accepted answers. The question as to what modern citizenship is becoming is one that many people are also answering, but they are doing so in ways that go well beyond what scholars can hope to determine, either in theory or practice. That is essentially as it should be, I believe; but I shall nonetheless seek to say something about where modern citizenship may be going.

FOUR MEANINGS OF CITIZENSHIP

To grasp what citizenship has come to mean in the contemporary world, it may be helpful to begin by identifying some different definitions of the term.

The first and perhaps the most familiar meaning of citizenship is in fact the seminal one. In both ancient and modern republics and democracies, a citizen has been a person with political rights to participate in processes of popular self-governance. These include rights to vote; to hold elective and appointive governmental offices; to serve on various sorts of juries; and generally to participate in political debates as equal community members.

Secondly, especially in the modern world, we also commonly speak of 'citizenship' as a more purely legal status. 'Citizens' are people who are legally recognized as members of a particular, officially sovereign political community. They therefore possess some basic rights to be protected by that community's government, whether or not those rights include rights of political participation. In this meaning, possessing 'citizenship' is understood to be effectively equivalent to possessing 'nationality' under a particular modern state, even if there remains some sense that 'citizens' are presumptively more entitled to full political rights than mere 'nationals.'

In the last century or so, moreover, it has become increasingly customary to use 'citizen' in a third way, as referring to those who belong to almost any human association, whether a political community or some other group. I can be said to be a citizen of my neighborhood, my fitness club, and my university as well as my broader political community. To be sure, this type of usage is far from strictly modern. St Augustine's fifth-century masterpiece, *City of God*, was premised on the idea that the saved are 'citizens of the heavenly City,' rather than simply citizens of earthly cities or indeed of 'the world community' (Augustine, [413–427] 1958: 326). Today this sort of deployment of the term 'citizenship' is still often understood to be at least partly metaphorical, as it was in Augustine's formulation. Yet now the use of 'citizenship' to refer to membership in virtually any association is so ubiquitous that many treat such non-political 'citizenship' as an alternative but equally valid meaning of the word.

Fourthly, as a result of, especially, both the first and third meanings, today we often use 'citizenship' to signify not just membership in some group but certain standards of proper conduct. Some people – those who contribute to the well-being of their political community, church, lunch club, or other human association, and do so frequently, valuably, at some cost to themselves – are understood to be the 'true' citizens of those bodies. Others who free-ride on their efforts are mere members who do not seem to understand, embrace, or embody what citizenship really means. When communities, public or private, give 'citizenship' awards to some of their members, it is this usage they invoke. It obviously implies that only 'good' citizens are genuinely citizens in the full meaning of the term. This meaning represents a merger of the republican conception of participatory citizenship with the now common practice of using citizenship to refer to membership in any of an almost infinite variety of human groups.

Note that the latter three of these meanings have emerged especially over the last several centuries, with the last two probably most prevalent in the last 100 years. What happened in the course of modern history to generate this proliferation of usages? The answers, I believe, reveal much about what citizenship has become and where it may be going.

THE PATH TO MODERN CITIZENSHIP

Perhaps necessarily, the oldest meaning of citizenship, participation in political self-governance, has survived in the modern world only in greatly modified form. The word 'citizen' derives from the Latin *civis* or *civitas*, meaning a member of an ancient city-state, preeminently the Roman republic; but *civitas* was a Latin rendering of the Greek term *polites*, a member of a Greek polis. Innumerable scholars have told how a renowned resident of the Athenian polis, Aristotle, defined a *polites* or 'citizen' as someone who rules and is ruled in turn, making 'citizenship' conceptually inseparable from political governance (Aristotle, [350 BCE] 1968: 1275a23). Though most inhabitants of Athens, including the foreigner Aristotle himself, were ineligible to participate in citizenship thus understood, this ideal of citizenship as self-governance has often served since as an inspiration and instrument for political efforts to achieve greater inclusion and democratic engagement in political life. It continues to play that role in modern political discourse.

But for that very reason, this ancient idea of citizenship has often seemed politically threatening to many rulers, who have abolished or redefined the category. It was for this sort of political reason – because the regimes that had created citizenship succumbed to conquest by Alexander's monarchical empire – that ancient Greek citizenship disappeared. And it was for a similar political reason – because the Roman republic gave way to imperial rule generated from within – that Roman citizenship came to have a different meaning than the one Aristotle articulated. In principle, Roman citizenship always carried with it the right to sit in the popular legislative assembly that had been the hallmark of Athenian citizenship. But as participation in that assembly became increasingly meaningless as well as impractical for most imperial inhabitants, Roman citizenship became essentially a legal status comparable to modern nationality (Pocock, 1995). It provided rights to legal protection by Roman soldiers and judges in return for allegiance to Rome. It no longer had any strong connection to actual practices of self-governance.

'Citizenship' was then eclipsed in the West by the various feudal and religious statuses of the medieval Christian world, but it did not vanish entirely. 'Burghers' or the 'bourgeoisie' were citizens of municipalities that often had some special if restricted rights of self-governance within feudal hierarchies. It was in fact in reference to this class of persons that the term 'citizen' first came to be commonly used in English, according to the *Oxford English Dictionary*. Such burghers remained, however, fundamentally subjects of some ruling prince or lord, with their 'citizenship' chiefly providing legal rights of protection in the manner of Roman imperial citizenship. In contrast, during the Renaissance some Italian cities achieved both independence and a meaningful measure of popular self-governance. They invoked ancient 'republican' ideals of participatory citizenship to define and defend their regimes. Their experiences in turn fed into the anti-monarchical revolutions that created the first modern republics, including the short-lived seventeenth-century English Commonwealth and late eighteenth-century French Republic, as well as the still enduring United States (Pocock, 1975). It was here that modern citizenship took its basic form.

In complex fashion, those revolutions inaugurated transformations 'from subjectship to citizenship' across much of the globe that are still ongoing today, when most of the world's governments proclaim themselves to be 'republics' of some sort populated by 'citizens.' In eighteeenth-century North America and France, to be a 'citizen' was once again understood to be someone who shared in political self-governance, as in the ancient and Renaissance Italian city-states. Unlike the medieval European burghers, then, these modern 'citizens' were people who were emphatically not 'subjects.' They rejected rule by hereditary monarchical and aristocratic families in favor of a much broader community of political equals. But in these modern republics, self-governance by 'citizens' no longer took place chiefly in 'cities.' Rather, it occurred within 'nations.' These were substantially larger populations who could not possibly have face-to-face knowledge of each other, only some form of 'imagined community,' in Benedict Anderson's valuable phrase (Anderson, 1983).

These 'imagined communities' could engage in self-governance, if at all, only through more extensive reliance on systems of representation – a reliance that became to many the distinguishing feature of modern republics. The authors of the *Federalist Papers* argued for the proposed US Constitution by applauding such representative systems as means to check the dangers of direct popular self-governance (Hamilton et al., [1788] 1987: 126, 372–3). Some French radicals influenced by Rousseau instead regarded elaborate structures of representation as dangers to true republican freedom (Higonnet, 1988: 220–8, 235). Still, those Rousseauean revolutionaries did not favor the creation of decentralized self-governing French city-states. Rather, they vigorously championed the concept of a large French nation, whom they claimed to represent directly. As that fact shows, in modern large-scale republics, there has simply been no practical alternative to extensive reliance on representative systems of self-government, except for effective abandonment of any meaningful self-governance at all.

Today, then, the core meaning of citizenship is membership with at least some rights of political participation in an independent republic that governs through some system of elected representatives – parliamentary, presidential, bicameral, unicameral, or some other variation. Such citizenship is understood to embrace not only various rights and privileges, including rights to participate politically, but also an ethos of at least some willingness to exercise these rights in ways that contribute to the common good. But the polity-wide assembly in which all citizens sit, deliberate and vote has effectively vanished from the modern world, as much or more than the hereditary aristocracies and monarchies that the American and French revolutionaries first assaulted. Only a few rare vestiges of direct, active, collective self-governance by the whole body of relevant citizens now exist, within sub-units such as small towns, counties, and school districts. And with the demise of the all-citizens assembly, expectations that most citizens will in fact be extensively involved in activities of political self-governance have also faded. As many have argued, citizenship in most modern societies rarely involves a strongly participatory public ethos or vigorous democratic practices (e.g. Barber, 1984, 1995).

How should we understand this transformation? How it has been bound up with the spread of the other meanings of modern citizenship that I have listed? Sheer logistical burdens in engaging in civic participation under the conditions that characterize large-scale modern republics surely provide a good portion of the answer; yet certain related political developments have also been more important than may first meet the eye.

THE POLITICS OF MODERN APOLITICAL CITIZENSHIP

To show why, let me first make another run at the pertinent history. Men created the early modern republics, first the American, then the French, and then others, in an international realm that had been organized by the 1648 Treaty of Westphalia into a system of mutual recognition among overwhelmingly monarchical nation-states. In gaining acceptance within that system, the new republics defined their citizens as having the same international status as national monarchical subjects. For international purposes, these citizens, too, were simply persons who owed allegiance to and could claim protection from particular sovereign governments. Whether those sovereigns were the representatives of the 'sovereign people' or were instead individual hereditary rulers, usurpers, or conquering despots made no difference to this legal status. Thus Westphalian international law gave no official recognition or significance to the ideological connection of modern republican citizenship with active self-governance, treating it instead as akin to the legalistic, protection-oriented, imperial version of Roman citizenship (Held, 1995: 74–83).

Furthermore, the first enduring modern republic, the United States, was forged amidst racial and gender hierarchies that few revolutionaries sought to challenge. Hence early American leaders felt compelled to argue that, though free blacks and women might be citizens, citizenship did not in fact inherently entail rights of political participation. It guaranteed, once again, only more limited rights to certain judicial and executive protections. Perhaps the most revealing example of this phenomenon in US law is the post-Civil War case of *Minor* v. *Happersett* (88 US 162, 1874). There a suffrage activist, Virginia Minor, argued that her citizenship in the American Republic under the Fourteenth Amendment of the US Constitution logically required that she be granted voting rights, since voting was inherent in the core meaning of such citizenship. Chief Justice Morrison Waite of the United States Supreme Court ruled, however, that republican citizenship actually meant only 'membership of a nation and nothing more.' Later courts invoked this reasoning to justify restrictions on the franchise for other classes of citizens as well (R.M. Smith, 1997: 341–2, 408, 432). Parallel understandings of citizenship can be found in the law of other modern republics, most of which denied women and some other free adult citizens the franchise until the twentieth century, for similar reasons. For long stretches of time, then, both international and national politics worked to strengthen legalistic as opposed to more participatory conceptions of citizenship in many modern societies, despite the rise of modern republicanism.

But if lawyers have tended to treat modern 'citizenship' and 'nationality' as fundamentally identical terms, many contemporary political theorists and historians of political thought have analyzed the apparent declining emphasis on participatory citizenship in modern regimes in another way. They often distinguish between 'liberal' conceptions of citizenship, usually traced back to the seventeenth-century political tracts through which John Locke shaped the English and later the American Revolutions, and 'republican' conceptions of citizenship, often traced back to the eighteenth-century writings of Jean-Jacques Rousseau, if not to Machiavelli and Aristotle (Hutchings, 1999). 'Liberal' conceptions are said to present civic membership basically as an instrument of a diverse range of self-interested personal life plans, with the emphasis generally on seeking economic, religious, and familial fulfillment. The guarantees of basic protections from one's regime contained in international law notions of citizenship are thought to be generally consonant with this 'liberal' view of citizenship, so long as basic human rights are not violated. In contrast, 'republican' conceptions still insist that citizenship must involve rights and practices of political participation to achieve common goods. Many modern regimes are then analyzed as combining 'liberal' and 'republican' civic elements. The resulting argument is that, for good or bad reasons or both, modern societies have simply moved toward more 'liberal' than 'republican' civic conceptions (e.g. Sandel, 1996).

These arguments are fine as far as they go, but there is much they omit. Not just the United States, but in fact most modern societies display not only liberal and republican civic traditions, but also long histories of governmental use of gendered, racialized, religious, nativistic, and other ascriptive categories to assign quite different civic statuses to different sets of people. Many of these categories are openly inconsistent with the requirements of respect for human rights built into most theoretical depictions of genuinely 'liberal' citizenship. Similarly, though republican views of citizenship often favor civic homogeneity as a means to strengthen civic commitments, they do not by themselves include or endorse notions of racial, ethnic, or religious superiority. Sociologists and historians, especially, have therefore often distinguished between two types of modern nations. 'Civic' nations base citizenship on acceptance of certain political principles and procedures, usually some combination of liberal and republican ones. 'Ethnic' nations instead stress hereditary ethnic, racial, or religious identities (e.g. Brubaker, 1992; Greenfeld, 1992; Ignatieff, 1993).

Though useful for some purposes, all these classifications fail, I believe, to recognize how modern forms of citizenship have emerged from political processes that predictably generate societies that do not fit readily into any of these pigeonholes. From the eighteenth through the twentieth centuries, modern nations arose chiefly in struggles against preexisting monarchical regimes and against European colonial regimes, whether monarchical or not. In those political contests many revolutionaries found liberal notions of human rights and republican notions of popular sovereignty (along with later Marxist notions of proletarian destiny) useful in defining and legitimating their causes. Yet logically, many of those ideals threatened systems of political and economic power and status in which the revolutionaries were themselves invested, such as gender and ethnic hierarchies. Furthermore, doctrines of a liberal, republican, or workers' state do not by themselves explain why people should embrace one particular liberal republic or workers' state rather than another.

As a result of these political problems, the architects of modern forms of nationhood and citizenship have regularly blended liberal, republican, or Marxian elements with forms of nationalism and patriarchy that build on and adapt prevalent notions of ethnic, racial, religious and gender as well as class identities. In so doing they add to their notions of membership what I have termed politically useful 'constitutive stories,' accounts that make citizenship in a particular society seem intrinsic to the identities of their putative members. Racial, ethnic, gender, cultural, and religious 'constitutive stories' purport to define who we essentially are. They can readily be blended into accounts that present membership in a specific regime as our natural or divine destiny. If citizens accept such accounts, they are likely to be quite loyal to their regime. That is one reason why would-be leaders regularly propagate such stories; and in so far as the stories help to sustain regimes that express and advance the identities, interests, and ideals of those whom they valorize, many citizens also have strong incentives to embrace them (R.M. Smith, 2001).

When we attend to the political processes through which senses of peoplehood have been shaped, then, it seems less surprising that in reality there simply have never been *any* purely 'liberal,' 'republican,' or 'liberal republican' modern republics; and existing regimes have *always* mixed elements of 'civic' and 'ethnic' nationhood (cf. A.D. Smith, 1991). They still do. Even today, for instance, most people acquire their political citizenship through unchosen, often unexamined, hereditary descent, not because they explicitly embrace any political principles, liberal, republican, civic, or otherwise. Immigration policies in western Europe, the USA, and elsewhere generally include some sort of favoritism for those who can claim kinship with current citizens, without any effort to ascertain if their commitment to civic principles is really stronger than those of applicants with no citizen relatives. National and international courts in the USA and elsewhere also continue to make the narrower, protection-centered view of citizenship legally authoritative in many contexts, even when clearly illiberal, unrepublican ethnic nations are involved. Many more examples could be cited.

It remains true, however, that the citizenship laws of most modern societies have been altered over time in more 'liberal,' 'republican,' and 'civic' directions, with explicit racial, ethnic, gender, and religious bars to full citizenship being dropped. In the political contests that have produced these changes over the last two centuries, the notion that genuine citizenship involves rights of political participation has been a resonant rhetorical tool for legislative and constitutional reformers and revolutionaries. Those ideological arguments have been combined with active, sometimes violent, domestic protests and international pressures, especially the need for broad support in wartime, to produce dramatic changes. By the late twentieth century, reformers had used these means to achieve the extension of the franchise to all adult citizens, in the USA and most of the Western world. In America, blacks won both citizenship and voting rights after the Civil War, even though most came to be effectively disfranchised in the 'Jim Crow' era of racial segregation; and women gained the franchise after World War I. In both cases, arguments appealing to their public service, especially in wartime, and to the idea that true citizenship must include the franchise, played key roles in their successes (Foner, 1988; Flexner, 1973). World War II, the Cold War, and the civil rights movement also all contributed to the ending of Jim Crow segregation and disfranchisement and also US racial restrictions on naturalization and immigration during the 1950s and 1960s (Daniels, 1990). Other nations that had versions of some or all of these policies, such as Australia and South Africa, have since generally followed suit.

In Britain and to some degree in other Western European nations that had been politically configured essentially by feudal and industrial class systems, modern citizenship was wrought out via somewhat different struggles. As T.H. Marshall famously argued, first middle and then working class political pressures resulted in the expansion of civil rights of property and protection, then in near-universal rights of political participation, and finally and incompletely, in 'social rights' for all national citizens that included income, housing, medical, and educational guarantees (Marshall, 1950). Marshall's argument has been so influential that many scholars and some political activists, especially in Europe, today equate genuine citizenship with full possession of all three types of rights: civil, political, and social. As a normative matter, that argument has power. But as a matter of historical analysis, Marshall's class-centered account is not well equipped to explain many civic developments, including the back-and-forth pattern of racial and ethnic voting rights in US history and the battles over gender discrimination and representation that are still ongoing in both the US and Europe. Today, moreover, different modern states define the content and extent of Marshall's three types of citizenship rights in ways that vary too greatly for his account to depict very concretely either the formal laws of citizenship or the broadly shared understandings of citizenship that prevail in most of the modern world (Turner, 1986).

Even so, Marshall's analysis can help to highlight some striking features in the evolution of modern citizenship, and the apparent decline in participatory civic ideals, that I have been reviewing. Even as the franchise was broadened in the USA, Europe, and elsewhere, even as old class, racial, gender, religious, and other barriers to full and equal membership were increasingly discredited, the rise of 'social rights' of citizenship provided new arenas for what were in many cases continuing conflicts over genuine civic equality. In the USA, for example, New Deal social programs of poverty relief, unemployment assistance, job training, and social insurance often reflected and reinforced beliefs that women and racial minorities still played distinctive and lesser roles in the market place and political processes. They did so by giving women and minorities different and lesser benefits (Mettler, 1998; Lieberman, 1998). In the civil rights era of the 1950s and 1960s, national and state legislators made many of those programs more inclusive; and in the Great Society years of the mid-1960s, new forms of educational and economic assistance, sometimes targeted at racial and ethnic minorities and women, were enacted. But from the late 1960s on, programs that were perceived as disproportionately aiding poor racial and ethnic minority members came under attack as inefficient and counterproductive, while measures explicitly aimed at aiding such groups were criticized as violating norms of equal citizenship (Quadagno, 1994).

The rise to power of Ronald Reagan in the USA and Margaret Thatcher in Britain made the 1980s an era in which many 'social rights' were reduced in these countries and, usually to lesser degrees, in many other advanced industrial societies as well. In some ways these developments 'strengthened' citizenship, as efforts mounted to prevent aliens from entering modern welfare states or from receiving full social benefits when they were present. But at the same time, these cutbacks in 'social rights' threatened to help perpetuate the more privileged statuses of higher-class, native-born, ethnically dominant groups and their political allies – privileged statuses to which modern citizenship laws had long contributed (Schuck, 1998). Partly as a result, many analysts have argued for increased representation of the interests of various sorts of disadvantaged groups, sometimes via official systems of 'differentiated' or 'multicultural citizenship' (Young, 1990, 2000; Kymlicka, 1995). Such advocacy has especially contributed to enhanced legal and political rights for native peoples and for women in a number of nations; but after the 1970s, the political tides were generally flowing against openly 'differentiating' civic policies in most locales.

These battles over the extension of various forms of social and political assistance to long disfranchised groups may also have contributed to the apparent increased modern apathy toward citizenship conceived as active participation in meaningful self-governance. Many have contended that when citizenship laws explicitly express racial, ethnic, gender, or religious identities (as, in fact, they have throughout most of modern history), they work against a strong sense of common citizenship (e.g. Lind, 1995). People are said to retreat instead into the lives of their multiple 'cultural' communities, in Balkanized fashion. Others contend that the movements against policies aiding the disadvantaged have worked to discredit the whole sphere of government in the minds of many of the better off, while these developments have simultaneously generated heightened political alienation and disaffection among the worse off. Both responses could well be working to foster widespread disengagement from active politics, by rich, poor, and middle classes alike. And even apart from their possible contributions to negative attitudes toward government, the economic and cultural developments that have led to a focus on activities in various social spheres may have also made traditional political activism simply seem less important. To many modern citizens, involvement in their social, economic, and cultural organizations may well appear more pressing.

For all these reasons, then, the term 'citizenship' may have become common in so many contexts beyond political self-governance because today it is in these other contexts that people find the memberships that mean the most to them, and in which they can act most effectively. It is there, too, that many now think citizenship understood as 'good' citizenship matters most. If so, then the inevitable corollary is that citizenship understood as political self-governance has indeed become quite secondary to the conscious concerns and activities of many modern citizens. Ironically, it seems that as citizenship has become ubiquitous, it has also become depoliticized, at least in so far as participation in formal self-governance is concerned. It is now more and more understood purely in terms of the latter three meanings with which we began – as an entitlement to legal protections and rights, of which political rights are the least important; as a label for membership in a whole variety of human associations; and as a normative conception of what good membership in all those groups involves. Citizenship as a political vocation is not an unknown concept today, to be sure; but it seems to be a vocation that relatively few now follow.

Political leaders frequently deplore this state of affairs when they wish for their citizens to provide more in the way of support and civic service. Still, few really try hard to combat it. It is probable that like their predecessors in other regimes, many who wield power in modern republics are content when those they govern think of citizenship chiefly in terms of subnational, often nongovernmental associations, and in terms of the 'good citizen's' civic service rather than vigorous political activism.

Yet even if few policies within modern republics do much to enhance the feasibility and potency of such activism, it is not clear that this fact is to be wholly regretted. If various economic, social, and cultural groups represent the forms of association and activity that people value most, then respect for persons and their free choices may well mean accepting the modern minimization of participatory republican or democratic citizenship. On the other hand, if such acceptance also means embracing policies that effectively perpetuate or even deepen the class, racial, gender, ethnic, and religious inequalities that have been central to the civic lives of most modern regimes, even those who are not advocates of strongly participatory ideals may have cause for concern. Hence the question of whether political life can be conducted successfully in modern republics with diminishing levels of civic involvement is one that these developments in modern citizenship have inescapably placed on the agenda today.

THE PROSPECT OF POSTNATIONAL CITIZENSHIPS

The circumstances of the twenty-first century, however, increasingly cast a new light on all these matters. Though some scholars and democratic activists lament what they see as the eclipse or decline of modern republican national citizenship, others react quite differently. They stress that the heightened transnational economic, transportation, and communication systems that we call 'globalization' are in any case making traditional notions of national citizenship obsolete (Soysal, 1994; Jacobson,

1996; cf. Miller, 1995). The old sovereign nation-state, such writers insist, is on the way out. Regional associations, international legal institutions, and transnational economic, cultural, and political organizations, all 'semi-sovereign' in some spheres of some people's lives, are said to be more likely to shape humanity's future than existing national regimes. Hence membership in such bodies will rightly represent the most important forms of 'citizenship' in the twenty-first century. The redirection of participation toward 'good citizenship' in a grand plethora of human associations, in a manner akin to the democratic vision of John Dewey, can be understood as the appropriate realization of ancient participatory ideals in the new millennium.

There is much to these arguments. The fact that such 'globalizing' trends exist is undeniable; though it must quickly be added that usually, national governmental actors remain the central players even in transnational or international organizations and institutions. Despite advances in communication and transportation, moreover, meaningful participation in the governance of such populous and geographically far-flung entities can seem even more chimerical for most people than it is within existing nation-states. Advocates of 'global citizenship' or 'cosmopolitan citizenship' respond that such concerns fail to appreciate the democratic opportunities that emerge when old forms of national sovereignty are shattered and governance is performed at many levels. Some supranational organizations may be beyond the reach of most of those they affect, but some transnational groups will not be massively populated and may be more electronically interconnected on a daily basis. Furthermore, these advocates stress that governmental power can often safely be decentralized, going down and out as well as up, with a great number of important decisions being made henceforth in local communities that can in some regards approximate the old ideal of democratic city-states (Held, 1995; Linklater, 1999). To varying degrees, such devolution is indeed visible in the modern policies of many modern Western states, including Canada, the United States, and most dramatically in the United Kingdom, where the Welsh and Scots now have their own national legislatures. Thus there is a real prospect that the idea of 'citizenship' will increasingly be severed not only from engagement in traditional forms of self-governance, but even from membership in some single, titularly sovereign political community. The term 'citizenship' may instead become all the more ubiquitous, but now with its dominant meaning referring to all memberships in any of a wide variety of human groups, to many of which persons will belong simultaneously.

There are, however, both normative and empirical reasons to raise doubts about this scenario. Normatively, skeptical analysts ask pointedly where the motivation for constructive participation in public life will arise when people feel themselves only partial members of many political associations, most of which they join only for narrow instrumental reasons, having only the faintest sense of shared identity with their fellow 'citizens' (Miller, 1999). And as a matter of empirical political behavior, history suggests that the leaders of political communities rarely give up power willingly. Therefore it is not surprising that efforts to resist globalizing trends and reinvigorate loyalties to existing nations and regimes are also visible players in modern 'citizenship politics,' particularly in regard to immigration policies. Under conditions of economic hardship, international conflict, or simply increased governance by remote supranational bureaucracies, moreover, it is possible that many more people will come to feel concerned about the decline in forms of citizenship through which they can exercise some genuine control over their collective lives. The fact that political and social reform movements have often gained wide support by insisting that citizenship means sharing in governance shows that such feelings can be politically powerful fuel driving quite important changes. Given the incentives and the skills political leaders have to channel such feelings into support for existing forms of political community, these circumstances may well mean that radical changes will come less rapidly than some analysts now expect. The enormous difficulties in creating a truly all-encompassing global government mean, moreover, that memberships in particular political communities of some sort are likely to remain important features of human life, even if those communities do come to be constituted in new ways, as they frequently have been in the past.

Thus we cannot rule out the possibility that both existing political memberships and older notions of participatory citizenship will continue to play important roles in the recrafting of political institutions and communities that the twenty-first century will inevitably see. Whether those recraftings will go so far as to mean the end of the nation-state or whether they instead produce some less radical transformations remains to be seen. But whatever forms of citizenship result, they will almost certainly be the ongoing products of intense political contests that distribute powers and memberships to some people and not others. These distributions will be all the more controversial because they will also convey to citizens only some sorts of civil, political, and social rights, protections, and resources, and not others. Hence though citizenship in the twenty-first century may in some respects look sharply different than citizenship today, just as modern citizenship is different than medieval or ancient citizenship, in some fundamental regards citizenship will probably remain what it has long been: a political status of profound importance for the well-being both of those who fully and securely possess it, and of those who do not.

REFERENCES

Anderson, B.R.O. (1983) *Imagined Communities: Reflections on the Origin and Spread of Nationalism*. London: Verso.

Aristotle, ([350 BCE] 1968) *The Politics of Aristotle*. ed. E. Barker, New York: Oxford University Press.

Augustine, Bishop of Hippo ([413–427] 1958) *City of God*. ed., V.J. Bourke New York: Image Books.

Barber, B.R. (1984) *Strong Democracy: Participatory Politics for a New Age*. Berkeley: University of California Press.

Barber, B.R. (1995) *Jihad v. McWorld: How Globalism and Tribalism Are Reshaping the World*. New York: Crown Publishing Group.

Brubaker, W.R. (1992) *Citizenship and Nationhood in France and Germany*. Cambridge, MA: Harvard University Press.

Daniels, R. (1990) *Coming to America: A History of Immigration and Ethnicity in American Life*. New York: HarperCollins.

Flexner, E. (1973) *Century of Struggle: The Woman's Rights Movement in the United States*. New York: Athaneum.

Foner, E. (1988) *Reconstruction: America's Unfinished Revolution, 1863–1877*. New York: Harper & Row.

Greenfeld, L. (1992) *Nationalism: Five Roads to Modernity*. Cambridge, MA: Harvard University Press.

Hamilton, A., Madison, J. and Jay, J. ([1788] 1987) *The Federalist papers*. ed. I. Kramnick, New York: Smith Peter.

Held, D. (1995) *Democracy and the Global Order: From the Modern State to Cosmopolitan Governance*. Stanford, CA: Stanford University Press.

Higonnet, P.L. (1988) *Sister Republics: The Origins of French and American Republicanism*. Cambridge: Harvard University Press.

Hutchings, K. (1999) 'Political Theory and Cosmopolitan Citizenship,' In K. Hutchings and R. Dannreuther (eds), *Cosmopolitan Citizenship*. New York: St Martin's Press.

Ignatieff, M. (1993) *Blood and Belonging: Journeys into the New Nationalism*. New York: Farrar, Strauss and Giroux.

Jacobson, D. (1996) *Rights across Borders: Immigration and the Decline of Citizenship*. Baltimore: John Hopkins Press.

Kymlicka, W. (1995) *Multicultural Citizenship: A Liberal Theory of Minority Rights*. New York: Oxford University Press.

Lieberman, R.C. (1994) *Shifting the Color Line: Race and the American Welfare State*. Cambridge, MA: Harvard University Press.

Lind, M. (1995) *The Next American Nation: The New Nationalism and the Fourth American Revolution*. New York: Free Press.

Linklater, A. (1999) 'Cosmopolitan Citizenship,' In K. Hutchings and R. Dannreuther, (eds), *Cosmopolitan Citizenship*. New York: St. Martin's Press.

Marshall, T.H. (1950) *Citizenship and Social Class and Other Essays*. Cambridge: Cambridge University Press.

Mettler, S. (1998) *Dividing Citizens: Gender and Federalism in New Deal Public Policy*. Ithaca, NY: Cornell University Press.

Miller, D. (1995) *On Nationality*. Oxford: Clarendon Press.

Miller, D. (1999) 'Bounded Citizenship,' in K. Hutchings and R. Dannreuther (eds), *Cosmopolitan Citizenship*. New York: St. Martin's Press.

Pocock, J.G.A. (1975) *The Machiavellian Moment: Florentine Political Thought and the Atlantic Republican Tradition*. Princeton: Princeton University Press.

Pocock, J.G.A. (1995) 'The Ideal of Citizenship since Classical Times', in *Theorizing Citizenship* ed. R.S. Beiner. Albany: State University Press of New York.

Quadagno, J.S. (1994) *The Color of Welfare: How Racism Undermined the War on Poverty*. New York: Oxford University Press.

Sandel, M. (1996) *Democracy's Discontent: America in Search of a Public Philosophy*. Cambridge, MA: Harvard University Press.

Schuck, P.H. (1998) *Citizens, Strangers, and In-Betweens: Essays on Immigration and Citizenship*. Boulder CO: Westview Press.

Smith, A.D. (1991) *National Identity*. London: Penguin Books.

Smith, R.M. (1997) *Civic Ideals: Conflicting Visions of Citizenship in U.S. History*. New Haven Conn.: Yale University Press.

Smith, R.M. (2001) 'Citizenship and the Politics of People-Building,' *Citizenship Studies* 5: 73–96.

Soysal, Y.N. (1994) *Limits of Citizenship: Migrants and Postnational Membership in Europe*. Chicago: University of Chicago Press.

Turner, B.S. (1986) *Citizenship and Capitalism: The Debate over Reformism*. Boston: Allen & Unwin.

Young, I.M. (1990) *Justice and the Politics of Difference*. Princeton, NJ: Princeton University Press.

Young, I.M. (2000) *Inclusion and Democracy*. New York: Oxford University Press.

7

Citizenship after Orientalism

ENGIN F. ISIN

At the root of the 'Western' conception of citizenship are two fundamental perspectives: orientalism (a way of dividing the world into essentially two 'civilizational' blocs, one having rationalized and secularized and hence modernized, the other having remained 'irrational', religious and traditional), and synoecism (a way of seeing the polity as embodying spatial and political unification). Orientalism mobilized images of citizenship as a unique occidental invention that oriental cultures lacked and of the citizen as a virtuous and rational being without kinship ties. Synoecism generated images of citizenship as fraternity, equality, liberty, expressing a unified and harmonious polity, and of the citizen as a secular and universal being without tribal loyalties. Both political and theoretical events in the last two decades have called these perspectives into question. These events have also mobilized new images of citizenship, opening up new possibilities but spawning new dangers. The most promising possibilities among these are images of citizenship as agonistic and contested processes of becoming political that generate rights claims and articulate responsibilities for multiple identities, polities, and practices. Groups based upon ethnic, 'racial', ecological and sexual identities have articulated such claims for citizenship to include group-differentiated rights at various scales from local to cosmopolitan. Yet, among the dangers are the tendencies to essentialize or relativize identities eventuating either violent encounters or reactions such as xenophobia, exclusions, expulsions and other forms of alienation. Without returning to orientalism and synoecism, is it possible at least theoretically to avoid these dangers while encouraging the possibilities of these new images of citizenship?

This chapter does not address that question. Instead, it discusses the origins of the occidental sociology of citizenship and argues that orientalism and synoecism constitute fundamental impediments for developing group-differentiated citizenship and rights. Since Max Weber was the main proponent of an occidental conception of citizenship, juxtaposing it against a 'cluster of absences' in oriental societies, a critical discussion of his conception of citizenship as the foundation of the modern idea of citizenship is the subject of the first section. The following section suggests that with the experience of pluralization and fragmentation of Western societies and polities, synoecism and orientalism have become problematic perspectives from which to view citizenship. The final section argues that this has become evident especially in the new Western views on ostensibly Islamic states and their incompatibility with democracy.

OCCIDENTALIZING CITIZENSHIP: ORIENTALISM AND SYNOECISM

While Weber's work has been associated with what may be called sociological orientalism, his emphasis on synoecism has never been made an issue. An important reason for this is that his sociology of citizenship as the unique aspect of occidental capitalism has been far less discussed and emphasized than his emphasis on rationalization and religion. Among his critics, Weber's designation as the major sociological progenitor of orientalism rests on three assumptions: first, that he shared the orientalist view of the superiority of the occident over the orient; second, that his comparative causal account of the uniqueness of the occident rested on an internalist research programme which discards or downplays the role of colonialism and imperialism in blocking the development of the orient; and, third, that the religion-based civilizational aspect of Weber's comparative sociology ascribed a unity, autonomy and primacy to religion and culture which drew him to the orientalist perspective (Nafissi, 1998: 98).

From Rodinson (1966: 99–117) and Said (1978: 259) to Dean (1994: 79–89) and Turner (1974; 1996: 257–86), the critics of Weber have focused on his theses on the origins of modern capitalism and his interpretation of why the oriental societies 'failed' to develop modern capitalism. The critics have invariably converged on issues of the rationalization of law, state administration and commerce, an ethic of acquisition, and an ethic of ultimate values as the essential differences between the oriental and occidental cultures, religions, societies and economies, issues which originally appeared in Weber's celebrated *The Protestant Ethic and the Spirit of Capitalism* (1905). While this critique has been useful in highlighting how Weber's work connects with broader themes of orientalism, Weber's later argument that the city as a locus of citizenship was the unique character of the occident that led to the development of capitalism has remained unexplored. This theme is also remarkably absent among sympathetic discussions of Weber's work on the city such as those by Momigliano (1970), Finley (1981), Murray (1990) and Colognesi (1995). More recently, Love (2000a, 2000b) also fails to discuss the importance for Weber of the relationship between the city and citizenship in constituting the uniqueness of the occident. Thus, the elective affinities between synoecism and orientalism that constitute the basis of Weber's conception of the difference between the occidental and oriental cities remain curiously unexplored. That for Weber the absence of autonomous cities and citizenship was the root cause of the failure of oriental societies to develop capitalism and that this was connected with synoecism is what we need to explore in further detail.

By always defining the city in terms of five essential characteristics (fortification, market, autonomous law and administration, association, and autocephaly), Weber argued that what made the occidental city unique was that it arose from the establishment of a fraternity, brotherhood in arms for mutual aid and protection, and the usurpation of political power (Weber, [1927a] 1981: 319). In this regard, Weber always drew parallels between the medieval 'communes' and ancient 'synoecism'. For Weber:

> The polis is always the product of such a confraternity or synoecism, not always an actual settlement in proximity but a definite oath of brotherhood which signified that a common ritualistic meal is established and a ritualistic union formed and that only those had a part in this ritualistic group who buried their dead on the acropolis and had their dwellings in the city. (p. 320).

As we shall see below, while Weber consistently emphasized that some of these characteristics emerged in China, Japan, the Near East, India and Egypt, he insisted that it was only in the occident that all were present and appeared regularly. From this he concluded that 'Most importantly, the associational character of the city and the concept of a burgher (as contrasted to the man from the countryside) never developed [in the orient] at all and existed only in rudiments' (Weber, [1921] 1978: 1227). Therefore '... a special status of the town dweller as a "citizen", in the ancient medieval sense, did not exist and a corporate character of the city was unknown' (p. 1227). He was convinced that '... in strong contrast to the medieval and ancient Occident, we never find the phenomenon in the Orient that the autonomy and the participation of the inhabitants in the affairs of local administration would be more strongly developed in the city ... than in the countryside. In fact, as a rule the very opposite would be true' (p. 1228). For him this difference was decisive: 'All safely founded information about Asian and oriental settlements which had the economic characteristics of "cities" seems to indicate that normally only the clan associations, and sometimes also the occupational associations, were the vehicle of organized action, but never the collective of urban citizens as such' (p. 1233). Above all, for Weber only 'in the Occident is found the concept of *citizen* (*civis Romanus*, *citoyens*, *bourgeois*) because only in the Occident does the *city* exist in the specific sense of the word' (Weber, [1927b] 1981: 232).

Broadly speaking, Weber provided two reasons why the city as confraternity arose only in the occident. First, since the occidental city originally emerged as a defence mechanism, the group that owned the means of warfare dominated the city. For Weber whether a group owned the means of warfare or was furnished by an overlord was as fundamental as whether the means of production were the property of the worker or the capitalist (Weber, [1927a] 1981: 320). Everywhere in the orient the development of the city as brotherhood in arms was prevented by the fact that the army of the prince or overlord dominated the city (Weber, [1918] 1994: 280). Why? Because in their origins and development, for India, China, the Near East, Egypt and Asia the question of irrigation was crucial. 'The water question conditioned the existence of the bureaucracy, the compulsory service of the dependent classes, and the dependence of subject classes upon the functioning of the bureaucracy of the king' (Weber, [1927a] 1981: 321). That the king expressed his power in the form of a military monopoly was the basis of the distinction between the orient and the occident. 'The forms of religious brotherhood and self equipment for war made possible the origin and existence of the city' (p. 321). While elements of analogous developments occur in India, China, Mesopotamia and Egypt, the necessity of water regulation, which led to the formation of kingship monopoly over the means of warfare, stifled these beginnings.

The second obstacle, which prevented the development of the city in the orient, was the persistence of magic in oriental religions. These religions did not allow the formation of 'rational' communities and hence the city. By contrast, the magical barriers between clans, tribes and peoples, which were still known in the ancient *polis*, were eventually set aside and so the establishment of the occidental city was made possible (Weber, [1927a] 1981: 322–3). What makes the occidental city unique was that it allowed the association or formation of groups based on bonds and ties other than lineage or kinship the basis of which was 'rational contract'.

In various studies between *The Agrarian Sociology of Ancient Civilizations* (1909) and *Economy and Society* (1921), Weber's argument that the city as a locus of citizenship was the characteristic that made the occident unique and his reliance on synoecism and orientalism appeared more consistently than his emphasis on rationalization and with an increasing urgency (Käsler, 1979: 42). That is why we need a more detailed analysis before we develop a critique.

For Weber, at first glance, the occidental city presented striking similarities to its Near and Far Eastern counterparts (Weber, [1921] 1978: 1236). Like the oriental city, it was a market place, a centre of trade and commerce and a fortified stronghold. Merchant and artisan guilds could also be found in both cities (Weber, [1917a] 1958: 33–5). Even the creation of autonomous legal authority could be found in both cities, though to varying degrees. Moreover, all ancient and medieval cities, like their oriental counterparts, contained some agricultural land belonging to the city. Throughout the ancient world the law applicable in cities differed from rural areas. However, particularly in the occidental medieval city, such difference was essential, while it was insignificant and irregular in the ancient oriental city. The ancient city almost always arose from a confluence and settling together of strangers and outsiders. While Weber used this as evidence of why the city always manifested a social and cultural differentiation, he often underlined its unity over diversity (Weber, [1921] 1978: 1237). While he recognized that the urban population consisted of very diverse social groups, what was revolutionary in the occidental city was the free status of this distinct population. The fact that the city was a centre of trade and commerce led rulers to free bondsmen and slaves to pursue opportunities for earning money in return for tribute (p. 1238). The occidental city arose as 'a place where *the ascent from bondage to freedom* by means of monetary acquisition was possible' (p. 1238). The principle that 'city air makes man free', which emerged in central and north European cities, was an expression of the unique aspect of the occidental city. 'The urban citizenry therefore usurped the right to dissolve the bonds of seigniorial domination; this was the great – in fact, the *revolutionary* – innovation which differentiated the medieval occidental cities from all others' (p. 1239). The common quality of the ancient polis and the medieval commune was therefore an association of citizens subject to a special law exclusively applicable to them. In ancient Asia, Africa or America similar formations of polis or commune constitutions or corporate citizenship rights were not known.

Despite his emphasis on the internal differentiation of the occidental city, however, when Weber made comparisons with the oriental city, he overlooked its differentiation in favour of a unity signified by its corporate status: 'The fully developed ancient and medieval city was above all constituted, or at least interpreted, as a fraternal association, as a rule equipped with a corresponding religious symbol for the associational cult of the citizens: a city-god or city-saint to whom only the citizens had access' (Weber, [1921] 1978: 1241). A significant difference between the occidental city and the ancient oriental city was that in the former there was no trace of magical and animistic castes. It was the belief of ancient citizens that their cities originated as free associations and confederations of groups, which were partly clans (p. 1242). But Weber never explained why the beliefs of the ancient Greeks should be taken at their face value. For them the ancient Greek polis was, for example, a settling together of clans and tribes. Its membership was neither occupational nor spatial but by birth in a clan. The *polis* was a confederation of noble families and was religiously exclusive. The European medieval city too, especially in the south, was a federation of noble families. The entry of the plebes into citizenship, however, lessened the significance of membership in clans or tribes; rather, membership was defined along spatial and occupational lines. The ancient *polis* was on the way to becoming a medieval association but it was incorporated into the Hellenistic and Roman systems of rule. 'The medieval city, by contrast, was a commune from the very beginning, even though the legal concept of the "corporation" as such was only gradually formulated' (p. 1243).

Thus, Weber argued that in the ancient oriental city kinship ties persisted regularly while in Greek *poleis* and medieval cities they progressively dissolved and were replaced by spatial and occupational relationships. In Greek *poleis* this becomes visible beginning with colonization, which required the settling together of strangers and outsiders to become citizens. In addition, the change in the military organization of the *polis* from heroic warfare to hoplitic warfare intensified the dissolution of clan ties. Although many Greek poleis maintained such ties for a long time, they became more ritualistic and less significant in the everyday life of politics. Similarly, the warrior associations of the wandering Germanic tribes in Europe after the fall of the Roman Empire were organized around leadership and military prowess rather than clan ties. The development of spatial units such as the 'hundreds' as a method of distributing obligations impeded a clan development.

> When Christianity became the religion of these peoples who had been so profoundly shaken in all their traditions, it finally destroyed whatever religious significance these clan ties retained; perhaps, indeed, it was precisely the weakness or absence of such magical and taboo barriers which made the conversion possible. The often very significant role played by the parish community in the administrative organization of medieval cities is only one of many symptoms pointing to this quality of the Christian religion which, in dissolving clan ties, importantly shaped the medieval city' (Weber, [1921] 1978: 1244).

By contrast, the oriental city never really dissolved the tribal and clan ties.

For Weber all cities in world history were founded by the settling together of strangers and outsiders previously alien to that space. Chinese, Mesopotamian, Egyptian, Mycenaean, Minoan kings founded cities, relocated them, and settled in them immigrants and recruited people. In such cities the king who controlled the warfare apparatus retained absolute power. An association failed to develop and the urban residents maintained their tribal identities (Weber, [1921] 1978: 1244). 'Under such circumstances no legal status of urban citizenship arose, but only an association for sharing the burdens and privileges of those who happened to inhabit the city at any given time' (p. 1245). In the ancient polis membership in one of the tribal associations remained a distinguishing mark of the citizen with full rights, entitled to participation in the religious cult and qualified for all offices which required communication with the gods. The ancient tribe remained an association in so far as it was artificially created rather than being an expression of descent or lineage. The north European medieval cities were different. The resident joined the citizenry as an individual, and as an individual swore the oath of citizenship (p. 1246). His membership was not in a tribe or clan but a city association. All the same, both ancient and medieval cities were able to extend citizenship to outsiders. 'In all Asian cities, including the Near Eastern ones, the phenomenon of a "commune" was either absent altogether or, at best, present only in rudiments which, moreover, always took the form of kin-group associations that extended also beyond the city' (p. 1248).

The majority of Weber's interpretations of India, Judea, China and the Near East rely on separate studies he undertook on these cultures, and thus each requires more detailed discussion. Since I have discussed these studies elsewhere (Isin, 2002), it will suffice to conclude that for Weber the occidental city was a sworn confraternity and this *was* the decisive basis for the development of citizenship. Everywhere the city became a territorial corporation and officials became officials of this institution. The occidental city was an institutionalized association in which the citizen was an active creator of law to which he was subject.

That the development of the city was impeded in the orient by the presence of kinship ties was as much Weber's conclusion as his premise. He approached ancient China already 'knowing' that the sibs were the bearers of central religious concerns and were very powerful. He approached ancient India already assuming that the castes were carriers of a specific style of life, and determined the individual's fate. While he recognized that the clan and sib ties were not as powerful in the ancient Near East as they were in ancient India and China, he still saw them as impediments to the emergence of confraternity. As Turner (1996: 268) argued, Weber's studies on Islam, India, China and Judea were not isolated, original or innovative researches but developed from the perspective of early twentieth-century orientalism. Weber's increasingly urgent and obstinate search for the origins of modern capitalism was situated in a general understanding of an ontological difference between the orient and the occident. Orientalism guided Weber to draw sharper and sharper distinctions between occidental and oriental cities and, in the process, provided a unified and homogeneous account of both. Citizenship became both the embodiment and the expression of the uniqueness of the occidental city. This ontological orientation meant that Weber never acknowledged that kinship and magic ties were never fully dissolved in either ancient *poleis* and *civitates* or medieval cities and that factionalism and fissiparousness were endemic conditions in both (Springborg, 1992: 247, 267). The ancient Greek *poleis* and Roman *civitates* as well as medieval cities maintained their clans and tribes. Even in later stages membership was a mixture of clan and kinship ties as well as occupational and spatial ones. Ultimately, the intensity of familial and religious ties persisted in the occidental city. The European medieval city too, especially in the south, was essentially a federation of noble families. The harmony and unity attributed to the ancient polis and medieval corporations in Weber's work overlooked the otherness of citizenship, its strangers and outsiders. Being a quintessential citizen himself – for Weber described himself as a bourgeois citizen – perhaps he was not nearly as sceptical and questioning about the narratives passed down to him by citizens and so did not consider it a problem to bequeath the same. He savagely criticized the Junker aristocracy who wanted to 'resurrect' historical forms of citizenship as belonging to groups by arguing that 'the modern state is the first to have the concept of the *citizen of the state*' according to which 'the individual, for once, is *not*, as he is everywhere else, considered in terms of the particular professional and family position he occupies, not in relation to differences of material and social situation, but purely and simply *as a citizen*' (original emphases Weber, [1917b] 1994: 103). This is, of course, a normative ideal as Weber saw the meaning and purpose of modern citizenship as a 'counterbalance to the social *inequalities* which are *neither* rooted in natural differences nor created by natural qualities but are produced, rather, by social conditions (which are often severely at variance with nature) and above all, inevitably, by the *purse*' (original emphases p. 103). To be sure, this normative ideal of modern liberal citizenship differed from the aristocrats of German constitutional liberalism. Nonetheless, this ideal did not exactly fit either historical or modern forms of citizenship in practice despite Weber's claim to historical accuracy (p. 91).

Throughout the twentieth century, orientalism and synoecism have mobilized various theories of modernization that anticipated or urged that the oriental (or in a more innocuous language, developing or developing societies) would eventually evolve or modernize by eliminating their irrational and fissiparous polities and values and develop democratic forms of citizenship. Theories of modernization also formed the bedrock theories of government, citizenship and democracy, constituting the universal citizen as their measure.

POSTMODERNIZING AND GLOBALIZING CITIZENSHIP

The events in the last two decades of the twentieth century that have been captured by the notions of 'postmodernization' and 'globalization' have challenged synoecism, and by extension, orientalism, as credible perspectives on citizenship (Isin and Wood, 1999). If we define postmodernization as both a process of fragmentation through which various group identities have been formed and discourses through which 'difference' has become a dominant strategy, its effect on citizenship has been twofold. On the one hand, various groups that have been marginalized and excluded from *modern* citizenship have been able to seek recognition (Fraser, 1997; Young, 1990; Young, 1993). Groups based upon ethnic, 'racial', ecological and sexual concerns have articulated claims for citizenship to include group-differentiated rights. Women have fought to expand their citizenship rights to include social rights such as access to childcare, pay equity, and rights to safe cities; ethnic and racialized groups have sought recognition and representation; aboriginal peoples have sought representation and self-government rights; gays and lesbians have struggled to claim rights that are already extended to heterosexual couples, such as spousal benefits and common-law arrangements; diasporic groups have struggled for naturalization and political rights; and various ability groups have demanded recognition of their needs to become fully functional citizens of their polities. These struggles of recognition as claims to exercise citizenship rights, challenged one of the most venerable premises of modernization – universalization – by exposing its limits. These struggles demonstrated that being a universal subject (Weber's pure citizen) did not necessarily guarantee rights let alone articulated duties. On the other hand, these various claims have strained the boundaries of citizenship and pitted group against group in the search for identity and recognition. As a result, while ostensibly making claims to citizenship and recognition, some members of these groups have become trapped or encased within essentialized specific identities, unable to move beyond the straitjacket that they have unintentionally created. The invention or persistence of such identities called into question another venerable premise of modernization that would have us believe in the disappearance of such allegiances. Either way, postmodernization of politics has, therefore, stressed the capacity of the modern conception of universal citizenship to accommodate and recognize these diverse and conflicting demands.

But it also forced rethinking of fundamental categories of political discourse by critiquing totality, universality, unity and homogeneity that have been attributed to polities. New valorizations of multiplicity, diversity, heterogeneity, hybridity and syncretism in social and political discourse were neither consequences nor causes of 'deeper' changes or transformations but were themselves such changes or transvaluation of values. As such, they were also intimately connected with 'globalization'. If we define globalization as both a process by which the increasing interconnectedness of places becomes the defining moment and as a discourse through which 'globalism' becomes a dominant strategy, its effect on citizenship has also been twofold. On the one hand, with the rise of global flows of capital, images, ideas, labour, crime, music, and regimes of governance, the sources of authority of citizenship rights and obligations have expanded from the nation-state to other international organizations, corporations and agencies such as the World Bank, IMF, IBM, the Internet, Greenpeace, Amnesty International, Microsoft, and Coca Cola. With growing flows, cities as cosmopolises have become accretions of unprecedented forms of multiplicity in 'lifestyles', cultures, religions, languages, values, and rationalities becoming worlds unto themselves (Isin, 2000). In fact, much of what we defined as 'postmodernization' has undoubtedly been concentrated in cosmopolises, simultaneously emanating from and producing them. On the other hand, the dominance of such cosmopolitan agents and cities has issued challenges to the sovereignty principle of the nation-states. In a very complex relay of events, nation-states withdrew certain citizenship rights and instead imposed new obligations on their citizens, which intensified tensions within states where citizenship rights that had been taken for granted began to disappear (e.g. unemployment insurance, welfare, or right to legal counsel) and new obligations (e.g. workfare) were implemented. Similarly, increased international migration has raised the question of 'citizenship' rights and duties of aliens, immigrants, and refugees.

While some believe that globalization means the rise of the world as one single place, others dispute whether globalization has become as widespread as claimed and point to increased postmodernization of culture and politics where diversity, fragmentation and difference dominate. But few would disagree that postmodernization and globalization are occurring simultaneously and are engendering new patterns of global differentiation in which some states, societies and social groups are becoming increasingly enmeshed with each other while others are becoming increasingly marginalized. A new configuration of power relations is crystallizing as the old geographic divisions rapidly give way to new spaces such that the familiar triad of core–periphery, North–South, and First World–Third World no longer represents these new spaces (Dirlik, 1997). Globalization has recast modern patterns of inclusion and exclusion between nation-states by forging new hierarchies, which cut across and penetrate all regions of the world (Held et al., 1999: 8). North and South, First World and Third World, are no longer 'out there' but nestled together within different nodes of capital, labour and commodities. It appears more questionable every day whether we can divide the world into discrete, contiguous and contained zones as a representation of reality. Instead, a new critical geopolitics seems to be crystallizing as overlapping networks of various flows of intensity in which certain spaces are the primary nodes. These complex overlapping networks connect the fate of one agglomeration to the fate of another in distant parts of the world. The powerful critique of orientalism that occasioned the emergence of postcolonial forms of discourse is undoubtedly both a product and a catalyst of this reconfigured world (Chakrabarty, 2000; Said, 1978, 1993; Spivak, 1999).

As such, postmodernization and globalization are implicated in and produce new regimes of accumulation and modes of regulation (Hoogvelt, 1997). This has further eroded the credibility of modernization theories that would have us believe in national trajectories that will follow the disappearance of religion, tradition and particularism. If a critique of Weber and his orientalism and synoecism does not appear radical or unreasonable it is because the world in which we write and think has been so transformed that we are no longer easily able to make his assumptions of occidental uniqueness, universality and unity. The intellectual task ahead of us in this century for developing new conceptions of citizenship after orientalism involves two moves. First, we will need to develop much more sophisticated conceptions of citizenship that will do justice to struggles of recognition and redistribution. The question facing us today, therefore, is not *whether* to recognize different ethnic identities or to protect 'nature' or to enable access to cultural capital or to eliminate discrimination against women and gays or to democratize computer-mediated communications, but *how* to do them all at the same time. Whether we like it or not, all this 'strange multiplicity' (Tully, 1995) is upon us, in all its forms at once. The question is how to imagine a postnational form of citizenship in which sovereignty is intersecting, multiple and overlapping. Of course, this work has begun with impressive results but this is just a beginning (Kymlicka and Norman, 2000). Second, we will need new historical investigations that will approach other cultures and cities such as those of India, the Ottoman Empire and China, with a 'hermeneutic difference'. That is, without implying either superiority or inferiority but recognizing difference that strives for a deeper understanding of both 'ourselves' and the other (Dallmayr, 1996). Instead of trying to demonstrate a cluster of absences that set the orient apart, we will need to investigate historical cities around the world with their radical specificities and multiplicities. Of course, this work has been ongoing but so much more lies ahead (Çelik, 1986;

Eldem et al. 1999). The road ahead is not straightforward and I shall conclude this paper with an illustration of how forms of 'new orientalism' and 'new synoecism' block understanding of political transformations taking place in diverse Islamic societies and the new conceptions of citizenship that are incipient in them.

ISLAMIZATION AND THE NEW ORIENTALISM

As the processes of postmodernization and globalization have unfolded in bewildering and exhilarating ways in the 'occident', fragmentation and pluralization have also continued apace in the oriental societies and call into question the theories of modernization. The rise of political Islam has most dramatically been the arena of confrontation, contest and conflict of competing theorization of modernization. The rise of political Islam as a social movement, its organization through political parties, and its substantial electoral successes in diverse countries were among the most important factors for the rise of new orientalism in the last two decades of the twentieth century (Esposito and Voll, 1996; Mayer, 1999; Roy, 1994). Remarkably, new orientalism has constructed the 'orient' and its lack of democratic institutions in a similar fashion to earlier orientalism but, ironically, for the opposite reasons (Sadowski, 1997). While nineteenth-century orientalism considered Islam to lack civic identity and collective spirit, new *fin de siècle* orientalism finds too much of both, expressed in 'fundamentalism'.

When compared with other world religions and civilizations, Islam has had the unique if dubious distinction of having always been regarded by the occident as a cultural 'other', an adversary. While rivalry over exclusive claims to one indivisible transcendent God and the share of their respective Holy Land and their geographic proximity partially explain this relationship, the occidental civilization has become dependent upon this other to articulate its own identity. As Hoogvelt (1997) argued, as much as 'orientalism' may be a product of occidental culture, as Said (1978) argued, it is also a product of its search of itself. It is this dependency that perhaps explains the occidental fear of Islam. Be that as it may, in their intertwining histories, the nineteenth century stands apart with the emergence of a special scientific discipline, 'orientalism', which inexorably links the difference of Islam as the anchor that defines the nature of the occident. While buttressing the confidence of Europe in its own cultural superiority, it cast Islam in the role of contemptible victim, in need of correction. The discipline linked itself up with broader interpretations that explained the trajectories of Islam on the basis of race, language and religion. I have shown above how orientalism penetrated into social scientific explanations of the lack of citizenship in the orient in the work of Weber and the subsequent theories of modernization. I would like now to return to Weber and discuss his approach to Islamic cities.

Although Weber did not undertake a special study on Islam comparable to those of Judaism, China and India, he made several scattered but significant comments on Islamic cities (Huff and Schluchter, 1999). Bryan Turner (1974) has undertaken the most penetrating analysis of these scattered comments. For Weber, it was the urban piety of certain status groups – artisans and merchants – in autonomous cities that was characteristic of the rise of European capitalism (Turner, 1974: 94). While Christianity played a fundamental part in the development of the associational character of the occidental city, Islam impeded the development of such a character with its emphasis on clan and kinship (Turner, 1974: 97). So, in oriental cities one finds a collection of distinct and separate clan and tribal groups which do not join common action, a tribalism which Christianity helped break in Europe. 'The internal development of a rich and autonomous guild and associational life within the city was closely connected with the legal and political freedom of the city from the interference of the patrimonial or feudal officials. Not only were cities legal persons, they were also independent political agents' (Turner, 1974: 97). They fought wars, concluded treaties and made alliances. Their autonomy was fundamentally connected with their military independence.

> It was in the city that urban piety, legal autonomy, occupational associations and political involvement developed; hence, the autonomous city had very important connections with the rise of European capitalism. In Islam, Weber argued, it was the combination of a warrior religiosity with patrimonialism which limited the growth of autonomous cities and which in consequence precluded the growth of urban piety within the lower middle classes. (Turner, 1974: 98)

Nonetheless, Turner, while admitting that Weber mistakenly overstated the importance of the warrior nobles in shaping Islamic ethos, argued that contemporary historical research gives ample evidence for Weber's thesis that Islamic cities were internally fissiparous and externally controlled by patrimonial rulers. 'The result was that Islamic cities did not produce a rich life of independent burgher associations' (Turner, 1974: 98). More recent research, however, has called this argument into question. The ostensible fissiparousness of the Islamic city was no more divisive than the factionalism of the *polis* or the medieval city. Turner's agreement with Weber focused on the fact that Islamic cities were aggregates of sub communities rather than socially unified communities. This was ostensibly illustrated by the very geography of cities of the great cities of Islam, Cairo, Damascus, Aleppo and Baghdad. These cities were divided into quarters or districts and each district had its homogeneous community and markets. The social solidarity of these districts or 'villages' within cities sometimes reflected the religious identity of its inhabitants (Turner, 1974: 99–100). 'As Weber rightly observed, the continuity of clan and tribal organization within the city context imported rural feuding arrangements into urban life' (Turner, 1974: 100). The city was the focal point of Islamic government, trade and religion; yet this focal point of Islamic culture lacked corporate institutions, a civic culture and a set of socially binding forces. Urban life was a precarious balance of social forces, a balance of contending quarters, sedentarized tribes, sects and legal schools (Turner, 1974: 103). 'Islamic guilds were not, therefore, organizations created by workmen to protect themselves and their craft; they were organizations created by the state to supervise the craft and workmen and above all to protect the state from autonomous institutions' (Turner, 1974: 103). The guilds were a facet of patrimonial control. The Islamic City lacked 'group feeling' and also failed to provide corporate institutions that would protect individuals (Turner, 1974: 104). Yet, as Southall (1998: 228–9) emphasizes in a recent overview of new research, this sharp distinction overlooks some structural similarities between Islamic guilds and their occidental counterparts. While guilds as self-governing and self-regulating bodies, controlling standards of production, conditions of work and criteria of entry, did not exist in Islamic cities, local authorities, on behalf and by appointment of the ruler, were required to control occupations by enlisting the help of guild leaders and notables (Southall, 1998: 228). In many cities this led to craft and merchant guilds in which local notables, just like their occidental counterparts, exercised power and exerted control. Similarly, Eldem, Goffman and Masters (1999) argue against Weber's typology of cities in the context of the Ottoman city. In their studies they have found that 'there does not exist a *typical* Ottoman, Arab, or Islamic city that imposes fundamentally unique and thus ghettoizing characteristics upon all such urban centres and their inhabitants' (Eldem et al., 1999: 15). Moreover, they also found that the civic unity that was ostensibly missing in the Ottoman city was present albeit in different forms and there were already syncretic and hybridized civic cultures: 'The colonies of Europeans in early modern Istanbul (the labyrinthine

Galata and Pera), Izmir (the exposed Street of the Franks), and Aleppo (the semi-fortified khans) each took different forms as they followed the distinctive cultural contours of their particular milieus' (Eldem et al., 1999: 15). As a result, such outsider groups not only enriched each of these Ottoman cities but also contributed to the formation of a particular civic culture. As more studies become available, clearly the orientalist picture of Islamic cities will undergo radical transformation.

At the end of the twentieth century, Islam was also at the centre of a new orientalism that cast Islamic societies as incapable of developing democratic institutions. While many scholars have argued that the characteristics attributed to 'Islam' by the new orientalism do not exist in any unity, such characterizations continue as discursive strategies of othering. By contrast, Mayer has argued that the distribution of citizenship rights derives more from political contingencies and trajectories of Muslim states than any specificity of Islam (Mayer, 1999). Since the 1980s the West has chosen to confront Islam, considering cultural issues the trigger of conflict. The fact that much of the Muslim world is undergoing a process of Islamization, which, far from being strictly religious, is closely linked to the need to find its own political and cultural language, cannot be divorced from either the experience of colonialism and imperialism or the failure of modernization and secularization processes set in motion by postcolonial intellectuals and intelligentsia during the 1960s and 1970s. Similarly, far from superficial interpretation, which associates the veiled woman with submission and the unveiled woman with liberation, the issue of dress conceals a diverse world full of signs and symbols that must be decoded (Göle, 1996). Citizenship, or rather its alleged incompatibility with the culture of 'Islamic' countries, is, therefore an issue that often conveys a distorted image of Islam in the occident. Islam has been found to be inhospitable to citizenship. If we transfer the meaning of submission as understood in religious terms in Islam, to the political sphere, some would conclude that Islam, therefore, promotes despotic rule and passive acceptance amongst the faithful. These orientations, while problematic, have increasingly become prevalent amongst not only 'intellectuals' but also political and policy intelligentsia in the West. As Esposito and Voll (2001) illustrate, influential Islamic intellectuals have been articulating conceptions of citizenship and democracy that go beyond fundamentalist and modernist ideas (see also Filali Ansary, 1996; Hamdi, 1996; Kubba, 1996; Lewis, 1996; Wright, 1996). New sociologies of citizenship in the occident and the orient that incorporate struggles for recognition, recognize group-differentiated identities, and develop new sensibilities toward otherness are complementary political and cultural developments that may well end a fundamental ontological difference between the occident and the orient without at the same time reducing various cultural zones to an equally fundamental sameness.

REFERENCES

Çelik, Zeynep (1986) *The Remaking of Istanbul: Portrait of an Ottoman City in the Nineteenth Century*. Seattle: University of Washington Press.

Chakrabarty, Dipesh (2000) *Provincializing Europe: Postcolonial Thought and Historical Difference*. Princeton, NJ: Princeton University Press.

Colognesi, L. Capgrossi (1995) 'The Limits of the Ancient City and the Evolution of the Medieval City in the Thought of Max Weber', in T. Cornell and K. Lomas (eds), *Urban Society in Roman Italy*. New York: St Martin's Press.

Dallmayr, Fred R. (1996) *Beyond Orientalism: Essays on Cross-Cultural Encounter*. Albany: State University of New York Press.

Dean, Mitchell (1994) *Critical and Effective Histories: Foucault's Methods and Historical Sociology*. London: Routledge.

Dirlik, Arif (1997) *The Postcolonial Aura: Third World Criticism in the Age of Global Capitalism*. Boulder, CO: Westview Press.

Eldem, Edhem, Goffman, Daniel and Masters, Bruce Alan (1999) *The Ottoman City between East and West: Aleppo, Izmir, and Istanbul*. New York: Cambridge University Press.

Esposito, John L. and Voll, John Obert (1996) *Islam and Democracy*. Oxford: Oxford University Press.

Esposito, John L. and Voll, John Obert (2001) *Makers of Contemporary Islam*. Oxford: Oxford University Press.

Filali Ansary, A. (1996) 'Islam and Liberal Democracy: The Challenge of Secularization', *Journal of Democracy*, 7 (2), 76–80.

Finley, M.I. (1981) 'The Ancient City: From Fustel De Coulanges to Max Weber and Beyond' in *Economy and Society in Ancient Greece*. New York: Viking.

Fraser, Nancy (1997) *Justice Interruptus: Critical Reflections on the 'Postsocialist' Condition*. New York: Routledge.

Göle, Nilüfer (1996) *The Forbidden Modern: Civilization and Veiling*. Ann Arbor: University of Michigan Press.

Hamdi, M.E. (1996) 'Islam and Liberal Democracy: The Limits of the Western Model', *Journal of Democracy*, 7 (2), 81–5.

Held, David, McGrew, Anthony, Goldblatt, David and Perraton, Jonathan (1999) *Global Transformations: Politics, Economics and Culture*. Cambridge: Polity.

Hoogvelt, Ankie (1997) *Globalisation and the Postcolonial World: The New Political Economy of Development*. Basingstoke: Macmillan.

Huff, Toby E. and Schluchter, Wolfgang (eds) (1999) *Max Weber and Islam*. New Brunswick, NJ: Transaction.

Isin, Engin F. (ed.) (2000) *Democracy, Citizenship, and the Global City*. London: Routledge.

Isin, Engin F. (2002) *Being Political: Genealogies of Citizenship*. Minneapolis: University of Minnesota Press.

Isin, Engin F. and Wood, Patricia K. (1999) *Citizenship and Identity*. London: Sage.

Käsler, Dirk (1979) *Max Weber: An Introduction to His Life and Work*. Oxford: Blackwell.

Kubba, L. (1996) 'Islam and Liberal Democracy: Recognizing Pluralism', *Journal of Democracy*, 7 (2), 86–9.

Kymlicka, Will and Norman, Wayne (eds) (2000) *Citizenship in Diverse Societies*. Oxford: Oxford University Press.

Lewis, B. (1996) 'Islam and Liberal Democracy: A Historical Overview', *Journal of Democracy*, 7 (2), 52–63.

Love, John (2000a) 'Max Weber's *Ancient Judaism*', in S.P. Turner (ed.), *The Cambridge Companion to Weber*. Cambridge: Cambridge University Press.

Love, John (2000b) 'Max Weber's Orient', in S.P. Turner (ed.), *The Cambridge Companion to Weber*. Cambridge: Cambridge University Press.

Mayer, Ann Elizabeth (1999) 'Citizenship and Human Rights in Some Muslim States', in G.M. Muñoz (ed.) *Islam, Modernism and the West: Cultural and Political Relations at the End of the Millennium*. London: I.B. Tauris.

Momigliano, Arnaldo ([1970] 1977) 'The Ancient City of Fustel De Coulanges', *Essays in Ancient and Modern Historiography*. Oxford: Blackwell.

Murray, Oswyn (1990) 'Cities of Reason', in O. Murray and S. Price (eds), *The Greek City: From Homer to Alexander*. Oxford: Oxford University Press.

Nafissi, M.R. (1998) 'Reframing Orientalism: Weber and Islam', *Economy and Society*, 27 (1), 97–118.

Rodinson, Maxime (1974) *Islam and Capitalism* tr. B. Pearce. London: Penguin.

Roy, Olivier (1994) *The Failure of Political Islam* tr. C. Volk, Cambridge, MA: Harvard University Press.

Sadowski, Yahya (1997) 'The New Orientalism and the Democracy Debate', in J. Beinin and J. Stork (eds) *Political Islam*. Berkeley and Los Angeles: University of California Press.

Said, Edward S. (1978) *Orientalism*. New York: Random House.

Said, Edward S. (1993) *Culture and Imperialism*. New York: Vintage Books.

Southall, Aidan William (1998) *The City in Time and Space*. Cambridge: Cambridge University Press.

Spivak, Gayatri Chakravorty (1999) *A Critique of Postcolonial Reason: Toward a History of the Vanishing Present*. Cambridge, MA: Harvard University Press.

Springborg, Patricia (1992) *Western Republicanism and the Oriental Prince*. Cambridge: Polity Press.

Tully, James (1995) *Strange Multiplicity: Constitutionalism in an Age of Diversity*. Cambridge: Cambridge University Press.

Turner, Bryan S. (1974) *Weber and Islam: A Critical Study*. London: Routledge & Kegan Paul.

Turner, Bryan S. (1996) *For Weber: Essays on the Sociology of Fate*. 2nd edition, London: Sage.

Weber, Max ([1905] 1930) *The Protestant Ethic and the Spirit of Capitalism* tr. T. Parsons. London: Unwin.

Weber, Max ([1909] 1976) *The Agrarian Sociology of Ancient Civilizations* tr. R.I. Frank. London: New Left Books.

Weber, Max ([1917a] 1958) *The Religion of India* tr. H.H. Gerth and D. Martindale. New York: Free Press.

Weber, Max ([1917b] 1994) 'Suffrage and Democracy in Germany', in P. Lassman and R. Speirs (eds) *Political Writings*. Cambridge: Cambridge University Press.

Weber, Max ([1918] 1994) 'Socialism', in P. Lassman and R. Speirs (eds), *Political Writings*. Cambridge: Cambridge University Press.

Weber, Max ([1921] 1978) *Economy and Society: An Outline of Interpretive Sociology* tr. G. Roth and C. Wittich. Berkeley: University of California Press.

Weber, Max ([1927a] 1981) 'Citizenship', *General Economic History*. London: Transaction Publishers.

Weber, Max ([1927b] 1981) *General Economic History*, tr. F.H. Knight. London: Transaction Publishers.

Wright, R. (1996) 'Islam and Liberal Democracy: Two Visions of Reformation', *Journal of Democracy*, 7 (2), 64–75.

Young, Iris Marion (1990) *Justice and the Politics of Difference*. Princeton, NJ: Princeton University Press.

Young, Iris Marion (1993) 'Together in Difference: Transforming the Logic of Group Political Conflict', in J. Squires (ed.) *Principled Positions: Postmodernism and the Rediscovery of Value*. London: Lawrence and Wishart.

Part Three

APPROACHES

8

Liberal Citizenship

PETER H. SCHUCK

The constitutive elements of a distinctively liberal conception of citizenship are clear enough in theory. It is far less clear how liberal citizenship can be achieved, and what its political consequences are likely to be. Indeed, those questions remain both open and profoundly elusive more than three centuries after liberal citizenship was first theorized in any systematic way – and despite our increasing knowledge growing out of an intensive quest for liberal citizenship.

This chapter first traces the essential principles upon which liberal citizenship is conceived. These principles speak to the nature of individuals, groups, civil society, the state, and supranational regimes, and to the relationships among them. The chapter then considers certain problematics of liberal citizenship – the challenges that confound it conceptually, politically, and institutionally. These challenges arise out of enduring social conditions, including the privatistic and materialistic tendencies of liberal citizens, the inequalities endemic even to relatively egalitarian liberal societies, the decentralizing tendencies of pluralistic politics, and the permeability, incapacities, and attempted neutrality of liberal states. The chapter concludes with a brief and frankly normative assessment of the aspirations and achievements of liberal citizenship.

Several preliminary definitions, observations, and qualifications are in order. Contemporary political discourse uses the term 'citizenship' very loosely, often treating it as little more than an empty vessel into which speakers may pour their own social and political ideals (Schuck, 1998: Ch. 8). Citizenship has become the normative category of choice, invoked by critics of the status quo – on both the Left and the Right – as a vehicle for demanding that the state do more, or less, to advance equality, justice, and participation in the civil society, economy, or polity.

By using 'citizenship' here to denote the status of full membership in a society, I effect only a slight improvement. After all, this definition, like others, begs two key questions: what are the relevant determinants of membership? and what are the indicia of fullness? In his magisterial approach to these two questions, T.H. Marshall emphasized the political, social, and economic dimensions of membership and elaborated his own understanding of the conditions necessary to fully achieve them (Marshall, [1950] 1992). But Marshall's idea of citizenship, published in 1950 at a time of heady enthusiasm about the welfare state among many intellectuals and others, has achieved no more canonical status than has any other.[1] Indeed, given the high stakes in how a society conceives of citizenship, any particular formulation – especially in a discussion as brief as this one must be – is readily contestable.

By 'liberal citizenship,' I mean a distinct conception and institutionalization of citizenship whose primary value is to maximize individual liberty. Needless to say, different liberal theorists have defined the nature and requirements of liberty rather differently, and the incidents of liberal citizen turn on which particular version is being invoked. In Isaiah Berlin's canonical formulation, one can view different accounts of liberalism as ranging from 'negative liberty' ideals that emphasize individuals' right to be left alone and to pursue their own projects free of state compulsion, all the way to 'positive liberty' notions. Common to positive liberty accounts is the claim that the state should act affirmatively to create or secure those substantive entitlements (e.g. income, health care, and education) that individuals need in order to lead the dignified, independent lives essential to their freedom (Berlin, 1969).

Different versions of contemporary liberal theory employ different methodologies for deriving principles of justification for state action and citizenship. Theorists defend these principles as being neutral, consensual, or otherwise consistent with liberal values, if not being required by them. Some of these methodologies are neo-contractarian (Nozick, 1977). Other versions are discursive or dialogic in nature; they rely upon propositions defining the particular, constrained forms of argument that might be capable of justifying assertions of power over free individuals (Ackerman, 1980). Still others are hybrid theories, employing a mix of approaches (Rawls, 1971).

The discussion here draws largely upon the debates over liberal citizenship in the United States, where the individualist and state-limiting aspects of liberalism have been most fully reified and the consequences of these aspects most severely criticized (Hartz, 1955; Smith, 1997). The word 'liberalism,' to be sure, has acquired a malodorous quality among politicians and many political commentators in the USA since the 1960s. Nonetheless, the fact remains that almost all mainstream political discourse in the USA, regardless of the speaker's party, proceeds as if the traditional liberal values of individual freedom, autonomy, consent, and limited state power were universally embraced, with the only differences being the means for achieving them. Indeed, disputants who advance non-liberal visions such as communitarianism and state-expanding ideals of social justice often redefine them in order to make them compatible with liberal discourse.

This overwhelmingly liberal discursive consensus, of course, has long been a profound source of frustration and criticism by liberalism's opponents, especially on the left, who seek more radical change than they think liberalism can deliver (Wolff, 1969; Marcuse, 1991). Other chapters of this book, in elaborating non-liberal notions of citizenship, address explicitly or implicitly many of the most important of liberalism's perceived limitations. Hence, I can limit my review of the challenges to liberal citizenship accordingly.

THE LIBERAL CONCEPTION OF CITIZENSHIP

Liberal theory, whether of citizenship or of anything else, begins with the individual. Liberalism's view of the individual shape its views of all other social aggregations, including the state. Yet its (and our) understanding of the nature of individuals is both dynamic and woefully incomplete. In particular, new advances in the fields of psychology, evolutionary biology, human genetics, and social science constantly unsettle received understandings about how individuals apprehend the world, about their motivations, rationality, spirituality, and behavior, and about the causal relationships that determine how these factors operate, and with what effects, in the real world. Partly for this reason, liberal theory has had to take individuals much as it finds them on the surface, while the scientists proceed with deeper investigations. This inability of liberal theory to advance an authoritative and convincing account of the individual poses a fundamental challenge to its coherence, one that I discuss below.

The most influential early expositors of systematic liberal theory were John Locke and John Stuart Mill. Locke ([1690] 1960) viewed individuals as endowed with and animated by reason, characterized as the 'Voice of God,' through which they can discern and act upon the dictates of divinely given natural law. From birth, all are equally endowed with this reason, which is the basis for their decisions to leave the state of nature, to enter into civil and political society, and to act in the community. Individuals may and often do act irrationally – that is, they debase their natural faculties and misapprehend what natural law requires – but Locke seems to suppose that most people most of the time will exercise their reason, making a just law and government possible. Indeed, natural law and the reason to apprehend it incline individuals to consider not only their own interests but those of others and thus to value social cooperation and self-restraint. In this way, they exhibit a kind of natural political virtue not altogether derivable from simple self-interest. Freedom under government, to Locke, is not simply the absence of external restraint but also living in conformity with a predictable, non-arbitrary law to which one has directly or indirectly consented. It is 'to have a standing Rule to live by, common to every one of the Society, and made by the Legislative Power erected in it ...' (Locke, [1690] 1960: 324).

To Locke and to the liberal theorists who followed him, private property is an essential condition for individual freedom, as well as a principal goal of its exercise. Locke's theory of property, which has received much attention from commentators, need not detain us beyond a recognition of three elements that are central to liberal citizenship. First is the notion that individuals create property (which Locke defines broadly as 'Lives, Liberties, and Estates' ([1690] 1960: 395)) and gain dominion over it by investing it with their labor; second, the protection of property against public and private invasion is the most important function of law and government. Third the lawful exercise of property rights naturally produces inequalities without injustice.

These elements together constitute the Lockeian version of what C.B. Macpherson has called a theory of 'possessive individualism.' Under this theory, individuals define themselves, attain social status, and relate to others largely through the institutions of private property, contract, and market that help to create wealth but also generate and legitimate persistent inequalities (Macpherson, 1962). On the other hand, Locke believed, as already noted, in a natural human sociability and concern for the interests of others that might mitigate these inequalities. Peter Laslett, describing Locke's theory of property as 'incomplete, not a little confused and inadequate to the problem as it has been analysed since his day,' has viewed that theory as quite consistent with state-mandated regulation and redistribution, perhaps even nationalization, of private property and wealth. More generally, according to Laslett, Locke was perhaps the first philosopher to regard 'citizenship ... as a specific duty, a personal challenge in a world where every individual either recognized his responsibility for every other, or disobeyed his conscience' (Locke [1690] 1960: 117–20, 135).

John Stuart Mill, writing in the mid-nineteenth century, advanced Locke's liberal philosophical project with a more systematic theory of liberty – its nature, the manner of its exercise, its relation to human welfare and to the discovery of truth, and the role of the state in limiting the freedom of individuals. Mill's theory, even more than Locke's, regarded individuality and self-interest, properly understood, as the source of social, not just personal, progress and well-being. Mill insisted that untrammeled freedom of individual thought, inquiry, worship, and expression is the surest path to truth and social improvement. And while Mill readily conceded that individuals' freedom of action could be limited more than their freedom of thought, he proposed a rule that would create and defend a very broad domain of individual autonomy and self-promotion, while minimizing the scope of government intervention.

Mill's theory of the relationship between individual liberty and the state can be generally summarized in a few propositions, albeit with considerable oversimplification. First, individual liberty and state action tend to be opposed; increasing the latter reduces the former. Mill does identify categories of situations in which state action can in fact enhance individual liberty – law enforcement and public goods, for example – but the conflict is in his view endemic. This tendency reflects several factors: the myopia, corruptibility, and other defects of state officials exercising coercive powers, the better outcomes when individuals pursue their own ends, and the natural sociability of private actors in a liberal culture. Spontaneity and free choice, in the Millian view, are the instruments of individual liberty; as spurs to action, they are more socially desirable than legal compulsion or other forms of coercion.

Mill's second, and closely related, proposition is based on a fundamental distinction between activities that affect 'chiefly' individuals' own interests and those that also affect the interests of others beyond those (e.g. one's own children) who are not yet regarded as independent, autonomous beings. In a liberal society, he insists, the pursuit of one's own interests that do not affect others is entirely the province of the individual, within which one must be free to do as one pleases without the law's interference. Where others' interests are affected, however, the state may be justified in regulating the activity – although even there it should recognize the presumptive superiority of private ordering and often stay its hand, out of prudence and a concern for individual liberty (Mill, [1859–61] 1951). Obviously, these two domains of the private and public are neither self-defining nor easy to measure empirically. More to the point, the permissible scope of the modern state turns on precisely where and how the boundary line between them is to be drawn, an issue discussed more fully below.

These, then, are the bedrock principles of classical liberal theory: the primacy of individual liberty understood primarily as freedom from state interference with one's personal development and projects; a very broad protection of freedom of inquiry, speech, and worship; a deep suspicion of state power over individuals; the restriction of state coercion to those areas of activity in which individuals' conduct affects others; and a strong though rebuttable presumption in favor of privacy, markets, and other forms of private ordering. In the last century and a half, of course, countless political, social, and economic theorists have built upon the foundations laid by Locke and Mill while glossing, challenging, or refining virtually all of their claims. In applying the principles of classical liberal theory to questions of citizenship, I shall discuss some of the contemporary critics.

GROUPS, CIVIL SOCIETY, THE STATE, AND SUPRANATIONAL FORMATIONS

We have already seen both that the individual is the cynosure of classical liberal theory, and that the nature and determinants of individuality are elusive and, given the limits of science, are likely to remain so. Indeed, poets like Walt Whitman and novelists like Henry James have artfully plumbed and explored this mystery of personality, and some theorists recognize this as among the most important justifications of liberal principles.

The strong propensity of individuals to combine into groups, and of groups to constitute a civil society that is more or less distinct from both individuals and the state, or at least stands between them, is a fact to which liberal theory has given much prominence, especially recently. This propensity is part of what it means to be an individual in society, and nothing in liberal theory suggests otherwise. Profound tensions arise within the liberal tradition, however, when the state accords legal rights or duties to groups *qua* group that may override those of individuals, or when it grounds individuals' rights or duties on their group membership, especially membership that the state imputes to them without their consent (Kymlicka, 1995). These tensions are further discussed toward the conclusion of this chapter.

Groups affect the process, outcomes, and all other aspects of a liberal state, thereby affecting in turn citizens and non-citizens in the polity. James Madison was perhaps the first thinker in the United States to write about the role of groups in politics; his Federalist #10 is today a canonical commentary on the subject[2] (Madison, [1787] 1992).

Early in the twentieth century liberal sociologists and political scientists began to develop systematic theoretical and empirical accounts of the formation and behavior of social groups, especially in politics. These 'pluralist' scholars noted the ease with which individuals sharing common interests and values coalesce into groups, classified the varied resources available to groups in politics, and traced the fluidity of the group bargaining processes that shape governmental decisions. Many of these accounts were normative as well as descriptive. Viewing pluralist bargaining as successful in integrating even marginal groups into the social and political mainstream, these analysts came to define the public interest in politics in processual not substantive terms, in effect legitimating whatever bargains emerged. According to the pluralist logic, if the process is fair then its outcomes should be regarded as democratically acceptable, if not necessarily just. The state, in this view, is simply one more group, albeit one with special rules of membership and unusual powers to enforce its bargains.

Especially in the USA, the broad consensus applauding this pluralist system – what political scientist Theodore Lowi called 'interest group liberalism' (Lowi, 1979) – came under enormous stress with the civil rights, welfare rights, anti-war, and environmental movements of the 1960s, and many academics attacked the system on both descriptive and normative grounds. Those on the left, like Lowi, emphasized the inequalities that the process preserved and promoted, while those on the right (led by economists such as George Stigler and James Buchanan) emphasized the distortions that interest-group incentives and behavior created in the polity and economy. This odd intellectual alliance of Left and Right was soon joined by the egalitarian, often populist critical legal studies movement, which argued that legal doctrine was deformed by some of the same organizational and political incentives and dynamics identified by the political scientists and economists. In the 1970s, these 'public choice' critiques of the role of interest groups began to dislodge pluralism as the ruling academic paradigm, while discrediting its procedural, functionalist, and often reductionist conception of the public interest. Such critiques, however, generally failed to offer a convincing alternative. And there the debate rests, both within liberalism and against it.[3]

During the late 1980s and 1990s, much concern among both liberal and non-liberal theorists shifted from a focus on group formation and the integrity of pluralist politics to a widespread anxiety about the role and quality of the social groups and institutions that stand between isolated individuals and the state – what are termed 'mediating' groups and institutions or (in a bow to Hegel) 'civil society.' These anxieties have prompted a flood of theoretical and empirical analyses directed at several issues that are highly salient to the character of liberal citizenship. Some analysts, led by political scientist Robert Putnam, claim that the number of informal groups through which democratic citizens can come to know one another, develop political skills, identify their interests, and engage in common efforts to pursue those interests has declined, along with the frequency and quality of their interactions (Putnam, 2000). Others emphasize the importance to an effective democratic polity of what has come to be called 'social capital' – the accumulation of trust among citizens who can view each other sympathetically as co-venturers and cooperate in joint projects rather than succumb to cynicism, isolation, and free-riding incentives – and to lament its erosion in contemporary society (Fukuyama, 1999). Still others maintain that certain other social developments have undermined the foundations of liberal citizenship, particularly the ideal of individual responsibility and efficacy, the rule of law, and the principle of limited government. A long list of possible causes is offered: mass media, soulless markets, mindless consumerism, the legalization and bureaucratization of traditionally informal relationships, a weakening of family and religious ties, a coarsening of politics, judicial activism, and the intrusion and blandishments of the contemporary welfare state.

This last – the state[4] – is especially important in the characterization of liberal citizenship. According to liberal theory, state power's inevitable diminution of individual liberty is the dread disease, for which the only preventative and cure is a robust and vigilant civil society. Liberalism holds that the state, while necessary for many social ends, constantly and remorselessly seeks to expand its authority and resources, driven by the self-interest of politicians, bureaucrats, and private groups that stand to gain by increasing state power. The task of liberal constitutionalism is to confine that power through public institutions and public values, and the task of a liberal civil society is to vindicate and reify that constitutionalism by nurturing an independent citizenry capable of resisting state power grabs, solving problems with minimal government intervention, and maintaining close oversight of its necessary activities. Liberalism's difficulties in meeting these challenges occupy most of the rest of this chapter.

Before turning to these difficulties, however, we must consider a final level of affiliation that increasingly confronts the liberal citizen: supranational regimes. Since World War II, states have increasingly created supranational formations such as the United Nations, European Union, General Agreement on Tariffs and Trade, North American Free Trade Agreement, the International Criminal Court, and many others. In most cases, these formations have entailed the surrender by member states of some of their national sovereignty. Some supranational regimes, however, are not state-created at all. Non-governmental actors concerned with human rights, international standards, cultural issues, and so forth now play an increasingly prominent role, constituting what some view as a kind of 'international civil society' (Spiro, 1996).

What is the relationship of the liberal citizen to these regimes? Do citizens owe a legal duty only to their national state or does their obligation extend to the larger formation as well? In most if not all cases, the regime's rules are binding on the citizens of the member states either directly or indirectly (i.e. through their own state); enforcement of the regime's rules, however, is almost always left to the member states, which have to enforce rules against their own citizens. The situation is somewhat clearer with respect to rights created by the supra-national regime. Some of these rights – for example, under the European Charter of Human Rights and similar instruments – are enjoyed directly by citizens (or legal aliens) of member states, who can enforce them against their states. Apart from legal duties and rights, is the liberal citizen likely to feel a growing sense of loyalty or affective identification with the supra-national regime, as many young and cosmopolitan Europeans are said to feel toward the EU? Answers to this question will only emerge over time (Caporaso, 2000).

THE PROBLEMATICS OF LIBERAL CITIZENSHIP

The advantages of liberal citizenship – at least for those who regard them as advantages – are easy to see. Individuals' ability to be free to form their own opinions, pursue their own projects, and transact their own business untrammeled by the state's political agenda and coercive power, except in so far as individual actions implicate the interests of other members of society, has been an enormously powerful wellspring of human progress, prosperity, and creativity. Although the precise causal pathways linking liberal cultures, market economies, and democratic politics remain uncertain, it is clear that the linkages are powerful and enduring. Liberal democratic polities tend to be relatively stable and tolerant regimes internally, while also peacefully co-existing with other liberal states – perhaps because their citizens' aggressive and competitive urges are channeled into more productive and pacific realms, especially the pursuit of wealth.

Liberal citizens are thus left to their own devices without much guidance from the state. They must decide for themselves how to use their constitutionally secured freedoms. Along with their fellow citizens – subject to their influence, perhaps, but not their coercion – they must make up their own minds about what to think, what to value, whether and how to worship, and how to structure their relationships with other individuals, groups, and the state itself. In short, they must decide what kind of citizen to be – including the possibility that they will decide to forswear any political activity at all, preferring to retreat into an entirely private world of family, friends, market transactions, and self-absorption and gratification, into a world largely indifferent to any public goods not generated within these parochial domains.

This picture of the liberal citizen, in at least one of the many possible incarnations, will have its attractions to many people. In a liberal culture, after all, politics is only one particular expression of human value, striving, or possibility. A few liberal citizens of a certain inclination will feel a genuine vocation in politics. A larger number will devote some time to political activity but it will not be a dominant aspect of their lives. Others will exhaust their political interest in voting in key elections, joining the local PTA, and watching the evening news. Still others will not even bother to register to vote or join a community group.

In appraising liberal citizenship, an important empirical question is what the proportions of these groups are in liberal polities. If the vast majority of citizens viewed politics as their vocation – if they derived most of their pleasure and income from imposing or exercising coercive authority over others – there might be good reason to doubt whether their society would continue to be liberal or even democratic (though this last is more uncertain). On the other hand, if few citizens are willing to devote much time or attention to politics, power will become an instrument of the few rather than of the many, and the polity's very survival in a democratic form will be endangered. In reality, and certainly in any robust democracy, the distribution of interest in politics falls somewhere in between these two extremes. In the United States, for example, citizens participate intensively in non-governmental organizations, many of which are politically active, but voting in elections, especially at the local level, is comparatively low. The pattern in most other nations is generally the reverse.

It may be that liberal cultures tend to discourage certain forms of political participation as compared with more communitarian cultures. Liberal polities do not merely permit their citizens to retreat into their private pursuits if they wish; liberal ideology, as we have seen, affirmatively valorizes the privatization of personality, commitment, and activity. Liberal market economies, moreover, facilitate the pursuit of wealth and the indulgence of material pleasures. This not only leaves less time available for politics and other public-regarding activities but also diminishes the social prestige that such activities enjoy relative to wealth-seeking and consumption.

Liberal societies tend to be less egalitarian than more communitarian ones – both as a matter of fact and as a matter of preference. This is particularly true in the USA, where income and wealth are less equally distributed than in other postindustrial economies. In fact, Americans value economic equality less than Western Europeans do, preferring higher absolute levels of consumption to lower but more equal ones. Such attitudes toward economic equality help to explain why liberal societies view consumption of private goods as socially desirable while more communitarian ones sometimes impose high taxes on income and wealth and use sumptuary laws to discourage conspicuous, envy-inducing opulence. The different taxation practices of different societies, of course, have complex effects on both economic behavior and public values, making it almost impossible to disentangle cause and effect. For example, low tax rates help to generate more wealth, which permits a privatistic society to maintain lower tax rates, tolerate greater inequality, and enjoy higher absolute consumption, which in turn cultivates a political culture that supports these practices.[5] In this way, policies and institutions shape citizens' values, as well as the other way around.

These observations suggest neither that liberal societies are wholly privatistic, materialistic, and indifferent to inequalities, nor that more communitarian ones are the opposite. Both cultures and ideologies are far more complicated than this. The human impulse to enjoy life's physical goods and comforts, although gratified in relatively few societies, appears to be nearly universal, as is the primacy of family, religion, and other private domains. By the same token, politics, broadly understood, is a natural activity and disposition that in all societies affects the lives and interests of everyone, even the most privatistic liberal. At least in postindustrial political cultures, the differences between liberal and communitarian citizens with regard to their values, interests, and activities are largely differences in degree – although in the aggregate these differences produce recognizably distinct civil and political societies. The political cultures and economies of USA, Sweden, and Japan, for example, have much in common but are also strikingly different from one another.

For all of these reasons (and others), liberal citizenship is easier to acquire and harder to lose, and demands less from both the individual and the state than other kinds of citizenship. US citizenship, for example, can be acquired through birth on US territory, descent from US citizen parents, or naturalization. In each case, the requirements for citizenship are relatively easy to satisfy.

Birthright citizenship (*jus soli*) is a right protected by the Citizenship Clause of the Fourteenth Amendment to the US Constitution. Judicial interpretation of this Clause has long been understood as extending this status to native-born children of aliens who are in the country, even if present illegally or on a temporary visa. This interpretation has never been seriously questioned in the courts, although it has recently come under scrutiny, and some criticism, from politicians, commentators, and scholars[6] (Schuck and Smith, 1985). Citizenship through descent (*jus sanguinis*) has steadily expanded over time, and the US Supreme Court has invalidated a number of gender-specific limitations on parents' ability to transmit it to their birth-, adoptive, and illegitimate children. (Nguyen v. I.N.S., 2001). Naturalization is also relatively easy; it requires only that a legal permanent resident have resided in the USA with that status for five years, be of good moral character, demonstrate an ability to speak, read, and write English, and demonstrate a basic knowledge of US government and history (Schuck, 1998: 185).

Plural citizenship is quite common in the USA due to the combination of the American *jus soli* rule with the various *jus sanguinis* rules of other countries. Although aliens who naturalize in the USA must renounce their prior allegiance, this renunciation may or may not actually terminate the individual's foreign citizenship under the foreign state's laws, and US naturalization law does not require that the renunciation actually be legally effective. In an important trend most countries of origin from which the largest groups of immigrants to the USA come recognize as citizens, children born to their nationals abroad. As a result plural citizenship among Americans is rapidly increasing. Following several US Supreme Court decisions, citizens cannot lose their American citizenship without their express consent, unless they have procured their naturalization wrongfully (Schuck, 1998: 185–6).

The USA is by no means alone in adopting inclusive citizenship acquisition rules. Indeed, something of a convergence toward the US model has recently occurred as traditionally more restrictive states have moved toward easier preconditions for naturalization, greater acceptance of dual nationality, and broader *jus soli* and *jus sanguinis* rules. The most notable examples of this development in Europe are France and Germany, which both liberalized their citizenship laws in the late 1990s.[7] Even earlier, a number of states in Asia and Latin America whose nationals migrate to the USA in large numbers also eased their restrictions on dual nationality in order to facilitate the migrants' naturalization in the USA and to maintain the states' ties with those migrants and their descendants living in the USA (Weil, 2001; Schuck, 1998: Ch. 10).

The USA, like most liberal polities, imposes few *duties* on its citizens other than a general obligation to obey the law (which of course applies to aliens as well) and jury duty. Voting is not required (unlike in Australia, for example), and compulsory military service was abolished in the 1970s. By the same token, almost all of the *rights* of US citizens are also enjoyed by legal resident aliens. The main exceptions – rights that attach to citizens only – are the right to remain in the USA without fear of possible deportation; the right to vote (although some localities have extended the franchise to aliens as well); citizens' greater right to sponsor alien relatives for immigration to the USA; access to certain high-level appointive and elective governmental positions; and the right to certain public welfare benefits denied to legal aliens (although most of these have been restored to those who resided legally in the USA in August 1996 when Congress limited aliens' benefits) (Schuck, 1998: 186–90).

Many commentators have denounced this disparity between the generous endowment of rights enjoyed by citizens (and aliens) and the imposition of only the most minimal duties on them. In criticizing liberal citizenship as too thin to support a healthy social order, these critics would de-emphasize individual rights and protect the larger society's more diffuse interests by cultivating a spirit of social solidarity – in part, through imposition of common civic duties and limits on deviant behavior in public places (Mead, 1986; Glendon, 1991; Etzioni, 1999). The fact that strong social forces oppose imposing on individuals even modest new duties reveals how pervasive the privatism, individualism, and anti-statism of liberal culture has become. Requiring work (or a genuine effort to find it) in lieu, or as a condition, of receiving welfare benefits was perhaps the most controversial element of the 1996 welfare reform law. Compulsory public service for young people has never been politically acceptable. Laws that mandate AIDS testing even of exposed pregnant women and informing of sex partners have been highly controversial and, when enacted, weakly enforced. Curbing the rights of individuals to use parks, subways, libraries, and other public spaces in ways that the vast majority of people find offensive has proved to be very difficult due to civil liberties and other constitutional values protected by the courts (Ellickson, 1996).

I have already noted that the USA and other liberal polities tolerate inequalities in wealth and income that more communitarian societies might find unacceptably large. As economic disadvantages express themselves in the social and political realms as well, these inequalities among citizens are extended and compounded. Liberal states, moreover, attract migrants, both temporary and permanent, legal and illegal, for reasons relating to the liberal cultures and markets of such states. These migrants tend to be poorer than citizens (at least for some time after their arrival), which creates additional inequalities that are often ethnically defined and hence exacerbate social divisions. This greatly complicates the political and administrative problems surrounding ethnically-based preferences and other rectification policies (Schuck, 1998: Ch. 14).

Precisely because of the persistence of inequalities among liberal citizens and between them and aliens, however, they are bound to engender much social and political conflict. Indeed, this persistence tends to dispirit and even de-legitimate a liberal polity that prides itself on the existence of genuine equal opportunity for individuals. This is not as paradoxical as it might seem. We have seen that liberalism tends to justify inequalities that arise out of differences in individual talents, values, and choices – differences, moreover, that the state cannot seek to efface without endangering citizens' liberties. On the other hand, liberalism's legitimation rests on society's conviction that individuals in fact enjoy an equal opportunity to develop their talents, acquire good values, and exercise free choices. Equality, however, is always incomplete, often glaringly so, and the gap between the pretense and the reality may become too large to sustain the ideological consensus. And technology constantly generates new kinds of inequalities; an example is the current concern about unequal access to the Internet. Indeed, social science evidence suggests that as differences diminish, those that remain become more intolerable than before, a phenomenon sometimes referred to as the 'narcissism of small differences' (Horowitz, 1985: 182–3). This has certainly been the American experience; doubtless, it is more universal (Fogel, 2000).

Perhaps the most daunting challenge to liberalism, then, is to reduce inequalities to levels and kinds that the society, and especially those who suffer relatively disadvantage, view as socially acceptable and politically sustainable, if not altogether just – while at the same time vindicating the liberal commitment to the protection of individual liberties. For several reasons, however, liberalism may actually increase economic and certain other kinds of inequalities rather than reduce them – unless and until the benefits of market-driven economic growth 'trickle down' to the socially disadvantaged. Liberalism extols free markets, which reward values and skills that are unequally distributed in the population. It does not merely produce the inequalities that arise from such differences; it justifies them so long as it can sustain the belief that they result from individuals' free choices, not from coercion (Sowell, 1975). Liberal citizens, inured to such inequalities and inclined to devote their energies to private pursuits, may not support changes designed and executed by the state rather than occurring through the decentralized, less self-conscious dynamics of civil society and markets.

Structurally, as well as ideologically, liberal states make redistributive policies difficult to enact, implement, and legitimate. In a liberal social system, the private sector controls most of the incentive systems that drive and shape individual and group behavior; these systems are largely immune from state control. More fundamentally, liberalism contrives to keep the state weak and permeable to private interests, institutionalizing its endemic fear of state power through political structures and practices that widely disperse and carefully confine the state's influence. In the USA, these include independent courts exercising legislative review, separation of powers, constitutional protection of private property and individual rights, federalism, and many others. Together, they make it difficult for the state to effect large social changes in the absence of a broad national consensus or sense of crisis. These power-dispersing structures of the American liberal state bespeak a conception of the public interest not as a set of independent substantive outcomes but as the competitive processes of those interests as they work to bend the state to their purposes (Lowi, 1979). This primacy of private interests in turn magnifies the risk that state intervention should it occur, will produce unforeseen and often perverse consequences (Schuck, 2000a: Ch. 13).

Certain kinds of inequalities plague liberal states in another, more threatening way. Where inequalities within a state are distributed along ethnic or geographical lines and those ethnic or geographic groups come to identify themselves as such, groups that think of themselves as being advantaged or disadvantaged relative to other groups in the state often demand some level of autonomy or even independence (Horowitz, 1985). Liberal states may be especially vulnerable to this threat; more than communitarian or republican polities, liberal ones facilitate, tolerate, and perhaps even encourage their citizens to identify with multiple values, traditions, or even states. For example, liberal polities should in principle be more willing to permit their members to acquire multiple citizenships than states that require of their citizens a more exacting, exclusive, and 'thick' allegiance (Schuck, 1998: Ch. 10). In any event, inequality-driven group demands may force a state to fragment its citizenship, creating rights that some citizens enjoy but others do not. Such discriminations among citizens, however, may not be an enduring solution; instead, it may simply presage the division of the state itself, as in the cases of Pakistan–Bangladesh and Ethiopia–Eritrea. Alternatively, the state may create a federal system, as in the USA, in which members possess both national and subnational citizenships. This too may turn out to be a mere prelude to division and independence (Schuck, 2000b).

Finally and relatedly, classic liberalism posits a state that maintains substantial normative neutrality. In this conception, the liberal state should neither choose among competing visions of the good society nor place its thumb on the scales in other ways, such as redistributive policies, that favor particular visions. It should instead play a far more modest, suppletive role, facilitating individuals' pursuit of their own projects or visions. Just how modest the liberal state's role should be has always been, and certainly remains, a matter of great controversy. At the most minimal, libertarian end of the philosophical spectrum is Robert Nozick's 'watchman state,' which should confine itself largely to enforcing the criminal law and private law entitlements. More interventionist, efficiency-minded conceptions would have the state also provide public goods and regulate externalities. At the most activist end of the spectrum are egalitarian visions that justify state efforts, more or less constrained, to employ wealth transfers and regulation to secure to individuals equal dignity, life chances, and opportunity (Rawls, 1971; Ackerman, 1980; Ackerman and Alstott, 1999; Dworkin, 1977).

In the event, it has proved impossible for the state to maintain neutrality. In the USA, for example, state action and inaction inevitably ignites political disputes reflecting the tension between the liberal commitments to individual liberty, autonomy, and constrained state power, on the one hand, and people's equally ardent convictions about the social conditions necessary to maximize that liberty and autonomy, on the other. They often regard these conditions as the state's responsibility to establish and maintain. The state, responding to political entrepreneurship, group pressures, ideological impulses, and genuine concerns about programmatic effectiveness, seeks to pursue its equalization project at wholesale rather than retail, using the group and not just the individual as the site of legal rights, subsidies, and other forms of advantage. And when the state confers advantages on groups, it is impelled to regulate them, if only to assure political accountability to the public for how the groups are using those advantages. This regulation inevitably entangles the state, groups, and individuals in ways that may threaten the autonomy and integrity of individuals and groups and hence endanger the liberal project itself.

Whether the policy in question is the curriculum in public schools, the regulation of hate speech, taxation, welfare reform, foreign affairs, affirmative action, vouchers redeemable in private religious schools, or countless other issues, the state is widely viewed as taking sides, promoting certain values and groups over others, and arrogating to itself the political authority and resources needed to implement that policy. The more diverse the society, the more controversial its policies (Schuck, 2003). The more ambitious and redistributive the agenda for state action, the more it strains against the ideological and institutional limits of the traditional liberal settlement with politics. Liberal citizens who come to regard the principled neutrality that constitutes the state's *raison d'être* as a pretense and an illusion will view politics as little more than a series of power plays by the dominant interests, decisions to which the losers may perforce have to submit but that enjoy no legitimacy.

CONCLUSION

These struggles over the role of the state constantly re-shape the contours of liberal citizenship. In the USA, citizens value social and economic equality but value market and other individual liberties even more. Believing that the state threatens these liberties, Americans seek to keep it permeable, weak, and neutral. In other liberal polities, of course, the balance among these values is different, as are their definitions and their views about the state's capacity and legitimacy.

Environmental pressures and humanitarian emergencies, including the spasmodic immigration flows discussed earlier, pose great challenges to liberal states, demanding a larger state role in allocating scarce resources, rights, and statuses among competing interests often bearing compelling moral claims. But what is truly transforming liberal citizenship in all societies is the growing crisis of the welfare state. This crisis is especially grave in Western Europe and other states whose welfare commitments are both deeply entrenched and steadily expanding under pressure from militant trade unions, strong socialist parties, and even centrist and conservative groups moved by collectivist and egalitarian traditions. Yet rapidly aging populations, slow economic growth, rigid labor markets, growing global competition from low-wage producers, and other conditions mean that this problem will only grow worse in these societies, while widespread xenophobia rules out large-scale legal immigration as a possible solution.

The promise of liberal citizenship – its vision of social and political membership based on the paramount value of individual freedom and the need to limit state power – continues to inspire many throughout the world. At the same time, the materialism, inequality, and normative neutrality that are often associated with liberalism are often repellent, even to some of the same people who admire its achievements. The rise of religious fundamentalism coupled with arbitrary and autocratic state power poses a particularly acute threat to liberal citizenship In the end, the allure of liberal citizenship. will be assessed – at least by those polities whose politics and economies leave them free enough to consider it – according to how effectively and fairly their states govern, their markets create and distribute wealth, and their societies define and value freedom.

NOTES

1. Marshall's essay was the subject of an American Political Science Association annual meeting panel, dated 31 August, 2000, on 'The 50th Anniversary of T.H. Marshall's "Citizenship and Social Class"', in which several commentators spoke. My remarks focused on Marshall's failure to anticipate three developments significantly affecting the concept of citizenship: (1) the challenge to the modern social welfare state, (2) the rise of multi-ethnic societies in postwar Europe, and (3) the changing understanding of the public and private realms and of the boundaries and relationships between them.

2. The significance of Madison's analysis is discussed in Schuck, 2000a: Ch. 7. Kramer (1999) demonstrates that the celebration of Federalist #10 is a relatively recent phenomenon.

3. The leading analyses by the pluralists and their critics are summarized and cited in Schuck, 2000a: 210–15.

4. For present purposes, we can assume that the state is a unitary nation-state in which the citizen belongs neither to a substate polity, as in a federal system, nor to an ethnic nation within the state, as with Indian tribes in the United States. See generally Schuck (2000b).

5. Most economists accept this account, not merely 'supply-siders'; the real difference among economists – and it is a crucial difference – concerns the magnitudes (or elasticities) of the economic effects and the way one should evaluate those effects.

6. Whether *jus soli* citizenship is liberal or not is an interesting and controverted question. For opposing views, see Schuck and Smith (1985), Neuman (1994: 248–9), Schuck (1994: 324–5).

7. In the German case, much political opposition to the new law persists among the conservative parties. See Cohen (2000).

REFERENCES

Ackerman, Bruce A. (1980) *Social Justice and the Liberal State*. New Haven, Conn.: Yale University Press.

Ackerman, Bruce A. and Alstott, Anne. (1999) *The Stakeholder Society*. New Haven, Conn.: Yale University Press.

Berlin, Isaiah (1969) *Four Essays on Liberty*. London: Oxford University Press.

Caporaso, James A. (2000) *The European Union: Dilemmas of Regional Integration*. Boulder, Colo.: Westview Press.

Cohen, Roger (2000) 'Germany's Financial Heart Is Open but Wary', *New York Times*, Dec. 30, 2000, p. A1.

Dworkin, Ronald M. (1977) *Taking Rights Seriously*. London: Duckworth.

Ellickson, Robert C. (1996) 'Controlling Chronic Misconduct in City Spaces: Of Panhandlers, Skid Rows, and Public Space Zoning', *Yale Law Journal*, 105: 1165.

Etzioni, Amitai (1999) *The Limits of Privacy*. New York: Basic Books.

Fogel, Robert W. (2000) *The Fourth Great Awakening and the Future of Egalitarianism*. Chicago: University of Chicago Press.

Fukuyama, Francis (1999) *The Great Disruption: Human Nature and the Reconstitution of Social Order*. New York: Free Press.

Glendon, Mary Ann (1991) *Rights Talk: The Impoverishment of Political Discourse*. New York: Free Press.

Hartz, Louis (1955) *The Liberal Tradition in America*. New York: Harcourt Brace.

Horowitz, Donald L. (1985) *Ethnic Groups in Conflict*. Berkeley. University of California Press.

Kramer, Larry D. (1999). 'Madison's Audience', *Harvard Law Review*, 112: 611–79.

Kymlicka. Will (1995) *Multicultural Citizenship*. Oxford: Oxford University Press.

Locke, John ([1690] 1960) *Two Treatises of Government*, ed., Peter Laslett. New York: New American Library, revised ed.

Lowi, Theodore J. (1979) *The End of Liberalism: the Second Republic of the United States*. 2nd edition, New York: W.W. Norton & Co.

Macpherson, C.B. (1962) *The Political Theory of Possessive Individualism: Hobbes to Locke*. Oxford: Oxford University Press.

Madison, James ([1787] 1961) 'Federalist # 10', in Clinton Rossiter (ed.), *The Federalist Papers*. New York: New American Library.

Marcuse, Herbert (1991) *One-Dimensional Man: Studies in the Ideology of Advanced Industrial Society*, 2nd edition, New York: Routledge.

Marshall, T.H. ([1950] 1992) *Citizenship and Social Class*. London: Pluto Press.

Mead, Lawrence M. (1986) *Beyond Entitlement: The Social Obligations of Citizenship*. New York: Free Press.

Mill, John Stuart ([1859–61] 1951) *Utilitarianism, Liberty, and Representative Government*. New York: E.P. Dutton & Co.

Neuman, Gerald L. (1994) 'Justifying U.S. Naturalization Policies', *Virginia Journal of International Law*, 35: 237–78.

Nguyen v. I.N.S. No. 99–2071. 121 S.Ct. ___ (2001).

Nozick, Robert (1977) *Anarchy, State, and Utopia*. New York: Basic Books.

Putnam, Robert D. (2000) *Bowling Alone: The Collapse and Revival of American Community*. New York: Simon & Schuster.

Rawls, John (1971) *A Theory of Justice*. Cambridge, MA: Harvard University Press.

Schuck, Peter H. (1994) 'Whose Membership Is It, Anyway? Comments on Gerald Neuman', *Virginia Journal of International Law*, 35: 321–31.

Schuck, Peter H. (1998) *Citizens, Strangers, and In-Betweens: Essays on Immigration and Citizenship*. Boulder, Colo.: Westview Press.

Schuck, Peter H. (2000a) *The Limits of Law: Essays on Democratic Governance*. Boulder, Colo.: Westview Press.

Schuck, Peter H. (2000b) 'Citizenship in Federal Systems', *American Journal of Comparative Law* 48: 195–226.

Schuck, Peter H. (2003) *Diversity in America: Keeping Government at a Safe Distance*. Cambridge, Mass: Harvard University Press.

Schuck, Peter H. and Smith, Rogers M. (1985) *Citizenship Without Consent: Illegal Aliens in the American Polity*. New Haven, Conn.: Yale University Press.

Smith, Rogers M. (1997) *Civic Ideals: Conflicting Visions of Citizenship in U.S. History*. New Haven, Conn.: Yale University Press.

Sowell, Thomas (1975) *Race and Economics*. New York: Longman.

Spiro, Peter J. (1996) 'New Global Potentates: Non-governmental Organizations and the "Unregulated" Marketplace', *Cardozo Law Review*, 18: 957–69.

Weil, Patrick (2001) 'Endowment for cultural international peace', in Alexander, T. and Aleinikoff, D.K., *Citizenship Today: Global Perspectives and Practices*. Washington D.C.: Carnegie Endowment for International Peace.

Wolff, Robert Paul (1969) *The Poverty of Liberalism*. Boston: Beacon Press.

9

Republican Citizenship

RICHARD DAGGER

To speak of republican citizenship is to risk confusion, at least in the United States, where it is often necessary to explain that one is referring to 'small-r' republicanism rather than a position taken by the Republican Party. But just as one may be a democrat without being a Democrat, so one may be a republican without being a Republican. The ideas of democracy and the republic are far older than any political party and far richer than any partisan label can convey – rich enough to make the use of 'republican' here worth the risk of some initial confusion.

'Republican' and 'citizen', in fact, are old and intertwined words – so old that some may wonder at their relevance in the brave new world of the twenty-first century, and so intertwined that the phrase 'republican citizenship' seems almost redundant to others. There is no republic without citizens, after all; and, according to the classical republican thinkers, there is no citizenship, in the full sense of the word, except among those who are fortunate enough to inhabit a republic. But this view of citizenship's connection to republicanism no longer seems to prevail. If it did, there would be no need for a chapter on republican citizenship in this volume of essays on citizenship, for the authors would simply assume that citizenship entails republicanism and go on to other matters.

There might also be no need for this chapter if it were not for the revival of scholarly interest in republicanism in recent years. Such a revival has definitely occurred, though, and occurred simultaneously with a renewed interest in citizenship. This coincidence suggests that *republican* citizenship is well worth our attention, not only for purposes of historical understanding but also as a way of thinking about citizenship in the twenty-first century. Why this revival has occurred and whether republican citizenship truly offers anything of relevance or value today are thus the subjects of this chapter.

The first subject, however, must be republicanism itself. Rather than attempt to survey the long, varied, and often contested history of republicanism – a task undertaken recently by Oldfield (1990), Rahe (1992), Sellers (1998) and others – I begin by trying to distill something of the spirit and forms of republicanism into a brief but historically sensitive account. The second part of the chapter then shifts the emphasis to citizenship by explaining, from the republican standpoint, its value. Part three takes up the revival of interest in republicanism and citizenship in the last quarter century or so, and the fourth section concludes the chapter with a defense of the continuing relevance of the republican conception of citizenship.

REPUBLICANISM

'Republic' derives from the Latin *res publica*, the public thing, matter, business, or property, with the implication that a republic differs from a state or society in which the rulers regard everything, including the people who inhabit it, as their property.[1] In a republic, that is, the government of the state or society is a public matter, and the people rule themselves. *Publicity* – the condition of being open and public rather than private or personal – and *self-government* thus seem to be the essential elements of republicanism.

But what exactly do publicity and self-government entail? What is 'the public', and how are its members to govern themselves? There is no single republican answer to these questions. In ancient times, and long beyond, republicans typically assumed that the public comprised the citizenry, and only property-owning, arms-bearing men could be citizens. Contemporary republicans define the public and citizenship more expansively, however, to include women and people without property, and nothing in the idea of republicanism prevents them from doing so. Similar shifts have occurred with regard to self-government. When they designed representative institutions for the new republic, for example, the men who drafted the US Constitution knew that they were departing from the classical conception of self-government as direct participation in rule; yet they saw this as an improvement within, not an abandonment of, republican practice. Whether they were right to think so, or whether they sacrificed too much participation and relied too heavily on representation, remains a point of contention. But it is the commitment to publicity and self-government that generates this and other intramural disputes among republicans. For republicans, the question is not whether publicity and self-government are good things; it is how best to achieve them.

One could say the same, of course, about liberals, conservatives, socialists, and others who claim to promote government of the people, by the people, and for the people. Publicity and self-government may be the essential elements of republicanism, but they are not peculiar to it. To the extent that they stress the importance of publicity and self-government, however, modern political theories do so because they draw upon the legacy of classical republicanism. To the extent that they differ from one another – and from republicanism – it is because they pursue the implications of publicity and self-government in different ways. Thus writers such as William Sullivan (1986), Michael Sandel (1996), and Philip Pettit (1997) maintain that liberalism gives too much attention to privacy and individual rights and too little to fostering the public virtues that lead people to do their duties as citizens. Liberals and republicans both want to promote self-government, according to Pettit, but liberals make the mistake of thinking that all forms of restraint deprive people of freedom – even, as we shall see, the restraints imposed by a legal system that prevent some people from ruling or dominating others. There is, then, a neo-republican school of thought that sees liberalism as a misguided rival of republicanism. To others with republican sympathies, these differences are more a matter of emphasis than of fundamental commitments. One may be a republican *and* a liberal, on this view, and there are reasons to think that republican liberalism is an especially attractive political philosophy.[2] Still, to speak of *republican* liberalism is to acknowledge, first, that republicanism and liberalism are not one and the same, and, second, that there are more and less republican forms of liberalism. To understand what is distinctive about republicanism, then, we must look more closely at the implications republicans draw from publicity and self-government.

In the case of publicity, the implications are twofold. The first is that politics, as the public's business, must be conducted openly, *in public*. The second is that 'the public' is not only a group of people but an aspect or sphere of life with its own claims and considerations, even if it is not easily distinguished from the private. What makes something public is that it involves people as members of a community or polity – as people joined by common concerns that take them out of their private lives and beyond, as Tocqueville put it in *Democracy in America* ([1835] 1969: 506), 'the circle of family and friends'. One need not go as far in this regard as Aristotle – or as Aristotle as read by Hannah Arendt (1958: esp. Part II) – but all republicans believe that there is something enriching about public life, regardless of how wearisome it sometimes may be. Public life draws people out, and it draws them together. It draws out their talents and capacities, and it draws them together into community – into connection and solidarity, and occasionally conflict, with other members of the public.[3] No matter how desirable they may seem to others, neither a life of unfettered individualism nor one devoted exclusively to family and friends will appeal to a republican.

From these aspects of publicity follow the republican emphasis on *the rule of law* and, perhaps most distinctively, *civic virtue*. The public business must be conducted in public not only for reasons of convenience – literally, of coming together – but also in order to guard against corruption. As members of the public, people must be prepared to overcome their personal inclinations and set aside their private interests when necessary to do what is best for the public as a whole. The public-spirited citizens who act in this way display public or civic virtue. If they are to manifest this virtue, furthermore, the public must be bound by the rule of law. Because it is the public's business, politics requires public debate and decisions, which in turn require regular, established procedures – that is, rules about who may speak, when they may speak, and how decisions are to be reached. Decisions must then take the form of promulgated rules or decrees that guide the conduct of the members of the public. From the insistence on publicity, the rule of law quickly follows.[4]

The connection of self-government to the rule of law is at least as strong and immediate. If citizens are to be self-governing, they cannot be subject to absolute or arbitrary rule. If the citizen is to be *self*-governing, then he or she must be free from the absolute or arbitrary rule of others. To avoid this arbitrariness, citizens must be subject to the rule of law – the government of laws, not of men, in what was the standard formula.[5] But it is also important to note that self-government requires self-*governing*. The republican citizen is not someone who acts arbitrarily, impulsively, or recklessly, but according to laws he or she has a voice in making. Again, the need for the rule of law is evident.

As with publicity, the republican commitment to self-government leads to characteristic republican themes, such as the republican conception of freedom and, again, of civic virtue. Self-government is, of course, a form of freedom. For republicans, it is the most important form, for other forms of individual freedom are secure only in a free state, under law. Freedom thus requires dependence upon the law so that citizens may be independent of the arbitrary will of others. In Pettit's terms, republicans are less concerned with freedom from interference than with freedom from domination (1997).[6] It is not interference as such that is objectionable but its arbitrariness. A slave and a citizen may both suffer interference when the former must bow to the will of the master and the latter must bow to the law, but their conditions are hardly equivalent. The master need not consider the slave's desires or interests, but the law, at least in the ideal, must attend to the interests of the citizen even when it interferes with his or her actions. Because it protects the citizen against arbitrary, unaccountable power, the law is 'the non-mastering interferer' that ensures the citizen's freedom (Pettit, 1997: 41).

The law only ensures the citizen's freedom, however, when it is responsive to the citizenry and when the republic itself is secure and stable enough for its laws to be effective. Sustaining freedom under the rule of law thus requires not only active and public-spirited participation in public affairs – the civic virtue of the republican citizen – but also the proper form of government. This will be some version of *mixed* or *balanced* government, so called because it mixes and balances elements of rule by one, rule by the few, and rule by the many. As Pocock (1975) and others have noted, writers from Polybius and Cicero to Machiavelli and the American founders celebrated the mixed constitution for its ability to stave off corruption and tyranny. Monarchy, aristocracy, and rule by the people are prone, according to these writers, to degenerate into tyranny, oligarchy, and mob rule, respectively; but a government that disperses power among the three elements could prevent either the one, the few, or the many from pursuing its own interest at the expense of the common good. With each element holding enough power to check the others, the result should be a free, stable, and long-lasting government.

If the mixed constitution is the characteristic form of the republic, civic virtue is its desired substance. Without citizens who are willing to defend the republic against foreign threats and to take an active part in its government, even the mixed constitution will fail. Republics must thus engage in what Sandel (1996: 6) calls 'a formative politics ... that cultivates in citizens the qualities of character that self-government requires'. Constitutional safeguards may be necessary to resist corruption in the forms of avarice, ambition, luxury, and idleness, but they will not suffice to sustain freedom under the rule of law in the absence of a significant degree of virtue among the citizens. Seeing to the continuing supply of civic virtue through education and other means will be, accordingly, one of the principal concerns of a prudent republic.

A prudent republic will also be a small one. That, at least, has been the conclusion – or presumption – of many republicans throughout the centuries. 'In a large republic', as Montesquieu explained in 1748 in *The Spirit of the Laws* (Book VIII, Chap. 16), 'the common good is sacrificed to a thousand considerations; it is subordinated to exceptions; it depends upon accidents. In a small one, the public good is better felt, better known, lies nearer to each citizen; abuses are less extensive and consequently less protected'. So widespread was this view in the late eighteenth century, and so fierce the insistence that only a small polity can sustain a republic, that the American authors of the *Federalist* found it necessary to point out that Montesquieu had also allowed for the possibility of a 'federal' – or 'CONFEDERATE', according to *Federalist* 9 – republic. Even then, the debate over the proposed constitution often turned on the question of whether the United States would become a 'federal' or a 'compound' republic – a republic comprising thirteen or more smaller republics – or whether it would become a 'consolidated' republic that could not long preserve its republican character.

A small republic or a large (con)federal republic: these seem to be the only alternatives that the republican tradition allows. The concern for size and civic virtue that these alternatives reflect testifies to the republican belief that citizens must have a strong attachment to their polity that grows out of a connection to their fellow citizens. This connection must work almost immediately, as in the city-republic, or in building-block fashion, with the higher and more remote layers of government resting on the local ones, as in the federal republic. Without some connection of this sort, civic virtue will not flourish and self-government will not survive. Neither will the form of citizenship that some have regarded as its only true form.

THE VALUE OF REPUBLICAN CITIZENSHIP

'We have physicists, geometricians, chemists, astronomers, poets, musicians, and painters in plenty; but we have no longer a citizen among us'. So wrote Jean-Jacques Rousseau in his *Discourse on the Arts and Sciences* (Rousseau, [1750] 1950: 169). His lament echoes today in the writings of those who deplore the decline or loss of 'real' or 'true' citizenship – especially in the United States and other countries where worries about declining electoral participation and eroding 'social capital' abound (e.g. Putnam, 2000). Consciously or not, these laments bespeak a desire for a revival of republican citizenship.

From the republican point of view, citizenship has an ethical as well as a legal dimension. If it did not, Rousseau's lament would make no sense in a world where more and more people hold the legal title of citizen. If the lament does make sense, it is because we continue to regard citizenship, in republican fashion, as an *ethos* – a way of life. Citizenship may be a matter of legal status that confers various privileges and immunities on the citizen, in other words, but it must be more than that. 'Real' or 'true' citizenship requires commitment to the common good and active participation in public affairs. It requires civic virtue.

That is not to say that republicans denigrate the legal aspect of citizenship. On the contrary, the citizen of a community governed by the rule of law must be someone who holds the legal rights and duties of membership. To say that Joan Smith or Juan Sosa is a citizen of a republic is to say that Smith or Sosa not only enjoys the protection of its laws but is also subject to them. It is also to say that, as a citizen, Smith or Sosa is supposed to be on an equal footing with other citizens. If Smith or Sosa is not treated equally under the law, then she or he may rightly complain of being a 'second-class citizen'. In these respects, legal status is as necessary to the republican conception of citizenship as to any other.

Necessary but not sufficient, for it requires the supplement of the ethical dimension. This ethical aspect of citizenship is evident in the theory and practice of the Greeks and Romans who bequeathed us the concepts of citizenship and republic. 'Citizen', of course, derives from the Latin *civis*, or member of the *civitas* (city-state); the Latin terms parallel the Greek *politēs* and *polis*. In ancient Greece and Rome the citizen was a full member of the community. Every other member – whether woman, child, slave, or resident alien – was subject to the laws, and might even enjoy some rights under them, but only the citizen had the right to take part in the government of the community. Not only was the citizen *entitled* to engage in civic affairs, he was *expected* to do so. In ancient Athens, this could mean that a citizen would have to devote the better part of his time and energy to public concerns, such as serving on a jury for a full year. Such devotion was necessary if he was to achieve the ideal of citizenship: to be a self-governing member of a self-governing community. Those who preferred a more private or less arduous life than the citizen's could find themselves mocked, as they were in Pericles' Funeral Oration, as 'good for nothing' (Thucydides, [431–411BCE] 1993: 42). Indeed, the Greeks drew a contrast between the *politēs*, the citizen expected to play a part in public affairs, and the *idiōtēs*, the private person who could not or would not meet this expectation.

That we no longer regard 'citizen' and 'idiot' as opposites may be a measure of how far we have departed from the classical ideal of citizenship. Even so, there is plenty of evidence to suggest that the ethical dimension of citizenship persists. There is, for instance, the fact that we sometimes characterize people as good or bad citizens. If citizenship were only a matter of legal status, we would not be able to distinguish 'good' citizens from 'bad', or 'true' citizens from those who are citizens 'in name only'. This point is brought home by those who insist that 'every citizen holds office' (Kennedy, 1961; Zwiebach, 1975: 87; van Gunsteren, 1998: 25). That is, citizens hold a position of public responsibility, just as mayors, senators, city councillors, and members of parliament do. The citizen who does not act responsibly may thus be said to betray a public trust, while the citizen who faithfully does his or her duty displays civic virtue. Citizenship has an ethical dimension, in short, because there are standards built into the concept of citizenship, just as there are standards built into the concepts of mayor, teacher, plumber, and physician. In the case of citizenship, moreover, these are republican standards, for they stress the public nature of citizenship.

This public nature manifests itself in two ways. The first is that the good citizen is a public-spirited person who places the interests of the community ahead of personal interests. Such a person will recognize that citizenship is a matter of responsibilities as much as rights, and the good citizen will discharge these responsibilities when called upon to do so – from the day-to-day demands of obeying traffic laws and respecting the rights of others to the more onerous burdens of paying taxes and providing military (or some alternative) service. The second way in which this commitment to the public good manifests itself is in civic involvement. Good citizens will undertake public responsibilities when called upon, as with jury duty, but they will not always wait for others to issue the call. Instead, they will take an active part in public affairs. They need not be 'political junkies' who have little interest in any other area of life; they may even share Oscar Wilde's concern that 'socialism [or any political cause] takes too many evenings'. But the good citizen will not think that an occasional evening devoted to public affairs is one too many, nor that politics is a nuisance to be avoided or a spectacle to be witnessed. Politics is the public's business, and the good citizen, according to the republican view, will try to play a well-informed and public-spirited part in the conduct of this business.

The republican standards embedded in the ethical dimension of citizenship thus provide an ideal of what a citizen should be. Like other ideals, however, republican citizenship can take more or less stringent forms. At its most stringent, the republican conception seems to demand unquestioning loyalty and total sacrifice from the citizen. The Spartan mother who supposedly told her son to come back a hero from the war or to come back on his shield gave voice to this view. In its less stringent forms, the republican conception acknowledges that even good citizens should not forsake self-interest altogether. Tocqueville articulated this position when he praised the doctrine of 'self-interest properly understood'. Paying taxes, serving on juries, obeying the law, and attending to public affairs require the sacrifice of time, attention, and treasure, but such sacrifices are necessary if we are to preserve republican government and continue to enjoy the rights of the citizen.[7] The doctrine of 'self-interest properly understood' may not inspire extraordinary deeds or heroic sacrifices, Tocqueville admitted, 'but every day it prompts some small ones; by itself it cannot make a man virtuous, but its discipline shapes a lot of orderly, temperate, moderate, careful, and self-controlled citizens. If it does not lead the will directly to virtue, it establishes habits which unconsciously turn it that way' ([1835–40] 1969: 526–7).

As Tocqueville's remarks suggest, the person who acquires the habits of the public-spirited citizen is also likely to become a better, more virtuous person in other respects. To appreciate how this can happen, we need to examine two further dimensions of republican citizenship: the *integrative* and the *educative*.

Republicans believe that citizenship provides 'an integrative experience which brings together the multiple role activities of the contemporary person and demands that the separate roles be surveyed from a more general point of view' (Wolin, 1960: 434). When we act as (republican) citizens, we cannot simply speak or vote as parents or workers or consumers or members of this group or that sect. A policy that will work to one's benefit as a consumer may work to one's detriment as a worker or parent, for instance, so the search for a more synoptic understanding of one's interests becomes necessary. According to Rousseau, one should simply set aside personal interests to follow the general will one has as a citizen – that is, as one who has no interests except as a member of the public ([1762] 1950, Book II, Chs. 1–4). But we cannot truly act as members of the public unless we have some understanding of the personal interests of the people involved. The activity of citizenship – the exchange of views, the give-and-take of debate – helps to provide this understanding. Indeed, the activity of citizenship performs an integrative function in two respects: it enables the individual to integrate the various roles he or she plays, and it integrates individuals into the community.

Assuming that citizenship does in fact provide this integrative experience, one may still wonder how this helps someone to become a better person. The answer is that it instills a more secure sense of self, of one's identity and integrity as a person. One of the most common complaints about modern society is that life tends to be divided into a series of almost discrete compartments. We leave home to go to work, where the division of labor often confines us to a narrow and repetitive task; we leave work to go shopping, where we encounter people we know only as clerks and customers; we leave the store to drive or ride home, seldom seeing a familiar face along the way. Modern, urban society presents a far greater range of opportunities than earlier forms of society, but it also separates people from one another and splits their lives into fragments (Wirth, 1938). To the extent that active citizenship requires people to see themselves as more than the sum of the various roles they play, it will work to establish a secure sense of self. Anyone who finds this desirable will thus have good reason to believe that the integrative aspects of citizenship will be, at least in the long term, of personal benefit.

Of course, there are other ways to deal with the multiplicity of roles and the fragmentation of identity characteristic of modern life. One way is to withdraw into a cave; another is to join an all-embracing community of like-minded people. Yet another is to concentrate, so far as the insistent demands of modern life will allow, on a single role – parent, perhaps, or soldier or scholar – to the virtual exclusion of all others. From the republican standpoint, however, citizenship offers a better alternative because it promises an educative as well as an integrative experience.

Perhaps the best way to make this point is in terms of a distinction Dennis Thompson draws between Rousseau's 'patriotic' and John Stuart Mill's 'enlightened' conception of citizenship (Thompson, 1976: 43–50). For Rousseau's austere republicanism, the true citizen puts the good of the community above all other considerations. Citizenship demands simplicity – a whole-hearted devotion to duty – rather than sophistication. For Mill's liberal republicanism, however, good citizens are people who develop their faculties through active engagement in public life. As Mill argues in *Representative Government*, the individual stands to gain from the intellectual growth, the practical discipline, and

> the moral part of the instruction afforded by the participation of the private citizen, if even rarely, in public functions. He is called upon, while so engaged, to weigh interests not his own; to be guided, in case of conflicting claims, by another rule than his private partialities; to apply, at every turn, principles and maxims which have for their reason of existence the common good: and he usually finds associated with him in the same work minds more familiarized than his own with these ideas and operations, whose study it will be to supply reasons to his own understanding, and stimulation to his feelings for the general interest. He is made to feel himself one of the public, and whatever is for their benefit to be for his benefit. (Mill, [1861] 1975: 196–7)

On Mill's account, then, active citizenship educates people by drawing out abilities that might otherwise remain untapped or unfulfilled. Because these abilities will prove valuable in other aspects of the citizens' lives as well, the educative dimension of citizenship clearly promises to work to their benefit.

Two other features of this educative dimension are noteworthy. Both pertain to 'the moral part of the instruction' afforded by participation in public affairs. The first is that this participation leads individuals to Tocqueville's doctrine of 'self-interest properly understood'. For reasons Mill set out, active citizenship widens individuals' horizons and deepens their sense of how their lives are involved with others', including the lives of people who are unknown to them. In this way participation works to overcome *individualism* as Tocqueville understood it: 'a calm and considered feeling which disposes each citizen to isolate himself from the mass of his fellows and withdraw into the circle of family and friends; with this little society formed to his taste, he gladly leaves the greater society to look after itself' ([1835–40] 1969: 506). Republican citizenship works to overcome this pernicious form of individualism by fostering the individual's sense of himself or herself as a part of, rather than apart from, the public.

It is also important to notice *how* participation encourages public-spirited citizenship. The legal dimension of citizenship inclines us to think of citizenship in categorical terms: either one is a citizen of a certain polity or one is not. From the ethical perspective, however, one can be more or less of a citizen – a 'real' citizen, a citizen 'in name only', or something in between. Mill's insight is that real citizenship can be cultivated by encouraging those who are citizens in name only to join in public life. From modest beginnings in occasional activities that require one to 'weigh interests not his own' and to look beyond 'his private partialities', political participation can transform the nominal citizen into one who, 'made to feel himself one of the public', is moved to act by the desire to promote the common good. Participation in public life thus seems to be a pathway to, as well as a defining feature of, republican citizenship.

REVIVING REPUBLICAN CITIZENSHIP

The belief that participation in public life is neither as extensive nor as intensive as it ought to be is largely responsible for the recent revival of interest in both citizenship and republicanism. The complaint is not so much that civic life in the advanced democracies has declined dramatically from some golden age as that it has failed to realize the promise of republican citizenship. This complaint, for instance, animated the work of Hannah Arendt in the middle of the twentieth century. Technology has eased the burdens of labor and freed people to act as citizens in the public realm, she argued in *The Human Condition* (1958), yet we turn away from public life and toward private consumption. We want governments to provide for the welfare of the citizenry, she declared in *On Revolution*, but we 'deny the very existence of public happiness and public freedom' as we 'insist that politics is a burden …' (1965: 273). We are, in short, squandering an opportunity to achieve what the republicans of ancient Greece and Rome thought impossible – a polity in which the freedom of republican self-government is available not only to the well-to-do few but to almost the entire people.

Similar concerns lie behind the republican revival of the last quarter-century or so. In this case, neo-republicans tend to place the blame on one, or both, of two theories they regard as pernicious. One of these is liberalism; the other is the tendency to reduce politics to the market place.

According to such critics as Sandel (1982, 1996), Sullivan (1986), Pettit (1997), and Barber (1984), the liberal emphasis on individual rights and liberties has worked to loosen civic bonds and undermine self-government. As Sandel puts it, 'the civic or formative aspect of our [American] politics has largely given way to the liberalism that conceives persons as free and independent selves, unencumbered by moral or civic ties they have not chosen' (1996: 6). This 'voluntarist' or 'procedural' liberalism, as found in the works of liberal philosophers such as John Rawls (1971, 1993) and the legal decisions of liberal jurists, has fostered a society in which individuals fail to understand how much they owe to the community. The chief purpose of the state, accordingly, is to arbitrate the conflicting claims of these individuals as they pursue their disparate conceptions of the good life. Such a society will be self-subverting, Sandel insists, for it 'fails to capture those loyalties and responsibilities whose moral force consists partly in the fact that living by them is inseparable from understanding ourselves as the particular persons we are – as members of this family or city or nation or people, as bearers of that history, as citizens of this republic' (1996: 14). Where such loyalties and responsibilities cannot be sustained, self-government cannot survive. Hence the need for a republican revival.

Others have reached this conclusion in reaction to the tendency of many political scientists and economists to think of politics as a form of economic activity. In politics and public affairs, according to this view (e.g. Schumpeter, 1962; Downs, 1957), the citizen is essentially a consumer. Political parties offer candidates and platforms in an attempt to win votes, and sensible consumer-citizens vote so as to strike the best bargain for themselves. If they decide that the political market place offers nothing appealing, or that their resources are better invested elsewhere, consumer-citizens will stay away from the ballot box and quite wisely forsake political activity. They may even find that it is rational for them to remain largely ignorant of public affairs. There is little that one vote can accomplish, after all, so why waste time studying the issues and assessing the candidates in order to cast a meaningless vote?[8]

This way of thinking about citizenship and politics is far removed from the republican ideal of civic virtue. Conceiving of the citizen as a consumer may capture the legal dimension of citizenship, but there is no room in this conception for the ethical, integrative, or educative aspects of citizenship. Indeed, one republican response is to say that the consumer-citizen is a citizen in name only: 'Market theories of political exchange which reduce the citizen to a "consumer" or "customer" are not so much amoral – although they are that too – as trivial: a *reductio ad absurdum*' (Selbourne, 1994: 14).[9]

Republican critics also point to other problems with the market model of politics, notably the problem of generating obedience and allegiance. If citizens are merely consumers and the political order, like the market, is merely a mechanism for coordinating and aggregating the citizens' preferences, there is no satisfactory answer to the question, 'What reason has anyone to accept the decision that emerges from the process of interest-aggregation?' (Miller, 1989: 257). Appeals to solidarity or civic virtue are not available to the advocates of the market model, of course. In such a 'resolutely individualistic' conception of politics, people 'are essentially competitors – rivals for space, for resources, for power ... The only bonds between citizens are contractual in nature, formed by agreements based on the self-interest of the parties involved' (Spragens, 1990: 139–40). Where self-interest does not dictate allegiance, there is simply no reason to obey the law or remain loyal.

To be sure, self-interest does dictate that people obey the law when they are likely to be punished if they do not. The proponents of the market model may thus argue that allegiance and cooperation are secured by the coercive force of the government. When obedience seems burdensome, however, the law and those who enforce it will be resented as obstacles, or even opponents, that block the satisfaction of the consumer-citizen's desires. Government and law soon appear to be alien forces imposed on one – not forms of self-rule but forces to be circumvented whenever possible. As law-breaking increases, and their own interests suffer, consumer-citizens have no recourse but to call for more police, more jails, and more coercion. This reliance on coercion reveals a most embarrassing problem for the market model of politics: its inefficiency. As Diego Gambetta observes, '[S]ocieties which rely heavily on the use of force are likely to be less efficient, more costly, and more unpleasant than those where trust is maintained by other means. In the former, resources tend to be diverted away from economic undertakings and spent in coercion, surveillance, and information gathering, and less incentive is found to engage in cooperative activities' (1988: 220–1). Such inefficiency demonstrates how the market model undermines itself. Citizens who think of themselves as consumers will surely prize efficiency. Yet the more citizens think of themselves as consumers, the more likely they are to rely on the inefficient means of coercion to secure compliance with the laws. On its own grounds, then, the conception of the citizen as consumer is inferior to a conception of citizenship that generates cooperation on the basis of solidarity and civic duty. Such a conception will be, at least to some extent, republican.

As with other revivals, in sum, the revival of interest in republicanism and in citizenship grows out of the sense that something valuable is in danger of being lost. That loss, in this case, will have grievous consequences for political stability and individual freedom, for one cannot be a free person, in the republican view, unless one is a citizen of a free, self-governing political community (Miller, 1991: 3). And such a community cannot be sustained unless a substantial number of citizens (in the legal sense) undertakes the active life of the public-spirited citizen.

THE RELEVANCE OF REPUBLICAN CITIZENSHIP

There is a sense in which all revivals are backward-looking, and one may wonder whether the attempt to revive the republican ideal of citizenship looks so far back – to the Greek *polis*, the Roman *civitas*, and the Italian city-republics of the Middle Ages – as to be irrelevant to life in the twenty-first century. Thomas Jefferson's agrarian republicanism is a case in point. Jefferson may have been right two hundred years ago to praise the small farmer as the model of the independent citizen who would rather live frugally on land he and his family worked than succumb to the luxury and corruption of urban life (Jefferson, 1999: 549–50, 28). Such praise, however, seems little more than nostalgia in today's world of global agribusiness and 'e-commerce'. What may be said, then, for the relevance of republican citizenship today? What may be said for it, moreover, in light of the biases implicit in the republican ideal of the property-owning, arms-bearing citizen?

We thus have two criticisms to consider by way of concluding the case for republican citizenship in this chapter. The first is that the republican conception of citizenship is no longer realistic, if ever it was; the second is that the conception poses a threat to an open, egalitarian, and pluralistic society. This second criticism is put forcefully by Iris Marion Young, who detects a denial of 'difference' in republican attempts to establish a 'civic public':

> This ideal of the civic public ... excludes women and other groups defined as different, because its rational and universal status derives only from its opposition to affectivity, particularity, and the body.... [I]n so far as he is a citizen every man leaves behind his particularity and difference, to adopt a universal standpoint identical for all citizens, the standpoint of the common good or general will. In practice republican politicians enforced homogeneity by excluding from citizenship all those defined as different... (1990: 117).

Space does not permit a full consideration of this criticism, but three points may be made here.[10] One is that there is a strong republican strain in the writings not only of pioneering feminists, such as Mary Wollstonecraft (1794), but also of some recent feminists (e.g. Dietz, 1985, 1990). A second point is that politics will be a tricky business indeed if concern for difference rules out attempts to find a common good. Young wants 'claimants to justify their demands before others who explicitly stand in different social locations' (1990: 190). But how is a decision to emerge from the conflicting claims of people in these 'different social locations' if no appeal to a common good or to the standpoint of the citizen is allowed? To be sure, Young's point is that the search for common ground serves to justify the dominance of a particular – and typically affluent, white, male – group. But if there is no common good or common ground, then it is difficult to see how *public* decisions, including those of the 'heterogeneous public' she recommends (1990: 190), can be justified.

The third point concerns the claim that citizenship involves a false ideal of impartiality. Here the republican response is to deny that the ideal is false. We should indeed strive to think and act, when establishing laws and policies, as members of the public rather than self-interested individuals. But this does not mean that we cannot take account of the particular needs and interests of the people – even people who 'stand in different social locations' – who compose the polity. Republican citizenship, again, is integrative. It requires us to bring together the facets of our individual lives as best we can. In working toward policies and laws that we can agree to despite our differences, citizenship also helps us to find unity in the midst of diversity. But it does not require that we surrender our particular identities or deny the value of diversity.

That is not to say that 'difference' and cultural pluralism do not present difficulties for a 'civic public', for they do. But difference and pluralism present difficulties for all kinds of polities, and republican citizenship at least has the virtue of confronting them head on by encouraging people to look for the common ground on which they stand, despite their differences, as citizens. In that respect, there is surely something to be said for the relevance of republican citizenship.

There is also something to be said in response to the first criticism – that republican citizenship is an irredeemably nostalgic ideal in this age of globalization. In this case the republican response is to point out that fear of dependence and hatred of corruption are still very much with us, and one need not be the yeoman farmer of Jefferson's vision to enjoy the kind of independence necessary to republican citizenship. The challenge is to find ways to adapt these enduring republican concerns to the circumstances of vast polities that are themselves entangled in a 'global economy whose frenzied flow of money and goods, information and images, pays little heed to nations, much less neighborhoods' (Sandel, 1996: 317). To those who would take up this challenge, republicanism offers guidance of both a general and a particular kind.

In general, the republican advice is to build community. Among other things, this means that a republican cannot be a wholehearted cosmopolitan (Miller, 1999; Dagger, 2001). To be a citizen, in the republican view, is to be a partner in a common enterprise, and people will be likely to put the common interest ahead of their own – to act as true citizens – only when they feel themselves to be part of such an enterprise. The Internet and satellite television are unlikely to inspire this sense of community on a global basis.

The republican, however, will also note that genuine communities come in many different forms, not all of which are hospitable to the republican ideal of self-government. Republicanism thus points toward particular characteristics to be cultivated in political communities. Indeed, we may say that the republican model of the good community exhibits the following five characteristics: fair treatment under the rule of law prevails; economic arrangements and the distribution of wealth promote citizenship rather than consumerism; preparing children for a life of responsible citizenship is a leading aim of education; civic design strengthens neighborhoods and public spirit; and opportunities for participation in public affairs, including programs of civic service, are abundant.

Much more needs to be said on each of these five points, of course, to clarify and bolster the case for republican citizenship. That so much may be said, however, and that neo-republicans and republican liberals are now beginning to say it, is perhaps the best testimony to the continuing relevance of the republican ideal of citizenship.

NOTES

1 Cicero made this point in his *Republic* when he asked (Book III, 43), 'So who would call that a republic, i.e., the property of the public, when everyone was oppressed by the cruelty of a single man...?' As the subsequent discussion, in his dialogue indicates, Cicero believed that rule by the few and rule by the many could also be tyrannical – and therefore not republican.

2 As I argue in Dagger (1997). For criticism of Sandel's and Pettit's attempts to distinguish republicanism from liberalism, see Dagger (1999 and 2000, respectively). Others who believe it is a mistake to divorce republicanism from liberalism include Terchek (1997) and Spragens (1999).

3 On this point note Spragens's (1999: 186–7) remarks on 'civic friendship':

> 'It is not only close friends who may share the common interests, common attachments, common purposes, and common values that generate the behavioral cohesion of amicable and cooperative association. Quite large groups of people may share these goods in common, and on the basis of pursuing them together they may form the quasi-erotic bonds of social concord Aristotle referred to as *homonoia*: 'friendship between the citizens of a state, its province being the interests and concerns of life'. [*Nichomachean Ethics*, Book IX, Chap. 6]

4 This connection is manifest in Cicero's famous definition (*Republic*, Book I, 39) of the republic as 'a numerous gathering brought together by legal consent [*iuris consensu*] and community of interest'. See also Book III, 45 – 'there is no public except when it is held together by a legal agreement' – and, for analysis and assessment, Schofield (1995).

5 Historians (Wirszubski, 1960: 9; Skinner, 1998: 45) trace this formula to the Roman writers Sallust, Livy, and Cicero.

6 On Pettit's account (1997: 80), 'freedom as non-domination' is the 'supreme political value' of the republican tradition.

7 Quentin Skinner (1991) makes a similar point with regard to Machiavelli and other republicans.

8 So, at least, went the argument before the closely contested US presidential election of 2000.

9 See also Ball (1988: Ch. 6) on the distinction between 'economic' and 'educative' democracy.

10 For more detailed discussion, see Miller (1995) and Dagger (1997: 176–81).

I am grateful to Terence Ball and Engin Isin for helpful comments on an earlier draft of this chapter.

REFERENCES

Arendt, Hannah (1958) *The Human Condition*. Chicago: University of Chicago Press.

Arendt, Hannah (1965) *On Revolution*. New York: Viking Press.

Ball, Terence (1988) *Transforming Political Discourse: Political Theory and Critical Conceptual History*. Oxford: Basil Blackwell.

Barber, Benjamin (1984) *Strong Democracy: Participatory Politics for a New Age*. Berkeley: University of California Press.

Cicero (1998) *The Republic and The Laws* tr. N. Rudd. Oxford: Oxford University Press.

Dagger, Richard (1997) *Civic Virtues: Rights, Citizenship, and Republican Liberalism*. New York: Oxford University Press.

Dagger, Richard (1999) 'The Sandelian Republic and the Encumbered Self', *Review of Politics*, 61 (2): 181–217.

Dagger, Richard (2000) 'Republicanism Refashioned: Comments on Pettit's Theory of Freedom and Government', *The Good Society*, 9 (3): 50–53.

Dagger, Richard (2001) 'Republicanism and the Politics of Place', *Philosophical Explorations*, 4 (3): 157–73. (Autumn 2001).

Dietz, Mary (1985) 'Citizenship with a Feminist Face: The Problem with Maternal Thinking', *Political Theory*, 13 (1): 19–37.

Dietz, Mary (1990) 'Hobbes's Subject as Citizen', in Mary Dietz (ed.), *Thomas Hobbes and Political Theory*. Lawrence, KS: University Press of Kansas.

Downs, Anthony (1957) *An Economic Theory of Democracy*. New York: Harper and Row.

Gambetta, Diego (1988) 'Can We Trust Trust?', in Diego Gambetta (ed.), *Trust: Making and Breaking Cooperative Relations*. Oxford: Basil Blackwell.

Jefferson, Thomas (1999) *Political Writings*. Joyce Applely and Terence Ball (eds). Cambridge: Cambridge University Press.

Kennedy John F. (1961) 'Every citizen holds office', *NEA Journal* 50 (October): 18–20.

Mill, John Stuart ([1861] 1975) *Three Essays: 'On Liberty', 'Representative Government', and 'The Subjection of Women'*. R. Wollheim. (ed) Oxford: Oxford University Press.

Miller, David (1989) *Market, State, and Community*. Oxford: Clarendon Press.

Miller, David (1991) 'Introduction', in David Miller (ed.), *Liberty*. Oxford: Oxford University Press.

Miller, David (1995) 'Citizenship and Pluralism', *Political Studies*, 43 (3): 432–50.

Miller, David (1999) 'Bounded Citizenship', in Kimberly Hutchings and Roland Dannreuther (eds), *Cosmopolitan Citizenship*. New York: St. Martin's Press.

Oldfield, Adrian (1990) *Citizenship and Community*. London: Routledge.

Pettit, Philip (1997) *Republicanism: A Theory of Freedom and Government*. Oxford: Clarendon Press.

Pocock, J.G.A. (1975) *The Machiavellian Moment: Florentine Political Thought and the Atlantic Republican Tradition*. Princeton, NJ: Princeton University Press.

Putnam, Robert (2000) *Bowling Alone: The Collapse and Revival of American Community*. New York: Simon and Schuster.

Rahe, Paul (1992) *Republics Ancient and Modern: Classical Republicanism and the American Revolution*. Chapel Hill, NC: University of North Carolina Press.

Rawls, John (1971) *A Theory of Justice*. Cambridge, MA: Harvard University Press.

Rawls, John (1993) *Political Liberalism*. New York: Columbia University Press.

Rousseau, Jean-Jacques ([1750; 1762] 1950) *The Social Contract and the Discourses*, tr. G.D.H. Cole. New York: E.P. Dutton.

Sandel, Michael (1982) *Liberalism and the Limits of Justice*. Cambridge: Cambridge University Press.

Sandel, Michael (1996) *Democracy's Discontent: America in Search of a Public Philosophy*. Cambridge, MA: Harvard University Press.

Schofield, Malcolm (1995) 'Cicero's Definition of *Res Publica*', in J.G.F. Powell (ed.), *Cicero the Philosopher: Twelve Papers*. Oxford: Clarendon Press.

Schumpeter, Joseph (1962) *Capitalism, Socialism, and Democracy*, 3rd ed. New York: Harper and Row.

Selbourne, David (1994) *The Principle of Duty: An Essay on the Foundations of the Civic Order*. London: Sinclair-Stevenson.

Sellers, M.N.S. (1998) *The Sacred Fire of Liberty: Republicanism, Liberalism, and the Law*. London: Macmillan.

Skinner, Quentin (1991) 'The Paradoxes of Political Liberty', in David Miller (ed.), *Liberty*. Oxford: Oxford University Press.

Skinner, Quentin (1998) *Liberty Before Liberalism*. Cambridge: Cambridge University Press.

Spragens, Thomas A., Jr. (1990) *Reason and Democracy*. Durham, NC: Duke University Press.

Spragens, Thomas A., Jr. (1999) *Civic Liberalism: Reflections on Our Democratic Ideals*. Lanham, MD: Rowman and Littlefield.

Sullivan, William (1986) *Reconstructing Public Philosophy*. Berkeley and Los Angeles: University of California Press.

Terchek, Ronald. (1997) *Republican Paradoxes and Liberal Anxieties*. Lanham, MD: Rowman and Littlefield.

Thompson, Dennis (1976) *John Stuart Mill and Representative Government*. Princeton, NJ: Princeton University Press.

Tocqueville, Alexis de ([1835–40] 1969). *Democracy in America*. tr. G. Lawrence, ed. J.P. Mayer. Garden City, NY: Doubleday.

Thucydides ([431–411BCE] 1993) *On Justice, Power, and Human Nature: Selections from 'The History of the Peloponnesian War'*. tr. P. Woodruff. Indianapolis, IN: Hackett Publishing.

van Gunsteren, Herman (1998) *A Theory of Citizenship: Organizing Plurality in Contemporary Democracies*. Boulder, Co and Oxford: Westview Press.

Wirszubski, Ch. (1960) *Libertas as a Political Idea at Rome During the Late Republic and Early Principate*. Cambridge: Cambridge University Press.

Wirth, Louis (1938) 'Urbanism as a Way of Life', *American Journal of Sociology*, 44: 1–24.

Wolin, Sheldon (1960) *Politics and Visions: Continuity and Innovation in Western Political Thought*. Boston: Little, Brown.

Wollstonecraft, Mary (1794) *A Vindication of the Rights of Woman*. Philadelphia: Matthew Carey.

Young, Iris M. (1990) *Justice and the Politics of Difference*. Princeton, NJ: Princeton University Press.

Zwiebach, Burton (1975) *Civility and Disobedience*. New York: Cambridge University Press.

10

Communitarianism and Citizenship

GERARD DELANTY

The idea of community has frequently been counterposed to society, as in Tönnies's famous treatise on *Gemeinschaft* and *Gesellschaft*, or to the state, as in the thought of modern communitarianism, the subject of this chapter. In this latter conception, community is rooted in something prior to the political order of the state and, in the former, it is based on something more substantive than the associational order of modern society (Tönnies, 1959). For many, community presupposes a social ontology which when examined closely turns out to be a non-social category and is frequently conceived of in cultural terms. Thus, political community is often seen to be rooted in a prior cultural community, for it is held neither the state nor society can provide enduring normative ties.[1] The appeal to community thus inevitably invokes a certain opposition to modernity and the liberal tradition of individualism with its too 'thin' understanding of community (see Walzer, 1994). In the debate on citizenship this is particularly apparent. Communitarians argue that citizenship is rooted in a culturally defined community, while liberals argue that citizenship rests on individuals and that therefore political community is derivative of its members, who are always individuals. Whether citizenship as membership of a political community rests on the individual or a prior cultural or moral community is what divides the protagonists in this debate.

It is noteworthy, however, that most of this debate – while harking back to classical sociological theory – has been fought out on the level of normative political theory and that, while communitarians claim to be more in tune with the social constitution of citizenship, there is a noticeable absence of a sociological analysis of the key terms in the debate, namely citizenship and community, which instead tend to be taken as given when in fact they are socially constructed. In this chapter I shall demonstrate that a sociological approach informed by recent developments in social theory offers advantages over a purely normative approach that is abstract and de-contextualized. My argument is that when viewed sociologically communitarianism does not offer a satisfactory alternative to the liberal conception of citizenship, and that at most it is a modification of it.[2] It is based on the same essentially normative understanding of what is in essence a volatile social process in which cultural structures – normative, cognitive, symbolic and aesthetic – are deeply bound up with different kinds of social agency. Community cannot be seen as a consensual resource from which citizenship can directly draw, but is a highly relational concept. The assumption in communitarianism that community provides a cultural foundation for citizenship distorts the nature of both citizenship and community in contemporary society. It has given a view of citizenship as pre-political and rooted in a consensual and spatially fixed understanding of the life-world. Against the assumption that a culturally and territorially defined community can offer a foundation for a politically defined conception of citizenship, I argue for a reflexive, internally differentiated and communicative understanding of community and citizenship that is more in tune with contemporary developments, allowing us to speak of a cosmopolitan institutionalization of communities of dissent. Thus against the communitarian appeal to a primordial cultural community as a foundation for liberalism's political community, I argue for a notion of communication community in the context of an increasingly global world. In order to link citizenship with community what is needed is a weak or 'thin' conception of the latter and a 'thick' version of the former.

In the first part of this chapter I outline what I take to be the four main conceptions of community in modern social and political thought. In the second part I look at the sociological theory of community suggested by recent social theory in order to find an alternative to the communitarian theory of community. By way of conclusion, I defend the continued use of the idea of community, but in a way that is tied to a more reflexive kind of communitarianism, which I call cosmopolitan communitarianism. The thesis defended here is that citizenship is rooted in community, which is to be understood in terms of essentially *social* as opposed to *cultural* or *moral* dynamics of group formation. In general, communitarian thought assumes a self-evident conception of group formation as consisting of an opposition of self and other. Rather than speak of community as something taken for granted, we need to see it in terms of a model of the group as internally differentiated.

THE APPEAL OF COMMUNITY IN MODERN SOCIAL AND POLITICAL THOUGHT

The communitarian debate on citizenship, while conducted within normative political theory, has recently taken on a more governmental form in public policy debates. The result is a very contested term. However, some basic assumptions can be discerned in these very diverse debates. There is a discredited functionalist understanding of community inherited from an earlier age of social and political thought, and not least from classical sociology. From this heritage has come a conception of community that emphasizes social order and a pre-established and relatively harmonious consensus based on shared cultural values and tradition. Community has thus come to stand for 'unity' and conflict for its absence.

Even when the emphasis is not on an underlying cultural community, there is the assumption that politics and citizenship must rest on an underlying moral order that is prior to the political. In the first section, I discuss this older tradition, in the second section I examine in detail the liberal communitarian debate, in the third section I look at the civic tradition of communitarianism and in the fourth section I look at the governmentalization of community.

The Modern Myth of Community

The concept of community in classical sociology is closely linked with a conservatively inclined functionalism, in the sense that community was seen as more functional than society. Ferdinand Tönnies's *Gemeinschaft und Gesellschaft*, published in 1887, pitted community and society against each other (Tönnies, 1957). 'Community' referred to the organic and cohesive traditional world while 'society' refers to the fragmented world of modernity with its rationalized, intellectualized and individualized structures. For Tönnies community was based on direct ties, while society was based on associational ties. Communities are allegedly culturally integrated totalities while society is defined by its parts. Tönnies regretted the passing of community – the world of the village and the rural community, and the arrival of society – the world of the city, believing that community could supply the individual with greater moral resources. His idea of community thus suggests a strong sense of place, proximity and totality, while society suggests fragmentation, alienation and distance.

This functionalist understanding of community is also present in Durkheim's sociology, where society is essentially a community based on common cultural values. Modernity for Durkheim is defined by the movement from mechanical forms of integration, characterized by ascriptive values and an immediate identification of the individual with the collectivity, to organic forms of integration, which are characterized by contractual relations and require cooperation between groups (Durkheim, 1960). He was critical of Tönnies's nostalgia for community as a lost totality, but nevertheless believed community was essential to citizenship in modern society. Durkheim was in fact the first classical communitarian theorist. In his liberal republican philosophy, society needs to re-create community in order to make a new kind of civic morality possible. He saw society as oscillating between integration and anomic, mechanical forms of integration on the one hand and the more functionalized organic forms of generalized communication on the other. Durkheim, unlike Tönnies who was a romantically inclined guild socialist, a positivist and a liberal, and had no difficulty in accepting the burden of modernity and its individualized and differentiated social organization, which was potentially liberating. In particular in his later work, he believed that occupational groups and a democratic political culture could provide a foundation for community compatible with the demands of modernity (Durkheim, [1893] 1957). Here there is a suggestion of a shift from a cultural to a moral understanding of community in the modern age. As with many of the thinkers of his era, Durkheim's vision of society was dominated by the belief that he was witnessing an epochal transition from tradition to modernity. While he reconciled himself to society, his vision of a functionalized social order bore the imprint of a fascination with community as an ontological and primordial reality and as a symbolic order.

The penchant for community in classical sociological theory was enhanced by the rise of anthropology, which perpetuated the myth of primitive society being a holistic fusion of culture and society around a symbolic order and primordial values. The early anthropologists called primitive societies 'cultures', preferring to reserve the word 'society' for their own allegedly superior scientific society. The anthropological vision had an enduring hold on the sociological mind, which tended to see cultural values and social practices as intertwined and underpinned by symbolic structures with a strong sense of group boundaries. Community in classical sociology came to be seen as modelled on primitive cultures, as small-scale and traditionally organized groups in which cultural cohesion is mirrored in social integration. Communities are also seen as territorially located, sharing a common territory as well as a set of primordial values. At a time when anthropology and sociology were not differentiated into separate disciplines, sociology – in particular the functionalist tradition – inherited this powerful myth of community as a lost totality rooted in place and proximity. It also entered political theory, providing it with a vision of community as a transcendental imaginary, as in, for example, the idea of a transnational political community (Deutsch et al., 1957).

As far as sociology was concerned, this led to a certain ambivalence with modernity, which it viewed as having brought about a rupture with tradition. Not only conservative functionalists adopted this position. The myth of community as a holistic fusion of culture and society was also behind liberal and Marxist interpretations of modernity (Nisbet, 1953, 1967). The search for community in the form of the utopian communist society at the end of history was central to Marxism. Few philosophies have been more successful in advocating a notion of community than Marxism, which conceived the communist society of the future as a perfect fusion of culture and society.

The Chicago School, too, was very much preoccupied with the idea of a tension between community and society. Their studies on the impact of industrialism and urban modernization on traditional communities greatly contributed to the myth of community as something destroyed by modernity. Other approaches saw a different kind of community – suggestive of the Christian *oecueme* – promising a more global kind of community beyond the social. Thus Parson's (1961: 10–1) functionalism was guided by the belief that modernity was ultimately regulated by the moral order of what he called the 'societal community'.

Despite some notable critiques, this appeal of community as an ontological and primordial set of values has endured throughout the twentieth century as a counterforce to society.[3] This was particularly prevalent in conservative sociology, which contrasted 'mass society' (with its weak symbolic resources and loose boundaries) with the more cohesive world of community. The vision of a recovery of a primordial totality has been a very powerful idea and ideal and has inspired many sociological and philosophical theories, as well as political ideologies (Cohen, 1985). It may be said that the twentieth century has witnessed the triumph of the spirit of community over the spirit of society. The ideologies of modernity – socialism, conservatism, nationalism, fascism, anarchism, kibbutz democracy – have all been inspired by the quest for community. Indeed, it may be suggested that the quest for community has been inspired precisely because of the failure of the social. While society has been associated with the negative aspects of modernity – rationalization, individualization, industrialism, disenchantment – community has been more successful in expressing the positive aspects of modernity. Yet, there is no denying its ambivalence with modernity.

In sum, classical sociological thought bequeathed a conception of community as embodied in a shared sense of place and cultural order based on consensus, primordialism and harmony. It led to a vision of society and of citizenship requiring the stable resources of community.

LIBERAL COMMUNITARIANISM

The concept of citizenship has not been central to sociological theory (Turner, 1993). The debate on citizenship has been more central to political theory, and to an extent in social policy, and has been traditionally dominated by liberal theory and its limits, as pointed out by T.H. Marshall in 1950 (Marshall, 1992). With the emergence of communitarianism since the 1980s, the debate on citizenship has been reopened around a more contextualized concept of citizenship as the expression of community. The liberal theory of citizenship (discussed in Chapter 8) reduced citizenship to the market, while Marshall relocated citizenship in the state, albeit the welfare state of the postwar era. It has thus been the fate of citizenship to be reduced either to the market or to the state. The republican tradition (discussed in Chapter 9 in this volume and briefly mentioned below) with its emphasis on civil society as a domain between the state and economy represented an alternative tradition, one that stressed the association order of civic life as the basis of citizenship and of community. However the liberal communitarian philosophy that emerged in the 1980s had a different project: one that was explicitly cultural in its conception of community. What is distinctive about communitarianism is the rejection of individualism and the contractualism. This move from 'contract to community' (Dallmayr, 1978) marks it off from liberalism, but also from social democracy, which in rejecting collectivism came to stand for a similar kind of privatism to liberalism.

The debate between liberals and communitarians is by all accounts a most confused debate.[4] The very premises of the debate are confused since the focus of the debate is the political theory of John Rawls, as outlined in his *A Theory of Justice*, originally published in 1971 (Rawls, 1981). As the title of the book suggests, his concern was with the foundations of a notion of justice rather than with citizenship as such. Rawls' liberalism is a left liberalism and is not too far removed from Marshall's concern with social justice. To an extent, then, communitarianism was a reaction, not to classical liberalism, but to a conception of citizenship based on social, civic and political dimensions of political community. Communitarianism stood for a deeper notion of community than its public phase in the democratic nation-state. It might be suggested that while liberalism was modified by social democracy, communitarianism has modified liberalism in yet another direction to produce liberal communitarianism, which may be called 'cultural democracy'.[5]

The communitarian thesis in political philosophy has been closely associated with Charles Taylor, Michael Sandel, Michael Walzer and Alisdair MacIntyre, the most famous proponents of communitarianism. Walzer's *Spheres of Justice* (1983), Sandel's *Liberalism and the Limits of Justice* (1982) and MacIntyre's *After Virtue* (1981) established the foundations of communitarianism.[6] The differences between communitarians and liberals must not be exaggerated, since what has often been at issue is less substantive differences than differences in metatheoretical justification and methodology; for this reason the communitarian position is perhaps best termed 'liberal communitarianism' since these are no longer exclusive positions (see Miller and Walzer, 1995; Mulhall and Swift, 1996). Today, the term liberal communitarianism is especially associated with the work of one of the best known communitarian thinkers, Charles Taylor, whose *Sources of the Self* (1989) has become a major statement of the mature political philosophy of communitarianism (see also Taylor, 1994). Taylor, a Canadian, represents a different kind of communitarianism to the brand associated with Sandel, also to be found in the work of such Americans as Phillip Selznick (Selznick, 1992) or Etzioni (see below).[7]

For communitarians, liberal conceptions of group membership, in particular rights, are too formalistic, neglecting the substantive dimensions of identity and participation, the real ties that bind members of a community together. Rejecting moral individualism for a group conception of citizenship, liberal communitarianism seeks to anchor political community in a prior cultural community. The kind of collectivism that is advocated is a moral collectivism and one that is less individualistic than cultural. In this it differs from socialist notions of collectivism since the values communitarians appeal to are essentially cultural rather than material. At issue is a particular conception of the self, one that is frequently defined in terms of minority or majority status within the polity. For communitarians the self is always culturally specific and for this reason communitarianism can be seen as a defence of cultural particularism against liberalism's moral universalism.

Communitarians object to the asocial concept of the self in liberalism. The self is not only socially constructed but is also embedded in a cultural context.[8] Rawls had not considered that different cultural groups might have different ideas of the common good. For communitarians, citizenship is about participation in the political community but it is also about the preservation of identity, and therefore citizenship is always specific to a particular community. Thus it would appear that the price paid for the introduction of a substantive dimension to citizenship has been the loss of the absolute commitment to universalism that has typified liberalism. Indeed, communitarianism can be seen as an attack on moral universalism, which is seen as an empty formalism and as potentially hegemonic. According to Taylor, who has become a major philosopher of citizenship as the recognition of cultural difference, the essential problem is not universalism but the integration of self and other (Taylor, 1994).[9] For him the crucial feature of social life is its dialogical character, for the encounter between self and other is embedded in a shared language. In this encounter what is of central importance is a discourse of recognition. With respect to the politics of recognition this can take the form of an emphasis on equality, for instance the equal dignity of all citizens with respect to their rights and moral worth, or an emphasis on difference, the need of the majority culture to make concessions to particular groups, generally minorities but also, and more importantly for communitarians, for the state to give official recognition to cultural community, be it that of the majority or minority: 'Where the politics of universal dignity fought for forms of nondiscrimination that were quite "blind" to the ways in which citizens differ, the politics of difference often redefines non-discrimination as requiring that we make these distinctions the basis of differential treatment' (Taylor, 1994: 39). In order for a cultural community to retain its integrity and flourish there must be some public recognition by the state of cultural community. This is particularly the case with minority cultures to which concessions must be granted by the majority culture. However, as is clear from the case of the Québecois politics, his main concern is with the cultural majority seeking to preserve their identity.

Taylor, however, is cautious about polarizing the principles of liberal equality and communitarian difference. He stands for a liberal communitarianism that seeks to modify liberalism by compelling it to accommodate the reality of cultural difference and the need for the preservation of cultural community. Yet the differences are quite strong. Because of the atomism underlying it, liberalism for Taylor has no sense of a common good in the narrow sense of a common way of life. 'Procedural liberalism cannot have a common good in the narrow sense, because society must be neutral on the question of the common good life' (Taylor, 1989: 172). Liberalism however does recognize a common good in the broader sense of a rule. But for Taylor there is also a common good in the more specific sense of 'patriotism', an identification with a political community which itself embodies a deeper cultural way of life. He is strongly supportive of patriotic causes, such as the demands of the French-speaking Quebecers for the official recognition of their language and francophone culture by the state as in the interests of the common good. It would appear that real recognition is recognition of a self-declared majority capable of defining the common good. So long as this culture respects diversity, it has a reasonable claim for official recognition. But this of course fails to take account of a plurality of cultures – which may entail a plurality of conceptions of the common good – and what may be a minority in one context may be a majority in another.

For political philosophers such as Taylor and Walzer, the contrast between liberalism and communitarianism is not quite so stark as having to choose between two fundamentally opposed positions. While their preference is clearly for liberal communitarianism – the need for a positive recognition of cultural community, this is anchored in a basic commitment to the liberal principle of equality. Liberal communitarianism is not a postmodernist theory of radical group difference. While liberals get around the problem of protecting minority groups by a commitment to group rights (Kymlicka, 1995), communitarians are on the whole more concerned with protecting the majority culture, which is not an issue for liberals, since this is largely taken for granted; or, as in a recent formulation of Rawls', it is a matter of looking for an 'overlapping consensus' (Rawls, 1987). It is this concern with reconciling cultural community to citizenship that allows communitarians to claim the liberal mantle. But as Bauman has argued, the liberal idea of 'difference' stands for individual freedom, while the communitarian 'difference' stands for the group's power to limit individual freedom (Bauman, 1993). The concept of community in communitarian discourse is the community of the dominant culture which is officially recognised by the state. Since political community, in which citizenship exists, rests on a prior cultural community, minorities and incoming groups must adapt to this community in order to participate in its political community. Thus, liberal communitarianism is simply forcing liberalism to make explicit the existence of the cultural community that underlies political community.

We can thus distinguish between two kinds of contemporary liberalism: Liberalism 1, 'political liberalism' (with a stress on social rights and political community), and Liberalism 2, 'communitarian liberalism' (with a stress on identity/cultural community). Within this latter category, as a result largely of feminism, communitarianism in recent times has expressed a growing sense of the group-differentiated nature of community (see Isin and Wood, 1999; Frazer, 1999; Frazer and Lacey, 1999; and Young, 1989[10]). Thus in the work of Marion Young, community is reconceived around group differences within the community whilst in the recent work of Michael Walzer there is a more nuanced recognition of 'thin' as opposed to 'thick' forms of community (Young, 1989; Walzer, 1994). The implications of this will be discussed in the second part of this chapter.

Civic Communitarianism[11] The roots of communitarianism lie deep in classical political theory. While much of recent communitarianism has been focused on the question of the survival of culturally defined groups in an age of multiplicity, others see it as the re-empowering of civil society. Instead of the preservation of cultural identity, what is at stake is social capital and participation in public life.

Participation in public life is the essence of the civic bond in the famous theories of Jean-Jacques Rousseau in *The Social Contract* in 1743, of Hannah Arendt (1958) and the work of Benjamin Barber (1984), Quentin Skinner (1978) and J. Pocock (1995). This republican version of communitarianism can be seen as a radical form of liberal individualism, differing from its classical liberal presuppositions in at least two respects. Firstly, that individualism reaches its highest expression in commitment to public life, as opposed to the liberal emphasis on the private pursuit of interest or personal autonomy. Rather than self-interest what is at stake is public interest. And secondly, while liberalism was based on negative freedom, the civic republican ideal of politics is one of positive freedom, the ideal of a self-governing political community. This is the true meaning of republicanism, as intended by the radical stream within the Enlightenment, though it was only in America that it became a real force, as Tocqueville recognized. In the radical variant, represented by Rousseau, this entailed a confrontation with liberal democracy, or constitutional democracy, in that the ideal of a self-governing political community was incompatible with representative government. It may be noted that historically liberal democracy had been tied to constitutional monarchy. But for theorists such as Hannah Arendt, civic republicanism was perfectly compatible with representative government (Arendt, 1958). The challenge rather lay in bringing politics out of the state and into the public domain. This was the republican challenge. One of the legacies of this tradition has been an ambivalent relationship with democracy. Classical republicanism, like liberalism, preceded the democratic revolution and to varying degrees accommodated democracy. But the original impetus of republicanism is a radical doctrine of citizenship as participation in the public domain of civil society. As is evidenced in the writings of Hannah Arendt, republicanism exhibits a deep distrust of the modern idea of democracy, which is associated with the intrusion of the social question into what is allegedly a purely political domain.

Much of civic communitarianism or republican discourse operates on the pre-political level, valuing associational participation for its non-political benefits. In one of the best known formulations of this 'neo-Tocquevillean' position, Robert Putnam relates civic engagement with what he calls 'social capital'. The value of civil society is not its ability to overcome conflicts but to promote values of trust, commitment and solidarity, values which allow democracy to flourish. In this version of republicanism, social responsibility primarily falls firmly on the shoulders of civil society rather than on the state, which can function only if civil society already speaks with one voice. In his study of modern Italy he thus found that what matters is not institutions but cultural traditions, in particular those that reinforce civil society (Putnam, 1993). It is civil society that makes for a better state and public institutions, not the reverse, he argues. Democracy is a social condition and can flourish without a state, according to Tocqueville (1969) in his classic work *Democracy in America*. Putnam takes up this Tocquevillean romanticism of American democracy but advances it one step further: a strong civil society will lead to a stronger state in which democracy will flourish. However, Putnam, like Tocqueville, does not consider the conflicts within civil society and the resolution of such conflicts in translating the demands of social capital into government policy (Whittington, 1998; Cohen, 1999). In general his model is one of the decline of social capital, as is evident from his recent *Bowling Alone* (Putnam, 1999). Another version of this kind of communitarianism, but with a more radical edge to it, is to be found in the writings of the American cultural critic, Christopher Lasch, who, in his final work, saw the decline of democratic values of citizenship as a consequence of the betrayal of democracy not by the masses but by the élites who have isolated themselves from community (Lasch, 1995).[12] He calls for a return to the virtues of community, religion and family.

GOVERNMENTAL COMMUNITARIANISM

So far I have argued that a notion of community as providing a kind of social ontology has pervaded classical sociological thought and is present in much of recent communitarism. An understanding of community as reflecting a cohesive and primordial group has been central to these conceptions of community. While liberal communitarianism, discussed in the previous section, was largely a modification of liberalism in its advocation of a politics of recognition for particular, and in fact culturally defined groups, communitarianism in recent times has become a more governmental stance on citizenship. This can be seen as a combination of the concerns of liberal communitarianism and civic communitarianism with identity and participation. Following Nikolas Rose, it is possible to point to a move towards government through community: 'in the institution of community, a sector is brought into existence whose vectors and forces can be mobilized, enrolled, deployed in novel programmes and techniques which encourage and harness active practices of self-management and identity construction, of personal ethics and collective allegiances' (1999: 176). This refers to the growing discourse of community in policy-making in recent years.

Communitarianism has become popular in Britain and North America, frequently becoming interchangeable with a civic kind of nationalism. It was central to the political rhetoric of the British Labour Party in the historic election campaign in 1997 when the terms 'nation' and 'society' became interchangeable. The appeal to trust and solidarity as particularly British civic values allowed the Labour Party to take over the Conservative Party's previous monopoly of the discourse of the nation. Thus what had been a nationalist populist rhetoric – focused on traditional nationalism: war, heritage, the cultural mystique of Englishness – became a communitarian discourse. The nation had become disengaged from patriotic nationalism and could be deployed for the purpose of social reconstruction. Communitarianism – as in Tony Blair's notion of a 'stakeholder society' – aided social reconstruction by social democracy against neo-liberalism by providing a crucial link with conservative values, which neo-liberalism appropriated for its project. The new technologies of community, to follow Nikolas Rose's characterization, are a diffuse set of practices that cut across government and civil society, linking citizens to the state. The governmentalization of community facilates this by the creation of a whole array of discourses about community, for instance community regeneration, community experts, local community initiatives such as community policing, community safety and community development (Rose, 1999: 189). It is important not to see this as merely the exercise of social control, for it can also be the reverse. The language of community and of morality is increasingly entering political discourse (ethical investment, ethical foreign policy). But as Rose points out, this can be a superficial moralizing of politics or it can offer new possibilities for empowerment for an ethico-politics. Not too surprisingly, then, we find the discourse of community in the manifestos of the Clinton and Blair governments emphasizing voluntarism, charitable works, self-organized care (Rose, 1999: 171).

This ambivalence is present in the influential work of Amitai Etzioni (1995). His advocation of community was an American reaction to the dominance of rational choice and neo-liberalism in the 1980s. It was a vision that was quite far from the philosophical concerns of Charles Taylor and what I have characterized as liberal communitarianism. His call for a recovery of community was designed to create a sense of responsibility, identity and participation in order to make citizenship meaningful to a society that had become highly depoliticized and to which the state had become irrelevant. Community, for Etzioni, is a moral voice; it is not just a question of entitlements that the state can satisfy. Though his appeal to community has a radical dimension to it, it lacks a political voice, for according to this vision politics has become exhausted of meaning. His formulation of citizenship has very little to say about the role of the state, and democracy hardly figures in it. Also there is little discussion on social citizenship, which in general has been absent from American debates on citizenship (Fraser and Gordon, 1994). John O'Neill argues that 'it is evident that communitarian action without state involvement merely represents another version of voluntarism' (1994: 13; see also O'Neill, 1997). Etzioni's concerns lie with schooling, family and policing.

Etzioni is not arguing for a romantic return to a golden age of the past: 'America does not need a simple return to *gemeinschaft*, to the traditional community. Modern economic prerequisites preclude such a shift, but even if it were possible, such backpedaling would be undesirable because traditional communities have been too constraining and authoritarian. Such traditional communities were usually homogeneous' (1995: 122). His version of community is intended to be compatible with diversity and social differentiation. Though he explicitly says he is not advocating a nostalgic return to the past, it is significant that he constantly uses the term a 'return' to community or a 'recovery' of community, thus making the assumption that community was a thing of the past and the present is all the poorer for letting it pass. The idea of community is expressed very much in terms of personal proximity. Community entails voice, a 'moral voice', and social responsibility rests on personal responsibility. A concern with responsibility articulates a core idea of Etzioni's communitarianism, as is clear from his quarterly, *The Responsive Community*. Etzioni's conception of responsive community is rooted in 'social virtues' and 'basic settled values' (1995: 1–5). The family and the school are the typical institutions which can cultivate the kind of citizenship required by responsive community.

While Etzioni recognizes that complex societies and cities with many different cultural traditions cannot easily form the basis of community, his model is ultimately based on the idea of the traditional community. He grants that modern economic structures make the return to the past impossible and that traditional communities were too homogeneous and have been too constraining and authoritarian (1995: 122). The city, not the village, is his concern. Yet his definition of community as a moral voice rooted in social virtues and personal responsibility does not square with his view of community as being also highly differentiated. It is ultimately a reappropriation of the traditional idea of community as a cohesive unity.

The communitarian position suffers from a relative neglect of democracy, being almost entirely a theory of citizenship as a self-empowering force. Though it has in many respects reconciled itself with cultural diversity, in its concern with voluntarism, it absolves the state from responsibility for society but at the same time allows the state to be present in the regulation of society. The present discussion has summarized the main strands in communitarian thought. Underlying the different conceptions of community discussed is an assumption of community as cohesive and consensual, and, in its most influential forms, as primordialism. The tendency seems to be to depoliticize community by reasoning that ignores its internally differentiated nature. In the second part of this chapter, drawing from recent social theory, I offer an alternative to this view, stressing the heterogeneous and relational nature of community and its reflexive relationship to community.

COMMUNITY BEYOND UNITY: THE NEW SOCIAL THEORY OF COMMUNITY

In many ways the postmodern era is the age of community (Bauman, 1991: 246; see also Bauman, 1993). If this is the case, the revival of community is far from the ethos of traditional rural communities that offered an alternative to modernity in classical sociological theory. Moreover, the concept of community in recent social theory offers an alternative to the concerns of liberal communitarianism with the recognition of group identities (Isin and Wood, 1999). But as Alain Touraine has argued, there is a latent authoritarianism in the idea of community in so far as it is disconnected from citizenship (Touraine, 1997, 2000).

Today, the idea of community is central to postmodern social thought (Lash, 1994; Mellos, 1994). The identity politics of nationalism, religious revivalism, neo-fascism, new age travellers and the whole range of media cultures, such as the idea of 'virtual communities', all revolve around the idea of community. Indeed the very idea of the 'global village' is based on the idea of community, which also enters the identity politics of many social movements and recent notions of cyber-community (Jones, 1995). What has been lost is the primordialism of the traditional community. As Gerd Baumann (1991) has argued in his analysis of multiethnic communities, the idea of community can accommodate a notion of contestation and must not be anchored in cultural consensus or a symbolic order. Lichterman (1996) demonstrates a similar argument in his study of community and commitment. In an important article on the idea of community, Craig Calhoun has argued against the identification of community with consensual value systems, claiming that community has been an important dimension to radical popular mobilizations (Calhoun, 1983). Cotterrell (1995) argues that geographical proximity is not an essential characteristic of community; he also rejects the communitarian emphasis on shared values. In his view, communities can be very varied in size and character. Drawing from Luhmann, Cotterrell elucidates how social complexity makes proximity impossible and ultimately shifts the burden of trust from culture onto law. Thus, law is placed in the foreground in the contemporary conceptualization of community. Community also has a connection with communication and this makes trust possible. Trust does not exist in a vacuum outside social interaction. Since social interaction is essentially communicative, we must view trust as a process of social communication.

In order to understand contemporary developments which point towards the revival of community in the world today, we must part company from the sociological and philosophical myth of community in communitarian discourse. This myth is fundamentally incapable of understanding the real significance of community today: the appeal of community cannot be explained by reference to the quest for a lost totality, a moral or primordial order. The political philosophy of communitarianism is also limited in its understanding of the discourse of community since the terms of its debates have been almost entirely shaped by two issues: the related problems of accommodating difference and individualism. The postmodernized communities of the global era are highly fragmented, contested and far from holistic collectivities; they are characterized more by aesthetic and communicative codes than by a moral voice rooted in the cohesive world of tradition. Communities have become more open. In the following discussion I draw from two conceptions of community beyond unity, first the idea of the postmodernization of community and, secondly, Habermas's theory of community as a communication community. Both of these conceptions, despite their obvious differences, share an understanding of community as essentially open and incomplete.

Postmodern Communities

Under the conditions of postmodern complexity, according to Maffesoli in *The Time of the Tribes* (1996a), the age of the masses is giving way to new social relationships and as a result we have entered the age of the 'tribes'.[13] The idea of the tribe suggests for Maffesoli an 'emotional community', which is defined by an affectual and aesthetic aura. Community mediated experience of everyday life which, according to Maffesoli, involves the constant flow of images and situations. Unlike the communities of the past, which were spatial and fixed, emotional community is unstable and open, a product of the fragmentation of the social and the disintegration of mass culture. People are increasingly finding themselves in temporary networks, or 'tribes', organized around lifestyles and images. Maffesoli sees community extrapolating a sense of 'sociability' from the 'social'. Community still involves proximity, but this is temporary and has no fixed purpose; it is characterized by 'fluidity, occasional gatherings and dispersal' (1996a: 76). Community serves to 're-enchant' the world and to provide a sense of solidarity that draws its strength from proximity. But the new proximity is located in urban-metropolitan spaces and is an expression of what he calls the vitality and creativity of action. For Maffesoli this all amounts to the end of modernity: 'While modernity has been obsessed with politics, it may be equally true that postmodernity is possessed by the idea of clan, a phenomenon which is not without its effect on the relationship to the Other and, more specifically, to the stranger' (1996a: 104). Community is then something radically open and unconstraining.

Jean-Luc Nancy in *The Inoperative Community* (1991) defends the idea of community as relevant not only to modern but also to postmodern society. Community is the basis of human experience and the identity of the self as a social being. However, his notion of identity is more that of non-identity: the experience of otherness as an absence. His approach is far from that of communitarianism in that he does not hanker after a lost community and insists that community is always based on the individual and the experience of the 'other': 'Community is what takes place always through others and for others' (Nancy, 1991: 15). Stressing finitude or present time as the key to community, Nancy opposes the attempt to locate community in the past or as a project for the future. Community cannot be reduced to an organic concept of social relations or to a place; it is something that always negates itself and is constituted in the differential relations of human beings. The 'inoperative community' is the tendency of community to undermine or 'interrupt' itself in the self-assertion of its members and in the struggle to define community: community is itself the experience of the loss of community. Nancy's idea of community is not unlike that of Maurice

Blanchot (1988) in *The Unavowable Community*, community as an incomplete project, a shared absence. Yet, for all his attempt to render community compatible with postmodernity (in the sense of the experience of difference), Nancy ultimately retreats into a kind of communitarianism for his conception of community, which is very much influenced by Heideggerian hermeneutics and a postmodemized and secularized Christianity, reflecting a concern with community as ontological in the sense of the expression of a human essence.

An example of a postmodern approach to community that avoids the dangers of essentialism and recognizes the political nature of community is William Corlett's (1993) *Community Without Unity*. Corlett aims to apply the deconstructionist philosophy of Derrida to community, arguing that difference is the essence of community. Community, he argues, must be understood as something more than the problem of collective unity versus individualism; it is the mutual appreciation of differences and does not require a holistic notion of culture, for there is always an excess of meaning which cannot be reduced to a particular moment. In this context Bill Readings's (1996: 180–93) notion of the 'community of dissensus' is relevant. For Readings the community of dissensus is best exemplified in the postmodern university. A dissensual community would be one that has abandoned any attempt to find a unified point of legitimation: 'the university will have to become one place, among others, where the attempt is made to think the social bond without recourse to a unifying idea, whether of culture or of the state' (Readings, 1996: 191). This notion of community is very much opposed to the Habermasian notion of a communication community: 'A distinction must be drawn between the political horizon of consensus that aims at a self-legitimating, autonomous society and the heteronomous horizon of dissensus. In the horizon of dissensus, no consensual answer can take away the question mark that the social bond (the fact of other people, of languages) raises' (Readings, 1996: 187). We thus have here a very important notion of community as a discursive entity that can never be reduced to identity or to unity.

Communication Communities

Habermas's recent social theory (Habermas, 1996) offers an important alternative to the mainstream conceptions of communitarism and builds upon postmodern thinking.[14] For Habermas, communitarianism emphasizes the existing community too much and reduces politics to the ethical. He criticizes these models of political community on the grounds that they see community as too holistic and do not see how community, in so far as it is to be a foundation for citizenship, involves the transcendence of particular cultural traditions. His alternative concept of discursive democracy has the merit, he believes, of incorporating the strengths of the liberal and communitarian perspectives while rejecting their disadvantages. Discursive democracy resides not in the ethical substance, or form of life, of a particular community, nor in universal human rights or compromised interests as in liberalism, but in the rules of discourse and forms of argumentation whose normative content derives from the structures of linguistic communication which can always in principle be redeemed. Discursive democracy is rooted in the public sphere, which provides it with an informal institutional reality in civil society. Habermas is centrally concerned with the social conditions of critical debate in society and how such public discourse can shape democracy, which involves a relationship to legal institutionalization. Law is rooted in democracy, which in turn is rooted in public debate. Habermas is less concerned with actual participation in decision-making than in the necessity to have decision-making mediated by communication. In his model communication is essentially about contestation. Habermas also breaks from communitarianism in another crucial respect: he strongly defends the possibility of a postnational society whose collective identity is defined by reference to the normative principles of the constitution rather than by reference to a cultural tradition, territory or loyalty to the state. Only what he calls a 'patriotism of the constitution' can guarantee a minimal collective identity today (Habermas, 1996, 1998). This all amounts to a notion of community as a communication community.[15]

While Habermas has established the basis of a non-communitarian theory of community, his own alternative runs the risk of being too decontextualized. We need to see how community actually operates in the sense of real and lived communities. Habermas speaks from the perspective of the observer, a position he insists is available to everybody. In other words, cultural traditions are not so constraining as to prevent people from critically reflecting on their otherwise taken-for-granted assumptions. But, in general, community is a problem for Habermas, for whom the discourse ethic is modelled on face-to-face dialogue (Delanty, 1997a). It is for this reason that several thinkers, such as Benhabib, have sought to reconstitute Habermas's project around a more rooted understanding of communication as contextualized in communities of difference (Benhabib, 1992, 1996).

CONCLUSION

The debate on community and citizenship in communitarian political philosophy, the principal focus of this chapter, presupposed the national state as the reference point for the revival of community. Cultural com munity was generally seen in terms of national, or subnational, ethnically defined groups. I have pointed out some of the limits of this reasoning, without dismissing the relevant of the concept of community for citizenship. Community is an important basis for citizenship. Citizenship as membership of political community must draw on something more basic than politics. In this the communitarian critique of liberalism is relevant, since citizenship is more than membership of the democratic state. But communitarianism runs aground in its search for a more primordial kind of community.

Against the alternative modes of communitarian reasoning – republicanism and governmental variants of communitarianism – I have tried to show how recent social and political thought offers an alternative vision. Taking a more sociological view of community – suggested by various postmodern theories and the social theory of Habermas – community can be conceived as essentially open and incomplete. Deepening the sociological implications of this, community in today's global age is highly dissensual, porous and contested. The most striking aspect of community today relates to the dynamics of group formation. It must be said that underlying the idea of community is a notion of the group. Communitarian thought tends to take for granted the existence of a relatively coherent and stable cultural group. A community is thus held to be a group conscious of itself as a culturally defined entity, and is generally either a minority or majority. However, when examined critically this becomes less evident, for groups in general are not so easy to define, especially in terms of their status as minorities or majorities. For instance, Catholics are a minority group in Northern Ireland while in the island of Ireland they are a majority.[16] Moreover, the internal divisions within the community can be more decisive than the standing of the larger group in respect of other groups, as is vividly apparent in the case of the Protestant community in Northern Ireland. The boundaries between groups are not as tightly drawn as communitarian thought suggest. Groups are temporary, deterritorialized and cross-cutting. Moreover, they are internally differentiated, fluid and dissensual. They are not based on primordial, or essentialist, categories but are highly relational, that is defined by relation to other groups. I believe these dynamics of group formation also apply to the concept of community, which cannot be reduced to the relatively fixed categories that are typical of communitarian thought.

The implication that this has for citizenship is a reflexive relationship to community. Political community cannot simply appeal to an underlying, cultural community that provides an ontological foundation. Political community is not then derivative of cultural community, but is reflexively shaped by it. In this sense community is more social than cultural, and it is also more cosmopolitan in its openess. Elsewhere I have used the term 'cosmopolitan community' to express the reflexivity of community in terms of the recognition of group difference within as well as across groups (Delanty, 2000b). In this view, communication is central to community in the global age, allowing us to conceive of a community beyond unity and the communication of difference.

NOTES

1 An exception to this is republican communitarianism, which clearly is more concerned with the associational order of public life and the mobilization of social capital as opposed to cultural capital.

2 Indeed, as the work of Will Kymlicka demonstrates, many communitarian arguments can be equally well stated from a liberal perspective (Kymlicka, 1989, 1995). However, though putatively a liberal theorist of multiculturalism, his position is closer to communitarianism in its strong advocacy for special rights for large-scale territorially defined communities.

3 See in particular Helmut Plessner's classic work on community, recently translated into English (Plessner, 1999).

4 The following is a revised version of parts of Chapter 2 of my *Citizenship in a Global Age* (Delanty, 2000b).

5 This use of cultural democracy is in contrast to other uses, e.g. Trend (1997). In the communitarian sense used here it refers to something closer to 'ethnic democracy'.

6 A further significant work is Phillip Selznick's *The Moral Community* (1992).

7 That this debate on membership of community has occurred largely in North America is not surprising since there the impact of social citizenship has been less pronounced. In the absence of a state historically committed to social rights, the debate on citizenship has tended to be posed in terms of membership of community. Community has appeared to many to hold out the promise of a utopia destroyed by both society and the state. Rather than retrieve the state project, communitarianism seeks to recover a lost dimension of community the utopia of which modernity promised but destroyed. Communitarians can be seen as liberals disenchanted by liberal individualism. However, Canadian communitarianism is different. While it is a project in Canada, in the United States it is a challenge to the status quo. Moreover, Taylor's communitarianism, with its concern with cultural community, is also a critique of American liberalism.

8 In his later works, *Political Liberalism* (1993) and *The Law of Peoples* (1999), Rawls recognized that some of the assumptions of his early position were untenable, in particular the assumption of cultural consensus on a common conception of the good.

9 This is despite the fact that his work displays little substantive concern with citizenship.

10 On radical and feminist conceptions of citizenship see chapter 12 in this volume.

11 See Chapter 10 for a more detailed discussion of this tradition, which also goes under the heading of republicanism.

12 See also Wuthnow (1994), where the emphasis is on community in terms of support groups.

13 Some of the discussion in this section borrows from Chapter 6 of my *Modernity and Postmodernity* (Delanty, 2000a).

14 While Habermas has been a critic of postmodern theory, his work in fact shares much with postmodern thought, in particular the question of the openness of discourse (see Delanty, 1999).

15 To use a formulation that in fact was used by Karl-Otto Apel (1980).

16 On the problem of defining minorities, see Packer (1999).

REFERENCES

Agamben, G. (1993) *The Coming Community*. Minneapolis: University of Minnesota Press.

Apel, K.O. (1980) 'The a priori of the Communication Community and the Foundation of Ethics: The Problem of a Rational Foundation of Ethics in the Scientific Age', in *Towards a Transformation of Philosophy*. Routledge & Kegan Paul: London.

Arendt, H. (1958) *The Human Condition*. Chicago: Chicago University Press.

Barber, B. (1984) *Strong Democracy: Participatory Politics for a New Age*. Berkeley: University of California Press.

Bauman, Z. (1991) *Modernity and Ambivalence*. Cambridge: Polity Press.

Bauman, Z. (1993) *Postmodern Ethics*. Oxford: Blackwell.

Baumann, G. (1991) *Contested Cultures: Discourses of Identity in a Muti-Ethnic London*. Cambridge University Press: Cambridge.

Benhabib, S. (1992) *Situating the Self*. Cambridge: Polity Press.

Benhabib, S. (ed.) (1996) *Democracy and Difference: Contesting the Boundaries of the Political*. Princeton: Princeton University Press.

Blanchot, M. (1988) *The Unavowable Community*. Barrytown, New York: Station Hill Press.

Calhoun, C. (1983) 'The Radicalness of Tradition: Community Strength or Venerable Disguise and Borrowed Language', *American Journal of Social Sociology* 88 (5): 886–914.

Castells, M. (1996) *The Rise of the Network Society* (*The Information Age:* Vol 1). Oxford: Blackwell.

Cohen, A. (1985) *The Symbolic Construction of Community*. London: Tavistock.

Cohen, J. (1999) 'Does Voluntary Association Make Democracy Work?' in Smelser, N. and Alexander, J.C. (eds), *Diversity and Its Discontents: Cultural Conflict and Common Ground in Contemporary American Society*. New Haven: Princeton University Press.

Cohen, J. and Arato, A. (1992) *Civil Society and Political Theory*. Cambridge, MA: MIT Press.

Corlett, W. (1993) *Community Without Unity: A Politics of Derridian Extravagance*, Durham: Duke University Press.

Cotterrell, R. (1995) *Law's Community*. Clarendon: Oxford.

Dallmayr, F. (ed.) (1978) *From Contract to Community: Political Theory at the Crosswords*. New York: Marcel Dekker.

Delanty, G. (1997) 'Habermas and Occidental Rationalism: The Politics of Identity, Social Learning and the Cultural Limits of Moral Universalism', *Sociological Theory*, 15 (3): 30–59.

Delanty, G. (1999) *Social Theory in a Changing World*. Cambridge: Polity Press.

Delanty, G. (2000a) *Modernity and Postmodernity: Knowledge, Power, and the Self*. London: Sage.

Delanty, G. (2000b) *Citizenship in a Global Age: Culture, Politics and Society*. Buckingham: Open University Press.

Deutsch, K. et al. (1957) *Political Community in the North Atlantic Area*. Princeton University Press: Princeton.

Durkheim, E. (1957) *Professional Ethics and Civic Morals*. London: Routledge & Kegan Paul.

Durkheim, E. ([1893] 1960) *The Division of Labor in Society*. Glencoe, Ill.: Free Press.

Etzioni, A. (1995) *The Spirit of Community*. London: Fontana.

Frazer, E. (1999) *Problems of Communitarian Politics: Unity and Conflict*. Oxford: Oxford University Press.

Frazer, E. and N. Lacey (1993) *The Politics of Communitarianism: A Feminist Critique of the the Liberal Communitarian Debate*. Brighton: Harvester Press.

Habermas, J. (1996) *Between Facts and Norms: Contributions to a Discourse Theory of Law and Democracy*. Cambridge: Polity Press.

Habermas, J. (1998) *The Inclusion of the Other: Studies in Political Theory*. Cambridge, MA: MIT Press.

Isin, E. and Wood, P. (1999) *Citizenship and Identity*. London: Sage.

Jones, S. (ed.) (1995) *Cybersociety: Computer Mediated Communication and Community*. London: Sage.

Kymlicka, W. (1989) *Liberalism, Community and Culture*. Oxford: Clarendon Press.

Kymlicka, W. (1995) *Multicultural Citizenship: A Liberal Theory of Minority Rights*. Oxford: Clarendon Press.

Lasch, C. (1995) *The Revolt of the Elites and the Betrayal of Democracy*. New York: Norton.

Lash, S. (1994) 'Reflexivity and its Doubles: Structures, Aesthetics, Community', in Beck, U., Giddens, A. and Lash, S. (1994) *Reflexive Modernization: Politics, Tradition and Aesthetics in the Modern Social Order*. Cambridge: Polity Press.

Lichterman, P. (1996) *The Search for Political Community: American Activists Reinventing Commitment*. Cambridge: Cambridge University Press.

MacIntyre, A. (1981) *After Virtue*. London: Duckworth.

Maffesoli, S. (1996a) *The Time of the Tribes: The Decline of Individualism in Mass Society*. Sage: London.

Maffesoli, S. (1996b) *The Contemplation of the World*. Minneapolis: Minnesota University Press.

Marshall, T.H. (1992) *Citizenship and Social Class*. London: Pluto Press.

Mellos, K. (1994) 'The Postmodern Challenge to Community', *History of European Ideas*, 19 (1–3): 131–6.

Miller, D. and Walzer, M. (eds) (1995) *Pluralism, Justice, and Equality*. Oxford: Oxford University Press.

Morris, P. (1996) 'Community Beyond Tradition', in Hellas, P., Lash, S. and Morris, P. (eds), *Detraditionalization*. Oxford: Blackwell.

Mulhall, S. and Swift, A. (1996) *Liberalism and Communitarianism*. 2nd edition Oxford: Blackwell.

Nancy, J.-L. (1991) *The Inoperative Community*. Minneapolis: Minnesota Press.

Nisbet, R. (1953) *The Quest for Community*. Oxford: Oxford University Press.

Nisbet, R. (1967) *The Sociological Tradition*. Heinemann: London.

Oldfield, M. (1990) *Citizenship and Community: Civic Republicanism and the Modern World*. London: Routledge.

O'Neill, J. (1994) *The Missing Child of Liberal Theory: Towards a Covenant Theory of Family, Community, Welfare and the Civic State*. Toronto: University of Toronto Press.

O'Neill, J. (1997) 'The Civic Recovery of Citizenship', *Citizenship Studies*, 1 (1): 19–32.

Packer, J. (1999) 'Problems in Defining Minorities' in D. Fottrell and B. Bowring (eds), *Minority and Group Rights in the New Millennium*. The Hague: Kluwer.

Parsons, T. (1961) *Societies: Evolvtionary and Comparative Perspectives*. Eaglewood Cliffs: Prentice-Hall.

Plessner, H. (1999) *The Limits of Community: A Critique of Social Radicalism*. New York: Humanities Press.

Pocock, J.G.A. (1995) 'The Ideal of Citizenship since Modern Times', in R. Beiner (ed.), *Theorizing Citizenship*. New York: SUNY Press.

Putnam, R. (1993) *Making Democracy Work: Civic Traditions in Modern Italy*. Princeton: Princeton University Press.

Putnam, R. (1999) *Bowling Alone*. New York: Simon and Schuster.

Rawls, J. ([1971] 1981) *A Theory of Justice*. Cambridge, MA: Harvard University Press.

Rawls, J. (1993) *Political Liberalism*. New York: Columbia University Press.

Rawls, J. (1999) *The Law of Peoples*. Cambridge, MA.: Havard University Press.

Readings, B. (1996) *The University in Ruins*. Cambridge, MA: Harvard University Press.

Rose, N. (1999) *Powers of Freedom*. Cambridge: Cambridge University Press.

Sandel, M. (1982) *Liberalism and the Limits of Justice*. Cambridge: Cambridge University Press.

Selznick, P. (1992) *The Moral Commonwealth: Social Theory and the Promise of Community*. Berkeley: University of California Press.

Skinner, Q. (1978) *The Foundations of Modern Political Thought*. 2 vols, Cambridge: Cambridge University Press.

Stewart, A. (1995) 'Two Conceptions of Citizenship', *British Journal of Sociology*, 46 (1): 63–78.

Taylor, C. (1989) *Sources of the Self*. Cambridge, MA: Harvard University Press.

Taylor, C. (1994) *Multiculturalism: Examining the Politics of Recognition*. Princeton: Princeton University Press.

Tocqueville, A. de ([1835–40] 1969) *Democracy in America*. New York: Doubleday.

Tönnies, F. (1957) *Community and Society*. East Lansing: Michigan State University Press.

Touraine, A. (1997) *What is Democracy*? Oxford: Westview.

Touraine, A. (2000) *Can We Live Together? Equality and Difference*. Cambridge: Polity Press.

Turner, B. (ed.) (1993) *Citizenship and Social Theory*. London: Sage.

Trend, D. (1997) *Cultural Democracy*. New York: State University of New York Press.

Walzer, M. (1983) *Spheres of Justice*. New York: Basic Books.

Walzer, M. (1994) *Thick and Thin: Moral Argument at Home and Abroad*. Notre Dame: Notre Dame University Press.

Whittington, K. (1998) 'Revisiting Tocqueville's America: Society, Politics, and Association in the Nineteenth Century', *American Behavioral Scientist*, 42 (1): 21–32.

Wuthnow, R. (1994) *Sharing the Journey: Support Groups and America's New Quest for Community*. New York: Free Press.

Young, I.M. (1989) 'Polity and Group Difference: A Critique of the Ideal of Universal Citizenship', *Ethics*, 99: 250–74.

11

Radical Democratic Citizenship: Amidst Political Theory and Geography

CLAIRE RASMUSSEN AND MICHAEL BROWN

WHAT AND WHERE IS CITIZENSHIP?

'Citizenship?' she cocked her head quizzically and looked beyond me, 'You mean like standing around on July 1 waving flags saying, "Yay Canada"?'[1]

'No,' I quickly replied. 'I mean how people are *being* political around AIDS – at various times and places in their daily lives. How doing things like participating in the AIDS Quilt display – whatever else it is – is about claiming rights, duties, and membership in a political community.'

'Oh, I see. Okay, sure, I'll talk to you about that.'

This awkward exchange took place in 1993, as Michael secured another interview in his participant observation research on radical democracy and AIDS politics in Vancouver, Canada (Brown, 1997). It exemplifies both the promise and dangers of reconceptualizing citizenship from a radical democratic perspective.

Radical democratic theory, a term that gained currency through the work of Ernesto Laclau and Chantal Mouffe, seeks to revive the centrality of citizenship: an identity believed to be enervated or eliminated in liberal and Marxist theory by limiting political relations to the realm of the state or the economy, ultimately reducing citizenship to inefficacious flag-waving. To expand the importance of citizenship, radical democracy seeks to put forward a conception of democracy as a way of life, a continual commitment not to a community or state but to the political conceived as a constant challenge to the limits of politics. The woman's activism around the Canadian AIDS Quilt display thus wasn't beyond or outside politics – nor could it be *completely* reducible to 'the political'. But the political was a situated moment or dimension in that space. The goal of radical democratic theory is to generate an anti-essentialist politics that continually attempts to redefine itself in order to resist the exclusion of individuals and groups in the formation of the social order. The theory takes up the mantle of democracy to embrace the commitment to equality and participation but includes the radicalization of politics through a commitment to constant social change – and actions like the quilt display *did* change things. Drawing from a broad spectrum of theoretical sources and a history of social movements, radical democratic theory has generated a wide-ranging debate about how to define politics and how it ought to be practiced. The discussion has brought together political theory and practice and has provided an alternative to Marxism and liberalism on the Left (see for instance Mouffe, 1992, 1993). The consequence has been a reinvigoration of citizenship and recognition of the complexity of political struggles by marginalized groups. The attempt to bridge the gap between theory and practice and a range of theoretical resources has initiated dialogue on the Left but, as the dialogue incorporates radical democracy, it continues to struggle with the same problems it identifies in other theories of citizenship.

As an urban political geographer, Michael sought to spatialize Mouffe's theoretical project, which is not to say that he was testing radical democratic theory. In his ethnographic research on geographies of Aids activism, he was interested in pressing Mouffe's claims about 'new spaces of politics' literally: to understand how the 'whereness' of these new forms of citizenship mattered to their constitution, efficacy, and failures. In this way, the premise is that radical democratic theory could aid in understanding new forms – and locations – of the political responses to Aids in Vancouver during the early 1990s. For this reason we narrate that research as a means of explicating radical democracy throughout this chapter.[2] Thus, in what follows radical democracy is placed both in terms of its theoretical underpinnings and through empirical practices. To understand both the commonalties in and the differences between radical democratic and other forms of citizenship, we trace its history from the early stages in which it attempted to redefine the category of 'political' in order to democratize the category of 'citizenship.' Second we examine how the redefinition of citizenship through radical democratic theory enables new forms of political resistance that avoid the exclusionary tendencies of other forms of citizenship. Finally we address the multiple theoretical perspectives now falling under the category of radical democracy, a project making ambitious attempts to unite diverse theoretical and practical political perspectives and practices.

BEGINNINGS: STAKING OUT TERRITORY IN THE ERA OF POST-ISMS

Laclau and Mouffe's *Hegemony and Socialist Strategy* (1985) may be arbitrarily identified as the text that inaugurated the theorization of radical democratic citizenship.[3] As the text's subtitle, *Towards a radical democratic politics* suggests, it was intended to stimulate a rethinking of both democratic and radical politics, and their potential combination. Published in 1985, it emerged at what Laclau and Mouffe identified as a 'crossroads' in left-wing thought and politics. In both theoretical and actual terms, Marxism had proved to be, to state the case mildly, a disappointment, and largely powerless to stop the rise of the right wing in the United States and Western Europe. In their introduction, Laclau and Mouffe stake out territory they called post-Marxist, a category they hoped would indicate their commitment to leftist politics while also engaging in emerging debates between Marxism and post-structuralist theory in continental theory, and in debates between liberals and communitarians in Anglo-American theory. What Marxism and other competing theories on the Left lacked was a thorough theoretical understanding of how to define politics and the activity of political subjects. The purpose of a radical democratic theory was to wed the radical project of social change and the democratic project of empowerment by expanding the field of the political, both theoretically and practically.

Radical democracy's continual commitment to the concept of citizenship announces both a relationship to and a break from Marxist commitments. Marx was skeptical of the emancipatory potential of citizenship, which he referred to as a 'political lion's skin' (Marx, 1977: 46). For Marx, the danger of universal citizenship was its false promise of equality masked by the formal equality accorded to the status of citizen. Writing specifically about the question of citizenship, Marx argued that to eliminate religious preference as a category of citizenship was to banish religion to the private realm as if it did not make a difference in actual political, power-laden relationships. The category of citizen drove a wedge between the public, political citizen and the private self within civil society, hiding the real sources of power within the sphere of the private. With respect to the emergence of Aids and the rise of lesbigay political identities by the early 1980s, Marxist theory would have an especially difficult time, ignoring them entirely, dismissing their relevance as bourgeois ideology, or prompting a necessary rethinking of the multiplicity of politics (e.g. Castells, 1983).

To retain the category of citizenship without falling prey to the depoliticization of social relations, Laclau and Mouffe began from both a theoretical and practical consideration of left-wing politics and a rethinking of the location of power within society. *Hegemony and Socialist Strategy* begins with a historiography of the concept of hegemony within Marxist thought. The Gramscian category of hegemony resisted the reduction of politics to a relationship with either the state or the economy and instead highlighted the everyday relationships of power that enabled systems of domination to function. Beginning with hegemony was an attempt to envision a bottom-up form of politics where power is located in and can be challenged not just at the institutional level but, potentially, everywhere.[4] Laclau writes:

> Hegemony is not a type of articulation limited to the field of politics in its narrow sense but it involves the construction of a new culture – and that affects the levels where human beings shape their identity and their relations with the world (sexuality, the construction of the private, forms of entertainment, aesthetic pleasure, etc.) (1990: 189).

The emphasis on everyday forms of power was in part a response to actual political engagements on the Left, including the rise of social movements such as feminist, anti-racist, and environmental. New social movements defied both the centrality of the working class to leftist projects and the public/private boundaries that had defined politics in relationship to a fixed coherent public sphere or a privileged geography. The theoretical conclusion drawn was that the terrain of the political must be expanded to consider a wider range of potentially political activities and locations because power operated at a range of sites and the definition of politics itself was the chief site of politics: 'the distinctions public/private, civil society/political society are only the result of a certain type of hegemonic articulation, and their limits vary in accordance with the existing relations of forces at a given moment' (Laclau, 1990: 185). With respect to Vancouver, this rethinking impelled the point that public and private 'spheres' are often materialized in material locations.[5] Thus where in the city people did their politics must be considered broadly, since a preordained map would be theoretically reductionist. This point has implications for scholars who are trying to make sense of 'new' and 'old' spaces of politics (Brown, 1999; Staeheli, 1994, 1996).

If in part inspired by actual political struggle, radical democracy was also a response and challenge to existing democratic political theory that could not explain why social movements had emerged at a particular historical juncture nor incorporate them into their boundaries of the political. The democratic element of the theory was the expansion of politics to enable a broader contestation of power in spheres beyond the state or the economy. However, Laclau and Mouffe also believed that democratic theory at present was inadequate to the task and therefore, they called for not just an expansion but a radicalization of democracy, a move they felt was both theoretically necessary and strategically sensible. On the one hand, previous conceptions of citizenship were exclusionary, based upon a definition of the political primarily in relationship to a state, a community or the economy. But more than a theoretical error, the Left's embrace of these models of citizenship was also a strategic mistake. The Right had long been engaging in cultural politics that recognized the key insight of radical democracy: power operates through hegemony, or identity-forming practices that require a politics attentive to forming, not just appealing to the interests of, political subjects. Therefore, the Left needed to develop similar theories and strategies that recognized the relocation of the political and worked to democratize it.

In seeking different ways to conceive democratic citizenship, Mouffe's *The Return of the Political* (1993) dealt with the contemporary debates within democratic theory, focusing primarily on debates between liberalism and communitarianism. Her text drew on Carl Schmitt's identification of the paradox inherent in liberal democracy, the tensions between the liberal emphasis on the autonomy of the individual subject and the democratic impulse toward unity/community (Schmitt, 1996). The tension could not be resolved through the privileging of the liberty of the individual subject above the public good or the primacy of the common good above that of the individual. Rather, for Mouffe (2000), the paradox was the solution. Rather than choosing between the options or resolving the tensions, she proposed that the conflict between the competing political principles was the location of the political. The subject of politics and the terrain of politics were mutually constitutive and engaged in a constant struggle. The inability to resolve political questions enabled a reinvigoration of the political sphere by making no questions uncontestable and all issues potentially political and enabling no a priori exclusions from the political sphere as either private or epiphenomenal.

Aids politics seems especially relevant to this theoretical attempt at holding these two longstanding perspectives on citizenship in tension. Because it was at once so enormous and thoroughgoing – but also so personal and immediate, Aids intensely prompted Vancouverites to prioritize the right over the good, and simultaneously the good over the right – often around the same specific issue. Consider safer sex campaigns, for instance (e.g. Brown, 1995). Volunteers would head out to public sex areas such as parks and beaches to distribute condoms, lubricants, and other safer sex materials promoting the individual's right to health and freedom. Yet sex in a public place was illegal according to the laws evocative of community morality. Simultaneously, a quarantine law was resurrected that allowed for the detention of individuals who knowingly spread HIV through sexual contact. The point is not whether or which time liberal arguments 'won' over communitarian ones. The point is that they were both at work *there* and their tension was never-ending, always in process.

Radicalizing the site of democracy required a rethinking of the place of citizenship within politics. Politicizing social relations and resisting the privileging of any particular positions, citizenship could not be defined as a fixed identity in relationship to a state or a community. Mouffe describes citizenship as central to political subjectivity and defines it as political activity involving a struggle for hegemony, possible at any site from an engagement with the state, in the economy, or in the everyday practices of identity formation. Citizenship shifts from being an identity to being an *activity*, or more precisely a dimension of an activity that is always already understood as something else, too. By expanding who is or can be included in the category of citizenship, radical democracy retains the democratic commitment to egalitarianism, seeing all subjects as political subjects and recognizing a broader range of activities as political and potentially valuable resources for struggle. The means and ends of democratic citizenship, however, are transformed from belonging to a community through prescribed means of participation, such as voting or debating, to any particular goal emergent within a context and any potential means of achieving that goal. So for example, 'buddies' were AIDS Vancouver volunteers who provided a broadly defined 'support' for people living with HIV and AIDS. Support could be emotional, practical, or even spiritual. Buddies' roles were impossible to pin down and therefore their citizenship could be theorized across a wide array of social relations: family, charity, social work, even state–client relations.

Radical democratic theory identifies three principles key to understanding contemporary politics. First, all political struggles are temporary and contextual, contingent upon particular power relations that become antagonistic at particular times and places. Second, citizenship or political agency is defined not as an achievement or possession but as a continual struggle within those contingent and therefore constantly shifting relationships of power. Third, the location of struggle is not just between the competing interests of citizens but at the site of subject formation, in the way citizens understand their relationship to the political world and themselves.

The expanded site of politics had several important effects in thinking about the practice of radical democratic politics. First was a renewed interest in cultural politics that in part reflected and shaped British cultural studies.[6] The emphasis on the particularity of specific conflicts as well as the importance of a democratization of cultural issues informed an interest in cultural politics that fell outside of the sphere of traditional politics. Taking aim at the ways that hegemonic representations of subordinate groups reinforced relationships of domination and identifying how counter-hegemonic cultural productions could challenge these power relations, cultural studies went to work identifying the multiple sites where power reproduced itself socially through the media, societal norms, language, etc. What radical democracy proposed was not a Marxist unmasking of the ideological content of everyday life, but a counter-hegemonic project of democratizing access to and possibilities for representation. Rather than seeking an essential truth about politics, the emphasis upon cultural dimensions of citizenship expanded membership in the category of 'citizen', broadening participation in and therefore responsibility for the polity.

The attention to the context of political struggle and the emergence of particular forms of conflict and resistance did not occur just within cultural studies (e.g. Anthias and Yuval-Davis, 1992) but also in an extended discussion of the conditions of emergence of particular struggles and how they played within local contexts. Radical democracy enabled a recognition that the terrain or space of politics was not predetermined and therefore theorization of a shifting object of politics needed to acknowledge the way radical democratic action emerged in real conflicts. Therefore, citizenship was not understood purely as a relationship among political agents but as an interaction between agencies embedded in historical and spatial contexts. Citizenship could not be understood as an abstract set of features or principles but was a concept continually reshaped through actual political engagement in context.

Other ways of conceiving citizenship required that citizenship be understood as a relationship among political agents within a particular public, political space, a homogenous container for political action. The space of the political was strictly bounded by who or what counted as citizenship, whether the *polis* of the Greek world or the rational sphere of modernism. Radical democratic citizenship did not consider these boundaries as predrawn but as the very object of contestation. If cultural studies concerned itself primarily with how particular identities became political, geographers have emphasized the importance of recognizing how hegemonic formations emerge within particular contexts that shape conflicts and what forms resistance can and does take.

In Vancouver, it became clear that spaces that enabled the sorts of agonistic citizenship that Mouffe proffers were those that hybridized political theory's classic tripartite map of state/civil society and family. In locations such as the emerging Aids service organizations (ASOs) relations of both state and civil society ebbed and flowed. Grassroots organizations of a gay neighborhood, these organizations were also tied to the state through funding arrangements, contracting, rules, and regulations. People's own homes became points of condensation for relations of state and family because of buddy volunteers. The 'eyes and ears of the state apparatus' they were also part of the 'families we choose.' Finally, locations such as the AIDS Quilt display were public spaces of memorial, but also private spaces of family grief. Activism – in the form of education, awareness, and fundraising – works because they were also spaces of grief and mourning for those we lost.

The initial stages of theorizing radical democratic practice included several key changes in conceiving citizenship. First is the changing definition of the political from a predetermined bounded sphere in which political subjects acted upon or formed their interests to an indeterminate sphere of contestation determined by the particular conflict. Therefore, any activity is potentially political, leading to a practice of politics attentive to the multiple sites of politics. Emerging from the redefinition of the political is an emphasis on the particularity of political contests, leading to an interest in the historical and spatial specificity of struggles and why specific social formations become antagonistic and therefore political. Beyond the empirical and theoretical claims that citizenship is practiced and must be understood as an everyday activity of struggle, radical democracy also endorses a normative claim that politics on the Left must endorse democracy and a version that resists ever achieving its own goal. Laclau describes the normative vision of radical democracy as follows:

> There is democracy as long as there exists the possibility of an unlimited questioning; but this amounts to saying that democracy is not a system of values and a system of social organization, but a certain inflection, a certain 'weakening' of the type of validity attributable to any organization and any value. (1990: 187).

The description of democratic citizenship as a way of life invokes an active citizen constantly engaged in political struggle at a variety of sites, even in one's own identity. If radical democracy promised the return of the political, what remained unclear was how to generate the conditions of possibility for the democratic ethos to prevail and sustain itself and could the promise of perpetual struggle provide a unified project for the Left?

FLESHING OUT THE CITIZEN: POST-STRUCTURALISM AND BEYOND

As radical democracy promised, democracy was an open and changing project theoretically and practically. The context, both intellectual and political, shifted in the 1990s, resulting in reconsideration and deepening of the project of radical democracy. The rise of neoliberalism threatened to engulf oppositional politics altogether. The disenchantment with institutional politics was heightened in the early 1990s with an apparent tempering of the politics of the Left in both the United States and Britain, with a New Left, characterized by the 'Third Way' in Britain. Post-cold war politics turned away from the dichotomy of Left/Right and sought out the middle in a politics of consensus-building. Rather than heralding the rise of the New Left, however, radical democratic theory has warned that middle-ground politics in fact is a further elimination of politics, attempting to eliminate disagreement rather than engage in struggle, and therefore is an undemocratic step in leftist politics.

Theoretically, the terrain had also changed with an increasing urgency to find leftist alternatives to Marxism, which many saw as inadequate to address the hegemony of neoliberalism and the new challenge of the Right. Many theorists turned to the language of *democracy* as a potential project for the Left, generating projects both similar to and antagonistic towards radical democracy as articulated in the mid-1980s. Drawing extensively from Kantian liberalism, Jürgen Habermas has become an increasingly important figure. For Habermas, social consensus is not based upon a priori grounds, such as community or individual liberty, but is constructed through social dialogue based upon agreed procedures of political decision-making that ensure equal and universal participation on the basis of rational agreement.

Against the view of democracy as consensus-building on the bases of universal rationality, other theorists drew from the post-structuralist emphasis upon a political sphere characterized by extreme difference. Jean-François Lyotard in particular proposed a politics predicated on the possibility of absolute difference and the lack of any universal unifying element that was not exclusionary and therefore violent (Lyotard, 1984). Others argue that a politics of difference must be preceded by an ethical commitment to difference and Otherness that also precludes any form of politics claiming a positive identity.[7] Both alternatives conflicted with radical democracy's opposition to the elimination of conflict via accommodation that characterized the depoliticization they also opposed in Third Way politics.

To formulate a theory that resisted both the emphasis upon achieved universalism in Habermasian politics and the depoliticizing potential of particularism in some versions of post-structuralism, Mouffe herself has turned to the resource of the philosophy of language, drawing from Wittgenstein. She follows the lead of James Tully, whose works argue that Wittgenstein offers a vision of a community of language-users that is constituted both by the formal rules of language usage (vocabulary, grammar, etc.) and the 'family resemblances,' defined as similarities between linguistic practices that enable communication to function, even if only on partial and uncertain terms (Tully, 1995). While no linguistic utterance ever fully represents the object it is meant to convey, the project of communication does not cease.

Mouffe believes Tully's use of Wittgenstein demonstrates that political action need not decide between a politics of universalism and one of particularity but instead can use the tension between the two principles as the ground of politics. As particular groups represent their interests as universal, a struggle ensues, as no particular interest ever becomes the universal. Rather than declaring the goal of universal representation, a Habermasian goal, or repudiating any attempt to represent, the Lyotardian solution, Mouffe argues for a consistent struggle amongst particularities. Mouffe calls her middle ground 'agonistic pluralism,' an alternative to deliberative democracy that, she suggests, implies a potential end point or solution. Agonistic pluralism, on the other hand, suggests the element of struggle – agonism – among different groups – pluralism – recognizing the value of both particularity and struggles amongst particular elements as their social positions conflict. Central to defining agonistic pluralism is the struggle over defining the community, the central activity of citizenship: 'a democratic system requires the availability of those contending forms of citizenship identification. They provide the terrain in which passions can be mobilized around democratic objectives and antagonism transformed into agonism' (Mouffe, 2000: 104).

Like Mouffe, Laclau has also been concerned with balancing the post-structuralist concerns with difference with a search for grounds for waging actual political struggles. Central to his work is the problem of how a commitment to radical democratic citizenship can lead to social change. Since *Hegemony and Socialist Strategy* Laclau has focused on two key issues for radical democratic theory. First, he addresses the question of how political subjectivity operates without a definite sphere of the political or a preconceived notion of agency. Second, he is concerned with the problem of how a politics based upon and dedicated to the preservation of difference can build coalitions or communities with real counter-hegemonic potential.

For answers Laclau has moved further away from Marxist theory towards psychoanalytic and post-structuralist theories of subjectivity and the social. The concern with theorizing political subjectivity centers on the problem presented around formulating an anti-essentialist politics compatible with the identity-focused projects that characterized the social movements inspiring radical democracy. As previously mentioned, citizenship was not to be considered an identity possessed by subjects but was an activity that constructed identity. Therefore, identity could not be understood as prepolitical, either an authentic essence or the private construction of the subject – the liberal subject, but nor could it be fully determined by the essence of the social structure – the Marxist version. Rather, identity must become the ultimate site of politics, determined neither by the agent nor by the structure but in a process of struggle.

Laclau has drawn extensively from psychoanalytic and post-structuralist theory, particularly the Lacanian concept of 'Lack'[8] (Laclau 1990, 1994; see also Laclau et al., 2000). Identity is not pregiven and is achieved through a process of identification. The subject is characterized by lack, an inability to represent itself, while identity represents objectivity, a representation. The agency of citizenship is the act of identification, of seeking identity in familiar forms of representation – ethnicity, nationality, race, gender, and sexuality – that shape but do not determine the identity of the subject. The representations available to the subject are contextually contingent upon particular hegemonic formations and are subject to change. Therefore politics is not about defending the intrinsic interests of a political subject but about a struggle to construct subjects, making identity a primary ground for the operation of politics. The possibility of different identifications and changing hegemonic representations results in the failure of any identity ever to be fully determined and therefore identity is always a location of potential contestation: 'whatever identity the political agents have can only result from precarious and transient forms of identification' (Laclau, 1994: 37).

In Vancouver, Laclau's insights compel us to understand how important issues of lack and identification were to the formation of sexual-gender identity. For many citizens, their activism was linked to their sexuality, because of the high proportions of gay men affected by HIV and the imbrication of homophobia through the responses to the virus by the city and state. Thus the declaration that was frequent in most interviews, 'I am gay', names an identity that structures the possibilities of that subject by placing it within a set of gendered social relations that articulate a relationship to the political world and to the self.

The commitment to anti-essentialism presents a second problem for radical democratic theory and practice, sustaining collective projects capable of confronting hegemony without repeating the exclusions it attempts to avoid. Marxists in particular felt radical democracy was a diversion from real political commitment on the Left.[9] As a means of understanding how identity/identification translated into political struggle, Laclau connected post-structuralist ideas about the 'emptiness' of signifiers with the Gramscian concept of articulation. According to theories of signification, specific signs (linguistic or social) acquire meaning, as we have seen, only through identification. So, for example, meaning becomes associated with words arbitrarily and has no necessary connection with their function within the linguistic system or any external, objective meaning. Over time, however, the meaning is sedimented by its shared usage. Laclau believes political identities function in the same manner. Without any necessary content, political identities are subject to change and therefore may become the object of struggle to change their position within the system. Just as a word may be mis-spelled or pronounced, or may be misused or even forgotten, so too can political identities be changed through different use within the system. Identity, therefore, becomes a function of the system in which it operates but is also liable to change through the agency of subjects who, by identifying with a particular identity, may change it.

To understand how identity becomes a site of collective political struggle, it is important to understand why the metaphor of language is central here. Just as language requires a language community to create meaning, so too do political identities imply a larger community whose meanings exist only in relationship to one another. The relations between meanings are such that often when one shifts, others are impacted. So, for example, gender and race acquire meaning in relationship to one another and their meanings, not moored to a determinate content, relate to one another in specific contexts. To understand how these relations can be transformed into political relationships, Laclau uses the Gramscian idea of articulation, the idea that specific commonalties, though not identical to one another, can become the basis of a shared project. Articulation enables a politics that operates at a variety of scales from individual identity formation to mass political movements.

A chain of signifiers that articulate with one another represents itself as unified with a common interest. The example Laclau often appeals to is in a moment of social unrest when a series of unrelated events, such as a factory workers' strike action, a university student protest and a civil rights action occur in proximity to one another. They are interpreted as shared resistance to economic hegemony and, for example, the initial strike is elevated to represent the shared opposition, a particular representing a common interest. The articulation of the demands together and the representation of a counter-hegemonic interest enable a collective political movement to form (Laclau, 1994). The interest is, of course, not universal but may represent itself as such to present a challenge to claims to universality by the hegemonic power. The emptiness of the signification – its emergence within a context and its arbitrary representation of a chain of identities – guarantees that the struggle will not succeed as a universal signification and will eventually itself come to be the grounds of struggle. The progressive stages of identification, articulation, and dissolution guarantee both a substantive challenge to hegemonic power and the promise of an ongoing struggle since any chain of articulations must eventually break. The emptiness of signification is both the possibility and impossibility of citizenship as an identity defined through struggle.

To return to the 'I am gay' performative as a site of political contestation, we may see the chains of empty signification at work. The signifier is already in circulation as a term of negativity but is reappropriated to come to signify a range of political exclusions on the basis of the norms of gender and sexuality. 'Gayness' articulates together a set of identities with a common relationship to exclusion on the basis of sexuality, those 'named' by the identity 'gay' and therefore generating a politicized community (see Brown, 2000). At the same time, however, Butler would remind us that the democratization of queer identity requires a persistent recognition of its own failure to achieve universal representation and 'to consider the exclusionary force of one of activism's most treasured contemporary premises' of the achievement of a positive identity (Butler, 1997: 227). And so, for example, while Aids organizations started out as upper middle class gay white men's organizations, the presence of women, lesbians, hemophiliacs, heterosexuals, drug users, children, homeless people, working class people, natives, Asians and other 'others' challenged the exclusions and fixity of a salient political identity through which citizenship had emerged. In Vancouver, Aids was a 'gay disease'; but it also was not. People who responded to Aids were gay; but they were not. The citizens they were trying to help were gay; but they were not. As Butler would have it, gays' response to Aids in Vancouver was always 'queered'.

If the early stages of radical democratic theory focused on seeing citizenship in a wider range of places, more recent work in radical democratic theory has attempted to sketch the outlines of how radical democracy ought to be practiced. Further placing citizenship amidst facets of identity, democratic citizenship requires a commitment to awareness of and engagement in a self-critical politicization of identity.

The core of radical democratic citizenship is an attempt to retain the egalitarian impulse in the idea of citizenship as a means of belonging to a political community without depoliticizing or excluding other elements of identity relevant to power relations. While sympathetic to Marx's fear that citizenship becomes an ideological veil for other modes of social inequality by declaring a universal political equality, radical democracy maintains that citizenship can be a liberatory identity by remaining an open site of struggle. The balance between the universalizing claims to citizenship and the particular demands to represent the content of citizenship can become the primary site of democracy. The very failure of citizenship to attain universality becomes its emancipatory potential as competing claims to the category of citizenship emerge through political struggle, allowing persistent challenges to any hegemonic forms of social order. As a consequence, the discussion of citizenship has been reinvigorated on the Left (see Shafir and Gershon, 1998).

The deployment of the category of citizen as an unfixed political signifier, not determined by any political or social border, has brought radical democratic theory into contact with a number of recent trends in political and social theory grappling the unique problems of globalization and persistent capitalist hegemony. By redefining citizenship as the site of subject formation, radical democracy has become a means of talking about identity politics not just as a particularistic struggle for access to the benefits of citizenship but as a shared movement to expand the political sphere and the meaning of citizenship through contingent and ongoing struggles.

Representative of the impact of radical democracy in defining citizenship is David Trend's 1996 collection *Radical Democracy*, bringing together theorists as different as bell hooks and Stanley Aronowitz and commitments ranging from feminism to socialism to post-colonialism. According to Trend, radical democracy has invigorated politics on the Left as a model that 'gives vitality to the impetus for democratic principles. The politicization of social spaces formerly considered neutral makes apparent the often unacknowledged power relations in everyday activities' (Trend, 1996: 5). The openness to multiple forms of political contestation provides theoretical and practical struggles under the banner of radical democracy. The language of citizenship has crept into numerous discourses about the political.

In feminism, theorists such as Iris Marion Young and Nancy Fraser have appealed to many of the theoretical resources of radical democracy to develop an anti-essentialist feminist politics. Young, Fraser and Butler all claim that identity categories such as 'woman' are fundamentally political identities that can be both the basis for hegemonic power and the basis of challenge themselves, without diminishing the power of identity-based politics. Young, for instance, argues that *groups* may make claims on the basis of exclusion from the category of citizen. Rather than basing those claims upon the shared universal qualities of individuals, thereby depoliticizing the characteristics of the group upon which the exclusion has been based, Young argues that groups rights may demand a counter-hegemonic ideal of community that contests existing boundaries of inclusion and exclusion (Young, 1992).

The multiple locations of citizenship have also enabled a broader discussion of how citizenship may operate on multiple scales, from the local to global (Brown, 1995). While the processes of globalization have modified the boundaries and importance of the nation-state, a concept of citizenship tied to the nation-state seems increasingly untenable. Calls for multicultural or global citizenship resonate with radical democratic emphases on the locating social power at sites beyond the macro levels of the state and the economy and at different scales, recognizing that power is dispersed throughout the social field and is actualized at particular locations. In Vancouver, for example, radical democracy was never simply or solely local politics.[10] Personnel and resources were exchanged with Guatemalan Aids activists. A toll-free helpline placed citizenship in cyberspace that spanned far beyond the city limits. Persons With Aids Society members in Vancouver pressed drug companies to make their products more affordable to PWAs in Africa and other extra-local sites. Immediately juxtaposing the dead individual with the national and international scope of the disease, the Quilt display poignantly 'glocalized' Aids. And the International Aids Conference of 1996 – including oppositional activism – was held in Vancouver, where local politics imbricated with global issues in multiple ways, not least of which were the glaring inequities between core and periphery in affordability and availability of the newly developed protease inhibitors and 'drug cocktails.'

Theoretically, radical democracy has deepened its attempts to draw from a variety of resources on the Left, deepening its engagement with both the post-structuralist and Anglo-American liberal traditions. A dialogue has ensued between radical democracy and American pragmatism primarily through Richard Rorty. Committed to a version of liberal democracy that does not require a foundational commitment to any universal qualities of citizens, such as rationality, Rorty argues that radical democracy may offer a non-foundational means of theorizing political identity (in Mouffe, 1996). While Rorty maintains a commitment to liberal values (though for pragmatic and political reasons, not on moral or ontological grounds), he notes the shared emphasis upon identity as contingent and strategic.

Radical democratic theory has also been influential within and influenced by debates about deconstruction. Most recently, Jacques Derrida, not known for endorsing political principles, has argued in favor of a 'democracy of the future,' that, like radical democracy, demands a commitment to a fundamental openness in the political field. Derrida's 'community without unity' outlines the ideal of a political community based upon an assumption of difference, without fixed borders and continually shifting (Derrida, 1994, 1998). While deconstruction should not be conflated with radical democracy, proponents have noted similarities in the emphasis upon difference, particularity, and context. The importance of subject formation in radical democracy maps onto deconstructive concerns with the emergence of identities within a context. The emergence of meaning – particularly the meaning of citizenship – within a particular time and place implies that these meanings are always subject to change and, therefore, power relations are always unfixed and a site of struggle. So for instance, many interviewees would bristle at Michael's imposition of 'citizenship' on their responses to AIDS in Vancouver (however locally sensitive and contextual he was being) through his published work, including this very chapter. For them, what they did was decidedly not 'citizenship', and who is Michael to appropriate their actions' meaningfulness? Similarly, by stressing specific relations (like buddies) as citizenship, that move does occlude and elide other ways of knowing that relationship. Citizenship is foregrounded, charity and compassion are backgrounded.

If radical democracy has become a common, almost hegemonic means of thinking about citizenship, its diversity is both its strength and its weakness. While it provides an alternative to socialism and liberalism on the Left, many critics argue that radical democracy is not a *radicalization* of either democratic or Marxist theory but represents an extension of liberalism not that different from the theories it critiques. The inclusionary impulse in radical democratic citizenship that wants to incorporate all elements of identity into the realm of politics repeats the very danger Marx warned about, a universalizing category that does not recognize its own exclusions. By locating politics potentially everywhere, the consequence may be to render the category meaningless or trivial.

A second problem presented by the openness implied in radical democracy is its vulnerability to the same critiques it makes of other versions of democratic theory. Mouffe's distinction between deliberative democracy and agonistic pluralism, presented in *The Democratic Paradox* (2000) leaves the reader with several puzzles. 'Agonistic pluralism' is presumably distinct from deliberative democracy in that it resists the arrival at a mutually agreed upon, rational consensus in favor of constant agonistic struggle towards democratic inclusion. The purpose of keeping the political open is to avoid the violence of exclusion of those outside of the sphere of citizenship. But the emphasis on struggle requires that *agonism* must remain distinct from *antagonism*, or disputes that dissolve into or are resolved via violence. While the liberal response to this problem is to exclude from the political intractable and potentially violent conflicts, radical democracy cannot make such a priori exclusions and therefore must find alternative ways to, in Mouffe's terms, transform enemies into adversaries. Radical democracy does not look to the liberal value of tolerance as a means of resolving political disputes, noting that universal tolerance requires the exclusion of those political issues that may cause intractable conflict.[11] As an alternative, it proposes that the instability of identity and the constant challenges to hegemonic and fixed identities can prevent the 'Balkanization' of difference, a move that seems already to presuppose the existence of competing political norms with which to identify and political subjects able to participate in and committed to the democratic project.

If radical democracy was premised upon attention to difference and particularity, the difficulty in distinguishing and mediating between democratic and anti-democratic forms of identity and politics continues to trouble the project both theoretically and practically. The anti-totalitarian and anti-universalist origins of the theory have left unanswered the question of how to challenge groups or movements that are specifically based upon exclusion and difference but still exercise power, often dominant power. The rise of militantly particularistic groups such as the religious Right raises questions about how to differentiate between and respond to different forms of anti-democratic politics.

The challenges facing radical democracy in its attempt to generate an active and context-based conception of citizenship resemble the very problems identified in the Marxist critique of the liberal citizen as too abstract and inattentive to real, material power relationships. The theoretical tendencies to overabstraction highlight the necessity of attention to the context in which political struggles emerge and are played out, in other words the practical grounding of democratic practice. If radical democracy highlights the importance of seeing the activity of citizens as potentially anywhere, spatializing democracy can concretely locate these political moments to continually reexamine the meaning of democratic commitments in certain struggles. For example, returning to the dialogue with which we opened this chapter, we might ask, who is Michael to label the woman's praxis as 'citizenship'? What if she disputes that claim and signifies it as charity instead? Isn't this imposition of meaning onto social relations ironically anti-democratic, since potentially Michael's framing has been rather more widely disseminated internationally through his writing and teaching? Keeping citizenship a contested and perpetually interrogated category works well in the abstract, but it becomes problematic when it is spatialized in real spaces and times amidst unequal power relations.

CONCLUSION

In this chapter we have sought to explain the discussions and debates over citizenship that are being reconceptualized as radical democracy and have invigorated political theory. We traced the history of the concept's origins in response to both Marxism and debates within classic political theory between liberalism and communitarianism and discussed its continual engagement with contemporary theory, most notably post-structuralism. By redefining and expanding the understanding of politics, citizenship is recognized as a practice relating political identities, everyday practices, and political communities. As Michael's work in Vancouver demonstrates, the lens of radical democracy sees a broader range of practices engaged in continual struggles over political meanings that cannot be confined to a single site. Citizenship understood as the struggle to define the terrain of the political broadens the theoretical and empirical possibilities for democracy. It remains to be seen, however, whether this innovative and in so many ways helpful theoretical turn can navigate the various rocks and hard places it charted for previous theories of democracy and politics.

NOTES

1 July 1st is Canada Day, the national holiday.

2 Other geographers have explored radical democracy (e.g. Massey, 1995; Jones and Moss, 1995). That work focused on importing its notions of de-centered identity into geographic thinking generally – rather than exporting geography into political theory.

3 The term 'radical democracy' is often associated with Rousseau's *Social Contract*. Although important differences exist between Rousseau's democracy and contemporary theories, they do share a commitment to radical egalitarian and primacy of political life. Another important theoretical point shared is recognition of the modern and/or liberal value of the autonomy of the individual, which both versions argue is possible only within the sphere of the political. Important differences, however, must be recognized, including Rousseau's belief in the possibility and desirability of a unified collective will and his privileging of the public over the private, views that differ from contemporary emphases upon difference and social antagonism.

4 The emphasis on 'micropolitical' relationships is shared with Foucault's theory of power, a relationship briefly mentioned by Laclau (1990) and Dyrberg. Gramscian hegemony, however, retains more of a focus upon how cultural politics reinforce larger structures of domination (specifically, capitalism). At times, radical democracy deploys both conceptions of power. However, the emphasis on relationships between universalism and particularity and coalition building (see below) indicates that radical democracy may remain closer to a Gramscian belief that micropolitics can and ought to engage with larger power structures.

5 This claim does not imply a simple equivalence between 'sphere' and 'location'. For instance, Staeheli (1996) prompts us to note the distinction between public–private spatial divides and public–private action divides. Michael's work in New Zealand (Brown, 1999) similarly deconstructs the unexamined assumptions in urban politics generally. Often groups contingently map these two axes against each other to stake political claims (e.g. bringing feminist equality arguments into the bedroom or same-sex couples kissing in public spaces of civil society).

6 British cultural studies are generally associated with the Birmingham program and Stuart Hall though it has expanded, particularly in the United States. Hall and others maintain an ambivalent relationship to Laclau and Mouffe's work but they generally share the wider definition of the political sphere and to leftist politics, especially social movements. Original cultural studies also drew extensively from Gramsci and used the idea of articulation, discussed below. The most explicit discussion of cultural studies' engagement with radical democracy can be found in 'On postmodernism and articulation: an interview with Stuart Hall', published in 1986 in the *Journal of Communication Inquiry*. For a thorough discussion of various engagements with radical democratic theory and social theory in Britain, see Smith (1998).

7 Mouffe (2000) groups together theorists such as Jacques Derrida, Emmanuel Levinas and Jean-Luc Nancy as the 'post-modern ethical theorists' who privilege the ethical over the political. Although Laclau and Mouffe have been critical of Lyotard, they both argue that radical democracy and deconstruction share a number of key commitments though deconstruction. Both authors express reservations about whether deconstruction offers an adequate political project (Mouffe 1993, Laclau 1996).

8 For discussion of radical democracy's relationship to post-structuralism, particularly in relationship to Foucault's theory of power, see Dyrberg (1998).

9 Following the publication of Hegemony and Socialist Strategy, (Laclau and Mouffe, 1985) a sustained debate on the merits of radical democracy was waged in the *New Left Review*, including an exchange between Norman Geras and Laclau and Mouffe in 1987.

10 For a fuller discussion see Brown (1995).

11 In liberal theory, the line is usually drawn between the public and the private, delineating which questions are political and which are not, a move which many, especially feminists and critical race scholars, have argued is already a political act (see Staeheli, 1995; Brown, 1999).

REFERENCES

Anthias, Floya and Nira Yuval-Davis (1992) *Racialized Boundaries: Race, Nation, Gender, Colour and Class and the Anti-Racist Struggle*. London: Routledge.

Brown, Michael (1995) 'Sex, scale, and "the new urban politics": HIV prevention strategies from Yaletown, Vancouver', in D. Bell and G. Valentine (eds), *Mapping Desire: Geographies of Sexualities*. London: Routledge, pp. 245–63.

Brown, Michael (1997) *RePlacing Citizenship: AIDS Activism and Radical Democracy*. New York: Guilford.

Brown, Michael (1999) 'Reconceptualizing public and private in urban regime theory: governance in AIDS politics', *International Journal of Urban and Regional Research*, 23: 70–87.

Brown, Michael (2000) *Closet Space: Geographies of Metaphor from the Body to the Globe*. London: Routledge.

Butler, Judith (1997) *Bodies that Matter*. New York: Routledge.

Castells, Manuel (1983) *The City and the Grassroots*. Berkeley: University of California Press.

Derrida, Jacques (1994) *Specters of Marx: the state of the debt, the work of mourning and the new international*. London: Routledge.

Derrida, Jacques (1998) *The Politics of Friendship*. London: Verso.

Dyrberg, Torben Bech (1997) *The Circular Structure of Power*. London: Verso.

Jones, J.P. and Moss, Pamela (1995) 'Democracy, identity, space', *Society and Space*, 12: 253–257.

Laclau, Ernesto (1990) *New Reflections on the Revolution of our Time*. London: Verso.

Laclau, Ernesto (1993) *Emancipation(s)*. London: Verso.

Laclau, Ernesto (ed.) (1994) *The Making of Political Identities*. London: Verso.

Laclau, Ernesto, Butler, Judith and Zizek, Slavoj (2000) *Contingency, Hegemony and Universality*: Contemporary Dialogs on the Left. London: Verso.

Laclau, Ernesto and Mouffe, Chantal (1985) *Hegemony and Socialist Strategy*. London: Verso.

Lyotard, Jean-François (1984) *The Postmodern Condition*. Minneapolis: University of Minnesota Press.

Massey, Doreen (1985) 'Thinking radical democracy spatially', *Society and Space*, 13: 283–8.

Marx, Karl (1977) *Selected Writings*. ed. D. McLellan, Oxford: Oxford University Press.

Mouffe, Chantal (ed.) (1992) *Dimensions of Radical Democracy*. London: Verso.

Mouffe, Chantal (1993) *The Return of the Political*. London: Verso.

Mouffe, Chantal (ed.) (1996) *Deconstruction and Pragmatism*. London: Verso.

Mouffe, Chantal (2000) *The Democratic Paradox*. London: Verso.

Shafir, Gershorn (1998) *The Citizenship Debates: A Reader*. Minneapolis: University of Minnesota Press.

Schmitt, Carl (1996) *The Concept of the Political* trans George Schwab. Chicago: University of Chicago Press.

Smith, Anne Marie (1998) *Laclau and Mouffe's Radical Democratic Imaginary*. London: Routledge.

Staeheli, Lynn A. (1994) 'Restructured citizenship in Pueblo, Colorado', *Environment and Planning A*, 26: 849–71.

Staeheli, Lynn A. (1996) 'Publicity, privacy, and women's political action', *Society and Space*, 14: 601–19.

Trend, David (ed.) (1996) *Radical Democracy: Identity, Citizenship, and the State*. London: Routledge.

Tully, James (1995) *Strange Multiplicity: Constitutionalism in an Age of Diversity*. New York: Cambridge University Press.

Young, Iris Marion, (1992) *Justice and the Politics of Difference*. Princeton: Princeton University Press.

Part Four

FORMS

12

Sexual Citizenship

RUTH LISTER

Until fairly recently, the notion of 'sexual citizenship' would have been dismissed as an oxymoron. As conventionally understood, citizenship transcends and is disconnected from the body and sexuality. The sexual pertains to the 'private' sphere, whereas citizenship is quintessentially of the 'public' sphere. The idea of 'sexual citizenship' thus defies and disrupts the public–private divide, which has traditionally underpinned citizenship.

The concept has appeared in the citizenship literature only relatively recently. It has two different, though overlapping, meanings. The first signals a shift in the terrain of what is considered relevant to citizenship to include 'the intimate' (Plummer, 1995). As such it acts as 'a sensitizing concept', highlighting 'new concerns, hitherto marginalized in public discourse: with the body, its possibilities, needs and pleasures; with new sexualized identities; and with the forces that inhibit their free, consensual development in a democratic polity committed to full and equal citizenship' (Weeks, 1998: 37–8).

The second concerns sexuality as a determining factor in the allocation of the rights (and to a lesser extent, responsibilities) associated with citizenship. This usage, in turn, takes two forms. One emphasizes access to the traditional triad of civil, political and social citizenship rights; the other, the articulation of new claims to 'sexual rights', understood as 'a set of rights to sexual expression and consumption' (Richardson, 2000a: 107). At issue, in particular, is the citizenship status of 'sexual minorities', namely those who do not conform to the patterns of institutionalized 'hegemonic heterosexuality' (Richardson, 1998: 83).

This chapter deploys 'sexual citizenship' as a broader umbrella term to include also a discussion of citizenship as a gendered concept. The latter has been the subject of a substantial, international, feminist citizenship literature, which is better established than the more recent literature on sexual citizenship. It should be noted, though, that gendered perspectives on citizenship are not normally discussed under the rubric of 'sexual citizenship'. Nevertheless, as we shall see, there are clear interconnections between the two. Moreover, people's lives as citizens (or partial citizens) and their relationship to citizenship are not lived in neat, separate compartments labelled 'gender', 'sexuality', 'race', 'disability' and so forth. Thus, many scholars would argue that, ultimately, both gendered and sexual citizenship need to be theorized as elements of a wider 'differentiated', pluralist, citizenship, which embraces diversity and addresses socio-structural divisions (see, for instance, Isin and Wood, 1999; Lister, 1997; Mouffe, 1992; Yuval-Davis, 1997a, and 1997b; Yuval-Davis and Werbner, 1999; Young, 1990, 2000).

The chapter will very briefly locate sexual citizenship within this broader framework. Its starting point is the history and roots of the exclusion from and partial inclusion into citizenship of women and 'sexual minorities', for this exclusion has been the catalyst for much of the literature and politics of gendered and sexual citizenship. It then analyses citizenship as a gendered and sexualized concept (including sexual rights), which leads into a discussion of strategies to achieve a more inclusive form of citizenship in gendered and sexual terms. In each case, these can be understood as strategies designed primarily to promote either 'equality' or 'difference', although the case will also be made for moving beyond this long-standing dichotomy.

FROM EXCLUSION TO PARTIAL CITIZENSHIP

Citizenship has been described as a 'contextualised concept' (Siim, 2000: 1. See also Molyneux, 2000). Both women and 'sexual minorities' experience exclusionary citizenship practices and fight for full inclusion 'from the vantage point of specific, differentiated cultures and practices of citizenship as they are consolidated in the countries in which they live, wish to live or are obliged to live' (Saraceno, 1997: 32). This needs to be borne in mind when reading an account written from a Western, and in particular British, perspective. That said, the underlying dynamics of exclusion and partial inclusion are sufficiently common, even if articulated in particular ways in different national and cultural contexts, to warrant a degree of generalization.

Women's exclusion from citizenship can be traced back to classical Greece where women, together with slaves, were non-citizens and only free men were deemed worthy to participate as citizens in the *polis* (Burchell, Chapter 5 in this volume). In the modern era, the triad of liberal citizenship rights identified by T.H. Marshall were typically won by women in Western societies later than men and not necessarily in the order identified by Marshall (Smith, Chapter 6 in this volume). In particular, as late as the nineteenth century, when civil rights were generally well established for men in many Western countries, married women still did not exist as independent individuals with civil rights but were subject to the will of their husbands. Full civil rights were not achieved until well after the franchise. Women also typically won the vote later than men in the West; in postcolonial societies, in contrast, they won the vote at the same time, often reflecting their involvement in liberation struggles, although this has not necessarily translated into effective equal political citizenship with men (Walby, 1994).

Today, women in some non-Western societies still do not enjoy full civil and political rights (Peters and Wolper, 1995). In Afghanistan, where citizenship has been described as 'radically unlike its Western counterpart in almost every conceivable sense', they were deprived of rights under the Taliban that they previously enjoyed (Pourzand, 1999: 89). In the West, women's admission to formal citizenship has been on male terms, which means that, in practice, they often continue to be lesser citizens. Thus, for example, although they have achieved the vote, they are grossly under-represented in most parliaments (the Nordic and Scandinavian countries, together with Scotland, being the shining exceptions to the rule) and access to social insurance benefits (a key element of social rights in most countries) is restricted where women do not comply with male employment patterns. Overall the greatest advances on both the political and social fronts have been in Scandinavia (Siim, 1999, 2000).

Women's struggle for citizenship as women dates back to the end of the eighteenth century in countries such as England and France. The claims of 'sexual minorities' are more recent, reflecting their lesser visibility, their initial less explicit exclusion from citizenship rights and their more recent emergence as a social movement.[1] Today, their citizenship is, in some ways, even more marginal than that of (heterosexual) women: 'Often as individuals, they remain oppressed (silenced, invisible or subject to harassment in public); as a group, the political legitimacy of their constituency and their claims of citizenship rights are regularly called into question' (Isin and Wood, 1999: 71). In some parts of the world, homosexuality is still criminalized and lesbians and gays are denied basic civil rights (*New Internationalist*, 2000; UNDP, 2000). Amnesty International has recorded the 'execution, torture, imprisonment, and other forms of persecution of lesbians and gay men' (Dorf and Perez, 1995: 332).[2]

Diane Richardson has analysed the partial citizenship of lesbians and gay men, in relation to Marshall's triad, in the British context. With regard to civil rights, she points to the exclusion, until very recently, from the right to serve in the armed forces, the former locus of citizenship.[3] The other most important example concerns the right to marry. Only the Netherlands has (recently) granted this right to same-sex citizens. A number of other countries, excluding Britain, now permit the civil registration of gay partnerships, which carry most of the legal rights associated with marriage.[4] Richardson also cites as an example of a denial of the right to justice 'the lack of protection in law from discrimination or harassment on the grounds of sexuality' (1998: 88).[5]

Politically, although in Britain lesbians and gay men are not formally excluded from political rights and despite an increase in the number of openly gay and lesbian MPs in recent years, it is still difficult to 'come out' in the formal political system. Without a legitimate public presence, full and effective citizenship cannot be said to exist. Representation of lesbian and gay concerns in the formal political process tends to be limited, marginalized and dismissed as 'political correctness', a label used by dominant groups in the West to ridicule and silence the claims of oppressed groups. In terms of social rights, in both the public and private sectors, same-sex partnerships are not normally recognized, creating particular difficulties on the death of one partner (but advantages with regard to social security cohabitation rules).[6] Richardson concludes that:

> lesbians and gay men are entitled to certain rights of existence, but these are extremely circumscribed, being constructed largely on the condition that they remain in the private sphere and do not seek public recognition or membership in the political community. In this sense lesbians and gay men, though granted certain rights of citizenship, are not a legitimate social constituency. This is a model of citizenship based on a politics of tolerance and assimilation (1998: 89; see also Evans, 1993; Foley, 1994; Palmer, 1995).

Even that limited model has only shallow roots in terms of the everyday experience of citizenship. Homophobic attitudes and practices can undermine the exercise of citizenship rights and create an atmosphere that is not conducive to their enjoyment. A Stonewall survey of 4,260 lesbian and gay respondents in 1996 found that 35 per cent of the men and 24 per cent of the women had experienced homophobic violence at least once in the previous five years. Transgendered people are also vulnerable to 'considerable victimisation, harassment and discrimination' (Foley, 1994: 58). There is no specific legislation against hate crimes against 'sexual minorities' in the UK unlike in, for instance, Canada and the majority of US states (*Guardian*, 6 June 1999).

THE ROOTS OF EXCLUSION

Although the patterns of exclusion from full citizenship of heterosexual women and of lesbians and gays may vary, their exclusion shares common roots: their association with the body and sexuality. In both the liberal and republican traditions, the citizen has stood as the abstract, *disembodied*, individual of reason and rationality. In the masculine citizenship community 'bodies and their appetites and desires are treated as loathsome, even inhuman, things that must be overcome if a man is to remain powerful and free ... individuals must separate themselves from and conquer the feelings and desires of the body' (Hartsock, 1985: 177–8).[7]

Feminist scholars have exposed the masculine nature of the mould from which the rational, disembodied citizen was cast (see, for instance, Benhabib, 1992; Cavarero, 1992; Gatens, 1992; Lloyd, 1984). Only male individuals were deemed capable of transcending the body; women as sexual beings and as bearers of children were not. Moreover, because of the weakness of their bodies, women were in need of the protection of male citizens (Jones, 1990). This is not just a Western construct. Writing from a Malaysian perspective, Aihwa Ong observes that the powerful *ummas* (Islamic scholars) tap into

> the popular Islamic belief that men tend to be ruled by reason, and women by passion ... to define the political relations of gender rights and citizenship under Islam. In their view, because men are constructed as more rational, and have certain God-given rights as men over women, they represent the normative citizens of the umma ... Morally [women] are second class citizens who derive their status through men (1999: 358).

The gendered dichotomy, which associates the disembodied male with reason and the embodied female with sexuality and the emotions, is a heterosexual construct. Cutting across it is a heterosexist categorization under which both female and male homosexuality are 'defined as essentially sexual' (Saraga, 1998: 175) and lesbians and gay men are 'defined primarily as sexual beings', while heterosexuality *qua* heterosexuality 'is rarely acknowledged as a sexuality' (Richardson, 1996: 13), Interestingly, in contrast to his homosexual counterpart, 'the category "gay man" is a more sexualised concept than "lesbian"' (Richardson, 1996: 13), although this may be less true today. In these sexual binaries, there is simply 'no social space for bisexual forms', which means no space for a bisexual citizenship identity or status (Evans, 1993: 148; Lorber, 1999; Saraga, 1998).

The inscription of sexuality onto male/female, heterosexual/homosexual is also inflected through other markers such as those of 'race', disability and age (Saraga, 1998). Iris Young analyses the exclusion from citizenship of a number of groups 'identified with the body and feeling' and with sexuality (1990: 10). Such groups represent:

> the Other. In everyday interactions, images, and decisions, assumptions about women, Blacks, Hispanics, gay men and lesbians, old people and other marked groups [notably disabled people] continue to justify exclusion, avoidance, paternalism, and authoritarian treatment. Continued racist, sexist, homophobic, ageist, and ableist institutions and behaviour create particular circumstances for these groups, usually disadvantaging them in their opportunity to develop their capacities. (1990: 164).

In other words, in the name of citizenship's professed universalism, these groups, representing the 'Other', have been unable 'to attain the impersonal, rational and disembodied practices of the modal citizen (Yeatman, 1994: 84).[8] This process of 'othering' has simultaneously cast some groups as too closely associated with the 'natural' (women in their association with their reproductive capacity) and other groups as 'unnatural' (lesbians and gays). In both cases, though, the heterosexual male has represented 'the human' against a process of 'dehumanisation' of others (Held, 1993: 45; Richardson, 1998: 93).

The male heterosexual human or citizen is firmly located in the public sphere, disassociated from the female private sphere, or the realm of necessity and the body. Indeed, public space has been described as 'male, heterosexual' (Pettman, 1996: 186). This public–private divide represents the very foundation stone of citizenship as traditionally conceived and practised. As such, it has both privileged male heterosexual access to the public sphere of citizenship and regulated the terms on which heterosexual women and lesbians and gays have been able to enter the public sphere as citizens. Few feminist and other critical citizenship theorists favour the complete dissolution of the categories of 'public' and 'private' and most would want to claim a sphere of privacy. Nevertheless, the contestation of a fixed, gendered and sexualized, public–private dichotomy, in which the two spheres are treated as separate, is a central move in the challenge to traditional gendered and sexualized notions of citizenship.[9] Heterosexual women's association with the private, domestic, sphere, and the failure or refusal to acknowledge the implications for public citizenship of what happens in the private sphere, have been identified as critical to their effective citizenship status and ability to act as citizens (Pateman, 1989).[10]

For lesbians and gays, the private sphere represents at best a grudging zone of tolerance predicated on the exclusion of overt homosexual identities and practices from the public sphere and at worst a sphere in which they are policed by the institutions of normative heterosexuality (Evans, 1993; Richardson, 1996, 1998). As Isin and Wood argue, for lesbians and gays, access to public space, which is central to the idea of citizenship, is about 'the right to participate in public processes *as a sexual person*, even if that sexuality is homosexuality' (1999: 85).

The rearticulation of the public–private divide is central to both a feminist and queer citizenship politics (Lister, 1997; Prokhovnik, 1998; Richardson, 1996). The public recognition of 'private' issues such as domestic violence and marital rape as concerns of public policy is a testament to their success. So is the emergence of what Ken Plummer has called 'gay and lesbian public spheres', in which alternative cultures have developed, in turn 'leaking' into the wider public sphere (2001: 245). The progress made in Scandinavia by women as political citizens means, according to Birte Siim, that 'the division between the public and private spheres ... has lost some of its gendered effects' (1999: 113; 2000). This acts as a reminder that what is a fluid divide operates in different ways in different societies and at different historical moments (Yuval-Davis, 1991; Einhorn, 1993). What remains constant is the gendered and sexualized nature of the divide even if its particular forms vary and its impact is attenuating in some societies.

Writing in the context of the Lebanon, Suad Joseph describes the public–private divide as 'constitutive of the will to statehood' and writes that 'the centrality of gender to contestations over government/non-government/domestic boundaries suggests that gender is at the heart of state-building enterprises. Elites imagining the state and nation not only must conceptualize women as a category but must articulate the gender-specific expectations of citizenship' (1997: 88–9). Women have been accorded a critical role in the reproduction of nations, not only in terms of physical reproduction and the transmission of culture but also as symbols of the nation, its spirit and honour, to be defended in war by male citizens (Anthias and Yuval-Davis, 1992; Walby, 1992; Yuval-Davis, 1997a). Their 'bodies are used to mark the boundaries of belonging in colonial and nationalist power relations and in other identity conflicts' (Pettman, 1996: 213).

Lesbians and gay men, on the other hand, 'are normally excluded from the construction of "nation" and nationality' and indeed have been regarded as a threat to the nation-state at times (Richardson, 1998: 90). Writing about state nationalism in Trinidad and Tobago and the Bahamas, M. Jacqui Alexander argues that embedded in the state's policing of the sexual are 'powerful signifiers about appropriate sexuality, about the kind of sexuality that presumably imperils the nation and about the kind of sexuality that promotes citizenship'. 'Having refused the heterosexual imperative of citizenship' to procreate, lesbian and gay 'bodies, according to the state, pose a profound threat to the very survival of the nation' (1994: 6). In this way, both the nation and citizenship embody heterosexuality.

Heterosexual men have been constructed as defenders of the nation, naturally linked to warfare and violence (Hearn, 1997; Yuval-Davis, 1997a). The citizen-soldier has been a prominent historical figure whose imprint on the citizenship template has been marked. This acts as a reminder of the need to theorize critically the relationship to citizenship of heterosexual men as well as of heterosexual women and lesbians and gay men. Jeff Hearn (1997) has called for an interrogation of 'the silence that has persisted on the category of men [as gendered actors] in both theory and practice around citizenship', but in a manner that both names and decentres men. By 'naming men as men', he argues, 'the gendering of citizenship is made explicit'. 'What is usually missing in both empirical studies and theoretical analyses of citizenship is explicit attention to the social construction and then deconstruction of the dominant. This is not just "men" as a general category but particular groups of men – often white, heterosexual, able-bodied men' (see also Carver, 1996).

CITIZENSHIP AS A GENDERED CONCEPT

Despite Hearn's reminder that men stand at the heart of citizenship as a gendered concept, it is women who stand at the heart of the literature on gendered citizenship. It is essentially a feminist literature, written from the perspective of women's interests and concerns, though increasingly acknowledging that these are not uniform, given the differences within the category 'woman'. It was feminist scholarship that demonstrated, contra contemporary 'malestream' citizenship theory, that women's historical exclusion from citizenship was far from accidental. Feminist scholarship has also analysed the gendered nature of the various components of citizenship and has debated the value to women of the main citizenship traditions and the contemporary 'vocabularies of citizenship' derived from them (Bussemaker and Voet, 1998).

Until recently, the (liberal/social liberal) vocabulary of rights has dominated modern Western citizenship discourses. It is a vocabulary that women have used in their struggle for equal citizenship with men in the civil, political and social spheres. They have also deployed it, since the late twentieth century, to frame claims for reproductive and bodily autonomy. Analytically, both historical and cross-national feminist analysis has demonstrated that a gendered analysis of women's role, as providers, users and shapers of welfare, is crucial to understanding the development and nature of social rights in different welfare regimes (see, for instance Bock and Thane, 1991; Lewis, 2000; Lister, 2000; Misra and Akins, 1998). The importance of these social rights to women, in weakening the hold of private patriarchal power and in strengthening women's position as political citizens, has been underlined by feminist commentators such as Wendy Sarvasy (1997) and Anna Yeatman (1994).

Nevertheless, there has been a considerable debate within feminism (reflecting its different strands) as to the utility and appropriateness of a rights discourse for women (for a discussion, see Bryson, 1999; Voet, 1998). Critics of a rights discourse point to the individualism, imbued with male values, that underlies most rights approaches and the patriarchal nature of the state and the law against which rights claims are made. A less oppositional, and more common, position is that of cautious and sceptical support. There is acknowledgement of 'the dual nature of the law – as an agent of emancipation as well as of oppression', which, for all its shortcomings, 'has played a vital role in securing for women the prerequisites of citizenship' (Vogel, 1988: 155). It also represents an important arena for feminist struggle, which can both yield tangible reforms and challenge dominant ideological constructions (Bryson, 1999).

An emphasis on rights as a site of struggle for their extension, reinterpretation and defence also underlines the limitations of a narrow conceptualization of citizenship rights as fixed and given. Some feminist citizenship theorists would go further and argue that, at best, rights should be regarded as a means to an end rather than an end in themselves. According to Rian Voet, for instance, 'instead of seeing citizenship as the means to realize rights, we should see rights as one of the means to realize equal citizenship. This implies that feminism ought to be more than a movement for women's rights; it ought to be a movement for women's participation' (1998: 73). She argues that, once women have acquired citizenship rights, the exercise of those rights, especially in the political sphere, is crucial to the full development of women as citizens as part of 'an active and sex-equal citizenship' (1998: Ch. 11).

Mary Dietz has put forward a particularly forceful exposition of participatory citizenship in opposition to the 'politically barren' construction of the 'citizen as bearer of rights' alone. Putting a feminist case for a civic republican model of citizenship, she argues that it is only when active political participation is valued as an expression of citizenship that feminists will 'be able to claim a truly liberatory politics of their own' (1987: 13–15). Other feminist scholars, sympathetic to Dietz's vision, such as Anne Phillips (1991, 1993) and Young (1990), nevertheless advise a critical engagement with civic republicanism. In particular, they point to its narrow, formalistic conception of politics and its failure to address the domestic constraints on many women's political participation (even if these are weakening in Scandinavian countries, see Siim, 1999).

Central to these domestic constraints is the unpaid care work, both for children and for older relatives, which many women still undertake in the home. Under dominant models of citizenship, which give prominence to paid work obligations, such work tends to stand outside the realm of citizenship obligations and responsibilities, with negative implications for access to social rights. This has led some feminists, such as Gillian Pascall (1993), to be wary of duties-based citizenship claims.

In contrast, Diemut Bubeck has seized on the increasingly hegemonic discourse of citizenship obligation (to be found in both neo-liberal and communitarian approaches) in order to subvert conventional constructions from a feminist perspective. She makes the case for 'a revised conception of citizenship in which the performance of her or his share of care has become a general citizen's obligation' (1995: 29). From a similar perspective, grounded in an ethic of care, feminist theorists such as Nancy J. Hirschmann (1996) and Selma Sevenhuijsen (1998, 2000) have challenged dominant discourses of obligation as rooted in an ontology of atomistic individuals. They have counterpoised:

> the feminist ethic of care [which] takes the idea of self-in-relationship as a point of entry for thinking about responsibility and obligation … The moral subject in the discourse of care always already lives in a network of relationships, in which s/he has to find balances between different forms of responsibility (for the self, for others and for relationships between them (Sevenhuijsen, 2000: 10).

This position opens up a reconceptualization of citizenship, grounded in an ethic of care and the responsibilities to which it gives rise. Increasingly it is being used in policy debates in a number of countries, for instance around the position of lone mothers, to challenge dominant constructions which privilege paid work obligations (see, for instance, Duncan and Edwards, 1999; van Drenth et al., 1999). From the slightly different angle of how we value different contributions to society, Young has, likewise, made the case for a broader conception of citizenship responsibilities. This embraces not just what she calls the 'dependency work' of caring for others, but also unpaid 'community organizing and service provision', much of which is undertaken by women (1995: 551–2).

The notion of citizenship obligations and responsibilities has also been developed by some feminist theorists in an internationalist context. Kathleen B. Jones, for instance, includes in a feminist perspective an emphasis on 'the global parameters of the responsible citizen's obligations' (1994: 269; see also Lister, 1997). Globalization as both a process and an ideology means that 'citizenship needs to be rethought as a possible tool for feminist use within a global frame' (Pettman, 1999; see also Werbner and Yuval-Davis, 1999). Kimberly Hutchings suggests that feminism is in sympathy with cosmopolitan conceptions of citizenship (see Linklater, Chapter 20 in this volume) because of 'the relevance of non-state/nation political constituencies for feminist political agendas (1999: 140).

That is not to say, as Hutchings acknowledges, that universalistic claims about humanity are 'uncontested within feminism' (1999:). Indeed, feminist debates about citizenship rights are paralleled by debates about the value of human rights discourses. Critics of such discourses question not just the value of a rights-based approach, but also Western hegemony in defining 'universalized notions of what it means to be human and what rights accompany this humanity' (Grewal, 1999: 340; for a response, see Zubaida, 1999). Werbner and Yuval-Davis, in contrast, argue that the discourses of human and citizenship rights imply each other 'so that national and transnational citizenships constitute two coexisting and interrelated modalities of citizenship' (1999: 3). In the same volume, Jacqueline Bhabha reminds 'critics of the Western universalist conception of human rights' that, notwithstanding the dangers of feminist human rights arguments being used to articulate 'simplistic anti-Islam positions':

> in the asylum context the application of a uniform standard can provide the basis for a defence of the right to differ and a critique of persecutory practices that a relativist perspective may preclude. It can also provide the consistency in the application of basic international protection that undermines narrowly nationalistic, anti-immigrant, even racist standards for public and foreign policy ... Relativist conceptions of human rights, while anti-imperialist in intent and rhetoric and sensitive to the need to contextualise social and cultural norms, in the asylum context easily become vehicles for a discriminatory hierarchisation of human rights protection and an uncritical reinforcement of exclusionary state practices (1999: 189).

Bhabha's statement points to another important strand in the feminist citizenship literature, which focuses on migration and asylum as a gendered phenomenon, the implications of which are largely ignored in the 'malestream' citizenship and migration literature.[11] Bhabha's main focus is the difficulties faced by women whose asylum claims are based on forms of persecution, generally deemed private, concerning their 'rights to control their own bodies, specifically their reproductive or genital organs, in opposition to prevailing norms'.[12] This she calls 'intimate violence: the territory of women's bodies' (Bhabha, 1999: 184; see also Peters and Wolper, 1995). This is the territory where gendered and sexual citizenship meet.

CITIZENSHIP AS A SEXUALIZED CONCEPT

Jeffrey Weeks locates the relatively novel concept of sexual citizenship in 'the new primacy given to sexual subjectivity in the contemporary world'. He heralds the 'sexual citizen' as 'a harbinger of a new politics of intimacy and everyday life' (1998: 35; see also Waites, 1996). Earlier, Plummer coined the term 'intimate citizenship' to refer to 'a cluster of emerging concerns over the rights to choose what we do with our bodies, our feelings, our identities, our relationships, our genders, our eroticisms and our representations' (1995: 17). He sees intimate citizenship as offering a more inclusive account of the personal life than do ideas of feminist and sexual citizenship alone (Plummer, 2001). Plummer regards the notion as extending our understanding of citizenship responsibilities as well as rights, thereby expanding traditional conceptions of citizenship. It does so by extending citizenship's territory beyond the public sphere into the most intimate corners of the private sphere: 'the body hence becomes a central site of concern for stories of intimate citizenship' (1995: 157). At the same time, intimate citizenship can also be traced at the global level, through, for example, global care chains and transnational concerns over genital mutilation (Plummer, 2001).

However, as Plummer (1999) himself has acknowledged, intimate citizenship is not to be confused with intimacy itself: it concerns public talk and action about the intimate. This supports my argument that 'intimate citizenship only constitutes a sphere of citizenship *practice* when its claims are made in the public sphere' (Lister, 1997: 128). In other words, 'the intimate' represents a proper object of citizenship struggles, but it is not the site of those struggles, which is not to deny the potential political nature of conflict within the intimate sphere.

Citizenship claims, made in the name of the intimate, are being theorized through the notion of 'sexual rights'. Such rights can be claimed by men as well as women, heterosexuals as well as homosexuals, but, among heterosexuals, it is primarily women rather than men who have had cause to lay claim to them and it is 'sexual minorities' for whom they hold a particular significance under conditions of heteronormalcy. Richardson (2000a) has outlined an analytic schema around three kinds of sexual rights claims, based on conduct or practice, identity and relationships, each of which is further subdivided into three categories.

Practice-based sexual rights claims, which often involve claims to civil rights, refer to the right to participate in sexual activity, to sexual pleasure and to sexual and reproductive autonomy. The right to sexual activity is a particular issue for 'sexual minorities' who may face legislation that permits consensual homosexual sexual contact of any form in private only (as in Britain for men) or that criminalizes all homosexual sexual intercourse (as in some US states and other parts of the world).

The right to sexual activity and sexual pleasure is also an issue for disabled people, who are often 'seen as asexual', without 'sexual needs' (Begum, 1992: 78; see also Shakespeare et al., 1996). Issues of sexual autonomy are likewise of particular importance for disabled women, whose bodies are 'policed' and reproductive rights denied (Meekosha and Dowse, 1997: 57). The denial of their sexuality has not 'exempted' them 'from the threat or actuality of male sexual violence'; indeed disabled women 'can be much more vulnerable to sexual abuse and victimization' (Begum, 1992: 81). Disabled women's reproductive rights are often in question, in particular in the case of women with learning difficulties, who may be sterilized without their direct consent (Williams, 1992). The unrestricted fertility of poor and/or black women, too, has in some instances been treated as problematic.

More generally, issues of sexual and reproductive autonomy and health have been identified as critical to women's citizenship, for bodily integrity and reproductive choice are a precondition of women's autonomy and full and free access to the public sphere (Doyal, 2000: see also Williams, 1999). At issue here are not just civil rights, for instance the right not to be raped by a marital partner, but also social rights, such as access to contraceptive and abortion facilities, necessary to ensure genuine reproductive choice and health (Shaver, 1993/94). Similarly, Aids has generated demands both for information about safer sex as integral to sex and health education on the one hand and for the curtailment of the civil rights of those who are HIV-positive, on the other (Watney, 1991).

(Explicitly) *identity-based claims* emerged in the late twentieth century, with the emergence of gay liberation movements. These are claims to public recognition as lesbians, gays, bisexuals or transgendered groups, as opposed to private tolerance of particular sexual acts. They involve the right to self-definition, to self-expression and to self-realization. Jan Pakulski cites such claims as 'the most interesting illustrative case' of the struggle for 'cultural citizenship' (see Miller, Chapter 14 in this volume). They involve among other things 'the right to a presence in the mainstream media, the right to be represented in a dignifying way, and the right to propagate gay identity and lifestyle' (Pakulski 1997: 81). For transgendered people, the right to self-definition is crucial, with implications for a range of other sexual rights. In the minority of countries under the Council of Europe which prohibit the alteration of a transgendered person's birth certificate (James, 2000):

> the lack of legal recognition of the fact that someone's true gender may not be that which is physically apparent at birth, means that a transgendered person's legal status will always be determined by the sex entered on the birth certificate. This has very wide-ranging effects on the lives of transgendered people, including denial of their right to marry. (Foley, 1994: 58; see also Evans, 1993).

Relationship-based rights concern: rights of consent, such as age of consent legislation (which in some countries such as the UK is set at different ages for young men and women and for heterosexuals and gay men); the right to choose sexual partners (which in some parts of the world such as South Africa and parts of the USA has, in the past, been a racialized right); and the right to publicly recognized sexual relationships.

Relationship-based rights provide a reminder that sexual citizenship is not just about individual rights but is about rights as exercised in relationships, involving responsibilities also. Their importance is underlined by Richardson, who points out that 'the assertion of rights does not guarantee protection from the harmful effects of various forms of sexual practices' (Richardson, 2000b: 155). Weeks writes that 'the emergence of "the paedophile", especially, indicates the limit case for any claim to sexual citizenship' (1998: 41; for a discussion, see Evans, 1993). While few would want to challenge the denial of sexual citizenship in this instance given the violation of children's rights at stake, more troubling is the disregard of paedophiles' civil rights by vigilante groups intent on their expulsion from their neighbourhoods. In such cases, paedophiles are being treated as having forfeited all claims to be a citizen.[13]

Particularly controversial among rights to publicly recognized relationships is the civil right to marry. Morris B. Kaplan underlines its wider, symbolic importance: 'ultimately at stake is acceptance of the moral legitimacy and ethical validity of the shared ways of life of lesbian and gay citizens' (1997: 209). The illegitimacy of those ways of life was underscored in Britain by first the passing of and then the resistance to the abolition of Section 28 of the Local Government Act 1988. This prohibited local authorities from 'the promotion' in schools of 'the acceptability of homosexuality as a pretended family relationship'. As Kath O'Donnell observes, this denial of 'any modicum of equal respect or legal recognition for lesbian and gay families epitomises the privileged nature of the heterosexual family unit' (1999: 79).

THE POLITICS OF GENDERED AND SEXUAL CITIZENSHIP

Section 28 has been a touchstone issue in British gay and lesbian politics at the turn of the twenty-first century. Some lesbian and gay activists deploy the language of citizenship, civil and human rights. Indeed, Stonewall, a UK lobby group that works to advance the rights of lesbian and gay men, has announced a major new project called Citizenship 21 'to challenge prejudice and homophobia, build links with other communities facing discrimination, and empower lesbians and gay men within the wider community' (Stonewall, 2000). Likewise, feminists in a number of countries 'have found the notion of "citizenship" to be the most appropriate political mobilization tool in the post-Beijing era' (Yuval-Davis, 1997b: 22), for it 'provides women with a valuable weapon in the fight for human, democratic, civil and social rights' (Werbner and Yuval-Davis, 1999: 28).[14] This has been particularly true of women in Latin America, where women's movements have been 'at the center' of citizenship struggles (Blacklock and Jensen, 1998: 129; *Social Politics*, 1998; Vargas and Olea, 1999. Molyneux 2000).

In both women's movements and lesbian and gay movements different stances have been taken in the politics of citizenship.[15] In both cases, it is possible, very crudely, to divide these into 'equality', 'difference' and 'pluralist' stances. In the context of women's citizenship, we can identify a process of 're-gendering' citizenship around the three normative images of the 'gender-neutral', the 'gender-differentiated' and the 'gender-pluralist' citizen (Lister, 2000; for alternative formulations see Hutchings, 1999; Prokhovnik, 1998; Voet, 1998). The first two of these find a parallel in lesbian and gay politics in Weeks' formulation of 'the moment of citizenship', in the name of equality, and of 'the moment of transgression', in the name of difference (Weeks, 1996, 1998). Hints at the third can be found in queer politics' 'disruption of [dichotomous] sex and gender identity boundaries' in the name of a plurality of sexualities (Gamson, 1995: 390; Storr, 1999).[16] Less radically, they also emerge in calls for 'choice and flexibility' and the recognition of 'a plurality of voluntary "intimate associations"' (Donovan et al., 1999: 706; Kaplan, 1997: 3).

In lesbian and gay politics, the 'equality' route, signposted at 'the moment of citizenship' is about inclusion and equal rights: 'the claim to equal protection of the law, to equal rights in employment, parenting, social status, access to welfare provision, and partnership rights, or even marriage, for same-sex couples' (Weeks, 1998: 37). One of its principal exponents has been Andrew Sullivan, albeit writing from a narrow conservative perspective (Kaplan, 1997). He sums it up in terms of 'a simple and limited principle: that all public (as opposed to private) discrimination against homosexuals be ended and that every right and responsibility that heterosexuals enjoy as public citizens be extended to those who grow up and find themselves emotionally different' (Sullivan, 1995: 6).

From the perspective of re-gendering citizenship, the 'gender-neutral' citizen is rooted in a belief in equal rights and obligations; gender should be irrelevant to their allocation. The priority is to enable women to compete on equal terms with men in the public sphere of the polity and the labour market. The latter, in turn, opens up access to the social rights of citizenship linked to labour market status through social insurance schemes. Although the main focus tends to be changes in the public sphere, contemporary champions of the 'gender-neutral' citizen, such as Susan Moller Okin (1989) and Phillips (1991, 1997) acknowledge the importance for citizenship of changes in the private sphere, notably in the sexual division of labour.

Phillips also concedes that until genuine gender-neutrality is achieved, gender-differentiated strategies are necessary in order 'to redress the imbalance that centuries of oppression have wrought' (Phillips, 1991: 7). Some feminists, nevertheless, remain sceptical. Ursula Vogel, for example, regards any attempts to insert women into the illusionary 'ready-made, gender-neutral spaces of traditional conceptions of citizenship' as 'futile' (1994: 86).

In contrast, the gender-differentiated citizen, personified in the mother, appeals to 'difference' in promoting women's claims as social and political citizens. Such a maternalist construction of citizenship has, though, attracted criticism for constructing what Kathleen B. Jones (1988: 18) has termed 'sexually segregated norms of citizenship' in which difference spells unequal and inferior. In response, a number of feminists, sympathetic to some of the values underlying the gender-differentiated model, are arguing for a non-maternalist conceptualization of difference around the broader notion of care and an ethic of care, which is, explicitly, not confined to women. The case for care as a resource for political citizenship has been put by Bubeck (1995) on the grounds that the private concerns, values, skills and understandings associated with the practice of caring can all enhance public practices of citizenship (see also Sevenhuijsen 1998, 2000).

This also points to different arenas and forms of politics, in particular informal community politics (often played out in poorer communities), in which women are often more active, bringing into the public sphere concerns derived from their caring responsibilities. This acts as a bridge to the social sphere, where some formulations deploy the concerns of the gender-differentiated model in order to move beyond it. Knijn and Kremer, for instance, make the case for the incorporation of 'care in the definition of citizenship, so the rights to time to care and to receive care are protected'. This they see as critical to an 'inclusive, degendered' approach to citizenship (1997: 357).

The case against a simple equality model for lesbians and gays has been put by Angelia R. Wilson:

> Surely we desire more than to be equal with heterosexuals. … Our struggle for liberation has not been a struggle for conforming equality. It has been a struggle in which we as a community, and as individuals, have grappled with difference. … The protesting cry for revolution, for change, cannot be one of equality alone. It must be accompanied by a politics of respect (1993: 188).

Weeks describes the 'moment of transgression' as 'the moment of challenge to the traditional or received order of sexual life: the assertion of different identities, different life-styles, and the building of oppositional communities' (1996: 82). Instead of integration and inclusion, it is above all about claiming a public gay identity. 'The rigid identity politics' of the 'moment of transgression' is, however, now being overtaken by those queer theorists who, in so far as they 'still speak the language of identity, … reconceive it as multiple, overlapping and, in process' (Dean, 1996: 57). In doing so, they move beyond the 'hetero/homo binary' to reconceptualize 'sexual categories, spaces and boundaries' (Isin and Wood, 1999: 89) through 'a politic of boundary disruption and category deconstruction' (Gamson, 1995: 392).[17] Here the deconstructed 'sexual-pluralist' citizen meets the deconstructed 'gender-pluralist' citizen who emerges from Chantal Mouffe's 'radical democratic conception of citizenship' (1992: 377). This is based on an understanding of the subject as 'constructed through different discourses and subject positions' as opposed to one whose identity is reduced 'to one single position – be it class, race or gender' (1992: 382).

Mouffe explicitly distinguishes her own radical pluralist position from that of Young, who proposes a 'group differentiated citizenship' (1990). A key criticism made of Young's position by Mouffe and others is that it runs the danger of freezing group identities, suppressing differences within groups and impeding wider solidarities (Mouffe, 1992; Phillips, 1993).[18] More fluid pluralist approaches, which attempt to guard against these dangers, have been articulated around the notions of a 'politics of difference' (Yeatman, 1993); a 'transversal politics' (Yuval-Davis, 1997a); a 'politics of solidarity in difference' (Lister, 1997) and a 'reflective solidarity' (Dean, 1996).

It is also possible to identify in lesbian and gay politics less deconstructionist pluralist citizenship models. One is that proposed by Donovan et al., who, as part of their research into 'families of choice' call for 'a concept of citizenship that is based on the creation of a package of social practices that facilitates inclusion, accommodates individual differences, is without a hierarchy of advantages attached to different living arrangements and allows people to adapt it to their own family of choice' (1999: 708; see also Kaplan, 1997).

Another model attempts to place the demands of lesbians and gay men into 'a wider ethical context' of citizenship which ensures 'constitutionally, that no other social constituencies will ever have to endure what gay men have been through' (Watney, 1991: 177). A similar stance has been adopted by the British radical gay rights activist, Peter Tatchell, who now makes the case for the integration of gay rights demands into a broader human rights agenda. 'The key to queer freedom', he argues, 'is a new, comprehensive, transformative politics for the emancipation of everyone' (Tatchell, 1999).

CONCLUSION

Approaches such as these acknowledge that neither gender nor sexuality can be understood as simple binaries and that they do not stand alone in shaping the contours of citizenship. Cross-cutting structural divisions of social class (and associated power and riches), 'race', ethnicity, disability and age mediate their relationship to citizenship. Such approaches also point to the need for a critical synthesis of 'equality', 'difference' and 'pluralist' approaches, in the interests of more inclusive and expansive forms of citizenship.

This chapter has discussed the contribution made by feminist and lesbian and gay theorists and activists to the development of more inclusive gendered and sexual perspectives on citizenship. It has therefore tended to focus mainly on the position of women and 'sexual minorities', particularly lesbians and gay men, and on the ways in which these groups have been excluded from and marginalized within hegemonic forms of citizenship. However, gendered citizenship is about men as well as women and heterosexuals as well as homo-, bi- and transsexuals are sexual beings with claims to sexual citizenship. In other words, citizenship is a profoundly gendered and sexualized construct. The issues raised here are critical to both the theorization and the practice of citizenship.

NOTES

1 In classical Athens, male homosexuality was an accepted practice, provided that it did not involve the penetration of citizens or young men who would become citizens (Rogers, 1999). It was, though, 'imbricated with pervasive inequality' in terms both of hierarchical age-based relationships and of a 'culture of misogyny' (Kaplan, 1997: 5).

2 Although lesbians and gay men are, for the most part, discussed together in this chapter, it should be noted that their experiences and politics sometimes differ, reflecting the intersection of sexual orientation with gender. Evans (1993: 90), for example, has noted that in some discourses 'the homosexual citizen is male'.

3 The right to serve in the armed forces was extended only after the British government lost a case in the European Court of Human Rights. Another area of discrimination, which has been addressed, at least partially, by the Labour government, concerns the rules governing the right to permanent residence of a foreign partner in a gay couple.

4 The right has existed in the Scandinavian and Nordic countries for a number of years and has been introduced more recently in Germany and, in a more limited way, in France. It also exists in some US states, although the majority have outlawed gay marriage as such.

5 A survey by the Trades Union Council found that 44 per cent of gay, lesbian or bisexual workers claimed they had suffered discrimination at work (*Independent on Sunday*, 2 July 2000). Progress can, however, be discerned in the European Union. Article 13 of the Amsterdam Treaty provides that action may be taken at European level 'to combat discrimination based on' a number of factors, including 'sexual orientation'. This has produced a Directive requiring the outlawing of discrimination on grounds of sexual orientation by 2003. Until this Directive is effective only three countries in the world (South Africa, Equador and Switzerland) outlaw discrimination against homosexuals (*New Internationalist*, 2000).

6 A House of Lords ruling that a homosexual couple in a stable relationship can be defined as a 'family' for the purposes of the right to inherit the tenancy of a flat was widely regarded as a breakthrough which could lead to a challenge in other areas of the law (*Guardian*, 29 October 1999; for a comment see Campbell, 1999).

7 An interesting example of how this may be changing is an interview given by the then leader of the British Conservative Party, William Hague, in which he boasted of his 'washboard stomach' and 'high definition pecs' (*Independent*, 9 August 2000).

8 In Western Europe, feminists have identified a similar process of 'othering' of Eastern and non-European women (Ferreira et al., 1998; Lutz, 1997).

9 For an interesting formulation of the private as a 'boundary', which heterosexual women and lesbians and gays can deploy to protect personal and sexual concerns, see Dean (1996).

10 A recent exploratory study of student teachers in Greece, Portugal, England and Wales points to the continued power of the gendered public–private dichotomy. It found that 'the sphere of politics and of economic life remain unambiguously marked as masculine' (Arnot et al., 2000: 163).

11 A gendered analysis of migration and asylum can be found in, for instance, Ackers (1998); Buijs (1993); Ferreira et al. (1998); Lutz (1997); Morokvasic (1984).

12 The UN High Commissioner for Refugees has urged countries to follow the USA and Canada in acknowledging the right to refugee status of women fleeing sexual persecution. New guidelines in the UK, announced in 2000, accept that such claims should be given full consideration ('Asylum rules eased for women', *Guardian*, 5 December 2000).

13 A study of welfare users' views about citizenship found that 'for many, the exclusion of convicted paedophiles, from not only social rights such as housing but also basic civil rights, was unproblematic' (Dwyer, 2000: 179). In summer 2000, the British media reported at length violent attacks on and demonstrations against anyone believed to be a paedophile by residents (particularly women and children) of a deprived housing estate. Such action, which was experienced as 'empowering' the women involved, perhaps also exemplifies the 'limit case' of active citizenship.

14 As an example, Shireen P. Huq, a member of a women's activist organisation in Bangladesh, has described how it 'mobilised around the conventions ratified by the government to advance the rights and citizenship of women' (2000: iii).

15 Differences between lesbian and gay politics are not explored here (see, for instance, Corrin, 1999: Ch. 6; Dean, 1996: Ch. 2; Evans, 1993).

16 For a discussion of bisexual politics, see Storr (1999).

17 Queer politics also sometimes involves assertion of the right to stand outside and challenge mainstream citizenship culture (Plummer, 2001).

18 Young's more recent work (2000) to some extent addresses such criticism, using the notion of the representation of 'perspectives' of oppressed or disadvantaged groups, which are acknowledged to contain a diversity of interests and positions.

REFERENCES

Ackers, L. (1998) *Shifting Spaces: Women, Citizenship and Migration within the European Union*. Bristol: Policy Press.

Alexander, M.J. (1994) 'Not just (any) body can be a citizen: the politics of law, sexuality and postcoloniality in Trinidad and Tobago and the Bahamas', *Feminist Review*, 48: 5–23.

Anthias, F. and Yuval-Davis, N. (1992), *Racialized Boundaries*. London: Routledge.

Arnot, M., Araújo, H., Deliyanni, K. and Ivinson, G. (2000) 'Changing femininity, changing concepts of citizenship in public and private spheres', *European Journal of Women's Studies*, 7 (2): 149–68.

Begum, N. (1992) 'Disabled women and the feminist agenda', *Feminist Review*, 40: 70–84.

Benhabib, S. (1992), *Situating the Self*. Cambridge: Polity Press.

Bhabha, J. (1999) 'Embodied rights: gender persecution, state sovereignty and refugees' in N. Yuval-Davis and P. Werbner (eds) *Women, Citizenship and Difference*. London and New York: Zed Books, pp. 178–91.

Blacklock, C. and Jensen, J. (1998) 'Citizenship: Latin American perspectives', *Social Politics*, 5 (2): 127–31.

Bock, G. and Thane, P. (eds) (1991) *Maternity and Gender Policies*, London: Routledge.

Bryson, V. (1999) *Feminist Debates*. Basingstoke: Macmillan.

Bubeck, D. (1995) *A Feminist Approach to Citizenship*. Florence: European University Institute.

Buijs, G. (ed.) (1993) *Migrant Women – Crossing Boundaries and Changing Identities*. Providence: Berg.

Bussemaker, J. and Voet, R. (1998) 'Citizenship and gender: theoretical approaches and historical legacies', *Critical Social Policy*, 18 (3), 277–307.

Campbell, B. (1999) 'Partners for life', *Guardian*, 1 November 1999.

Carver, T. (1996) '"Public man" and the critique of masculinities', *Political Theory*, 24 (4): 673–86.

Cavarero, A. (1992) 'Equality and sexual difference: amnesia in political thought' in G. Bock and S. James (eds), *Beyond Equality and Difference*. London and New York: Routledge, pp. 32–47.

Corrin, C. (1999) *Feminist Perspectives on Politics*. London and New York: Longman.

Dean, J. (1996), *Solidarity of Strangers*. Berkeley: University of California Press.

Dietz, M. (1987). 'Context is all: feminism and theories of citizenship', *Daedulus*, 116 (4): 1–24.

Donovan, C., Heaphy, B. and Weeks, J. (1999), *Journal of Social Policy*, 28 (4): 689–709.

Dorf, J. and Perez, G.C. (1995) 'Discrimination and the tolerance of difference: international lesbian human rights' in J. Peters and A. Wolper, (eds),

Women's Rights, Human Rights. London: Routledge, pp. 324–34.

Doyal, L. (2000) 'Focus on Reproductive Health', *Womankind Worldwide Newsletter*, Summer.

Duncan, S. and Edwards, R. (1999) *Lone Mothers, Paid Work and Gendered Moral Rationalities*. Basingstoke: Macmillan.

Dwyer, P. (2000) *Welfare Rights and Responsibilities*. Bristol: Policy Press.

Einhorn, B. (1993) *Cinderella goes to Market*. London: Verso.

Evans, D.T. (1993) *Sexual Citizenship*. London: Routledge.

Ferreira, V., Tavares, T. and Portugal, S. (eds) (1998) *Shifting Bonds, Shifting Bounds: Women, Mobility and Citizenship in Europe*, Oeiras: Celta.

Foley, C. (1994) *Sexuality and the State*. London: Liberty/Outrage!/Stonewall.

Gamson, J. (1995) 'Must identity movements self-destruct? A queer dilemma', *Social Problems*, 42 (3): 390–407.

Gatens, M. (1992) 'Power, bodies and difference' in M. Barrett and A. Phillips (eds) *Destabilising Theory*. Cambridge: Polity Press.

Grewal, I. (1999) '"Women's rights as human rights": feminist practices, global feminism, and human rights regimes in transnationality', *Citizenship Studies*, 3 (3): 337–54.

Hartsock, N. (1985) *Women, Sex and Power*, Boston: Northeastern University Press.

Hearn, J. (1997). 'Men and power: citizenship, welfare, nation and global relations', paper given at European Sociological Association Conference, University of Essex, August.

Held, V. (1993) *Feminist Morality*. Chicago and London: University of Chicago Press.

Hirschmann, N.J. (1996) 'Rethinking obligation for feminism' in N.J. Hirschmann and C. Stegano (eds), *Revisioning the Political*. Boulder, CA: Westway Press, pp. 157–80.

Huq, S.P. (2000) 'Gender and citizenship: what does a rights framework offer women?', *IDS Bulletin*, 31 (4): 74–82.

Hutchings, K. (1999) 'Feminist politics and cosmopolitan citizenship' in K. Hutchings and R. Dannreuther (eds), *Cosmopolitan Citizenship*. Basingstoke: Macmillan, pp. 120–42.

Isin, E.F. and Wood, P.K. (1999) *Citizenship and Identity*. London: Sage.

James, A. (2000) 'Everybody needs some body', Guardian, 19 January.

Jones, K.B. (1988) 'Towards the revision of politics', in K.B. Jones and A.G. Jónasdóttir (eds), *The Political Interests of Gender*. London: Sage, (pp. 11–32).

Jones, K.B. (1990), 'Citizenship in a woman-friendly polity', *Signs*, 15 (4): pp. 781–812.

Jones, K.B. (1994) 'Identity, action and locale: thinking about citizenship, civic action and feminism', *Social Politics*, 1 (3): 256–70.

Joseph, S. (1997) 'The public–private – the imagined boundary in the imagined nation/state/community', *Feminist Review* 57: 73–92.

Kaplan, M.B. (1997) *Sexual Justice: Democratic Citizenship and the Politics of Desire*. New York and London: Routledge.

Knijn, T. and Kremer, M. (1997) 'Gender and the caring dimension of welfare states: toward inclusive citizenship', *Social Politics*, 4 (3): 328–61.

Lewis, J. (2000) 'Gender and welfare regimes' in G. Lewis, S. Gewirtz and J. Clarke (eds), *Rethinking Social Policy*. London: Sage, pp. 37–51.

Lister, R. (1997) *Citizenship: Feminist Perspectives*. Basingstoke: Macmillan.

Lister, R. (2000) 'Gender and the analysis of social policy' in G. Lewis, S. Gewirtz and J. Clarke (eds), *Rethinking Social Policy*. London: Sage, pp. 22–36.

Lister, R. (2001) 'Citizenship and gender' in K. Nash and A. Scott (eds), *The Blackwell Companion to Political Sociology*. Oxford: Blackwell, pp. 323–32.

Lloyd, G. (1984) *The Man of Reason*. London: Methuen.

Lorber, J. (1999) 'Embattled terrain: gender and sexuality' in M.M. Ferree, J. Lorber and B.B. Hess (eds), *Revisioning Gender*. Thousand Oaks: Sage.

Lutz H. (1997) 'The limits of European–ness: immigrant women in Fortress Europe', *Feminist Review*, 57: 93–111.

Meekosha, H. and Dowse, L. (1997) 'Enabling citizenship: gender, disability and citizenship in Australia', *Feminist Review*, 57: 49–72.

Misra, J. and Akins, F. (1998) 'The welfare state and women: structure, agency and diversity', *Social Politics*, 5 (3): 259–85.

Molyneux, M. (2000) 'Comparative perspectives in gender and citizenship: Latin America and the former socialist states' in J Cook, J. Roberts and G. Waylen (eds) *Towards a gendered Political Economy*. Basingstoke: MacMillan.

Morokvasic, M. (1984) 'Birds of passage are also women', *International Migration Review*, xviii (4): 886–907.

Mouffe, C. (1992b), 'Feminism, citizenship and radical democratic politics' in J. Butler and J.W. Scott (eds), *Feminists Theorize the Political*. New York and London: Routledge.

New Internationalist (2000) 'Sexual Minorities', October.

O'Donnell, K. (1999) 'Lesbian and gay families: legal perspectives' in G. Jagger and C. Wright (eds), *Changing Family Values*. London and New York: Routledge, pp. 77–97.

Okin, S.M. (1989) *Justice, Gender and the Family*. New York: Basic Books.

Ong, A. (1999) 'Muslim feminism: citizenship in the shelter of corporatist Islam', *Citizenship Studies*, 3 (3): 355–71.

Pakulski, J. (1997), 'Cultural citizenship', *Citizenship Studies*, 1 (1): 73–86.

Palmer, A. (1995) 'Lesbian and gay rights campaigning: a report from the coalface', in A.R. Wilson (ed.),

A Simple Matter of Justice? Theorizing Lesbian and Gay Politics. London and New York: Cassell, pp. 32–50.

Pascall, G. (1993) 'Citizenship – a feminist analysis', in G. Drover and P. Kerans (eds), *New Approaches to Welfare Theory*, Aldershot: Edward Elgar, pp. 113–126.

Pateman, C. (1989) *The Disorder of Women*. Cambridge: Polity Press.

Peters, J. and Wolper, A. (eds) (1995) *Women's Rights, Human Rights*. London: Routledge.

Pettman, J.J. (1996) *Worlding Women*. London: Routledge.

Pettman, J.J. (1999) 'Globalisation and the gendered politics of citizenship', in N. Yuval–Davis and P. Werbner (eds) *Women, Citizenship and Difference*. London and New York: Zed Books, pp. 207–20.

Phillips, A. (1991) *Engendering Democracy*. Cambridge: Polity Press.

Phillips, A. (1993), *Democracy and Difference*. Cambridge: Polity Press.

Phillips, A. (1997) 'What has socialism to do with sexual equality?', in J. Franklin (ed.), *Equality*. London: IPPR, pp. 101–21.

Plummer, K. (1995) *Telling Sexual Stories*. London: Routledge.

Plummer, K. (1999) 'Inventing intimate citizenship', paper, Rethinking Citizenship Conference, University of Leeds.

Plummer, K. (2001) 'The square of intimate citizenship: some preliminary proposals' *Citizenship Studies* 5 (3): 237–253.

Pourzand, N. (1999) 'Female education and citizenship in Afghanistan: a turbulent relationship', in N. Yuval-Davis and P. Werbner (eds) *Women, Citizenship and Difference*. London and New York: Zed Books, pp. 87–99.

Prokhovnik, R. (1998) 'Public and private citizenship: from gender invisibility to feminist inclusiveness', *Feminist Review* 60: 84–104.

Richardson, D. (ed.) (1996) *Theorising Heterosexuality*. Buckingham: Open University Press.

Richardson, D. (1998) 'Sexuality and citizenship', *Sociology*, 32 (1): 83–100.

Richardson, D. (2000a) 'Constructing sexual citizenship', *Critical Social Policy*, 20 (1): 105–35.

Richardson, D. (2000b) 'Extending citizenship: cultural citizenship and sexuality', in N. Stevenson (ed.), *Culture and Citizenship*. London: Sage, pp. 153–66.

Rogers, B. 'Deviance, if you like', *Guardian*, 26 August 1999.

Saraceno, C. (1997) 'Reply: citizenship is context-specific', *International Labor and Working Class History*, 52 (Fall): 27–34.

Saraga, E. (1998) *Embodying the Social*. London and New York: Routledge.

Sarvasy, W. (1997) 'Social citizenship from a feminist perspective', *Hypatia*, 12 (4): 54–73.

Sevenhuijsen, S. (1998) *Citizenship and the Ethics of Care*. London and New York: Routledge.

Sevenhuijsen, S. (2000) 'Caring in the third way', *Critical Social Policy*, 20 (1): 5–37.

Shakespeare, T., Gillespie-Sells, K. and Davies, D. (1996) *The Sexual Politics of Disability: Untold Desires*. London: Cassell.

Shaver, S. (1993/94) 'Body rights, social rights and the liberal welfare state', *Critical Social Policy*, 13 (3): 66–93.

Siim, B. (1999) 'Gender, citizenship and empowerment', in I. Gough and G. Olofsson, (eds), *Capitalism and Social Cohesion*. Basingstoke: Macmillan, pp. 107–24.

Siim, B. (2000) *Gender and Citizenship*. Cambridge: Cambridge University Press.

Social Politics (1998) Special Issue, Citizenship: Latin American perspectives, 5 (2): 127–249.

Stonewall (2000) *Stonewall Update*, 1 (1).

Storr, M. (1999) 'New sexual minorities, opposition and power: bisexual politics in the UK', in T. Jordan and A. Lent (eds), *Storming the Millennium*. London: Lawrence and Wishart, pp. 51–67.

Sullivan, A. (1995) *Virtually Normal*. London: Picador, as extracted in the *Guardian*, 9–11 November 1995.

Tatchell, P. (1999) 'Let us cease these gay campaigns', *Guardian*, 24 June.

UNDP (2000) *Human Development Report: human rights and human development*. New York: United Nations Development Programme.

van Drenth, A., Knijn, T. and Lewis, J. (1999) 'Sources of income for lone mother families: policy changes in Britain and the Netherlands', *Journal of Social Policy*, 28 (4): 619–41.

Vargas, V. and Olea, C. (1999) 'An agenda of one's own: the tribulations of the Peruvian feminist movement' in N. Yuval-Davis, and P. Werbner (eds) *Women, Citizenship and Difference*. London and New York: Zed Books, pp. 246–61.

Voet, R. (1998) *Feminism and Citizenship*. London: Sage.

Vogel, U. (1988) 'Under permanent guardianship: women's condition under modern civil law', in K.B. Jones and A.G. Jónasdóttir (eds), *The Political Interests of Gender*. London: Sage, pp. 135–59.

Vogel, U. (1994) 'Marriage and the boundaries of citizenship' in B. van Steenbergen (ed). *The Condition of Citizenship*. London: Sage, pp. 76–89.

Waites, M. (1996) 'Lesbian and gay theory, sexuality and citizenship', *Contemporary Politics*, 2 (3): 139–49.

Walby, S. (1992) 'Women and nation', *International Journal of Comparative Sociology*, XXXIII (1–2): 81–100.

Walby, S. (1994) 'Is citizenship gendered?', *Sociology*, 28 (2), 379–95.

Watney, S. (1991) 'Citizenship in the age of AIDS', in G. Andrews (ed.), *Citizenship*. London: Lawrence and Wishart, pp. 164–82.

Weeks, J. (1996) 'The idea of a sexual community', *Soundings*, 2: 71–84.

Weeks, J. (1998) 'The sexual citizen', *Theory, Culture and Society*, 15 (3–4): 35–52.

Werbner, P. and Yuval-Davis, N. (1999) 'Introduction: women and the new discourse of citizenship', in N. Yuval-Davis, and P. Werbner (eds) *Women, Citizenship and Difference*. London and New York: Zed Books, pp. 1–38.

Williams, F. (1992) 'Women with learning difficulties are women too', in M. Langan and L. Day (eds), *Women, Oppression and Social Work*, London: Routledge, pp. 149–68.

Williams, F. (1999) 'Good-enough principles for welfare', *Journal of Social Policy*, 28 (4): 667–87.

Wilson, A.R. (1993), 'Which equality? Toleration, difference or respect' in J. Bristow and A.R. Wilson (eds), *Activating Theory: Lesbian, Gay, Bisexual Politics*. London: Lawrence & Wishart.

Yeatman, A. (1994), 'Voice and representation in the politics of difference' in A. Yeatman and S. Gunew (eds) *Feminism and the Politics of Difference*. St Leonards, Australia: Allen and Unwin, pp. 228–245.

Young, I.M. (1990), *Justice and the Politics of Difference*. Princeton NJ: Princeton University Press.

Young, I.M. (1995) 'Mothers, citizenship and independence: a critique of pure family values', *Ethics*, 105: 535–56.

Yuval-Davis, N. (1991) 'The citizenship debate: women, ethnic processes and the state', *Feminist Review*, 39: 58–68.

Yuval-Davis, N. (1997a) *Gender and Nation*. London: Sage.

Yuval-Davis, N. (1997b) 'Women, Citizenship and Difference', *Feminist Review*, 57: 4–27.

Yuval-Davis, N. and Werbner, P. (eds) (1999) *Women, Citizenship and Difference*. London and New York: Zed Books.

Zubaida, S. (1999) 'Contests of citizenship: a comment', *Citizenship Studies*, 3 (3): 387–90.

13

Citizenship and Indian Peoples: The Ambiguous Legacy of Internal Colonialism

ALAN C. CAIRNS

There are some 300 million indigenous people in the world (Niezen, 2000: 120) located in every continent. In Canada, about 800,000 individuals identify themselves as Aboriginal, distributed in three categories – Indian (69%), Inuit (5%), and Metis (26%) (Canada, 2001: 89 – 1996 figures). Making sense of how indigenous peoples in probably over a hundred countries are, or are not, accommodated by citizenship regimes would be a task of Toynbeean proportions that I concluded would defeat me even before I commenced.

'In structural terms,' according to Fleras and Maaka, 'most indigenous peoples occupy an encapsulated status as disempowered and dispersed subjects of a larger political entity' (2000: 114). In recent decades, they have emerged from the sidelines of history. There is a developing indigenous international, whose visibility and impact varies according to local circumstances, but which in general seeks to combat the systems of internal colonialism from which indigenous peoples seek an escape.

Escape from internal colonialism is, however, far more difficult than was escape from the overseas colonialism of yesterday's European empires (if we ignore, for purposes of comparison, neo-colonialism.) Indigenous peoples have to work out a co-living arrangement with their former oppressors who will be a majority within the same polity. The analysis of the Indian peoples of Canada, now called First Nations, illustrates how difficult that task is, even in a wealthy, liberal, capitalist democracy. Citizenship, the obvious vehicle for binding individuals to the state and to each other in bonds of civic solidarity, generates at best an ambivalent reaction from many Indian peoples. Their allegiance to a state that has victimized them is problematic, and an empathy toward and civic solidarity with the majority society are weakened by a nationalism which increases social distance from the society it is reacting against.

The following analysis, which focuses overwhelmingly on one small indigenous population – much less than 1% of the world's indigenous population – could be argued to have only idiosyncratic value. However, the issues it raises about the difficulties of crafting a version of citizenship which both positively accommodates indigenous diversity and forges bonds of civic solidarity with the majority population will almost certainly recur for most, perhaps all other indigenous minorities. The Canadian debate is framed against the bitter legacy of internal colonialism in a domestic context where independence is unavailable to separate indigenous and non-indigenous peoples from each other. That constraining context is not uniquely Canadian. It is inherent in the life situation of internal indigenous minorities. Fleras and Maaka unhappily but appropriately observe that the task of 'postcoloniz[ing] "from within"' presents a 'much more elusive [goal] than [was initially] imagined' (2000: 111). The Canadian debate, therefore, has much to offer to anyone groping for tentative answers in an emerging constitutional policy area that is reshaping the relations between states and peoples for much of humanity.

HISTORICAL BACKGROUND

The Imperial Background and Exclusion from Citizenship

Historically, from Confederation in 1867 to the 1960s, Indian policy was explicitly an instrument of exclusion. The treatment of Indians drew much of its inspiration from an imperial spirit of the times that originated outside Canada but washed over Canadian borders. Until World War II, the historic relationship was a domestic version of the imperial domination of much of humanity by the European powers. On the ground, and on a global scale, imperialism meant the denial of self-rule for hundreds of millions of non-Western peoples. To those who were in charge, it was simply the natural order, justified by the confident belief in their own cultural and/or racial superiority. They saw themselves as in the vanguard of humanity – in touch with the future for they were its creators.

Indians occupied a unique place in the post-Confederation federal system. They were kept outside the majority civic community, an administered people deemed incapable of deciding their own future. They were subject to special federal government legislation, which gave them a unique legal status – the Indian Act, enforced by field officers who had discretionary powers over much of the minutiae of daily living. With some exceptions they lacked the franchise until 1960, which not only powerfully symbolized their civic exclusion, but deprived them of the normal democratic influence individuals have over how they are governed. This underlined their identification as children in a world of adults. They lacked voice, because they were deemed incapable of effectively exercising it. They were dispossessed of their lands and routinely referred to as wards. Their unique relation to the federal government insulated them from provincial life. Unless they left the reserve, they in effect lived in a unitary state. Their isolation from the provincial arena and their status as wards had the consequence that they were deprived of many services and benefits routinely provided to non-Aboriginal Canadians. The policy of enfranchisement, the confusing label for giving up Indian status, however, had negligible appeal, and the numbers who took advantage of it were minimal. (For an estimate of numbers, see Johnston, 1993: 362, n. 59) 'Enfranchisement,' in the language of Darlene Johnston of the Chippewas of Nawash Band, 'involved. … rejection of the values that community membership represented. It meant standing outside the circle that contained one's ancestors, language, traditions, and spirituality' (1993: 362. See also Foster, 1999: 361).

The goal was clear. Its classic and frequently quoted expression was given by Duncan Campbell Scott, the Deputy Superintendent General of Indian Affairs (1913–32), in a 1920 presentation to a House of Commons Committee: 'I want to get rid of the Indian problem. … Our object is to continue until there is not a single Indian in Canada that has not been absorbed into the body politic and there is no Indian question, and no Indian Department …' (cited in Leslie and Macguire, 1979: 114).

Clearly for Scott the goal of Indian administration was not the preparation of Indian peoples for independence, or enhancing the capacity of future self-governing Indian nations (the word would have baffled him) to revitalize their cultures, but simply their disappearance into the majority society. Domestic imperialism, therefore, differed from its overseas counterparts in treating Indians as akin to immigrants who arrived early – and thus were destined for assimilation – not as members of nations in the making.

The traditional beliefs that had governed Indian policy since Confederation remained in place as late as the middle of the twentieth century. They included:

1 The coexistence of Indian peoples and the majority society was appropriately hierarchical, with the governments of the latter possessing legitimate authority over the former for a transition period of indeterminate length.
2 Policy assumed a certain historical direction. European civilization was in the vanguard of humanity, shaping the world into which others were to fit. Hence assimilation was a progressive policy, in tune with the way the world was going. For successive governments to pursue it was simply thought of as responsible leadership, a domestic example of the League of Nations Trusteeship Council mandate to be the teachers and guardians of 'people not yet able to stand by themselves under the strenuous conditions of the modern world.'

The Post-Imperial Era

If historic Indian policy in Canada had been sustained by the powerful symbolism and potent background reality of the globe-straddling European empires – as it was, the successor world of Indian nationalism, of the official repudiation of the previous policy of assimilation, and of the intensified debate about how we are to live together in mutual respect, is a spillover of the ending of overseas European colonial empires. The emergence of many dozen colonies to independence transformed the international system. The United Nations was no longer a primarily European club as a flood of non-white states, mostly small and poor, took over the United Nations General Assembly. The Commonwealth was no longer a club of white dominions (including the anomalous presence of South Africa), but a vast multiracial assemblage encompassing a cross-section of humanity. 'La Francophonie,' like the Commonwealth, is largely a non-white club of ex-colonies with only a handful of members of European background.

The formal ending of overseas colonialism abroad and the subsequent transformation of the international state system sent shock waves through settler colonies with indigenous minorities. In the United States, what the anthropologist Edward M. Bruner described as a new story line for American Indians, from the inevitability of assimilation to the 'future as ethnic resurgence,' was triggered, among other factors, by the 'overthrow of colonialism.' (Bruner, 1986: 139, 152). In Australia, the fear of international public opinion, channelled through the United Nations, induced the government to improve the treatment of Aborigines (Clark, 1998: 99–100, 109; Mansell, 1993: 169). Ward and Hayward speculate that positive government responses in New Zealand to Maori protests in the 1970s were facilitated by 'a changing national and international environment that was increasingly focused on the rights and management of indigenous peoples' (Ward and Hayward, 1999: 393–4). International norms now repudiated what they had formerly supported, overseas colonialism and domestic wardship for indigenous peoples (Webber, 1995: 14, 25).

The end of empire changed the nature of the Canadian debate. The Diefenbaker Conservative government extended the franchise to status Indians in 1960. This was not done because of irresistible pressure from Indian peoples, but rather because of the increasing difficulty, verging on impossibility, of defending Indian exclusion from the franchise at a Commonwealth conference in which white states were in the minority, or in the United Nations with its growing

Afro-Asian majority in the General Assembly (Cairns, 1995: 243). The 1969 unfortunately-named White Paper of the federal government, which proposed the rapid winding down of the policy of different treatment for Indian peoples, on the ground that it was the cause of Indian poverty, malaise, and other social ills, was also fed by the difficulty of justifying a system which, whether accurately or not, could be likened to apartheid (Martin, 1995: 191).

Although she notices important policy variations between Canada, New Zealand and Australia, Professor Catherine J. Iorns Magallanes observed that 'developments in all three countries have paralleled international developments, in that all have implicitly rejected assimilationist goals and conceded elements of self-determination' (Magallanes, 1999: 264). As the Canadian case illustrates, however, this rejection was not immediate. Assimilation did not go into official retreat until the early 1970s, slightly preceding similar retreats in the late 1970s in Australia and New Zealand (Havemann, 1999: 334; Fletcher, 1999: 342). Prior to that, in Canada it was considered a progressive policy, strongly supported by liberals, democratic socialists, humanitarians, and the good-will elements of the non-Aboriginal citizenry. Its redefinition as cultural imperialism was still to come.

Ambiguities of a Post-Imperial World in Transition

Recognition that the end of European overseas empires signalled the end of domestic empire, perhaps with a time lag, did not immediately provide an agreed sense of direction. The initial federal government response to a post-colonial climate, presented in the 1969 White Paper (Canada, 1969), assumed the appropriateness of the assimilation goal but not the historic means of separate treatment as the vehicle for reaching it. In fact, the system of reserves, the Indian Act, and a colonial type of administration were now held to reinforce the very sense of Indianness they were supposed to overcome. In addition, separate treatment was now viewed as an unacceptable badge of inferiority, no longer defensible in public, as well as being the explanation of the social malaise and depressing conditions characteristic of many Indian communities. The answer was to dismantle the machinery of separate treatment and, after a short transition period, to place Indian peoples in the same civic relationship to governments as other Canadians.

This approach, without saying so, equated Canadian Indians and Afro-Americans, with the suggestion that the former, unfortunately, had not yet found their Martin Luther King. When the federal government substituted itself for the absent leader with its 1969 assimilationist proposals, it implicitly assumed that the surviving Indian desire for separate status was based on a false consciousness, which would vanish when confronted with the opportunities held out by participation in the majority society.

The White Paper was appropriately named. It was, in a sense, the last great act of paternalism, driven by the goal of a common citizenship. Confronted with massive Indian opposition, Trudeau ruefully but candidly admitted: 'I'm sure that we were very naive … We had perhaps the prejudices of small "l" liberals and white men at that who thought that equality meant the same law for everybody, and that's why … we said, "well let's abolish the Indian Act and make Indians citizens of Canada like everyone else" … But … perhaps we were a bit too theoretical, we were a bit too abstract …' (Weaver, 1981: 185). The White Paper was withdrawn.

An alternative post-colonial response, more in tune with Third World anti-colonialism, was to think of wardship ending not by individuals entering the majority society, but by small Indian communities taking more control of their future. This vision gained legitimacy from the increasing international unacceptability of paternalism, graphically underlined by UN General Assembly Resolution 1514, Declaration on the Granting of Independence to Colonial

Countries and Peoples, which stated 'all peoples have the right to self-determination [and] inadequacy of political, economic, social and educational preparedness should never serve as a pretext for delaying independence.' The resolution was passed 89–0 in 1960 in the UN General Assembly, with nine abstentions (Jackson, 1993: 121, 124).

The goal of self-governing communities was perhaps implicit in the Indian rejection of the White Paper. That rejection, however, was not clothed in the language of nationalism, but rather in a phrase originally developed in the Hawthorn report of the mid 1960s 'citizens plus' – to describe the appropriate relationship of Indian peoples to the Canadian state (Hawthorn, 1966–67). To the Hawthorn research team, the term 'citizens' was intended to end the historic stigmatized exclusion of Indians from positive civic membership in the Canadian community, an exclusion that had facilitated their neglect and maltreatment. 'Plus' meant some version of differentiated citizenship – the wedding of a 'plus' component of special entitlements and Canadian citizenship. 'Plus' clearly included the survival of self-governing Indian communities as such into the future. These communities, however, were not yet thought of as nations. Hawthorn and his colleagues saw villages, not nations. Even the Indian Chiefs of Alberta, with Harold Cardinal as their spokesman, who led the attack on the White Paper with a lengthy brief titled *Citizens Plus*, thought of the future of Indian communities in municipal, not national terms (Indian Chiefs of Alberta, 1970: 14).

Both the White Paper view and the rival vision of distinct self-governing Indian communities, whether or not they were called nations, were compatible with the developing moral, intellectual climate of the post-imperial era. Both repudiated wardship. The former was the government view and probably the view of the majority society.

Indian leadership opted clearly for the latter, seeing the Trudeau proposals – what Rogers Smith called the 'greater inclusiveness in public life' option (Smith, 1997: 473) – not as the liberation of individuals, but as the suppression of community. Community survival, cultural reinvigoration, and self-government, by contrast, were emerging as the explicit goals of the Indian people. Future policy incorporating the Indian view of a desirable future would have to be negotiated, not simply announced as the White Paper had been. Once the premise of disappearance through assimilation was ended, irresistible incentives in the Canadian case drove Indian peoples to the language of nationalism and to the self-description of Indian peoples as belonging to nations.

TRANSFORMATION OF INDIAN CONSCIOUSNESS

The language of 'nation' was conspicuously absent from public discussion of Indian policy in the 1960s and early 1970s. In the mid 1960s, the Hawthorn Report, which grappled with the relation of Indian peoples to the larger society, did not use the label 'nation' for the Indian peoples whose lives it hoped to improve (Hawthorn, 1966–67). The word had no currency at the time. Although the report discussed treaties, it was not impressed with their significance. The 'rights and privileges guaranteed by treaty to some Indians,' it asserted, 'are insignificant in relation to both Indian needs and the positive role played by modern governments' (Hawthorn, 1966–67: vol. I, 247). The authors of the 1969 White Paper did not see Indian peoples as belonging to nations. Further, Prime Minister Trudeau found it inconceivable that one section of society could have a treaty with another section of society. The critique of the White Paper by the Indian Chiefs of Alberta was devoid of the language of nation and the rhetoric of nationalism (Indian Chiefs of Alberta, 1970). Concurrently, two successive publications on *Native Rights in Canada* (Indian-Eskimo Association of Canada, 1970; Cumming and Mickenberg, 1972), written by advocates of native rights, also made no mention of Indian nations in their analysis.

The debate between the assimilationist approach of the White Paper and 'citizens plus', proposed by the Hawthorn Report in 1966 and adopted by the Indian Chiefs of Alberta to do battle with the White Paper, was between two theories of belonging. To the then federal government, a uniform, standard version of citizenship would end the marginalization held to be the cause of so many of the ills of the Indian people. The message was clear – the bracing winds of competition on a level playing field would be the engine of socio-economic advance. From the 'citizens plus' perspective, by contrast, stand alone citizenship was not enough – it had to be coupled with a 'plus' component which simultaneously recognized the historical priority of Indian peoples in what became Canada, and the contemporary fact that most Indians still lived in politically organized communities which would survive into the indefinite future. 'Plus,' to be worked out in the political process, was not intended to displace citizenship, but to supplement it. In spite of their obvious difference, however, both 'citizens plus' and the White Paper agreed on the central importance of citizenship for the future of Indian peoples. 'Nation' played no part in the debate.

Peter Kulchyski, after noting how the concept of 'citizens plus' was a powerful weapon employed by Indian peoples to defeat the White Paper, suggests that the 'concept … continued to evolve [in the 1970s, and] as citizenship rights were secured the "plus" or additional rights became the focus of discussion' (Kulchyski, 1994: 5). By the late 1970s, he continued, the term '"Aboriginal rights" … replaced the term "citizens plus" in legal and political discourse and remains a focal concept for negotiating the boundary between Aboriginal and non-Aboriginal peoples' (Kulchyski, 1994: 5).

The transformation of Indian consciousness from the 1960s to the present brought in its wake a dramatic change in the tenor of Indian demands and the responses to them. The tone shifted from deferential to aggressive. The 1975 Dene Declaration on nationhood was a portent. 'We the Dene of the Northwest Territories insist on the right to be regarded by ourselves and the world as a nation' (Watkins, 1977: 3–4). The S. 35(1) recognition and affirmation of 'the existing aboriginal and treaty rights of the aboriginal peoples of Canada' in the 1982 Constitution Act was a powerful stimulus for Aboriginal leaders to define their 'political activities … in terms of nationhood rather than in terms of accommodation to the Canadian state. [This changed] negotiations and the whole structure of the language surrounding negotiations (even the whole idea of "nation")' (Sawchuk, 1998: 133). The renewed pride and activism of Indian nations in Canada was paralleled by what Stephen Cornell called *The Return of the Native*, the political resurgence of American Indians, which peaked in the 1970s (Cornell, 1988). Vine Deloria Jr. ushered in the decade with *We Talk, You Listen* (1970), which was followed three years later by the violent ten week siege of Wounded Knee in 1973. According to Stephen Cornell (1988: 4) Wounded Knee 'provided … sensational evidence … of the return of Native Americans to the political arena, of their defiant claim to the right once again to make their own choices.' Maori consciousness and claims underwent a similar evolution to a much more aggressive pattern of demands in this period (Sharp, 1990: 6–9).

In Canada, the emergence of Indian nationalism was stimulated by the recurrent bouts of constitutional introspection from the 1960s to the present, which raised the fundamental question of who Canadians were as a people. This introspection was triggered by the diminishing significance of the British connection, by the accelerating influence of the United States on Canadian life, by a centrifugal provincialism in the federal system, and in particular by the emergence of an aggressive Quebec nationalism seeking independence or enhanced powers for what was now called the state of Quebec. The pace and agony of this self-questioning accelerated after the 1976 parti québécois provincial election victory, with its powerful message that the label 'nation,' coupled with aggressive demands for recognition, compelled a degree of attention that could not be achieved with milder terminology. 'Nation' carried an emotional weight that 'Indians', or 'bands,' or 'peoples' did not. 'Nation,' for Indian peoples, especially when coupled with the adjective 'First,' performed 'an important political function' in communicating not only a desire for self-government, but a justification for its possession superior to that of the newcomers who already possessed it (Carens, 2000: 181).

From the Penner Report of 1983 (Canada, 1983) to the 1992 Charlottetown Accord (Canada, Consensus Report, 1992) and the 1996 RCAP Report (Canada, 1996), 'nation' drives each response to enhance the status of Indian peoples, enlarge their powers of self-government, and redress the stigmatization of their past treatment with a positive constitutional recognition of their special place in Canada. The Penner Report consistently used the phrase 'Indian First Nations' in response to the language of the witnesses before the House of Commons Special Committee, chaired by Keith Penner (Canada, 1983: 7). That Report argued that the self-government it advocated in ringing terms 'would mean that virtually the entire range of law-making, policy, program delivery, law enforcement and adjudication powers would be available to an Indian First Nation government within its territory' (Canada, 1983: 63). The Charlottetown Accord constitutional package, whose Aboriginal contents were heavily influenced by the presence of the major Aboriginal organizations at the bargaining table, not only recognized the inherent right of self-government, but proposed that 'virtually every major institution of the Canadian state would in future have a distinctive Aboriginal input or presence – Senate, House of Commons, Supreme Court (tentatively), first ministers' conferences, and amending formula' (Cairns, 2000: 83). Overall, the basic political theory of the Accord was parallelism, the side-by-side coexistence of Aboriginal and non-Aboriginal peoples. Four years later, the RCAP Report refined the concept of parallelism by defining Aboriginal and non-Aboriginal Canadians as members of separate nations to be linked by treaties. The self-governing Aboriginal nation was 'the core around which the Commission's recommendations are built' (Canada, 1996: vol. 2 (2), 1015). It is 'through the nation – the traditional historical unit of self-governing power, recognized as such by imperial and later Canadian governments in the treaty-making process – and through nation-to-nation relationships, that Aboriginal people must recover and express their personal and collective autonomy' (Canada, 1996: vol. 1, 610). Aboriginal rights, treaties and treaty rights, and nations became a tightly linked trilogy, a compact packaging of First Nations nationalism.

By the end of the twentieth century, 'nation' had become a standard term, although there was disagreement over how many nations there were. The main Indian organization changed its name from the National Indian Brotherhood to the Assembly of First Nations in 1980. By the late 1990s, nearly one-third of the more than 600 Indian bands had officially added nation to their titles (Canada, 1985, 1990, 1999). A burgeoning literature, triggered by Aboriginal nationalism and the proliferation of Aboriginal nations, defined Canadians as a multinational people (Cairns, 2001). Paul Chartrand, an influential RCAP commissioner of Métis background, suggested there were 35–50 distinct Aboriginal nations in Canada, 'meaning peoples in the usually accepted international sense of a group with a common cultural and historical antecedence – a feeling that we are distinct historical communities, social-political communities.' We need, he continued, a vision 'in which these historical indigenous nations *matter* and they're *included*. That ... means a *multinational* vision of Canada' (Chartrand, 1999: 104, 90). The RCAP Report agreed on the necessity of a multinational vision, recommended the consolidation of individual communities into 60–80 Aboriginal nations (Canada, 1996: vol. 1, xxiv.), and indicated that it would be a mistake to think of the Canadian community as a community of citizens. Indeed, the proposed nation-to-nation relationship regulated by treaties in a multinational federalism that it advocated was the antithesis of a community of citizens.

This remarkable evolution of a more aggressive public identity, which has transformed the discussion of how Aboriginal and non-Aboriginal peoples are to live together, has been little studied. However, the following factors clearly played a part (see also 'The Ambiguous Colonial Analogy' below.)

Nations Within

At a general level, as Walker Connor and numerous other authors have noted, ours is an era of substate nationalism. The boundaries of states and the boundaries of ethnic groups rarely coincide. Only about 15 of the more than 180 states in the world can be considered 'essentially homogeneous' (Connor, 1999: 164). The difficulty of accommodating this internal diversity is compounded when minority group quiescence is replaced by heightened consciousness and mobilization. When ethnic diversity is conceptualized in terms of 'nations within' (Fleras and Elliott, 1992), as now is true of Aboriginal nations in Canada, the psychological distancing from the majority society grows exponentially and a homogeneous citizenship is put on the defensive.

Indigenous International

There is now an indigenous international – a vehicle for exchanging views, and an emotional support for small nations who are given the reassurance that they are not alone, indeed that they are participants in a global movement. Formerly, although it was possibly seldom thought of as such, there was an imperial international – the solidarity that sprang from the tacit understanding that the peoples and states of Europe and their migratory cousins in Canada, Australia and elsewhere rightly held sway over much of humanity. That imperial international was challenged and overthrown in overseas colonies by a counter-international of anti-colonial nationalist movements that led to the contemporary international system dominated by non-Western states. By an inevitable contagion effect, the success of Third World anti-colonial nationalism in overthrowing imperial rule changed the moral and intellectual climate in settler polities with indigenous minorities. Indigenous peoples, relatively unaware as late as the 1950s of the 'widespread, almost global, nature of the crises they faced,' began to develop a global identity 'through an expansion of indigenous organizations and networks of communications between them in the 1960s and 1970s' (Niezen, 2000: 123). The indigenous international which developed and is active in international forums, especially the United Nations, is the Fourth World opposition party spawned in reaction to the settler majorities born of European migration. It contributes to an international indigenous identity which transcends particular states, while reinforcing demands for breathing space and recognition within those states.

Stigmatization and the Impact of Separate Treatment (Cairns, 1999)

Although it was not so intended, the past treatment of Indian peoples by the Canadian state almost appears as a deliberate attempt to reinforce a separate identity and to generate a distrust and suspicion of the majority society and its governments. They were a stigmatized people, subjected to a cultural assault by the Canadian state and, as one anthropologist put it, conditioned to see themselves as worthless (Dyck, 1991). The legal banning of cherished customs, the employment of residential schools to eradicate Indian cultures, their isolation from the majority community, and the constant reminders of their inferiority generated a counter-definition in which the Indian past is positively portrayed and the culture of the newcomers is denigrated (First Nations Circle on the Constitution, 1992). Such contrasts, which are pervasive, turn the justification for imperialism on its head, and respond to a profound 'hunger within the native community for an identity separate from the Canadian mainstream' (LaRocque, 1997: 88).

Multiculturalism

The implementation of the official Canadian policy of multiculturalism in 1971 generated an incentive for all Aboriginal peoples to distinguish themselves from more recent arrivals. 'Nation,' considered inapplicable to immigrant communities, was the obvious candidate, for it not only singled out Aboriginal peoples from ethnic groups, but it carried more clout, and put Aboriginal nations on a par with the two French and English founding nations. For Indian peoples who identified themselves as 'First Nations,' 'First' indicated that they had a special claim based on their prior presence in what became Canada.

Psychological and Bargaining Benefits

The 'nation' label was psychologically satisfying. It enhanced the self-esteem of Indian peoples when others applied it to them as a matter of course. It enhanced the bargaining power of those who successfully employed it. It deflected attention from the small size and limited resources of Indian communities. When 'nation-to-nation' became the preferred phrase to refer to future relations between Aboriginal and non-Aboriginal peoples, and when treaties became the preferred instrument to regulate those relations, the gratifying symbolic message was of a coexistence among equals.

The cumulative effect of the preceding is that Canadian citizenship has a low priority for many members of First Nation communities (Boldt, 1993: 50, 73–4, 83, 108); (Carens, 2000: Ch. 8). It receives limited attention from a host of analysts/commentators. The massive Report of the 1996 Royal Commission on Aboriginal peoples treated it almost as a distraction. Citizenship was dwarfed by the Report's reiterated thesis that the self-governing Aboriginal 'nation' exercising its inherent right was the fundamental solidary unit, and a nation-to-nation relationship regulated by treaties was the route to a dignified future for Aboriginal peoples.

Treaty federalism, most prominently associated with James (Sakej) Youngblood Henderson, has a similar thesis, arguing that First Nations, represented by 'Treaty Delegates,' should be directly represented in federal and provincial legislatures. Henderson criticized the 1960 extension of the federal franchise as an illegitimate attempt to justify 'the oppressive extension of ... [federal] powers over Aboriginal peoples' (Henderson, 1994: 321). Overall, he decries the electoral participation of individual Indians in heterogeneous constituencies as designed to legitimate the illegitimate legislative intrusion by the federal and provincial governments into matters reserved to the jurisdiction of Indian governments (Cairns, 2000a: 179–82). In a recent co-authored publication, Henderson and his colleagues elaborate on the direct representation of Aboriginal peoples as such alongside 'representatives of the Canadian people' (Henderson, et al., 2000: 449). This distinctive Aboriginal presence in legislatures will reflect, speak for, and protect the constitutionally guaranteed Aboriginal and treaty rights under S. 35 (1), and, it is argued, will facilitate a reconciliation (Henderson et al., 2000: 444–9).

A cohort of mostly non-Aboriginal scholars in the academic legal community, the lead discipline in the contemporary analysis of Aboriginal issues and the major academic contributor to a constitutional theory of Aboriginal/non-Aboriginal coexistence, overwhelmingly conducts itself as the vanguard of Aboriginal nationalism. Within the constitutional category 'aboriginal peoples' (Indian, Inuit and Métis), legal scholarship focuses overwhelmingly on

Indian peoples. Its self-defined task is to maximize the constitutional space available to First Nation governments exercising the inherent right of self-government. Macklem correctly observes that 'Canadian academic [legal] scholarship has been as creative as its American counterpart in providing arguments for the creation of constitutional spaces in which Indian forms of government can take root and flourish' (Macklem, 1993: 1366). Canadian citizenship concerns, by contrast, are almost invisible in the constitutional vocabulary of legal academics.

The triumph of 'nation' over citizen spills over into a widespread Aboriginal distrust of democratic politics and the existing system of representation. The RCAP Report speaks of the

> inherent ineffectiveness of the democratic political relationship as seen by Aboriginal peoples. There has been a profound absence of representation for Aboriginal peoples in Canadian democratic institutions. But more important, such representation, when cast in terms of conventional democracy, is itself regarded as illegitimate. Aboriginal peoples seek nation-to-nation political relations, and these cannot be achieved simply by representation in Canadian political institutions. (Canada, 1996: vol. I, 249)

Georges Erasmus, National Chief of the Assembly of First Nations from 1985 to 1991, and subsequently co-chair of the Royal Commission on Aboriginal Peoples, bluntly stated in 1987 that the 'bland assertion that First Nations and their governments are represented by non-Aboriginal politicians who have no interest, demonstrated or latent, in advocating our rights is bogus and without foundation in fact or action' (Canada, 1987: 2201). Not surprisingly, given these sentiments, voting turnout in federal and provincial elections based on heterogeneous constituencies is typically low. According to a recent study, which began by noting the historic tensions and suspicion in the relations between Aboriginal peoples and Canadian governments, 'natives do not place a high priority on voting in Canadian elections.' Many believed that voting and participation in legislatures 'gives unwarranted legitimacy to non-native governments' (Malloy and White, 1997: 60, 62; see also Schouls, 1996). Two other authors attribute low voting participation in the Maritime provinces to the 'little confidence [of Aboriginal people] in the likelihood of finding a comfortable domicile within the Canadian state' (Bedford and Pobihuschy, 1994: 35).

As the preceding suggests, the political representation of Indian peoples is a major site of contestation and ambiguity. Thirty years ago, the federal government began to fund Aboriginal political organizations, for the eminently laudable reason of giving greater voice to constituencies that lack the numbers and resources to make themselves heard. So successful has this system of support been that the major Aboriginal organizations participated with the heads of government in four constitutional conferences (1983–87) exclusively devoted to Aboriginal constitutional issues. Again, in the discussions that produced the 1992 Charlottetown Accord, Aboriginal organizations played a (perhaps the) leading role in crafting a remarkable package of constitutional change for their peoples which, along with other constitutional amendments, was defeated in the country-wide 1992 constitutional referendum.

According to Sanders, the strategy of funding Aboriginal political organizations 'in order to bring aboriginal people within the process of policy formation … was integrative … intended to facilitate participation and reduce isolation, frustration and confrontation' (Sanders, 2001: 33). The funding policy coexists, however, with the normal federal and provincial electoral process in which Aboriginal voters in individual constituencies help to select federal and provincial politicians who have the right and obligation to represent and speak for all members of their electorates.

Ideally, federal politicians should speak on behalf of the federal dimension of their Aboriginal constituents that they represent in Ottawa, and provincial politicians on behalf of the provincial dimensions they represent in the provincial capitals. Their capacity to do so, however, is challenged by Aboriginal organizations whose leaders claim that their own capacity to speak on behalf of nations has a superior legitimacy to the claims of elected non-Aboriginal legislators to speak on behalf of Aboriginal constituents. Support for this position is not restricted to Aboriginal leaders. Joseph Carens, a University of Toronto political theorist, says he cannot 'see how any non-aboriginal person could claim to speak politically on behalf of aboriginal people, unless directly authorized to do so by an aboriginal constituency, because the political salience of aboriginal identity is so apparent' (Carens, 2000: 176). What appears as disarray in the theory and practice of representation may only be a transitional problem, part of our groping toward a more normal situation, or it may be an anomaly that will survive because it fulfills functions that normal politics cannot. At the moment, it is an example of 'muddling through,' sheltered from examination by a tacit assumption that to seek answers to complex questions of constitutional theory at this time would be counter-productive.

Individual Aboriginal scholars deny that they are Canadian (Monture-Angus, 1999: 152). Antipathy to, indifference or tepid support are reported as widespread attitudes to Canadian citizenship (Johnston, 1993: 349). A recent article classified Aboriginal peoples as 'uncertain citizens' (Borrows, 2001). The application of the Charter, a powerful symbol of Canadianism, to the relations between Aboriginal governments and their citizens has been deeply divisive (Borrows, 1994: 21, 31), with Aboriginal opponents of the Charter decrying it as an alien document incompatible with Aboriginal values (Turpel, 1989–90; First Nations Circle on the Constitution, 1992). A recent volume with the title *We Are Not You* (Denis, 1997) underlined the psychological distance between First Nations and the majority society.

None of the preceding is surprising. There are deep psychological impediments to a ready embrace of Canadian citizenship. After all, historically the rights and obligations of citizenship were only available to Indians who gave up (or lost) their Indian legal status by a process unhelpfully called enfranchisement. Hence, Indianness and Canadian citizenship were incompatible. One could only assume the latter by giving up the legal status of the former (Carens, 2000: 185, 186, 188, 196). In that era, to opt for citizenship could be seen as an act of betrayal, as going over to the other side. Memories of that past lead to a view of linkage with Canada as little more than a 'regrettable necessity,' based on the need for transfers of resources and on the limited viability of small political units (Carens, 2000: 173).

The often reported ambivalence of members of First Nations to Canadian citizenship is overdetermined. There is an almost unavoidable psychological tension involved in the nationalist incentive to define the majority and its governments in negative terms as 'other,' in order to maximize the rationale for extensive self-governing powers and simultaneously to advocate enthusiastic citizen membership in and participation as individuals in the political affairs of the enveloping majority society. However, even this observation probably oversimplifies the complexities of and psychological dimensions of the relations of Indian peoples to the Canadian state. Speculatively, it is highly likely that the reportedly lukewarm attitude to Canadian citizenship is possible because its benefits – welfare state, for example – are nevertheless available to Indian peoples. In general, unless there is a conflict with Aboriginal or treaty rights, or the Indian Act, Indians have the same relation to the rights, privileges and obligations of Canadian law as other Canadians. Indifference to citizenship would almost certainly weaken if anyone suggested removal of the franchise, or withdrawal of Old Age Security benefits. As Kulchyski argued, once citizenship rights were secured by the 1970s, 'the "plus" or additional rights became the focus of discussion' (Kulchyski, 1994: 5). It may be, then, that citizenship rights can be accorded low priority because they are considered to be secure. Further, the historic link between giving up Indian status and accepting citizenship – the historic enfranchisement policy – suggests that a too overt support for citizenship status will be seen by some as an overt denial of Indianness.

Speculatively, again, the pallid public support for citizenship and the contrasting political rhetoric of nationalism reflects the communal reality of the 60% of the status Indian population that is reserve-based. If the Indian people were scattered throughout Canadian society with no land base to call their own, the Canadian debate would presumably have been a modified version of the American debate over the position of Afro-Americans intermingled in urban milieus with the non-Afro-American majority. Claims based on a common citizenship would have been more frequent and powerful. The contemporary dominant discourse, which privileges the Indian First Nation over the Canadian citizen, would probably have been rivalled and possibly surpassed by a rhetoric of participatory inclusion. In this hypothetical scenario, the urban Aboriginal population would have what it now lacks, a voice and visibility proportionate to its numbers.

The existence of individual communities with a territorial base and a chief and council structures debate around the issues of the cultural survival of Indian nations and the role of governments in fostering it. The debate portrays the Aboriginal nation and Canadian citizenship as rival modes of belonging. Claims on the majority society for justice are not made in the language of a shared citizenship but in the language of Aboriginal rights, of wrongs historically inflicted on their people, of treaty rights that have been violated (Sanders, 2001). The triumph of the language of nation over citizenship from an Aboriginal perspective is not dictated by numbers. The language of nation is much less persuasive for the more than half of the overall Aboriginal population (Indian, Inuit and Metis) that lacks a land base, and which constitutes a much more receptive constituency for the language of citizenship – 'We want in!' It is, however, less easily organized, very heterogeneous, especially in metropolitan centres, of less interest to the legal profession, and in the inner city cores Aboriginal peoples are 'seen but not heard,' as a recent volume described their condition (LaPrairie, 1995).

THE AMBIGUOUS COLONIAL ANALOGY

The widely employed colonial analogy is a natural migration from the largely vanished world of overseas empire to the domestic situation of numerically weak indigenous peoples surrounded by settler majorities. The demise of European empires and the emergence of formerly subject peoples to independence helped indigenous peoples in settler countries to see their own situation in terms of a history of colonialism from which they sought an escape. In each case, indigenous peoples were taken over and subordinated to the newly arrived Europeans. In the classic imperial setting, colonialism was an overseas venture, the ending of which required the transfer of governing authority to the indigenous majority. A new flag is raised. A new country enters the United Nations, and the international community of sovereign states acquires a new member.

In New World settler societies, the colonial analogy was an appropriate label for the historic subjugation of native peoples and their subsequent treatment as wards incapable of self-rule, a point repeatedly made by RCAP (Canada, 1996). Indians, in particular, see themselves as a colonized people (First Nations Circle on the Constitution, 1992). In both cases, overseas and domestic, the newcomers diverted indigenous peoples from the paths on which they had been traveling. They were subjected to distant authorities over which they had negligible influence. In both cases, equally deprived of self-rule, their situation and treatment was colonial. However, the ending of colonialism took them on different paths. The newly independent subjects of a former overseas colony meet yesterday's masters in the international community of states, where both meet formally as equals, clothed in the garments of independent statehood. For indigenous peoples in settler colonies – the 'nations within,' who had been similarly denigrated and humiliated by European peoples, the ending of colonialism could not culminate in independence. Small numbers and their scattering in the Canadian case into small communities preclude independence. The majority is not going to go home, and federal and provincial governments are disinclined to consider the dismemberment of the Canadian state. The realistic aspirations of small indigenous nations are limited to carving out whatever degree of autonomy they can, supplemented by a rapprochement in matters outside their indigenous jurisdiction with the surrounding majority society which had been the instrument of their oppression.

Their identity, as is commonly true of indigenous peoples, derives much of its content from nationalist histories of their victimization. It was almost inevitable, therefore, given their own past treatment, the independence outcome for former overseas colonies, their distrust of the majority society, and their own assertive nationalism, that constitutional theorizing by or on behalf of First Nations would largely be directed to the autonomy goal and much less to the rapprochement via a common citizenship with those who had built a flourishing society that had passed them by.

To interpret past treatment as colonial defines the counter-attack as nationalist; the community of belonging is the struggling nation, and the goal is escape by the maximum self-government possible. A colonial interpretation of the past creates a psychological impediment to a positive view of Canadian citizenship. Escape from a colonial past is conventionally seen as an act of collective emancipation, not as a series of individual citizen memberships in the society that historically excluded one's people as unworthy. If this psychological impediment triumphs, and the members of small self-governing nations have only a limited connection to the political institutions of the majority society, and limited enthusiasm for participation in settler political institutions as voters, legislators, or cabinet ministers, they will have minimal or no impact on the great affairs of state which will be handled outside of First Nations jurisdiction.

The necessary rapprochement to overcome a dangerous isolation is not easy, as First Nations members are unlikely to see the Canadian state in its federal and provincial embodiment as 'their' state. Even if wardship has been officially repudiated, members of First Nations encounter their former masters in a domestic setting, where the latter are still a decisive majority. At best, they continue to live in a halfway house, still minorities, albeit nations, in the midst of majorities on whom they remain dependent. Such a halfway house may still be experienced as a continuation of colonialism. The possibilities of escape even by some federal arrangement of constitutionally protected self-government are severely limited. This is especially so if individual nations have small populations, if they seek the goods and services available to the majority, and if many of the policies and decisions affecting them are outside the sphere of self-government – all of which applies to First Nations.

The introspective nationalism of small, scattered communities does not threaten the territorial integrity of Canada. 'Indigenism,' as Niezen observes, 'can … be distinguished from ethnic nationalism by the consistent reluctance of indigenous peoples … to invoke secession and independent statehood as desired political goals' (Niezen, 2000: 141; see also Sharp, 1990: 251 for general agreement for the Maori, but 256–65 for important exceptions). Nevertheless, indigenous nationalism in Canada weakens allegiance to and identification with the Canadian state, at least for a transition period of indeterminate length. Until a reasonable rapprochement at the psychological level between Indian nationalism and Canadian citizenship can be worked out, the former may lead to a kind of civic deficit for possibly hundreds of small communities that are geographically within Canada, but emotionally distant from it. The same point was made by Andrew Sharp about New Zealand in the 1980s, that 'it was ... obvious to all that the state as it was constituted and as it operated was hardly the object of devotion of many Maori and that it stood to lose the adherence of still more' (Sharp, 1990: 266).

If escape to independent statehood in the international system is impossible, one strand of constitutional theorizing redefines the domestic political system as if it were a quasi-international system. Participation in settler institutions is not then understood as participation with fellow citizens from heterogeneous constituencies, but rather as nations participating in an emerging multinational polity. As already noted, the RCAP Report privileges the Aboriginal nation as the primary unit of allegiance and solidarity, asserts that the Aboriginal non-Aboriginal relationship should be restructured in terms of nation-to-nation, that the relations between these nations should be regulated by treaty, and that Aboriginal peoples should be part of a 'multinational federalism' that practices a 'multinational citizenship' (Canada, 1996: vol. I, xxiv). Canada's 'true vision,' accordingly, is a partnership of nations held together by civic allegiance to the separate nations (Canada, 1996: vol. I, xxv). Given the triumph of 'nation' over 'citizen' in its Report, RCAP's dismissive attitude to a House of Commons based on heterogeneous constituencies is perfectly logical. When the Commission turns its attention briefly to representation in the federal government legislative arena, it opts for Aboriginal nations as the units to be represented in a new third chamber acting as a watchdog for Aboriginal interests (Canada, 1996: vol. II (1) 374–82). Given this image of Canada as an assemblage of nations, a suggestion by Mary Ellen Turpel makes sense: 'It may be helpful [in thinking about direct Aboriginal participation in legislatures] to conceptualize special indigenous representatives as ambassadors or international representatives of indigenous communities with a quasi-diplomatic function. This model helps to dispel the impression that indigenous peoples are seeking assimilation into dominant institutions' (Turpel, 1992: 600).

Possibly the royal commission vision of a multinational federalism that verges on being an international system, which is shared by other scholars and activists (Henderson, 1994; Henderson et al., 2000), is realizable. The demise of overseas colonialism fundamentally and unpredictably transformed the international state system. The demise of domestic colonialism now underway will unquestionably and also unpredictably transform the relations between states and the peoples they govern. Although a transition era is characterized by adventurous thinking and is thus perhaps a poor time to be categorical about possible futures, the impediments to implementing the royal commission vision, three of which are discussed below, are enormous.

Firstly, in the many positive discussions of self-government, the very small size of the populations that will handle governing responsibilities is typically (one is tempted to say 'almost systematically') overlooked. Only 5% of Indian bands, 30 out of 623, have on-reserve populations of more than 2000; 405 have on-reserve populations of less than 500. One hundred and eleven bands have on-reserve populations of less than 100 (Indian and Northern Affairs Canada, 1997: xvi) Even RCAP, that saw the serious governance problems dictated by small size and therefore recommended a broad-based consolidation of existing communities to achieve an average nation size of 5000–7000 for a self-governing nation, ends up with large villages. The inescapable limitations on the extent of the jurisdictions that can be managed by such communities means that individual members of self-governing nations, even if their resource base is expanded, will remain heavily dependent on policies and services from federal and provincial governments. The tendency to downplay this consideration is remarkable.

Secondly, the related tendency of indigenous nationalist thought to focus on self-government and minimize the significance of citizenship as the vehicle for positive civic identification with the majority society may erode the good will of the latter. If the majority hears a consistent refrain of 'We are not you,' it may respond with 'They are not us.' If this dialectic takes place, in which each party is acting logically in terms of its definition of the situation, First Nations exercising limited sovereignty over small populations may be seen as strangers to whom little generosity is owed – an unfortunate outcome for citizens of small nations with little capacity for escaping poverty in the absence of substantial ongoing external support. Self-government in these circumstances may be a recipe for frustration, rather than the route to a viable future blending usable traditions and the skill practices of modernity.

Possibly, of course, 60 to 80 nation-to-nation treaty relationships, as proposed by RCAP, along with monitoring arrangements and implementing tribunals, can be a functional alternative to citizenship, especially if the treaties are constantly upgraded. However, when the Canadian nation partner is 5000 times larger in numbers than the average Aboriginal partner – assuming the consolidations of communities proposed by RCAP – and RCAP builds in no alternative source of empathy or solidarity, this vision of the future appears as a high risk gamble. The problem is eloquently raised by Fleras and Maaka: 'Will the extension of indigeneity as principle and practice create a society that is bifurcated around two constitutionalisms, thus creating new forms of segregation?' (Fleras and Maaka, 2000: 115).

The challenge of constitutional transformation, accordingly, 'lies in acknowledging [indigenous peoples'] rights as original occupants and political communities, without undermining societal cohesion and national identity in the process' (Fleras and Maaka, 2000: 119. See also Sharp, 1990: 284 for agreement from a New Zealand perspective). In general, and unfortunately, this fundamental challenge receives negligible attention in the mushrooming Aboriginal policy literature in Canada.

Thirdly, the colonial analogy and the discourse of nation are ill-suited to the situation of urban Aboriginals – more than 50% of the total aboriginal population and 42% of the status Indian population. The dominant discourse on nation and focus on self-government has only a limited application to their situation. As a result, they receive neither the policy concern, nor the academic attention their numbers and social problems justify. This is an extremely serious omission. Numerous indicators suggest that major Canadian cities, especially in the three western prairie provinces, are beginning to experience a Canadian version of the American big city situation with an Afro-American (Aboriginal) middle class and an Afro-American (Aboriginal) ghetto, with high levels of unemployment, violence, youth gangs, drugs and alcoholism (Cairns, 2000b). The hegemony of a discourse with minimal capacity to encompass urban Aboriginal populations is unfortunate. They are marginalized by a discourse more suited to nations with boundaries. They may, in extreme cases, be viewed as having betrayed the nationalist cause, of having gone over to the other side.

These three concerns – very small nations, the limited attention paid to social cohesion in nationalist literature, and the under-inclusiveness of the rhetoric of nation which marginalizes the urban half of the Aboriginal population – suggest that the vision of a multinational Canada of 60 to 80 or more Aboriginal nations linked to Canada by treaty but only minimally by a common citizenship, is, at a minimum, problematic.

CONCLUSION

A nationalist discourse of indigeneity in white settler dominions strengthens the developing momentum behind a 'proposed paradigm shift … partly in response to escalating indigenous pressure and prolonged public criticism, in other part to deflect a growing crisis in state legitimacy' (Fleras and Maaka, 2000: 113; see also 124). In Canada, the major indicator of that paradigm shift is S. 35 of the 1982 Constitution Act, which respects and affirms Aboriginal and treaty rights. The diffusion of the concept of 'nation,' and even more so First Nation, enhances the status of the holders of these rights. The existence of a treaty process in British Columbia, following more than a century of denial of Aboriginal title by successive British Columbia governments, testifies to the power of the transformed moral and intellectual climate which gives Aboriginal claims a legitimacy beyond the capacity of previous generations to imagine. The establishment of a major royal commission on Aboriginal issues, with an Aboriginal majority among the commissioners, indicated both the question mark about where Canadians were heading, and that Aboriginal people would play a lead role in influencing the choice of direction (Canada, 1996). Transforming these and other indicators of a developing politics of positive recognition into healthy self-governing nations for the 60% of Indian peoples living in organized communities, nevertheless will not be easily achieved. (See Wilkins, 2000 and Hull, 2001 for the difficulties.) However, the direction of change and momentum behind it are undeniable.

Doug Sanders, a non-Aboriginal legal scholar with perhaps a longer uninterrupted involvement in Aboriginal issues than any of his colleagues, recently offered the following policy advice.

> There is a consensus that the justification for Aboriginal rights is respect for Aboriginal difference and separate Aboriginal identities. Respect for Aboriginal difference means that the larger society and its legal system should not vigorously police the minority. Minorities need space within the larger society. At the same time, they should not be artificially isolated from the life around them. Some balance is needed. (Sanders, 2001: 36; See also Havemann, 1999: Chap. 18.)

A rephrasing of Sanders for the explicit citizenship focus of this paper suggests two requirements for a viable long-run citizenship policy for the Indian peoples of Canada. Such a policy has to respond to the desire of Indian peoples for positive differential treatment/distinct status in terms of self-government and/or rights. It has to do so in such a way that Indian peoples and other Canadians feel and believe that we all belong to the same Canadian community. The first criterion is self-evident. The failure to recognize it led to the defeat of the 1969 White Paper. Now, however, it is no longer a matter of choice. It has constitutional status in S. 35 of the 1982 Constitution Act. The second is no less important, although it receives less attention in the literature.

The apparent simplicity of these two criteria – respect for and accommodation of difference, and psychological identification with other Canadians in a pan-Canadian citizenship – should not blind us to how far we are from meeting them. John Borrows has recently defined Aboriginal peoples as 'uncertain citizens' (Borrows, 2001), a labelling that reflects the impact of a lengthy history of maltreatment, deprivation, and especially for status Indians, a systematic exclusion for previous generations from civic membership in the encompassing Canadian society. Overcoming a deeply divisive history is not easy. Indeed Andrew Sharp, writing of New Zealand, but in language also applicable to Canada, after asserting that 'Maori and Pakeha have separate and often contradictory conceptions of what justice demands,' argues that 'sustaining a political society … means really living with difference, hence living with injustice, [while] continually negotiating its distribution' (Sharp, 1990: 1, 26) This means, of course, that 'uncertain citizens' is likely to be a long-lived status.

As already noted, the two comprehensive attempts to find a viable policy for a rapprochement – the 1969 White Paper and the 1996 Royal Commission on Aboriginal Peoples – both failed to meet the two criteria suggested above. The White Paper, addressed only to Indian peoples, failed to accommodate, indeed ignored, their desire for a continuing distinct status, albeit one that this time gave them a positive niche in the constitutional order. RCAP failed on the other dimension. Although its recommendations were not a recipe for independence, the Report was above all a document of Aboriginal nationalism ('Aboriginal' because its terms of reference included Inuit and Métis as well as the Indian peoples of Canada). It failed to address the issue(s) of common belonging, of a country-wide citizenship, and the need for some fellow-feeling to sustain empathy with non-Aboriginal Canadians. It is unclear whether the commissioners understood the significance of this consideration.

Helpful guidance in thinking our way through the ambiguities and complexities of this difficult policy area comes from Rogers Smith's historical analysis of US citizenship laws (Smith, 1997) and Charles Taylor's recent writings on the need for a degree of common identity and community cohesion for the effective functioning of a contemporary democracy (Taylor, 1996, 1999, 2001).

Historically, according to Smith, American citizenship laws have been home to illiberal, undemocratic exclusions at various times (Smith, 1997: 1, 2, 3, 15, 29). Similar patterns of exclusion, with that of status Indians being the most striking, have been pervasively present in the Canadian past (Cairns, 1995b). Smith's admonitions derived from American history that governments 'are more likely to use their powers to aid those who are their citizens than those who are not' (Smith, 1997: 31) could easily have been extracted as the lesson of Indian policy in the first century after Confederation. It has continuing relevance by suggesting that there are limits to differentiated citizenship, that at some point recognition of difference can so reduce the residual citizenship that it can no longer sustain a meaningful solidarity or empathy.

Smith underlines the volatility of American citizenship policy, tracking its zigzag route between universalism and exclusionist ascriptive criteria. No devotee of Whig history, he warns that 'neither the possession nor the fresh achievement of greater equality can guarantee against later losses of status due to renewed support for various types of ascriptive hierarchy' (Smith, 1997: 471). In practical terms, this suggests the imperative necessity of a sensitive balancing act so that the positive recognition of difference by, for example, a constitutionalized third order of Aboriginal government, does not contribute to a revived marginalization and outsider status.

Smith agrees with Charles Taylor (see below) that governments and leaders are driven by the necessities of political life to fashion a people, a community with sufficient solidarity to think of itself as a 'we' group – one for whom reciprocal responsibility for each other is natural. This, Smith asserts, is a huge problem, for contemporary states contain many peoples whose 'traits give them reason to decide that their primary political identity and allegiance is to some group other than that defined by the regime governing the territory in which they reside' (Smith, 1997: 32).

Similar points have recently and repeatedly been made by Charles Taylor. Free societies, based on citizen democracy, 'require a degree of cohesion, of willing loyalty and support from their members … [such] societies based on the legitimating idea of popular sovereignty have to be able to understand themselves as deciding together, and therefore deliberating together, and this presupposes a certain common focus, a common sense of what the society is concerned with, around which public debate takes its shape.'

We 'neglect at our peril,' he argues, '[such] goals like social harmony, a sense of solidarity, mutual understanding and a sense of civility' (Taylor, 2001: 4; see also Taylor, 1996, 1999; and Wilkins 2000).

Both Smith and Taylor are responding to what the Aboriginal law professor John Borrows described, following Kymlicka and Norman (2000: 39–40), as an essential component of a functional citizenship, its contribution to social cohesion, which 'facilitates empathy, common concern and compassion that are essential to the functioning of any civil society. It encourages the removal of barriers that restrict sharing and exchange, and thereby assists in the free flow of goods, services, affluence and assistance' (Borrows, 2001: 23). Conversely, of course, a weak overarching citizenship, one that is reluctantly adhered to by a discrete minority, would weaken empathy and compassion in the long run and discourage that flow of goods, services, affluence and assistance.

Borrows observes that the Canadian Supreme Court, which has become one of the leading players in the search for reconciliation between Aboriginal and non-Aboriginal Canadians, quite properly concerns itself with social cohesion in its decisions. He noted and applauded the Court's encouragement of negotiation, its efforts both to recognize rights and to develop a jurisprudence of when they might be restricted in the interest of 'societal stability … [thus] illustrat[ing] sensitivity to the interests of both Aboriginal and non-Aboriginal peoples' (2001: 29), and its thesis that the recognition of Aboriginal rights 'must be directed towards reconciliation … with the sovereignty of the Crown' (2001: 32), which translates into reconciliation with 'the broader political community of which they are part' (2001: 34).

The Court's concern for social cohesion is reinforced by the position of the federal government. The federal government has never wavered from its position that the inherent right of self-government is to be exercised 'within Canada'. It has been equally adamant that the Charter of Rights and the Canadian Human Rights Act must apply in self-government agreements (Sanders, 2001: 8, 10). The Aboriginal peoples whose Aboriginal and treaty rights are constitutionally recognized in S. 35 of the 1982 Constitution Act are 'aboriginal peoples of Canada'. (See Sharp, 1990: Ch. 14 for strong judicial and political (Pakeha) assertion of the sovereignty of the New Zealand state when confronted with Maori claims.)

The jurisdictional meaning of 'within Canada' is spelled out in the federal government 1995 policy statement *Aboriginal Self-Government* (Irwin, 1995). The statement is adamant that the recognition of self-government, even if inherent, is to be implemented within the Canadian constitutional framework. From the federal perspective, the jurisdiction of Aboriginal governments will likely extend to 'matters that are internal to the group, integral to its distinct Aboriginal culture, and essential to its operation as a government or institution' (Irwin, 1995: 5). In some areas neither integral to Aboriginal culture nor internal to the group, but where some Aboriginal jurisdiction might be negotiated, it will be subject to federal and provincial paramountcy. No deviation will be allowed 'from the basic principle that those federal and provincial laws of overriding national or provincial importance will prevail over conflicting Aboriginal laws' (Irwin, 1995: 11). Finally, there is a lengthy list of subject matters 'where there are no compelling reasons for Aboriginal governments or institutions to exercise law-making authority' (Irwin, 1995: 6). They include subject matters related to sovereignty, defence and external relations, and 'other National Interest Powers,' including management of the national economy, national law and order, health and safety, and specific federal undertakings such as aeronautics and the postal service.

This clearly indicates the federal government view of the limits to Aboriginal self-government. On the whole, the great affairs of state will remain in federal hands. Many of the services and policies that will apply to First Nations members will come from federal and provincial governments, and for off-reserve Indians also from municipal governments.

Perhaps if and when the constitutional system settles down a constitutional theory will emerge to describe what we have become. That First Nations and other Aboriginal peoples will have some special constitutional recognition and self-governing space in the constitutional framework may be assumed, given the interplay between Aboriginal nationalism and the recognition and affirmation of 'aboriginal and treaty rights' in the 1982 Constitution Act. That such recognition will be within Canada is also predictable. The federal government has indicated the subject matters it will reserve for itself.

We are in a transition phase in which competing positions are being staked out. The image that emerges is one in which the federal and provincial governments impose Canadian constraints and First Nations inject demands for recognition and jurisdiction into what is in effect an ongoing constitutional dialogue. Two high-profile questions are still without an answer. Can we and will we develop a second dialogue to address urban Aboriginal issues, one that is not simply a servant of the existing nation-to-nation theme? And will the outcome some decades hence meet Charles Taylor's requirement for a functioning contemporary democracy: a high degree of overall citizen commitment, mutual trust and a strong collective identity (Taylor, 1999)? The conditions necessary for their achievement, particularly for a strong collective identity encompassing the non-Aboriginal majority and Indian peoples, are lacking. A history of past exclusion and a litany of mistreatment and dispossession stored in collective memories generate a suspicious watchfulness. Taylor's thesis that Canadians must learn to share identity space (Taylor, 1999: 281) is a project still in its early stages. Carens underlines the 'paradox ... that the very concepts and institutions (aboriginal self-government, differentiated citizenship) that seem the most promising in terms of leading aboriginal people to feel as though they really belong to Canada as a political community are ones that may lead non-aboriginal Canadians to feel as though aboriginal people no longer belong' (Carens, 2000: 198, see also 193–4). The search is a for a coexisting balance in which recognition of difference and support for commonality are not seen as unremitting rivals, but as complementary, both at the level of institutions and civic identities.

The concerns of both sides are legitimate and understandable. The Canadian federal state seeks to ensure future positive links between itself and members of First Nations. This is not an easy task, given Canadian history. The state's authority is diminished if some of its peoples do not see it as their state. First Nations with a land base seek governing powers to increase their leverage against the overwhelming pressures from the majority society. Gaining reasonable leverage is immensely difficult given all the constraints imposed by small numbers and limited resources. Finding a workable compromise between these conflicting objectives remains a distant goal. Possibly Fleras and Maaka are right, that a 'degree of "standing apart"' may have to precede '"working together"' (Fleras and Maaka, 2000: 114). Borrows' description of Aboriginal peoples as 'uncertain citizens' (Borrows, 2001) should not, given the divided 'we' that Canadians have inherited from a colonial past, be viewed as a sign of failure but as a modest achievement.

REFERENCES

Bedford, David and Pobihuschy, Sidney (1994) 'Aboriginal Voter Participation', a paper presented at the Canadian Political Science Association Annual Meeting, University of Calgary, June 12, mimeographed.

Boldt, Menno (1993) *Surviving as Indians: The Challenge of Self-Government*. Toronto: University of Toronto Press.

Borrows, John (1994) 'Contemporary Traditional Equality: The Effect of the Charter on First Nation Politics', *University of New Brunswick Law Journal*, 43.

Borrows, John (2001) 'Uncertain Citizens: Aboriginal Peoples and the Supreme Court', *Canadian Bar Review*, 80.

Bruner, Edward M. (1986) 'Ethnography as Narrative', in Victor W. Turner and Edward M. Bruner (eds), *The Anthropology of Experience*, Urbana and Chicago: University of Illinois Press.

Cairns, Alan C. (1995a) 'Aboriginal Canadians, Citizenship and the Constitution', in *Reconfigurations: Canadian Citizenship and Constitutional Change: Selected Essays by Alan C. Cairns*, ed. Douglas E. Williams, Toronto: McClelland and Stewart.

Cairns, Alan C. (1995b). 'The Constitutional World We Have Lost', in *Reconfigurations: Canadian Citizenship and Constitutional Change: Selected Essays by Alan C. Cairns*, ed. Douglas E. Williams, Toronto: McClelland and Stewart.

Cairns, Alan C. (1999) 'Constitutional Stigmatization', in Patrick J. Hanafin and Melissa S. Williams (eds), *Identity, Rights and Constitutional Transformation*. Aldershot: Ashgate Publishing.

Cairns, Alan C. (2000a) *Citizens Plus: Aboriginal Peoples and the Canadian State*. Vancouver: UBC Press.

Cairns, Alan C. (2000b), 'The End of Internal Empire: The Emerging Aboriginal Policy Agenda', in David M. Hayne (ed.), *Governance in the 21st Century*, Transactions of the Royal Society of Canada, Series VI, vol. x., 1999 Toronto: University of Toronto Press.

Cairns, Alan C. (2001) 'Searching for Multinational Canada: The Rhetoric of Confusion', 2001 *Review of Constitutional Studies* 6 (1).

Canada (1969) *Statement of the Government of Canada on Indian Policy*. Presented to the First Session of the Twenty-eighth Parliament by the Honourable Jean Chretien, Minister of Indian Affairs and Northern Development, Ottawa: Department of Indian Affairs and Northern Development.

Canada (House of Commons) (1983) 'Indian Self-Government in Canada', *Minutes and Proceedings of the Special Committee on Indian Self-Government*, no. 40, 12 and 20, October 1983.

Canada (Department of Indian Affairs and Northern Development) (1985, 1990, 1999) *Schedule of Indian Bands, Reserves and Settlements Including Membership and Population Location and Acreage in Hectares*. June 1, 1985; December 1990; January 22, 1999, Ottawa: DIAND.

Canada (1987) *Debates*, Senate, 18 November.

Canada (1992) *Consensus Report on the Constitution, Charlottetown, August 28, 1992*. Final Text and Draft Legal Text, 9 October 1992.

Canada (1996) *Report of the Royal Commission on Aboriginal Peoples*. 5 vols, Ottawa: Canada Communication Group Publishing.

Canada (2001) *Canada Year Book*. Ottawa: Statistics Canada.

Carens, Joseph H. (2000) *Culture, Citizenship, and Community: A Contextual Exploration of Justice as Evenhandedness*. Oxford: Oxford University Press.

Chartrand, Paul (1999) 'Aboriginal Peoples in Canada: Aspirations for Distributive Justice as Distinct Peoples', in Paul Havemann, (ed.) *Indigenous Peoples' Rights in Australia, Canada, and New Zealand*. Auckland: Oxford University Press.

Clark, Jennifer (1998) 'The "Winds of Change" in Australia: Aborigines and the International Politics of Race, 1960–1972', *International History Review*, 20 (1).

Connor, Walker (1999) 'National Self-Determination and Tomorrow's Political Map', in Alan C. Cairns, John C. Courtney, Peter Mackinnon, Hans J. Michelmann and David E. Smith (eds), *Citizenship, Diversity and Pluralism: Canadian and Comparative Perspectives*. Montreal and Kingston: McGill-Queen's University Press.

Cornell, Stephen (1988) *The Return of the Native: American Indian Political Resurgence*. New York: Oxford University Press.

Cumming, Peter A. and Neil H. Mickenberg (1972) *Native Rights in Canada*. 2nd edition, Toronto: University of Toronto Press.

Deloria, Vine, Jr. (1970) *We Talk, You Listen*. New York: Macmillan.

Denis, Claude. (1997) *We Are Not You: First Nations and Canadian Modernity*. Peterborough: Broadview Press.

Dyck, Noel (1991) *What is the Indian "Problem"?* St. John's: Institute of Social and Economic Research.

First Nations Circle on the Constitution. (1992) *To the Source: Commissioners' Report*. Ottawa: Assembly of First Nations.

Fleras, Augie and Elliott, Jean Leonard (1992) *The "Nations Within"*. Toronto: Oxford University Press.

Fleras, Augie and Maaka, Roger (2000) 'Reconstitutionalizing Indigeneity: Restoring the "Sovereigns Within"', *Canadian Review of Studies in Nationalism*, xxvii (1–2).

Fletcher, Christine (1999) 'Living Together but Not Neighbours: Cultural Imperialism in Australia', in Paul Havemann (ed.), *Indigenous Peoples' Rights in Australia, Canada, and New Zealand*. Oxford: Oxford University Press.

Foster, Hamar (1999) '"Indian Administration" from the Royal Proclamation of 1763 to Constitutionally Entrenched Aboriginal Rights', in Paul Havemann (ed.), *Indigenous Peoples' Rights in Canada, Australia and New Zealand*. Oxford: Oxford University Press.

Havemann, Paul (ed.) (1999) *Indigenous Peoples' Rights in Australia, Canada and New Zealand*. Oxford: Oxford University Press.

Hawthorn, H.B. (ed.) (1966–67) *A Survey of the Contemporary Indians of Canada*. 2 vols, Ottawa: Queen's Printer.

Henderson, James (Sakej) Youngblood (1994) 'Empowering Treaty Federalism' *Saskatchewan Law Review*, 58 (2).

Henderson, James (Sakej) Youngblood, Benson, Marjorie L. and Findlay, Isobel M. (2000) *Aboriginal Tenure in the Constitution of Canada*. Scarborough, Ont.: Carswell.

Hull, Jeremy (2001), *Aboriginal People and Social Classes in Manitoba*. Winnipeg: Canadian Centre for Policy Alternatives.

Indian and Northern Affairs Canada (1997) *Indian Register Population by Sex and Residence 1996*. Ottawa: Department of Indian Affairs and Northern Development.

Indian Chiefs of Alberta (1970) *Citizens Plus: A Presentation by the Indian Chiefs of Alberta to Right Honourable P.E. Trudeau, June 1970*. Edmonton: Indian Association of Alberta.

Indian-Eskimo Association of Canada (1970) *Native Rights in Canada*. Toronto: Indian-Eskimo Association of Canada.

Irwin, The Honourable Ronald A., Minister of Indian Affairs and Northern Development. (1995) *Aboriginal Self-Government: The Government of Canada's Approach to Implementation of the Inherent Right and the Negotiation of Aboriginal Self-Government*. Ottawa: Department of Indian Affairs and Northern Development.

Jackson, Robert H. (1993) 'The Weight of Ideas in Decolonization: Normative Change in International Relations', in Judith Goldstein and Robert O. Keohane (eds), *Ideas and Foreign Policy: Beliefs, Institutions and Political Change*, Ithaca, N.Y.: Cornell University Press.

Johnston, Darlene (1993) 'First Nations and Canadian Citizenship', in William Kaplan (ed.), *Belonging: The Meaning and Future of Canadian Citizenship*. Montreal and Kingston: McGill-Queen's University Press.

Kulchyski, Peter, ed. (1994) *Unjust Relations: Aboriginal Rights in Canadian Courts*. Toronto: Oxford University Press.

Kymlicka, Will and Norman, Wayne (2000) 'Citizenship in Culturally Diverse Societies: Issues, Contexts, Concepts', in Will Kymlicka and Wayne Norman (eds), *Citizenship in Diverse Societies*. Oxford: Oxford University Press.

LaPrairie, Carol (1995) *Seen But Not Heard: Native People in the Inner City*. Ottawa: Department of Justice Canada.

LaRocque, Emma (1997) 'Re-examining Culturally Appropriate Models in Criminal Justice Applications', in *Aboriginal and Treaty Rights in Canada: Essays on Law, Equality, and Respect for Difference*. ed. Michael Asch. Vancouver: UBC Press.

Leslie, John and Macguire, Ron (eds) (1979) *The Historical Development of the Indian Act*. 2nd edition. Ottawa: Treaties and Historical Research Centre, Research Branch, Corporate Policy, Department of Indian and Northern Affairs.

Macklem, Patrick (1993) 'Distributing Sovereignty: Indian Nations and Equality of Peoples', *Stanford Law Review*, 45 (5).

Magallanes, Catherine J. Iorns (1999) 'International Human Rights and their Impact on Domestic Law on Indigenous Peoples' Rights in Australia, Canada, and New Zealand', in Paul Havemann (ed.), *Indigenous Peoples' Rights in Australia, Canada, and New Zealand*. Auckland: Oxford University Press.

Malloy, Jonathan and White, Graham (1997) 'Aboriginal Participation in Canadian Legislatures', in Robert J. Fleming and J.E. Glenn (eds), *Fleming's Canadian Legislatures, 1997*. 11th edition, Toronto: University of Toronto Press.

Mansell, Michael (1993) 'Australians and Aborigines and the Mabo Decision. Just Who Needs Whom the Most?', *Sydney Law Review*, 15 (2; June).

Martin, Lawrence (1995) *Chrétien: The Will to Win*. vol. 1, Toronto: Lester Publishing.

Monture-Angus, Patricia (1999) *Journeying Forward: Dreaming of First Nations Independence*. Halifax: Fernwood Publishing.

Niezen, Ronald (2000) 'Recognizing Indigenism: Canadian Unity and the International Movement of Indigenous Peoples', *Comparative Studies in Society and History*, 42 (1, January).

Sanders, Douglas (2001) 'Aboriginal Rights and Human Rights', April 29, mimeographed.

Sawchuk, Joe (1998) *The Dynamics of Native Politics: The Alberta Métis Experience*. Saskatoon: Purich Publishing.

Schouls, Tim (1996) 'Aboriginal Peoples and Electoral Reform in Canada: Differentiated Representation versus Voter Equality', *Canadian Journal of Political Science*, xxix (4 December).

Sharp, Andrew (1990) *Justice and the Maori: Maori Claims in New Zealand Political Argument in the 1980s*. Auckland: Oxford University Press.

Smith, Rogers M. (1997) *Civic Ideals: Conflicting Visions of Citizenship in U.S. History*. New Haven and London: Yale University Press.

Taylor, Charles (1996) 'Why Democracy Needs Patriotism', in *Debating the Limits of Patriotism, For Love of Country, Martha C. Nussbaum with Respondents*, ed. Joshua Cohen, Boston: Beacon Press.

Taylor, Charles (1999) 'Democratic Exclusion (and its Remedies?)' in Alan C. Cairns, John C. Courtney, Peter Mackinnon, Hans J. Michelmann and David E. Smith (eds), *Citizenship, Diversity and Pluralism: Canadian and Comparative Perspectives*. Montreal and Kingston: McGill-Queen's University Press.

Taylor, Charles (2001) 'How to be Diverse: The need for a looser "us" to accommodate "them", a review of Bhikhu Parekh, *Rethinking Multiculturalism*', *Times Literary Supplement*, April 20.

Turpel, Mary Ellen (1989–90) 'Aboriginal Peoples and the Canadian Charter: Interpretive Monopolies, Cultural Differences', *Canadian Human Rights Yearbook*, 6.

Turpel, Mary Ellen (1992) 'Indigenous Peoples' Rights of Political Participation and Self-Determination: Recent International Legal Developments and the Continuing Struggle for Recognition', *Cornell International Law Journal*, 25 (3).

Ward, Alan and Hayward, Janine (1999) 'Tino Rangatiratanga: Maori in the Political and Administrative System', in Paul Havemann (ed.), *Indigenous Peoples' Rights in Australia, Canada, and New Zealand*. Auckland: Oxford University Press.

Watkins, Mel (ed.) (1977) *Dene Nation – The Colony Within*. Toronto: University of Toronto Press.

Weaver, Sally M. (1981) *Making Canadian Indian Policy: The Hidden Agenda 1968–1970*. Toronto: University of Toronto Press.

Webber, Jeremy (1995) 'The Jurisprudence of Regret: The Search for Standards of Justice in Mabo', *Sydney Law Review*, 17 (1).

Wilkins, Kerry (2000) 'Take Your Time and Do It Right: *Delgamuukw*, Self-Government Rights and the Pragmatics of Advocacy', *Manitoba Law Journal*, 27 (2).

14

Cultural Citizenship

TOBY MILLER

Citizenship today takes a number of forms. Perhaps the most discussed are political and economic citizenship. In this chapter, I focus on cultural citizenship and its differences from these forms, examining in particular its enabling condition of existence – immigration – and its enabling intervention – governmental means of producing cultural subjects.

Political citizenship permits voting, appeals to representative government, and guarantees of physical security in return for ceding the right to violence to the state. Its founding assumption is that personal freedom is both the wellspring of good government *and* the authority of that government over individuals. In Jean-Jacques Rousseau's paradox, this involves 'making men free by making them subject' (Rousseau, [1762] 1975: 123). As developed through capitalism, slavery, colonialism, and liberalism, political citizenship has expanded its reach and definition exponentially since the eighteenth century, though it remains unevenly spread across the globe.

Economic citizenship covers employment, health, and retirement security through the redistribution of capitalist gains and the use of the state as an agent of investment. In the words of Australia's World War II Prime Minister John Curtin, 'government should be the agency whereby the masses should be lifted up' (quoted in van Creveld, 1999: 355). Economic citizenship emerged from the Depression and decolonization as a promise of full employment in the First World and economic development in the Third. Today, it is in decline, displaced by the historic policy renegotiations of the 1970s conducted by capital, the state, and their intellectual servants in economics that redistributed income back to bourgeoisies.

Cultural citizenship concerns the maintenance and development of cultural lineage via education, custom, language, and religion, and the positive acknowledgement of difference in and by the mainstream. It is a developing discourse, in response to the great waves of cross-class migration of the past fifty years and an increasingly mobile middle class culture-industry workforce generated by a new international division of cultural labor (NIDCL) that favors North over South and capital over labor, as film and television production, computing, and sport go global in search of locations, skills, and docile labor. Within the NIDCL, certain cosmopolitans embark on what Aihwa Ong (1999: 112–13) calls 'flexible citizenship,' a strategic making-do that seeks access to as many rights as possible whilst falling prey to as few responsibilities as possible. This conduct matches corporate trends of globalization. It alienates those who wish that others had an affective, allegedly non-sectarian relationship with the state as well as an instrumental one (though the latter might be regarded by institutionalist political science as an exemplary instance of interest-group pluralism, or lauded by neoclassical economists as market-style shopping!) (Aleinikoff, 2000: 132, 145). Meanwhile, away from the capitalist class and the salariat, those affected by the division of labor in manufacturing and agriculture need rights to communication in the new media. Of course, many migrant workers around the world are 'temporary' or 'undocumented' workers – neither citizens nor immigrants. Their identity is quite separate from both their domicile and their source of sustenance, and they are guaranteed equitable treatment not by sovereign states, but through the supranational discourse of human rights and everyday customs and beliefs that superintend the legal obligations of conventional citizenship (Shafir, 1998: 20, 19).

Put another way, we might say that where classical political theory accorded political representation to the citizen through the state, the distinctively modern economic addendum to this was that the state promised a minimum standard of living, provided that the citizen recognized a debt to the great institutions of welfare. The decisive postmodern guarantee is access to the technologies of communication. The latter promise derives its force from a sense that political institutions need to relearn what sovereignty is about in polymorphous sovereign states that are diminishingly homogeneous in demographic terms and increasingly heteroglossic in their cultural competence. Contradictory accounts of the citizen emerge from the presumption that the work of executive government is to tell the people why they should be faithful to it, whilst claiming their considered acceptance and support as the grounds for its own existence (Miller, 1993).

This is especially true in the multiple identity of the citizen-consumer. On the one hand, the government places great faith in the capitalist system, which necessarily produces inequalities of income and operates via the desiring machinery of utility maximization. Some confusion results from the need to yoke together the rational citizen, who thinks of the greater good of the greater number, and the rational consumer, who valorizes him- or herself. They are both called up inside the one subject, who must be taught to distinguish between public goods, where one person's consumption does not preclude another's, and private goods, where it does. Now that many forms of publicly expressed identity have emerged from a combination of expanded human and civil rights discourse and expanded niche marketing, globalizing and privatizing norms merge with forms of consumer targeting to produce new kinds of civic life. Opportunities for marginal groups to express themselves, and fears for legitimacy on the part of hitherto dominant social classes, amount to a double movement of renewal under the sign of citizenship within a civil society that 'exists over against the state, in partial independence from it' (Taylor, 1990: 95).

THEORIZING CULTURAL CITIZENSHIP

There have been three key sites for theorizing cultural citizenship activity, each with strong links to the public sphere. They emerged at the same time, but with seemingly minimal interaction. Since the late 1980s, Tony Bennett and colleagues in the cultural-policy studies movement have focused on a guaranteed set of cultural competences that government should give to its citizenry. Their primary interlocutor is the Australian federal government's cultural bureaucracy, and their admirers include others in search of influence beyond affective protest (*American Behavioral Scientist*, 2000; Bennett, 1998; Miller, 1998). Renato Rosaldo and colleagues in Californian, Texan, and New York Latino/a studies of the same period look to a guaranteed set of rights for minorities. Their primary interlocutor is Latino/a social movements, and their admirers include the *Fresno Bee* newspaper (Rosaldo, 1997; Flores and Benmayor, 1997; Rodriguez and Gonzales, 1995). Finally, Will Kymlicka and fellow liberal political theorists seek a rapprochement between collective minority cultures and individual majority culture. Their primary interlocutor is a series of states dealing with ethnic minorities, and their admirers include the *Wall Street Journal* (Kymlicka, 1995; Zachary, 2000). Where Rosaldo et al. seek to transform as well as to use citizenship for the purposes of their own culture and others marginalized by the majority, Bennett and Kymlicka seek to utilize it for a general purpose that takes account of minorities. For Rosaldo, US culture is distinguished by the Latino/a immigrant experience of disenfranchisement. As such, culture substantively trumps formal universalism. Kymlicka thinks similarly. For Bennett, culture is a set of tools for living that are deployed or not depending on their value for achieving specific purposes, rather than purely expressive ends in themselves. Rosaldo is critical of liberal government for its myths of the sovereign individual and assumptions of a shared language and culture. Kymlicka endorses liberalism provided that it allows for real protection to minorities – as a matter of justice and self-interest. Bennett endorses liberal government as a project of constituting, not drawing upon, the liberal individual, and is agnostic about its humanist claims.

Most proponents of cultural citizenship argue that identity is developed and secured through a cultural context. On this reading, collective senses of self are more important than monadic ones, and rights and responsibilities can be determined in accordance with cultural membership rather than the individual (Fierlbeck, 1996: 4, 6). For some critics, this flexibility can be achieved through a doctrine of cultural rights. For others, such as Amélie Oksenberg Rorty, it is a by-product of universal access to education, a 'primary condition of free and equal citizen participation in public life' (Rorty, 1995: 162). Rorty opposes public funding to sustain specific cultural norms of familial or religious origin, calling instead for a curriculum designed to generate cosmopolitans who learn about their country and its 'global neighbors' in a way that does not adjudicate between identities as workers, believers, or other forms of life that exist alongside one's culture of origin (Rorty, 1995: 164). Her argument is a collectivist flip-side to human-capital *données* about individuals maximizing their utility through investment in skills. It reunites cultural citizenship with liberalism. Each position is fundamentally concerned with efficient and effective social life and naturalization requirements. For instance, to become a citizen of the USA other than by birth or blood, one must reside there, know the country's basic political history, 'read, write, and speak words in ordinary usage in the English language', and neither consort with sex workers nor be repeatedly drunk in public. One must also renounce allegiance to other states (Aleinikoff, 2000: 130). These conditions reference the key crisis that has underpinned the clamor for cultural citizenship – immigration.

IMMIGRATION

Orthodox histories of citizenship postulate it as the Western outcome of 'fixed identities, unproblematic nationhood, indivisible sovereignty, ethnic homogeneity, and exclusive citizenship' (Mahmud, 1997: 633; also see Hindess, 1998). These histories ignore the fact that theories of citizenship were forged in relation to the imperial and colonial encounters of West and East as a justification of extra-territorial subjugation, followed by incorporation of the periphery into an international system of labor. These conditions led in turn to cultural policy concerns with language, heritage, and identity, expressed by both metropole and periphery as they exchanged people and cultures and governed by an overt logic of superiority whose legacies many see in the universalism of human-rights discourse (Mahmud, 1999: 1223). Western states derived an ethics from the bloodletting and conquest of war and nationalism that differentiated their forms of political organization from prior and alternative styles of governing. The West's model concentrated all such functions under its sovereign control, defined territorially to claim the right to govern conduct within its boundaries. In the process, the state established itself as an abstraction beyond embodiment in a monarch or a group, such that it could survive their expiration and engage in its own rites of personification and auto-anthropomorphism.

In turn, it opened these rites up to other non-human actors, such as corporations. That very non-human activism has latterly drawn into question the state's future, as multinational firms have grown in their economic reach and legal stature to attain the national and international status that was once only available to states (van Creveld, 1999: 415–16). In turn, they create and touch upon forms of cultural life that achieve an institutional personality. This is the current legacy of globalization. Of course, there are more valuable aspects to this legacy. In Argentina, for example, which has a migrant workforce from Bolivia and Paraguay to do menial jobs, leftists attempt to extend a more general rights-inflected citizenship to them by arguing that recently achieved rights in the aftermath of dictatorship should be extended to all residents. This promotes a multicultural framework, as in countries that do not have migrant workforces, e.g. Mexico and Colombia. Citizenship rethought as the struggles of social movements is strong in many other countries and in UNESCO.

In some sense we can see globalizing origins of cultural-citizenship discourse very far back. In 1513, one of the early major Spanish excursions to destroy pre-Columbian civilization was subject to serious ideological retooling by a theological committee. It provided the *conquistadores* with a manifesto that was translated for the Indians. It was a world history told through the anointing of Peter as Christ's vicar on Earth, which was used to justify later Popes dividing up the world. The document concluded with a chilling warning of what would happen in the event of resistance to imperial conquest: Indian women and children would be enslaved, their goods seized, and culpability laid at the feet of the vanquished. In its careful attention to ideology, its alibi in divine nomination, and its overtly political use of non-combatants as symbols, this is a remarkably modern text, so overt are its precepts. Of course, its superstition (Christianity) is non-modern, but the text's mode of address is incantatory and reasoned in its brutality – fire and the sword will prevail, so follow the direct line of reasoning from God and you will be spared. The Aztecs and Incas whom the Spanish subsequently overthrew had shown no such desire for cultural justification in destroying the civilizations *they* had found. And unlike other conquerors, the Spanish did not present themselves as superior – simply as selected by God's delegate (Brown, 2000: 203–5). Nevertheless, the result of this has been precisely to exclude other forms of culture from full citizenship – as the Economic Commission for Latin America and the Caribbean/Comisión Económica por America Latina has recently noted with reference to indigenous peoples, African Americans, and Afro-Caribbeans (Xinha News Agency, 2000).

This harsh link of soil and blood has remained central to citizenship rights. Most states confer these rights through *jus sanguinis*, or blood right, based on parentage. The USA is unusual in that it uses *jus sanguinis* only for children born overseas to its own citizens. A much older, medieval concept is dominant: *jus soli*, a right of the soil that is based on residence. This principle derives from the Fourteenth Amendment's anti-racist guarantee of citizenship to those born or naturalized in the USA. (Until 1865, white male immigrants could vote without being naturalized, but native-born women and people of color could not.) This history of racialization and deracialization has made US citizenship policy close to culture from day one (Aleinikoff, 2000: 124, 151, 151 n. 67).

Traditional views of naturalized citizenship have been thrown into confusion by late twentieth-century immigration and multiculturalism (Feldblum, 1997: 103). Liberal ideals assume a migrant subject who throws off prior loyalties in order to become a citizen. Alongside nationals of the same country, they put aside social divisions in the common interest. Liberalism assumes, with neoclassical economics, that people emerge into citizenship fully formed, as sovereign individuals with personal preferences. Multiculturalism, by contrast, blurs the lines between individualism and communitarianism. Multiculturalism assumes, with communitarianism, that group loyalties override this notion. But where communitarianism assumes people find their collective identity through political participation, multiculturalism assumes, with liberalism, that this subjectivity is ordained prior to politics (Shafir, 1998: 10–11).

The new conditions of citizenship may not locate fealty in the sovereign state, nor do they necessarily articulate with democracy, because subjects of the international trade in labor frequently lack the access to power of native-born sons and daughters (Preuss, 1998: 310). In Europe, the creation of 'supranational citizenship' in 1992 problematized coupling citizenship to national culture. At the same time that this recognized a new international division of labor, equivalent moves limited the rights of guest workers – a common move in supposedly liberal democracies. Consider the situation of those who, because of changed socioeconomic conditions, become officially acceptable migrant-citizens having previously been pariahs. For example, excluding and brutalizing Asians had been historically critical to white Australian citizenship and national identity for most of the twentieth century, until Asian economic power became clear in the 1970s. Asian Australians' latter-day take on citizenship is, not surprisingly, instrumental. They are concerned with rights, but they may not feel patriotic (Ip et al., 1997).

Bonnie Honig (1998) has shown that immigrants have long been the limit-case for loyalty, as per Ruth the Moabite in the Jewish Bible/Old Testament. Such figures are both perilous for the sovereign state (where does their fealty lie?) and symbolically essential (as the only citizens who make a deliberate decision to swear allegiance to an otherwise mythic social contract). In the case of the USA, immigrants are crucial to the foundational ethos of consent, for they represent alienation from their places of origin and endorsement of the New World. This makes a national culture all the more fraught, for just as the memory of what has been lost (by choice) is strong, so is the necessity to shore up the 'preference' expressed for US norms.

This becomes as much a pragmatic question as a moral one under present circumstances in the United States. In the post-1960s period, the rise of welfare, along with the state's incapacity to prevent undocumented immigration, has rendered *jus soli* extremely expensive for the middle class and hence contentious. We already know from the US Census of 2000 that in the past decade the country's Asian and Pacific Islander population increased by 43% and its Hispanic population by 38.8%. Between those two groups, African Americans, and Native Americans, 79.2 million US residents define themselves as minorities ('Hispanic', 2000). The foreign-born proportion of the population is 10% – double the figure from 1970. Similar numbers are becoming normal in large Western democracies. Non-citizens make up 6.3% of the French population and 8.5% of the German (Aleinikoff, 2000: 121, 126).

Some critics, such as Rosaldo, claim that the difficulty with encouraging minority groups in the USA to vote, and the low levels of naturalization for non-Asian minority immigrants (in the 1990s, 57.6% of immigrants from Asia became US citizens versus 32.2% of Hispanics [Aleinikoff, 2000: 130]) can be addressed by promoting cultural citizenship – that one can have multiple affinities, to 'former' languages, places, or norms *and* to adopted countries. The *Fresno Bee* says cultural citizenship is 'a concept sweeping America's universities', eschewing assimilation but demanding rights, including immigrant cultural maintenance. In support of this, the paper argues that a 'Salvadoran family ... is Salvadoran whether they live in Washington, D.C., or San Salvador' (Rodriguez and Gonzales, 1995). Perhaps – but if they are, what should happen to them if there is a military conflict between El Salvador and the United States, and they are called upon to fight for one side or both; or less spectacularly, which set of national laws should apply to them and those around them? (Consider the fate of Japanese Americans during World War II.) If, as the *Fresno Bee* asserts, this dualism is a matter of 'basic human rights', what if El Salavador and the USA adopt different positions on human rights – or similar ones, but they are infractions of the very concept as parlayed through the UN? The recent history of the two nations makes this debate far from abstract.

Citizenship can also bedevil internal migration. In China, the market reforms of the past decade and a half have had the historically typical capitalist effect of a huge demographic pull away from the countryside and toward the city. Because of China's complex system of household registration, ideas of citizenship are closely tied to regionalism and policing. As peasants are not registered municipally, those who have flooded the cities from the countryside since the mid-1980s are essentially denied citizenship rights such as education and health care, not to mention housing. There seems to be as little incentive for locals and the state to include them as there is a desire on their part to be incorporated. This dilemma problematizes the long-held liberal assumption of a fit between the spread of citizenship and the rise of capitalism or urbanism (Solinger, 1999: 1–5).

When the Soviet Union broke up, its former republics had two choices in dealing with their sizeable Russian-speaking minorities: either propound a cultural nationalism that marginalized the Russian language and set religious, racial, and linguistic criteria for citizenship (as per Estonia and Latvia); or adopt a civic policy that offered entitlements based on territory, fealty, and labor (which took place in Ukraine and Kazakhstan) (Laitin, 1999: 314–17). Today, the Estonian government has to deal with a sizeable Russian minority, which it initially alienated by adopting a hard-line nationalism. The government is trying to defuse the situation via Russian-language schools and cultural groups – courtesy of a Kymlicka consultancy (Zachary, 2000).

In both intra- and international environments, there are ongoing tensions between doctrines of cultural rights and liberal individualism. Consider the Salman Rushdie case, in which a person was sentenced to death *in absentia* by a country of which he was not a citizen and in which he had not been tried for any crime. And does a respect for different cultures mean that Saudia Arabia and Iran should respect the universalist claims of individualistic human rights discourse – or that Britain and the United States should respect the universalist claims of collectivist Islamic dignity discourse? The problems multiply with religions such as Buddhism, Confucianism, and Hinduism, which are atextual and non-transcendent by contrast with Islam, Christianity, and Judaism. What happens when the existence lived well and in accord with rigorous principles of loyalty or decency in public life bumps up against reincarnation and family values, which trump the notion of life as an individual project (Brown, 2000: 200, 206)? Cultural rights and human rights do not fit together easily: how, for instance, might the *New York Times* reconcile its seemingly absolutist support for protecting indigenous people from 'cultural extinction' with its ringing denunciations of ritualized female slavery in religious shrines as atonement for the crimes of others in West Africa (Johnson, 2000: 405, 410)? And what should be our attitude to the National Rifle Association of the United States taking up the cudgels (or whatever weapon was to hand) on behalf of resident aliens when Congress proposed limiting the right to own guns to citizens (Aleinikoff, 2000: 161 n. 97)?

Multiple affinities produce practical and ideological problems. The 1932 Hague Convention on nationality states that 'the international community' needs a system whereby 'every person should have a nationality and should have one nationality only' (quoted in Aleinikoff, 2000: 137). Dual citizenship's institutionalization of split subjectivity goes further than querying voting, military service, and diplomatic aid. It gets to the heart of an affective relation to the nation-state. For all that the USA calls for membership of just one polity, there are four ways of attaining dual nationality there: naturalization, having renounced one's original citizenship, then resumption of it with the USA none the wiser; naturalization, with renunciation not recognized by one's country of origin; birth in the USA to immigrant parents from a country that recognizes *jus sanguinis*; and birth outside the USA to a foreigner and a US citizen.

Mexico has been much more protectionist than the USA – not surprisingly, since its land was expropriated ('No crucé la frontera, la frontera me cruzó a mí' [I didn't cross the border, it crossed me]; 'young Chicana poet' quoted in Rosaldo, 1997: 31). To own land in Mexico, foreigners had to renounce the right to diplomatic protection by their countries of citizenship, and land ownership in coastal and border territories has been subject to additional restrictions. But now that the NICL sees so much money held by transnationals, the government has adopted a different position. Since NAFTA and California's Proposition 187, Mexico must deal with increased emigration to the USA and ensure that its nationals have political power over the border whilst retaining economic status at 'home'. As in the USA, all persons born in Mexico are nationals, and naturalizing aliens must renounce their citizenship of origin. Becoming a citizen of another nation once required renunciation of Mexicanness, although *jus sanguinis* made the latter genetically inalienable – adults could lose their own Mexican citizenship, but still transmit it to their progeny. Since 1997, dual nationality has been permitted. It can also be achieved retrospectively, though the right to vote remains the sole province of residents. The Dominican Republic enacted similar arrangements in 1994. So a Dominican American can act as a politician in both Santo Domingo and Washington Heights, and a non-resident South Asian naturalized in the USA can own a Pennsylvania hotel chain, then expand it to Mumbai. This transnational identity has both a practical and a normative aspect. Not only does it facilitate the NICL, but various romantic souls ascribe to it a cosmopolitan effect of exchange between cultures without the obliteration of difference – thousands of blooming, mutually respectful flowers (Bauböck, 2000: 306–7; Aleinikoff, 2000: 138–9, 142, 144, 162–3).

But as Eve Kosofsky Sedgwick (1990: 61) notes, even social movements that are founded on difference are bound up with practices of exclusion. United fronts adopted for the purposes of external conflictual engagement always conceal 'differences … raging behind' (Hall, 1991: 56). Paradoxically, the standardization of identity politics references the difference-crushing machines of universalism that it was designed to counter, because it can downplay or deny either particular traits of conduct or whole categories of person (Mouffe, 1992, 1993). Stuart Hall has demonstrated both the utility of the word 'Black' in the UK context as a reversed, renewing trope against racism, and its more negative coefficients: the exclusion of Asian people of color and black people who have other coordinates of collective identification. A respect for cultural difference founded in relativism can, on the other hand, amount to a rather bland version of functionalist thought – meaning and custom binding people together (Johnson, 2000: 411).

One crucial issue is whether, in ethnomethodological terms, cultures permit folks to say 'Please don't include me' – in other words, can Membership Categorization Devices (MCDs) be refused? This is where any culturalist project of radical democracy must, in my view, make some peace with liberal political philosophy (LPP). LPP argues that the state should recognize the right of individuals to be respected as citizens and as members of a culture, because deciding to participate in that culture may be in their interest for collective or personal identity (for example, exempting Sikhs from British motorcycle-helmet legislation because of their need to wear turbans). The state can and should intervene, however, when members of those cultures seek to opt out, when MCDs become oppressive (for example, when a British woman rejects her Muslim parents' plans for an arranged marriage). This is a double bind – cultures should be protected from *external* oppression, even as their members must be protected from *internal* oppression (Johnson, 2000: 406, 408).

David Birch (1998a and b) argues from such a position that the discourse of pan-Asian 'values' was invented within authoritarian states in South-East Asia across the 1970s and 1980s to protect oligarchical and monopolistic power structures that felt threatened by the popular-cultural corollaries of international capitalism and their message of social transcendence. 'Asian values' became a distinctive means of policing the populace in the name of an 'abiding' idea of personhood that was in fact a reaction to the growth of capitalism and participation in international cultural exchange, while press freedom was constrained in the name of nation-building. So 'Asianness' may be an alibi for domestic social control. Whether we explain, say, the Singaporean state's anxieties in terms of values or power, its object of concern remains the citizen, and its realm for articulating these concerns is cultural policy.

PRODUCING CULTURAL SUBJECTS

Rousseau ([1762] 1975: 130) insists that 'It is not enough to say to the citizens, *be good*, they must be taught to be so'. Since the nineteenth century, cultural policy has been the lever turned to by liberal-capitalist states to encourage their populations to '*be good*'. Cultural policy always implies the management of populations through suggested behavior. It is a normalizing power that sets an ideal for the subject which can never quite be attained, yet enjoins that subject to strive for it via a doctrine of ethical incompleteness (Miller, 1993). This notion is premised on instilling a drive towards perfection (as the best possible consumer, patriot, or ideologue). It inscribes a radical indeterminacy in the subject in the name of loyalty to a more complete entity – the nation. Cultural policy finds, serves, and nurtures a sense of belonging through educational and other cultural regimes that are predicated on an insufficiency of the individual against the benevolent historical backdrop of the nation. These regimes are the means of forming a collective public subjectivity via what John Stuart Mill termed 'the departments of human interests amenable to governmental control' ([1869] 1974: 68). Much of this is done in the name of maintaining culture, to preserve ways of being a person (or to retain control over a population) in terms of ethnicity, age, gender, faith, or class.

These regimes can also manage change, often by advancing new modes of expression. Some innovations prioritize indigenous cultural production, placing a premium on locally made meanings and their systems. Others embrace technological developments, producing the need for a citizenry equipped with the latest and the best. Whilst there are superficial differences between a collectivist ethos and Mill's individualistic utilitarianism, they share the precept that ethico-aesthetic exercise is a necessary prerequisite to developing the responsible individual (Lloyd and Thomas, 1998: 121). 'Good taste' becomes both a sign of and a means towards better citizenship. This ethico-aesthetic exercise also has a postmodern version: culture is the legitimizing ground on which particular groups (e.g., African Americans, gays and lesbians, the hearing-impaired) can make a claim for resources and inclusion in the national narrative, if only to decenter it (Yúdice, 1990). Normalization's performative force varies across time and space. It favors bourgeois manners for a circumscribed set of individuals in one period, and stratifying access to cultural and other material resources on the basis of divers demographic categorizations at another (e.g. the five pan-ethnic categories that characterize the US census, media and consumer markets, and political voting blocs).

Culture is connected to policy in two registers: the artistic and the everyday. Artistic output emerges from creative people and is judged by aesthetic criteria, as framed by the interests and practices of textual studies and cultural history. Everyday customs reference how we live our lives, the sense of place and person that makes us human. Cultural policy refers, then, to the institutional supports that channel both aesthetic creativity and collective ways of life. It is embodied in a systematic, regulatory guide to action that is adopted by an organization to achieve its goals. In short, cultural policy is bureaucratic rather than creative or organic. Organizations solicit, train, distribute, finance, describe, and reject actors and activities that go under the signs of artist or artwork, through the implementation of policies. Governments, trade unions, colleges, social movements, community groups, foundations, and businesses aid, fund, control, promote, teach, and evaluate creative persons; in fact, they often decide and implement the very criteria that make possible the use of the word 'creative.' This may be done through law courts that permit erotica on the grounds that they are works of art, curricula that require students to read plays on the grounds that they are uplifting, film commissions that sponsor scripts on the grounds that they reflect national concerns, entrepreneurs who print symphonic program notes justifying an unusual season on the grounds of innovation, or foundations that sponsor the community culture of minorities on the grounds of supplementing (mostly white) middle class culture with 'diversity.' In turn, these criteria may themselves derive, respectively, from legal doctrines, citizenship or tourism aims, the profit plans of impresarios, or philanthropic criteria. The second understanding of culture may appear in academic anthropology or journalistic explanations of the *Zeitgeist*. For instance, references to the cultures of indigenous peoples by anthropologists before land-rights tribunals are in part determined by the rules of conduct adopted by the state in the light of political power. Similarly, references to dot-com caffeine culture by newspaper feature writers are in part determined by the rules of conduct adopted by their editors/proprietors in the light of market segmentation. We hear about these lifestyle/ritual practices through policy.

There are inescapable contradictions in this model, and they become evident when cultural policy's favored method of animation – the creation of abstract subjects as objects of knowledge – is coupled with intervening in all areas of life. Whilst this enables training and surveillance, it simultaneously divides subjects up so carefully that they cease to be rallied under the clarion call of the abstract citizen. Instead, they look outside representative democracy for public definitions and political technologies of identity. That opportunity derives from the manifold activities of the state, which interpellate the subject beyond the technical role of the citizen: working, living, and birthing subjects are of more poignant, consistent, and pregnant moment on a diurnal basis. Governments may yearn for social efficiency, 'a happy, healthy, virile and integrated social body', but their policies and programs often uncover or generate a productively fractured sovereignty (Barron, 1990: 109, 116–17).

CULTURAL GOVERNMENTALITY

These contradictions are obvious in the case of sport. At times, the codification and expansion of sport in the USA as part of cultural governmentality encountered critique and engagement, for example, from those seventeenth-century north-eastern Puritans who devoted great efforts towards quelling such pleasures of the lower orders as cock-fighting and horse-racing. This spread to the classically modern abhorrence of cruelty to animals across the country in the nineteenth century, with associated state intervention. But the push towards Americanization of new immigrants in the late nineteenth and early twentieth centuries was embodied in the formation of voluntary sporting associations. In the two decades from 1881, the USA birthed national bodies to regulate tennis, golf, and college sports. Over the next twenty years, baseball, hockey, and football professionalized. During World War I, there was a major articulation of sporting values with militarism and citizenship – an internal Americanization equating national sports with patriotism. The American Legion sponsored baseball to counter working-class radicalism and encourage social and migrant integration. When feminist criticisms of sport emerged in the 1960s, part of their force concerned the claim to equitable public funding. Hence the Federal Government's 1972 Title IX Educational Amendments, which forced US colleges in receipt of Federal funds to allocate them across campus in accord with the proportions of men and women they enrolled. These were among the first women's legislative gains of the contemporary era, and they addressed the expenditure of state money on the body as a source of fitness – cultural citizenship at play (Houlihan, 1997: 62, 56, 63). And when we look back with some measure of distance on Eastern European and Third World state socialism of the 1980s, it may be possible to acknowledge the critical role that these nations played in finally persuading the West to follow an all-sports boycott of apartheid South Africa because it did not permit universal suffrage (Booth, 1998: 85–122).

Despite its mission of producing citizens, cultural policy is now linked by both the Left and Right sides of politics to citizenship. It offers radicals a means of tying social-movement claims to actionable policy, a newly valuable form of entitlement that is a guarantee against the excesses of both the market and state socialism. On the Right, culture is subject to privatization pressures. Citizens and consumers continue their uncertain dance in the rhetoric of political philosophy, neoclassical economics, and neoliberal policy mandarinism (Zolberg, 1996: 396). An additional division on the Right exists between those who consider that citizens' responsibilities go beyond the self, and those who do not. Cultural policy has seen a series of debates in which seeming polar opposites – the Right versus multicultural arts – appear to be logocentrically interdependent. Each group dismisses traditional aesthetics in favor of a struggle to use art to represent identity and social purpose (Yúdice, 1990: 130). Multiculturalism stresses the need for a grassroots and marginal arts activism, focused on civil rights, and a combination of demographic and artistic representation and representativeness. Conservatism calls for an arts practice that heralds Western values and progress while obeying the dictates of religious taste.

We need to reconceptualize the three forms of citizenship as interlocking zones, interdependent and equally important – not just in terms of individual access, but as measured by political participation, economic development, cultural norms, and tastes. Second, immigration and the NICL must be centered in deliberations that look to those who are disenfranchised from citizenship and consumption, via a global commitment to workers' rights inflected with questions of cultural exchange.

The technology of citizenship, of shared rights, has been the principal arguing point shared by modern movements of emancipation. The idea that political rights are granted to all through birth has animated the claims of every category of the oppressed since the eighteenth century. Even so, the struggle, once won, has rarely satisfied. Equal access to citizenship has not led to social justice for all, because of the propensity towards economic anarchy and political oligarchy, and because the discourse of justice increasingly presumes a space of autonomy between person, economy, and polity, rather than a policy of assurance by the last on behalf of the first, or some other variant. For this reason, Iris Marion Young (1990) proposes 'group-differentiated citizenship'. She acknowledges the value of universalism in terms of 'a general will and common life', but is critical of the exclusion from dialogue of a raft of groups under such totalities. Too often, the notion of citizenship functions as a 'demand for homogeneity'. This can be avoided if access to political decisions is institutionalized for all categories of person, however different (Young, 1990: 117–19, 126).

For marginal or resistive groups to function, they must clearly harness both a reformism that knows the subjectifying technologies of the cultural-capitalist state, and a means of fashioning their own technologies of the self. The state uses the concepts of the nation and the individual as tropes to engender fealty. But even these homogenizing categories may be usefully deployed by various subordinate groups, because the heterogeneous composition of populations necessitates a certain regard for difference. The state is ultimately a grid of governance that brings together some really quite distinct forces in the management of people. In particular, cultural-capitalist democracies specialize in 'action at a distance'. They seek to organize the social world not merely through institutional agencies of the state, but via a very broad band of knowledge across public health, social work, auditing, accountancy, and other modes of modulation. There are always opportunities for the expression of difference in so dispersed a set of actions. Such openings arise because the very act of government involves problematizing, bringing subjects into doubt, dividing them conceptually to render social issues manageable, but thereby creating more and more difficulties in need of resolution (Rose and Miller, 1992: 174–5, 180–1). For example, the fictions of racial democracy in Brazil and racial inclusiveness in the USA, as registered/reified in the census, have ironically provided social movements with the means of critique, because they can point to correlations of social division with inequality and then call for a full entry into modernity (Nobles, 2000: 4–5).

Cultural governmentality has mixed consequences. Attempts to look at reproductive ritual in Egyptian villages or Brazilian cities, for example, must think through the meaning of custom in the context of experiments in birth control sanctioned by the nation-state, international state organizations, and scientists accredited by state policing norms, while the recent US adoption market in white babies has made Romania a key supplier because of governmental opposition there to contraception (Ginsburg and Rapp, 1995: 2; Barroso and Corrêa, 1995; Kligman, 1995). It may even be that a form of international civil society is at play that 'works' the state into compliance with associational norms of socioeconomic development, citizenship rights, national science policy, justice, public health, and universal education – in short, responsibility for the population's progress that is as much about meeting international expectations expressed by academia, the media, and non-governmental organizations, as it is to do with rational, purposive action that is 'essential' to statehood (Meyer et al., 1997).

What of the issues raised by immigration? Instead of a binding, but not freely made, social contract, there might be a different engagement between state and person, one that eschews blood, soil, or travel – a quid pro quo based not on the notion that people pledge allegiance and practice obedience in return for rights, but that they do so by giving and receiving things. *Population* becomes a master signifier, displacing the mythic compact, and *demography* succeeds LPP as its principal interpretive method. This is equally a means of getting away from thinking of people as consumers, and of dealing with the complexities of the NICL's deterritorialization – we all end up in material space, however cosmopolitan we may be. Nor is this wish-fulfillment, for even under globalization, there is always already government. Even globally exploitative non-state actors, like US Major League Baseball or Nike, may be accountable under international law for their human-rights abuses (Marcano and Fidder, 1999: 557).

In any event, citizenship is no longer easily based on soil or blood. Rather, it is founded on some variant of those qualities in connection with culture and the capitalist labor market. The state is no longer the sole frame of citizenship in the face of new nationalisms and cross-border affinities that no single governmental apparatus can contain (Feldblum, 1997: 96, 98–9, 101, 110). Supranational citizenship and identity are not only tied to a new international division of labor, but also to a new trading order, in which juridically established trading blocs like North American Free Trade Agreement/ Trato de Comercio Libre, the Mercado Común del Sur, and the European Union make decisions that override national laws. In fact, awareness that the rule of law transcends the nation-state can lead to a more compelling supranational identity, as witnessed by the number of cases brought by individuals to the European Court of Justice and the European Court of Human Rights (Cohen, 1991). These actions were feasible because of cultural citizenship's uptake as a crucial site of governmentality. Therein lies promise for a radical democratic politics.

ACKNOWLEDGEMENT

1 Thanks to Marie Leger, Engin F. Isin, and participants in the seminar of the Privatization of Culture Project on Cultural Policy for their comments.

REFERENCES

Aleinikoff, T. Alexander (2000) 'Between principles and politics: U.S. citizenship policy', in T. Alexander Aleinikoff and Douglas Klusmeyer (eds), *From Migrants to Citizens: Membership in a Changing World*. Washington: Carnegie Endowment for International Peace, pp. 119–72.

American Behavioral Scientist (2000) 'Citizenship and cultural policy', 43 (9).

Barron, Anne (1990) 'Legal discourse and the colonisation of the self in the modern state', in Anthony Carty (ed.), *Post-Modern Law: Enlightenment, Revolution and the Death of Man*. Edinburgh: Edinburgh University Press, pp. 107–25.

Barroso, C. and Corrêa, S. (1995) 'Public servants, professionals, and feminists: The politics of contraceptive research in Brazil', in Faye D. Ginsburg and Rayna Rapp (eds), *Conceiving the New World Order: The Global Politics of Reproduction*. Berkeley: University of California Press, pp. 292–306.

Bauböck, Rainer (2000) 'Introduction', in T. Alexander Aleinikoff and Douglas Klusmeyer (eds), *From Migrants to Citizens: Membership in a Changing World*. Washington: Carnegie Endowment for International Peace, pp. 305–11.

Bennett, Tony (1998) *Culture: A Reformer's Science*. London: Sage.

Birch, David (1998a) 'An "open" environment: Asian case studies in the regulation of public culture', *Continuum*, 12 (3): 335–48.

Birch, David (1998b) 'Constructing Asian values: National identities and "responsible" citizenship', *Social Semiotics*, 8 (2–3): 177–201.

Booth, Douglas (1998) *The Race Game: Sport and Politics in South Africa*. London: Frank Cass.

Brown, Chris (2000) 'Cultural diversity and international political theory', *Review of International Studies*, 26 (2): 199–213.

Carens, Joseph H. (2000) *Culture, Citizenship, and Community: A Contextual Exploration of Justice as Evenhandedness*. Oxford: Oxford University Press.

Cohen, Robin (1991) *Contested Domains: Debates in International Labor Studies*. London: Zed.

Economist (2000) 'Sins of the secular missionaries', 29 January, pp. 25–27.

Feldblum, M (1997) '"Citizenship matters": Contemporary trends in Europe and the United States', *Stanford Humanities Review*, 5 (2): 96–113.

Fierlbeck, K. (1996) 'The ambivalent potential of cultural identity', *Canadian Journal of Political Science/Revue canadienne de science politique*, 29 (1): 3–22.

Flores, William V. and Benmayor, Rina (eds) (1997) *Latino Cultural Citizenship: Claiming Identity, Space, and Politics*. Boston: Beacon Press.

Ginsburg, Faye D. and Rapp, Rayna (1995) 'Introduction: Conceiving the New World Order', in Faye D. Ginsburg and Rayna Rapp (eds), *Conceiving the New World Order: The Global Politics of Reproduction*. Berkeley: University of California Press. pp. 1–17.

Hall, Stuart (1991) 'Old and new identities, old and new ethnicities', in Anthony D. King (ed.), *Culture, Globalization and the World-System: Contemporary Conditions for the Representation of Identity*. Basingstoke: Macmillan, pp. 41–68.

Hindess, Barry (1998) 'Divide and rule: The international character of citizenship', *European Journal of Social Theory*, 1 (1): 57–70.

Hispanic and Asian populations expand', *New York Times* 30 August 2000.

Honig, Bonnie (1998) 'Immigrant America? How foreignness "solves" democracy's problems', *Social Text*, (56): 1–27.

Houlihan, Barrie (1997) *Sport, Policy and Politics: A Comparative Analysis*. London: Routledge.

Ip, D., Inglis, C. and Wu, C.T. (1997) 'Concepts of citizenship and identity among recent Asian immigrants to Australia', *Asian and Pacific Migration Journal*, 6 (3–4): 363–84.

Johnson, James (2000) 'Why respect culture?', *American Journal of Political Science*, 44 (3): 405–18.

Kligman, G. (1995) 'Political demography: The banning of abortion in Ceaucescu's Romania', in Faye D. Ginsburg and Rayna Rapp (eds), *Conceiving the New World Order: The Global Politics of Reproduction*. Berkeley: University of California Press. pp. 234–55.

Kymlicka, Will (1995) *Multicultural Citizenship: A Liberal Theory of Minority Rights*. Oxford: Oxford University Press.

Laitin, David D. (1999) 'The cultural elements of ethnically mixed states: Nationality re-formation in the Soviet successor states', in George Steinmetz (ed.), *State/Culture: State-Formation After the Cultural Turn*. Ithaca: Cornell University Press, pp. 291–320.

Lloyd, David and Thomas, Paul (1998) *Culture and the State*. New York: Routledge.

Mahmud, Tayyab (1997) 'Migration, identity, and the colonial encounter', *Oregon Law Review*, 76 (3): 633–90.

Mahmud, Tayyab (1999) 'Colonialism and modern constructions of race: A preliminary inquiry', *University of Miami Law Review*, 53 (4): 1219–46.

Marcano, Arturo J. and Fidder, David P. (1999) 'The globalization of baseball: Major League Baseball and the mistreatment of Latin American baseball talent', *Indiana Journal of Global Legal Studies*, 6: 511–77.

Meyer, J., Boli, J., Thomas, G.M. and Ramirez, F.O. (1997) 'World society and the nation-state', *American Journal of Sociology*, 103 (1): 144–81.

Mill, John Stuart ([1869] 1974) *On Liberty*. Harmondsworth: Penguin.

Miller, Toby (1993) *The Well-Tempered Self: Citizenship, Culture, and the Postmodern Subject*. Baltimore: The Johns Hopkins University Press.

Miller, Toby (1998) *Technologies of Truth: Cultural Citizenship and the Popular Media*. Minneapolis: University of Minnesota Press.

Mouffe, Chantal (ed.) (1992) *Dimensions of Radical Democracy: Pluralism, Citizenship, Community*. London: Verso.

Mouffe, Chantal (1993) *The Return of the Political*. London: Verso.

New York Times (2000) 'Hispanic and Asian populations expand', 30 August, p. A16.

Nobles, Melissa (2000) *Shades of Citizenship: Race and the Census in Modern Politics*. Stanford: Stanford University Press.

Ong, Aihwa (1999) *Flexible Citizenship: The Cultural Logics of Transnationality*. Durham: Duke University Press.

Preuss, U.K. (1998) 'Migration – A challenge to modern citizenship', *Constellations*, 4 (3): 307–19.

Rodriguez, Roberto and Gonzales, Patrisia (1995) 'Cultural idea for citizenship is catching on', *Fresno Bee*, 15 May, p. B5.

Rorty, Amélie Oksenberg (1995) 'Rights: Educational, not cultural', *Social Research*, 62 (1): 161–70.

Rosaldo, Renato (1997) 'Cultural citizenship, inequality, and multiculturalism', in William V. Flores and Rina Benmayor (eds), (1997) *Latino Cultural Citizenship: Claiming Identity, Space, and Politics*. Boston: Beacon Press, pp. 27–38.

Rose, Nikolas and Miller, Peter (1992) 'Political power beyond the state: Problematics of government', *British Journal of Sociology*, 43 (2): 173–205.

Rousseau, Jean-Jacques ([1762] 1975) *The Social Contract and Discourses*. tr. G.D.H. Cole. London: J.M. Dent.

Sedgwick, Eve Kosofsky (1990) *Epistemology of the Closet*. Berkeley: University of California Press.

Shafir, Gershon (1998) 'Introduction: The evolving traditions of citizenship', in Gershon Shafir (ed.), *The Citizenship Debates: A Reader*. Minneapolis: University of Minnesota Press, 1998, pp. 1–28.

Solinger, Dorothy J. (1999) *Contesting Citizenship in Urban China: Peasant Migrants, the State, and the Logic of the Market*. Berkeley: University of California Press.

Taylor, Charles (1990) 'Modes of civil society', *Public Culture*, 3 (1): 95–118.

van Creveld, Martin (1999) *The Rise and Decline of the State*. Cambridge: Cambridge University Press.

Xinha News Agency (2000) 'CEPAL: Discrimination creates suffering among indigenous peoples', 6 December.

Young, Iris Marion (1990) 'Polity and group difference: A critique of the ideal of universal citizenship', in Cass R. Sunstein (ed.), *Feminism and Political Theory*. Chicago: University of Chicago Press, pp. 117–41.

Yúdice, George (1990) 'For a practical aesthetics', *Social Text*, (25/26): 129–45.

Zachary, G. Pascal (2000) 'A philosopher in red sneakers gains influence as a global guru', *Wall Street Journal*, 28 March, pp. B1, B4.

Zolberg, Vera L. (1996) 'Paying for art: The temptations of privatization à l'Américaine', *International Sociology*, 11 (4): 395–408.

15

Multicultural Citizenship

CHRISTIAN JOPPKE

On the list of hyphenated citizenships the 'multicultural' one certainly takes a prominent place. It signals a general concern for reconciling the universalism of rights and membership in liberal nation-states with the challenge of ethnic diversity and other ascriptive 'identity' claims. In this chapter, I first discuss multicultural citizenship in theory, pointing to the shortcomings of both 'radical' and 'liberal' approaches to justifying minority rights under the generic, and paradoxical, notion of multicultural citizenship. Secondly, I look at the ways in which multicultural citizenship has been practiced in liberal nation-states. This investigation reveals a gap between the theory and the practice of multicultural citizenship: a mechanism to accommodate ethnic, national, and other minorities in theory, multicultural citizenship in practice has been a variant of nation-building in a few new settler societies without independent founding myths. In addition, I argue that the state-centered notion of multicultural *citizenship* deflects from the decentered accommodation of multicultural minority claims in functionally differentiated societies, which remains short of official state recognition. Considering the difficulties of grounding multicultural citizenship in theory, and considering the diverse and often contested practices that it seeks to encompass, I conclude that the notion of multicultural citizenship is too vague and multifaceted to be a useful tool of sociological analysis. It also runs counter to a trend toward de-ethnicization in liberal states, in which the cultural impositions of the majority on minority groups are growing thin, thus removing the case for minority rights.

MULTICULTURAL CITIZENSHIP IN THEORY

A good way of approaching multicultural citizenship is to explicate its critiqued or modified opposite. One influential author has identified the latter as 'universal citizenship' (Young, 1989). Universal citizenship refers to the equality of rights and status that have come to define membership in liberal-democratic nation-states: 'citizenship for everyone, and everyone the same qua citizen' (Young, 1989: 250). Universal citizenship, product of the French and American revolutions, has its own historical opposite: the tiered and multiple subject statuses and the particularistic rights and duties attached to them under feudalism. In fact, 'universal citizenship' is a pleonasm, because universalism as the rejection of particularistic rights and statuses is constitutive of citizenship as such. Accordingly, universal citizenship is meaningful only if viewed as the opposite of multicultural citizenship. The latter is thus paradoxical, because it seeks to (re)particularize a form of membership that is inherently universalistic.

From a different point of view, the notion of universal citizenship is not a pleonasm, but an oxymoron. As long as there is no world state, citizenship means membership of a particular state. Citizenship as state membership is 'inherently group-differentiated' (Kymlicka, 1995: 124), and thus the exact opposite of 'universalist.' This ambivalence of 'universal citizenship,' to be either pleonasm or oxymoron, reflects the dual nature of citizenship as both 'internally inclusive' and 'externally exclusive' (Brubaker, 1992: Ch. 1). The distinction between internal and external aspects of citizenship points to an important limitation of the meaning of multicultural citizenship: to the degree that the latter is a commentary on the shortcomings of universal citizenship, it focuses only on the internal rights dimension, and takes no account of the external state-membership dimension of citizenship.

The abstraction from the external dimension of citizenship in most discussions of multicultural citizenship is puzzling. After all, the multiplication of cultures and ethnic groups within contemporary nation-states is largely the result of cross-border migrations, which is partially shaped by (and, in turn, impacts on) a state's formal citizenship laws and policies. In multicultural citizenship's most concise formulation (Kymlicka, 1995), special group rights (for immigrants, for example) are compensation for axiomatically assumed strong nationalizing practices even in contemporary liberal states, which are said to have a discretionary 'right … to determine who has citizenship' (Kymlicka, 1995: 124). As Kymlicka provocatively argues, this right of states 'rests on the same principles which justify group-differentiated citizenship within states,' and 'accepting the former leads logically to the latter' (1995:).

Following the same logic, a relaxing of the axiomatically assumed state discretion on citizenship would remove the main justification for group rights. In light of a liberalization of citizenship law across immigrant-receiving Western states (see Weil, 2001), which is part of a larger trend toward de-ethnicization in such states (see Joppke and Morawska, forthcoming: Ch. 1), there is evidence that this is actually happening. However, by focusing only on the internal rights and ignoring as an invariable parameter the external state-membership dimension of citizenship, Kymlicka has ruled out by design the possibility of changes in the external aspect of citizenship impacting on its internal rights dimension. In sum, a proper assessment of multicultural citizenship has to take account of both the internal and the external dimensions of citizenship.

Before elaborating on this, it is important to note that current versions of multicultural citizenship differ in their relationship to universal citizenship. For feminist and (post)Marxist radicals, the relationship is one of critique and substitution (Young, 1989, 1990); for liberals, it is one of complementarity and linear addition (Kymlicka, 1995; Carens, 2000). The thrust of Iris Marion Young's radical formulation is to denounce the 'universal' in universal citizenship as the disguised particularism of the dominant group(s). 'Oppression' is key to her scenario: society is seen as composed of 'social groups,' which are either dominant or oppressed. Not much is said about the dominant group(s) (is it one or several?), despite occasional reference to 'white middle-class men' (Young, 1989: 268). This omission is perhaps not accidental, because the dominant can hide their groupness under the cloth of universalism. 'Differentiated citizenship,' which for Young is mostly about special representation rights in the polity, is reserved for 'oppressed' groups, whereby oppression is defined rather broadly as including anything from economic exploitation to cultural discrimination.[1] From this broad definition of oppression follows a long list of groups entitled to differentiated citizenship: 'Women, blacks, Native Americans, Chicanos, Puerto Ricans and other Spanish-speaking Americans, Asian Americans, gay men, lesbians, working-class people, poor people, old people, and mentally and physically disabled people' (Young, 1989: 261). Without any commentary, a second list adds 'young people,' while dropping 'Asian Americans' (1989: 265). The underlying reasoning is apparently ad hoc; and 'differentiated citizenship' for what turns out to be the vast majority of the US population seems a rather impracticable idea.

Young's failure to come up with a more concise definition and elaboration of what constitutes an 'oppressed group' is instructive.[2] It shows the difficulty of building a theory of multicultural citizenship around the notion of 'oppression.' This notion is too vague and simplistic to account for the asymmetries of power and resources in complex societies. As an inherently polemical (or 'critical') concept, oppression thrives on its (utopian) opposite, the absence of oppression. Has it ever existed? Can it exist at all, particularly if group differentiation is not only an inevitable but a 'desirable process' in modern societies (Young, 1989: 261)? Why should oppression stop when The Others are in charge? Finally, there is a systematic ambivalence about the inclusive or exclusive thrust of differentiated citizenship, and thus about its relationship to its critiqued opposite, 'universal citizenship.' If 'universal' is just a smokescreen for dominant group interests, the purpose cannot be inclusion into this false universal (as it had been in the – negatively evaluated – 'emancipatory momentum of modern political life' 1989: 250). Accordingly, the quest for differentiated citizenship is presented as a 'politics of difference' that rejects traditional 'inclusion' (Young, 1990: Ch. 6). However, in other places the whole point of differentiated citizenship is still seen as 'mak[ing] participation and inclusion possible' (Young, 1989: 273). Inclusion into what, one is inclined to ask, if existing institutions and representations (such as 'universal citizenship') are just instruments of dominant groups.

The notion of oppression does not figure centrally, in fact, hardly appears at all, in Kymlicka's (1995) liberal alternative of multicultural citizenship. Furthermore, for Kymlicka the relationship between universal and multicultural citizenship is not one of critique and substitution, but of simple addition. Rather than being subjected to a radical critique, universal rights are fine; the problem is that they are not enough for certain groups: 'A comprehensive theory of justice in a multicultural state will include both universal rights, assigned to individuals regardless of group membership, and certain group-differentiated rights or "special status" for minority cultures' (Kymlicka, 1995: 6).

Whereas Young's key concept was oppression, Kymlicka's is 'societal culture.' Individuals need societal culture as a context of meaningful choices: without it there is no freedom (Kymlicka, 1995: Ch. 5). In addition, access to a societal culture can become an issue of equality and justice under certain circumstances (1995: Ch. 6). No state, not even liberal states, can be culturally neutral; for example, in its selection of an official language a state inevitably promotes the majority culture, at the cost of the culture of minority groups that may reside in the same territory. Given the inevitable nexus between state and majority culture, the traditional liberal answer to ethnic and cultural difference, 'benign neglect,' is not enough: liberal justice requires special rights recognizing and protecting the cultures of minority groups.

Kymlicka's distinctive contribution has been the liberal mainstreaming of minority rights. After Kymlicka, the earlier confrontation between liberal defenders of universal citizenship and radical proponents of multiculturalism and group rights has lost its basis: it is not a radical critique of existing institutions, but those liberal principles on which existing institutions are built that require multicultural citizenship.

It is therefore worth scrutinizing this theory in more detail. A crucial difference to Young is the drastic narrowing of the minority groups entitled to special rights: only ethnic and national minority groups qualify. This is due to a narrow definition of the conditioning factor of group rights, 'societal culture.' Kymlicka defines societal culture as shared history, language, and territory, making it 'synonymous with "a nation" or "a people" – that is, ... an intergenerational community, more or less institutionally complete, occupying a given territory or homeland, sharing a distinct language and history' (Kymlicka, 1995: 18). This definition excludes non-ethnic groups, such as gays and lesbians, the disabled, or lifestyle groups, as multicultural claimants (see Kymlicka, 1998: Ch. 6).

However, the claims of the only two legitimate multicultural groups in Kymlicka's liberal scenario, national minorities and immigrants, differ in significant ways. And, as I would like to add critically, they differ in ways that ultimately militate against the very notion of multicultural citizenship. National minorities, such as the Catalans in Spain, the Quebecois in Canada, or the Aborigines in Australia, have the strongest claims within Kymlicka's scheme. All of them have 'institutionally complete' cultures, that is, cultures that cover the full range of human activities, needs, and functions (1995: 78). Moreover, as the victims of nation-state building, they are forced to reside in states that do not carry the marks of their culture (most notably, their language). To accommodate the always potentially secessionist national minorities within multinational states, strong 'self-government rights' are required, and also justifiable from a liberal point of view. Kymlicka does not hide the fact that these rights pose a serious threat to the integrative function of citizenship, because their thrust is separation, not integration (1995: 188).

By the same token, the nationalist, state-seeking ambition of national minorities is imperfectly captured, even trivialized, by the notion of multicultural citizenship. The very case of Quebec, which partially motivated Kymlicka's theory, demonstrates this. The Quebecois have always fiercely rejected Canada's multiculturalist policies, because Canada's binational founding structure is insufficiently visible in them. In fact, Canadian official multiculturalist policy was introduced just two years after the Official Languages Act of 1969 had made French the second official language of Canada, and it was an obvious attempt to make this concession to the francophone community acceptable to the country's other minorities, the immigrants and the Aborigines. The Quebecois understood this symmetrizing, levelling function of official multiculturalism, and refused to be considered just a minority among other minorities in a multicultural Canada. It is astonishing that Kymlicka, who is perfectly aware of the stern aspirations of (some) national minorities, and who has argued in particular that only an 'asymmetrical' understanding of Canadian federalism could accommodate Quebec (Kymlicka, 1998: Ch. 10), has distorted the asymmetrical, monocultural pretensions of national minorities in the symmetrical and pluralist notion of multicultural citizenship.

The pluralist thrust of multicultural citizenship is more plausible in the case of immigrants, the second legitimate claimant in Kymlicka's scheme. In fact, all official multiculturalist policies, starting with Canada and Australia in the early 1970s, have prominently (though not exclusively) targeted immigrants. However, immigrants pose their own difficulties for Kymlicka's scheme. In contrast to strong self-government rights for national minorities, immigrants are due only more moderate 'polyethnic rights' – examples being exemptions from some general laws that discriminate against minority beliefs and practices, or special benefits (like support for ethnic organizations or mother-tongue instruction and services) that accrue to the majority population automatically. However, qualifying these measures as 'rights' is misleading, and it would be more appropriate to call them contingent policies – even within Kymlicka's scheme. Why? The purpose of minority rights is to secure access for minority groups to their own societal culture. However, immigrants, in voluntarily leaving their country of origin, have 'waived' the right to their culture (Kymlicka, 1995: 96). Accordingly, the thrust of 'polyethnic rights' is integration into the majority culture. Kymlicka's low-key stance on immigrant rights is healthily realistic:[3] no state would continue admitting immigrants if they arrived with the right to recreate their homelands; and immigrant groups are usually 'too small and dispersed' to form viable societal cultures (Kymlicka and Rubio Marin, 1999: 146). However, this realism can be turned against the theory itself. If immigrants have 'waived' the right to their societal culture, there is no ground within this theory to endow them with any special 'right' at all. To call those immigrant integration policies of states that are more contingent and public order-oriented than rights-based an instance of 'multicultural citizenship' seems to be overstated, even misleading.

Most critics of Kymlicka's theory of multicultural citizenship have zeroed in on its key concept of societal culture (e.g. Benhabib, 1999: 53–6). Joseph Carens rightly detects in its monolithic contours the 'old logic of the nation-state' (2000: 66), making it 'much better suited to a monocultural conception of citizenship than to a multicultural one' (2000: 65). Most national minorities, particularly the decimated and beaten ones, could never venture on the building of an institutionally complete nation-like culture, from schools to media and hospitals, leaving the basis of their rights claims unclear; and for immigrants 'it is not clear why (they) are entitled to any special rights to maintain their distinctive cultural commitments' (2000: 57). There is indeed a tension in Kymlicka's concept of culture between being either too thick or too thin: 'too thick' to give a realistic account of the relationship between liberal states and culture; 'too thin' to justify any minority rights at all, particularly for immigrants. Let me develop both lines of criticism in turn.

On the one hand, states are axiomatically presented in Gellnerian terms as strong and tireless nation-builders, as guardians of a thickly conceived majority culture, now as in the nineteenth century, the high point of industrialism and nation-building in the West (Kymlicka, 1995: 76f.). This is not a realistic picture for contemporary liberal states. Consider their treatment of immigrants. If one takes the nationalizing practices of states as variable rather than parameter, one sees that in contemporary liberal states there is very little that these states expect of and impose on their newcomers, even at the point of acquiring citizenship. If this is the case, it is not clear why these states should concede minority rights in return for their (very minimal) cultural impositions. Immigrant integration policies are everywhere clothed in multicultural rhetoric, shunning the 'assimilation' of immigrants (see Joppke and Morawska, forthcoming). Even in an extreme case of nation-building, like Quebec, the only nationally distinct imposition is the requirement to adopt French language in public life. The other integration requirement in Quebec's immigrant policy is a dual commitment to democracy and pluralism, which is not specific to Quebec but generic to all liberal democracies (Carens, 2000: 113).

Language, in fact, boils down to the one substantive, and not just procedural, imposition on immigrants. Partially in response to immigration, liberal states have gone a long way toward tilting all (however implicit) ethnic preferencing in their policies and institutions – the shrill Foulard affair in France has been the exception to the generally smooth and noiseless adaptation of European states to the Islamic religion imported by some of their immigrants (see Bauböck, forthcoming). Language is different, because the state has to rely on it in its very functioning – the state can distance itself from religion (and it has actually done so), but not from language. However, language differs from religion in that a person can speak several languages, but can adhere to only one religion. This suggests that the identitarian implications of language use are less than those for religious practice. At least it is not clear why the adoption of another language would deprive a person of a meaningful context of choice.

The relaxing of liberal states' nationalizing practices is equally visible in the attribution of citizenship. While in international law states have the sovereignty to determine their nationality laws, a creeping rights-logic has rendered this a sovereignty on paper only. This is especially visible in Europe, whose *jus sanguinis* tradition had at first erected high hurdles to citizenship for immigrants. To better integrate their later-generation labor and postcolonial immigrants, most European states have in the meantime added *jus soli* elements to their blood-centered nationality laws. With the exception of Luxembourg, Greece, and Austria, all member states of the European Union now provide a right to citizenship to their second- and third-generation immigrants (see the overview in Weil and Hansen, 1999). In addition, most European states have significantly lowered the requirements for naturalization. Germany, for instance, which was until its recent citizenship reform the proverbially ethnic state, in the early 1990s introduced non-discretionary as-of-right naturalization for later-generation immigrants of legal residence and in effect no longer required these citizenship applicants to be culturally assimilated (Joppke, 2000).

These recent changes of immigrant integration policies and nationality laws in liberal states have important implications for multicultural citizenship: if minority rights are compensation for states' strong nationalizing practices, the weakening of these nationalizing practices removes the case for (this type of) minority rights.

On the other hand, in response to Waldron's 'cosmopolitan' alternative multiculturalism (Waldron, 1992), Kymlicka has admitted to a rather 'thin' picture of societal cultures in modernized societies. Citing the case of modern Quebec, Kymlicka finds that all have a place in it, 'e.g. atheists and Catholics, gays and heterosexuals, urban yuppies and rural farmers, socialists and conservatives, etc.' (Kymlicka, 1995: 87). In fact, to be Quebecois today 'simply means being a participant in the francophone society of Quebec' (ibid) – this indicates again the unique position of language in the contemporary liberal state's cultural impositions. If this is the case, it is not clear why the state's inherent alignment with this thin and pluralistic culture, which excludes virtually no one, should necessitate compensatory minority rights.

MULTICULTURAL CITIZENSHIP IN PRACTICE

Whatever the difficulties of justifying multicultural citizenship at the theoretical level, does it exist anywhere in the real world? Here it is important to distinguish between *explicit* multicultural citizenship, in which the latter is an official state program, and *implicit* multicultural citizenship, in which diversity claims have widely diffused without being written on the forehead of the state concerned. Explicit multicultural citizenship can be found in less than a handful of Western states. The most prominent examples are Canada and Australia, where the very notion of multiculturalism originated in the early 1970s. Canada made a start in 1971 with its policy of 'multiculturalism within a bilingual framework' (quoted in Kymlicka, 1998: 55). As indicated above, this multiculturalism is compensation for accommodating the francophone national minority of Quebec, and thus rather separate from the concerns of the latter. Interestingly, its underlying concern is not so much minority recognition as state neutrality, or, in Kymlicka's terms (1998: 57), '(to) separate the ... dominance of ... common languages ... from the historical privileging of the interests or lifestyles of the people descended from the historically dominant groups.' In line with this de-ethnicizing function, Canadian multiculturalism is an integrative offer for the whole society, not just for minorities. This is explicit in the Canadian Multiculturalism Act of 1988, which 'acknowledges the freedom of *all members* of Canadian society to preserve, enhance and share their cultural heritage' (quoted in Kymlicka, 1998: 185; emphasis added).

The nation-building function of multiculturalism is even more visible in Australia.

One of its central documents, the National Agenda for a Multicultural Australia, passed by a Labour government in 1989, stresses that multiculturalism is a 'policy for managing the consequences of cultural diversity *in the interests of the individual and society as a whole*' (quoted in Castles and Davidson, 2000: 166; emphasis added). More than its Canadian precursor, Australian multiculturalism stresses the limits of diversity: 'Multicultural policies are based on the premise that all Australians should have an overriding and unifying commitment to Australia, to its interests and future first and foremost' (quoted from the National Agenda, in Castles and Davidson, 2000).

Canadian and Australian multiculturalist policies have gone along with a liberalization of citizenship laws, which had previously been tainted by racial selectivity. The Australian Citizenship Act of 1973, for instance, considerably lowered the residence and language requirements for naturalization, and no longer asks for a 'transfer of cultural attachments,' only for a procedural commitment to liberal democratic values (Castles and Davidson, 2000: 168). Castles and Davidson therefore conclude that 'Australia's citizenship rules are now multicultural rather than national' (2000: 169). More correct would be to say that multicultural citizenship in Australia (as well as in Canada) is a distinct way of conceiving of national citizenship.

The few explicitly multiculturalist policies in Europe, notably those of Sweden and the Netherlands, look rather different. They are not identity options for society as a whole, but target immigrants only. In this sense, they are closer to 'multicultural citizenship' in Kymlicka's sense. However, it is also misleading to couch European multiculturalism policies in the language of citizenship, because one of their initial purposes was to protect the status of immigrants *qua* aliens and not to impose on them the citizenship of the receiving state.

It is worth referring here to the rather curious Swedish experience. A key purpose of Sweden's multicultural Immigrant and Minority Policy launched in 1975 was to give immigrants the 'freedom of choice' between maintaining their ethnic identity or adopting a (obviously ethnically conceived) Swedish identity (see Wieviorka, 1998: 686). This implied that immigrants would not be forced into Swedish citizenship (though citizenship was easier to acquire in Sweden than in most other countries of Europe). Expressions of the upgrading of alien status were the introduction of local and regional voting rights for immigrants in 1975, and – most important – the inclusion of a clause on ethnic and linguistic minority protection in the Swedish constitution in 1976. However, a parliamentary inquiry in the early 1980s correctly noted that in international law only autochthonous minorities – that is, long-settled, territorially concentrated minorities with citizenship status – were entitled to minority protection. In addition, the inquiry suggested that the proper meaning of 'freedom of choice' could not be the state's active furthering of ethnic minority identities, but its adopting a 'neutral position' and desisting from forced cultural assimilation (Soininen, 1999: 690). The government heeded this advice, renaming its 'immigrant and minority policy' 'immigrant policy.' This was but a step in Sweden's gradual withdrawal from its explicitly multiculturalist policy. In the 1990s, escalating unemployment among immigrants moved the attention from cultural to economic issues. The multicultural society was no longer a desirable project for the future but an unavoidable reality that had to be mastered by a centrist rather than difference-oriented state policy. Now the Swedish government even tilted the 'immigrant' reference from its immigrant-related policy, calling the latter simply 'integration policy'. Its stress is no longer to protect immigrants as ethnic groups, but to enable them as individuals to 'acquire the Swedish tools which can be needed to manage on one's own in Swedish society' (a government statement of 1995, quoted in Soininen, 1999: 692).

The Dutch withdrawal from explicit multiculturalism has been even more extreme (see Entzinger, 1999). The Dutch

Minderhedennota (ethnic minorities policy) of 1983 earmarked eight official immigrant minorities for 'emancipation,' not within Dutch society, but within state-supported ethnic parallel societies, reminiscent of the 'pillar' tradition in this religiously and ideologically divided country (see Lijphart, 1968). This most multicultural of all European immigrant policies soon ran into problems. First, the ethnic diversification of migrant streams in the age of asylum-seeking made it simply impracticable to provide each ethnic group with its own infrastructure, including ethnic schools, media, and social services. Second, the focus on cultural autonomy proved inadequate for the most pressing problem facing immigrants: unemployment and socioeconomic marginalization. In response, much as in Sweden, there has been a reorientation toward 'open[ing] up the existing institutional arrangements to immigrants, rather than aiming at the development of new, parallel institutions' (Entzinger, 1999: 10). All references to ethnic minorities, even the very notion of immigrant, were erased from the state's new 'integration policy,' and the new emphasis was on integrating newcomers as individuals rather than as members of groups. The Dutch withdrawal from explicit multiculturalism culminated in the 1998 Law on the Civic Integration of Newcomers, which requires new (non-EU) immigrants to take 600 hours of civics and Dutch language classes.

The demise of official multiculturalist policies in Europe is not the result of a right-wing backlash. As in the Netherlands, impeccable liberals have driven the change.[4] The insight took hold that it was counterproductive to fuel the centrifugal thrust of ethnically diversifying societies with explicitly multiculturalist policies. This implies a fundamental re-evaluation of multiculturalism, which is no longer seen as a normative goal but as an empirical exit-condition of state policy.

In contrast to the precarious nature of explicitly multiculturalist policies, implicit multiculturalism is deeply entrenched throughout immigrant-receiving Western states. It reflects the simple fact that liberal states cannot but sit on top of pluralizing societies. A good example of this is the United States. Unlike the other new settler nations, (Canada and Australia), the United States does not officially consider itself a multicultural society. Nathan Glazer, who captured the pervasive reality of American multiculturalism in the happy notion that 'we are all multiculturalists now' (1997), also pointed to the fact that there was 'nothing multicultural yet' about US naturalization law, which requires citizenship applicants to swear an oath of allegiance to their new country (Glazer, 1999: 196). Unlike Canada and Australia, which are still today part of the British Commonwealth, the United States has its own founding myth, one that invites ethnic pluralism through its exclusively political content, but also checks such pluralism through its very existence. The recent 'Americanization' campaign of the federal government invokes this distinct founding myth of 'liberty, democracy and equal opportunity' (US Commission on Immigration Reform, 1997: 26),[5] which is not available in Canada or Australia, and substituted there by their post-British nation-building commitment to multiculturalism.

American multiculturalism rests on the dual pillars of affirmative action and public education (see Joppke, 1999: Ch. 5). Affirmative action is an example of the 'special representation rights' identified by Kymlicka (1995: 31–3) as an intermediate, third category of minority rights. Its purpose (though not its reality) is to be temporary only, and to redress discrimination on the basis of race (as well as sex and other ascriptive markers, such as, more recently, physical handicaps). However the state has not carved out official racial categories in order to give them public recognition; rather, racial categorizing is an unintended consequence of anti-discrimination laws and policies, originally color-blind, that were driven towards color-consciousness by concerns of administrative efficiency (see Skrentny, 1996). Accordingly, classifying affirmative action as an instance of multicultural citizenship may appear to be stretching the meaning of the term, if the latter is meant to be recognition and protection of minority cultures. However, affirmative action is a policy with many faces (see Skrentny, 1998). One of them is the quintessentially multicultural idea of mirror representation, which sees society as a composite of 'groups' and calls for their proportional representation in key sectors such as the polity, higher education, and the workplace (on the idea of mirror representation, see Phillips 1995).

The main site of American multiculturalism is the 'world of education' (Taylor, 1992: 65), where it has appeared as the claim for non-Western-centered public school and college curricula. If minority cultures have found public recognition in the USA, it is mostly through their successful entry into the curriculum – up to a point, as Charles Taylor critically remarks, where the 'presumption' of the equal value of the creative expressions of minority cultures is replaced by the 'peremptory demand for favorable judgments of worth' (Taylor, 1992: 71). This has been exhaustively discussed under the rubrics of 'culture wars,' 'political correctness,' etc. It is more interesting for our purposes that this form of multicultural citizenship is thoroughly entrenched yet has remained short of official state recognition – also because in the federal US polity the responsibility for public education is multiply divided, horizontally between public and private actors and organizations, and vertically between the federal, state, and substate levels.

The American case points to a central shortcoming of the idea of multicultural citizenship: its fixation on the state. This fixation is perhaps unavoidable because citizenship refers to a relationship between the individual and the state. However, it has obscured the multiple entry points of multicultural claims in the fabric of functionally differentiated societies. To catch the pervasive reality of implicit multiculturalism, we have to change the root image of modern society: not (exclusively) bounded and steered from the top or by a state, but (also) composed of a multiplicity of autonomous subsystems. Among the latter the political system is only one, and not one that could claim to be more central than the others – in Luhmann's diction, modern societies have 'neither peak nor center' (1986: 167–182).

One important sphere in which implicit multiculturalism has quickly taken hold is markets. Because of the 'Hispanic market,' Spanish has established itself as the unofficial second language in certain (southwestern and southeastern) parts of the United States – automatic bank tellers in California give customers the choice of English or Spanish; large billboards on Los Angeles' glamorous Wilshire Boulevard advertise their products in Spanish; the leading newspapers in Los Angeles and Miami now publish Spanish-language editions. An advertisement in the business section of the *New York Times* has the obvious answer to the question, 'Why Hispanic?': 'Because in the next 15 years Hispanic buying power in New York will double to $89.9 billion dollars!' (quoted in Zolberg and Woon, 1999: 37, fn.74). As Zolberg and Woon (1999: 26) conclude their important observations, there is now a 'market-driven multiculturalism' in the USA, 'quite independently of any public policy choices.'

A second sphere in which implicit multiculturalism has found entry is the legal system. A staple in multicultural-citizenship reasoning is that the individual-rights principle of non-discrimination is not enough to protect minorities.[6] This underestimates the teeth of this legal principle. In Europe, for example, general constitutional provisions on family rights and religious freedoms have been sufficient to exempt a particularly vulnerable group, Muslim girls, from parts of the public-school curriculum that their parents deem incompatible with Islamic norms (see Albers, 1994). In Germany, a landmark decision by the Federal Administrative Court in early 2000 forced the Senate of Berlin to recognize an Islamic sect (Milli Görüs) as an official religious organization, with the right to teach Islam in Berlin's public schools. Not explicit minority rights, but universal legal principles seem to be sufficient to put Islam on the path to establishing itself as the fourth official religion in Germany.[7]

Sometimes multicultural recognition claims are not only indirectly satisfied by the law's individual non-discrimination principle, but have come to shape legal strategies and principles directly. An example of the latter is the recent 'cultural defense' strategy in American criminal law (see Coleman, 1996). It builds on a long-standing trend in American criminal law toward 'individualized justice.' Departing from the previous principle that every offense in a like legal category calls for identical punishment, individualized justice takes into account mitigating circumstances and the individual character and propensities of the offender in the assessment of guilt and punishment. Cultural defense injects the defendant's culture as one such mitigating and individualizing circumstance into the criminal process. It argues that someone raised in a foreign culture should not be held fully accountable for conduct that violates domestic law if that conduct would be acceptable under his or her native law. Successfully invoked by immigrant defendants in California, New York, Georgia and Minnesota, the cultural defense strategy has led some courts to reinterprete rape among Hmong refugees as part of their traditional courtship customs; to consider wife-beating and killing among Chinese as conditioned by 'traditional Chinese values about adultery and loss of manhood' (quoted in Coleman, 1996: 1109); and to exonerate from manslaughter charges a Japanese mother who had drowned her three children because in Japanese culture mother-child suicide is an accepted method for betrayed wives to escape shame. As Coleman points out, there is a tension between cultural defense and individualized justice, because in the former the question of moral culpability is not answered by resort to the particular individual's beliefs, but by summarily invoking his or her subgroup's cultural standards (1996: 1126f).

More disturbingly, this 'clearest example of how multiculturalism has influenced the law' (Coleman, 1996: 1100) violates the equal protection doctrine and anti-discrimination principle, the cornerstones of US civil rights law, because it denies justice to the immigrant women and children harmed by immigrant offenders. Multicultural criminal law thus poses a 'Liberals' Dilemma' (1996: 1096): the liberal impulse in criminal law to protect the offender (see Dworkin, 1978: 135f.) leaves unprotected the victims of immigrant crimes. Moreover, the liberal's multicultural defense of the immigrant offender 're-institutes a bifurcated criminal code that is frighteningly similar to the old slave codes and to the black codes that briefly existed after the Civil War' (Coleman, 1996: 1144) – to undo what had been whole point of the 14th Amendment's equal protection clause.

The example of multicultural criminal law raises a larger problem for advocates multicultural citizenship: the question of how to deal with illiberal minority cultures. Feminist authors in particular have pointed to the fact that endorsing (very often chauvinist and authoritarian) minority cultures may amount to the suppression of women and internal dissidents (e.g. Shachar, 1999). This is a very serious charge that, in my view, has not been convincingly rebutted by defenders of multicultural citizenship.[8] Kymlicka (1995: Ch. 8) distinguishes in this context between minority rights as 'external protections' (which secure equality between minority and majority groups in society and are therefore legitimate from a liberal point of view) and minority rights as 'internal restrictions' (which suppress the autonomy of the members of minority groups and therefore cannot be endorsed by a liberal). Building his theory of minority rights on the principle of individual autonomy (rather than toleration) allows Kymlicka to be more critical of illiberal minority groups than some liberals who reject group rights but allow for internal restrictions in the name of toleration (e.g. Kukathas 1992). However, the liberal theorist's rejection of minority rights that restrict the autonomy of minority individuals does not mean, according to Kymlicka (1995: 171), that liberals can impose their principles on illiberal groups: 'Liberals have no automatic right to impose their views on non-liberal national minorities.' Much as in the world of interstate relations, where the principle of non-intervention is firmly established, all that liberals can hope for in their dealings with illiberal national minorities is the soft power of 'dialogue' – in a word, much as we might despise illiberal minority practices, we have to let them go. Note, however, that this hands-off approach may be relaxed in the case of voluntary immigrants, where 'it is more legitimate to compel respect for liberal principles' (Kymlicka, 1995: 170) – only, 'how' legitimate this is and where the margin of the tolerable ends even this most succinct account of the limits of toleration does not say.

CONCLUSION

Where does this discussion of the theory and practice of multicultural citizenship leave us? At the level of theory, attempts to ground minority rights in 'oppression' (Young, 1989) and 'societal culture' (Kymlicka, 1995) have run into difficulties. With the vague concept of 'oppression,' all of society is turned into a composite of minorities, in a kind of apartheid in reverse. The more concise concept of 'societal culture' prudently narrows the range of legitimate multicultural claimants, one of which, however, sees its monocultural, nationalist ambitions trivialized and distorted by the pluralist notion of multicultural citizenship (national minorities), while the other's rights claims are left without a basis (immigrants).

Kymlicka's liberal theory has the advantage over Young's radical theory of being more closely aligned with actual state practices regarding minorities – no abstract principles are held against states from the outside, but liberal states are confronted with the normative implications of some of their own time-tested practices regarding minorities. However, the central shortcoming of Kymlicka's theory is its exclusive focus on the internal rights dimension, disregarding as an unchangeable parameter the external state-membership dimension of citizenship. If the argument is that axiomatically assumed strong nationalizing practices on the external citizenship dimension justify minority rights, this nexus is empirically rendered obsolete by the trend toward de-ethnicization in liberal states. Particularly in response to immigration, liberal states have excised most ethnic references from their citizenship laws and integration policies – it is *de rigueur* in all of them not to 'assimilate' immigrants, even at the point of citizenship acquisition. As liberal states, in response to ethnically diversifying societies, are busily tilting all ethnic majority preferencing and referencing, it would be strange to demand that they reverse this trend for ethnic minorities (except in the rare and serious cases of state-seeking national minorities).

Michael Walzer (1992: 100f.), in a stridently liberal rejection of multiculturalism, has drawn a distinction between the ethnically neutral American 'nation of nationalities,' where 'there is no privileged majority and there are no exceptional minorities,' and the ethnic 'nation-states' of Europe, whose 'governments take an interest in the cultural survival of the majority nation.' Since state neutrality is realized in the United States, there is no point in granting minority rights here; in the ethnic states of Europe, according to Walzer, minority rights are more appropriate, even though these states may find such rights impracticable. Walzer is both right and wrong: right in his intuition that liberal states can (and do) live up to the ideal of neutrality, thus rendering the idea of minority rights pointless; but wrong in his belief that striving for public neutrality is a privilege of the United States. The United States is not different in kind from European states. All European immigrant-receiving states are moving in the same, American direction of politically constituted nationhood and territorial citizenship.

The trend towards state neutrality also in Europe is perhaps best documented in the recent controversy in Germany over a '*deutsche Leitkultur*' (German dominant culture) that immigrants should adopt. The notion was introduced by the conservative opposition party in parliament (CDU), as an antidote to Germany's current opening toward new labor migration. Interestingly, when pressed to define it, its proponents could not say what exactly the *deutsche Leitkultur* was. For the CDU parliamentary leader, it consisted of the 'constitutional tradition of our Basic Law,' the 'European idea,' equality of women, and the German language – in that order, with the only specifically 'German' marker appearing last, and overlapping with the functional language requirement.[9] This was also precisely how the SPD Chancellor, like most in the political élite an opponent of the notion of *Leitkultur*, defined the criteria of immigrant integration.[10] A CDU position paper on immigration, notable also for the party's retreat from its long-held mantra that Germany was 'not a country of immigration,' finally included the contested notion of *Leitkultur*.[11] It identifies as 'Christian-occidental culture' the value added by *Leitkultur* to the constitutional and language obligations that are agreed by all. However, this 'culture' is already circularly interwoven with Germany's laws and constitution, and – most disturbingly – it does not contain anything that is particularly 'German': every country in Europe, and many countries beyond Europe too, share this 'culture.'

David Miller, philosophical proponent of liberal nationalism, defined national identity, among other things, as a 'distinct public culture' (1995: 27), which is meant to be more than the 'common currency of liberal democracies,' because it provides an answer to the question 'why the boundaries of the political community should fall here rather than there' (1995: 163). Germany's inconclusive wrangling over *Leitkultur* shows that a liberal state cannot formally commit its immigrants to anything that exceeds the procedural canon of liberal democratic rules. This creates the paradox that the political community that immigrants are to be socialized into has to remain unnamed. And, for our purposes, it leaves unclear what exactly 'multicultural citizenship' is supposed to remedy.

At the level of practice, multicultural citizenship as written on the forehead of the state has remained exceedingly rare. As the few European states that once practiced multicultural policies (though not: multicultural *citizenship* policies) are moving away from them, perhaps only Canada and Australia qualify – though their multicultural citizenship differs from that of the theorist by being a citizenship for all, not just for minorities. At the same time, the state-centered 'top-down' notion of multicultural citizenship has deflected from the multiple 'bottom-up' successes of multicultural claims in the decentered subsystems of differentiated societies, which have remained short of official state recognition. Considering that multiculturalism is *de facto* everywhere in liberal societies, whereas it is explicit policy only in some countries (and for some groups therein), it may be better to use a diverse vocabulary to capture a diverse reality – and not to swallow the latter under the general and in important respects misleading rubric of 'multicultural citizenship.'

NOTES

This chapter was first published as 'Multicultural Citizenship: A Critique' in *Archives européennes de sociologie* (May 2001). It is reprinted here with the kind permission of Cambridge University Press.

1 Young (1990: Ch. 2) lists 'five faces of oppression': exploitation, marginalization, powerlessness, cultural imperialism, and violence.

2 A better but metacritical attempt is Offe (1998).

3 See, by contrast, Parekh's (1994) stronger claim that immigrants, as 'probationary citizens', have a 'moral right' to preserve their difference.

4 The liberal sociologist Han Entzinger masterminded the 1998 Dutch Law on Civic Integration.

5 'The Commission reiterates its call for the Americanization of new immigrants, that is the cultivation of a shared commitment to the American values of liberty, democracy and equal opportunity' (US Commission on Immigration Reform, 1997: 26).

6 See Kymlicka's critique of 'benign neglect' (1995: 3f).

7 See 'Das Recht auf Unterricht', *Die Zeit*, 2 March 2000: 32.

8 A sensible contextual approach to 'the limitations of liberal toleration' is given by Carens (2000: Ch. 6).

9 Friedrich Merz (CDU), in *Die Welt*, 25 October 2000.

10 Gerhard Shröder (SPD), in *Frankfurter Allgemeine Zeitung*, 6 November 2000: 1.

11 *Arbeitsgrundlage für die Zuwanderungs-Kommission der CDU Deutschlands*, 6 November 2000, Berlin (http://www.cdu.de).

ACKNOWLEDGEMENT

The text of the above article has been previously printed in the *European Journal of Sociology*, XLII (2001), 431–447. Reprinted with permission.

REFERENCES

Albers, Hartmut (1994) 'Glaubensfreiheit und schulische Integration von Ausländerkindern', *Deutsches Verwaltungsblatt*, 1 September, pp. 984–90.

Bauböck, Rainer (forthcoming). 'Cultural Minority Rights in Public Education', in A. Messina (ed.), *Europe: The New Melting Pot?* Boulder: Westview Press.

Benhabib, Sheila (1999) '"Nous et les autres"' in C. Joppke and S. Lukes, (eds), *Multicultural Questions*. Oxford: Oxford University Press.

Brubaker, Rogers (1992) *Citizenship and Nationhood in France and Germany*. Cambridge: Harvard University Press.

Carens, Joseph (2000) *Culture, Citizenship, and Community*. Oxford: Oxford University Press.

Castles, Stephen and Davidson, Alastair (2000) *Citizenship and Migration*. Basingstoke: Macmillan.

Coleman, Doriane Lambelet (1996) 'Individualizing Justice Through Multiculturalism', *Columbia Law Review*, 96 (5): 1093–1167.

Dworkin, Ronald (1978) 'Liberalism', in Stuart Hampshire (ed.), *Public and Private Morality*. Cambridge: Cambridge University Press.

Entzinger, Han (1999) 'Towards a Model of Incorporation: The Case of the Netherlands', unpublished manuscript.

Glazer, Nathan (1997) *We Are All Multiculturalists Now*, Cambridge: Harvard University Press.

Glazer, Nathan (1999) 'Multiculturalism and American Exceptionalism', in C. Joppke and S. Lukes (eds), *Multicultural Questions*. Oxford: Oxford University Press.

Joppke, Christian (1999) *Immigration and the Nation-State: The United States, Germany, and Great Britain*. Oxford: Oxford University Press.

Joppke, Christian (2000) 'Mobilization of Culture and the Reform of Citizenship Law', in R. Koopmans and P. Statham (eds), *Challenging Immigration and Ethnic Relations Politics*. Oxford: Oxford University Press.

Joppke, Christian and Ewa Morawska (eds) (forthcoming) *Toward Assimilation and Citizenship*. Basingstoke: Palgrave.

Kukathas, Chandran (1992) 'Are There Any Cultural Rights?', *Political Theory*. 20 (1): 105–39.

Kymlicka, Will (1995) *Multicultural Citizenship*. Oxford: Oxford University Press.

Kymlicka, Will (1998) *Finding Our Way*. Toronto: Oxford University Press.

Kymlicka, Will and Rubio Marin, Ruth (1999) 'Liberalism and Minority Rights: An Interview', *Ratio Juris*, 12 (2): 133–52.

Lijphart, Arend (1968) *The Politics of Accommodation*. Berkeley: University of California Press.

Luhmann, Niklas (1986) *Ökologische Kommunikation*. Opladen: Westdeutscher Verlag.

Miller, David (1995) *On Nationality*. Oxford: Clarendon Press.

Offe, Claus (1998) '"Homogeneity" and Constitutional Democracy', *Journal of Political Philosophy*, 6 (2): 113–41.

Parekh, Bhikhu (1994) 'Cultural Pluralism and the Limits of Diversity', *Alternatives*, 20 (3): 431–57.

Phillips, Anne (1995) *The Politics of Presence*. Oxford: Oxford University Press.

Shachar, Ayelet (1999) 'The Paradox of Multicultural Vulnerability', in C. Joppke and S. Lukes (eds), *Multicultural Questions*. Oxford: Oxford University Press.

Skrentny, John (1996) *The Ironies of Affirmative Action*. Chicago: University of Chicago Press.

Skrentny, John (1998) 'Affirmative Action', *American Behavioral Scientist*, 41 (7): 877–85.

Soininen, Maritta (1999) 'The "Swedish Model" as an Institutional Framework for Immigrant Membership Rights', *Journal of Ethnic and Migration Studies*, 25 (4): 685–702.

Taylor, Charles (1992) *Multiculturalism and 'The Politics of Recogniton'*. Princeton: Princeton University Press.

US Commission on Immigration Reform (1997) *Becoming an American*. Washington, DC: Government Printing Office.

Waldron, Jeremy (1992) 'Minority Cultures and the Cosmopolitan Alternative', *University of Michigan Journal of Law Reform*, 25 (3&4): 751–93.

Walzer, Michael (1992) 'Comment', in Charles Taylor *Multiculturalism and 'The Politics of Recognition'*. Princeton: Princeton University Press.

Weil, Patrick (2001) 'Access to Citizenship', in T.A. Aleinikoff and D. Klusmeyer (eds), *Citizenship: Comparisons and Perspectives*. Washington, DC: The Brookings Institution.

Weil, Patrick and Hansen, Randall (eds) (1999) *Nationalité et citoyenneté en Europe*. Paris: La Decouverte.

Wieviorka, Michel. (1998) 'Is Multiculturalism the Solution?', *Ethnic and Racial Studies*, 21 (5): 881–910.

Young, Iris Marion (1989) 'Polity and Group Difference: A Critique of the Ideal of Universal Citizenship', *Ethics*, 99: 250–74.

Young, Iris Marion (1990) *Justice and the Politics of Difference*. Princeton: Princeton University Press.

Zolberg, Aristide and Long Litt Woon (1999) 'Why Islam is Like Spanish', *Politics and Society*, 27 (1): 5–38.

16

Religion and Politics: The Elementary Forms of Citizenship

BRYAN S. TURNER

WEBER, SOCIOLOGY AND CITIZENSHIP

Religion and politics would appear to be different and antagonistic spheres of activity. In a variety of Romance languages that derive their etymological roots from classical Latin, religion or *religio* refers to those institutions that bind individuals together into communities. Religion is expressive of those practices that create and maintain community. Politics is the art or science of government, the core of which is the state as an instrument of collective force. Politics refers to the division of interests in a society and the management of conflict that results from such divisions. The *Oxford English Dictionary* notes that the term 'politic' referred in the eighteenth century to somebody who was indifferent to religion. This contradiction between politics and religion has been a productive and creative force in society. Religious visions and utopian mentalities have produced powerful political ideologies of revolutionary change. In the Christian West, the vision of a 'new Jerusalem' has been a powerful political motivation. Millenarian ideologies of transformation and political change have driven social revolution in Buddhism, in so-called nativistic movements, in cargo cults and in fundamentalist Islam. The religious utopias of the oppressed have been the imaginative driving force of much political change (Lanternari, 1963). It was for these reasons that Karl Marx, following Ludwig Feuerbach, regarded religion as 'the opium of the people' and assumed that socialism would come eventually to replace religious fantasy as the driving force of a universal politics (Turner, 1991). Although these social movements are relevant to the sociological study of politics and religion, the question of this chapter is relatively specific, namely how has religion contributed to the growth of secular citizenship?

The relationship between religious traditions and the institutions of a citizenship is a large and complex issue. In order to provide this topic with some historical focus, my analysis is presented within the framework of the political sociology of Max Weber. Weber's sociology is particularly pertinent to my project, given his keen understanding of the culturally creative tensions between religious and political modes of domination. Weber was the first sociologist to tackle the origins of modern citizenship directly. It is commonly recognised that the historical study of the relationship between the economic ethics of the world religions and the rise of rational capitalism provided the core of Weber's sociology as a whole (Tenbruck, 1980; Turner, 1992). As a result, Weber's political and historical sociology of citizenship has been somewhat neglected in Weber studies. The historical roots of citizenship were explored in his study of the city (Weber, [1921] 1958), economic history (Weber, [1923] 1981) and democratisation and its failures, such as the Russian revolutions (Weber, [1906] 1995).

Weber's sociology of religious worldviews and citizenship is based on a paradox that the greater the ascetic rejection of this world, the more religion has contributed to the rise of democratic citizenship. The unintended consequence of religious rejections of this world has been to create a sharp separation between the sacred and the profane that in turn created institutional means for the development of secular politics. As a result of his sociology of religion, Weber pointed towards an innovative theory of the origins of modern politics, that nevertheless remains implicit in his work. One might say that for Weber, if the unintended consequence of religious asceticism was the spirit of capitalism, then the unintended consequence of the rejection of the world was the spirit of liberal democracy. The argument is contentious, but it is also illuminating.

Weber's analysis of power was grounded in a basic dichotomy between secular and spiritual domination. Weber defined the state as that institution that exercises a monopoly of violence within a given territory, but his conceptualisation of the state makes little sociological sense without the corresponding study of the Church. In *Economy and Society* (Weber, [1922] 1978: 50), the Church is defined as a compulsory hierocratic organisation that claims a monopolistic authority over spiritual services. It is a 'system of spiritual domination over human beings' ([1922] 1978: 56). The Church involves the institutionalisation or routinisation of charismatic force in a set of ecclesiastical, specifically episcopal, offices. The Church hierarchy has a monopoly over institutionalised charisma through the means of grace such as baptism, marriage, eucharist and confession. The Christian Church, unlike the Islamic *ulama* (religious leaders) or the Buddhist *sangha* (community), requires a sacerdotal priesthood. Because the priesthood has a monopoly, it can in principle exercise domination over the laity. Religious leaders in Islam, Judaism and Buddhism were essentially teachers of religious knowledge and did not, in the technical sense, necessarily have a priestly role (Weber, [1922] 1966: 27–8). Sacramentalism in the Christian Church is important for understanding the sociological differentiation between religious and political powers.

Unlike the state, the Church had historically little interest in sovereignty over territory as such; its power was expressed through a monopoly of institutional means of grace. Society, for Weber, was thus structured around two forms of domination – the secular domination of the state and the spiritual domination of the Church. In principle, this division gave rise to two contrasted forms of citizenship. There existed a spiritual citizenship within the body of Christ and a profane citizenship within the political community. As a millenarian religion with a dramatic and comprehensive eschatology, Christianity regarded this world (the City of Man) and its powers as worthless and hence this world is merely a preparation for a future citizenship in the City of God. As Christianity adjusted to a post-millenarian environment, it came to elaborate a theory of good citizenship in this world. However, where these two patterns of citizenship remained separate and antagonistic, there was a social space within which social rights could evolve. Political and civil rights emerged as claims against the state, and hence civil society provides a set of intermediary institutions that limits the absorption of the citizen within the state.

In this account of citizenship, my Weberian argument is firstly that in the West the division between the City of God and the urban politics of the worldly city provided an important foundation for democratic citizenship. St Augustine's political writings therefore promoted the possibility of citizenship through this critical division between a sphere of love (*caritas*) and a sphere of cupidity, or self-regarding actions (*cupiditas*). Secondly, modern citizenship has drawn considerable inspiration from the congregational polities that were products of the Reformation and its struggle with the state. Thirdly, secular citizenship in the modern polity was a product of the English Civil War and the American Revolution, the inspiration for which was a religious vision of society. Finally, world religions provide an important element of universalism, that one can detect behind the contemporary debate over cosmopolitan democracy. These arguments are clearly controversial, and raise critical problems about the legacy of the ancient world for democracy. Furthermore, Weber's account of the city and citizenship has characteristic difficulties that are associated with the problem of Orientalism (Turner, 1978). It will be necessary to turn to these problems towards the conclusion of this argument.

Weber's account of the historical roots of democracy and citizenship has created the dominant paradigm within which citizenship has been analysed by sociologists. Two aspects of Weber's argument have remained influential. Firstly, in *The City* ([1921] 1958) Weber regarded the medieval and renaissance city as an important location for Western democracy, because the independent guilds, the decline of slavery, the growth of independent legal institutions and the creation of an urban militia all favoured the growth of social rights. In the towns, merchant and artisan classes arose that were independent of feudal knights, and hence democracy has its origins in the *plebs* and the *popolo*. In particular *Bürgerschaft* does not follow the life-order of knights. Secondly, the

> basis of democratization is everywhere purely military in character; it lies in the rise of disciplined infantry, the hoplites of antiquity, the guild army of the middle ages. … Military discipline meant the triumph of democracy, because the community wished and was compelled to secure the co-operation of the non-aristocratic masses and hence put arms, and along with the arms political power, into their hands' (Weber, [1923] 1981: 324–5).

Changes in the technology of warfare that encouraged the routinisation of military activity, namely taking military prowess out of 'the battle between heroes' (Weber, [1923] 1981: 325), also promoted the growth of democratic institutions. The notion that the unintended consequence of the democratisation of military organisation has been to favour the general democratisation of society has been common to many accounts of citizenship from Richard Titmuss (1962) to Michael Mann (1986). Military democratisation produced the citizen-soldier as a key pillar of civil society (Turner, 2001).

Alongside this core theory of democratic citizenship, we can note Weber's interest in the impact of religion, specifically Christianity, on the development of citizenship. First, he argued that the Christian notion of a community based on faith rather than blood had the effect of undermining ethnic and kinship conflicts within the city, and hence allowed the formation of urban associations that transcended blood as a principle of social alliance. Weber claimed that 'the city Church, city saint, participation of the burghers in the Lord's Supper and official Church celebrations by the city were all typical of the Occidental cities. Within them Christianity deprived the clan of its last ritualistic importance, for by its very nature the Christian community was a confessional association of believing individuals rather than a ritualistic association of clans' (Weber, [1921] 1958: 102–3). The magical barriers between clans, tribes and people were set aside (Weber, [1923] 1981: 322–3). Secondly, Weber's analysis of the relationship between secular and religious powers in *Economy and Society* was organised around a discussion of the limits of

'Caesaro-papism', namely the subordination of priestly to earthly powers (Weber, [1922] 1978: 1161). Weber noted that the division between sacred and profane power was frequently compromised by Caesoro-papism as for example in the Carolingian empire, the Holy Roman Empire, in the Counter-Reformation, in Turkey and Persia. The Church as an independent hierocratic power required a priesthood, universal domination, dogma and rites, and a compulsory organisation. A fully developed ecclesiastical hierarchy with the backing of a systematic theology and priesthood cannot be easily uprooted and acts as a check on political power (Weber, [1922] 1978: 1175). Finally, Weber followed Ernst Troeltsch ([1911] 1931) in recognising the democratic thrust of the church–sect typology, in which sectarian opposition to ecclesiastical powers created an opportunity for democratic debate. The sects insisted on direct democratic administration of the congregations, often treating clerical officials as merely servants of the congregation. Freedom of conscience in the interpretation of scriptures was also important in creating a democratic culture. Because the sect is a radical voluntary association, it insisted on the separation of Church and state, and hence rejected a sacerdotal priesthood in favour of the doctrine of the priesthood of all believers (Weber, [1922] 1978: 1208).

It is obviously the case that Christian theological understanding of the political was shaped by Greek views of the *polis*. This Greek legacy shaped early Christian theory of the relationship between politics and religion through the theology of writers like St Augustine, Eusebius and Theodosius. While we can trace these components of citizenship from the Greek *polis* and the early Church, citizenship is most appropriately regarded as a modern concept that first emerged with the creation of autonomous cities in medieval Europe, but came to fruition with the revolutions that created the modern world, namely the American and French Revolutions. In European culture, 'citizen' is made possible by the rise of 'civil society' (*die bürgerliche Gesellschaft*), and they are both dependent on the emergence of a bourgeois civilisation.

Weber's insistence on the importance of religion in the rise of urban citizenship runs counter to the conventional view that religion has been hostile to the rise of democratic politics. The typical assumption is that the rise of secular citizenship requires, almost by definition, an erosion of the authority of institutional religion. This view of citizenship would further assume that the principal ideological themes of the French Revolution prepared the way for modern politics, in which religion has become a matter of private faith and ritual activity. The dramatic decline of institutional religion in the twentieth century also appears to support the view that the claims of modern citizenship require a process of secularisation. Indeed, the secularisation thesis has become an important component of a more general interpretation of the modernisation of society (Wilson, 1966). The contrast between the United States, where religion has continued to flourish, and the secularity of most European societies has as a result been a topic of considerable interest. In twentieth-century America, the consequence of postwar migration was to convert religious identity into a sign of American membership (Herberg, 1955), whereas in Europe religious affiliation was more persistently associated with class membership (Thompson, 1963). In Europe, religion had to become a matter of private devotion because its public manifestations produced civil conflict. This view has been the dominant historical interpretation of the effects of the Thirty Years War on the institutional division between the Church and the state, and the exclusion of religious controversy from the public domain.

This conventional view of the connection between the rise of citizenship and the impulse of secularisation, that has drawn its ideological inspiration from the French Revolution, often fails to make a further connection between the rise of nationalism and national citizenship. During the nineteenth century, citizenship functioned as a 'civil religion' that provided the social glue of industrial capitalism where social class divisions were increasingly important for politics and political identity. The historical tensions between religion and politics were submerged within a common national identity that used citizenship rituals and institutions as the conduit of national pride. With the decline of kingship and religion as principles of national unity, national citizenship and an imperial state developed as carriers of national consciousness. National rituals of political unity were religious in the sociological sense of creating collective representations of a national spirit, but monarchy and Christianity were either submerged in this development or employed to articulate a national mission (Durkheim, [1912] 1954). At the same time, the state acquired an identity around gender to articulate an imagined fraternity of common purpose (Nelson, 1998).

The main burden of my argument is to challenge this version of the secularisation thesis, namely the view that citizenship can only arise as a consequence of the decline of religion, or more specifically that citizenship requires the liberation of society from religious hegemony. In short, it is to question the simple proposition that citizenship is *par excellence* a product of secularism. There is a commonly held view that citizenship evolves with the Enlightenment, the spread of social contract theory, the triumph of science and the disenchantment of culture. The secularisation of the public sphere and the development of social rights prepare the groundwork for the triumphal emergence of the active citizen from the French and American revolutions. The secularisation thesis thus stands behind a theory of the modernisation of politics, wherein the creation of the citizen is an essential component. If one were to accept the claim that citizenship had its cultural origins in the Enlightenment and came to institutional maturity as a consequence of the political turmoil of the French Revolution, then citizenship and religion would appear to stand in a contradictory and corrosive relationship. If citizenship emerges with the growth of secular modernity, then the secularisation of culture is a necessary requirement for the development of an elaborate form of citizenship rights and institutions. This interpretation has considerable force, but it is incomplete.

The point of this chapter is to demonstrate the complexity of the relationship between religion and citizenship. The argument is that the tensions between religion and politics, between Church and state, and between Jerusalem and Athens (Strauss, 1995) have been productive of early or primitive versions of opposition to government that is important for active citizenship. Where citizenship is a product of political and social struggles, it assumes an active rather than passive form (Turner, 1993), but active citizens require a vision of politics that can transcend the everyday world of their existence. Religious objections to secular power ('idolatry' or 'false gods') have created the foundation of a utopian vision (Mannheim, 1936) against secular powers. On the basis of this structural principle (the separation of religion and politics), I attempt to trace the origins of western citizenship in the theological division between faith and politics, in Protestant congregationalism, in religious notions of equality (the priesthood of all believers), and in religious objections to arbitrary power. This argument about the theological strands in the history of citizenship, that regards St Augustine's political theory as a pivotal event in this trajectory of European society, is consequently a reflection on Weber's embryonic sociology of citizenship, as specifically outlined in his analysis of associations and city life (Weber, [1921] 1958).

Weber's account of urban institutions has to be understood in the context of his sociology of religion. For example, the peculiar contribution of Christianity to the city was to create a basis for social solidarity that was based on faith rather than blood. In short, the medieval city could evolve without the divisive complication of ethnic identity. The militia and urban trading associations were essentially fraternal associations based on common belief rather than tribal loyalty. This aspect of Weber's argument is well understood (Turner, 1998). We also need to read Weber's view of politics through the lens of his sociology of religion, namely the distinction between this-worldly and other-worldly soteriological systems. Any religion that has a this-worldly soteriology, especially an ascetic salvational orientation, will create a dialectic between the sacred and the secular, between for example a religion of brotherly love and the mundane necessity for violence in political life. This tension, as we know, was the privotal argument of Weber's account of the rise of rational capitalism (Weber, [1905] 1930). In this discussion of religion and citizenship, I argue that the religious dialectic between the two kingdoms (of love and violence) was a constitutive force in the rise of modern citizenship. The communal basis of the Church provided a model of human association as a non-coercive association that was influential in the development of early forms of secular citizenship. This theme was fundamental to both Augustinian political theory and Hannah Arendt's vision of public space (Scott and Stark, 1996). This aspect of the argument has a clear dependence on the sociology of knowledge of Karl Mannheim (1936) in which the Christian vision of history forged a utopian notion of community as an alternative to the state and empire.

THE WORLD AND THE SACRED IN THE ABRAHAMIC TRADITION

There is an important tension between the sacred and politics within any religious culture that has an evangelical relationship to the world. As a result, the history of citizenship is closely connected with the institutionalised forms of charismatic and secular power in human societies. This conflict between religious values and worldly institutions is brought about by the presence of charisma in social relationships. 'Charisma' (*kharisma* or *kharis*) or 'gift of grace' is a theological notion that has been widely used in the social sciences to describe the basis of authority and leadership in society generally. Charismatic power is associated with the idea of the sacred as a disruptive and violent force in human affairs. In its religious context, it means a divinely conferred power (Weber, [1922] 1966).

The different ways in which societies manage the challenge of charismatic powers has an important relationship to the rise of citizenship, because institutional routinisation established the division between the charismatic authority of ecclesiastical institutions and the secular power of kings. In this discussion, I shall be primarily concerned with the division between Church and state, but similar arguments also apply to Judaism and Islam, and to a lesser extent to so-called Asiatic religions such as Buddhism. In Islam, the death of the Prophet in 661 CE created similar problems of succession, resulting in the split between Shi'ism and Sunni Islam with respect to the source of authority and leadership within the Islamic community. The evolution of Shi'ism into a separate but suppressed religious movement produced the doctrine of the Hidden Imamate in which the secular state had no ultimate authority over the community. This doctrine (the Occultation of the Hidden Imam) provided the radical seed of the Iranian revolution in which the modernising government of the Pahlavi Shah was condemned as heretical. The authority of the Ayatollah Khomeini provided a charismatic challenge to the secular institutions of the modern state. By contrast Sunnism accepted the caliphates of the Umayyad and Abbasid dynasties as a legitimate form of government. Fundamentalist Islam in the twentieth century challenged this traditional compromise between the private sphere of religious devotion and the public arena of social institutions, and between the religious leadership of the community (*umma*) and the secular authority of the state. Thus the routinisation of charisma in religious movements forces religious authorities to develop a compromise with secular power. When a messianic religion becomes domesticated, there is a parallel evolution of religious citizenship within the religious community and political citizenship within the state. Because the religious community was an institution of consent, it often happened that the participation of the laity within the church provided a primitive model of secular citizenship.

Weber's contrast between priestly and prophetic authority was not a minor part of his sociology of religion, but an essential aspect of his understanding of modern politics, the state and political vocation. In the extended discussion of charisma in *The Sociology of Religion* (Weber, [1922] 1966; Ch. 4), he outlined the ideal typical contrasts between prophets, magicians and priests. Although the discussion is broad-ranging, his real focus was on the Judaic prophets of the classical period of the eighth century BC that formed much of the basis of the Old Testament. He distinguished between the prophet who, as a charismatic figure, has a personal call to prophesy, and the priest who has authority by virtue of his appointment to office and training in a sacred tradition. The prophets, who occasionally emerge from the ranks of the priesthood, are unremunerated, and depend on gifts from followers. Their calling to prophesy involves an involuntary acceptance of a divine commandment. Weber also distinguished two forms of prophesy as represented on the one hand by Buddha and on the other by Zoroaster, Jeremiah and Muhammad. The latter are involved in 'ethical prophesy' and are conceived as instruments of God. In *Ancient Judaism* ([1917] 1952) Weber argued that these prophets receive a commission from God to preach a revelation and demand obedience from their disciples as an ethical duty. By contrast exemplary prophets demonstrate to their followers a salvational path through the example provided by their own lives. Exemplary prophesy was, according to Weber, characteristic of Asia; ethical prophesy, of the Abrahamic religions of the Middle East. Weber's analysis of charisma with respect to ethical prophesy in the Old Testament has been subject to considerable criticism (Zeitlin, 1984), but his conceptual framework continues to influence both sociology and anthropology (Lindholm, 1990).

Judaic prophesy was a function of the rise of ethical monotheism around the God Yahweh among an unstable tribal confederacy. The Jews became a chosen people as a result of a contractual relationship that involved rights and obligations with respect to this jealous, unseen and universal god who rejects fertility cults and local deities. He is a god of the collectivity and not the individual. In return for complete obedience, Yahweh formed a social contract with the Jewish tribes. This contract required the complete rejection of the false gods of nature, the elimination of polytheism, and eventually devotion to the Law. The prophetic tradition in Judaism was a product of this fundamental contract where the Old Testament prophets of the wilderness denounced the corruption of the earthly city in the name of Yahweh who had promised to deliver his People from this-wordly tyranny. The prophets are the champions of the poor and downtrodden against the pomp and pride of earthly rulers. While Weber accepted this view of the prophets as anti-royalists, he did not accept the Marxist interpretation of writers like Karl Kautsky of the prophets and early Christianity as working class movements against the rich (Turner, 1991). The real point of the Old Testament prophets was that they were alone and isolated voices in the desert.

Weber's appreciation of the role of the prophets in the political imagination of Western philosophy was an important component in his analysis of Caesarism and Caesaro-papism. In Weber's political sociology, Caesarism is a form of primitive democracy in which as a result of military conquest soldiers elect one of their leaders to be a ruler. Such authoritarian rule may often be supported by adopting the local gods who are associated with the local territory. This convergence of religious and political authority can provide a powerful form of despotic rule in which sacred and profound forces are united into Caesaro-papism. Weber argued that this pattern of rulership was to be found at various times in the late Moscovite empire, the Islamic caliphs, the Eastern Church and Catholicism. While Weber was critical of the historical legacy of religio-political leadership, he was attracted to Caesarism as a solution to the lack of leadership in post-Bismarckian Germany. The peculiarities of the late development of a centralised nation-state in Germany had produced a special path (*Sonderweg*) and required an unusual political intervention, and hence Weber advocated a limited democracy (plebiscitary democracy) and decisive leadership. In short, only a charismatic leader could break through the limitations of German democratic politics.

This discussion of charisma with respect to different social roles should be seen as part of a larger sociological debate about the forms of association that characterise the social organisation of religious belief and practice. Weber wanted to argue that any group that is subject to charismatic authority forms a charismatic community (*Gemeinde*) and that such a community is inherently unstable. With the death of the leader, the group either dissolves or charisma undergoes a process of routinisation. The disciples have no career, no formal hierarchy, no offices and no qualifications. The Church that provides the organisational context of the priesthood is very different. Ecclesiastical organisations require a hierarchical administration of the 'charisma of office' in which there are definite stages in clerical and administrative careers. It is clearly the case that Weber's sociology of charisma should be understood as an application of the 'church–sect typology' (Troeltsch, [1911] 1931), in which there is a historical oscillation between the evangelical sects and the bureaucratic churches. Because Weber believed that in modern societies legal rational authority would become dominant, tradition and charisma were regarded as 'pre-rationalistic' and thus as characteristic of pre-modern societies. The notion that charismatic authority was not a resilient aspect of modern society was in turn a function of Weber's pessimistic understanding of social change in terms of secular rationalism and the erosion of religious meaning.

What was the legacy of early and medieval Christianity for the rise of Western citizenship? As we have seen, Christian theology developed a very clear view of the political, namely that politics was a secular activity between competitive men who sought domination over their societies. Politics was essentially about coercion and conflict between sinful beings. The Church by contrast was, from the standpoint of normative theory, a non-coercive association of people in search of salvation. The Augustinian theory had established a perspective on the state as a necessary evil. The main justification for the state was its ability to create order, but such an order could never be just. The Church was a non-coercive community or a corporation, not of kinship, but of common ends. The Church was an institution based not on blood but on a shared belief and ritual. Religious values functioned as a check on this-worldly powers. The evolution of asylum and immunity are two examples of how the church checked the power of the state. These immunities evolved out of two episcopal duties, namely intercession of sins and the administration of penance. Lay people sought refuge within the Church on the assumption that they would repent their sins and request clemency (Rosenwein, 1999). The concept of immunity developed out of the Church's historical role in human salvation. The Church had created a view of history as a linear history of salvation and so the Church was seen as a universal community of natural law.

RELIGION AND ASSOCIATIONAL DEMOCRACY

While in European societies there is clear evidence of secularisation, American history appears to contradict a simple secularisation thesis. The American colonies were created as religious experiments whose leadership sought to escape both secular and religious tyranny. The separation of Church and state in the Constitution recognised denominationalism as a major platform of American democracy. The significance of American religious pluralism was further recognised by Alexis de Tocqueville (1805–59) in *Democracy in America* (1968) that appeared in 1835 and 1840, and has remained axiomatic in the analysis of the connections between social capital, trust and participatory democracy. Independent congregations as illustrations of the basic principle of voluntary association are fundamental features of a vibrant civil society, because they protect individuals from mass opinion and the anomie of industrial capitalism. Talcott Parsons (1974) saw denominational pluralism as the final point of the processes of social differentiation that were necessary for the adaptive capacity of a modern social system. The Tocquevillian version of democracy as an associational politics of local participation has become central to any account of the relationship between civil society and modern citizenship. Churches as congregations of lay believers are voluntary associations and provide an experience of local democracy, lay leadership and participation that involves a process of schooling in democracy.

How then did the Protestant Reformation relate to the development of citizenship in Europe? I have already noted that 'citizenship' is a political status closely associated with the growth of independent cities in northern Europe. The argument that modern citizenship emerged from the independent associations and guilds of traders and artisans in medieval cities in the absence of effective patrimonial bureaucracy was the cornerstone of Weber's urban sociology. In England, the boroughs were the public context of burgher independence and throughout Europe bourgeois culture was a precondition of citizenship. It is hardly surprising that there is a strong etymological connection between civil, civility and civilisation. Citizenship civilises capitalism. Weber's historical viewpoint can be elaborated to argue that liberal democracy has flourished where the peasantry disappeared early in the development of capitalism and where the bourgeoisie was strong enough to block any reactionary alliance between aristocracy and peasantry in the context of the collapse of a feudal agrarian economy (Moore, 1967). The Protestant Reformation was a necessary condition of the emergence of a bourgeois culture as the cultural framework of bourgeois democracy. The Protestant sects contributed directly to the rise of the middle class and to its cultural outlook.

There is a conventional view that locates the origins of the modern public sphere in the formal doctrines of the French Enlightenment, but an alternative argument is that modern democratic discourse emerged in the religious debates of the Puritans. These religious debates were in turn dependent on the emerging printing industry in England prior to the Civil War (Zaret, 2000). The English Civil War provides 'the model case' of the growth of a public sphere and hence it is directly relevant to an understanding of the origins of modern civil society. It was practical innovations in communication that eventually prepared the way for the maturation of democratic theory towards the end of the seventeenth century in the work of writers such as John Locke.

These religious debates were facilitated by innovations in printing and had the consequence of undermining the conventional norms of secrecy and privilege that had hitherto dominated political decision-making. In Stuart England, the privilege of royal power ruled out any public discussion of government and supported 'council' (such as the Crown's Privy Council or Parliament) as the only legitimate channel for debate. The religious authority of Calvin and Hooker was frequently invoked to justify the view that 'private men' had no right to discuss the public affairs of state. The point of discussion in council was to better advise the monarch on matters of government and to provide an opportunity for petition and redress of grievances. Council did not exist to create opinion as an end in itself and communication between monarch and people was typically undertaken through church rituals, preaching and public ceremonies such as coronations, royal marriages and funerals. Within Anglicanism, the Establishment saw the pulpit as a political resource for communicating the king's pleasure.

The political effect of print presupposed important social changes, the most important being literacy, which was a consequence of the Puritan emphasis on individualism, the authority of the biblical text and the education of the laity. Public opinion was not simply the creation or the invention of print technology. Print culture was a contingent alliance between religious controversy and capitalist commerce that was brought about by the interests of authors and stationers. Political texts legitimated a legislative agenda, but they also thereby influenced the opinion of readers.

To what extent did the print revolution depend on Lutheran theology, which, through the doctrine of the priesthood of all believers, created the ideological conditions for a reading public? Puritans came to provide the cultural acid for the erosion of priestly (and later monarchical) authority, despite their deeply conservative view of the importance of social order and distrust of vulgar opinion. Thus, public opinion was distrusted by the very social groups that had unleashed it. The masses were seen to be a many-headed monster and irrationality was inversely connected to social rank, such that reasonableness increased with status. But this was a characteristic unintended consequence of the political radicalism of Puritan political and social teaching. The doctrine of the priesthood of all believers needed the iron discipline of the state to regulate sinful men, and therefore Lutheranism had a profoundly conservative message about the importance of the state. This ironic message is deeply Weberian, because the inner-worldly asceticism that was the real foundation of Puritan activism created not only the spirit of capitalism but also the spirit of print. Both capitalism and print have stood in a cancerous relationship to the ethic of Protestantism.

Before the outbreak of the Civil War in seventeenth-century England, Puritanism had created a reading culture and a public space for (theological) debate. The Puritan leadership expected that children would receive adequate religious instruction within the household and this expectation further elevated the status of the head of the household over the clergy. In homes, but also in taverns and barns, religious debate through printed texts flourished. A nascent public sphere was evolving that brought with it the implication of a democratic debate that undercut the traditional authority of the conservative clergy. We could argue that this thesis is a specifically political interpretation of *The Protestant Ethic and the Spirit of Capitalism* (Weber, [1905] 1930). Puritan individualism, combined with congregational independence, literacy, a linear view of history and a profound distrust of the state, proved to be an ideal breeding ground for the political culture of citizenship.

This discussion of the cultural impact of Protestant sects on the evolution of the working class introduces a more general question, namely the relationship between Christianity and socialism in the modern history of capitalist society. There has been a definite tradition of historical sociology that has noted that Protestantism was a 'revolutionary ideology' and detected a close parallel between Puritan moral criticism and the ascetic components of socialist doctrine (Walzer, 1964). In a peculiar fashion, Marx would have also agreed that Protestantism had an elective affinity with citizenship, primarily because he saw liberal democracy and individualism as a bourgeois legacy. In *Capital* volume one, Marx argued that, in a society based on the production of commodities, Christianity 'with its cultus of abstract man, more especially in its bourgeois developments, Protestantism, Deism, etc., is the most fitting form of religion' (Marx, 1970, [1867] vol. 1: 83). In the theory of alienation, Christianity expressed the isolation and estrangement of human beings, because, following Ludwig Feuerbach and David Strauss, Marx argued that religion inverted the real world by attributing causal powers to divine beings. Protestantism was an inverted truth about the abstract nature of social relations in capitalism (Turner, 1991: 66). The argument about the connections between Christianity and conservative politics has raged across political theory ever since.

For many political theorists, citizenship was historically a 'ruling-class strategy' the purpose of which was to incorporate the working class into nascent capitalism through the creation of social rights to welfare (Mann, 1987). Welfare capitalism achieved the pacification of the working class with relatively little concession to the fundamental issues of inequalities in wealth and political power. Citizenship left the class structure of capitalism intact, but avoided the revolutionary conflicts of the class system. This thesis can be criticised, because it fails to distinguish different forms of democratic citizenship, some of which are more radical than others. Citizenship that is grasped from below tends to be more active and radical than citizenship that is handed down by the ruling class through the state apparatus (Turner, 1990). The English Civil War and the American and French revolutionary experience produced an active form of citizenship. In fact the notion of 'active citizenship' is primarily a product of the public debates of the French Revolution. It was Rousseau who defined the object of morality and politics as the citizen not man. By contrast, the Glorious Revolution that brought English radicalism to a close promoted a passive and individualistic version of liberal citizenship. In England, Anglicanism for obvious reasons supported the establishment and provided the cultural ingredients of political gradualism. Anglicanism, which is essentially a political and theological compromise, provided the cultural glue of Britain and its empire within which the British citizenship was a subject of the monarch. The religious sects that opposed Anglicanism were often themselves quietist and thus the Arminian theological of the Wesleyan chapels was well suited to a benevolent and patronising attitude toward the disenchanted underclass.

CRITICAL EVALUATION OF WEBER'S THEORY

Weber's analysis of the European origins of civil society and citizenship raises some controversial issues with respect to the traditional problem of Orientalism (Turner, 2000a). A full analysis of this problem would require an extensive discussion of Weber's writings, for example on religion in China and India as well as Judaism and Islam. Weber's analysis of Islam has been supported by writers, like S.M. Lipset (1960 [1994]) who have argued that the fusion of religion and politics in early Islam provided no source of legitimation outside the state. Hence, there was little social leverage to exert criticism of the state. The Four Rightly Guided Caliphs who created the golden age of Islam followed the leadership of the Prophet, within which religious and political power was combined. As Islamic empires became Caesaro-papist, loyalty to the state became a matter of religious conviction. One problem with this view of Islam is that it fails to recognise important differences between Sunni and Shi'ite Islam (Arjomand, 1984). Shi'ism broke with the Sunni traditions of leadership and came to assert the infallible authority of an Imam who is pure, perfect and knowledgeable. With the death of the Twelfth Imam, Shi'ites came to believe in the historical role of a Hidden Imam, whose very absence renders current regimes illegitimate. The development of a doctrine of the Imamate, the Occultation of the Imam and the celebration of martyrdom produced a radical doctrine of political activism and social equality (Richard, 1995). In the revolutionary struggles against the modernising regime of the Shah, Shi'ite radicalism produced the ideological framework for radical politics for figures as diverse as Khomeini and Ali Shari'ati.

Weber's criticism of Islam and politics has been questioned by much contemporary scholarship. It is commonly argued that Weber's characterisation of Islam is too general to be reliable, and that scholarship should concentrate on specific, clearly defined cases (Huff and Schluchter, 1999). In the twentieth century, Islam was specifically associated with radical political movements against Western capitalism and hence against Weber's liberalism. It has been claimed that Islamic politics can support radical and progressive social movements. Radical fundamentalism provides political movements in the Third World with a revolutionary ideology that is anti-capitalist and therefore specifically anti-American. Liberal politics in the West has assumed, particularly since the fall of communism, that social and political affairs are best managed through the neutral mechanism of the market. The role of politics is only to protect the free operation of exchange in the market place, where conflicts of interest can be resolved, if only temporarily, through the blind exchange of goods. A market place does not, according to this perspective, require social or moral connections. In fact, culture and religion are 'noise' that disturbs the flow of goods. Liberals have been particularly hostile to fundamentalism, which is regarded as an irrational response to modernity. These debates have, however, only served to make Weber's question more urgent: what is the relationship between religion and modern politics? Weber's basic criticism of Caesaropapism can be supported on the grounds that the division between religion and politics offers a space for critical reflection on and opposition to repressive politics. Radical movements in Islam in the 1970s have themselves been hostile to the state monopolisation of religion through ministries of religious affairs that employed religious jurists to issue decrees in favour of state policies (Zartman, 2001).

Weber's analysis of the city has also been criticised because it implies the absence of an urban civil society in Islam, namely the absence of a set of intermediary associations between the individual and the state. For Weber, the Islamic city was merely a military camp that could achieve no independence from a patrimonial ruler. In general, Weber's argument that the social carrier of Islam was the warrior is defective, because it underestimates the importance of trade in the dissemination of the Islamic faith. Furthermore, it is difficult to argue that tribal loyalties were not questioned by Islam, since Muhammad's teaching specifically promoted the idea of a single *umma* (community) over local loyalties (Levy, 2000: 273). More recent scholarship on Islamic civil society has argued that there was a rich density of civil associations in the Islamic city (Kamali, 1998). The Shi'ite opposition to western-style industrialisation has precisely the characteristics of a religiously motivated utopian vision against secular powers that Weber assumed were important in creating revolutionary politics.

Weber's perspective on the origins of citizenship in the democratic institutions of early Greek society is also problematic. Clearly, the rise of literacy, the formulation of written laws and the institutionalisation of ostracism through a popular vote laid the foundations of Greek democracy. It is thus conventional to locate the origins of democracy in the classical Greek world, but the exclusion of women from public debate and the dependence on slave labour present serious problems for the modern search for the classical roots of democratic politics. Political theory has derived a view of democracy in terms of the political contest that shaped the public sphere in Athens, but the heroic legacy of Athenian military conflict produced a narrow and exclusive definition of the political community (Deneen, 2000; Saxonhouse, 1992). There is obviously a wealth of historical evidence to measure the rise of democracy and the decline of an aristocratic stratum of warriors in seventh-century BC Athens. These developments are often referred to in terms of the rise of citizenship (Bryant, 1996), but these are precocious foundations. Similar problems arise in general with the quest for the historical roots of citizenship in Roman antiquity (Turner and Hamilton, 1994). The historical research of Moses Finley (1991: 9) showed that Greek society in particular was dependent on a slave economy, that access to citizenship was severely limited and that women were excluded from participation in the public sphere. It was for this reason that the private or domestic sphere was an area of privation, and that both Greek and Roman society made a clear distinction between citizens who could vote and decide, and those who could not. There was a clear division between *boni* and *optimi*, and the rest (*plebs*, *multitudo*, and *improbi*). The full development of democratic citizenship presupposes the era of revolutionary politics that shaped modernity, and created a civil society that was open, at least in principle, to all social classes (Moore, 1967).

One further problem with Weber's approach is that it does not clearly differentiate between types of citizenship. While the early development of citizenship is associated with the growth of the city, a fully elaborated vision of modern citizenship has been the product of the American and French Revolutions. It is possible to argue, however, that the inspiration for these two revolutions was very different. The idea that revolutions involve an assault on religion is a product of the conditions that produced the French Revolution, where there was a specific attempt to replace the rites and doctrines of Catholicism with a secular culture. By contrast, the American Revolution was in part dependent on the revolutionary doctrines of the English Puritans, and developed an ideology that had obvious religious dimensions.

The English Civil War was a complex social and political movement concerned with freedom from arbitrary rule and fickle taxation, and freedom of religious expression in opposition to Roman and Anglican notions of kingship. English revolutionary fervour owed much to the commentaries of writers like John Milton, who, in 1659 to 1660 in ' The Ready and Easy Way to establish a Free Commonwealth and the Excellence thereof compared with the Inconveniences and Dangers of Re-Admitting Kingship in this Nation', compared the monarchical principle to idolatry in the Old Testament. For Milton, royalty was 'a gilded yoke' (Milton, [1644] 1927: 179). The execution of the king was therefore not an act of folly or fury, but a just defence of English liberties and religion. In his *Defence of the People of England* in 1651, the protection of the commonwealth of men meant that love of country was not incompatible with either natural law or religion. While religious and earthly loyalties were separate, the legacy of the classical notion of *respublica* was not incompatible with Christian duty (Viroli, 1995).

The Puritans carried these sentiments to the American colonies where they sought to create a commonwealth free of an established Church and the burden of arbitrary taxation without representation. American political culture has been shaped by the settlement of the colonies by Puritans who had escaped from religious persecution and hence the separation of Church and state became a primary premise of the Constitution. The revolution had itself been understood in terms of the Old Testament as a struggle to establish a righteous community. The American civil war was a religious trial in which the new nation was tested (Bellah, 1967). In short, there are major differences between French republicanism and American liberalism, where revolutionary sentiment in France is by definition secular. Religious values by contrast have remained central to American notions of citizenship. These different models of revolution have produced very different forms of citizenship.

In broad terms, we might distinguish three separate traditions of citizenship. In the Anglo-American legacy, religion and politics are sharply differentiated and citizenship rights are essentially political rights of individual freedom from the state to hold opinions, to practise religion freely, and to pursue economic self-interest without hindrance from the state. Religious differences are matters of private belief that need not impinge on the free market. A second tradition from French republicanism has a more positive and elaborate view of the citizen, whose liberties should be fully protected and cultivated by the state. Republicanism is less concerned with individual difference and more committed to the achievement of equality through universal provision. French republican traditions of citizenship are hostile to religious differences in civil society because they corrode the unity of the citizenry. Wearing a veil can be interpreted as a hostile rebuff of secular universalism. Finally there is a German tradition of citizenship in which the principal aim of social rights and civil society is to develop the character and moral status of the citizen. Education of the citizen is an essential condition of a good society. State interference in society is necessary to protect the citizen and enhance the full moral development of personality. Citizenship and civility are components of a more general process of civilisation. This perspective was associated with the notion of *Bildung* and hence with the *Bildungsbürgertum*. This tradition can be hostile to capitalism because it is not a force of moral development, and hence there is a certain compatibility between the aims of the church and the state. Weber's historical sketch of the origins and conditions of citizenship does not explicitly take into account these differences, but these three ideal types are nevertheless present in his work.

Finally, there is a further possible criticism of Weber's political sociology, namely that it was based on an outdated set of assumptions about the permanence of the nation-state. Some sociologists (Giddens, 1990) have dismissed Weber because his sociology cannot grasp the importance of globalisation. The effects of globalisation are politically complex but it can be claimed that it has created new opportunities for the spread of democratisation through the creation of electronic communities. At the same time, the global media have created the conditions for traditional 'world religions' to become truly global religions. There is however a serious problem about how citizenship can function as a progressive form of social inclusion in a context of competition between religions. National citizenship involves a specific principle of exclusion on the basis of national identity and membership, and therefore there are problems about citizenship as a political framework in societies that are multicultural and in a context of global governance. Perhaps human rights offer a mode of legal inclusion that is not tied to the nation-state. Although religion has been deeply involved in ethnic violence for centuries, the world religions provide one source for the development of a vision of a common humanity, and universalistic religious assumptions about humanity have underpinned human rights discourse. Religion provides a metaphysical framework for the doctrine of human rights against relativism and secularity (Turner, 2000b, 2000c). It is possible that religious universalism could contribute to the emergence of a cosmopolitanism that would foster the development of global democracy and human rights.

CONCLUSION: THE MARKET, POLITICS AND RELIGION

The argument of this chapter has followed the conventions of a liberal or Weberian interpretation of the religious origins of citizenship. Protestant institutions have contributed to the evolution of pluralism and free speech through an emphasis on individual responsibility. The doctrine of the priesthood of all believers has been a basis of egalitarianism, and religious congregationalism fostered communal autonomy, local involvement and individual development (Maddox, 1996: 200). The failure of the division between religion and politics resulted in a monopolistic authority, namely Caesaro-papism. A tension between Athens and Jerusalem, between reason and revelation, and between politics and religion has been a productive basis for the evolution of democratic cultures (Strauss, 1995).

Weber's vision of politics and religion was liberal, although of a rather tough and demanding character. His vision of politics was far removed from that of Locke or Mill. His arguments about the relationship between the state and the Church, his sympathetic treatment of the German Protestant tradition, his hostility towards mass democracy and party machines, his opposition to the German *Junkers* and his endorsement of individualism were part of the legacy of German liberalism. Partly because Weber's cultural and political sympathies were with liberal Protestantism, the cultural role of Roman Catholicism in the global history of economics and politics is missing from Weber's macro-history. His nationalism and his support for the World War I were shared by political and religious liberals in the German high bourgeoisie. The notion that Germany had a special role to play in European history as a force against the standardisation of culture by a technological civilisation was a perspective that Weber shared with writers like Thomas Mann (1987). Weber did not embrace a positive or full-blooded theory of democracy. He was committed to plebiscitary democracy that was a method of selecting a leader rather than a theory of radical political participation through parliamentary means.

While Weber admired the democracies of America and Britain, he recognised that the political difficulties of German society required determined leadership. It was not clear that such a leadership could come from a mass democracy grounded in universal citizenship. What was required was 'leadership-democracy', not Anglo-American parliamentary politics. One specific problem for Germany was to manage the political vacuum that had been caused by the departure of Bismarck. Weber's sociology has been said to have anticipated the rise of fascism, because Hitler's national socialism was an example of leadership-democracy that offered a response to the threat of communism and the growth of Anglo-American global dominance. There are therefore certain similarities between Weber's view of charismatic politics, politics as a vocation and the concept of the political in the work of Carl Schmitt (1996). If the historical struggle and tension between the religious and the political has been essential to the development of Western politics, then the rise of a secular liberalism and universal citizenship does suggest paradoxically the end of the political. Liberal notions of freedom are under attack, because the logical conclusion of liberal individualism is a society that is held together only by the market place, where isolated individuals exchange commodities. Liberalism ironically dilutes notions of civil society and active citizens involved in political struggles to maintain public space within which civic virtues can be exercised.

This conclusion is compatible with Weber's pessimistic analysis of the iron cage of capitalism, but it is not a conclusion we are compelled to accept (Habermas, 1989). Schmitt's attack on liberalism treats the political as the necessary conflict between friend and foe. It suggests that liberal compromise within civil society is also a compromise of virtue because it destroys the creative tension of politics, thereby making a moral life impossible. Schmitt and Weber are similar in treating politics as a domain of violent conflict. The notion of citizenship is seen to be part of this liberal legacy in which compromise within civil society is necessary to permit the free exchange of commodities.

These contemporary interpretations of Schmitt and Weber emphasise conflict (the presence of a foe) but they have little to say about social solidarity (the presence of a friend). In response to (authoritarian) critics of liberal citizenship, we might argue that citizenship is essential to building up friendship, and that without the affective ties of solidarity civility could not exist. In this respect, T.H. Marshall was correct to argue that citizenship establishes the basic framework for a civilised life within society. Citizenship is the expression of a commonwealth and that without love of this commonwealth society cannot flourish. This vision of a commonwealth has, often paradoxically, drawn its inspiration from the religious vision of a heavenly commonwealth within which cupidity, hatred and violence have been replaced by charity.

REFERENCES

Arjomand, S.A. (1984) *The Shadow of God and the Hidden Imam: Religion, Political Order and Societal Change in Shi'ite Iran from the Beginning to 1890.* Chicago: University of Chicago Press.

Bellah, R. (1967) 'Civil religion in America', *Daedalus*, 96: 1–21.

Bryant, J.M. (1996) *Moral Codes and Social Structure in Ancient Greece.* Albany: State University of New York Press.

Deneen, P.J. (2000) *The Odyssey of Political Theory. The Politics of Departure and Return.* Lanham: Rowman and Littlefield.

Durkheim, E. ([1912] 1954) *The Elementary Forms of the Religious Life.* London: Allen & Unwin.

Finley, M.I. (1991) *Politics in the Ancient World.* Cambridge: Cambridge University Press.

Giddens, A. (1990) *The Consequences of Modernity.* Cambridge: Polity Press.

Habermas, J. (1989) 'The horrors of autonomy: Carl Schmitt in English' in *The New Conservatism.* Cambridge: Polity Press, pp. 128–39.

Herberg, W. (1955) *Protestant Catholic Jew.* New York: Doubleday.

Huff, T.E. and Schluchter, W. (eds) (1999) *Max Weber and Islam.* New Brunswick, NJ: Transaction.

Kamali, M. (1998) *Revolutionary Iran: Civil Society and State in the Modernisation Process.* Aldershot: Ashgate.

Lanternari, V. (1963) *The Religions of the Oppressed: A Study of Modern Messianic Cults.* London: MacGibbon and Kee.

Levy, R. (2000) *The Social Structure of Islam.* London: Routledge.

Lindholm, C. (1993) *Charisma.* Oxford: Blackwell.

Lipset, S.M. (1994) 'The Social Requisites of Democracy Revisited' *American Sociological Review*, 59 (1): 1–22.

Maddox, G. (1996) *Religion and the Rise of Democracy.* London and New York: Routledge.

Mann, M. (1986) *The Sources of Social Power. vol. 1: A history of power from the beginning to A.D. 1760.* Cambridge: Cambridge University Press.

Mann, T. (1987) *Reflections of a Nonpolitical Man.* New York: Ungar.

Mannheim, K. (1936) *Ideology and Utopia.* London: Routledge & Kegan Paul.

Marx, K. (1970) [1867] *Capital.* London: Lawrence and Wishart, Volume one.

Milton, J. ([1644] 1927) *Areopagitica and Other Prose Works.* London: Dent.

Moore, B. (1967) *Social Origins of Dictatorship and Democracy: Lord and Peasant in the Making of the Modern World.* London: Allen Lane.

Nelson, D. (1998) *National Manhood: Capitalist Citizenship and the Imagined Fraternity of White Men.* Durham: Duke University Press.

Parsons, T. (1974) 'Religion in Postindustrial America: the Problem of Secularization', *Social Research*, 41 (2): 193–225.

Richard, Y. (1995) *Shi'ite Islam: Polity, Ideology and Creed.* Oxford: Blackwell.

Rojek, C. and Turner, B.S. (2001) *Society and Culture.* London: Sage.

Rosenwein, B.H. (1999) *Negotiating Space: Power, Restraint and Privileges of Immunity in Early Medieval Europe.* Manchester: Manchester University Press.

Saxonhouse, A.W. (1992) *Fear of Diversity: The Birth of Political Science in Ancient Greek Thought.* Chicago and London: University of Chicago Press.

Schmitt, C. (1996) *The Concept of the Political.* Chicago and London: University of Chicago Press.

Scott, J.V. and Stark, J.C. (eds) (1996) *Love and Saint Augustine.* Chicago: University of Chicago Press.

Strauss, L. (1995) 'Jerusalem and Athens: Some Preliminary Reflections' in S. Orr, *Jerusalem and Athens. Reason and Revelation in the Works of Leo Strauss.* Lanham: Rowman and Littlefield.

Tenbruck, F. (1980) 'The problem of the thematic unity in the works of Max Weber', *British Journal of Sociology*, 31 (3): 316–51.

Thompson, E.P. (1963) *The Making of the English Working Class.* Harmondsworth: Penguin.

Titmuss, R. (1962) *Income Distribution and Social Change. A Case Study in Criticism.* London: Allen & Unwin.

Tocqueville, A. de ([1835–40] 1968) *Democracy in America.* Glasgow: Collins.

Touraine, A. (2000) *Can We Live Together? Equality and Difference*. Cambridge: Polity Press.

Troeltsch, E. ([1911] 1931) *The Social Teaching of the Christian Churches*. New York: Macmillan.

Turner, B.S. (1978) *Marx and the End of Orientalism*. London: George Allen & Unwin.

Turner, B.S. (1990) 'Outline of a theory of citizenship', *Sociology*, 24 (2): 189–217.

Turner, B.S. (1991) *Religion and Social Theory*. London: Sage.

Turner, B.S. (1992) *Max Weber: From History to Modernity*. London: Routledge.

Turner, B.S. (ed.) (1993) *Citizenship and Social Theory*. London: Sage.

Turner, B.S. (1994) *Orientalism, Postmodernism and Globalism*. London and New York: Routledge.

Turner, B.S. (1998) *Weber and Islam*. London: Routledge/ Thoemmes Press.

Turner, B.S. (2000a) 'Islam, civil society and citizenship' in N.A. Butenschon, U. Davis and M. Hassassian (eds), *Citizenship and the State in the Middle East: Approaches and Applications*. New York: Syracuse University Press, p. 28–48.

Turner, B.S. (2000b) 'Liberal citizenship and cosmopolitan virtue' in A. Vandenberg (ed.) *Citizenship and Democracy in a Global Era*. Basingstoke: Macmillan, pp. 18–32.

Turner, B.S. (2000c) 'Cosmopolitan virtue: loyalty and the city' in E. Isin (ed.), *Democracy, Citizenship and the Global City*. London: Routledge, pp. 129–47.

Turner, B.S. (2001) 'The erosion of citizenship', *British Journal of Sociology*, 52 (2): 189–209.

Turner, B.S. and Hamilton, P. (eds) (1994) *Citizenship: Critical Concepts*. London: Routledge.

Viroli, M. (1995) *For Love of Country: An Essay on Patriotism and Nationalism*. Oxford: Clarendon Press.

Walzer, M. (1964) 'Puritanism as a revolutionary ideology', *History and Theory*, 3: 61–90.

Weber M. ([1905] 1930) *The Protestant Ethic and the Spirit of Capitalism*. London: Allen & Unwin.

Weber, M. ([1917] 1952) *Ancient Judaism*. New York: Free Press.

Weber, M. ([1921] 1958) *The City*. New York: Free Press.

Weber, M. ([1922] 1966) *The Sociology of Religion*. London: Methuen.

Weber, M. ([1922] 1978) *Economy and Society: An Outline of Interpretive Sociology*. 2 vols, Berkeley University of California Press.

Weber, M. ([1923] 1981) *General Economic History*. New Brunswick: Transaction Books.

Weber, M. ([1906] 1995) *The Russian Revolutions*. Cambridge: Polity Press.

Wilson, B. (1966) *Religion in Secular Society*. London, Watts.

Wolin, S.S. (1961) *Politics and Vision: Continuity and Innovation in Western Political Thought*. London: George Allen & Unwin.

Zaret, D. (2000) *Origins of Democratic Culture: Printing, Petitions, and the Public Sphere in early-modern England*. Princeton, New Jersey: Princeton University Press.

Zartman, I.W. (2001) 'Islam, the state and democracy: the contradictions', in C.E. Butterworth and I.W. Zartman (eds), *Between the State and Islam*. Cambridge: Cambridge University Press, pp. 231–44.

Zeitlin I. M. (1984) *Ancient Judaism: Biblical Criticism from Max Weber to the Present*. Cambridge: Polity Press.

17

Towards Post-National and Denationalized Citizenship

SASKIA SASSEN

Most of the scholarship on citizenship has claimed a necessary connection to the national state. The transformations afoot today raise questions about this proposition in so far as they significantly alter some of those conditions which in the past fed that articulation between citizenship and the national state. If this is indeed the case, then we need to ask whether is exclusively centred in the nation state and whether this is the only legitimate form of the institution. This chapter examines these possibilities and in so doing underlines the historicity of both the institution of citizenship and that of national state sovereignty. It is becoming evident today that far from being unitary, the institution of citizenship has multiple dimensions, only some of which might be inextricably linked to the national state. This chapter discusses the rapidly growing literature that is documenting and conceptualizing these issues, with particular attention to post-national conceptions of citizenship.

The context for this possible transformation is defined by two major, partly interconnected conditions. One is the change in the position and institutional features of national states since the 1980s resulting from various forms of globalization. These range from economic privatization and deregulation to the increased prominence of the international human rights regime. The second is the emergence of multiple actors, groups and communities partly strengthened by these transformations in the state and increasingly unwilling to automatically identify with a nation as represented by the state. The growth of the Internet and linked technologies has facilitated and often enabled the formation of cross-border networks among individuals and groups with shared interests that may be highly specialized, as in professional networks, or involve particularized political projects, as in human rights and environmental struggles. This has engendered or strengthened alternative notions of community of membership. These new experiences and orientations of citizenship may not necessarily be new; in some cases they may well be the result of long gestations or features that were there since the beginning of the formation of citizenship as a national institution, but are only now evident because enabled by current developments.

One of the implications of these developments is the possibility of post-national forms of citizenship (Soysal, 1994; Jacobson, 1996; Feldblum, 1998; see multiple chapters in Isin, 2000). The emphasis in this formulation is on the emergence of locations for citizenship outside the confines of the national state. The European passport is, perhaps, the most formalized of these. But the emergence of a reinvigorated cosmopolitanism (Turner, 2000; Nussbaum, 1994) and of a proliferation of transnationalisms (M. Smith and Guarnizo, 1998; R. Smith, 1997; Basch et al., 1994) have been key sources for notions of post-national citizenship. As Bosniak (2000) has put it, there is a reasonable case to be made that the experiences and practices associated with citizenship do, in variable degrees, have locations that exceed the boundaries of the territorial nation-state. Whether it is the organization of formal status, the protection of rights, citizenship practices, or the experience of collective identities and solidarities, the nation-state is not the exclusive site for their enactment. It remains by far the most important site, but the transformations in its exclusivity signal a possibly important new dynamic.

A second dynamic is becoming evident which, while sharing aspects with post-national citizenship, is usefully distinguished from it in that it concerns specific transformations inside the national state which directly and indirectly alter specific features of the institution of citizenship. These transformations are not predicated necessarily on a relocating of citizenship components outside the national state, as is key to conceptions of post-national citizenship. Changes in the law of nationality entailing a shift from purely formal to effective nationality, and enabling legislation allowing national courts to use international instruments, are two instances that capture some of these transformations inside the national state. More encompassing changes, captured in notions of privatization and shrinking welfare states, signal a shift in the relationship of citizens to the state. These and other developments all point to impacts on citizenship that take place *inside* formal institutions of the national state. It is useful to distinguish this second dynamic of transformation inside the national state because most of the scholarship on these issues is about post-national citizenship and has either overlooked these trends or interpreted them as post-national. In my own work (Sassen, 1996, 2003) I have conceptualized these trends as a denationalizing of particular aspects of citizenship to be distinguished from post-national developments. I return to this in a later section.

CITIZENSHIP AND NATIONALITY

In its narrowest definition citizenship describes the legal relationship between the individual and the polity. This relation can in principle assume many forms, in good part depending on the definition of the polity. In Europe this definition of the polity was originally the city, both in ancient and in medieval times. But the configuration of a polity reached its most developed form in the national state, making it eventually a dominant form worldwide. It is the evolution of polities along the lines of state formation that gave citizenship in the West its full institutionalized and formalized character and that made nationality a key component of citizenship.

Today the terms citizenship and nationality both refer to the national state. In a technical legal sense, while essentially the same concept, each term reflects a different legal framework. Both identify the legal status of an individual in terms of state membership. But citizenship is largely confined to the national dimension, while nationality refers to the international legal dimension in the context of an interstate system. The legal status entails the specifics of whom the state recognizes as a citizen and the formal basis for the rights and responsibilities of the individual in relation to the state. International law affirms that each state may determine who will be considered a citizen of that state.[1] Domestic laws about who is a citizen vary significantly across states and so do the definitions of what it entails to be a citizen (see various chapters in this volume). Even within Europe, let alone worldwide, there are marked differences in how citizenship is articulated and hence how non-citizens are defined.

To understand the nature of the transformations we seek to capture through terms such as post-national and denationalized citizenship it is helpful to situate the nationalizing of citizenship. The shift of citizenship into a national state institution and away from one centred in cities and civil society was part of a larger dynamic of change. Key institutional orders began to scale at the national level: warfare, industrial development, educational and cultural institutions. These were all at the heart of the formation and strengthening of the national state as the key political community and crucial to the socialization of individuals into national citizenship. It is in this context that nationality becomes a central constitutive element of the institution of citizenship in a way that it was not in the medieval cities described by Weber.

The evolution of the meaning of nationality captures some of these transformations. Historically, nationality is linked to the bond of allegiance of the individual to the sovereign. It dates from the European state system even in some of its earliest elementary forms and describes the inherent and permanent bond of the subject to the sovereign: 'No man may abjure his country.' Traditionally this bond was seen as insoluble or at least exclusive. But while the bond of insoluble allegiance was defensible in times of limited individual mobility, it became difficult in the face of large-scale migration which was part of the new forms of industrial development. Insoluble was gradually replaced by exclusive, hence singular but changeable, allegiance as the basis of nationality. Where the doctrine of insoluble allegiance is a product of medieval Europe, the development of exclusive allegiance reflects the political context in the second half of the nineteenth century (Rubenstein and Adler, 2000). This is when state sovereignty becomes the organizing principle of an international system – albeit a system centred on and largely ruled by Europe.[2]

Dual nationality was incompatible with the absolute authority of the state over its territory and its nationals (Brubaker, 1989). Indeed, we see the development of a series of mechanisms aimed at preventing or counteracting the occurrence of de facto dual nationality, such as the redrawing of borders after wars or the imposition of a new nation-state on an underlying older one (Marrus, 1985). There were no international accords on dual nationality, a sharp contrast with the 1990s, which have seen a proliferation of such accords. This negative perception of dual nationality continued into the first half of the twentieth century and well into the 1960s. The main effort by the international system was to root out the causes of dual nationality by means of multilateral codification of the law on the subject (Rubenstein, and Adler, 2000).

The major transformations over the last two decades have once again brought conditions for a change in the institution of citizenship and its relation to nationality, and they have brought about changes in the legal content of nationality. It is probably the case that the particular form of the institution of citizenship centred on exclusive allegiance reached its high point in the twentieth century and has, over the last decade, begun to incorporate formal and non-formal qualifications that contribute to dilute that particular formalization. The development in international law of nationality has moved to more flexible forms. The long-lasting resistance to dual or multiple nationality is shifting towards a selective acceptance. According to some legal scholars (Rubenstein and Adler, 2000), in the future dual and multiple nationality will become the norm. Today more people than ever before hold dual nationality (Spiro, 1997). For Spiro this possibility of multiple allegiances indicates that national citizenship might be less important than it once was.[3] In so far as the importance of nationality rests on the central role of states in the international state system, a decline in the importance of this role and of this system will affect the value of nationality. This would parallel the devaluation of nation-state-based sovereignty (Sassen, 1996: Ch. 1).

Some of the major transformations occurring today under the impact of globalization may give citizenship yet another set of features as it continues to respond to the conditions within which it is embedded. The nationalizing of the institution which took place over the last several centuries may today give way to a partial denationalizing. A fundamental dynamic in this regard is the growing articulation of globalization with national economies and the associated withdrawal of the state from various spheres of citizenship entitlements. One could posit that this thinning if not decline of Marshall's concept of evolving citizenship towards social rights raises the possibility of a corresponding dilution of loyalty to the state. In turn, citizens' loyalty may be less crucial to the state today than it was at a time of intense warfare and its need for loyal citizen-soldiers (Turner, 2000).[4] Masses of troops today can be replaced by technologically intensive methods of warfare. In the highly developed world, warfare has become a less significant event partly due to economic globalization, that is to say, the fact that crucial economic systems and dynamics scale at the global level. One key aspect is the impact of increasingly strong supranational institutions that challenge the authority of nation-states; the EU, IMF, World Bank, WTO, and other such supranational institutions can determine key features of domestic economic performance. Global firms and global markets do not want the rich countries to fight wars among themselves. The 'international' project is radically different from what it was in the nineteenth and first half of the twentieth centuries.

DECONSTRUCTING CITIZENSHIP

Though often talked about as a single concept and experienced as a unitary institution, citizenship actually describes a number of discrete but related aspects in the relation between the individual and the polity. Current developments are bringing to light and accentuating the distinctiveness of these various aspects, from formal rights to practices and psychological dimensions. These developments also bring to the fore the tension between citizenship as a formal legal status and as a normative project or an aspiration. Current conditions have led to a growing emphasis on claims and aspirations that go beyond the formal legal definition of rights and obligations. Most recently there has also been a reinvigoration of theoretical distinctions: communitarian and deliberative, republican and liberal.

Yet more often than not the nation-state is the typically implicit frame within which these distinctions are explored. In this sense, much of this literature cannot be read as post-national even when it seeks to locate citizenship in areas that go beyond the formal political domain. Nonetheless, this deconstruction of citizenship has also fed a much smaller but growing scholarship which begins to develop notions of citizenship not based on the nation-state, whether understood in narrow political terms or broader sociological and psychological terms. The growing prominence of the international human rights regime has played an important theoretical and political role in strengthening post-national conceptions even as it has underlined the differences between citizenship rights and human rights.

Recently there have been several efforts to organize the various understandings of citizenship one can find in the scholarly literature: citizenship as legal status, as possession of rights, as political activity, as a form of collective identity and sentiment. (Kymlicka and Norman, 1994; Carens, 1989; Kratochwil, 1994; Vogel and Moran, 1991; Conover, 1995; Bosniak, 2000). Further, some scholars (Turner, 1993; Taylor, 1994; see also generally van Steenbergen, 1994) have posited that cultural citizenship is a necessary part of any adequate conception of citizenship, while others have insisted on the importance of economic citizenship (Fernandez Kelly, 1993) and yet others on the psychological dimension and the ties of identification and solidarity we maintain with other groups in the world (Conover, 1995; Carens, 1989; Pogge, 1992).

It is important to recognize that while many of these distinctions deconstruct the category of citizenship and hence are helpful for formulating novel conceptions, they do not necessarily cease to be nation-state-based. For the development of notions of post-national citizenship it is important to question the assumption that people's sense of citizenship in liberal democratic states is fundamentally characterized by nation-based frames. These questions of identity need to be taken into account along with formal developments such as European Union citizenship and the growth of the international human rights regime. Because legal and formal developments have not gone very far, a focus on experiences of identity emerges as crucial to post-national citizenship.[5]

The scholarship that critiques the assumption that identity is basically tied to a national polity represents a broad range of positions, many having little to do with a post-national conception. For some, the focus is on the fact that people often maintain stronger allegiances to and identification with particular cultural and social groups within the nation than with the nation at large (Young, 1990; Taylor, 1994). Others have argued that the notion of a national identity is based on the suppression of social and cultural differences (Friedman, 1989). These and others have called for a recognition of differentiated citizenship and incorporation not only as individuals but through cultural groups (Young, 1990; Kymlicka and Norman, 1994; Taylor, 1994; Conover, 1995). As Torres (1998) has observed, the 'cultural pluralist' (Kymlicka and Norman, 1994) or multiculturalist positions (Spinner-Halev, 1994) do posit alternatives to a 'national' sense of identity, yet continue to use the nation-state as the normative frame and to understand the social groups involved as parts of national civil society. This holds also for proposals to democratize the public sphere through multicultural representation (Young, 1990; Kymlicka, 1995) since the public sphere is thought of as national. Bosniak (2000) observes that they reject notions of citizenship as unitary, but the fragments continue to be located within national boundaries.

Clearly, some of these critical literatures do not actually go beyond the nation-state and thereby do not fit into post-national conceptions of citizenship, even though they may fit into a conception of citizenship as partly or increasingly denationalized.

Critical challenges to statist premises can also be found in concepts of local citizenship, typically at the urban level (e.g. Magnusson, 1996, 2000; Isin, 2000), or by reclaiming domains of social life, often excluded from conventional conceptions of politics, as sites for citizenship (Chinchilla and Hamilton, 2002). Examples of the latter focus on recognition of citizenship practices in the workplace (Pateman, 1988), in the economy at large (Dahl, 1989), in the family (Jones, 1998), in new social movements (Tarrow, 1994; Magnusson, 2000). These are more sociological versions of citizenship, not confined by narrowly defined formal political grounds for citizenship. Again, most of the literature on civil society is nationally demarcated. As for the literature on local citizenship, it contains important indications of trends that are of interest to post-national and denationalized conceptions of citizenship, as discussed in a later section (See also Yuval-Davies and Werkner, 1999).

Partly influenced by these various critical literatures and partly originating in other fields, there is a rapidly growing literature today that is beginning to elaborate notions of transnational civil society and citizenship. It focuses on new transnational forms of political organization emerging in a context of rapid globalization and proliferation of transnational activity through NGOs (Smith and Guarnizo, 1998; Keck and Sikkink, 1998; Bonilla et al., 1998; Wapner, 1995), including cross-border struggles around human rights, the environment, arms control, women's rights, labor rights, rights of national minorities. For Falk (1993) these are citizen practices that go beyond the nation. Transnational activism emerges as a form of global citizenship which Magnusson (1996: 103) describes as 'popular politics in its global dimension.' Wapner (1995: 312–13) captures these emergent forms of civil society as 'a slice of associational life which exists above the individual and below the state, but also across national boundaries.'

A growing number of scholars concerned with identity and solidarity posit the rise of transnational identities (Torres, 1998; Cohen, 1996; Franck, 1997) and translocal loyalties (Appadurai, 1996: 165). Bosniak (2000: 482) finds at least four forms taken by transnationalized citizenship identity claims. One is the growth of Europe-wide citizenship said to be developing as part of the EU integration process, and beyond the formal status of EU citizenship (Soysal, 1994; Howe, 1991; Isin, 2000: 1–22; Delanty, 2000). Turner has posited a growing cultural awareness of a 'European identity' (2000). A second focus is on the affective connections that people establish and maintain with one another in the context of a growing transnational civil society (Cohen, 1994; Lipschutz, 1996; Lister, 1997). Citizenship here resides in identities and commitments that arise out of cross-border affiliations, especially those associated with oppositional politics (Falk, 1993), though it might include the corporate professional circuits that are increasingly forms of partly deterritorialized global cultures (Sassen, 2001).

A third version is the emergence of transnational social and political communities constituted through transborder migration. These begin to function as bases for new forms of citizenship identity to the extent that members maintain identification and solidarities with one another across state territorial divides (Portes, 1996; Basch et al., 1994; R. Smith, 1997; M. Smith and Guarnizo, 1998; Soysal, 1997). These are, then, citizenship identities that arise out of networks, activities, ideologies that span the home and the host society (Basch et al., 1994). A fourth version is a sort of global sense of solidarity and identification, partly out of humanitarian convictions (Pogge, 1992). Notions of the ultimate unity of human experience are part of a long tradition. Today there are also more practical considerations at work, as in global ecological interdependence, economic globalization, global media and commercial culture, all of which create structural interdependencies and senses of global responsibility (Falk, 1993; Hunter, 1992; Held, 1995; Sassen, 1996).

TOWARDS EFFECTIVE NATIONALITY AND INFORMAL CITIZENSHIP

Some of these issues can be illustrated by two contrasting forms of localized citizenship.

Unauthorized Yet Recognized

Perhaps one of the more extreme instances of a condition akin to effective as opposed to formal nationality is what has been called the informal social contract that binds undocumented immigrants to their communities of residence (Schuck and Smith, 1985). Thus, unauthorized immigrants who demonstrate civic involvement, social deservedness, and national loyalty can argue that they merit legal residency. To make this brief examination more specific, I will focus on one case, undocumented immigrants in the USA. Individuals, even when undocumented immigrants, can move between the multiple meanings of citizenship. The daily practices by undocumented immigrants as part of their daily life in the community where they reside (raising a family, schooling children, holding a job) earn them citizenship claims in the USA even as the formal status and, more narrowly, legalization may continue to evade them. Certain dimensions of citizenship, such as strong community ties and participation in civic activities, are being enacted informally through these practices. These practices produce an at least partial recognition of the individuals as full social beings. In many countries around the world, including the USA, long-term undocumented residents often can gain legal residence if they can document the fact of this long-term residence and 'good conduct.' US immigration law recognizes such informal participation as grounds for granting legal residency. For instance, prior to the new immigration law passed in 1996, individuals who could prove seven years of continuous presence and good moral character, and that deportation would be an extreme hardship, were eligible for suspension of deportation, and thus, US residency. NACARA[6] extended the eligibility of this suspension of deportation to some 300,000 Salvadorans and Guatemalans who were unauthorized residents in the USA.

The case of undocumented immigrants is, in many ways, a very particular and special illustration of a condition akin to 'effective' citizenship and nationality. One way of interpreting this dynamic in the light of the discussion in the preceding sections is to emphasize that it is the fact of the multiple dimensions of citizenship which engenders strategies for legitimizing informal or extra-statal forms of membership (Soysal, 1994; Coutin, 2000). The practices of these undocumented immigrants are a form of citizenship practices and their identities as members of a community of residence assume some of the features of citizenship identities. Supposedly this could hold even in the communitarian model where the community can decide on whom to admit and whom to exclude, but once admitted, proper civic practices earn full membership.

Further, the practices of migrants, even if undocumented, can contribute to recognition of their rights in countries of origin. During the 1981–92 civil war, Salvadoran migrants, even though citizens of Salvador, were directly and indirectly excluded from El Salvador through political violence, enormous economic hardship, and direct persecution (Mahler, 1995). They could not enjoy their rights as citizens. After fleeing, many continued to provide support to their families and communities. Further, migrants' remittances became a key factor for El Salvador's economy – as they are for several countries around the world. The government of El Salvador actually began to support the emigrants, fight to obtain residency rights in the USA, even as they were joining US-based opposition organizations in this effort. The Salvadoran government was thus supporting Salvadorans who were formerly excluded citizens – they needed those remittances to keep coming and they needed the emigrants to stay out of the Salvadoran workforce, given high unemployment. Thus the participation of these undocumented migrants in cross-border community, family and political networks has contributed to increasing recognition of their legal and political rights as Salvadoran citizens (Coutin, 2000; Mahler, 1995; see Sassen, 2003 for the case of several other countries).

According to Coutin (2000) and others, movements between membership and exclusion, and between different dimensions of citizenship, legitimacy and illegitimacy, may be as important as redefinitions of citizenship itself. Given scarce resources, the possibility of negotiating the different dimensions of citizenship may well represent an important enabling condition. Undocumented immigrants develop informal, covert, often extra-statal strategies and networks connecting them with communities in sending countries. Home towns rely on their remittances and their information about jobs in the USA. The sending of remittances illegally by an unauthorized immigrant can be seen as an act of patriotism, and working as an undocumented immigrant can be seen as contributing to the host economy. Multiple interdependencies are thereby established and grounds for claims on the receiving and the originating country can be established even when the immigrants are undocumented and laws are broken (Basch et al., 1995; R. Smith, 1997).

Authorized yet Unrecognized

At perhaps the other extreme of the undocumented immigrants whose practices allow them to become accepted as members of the political community is the case of those who are full citizens yet not recognized as political subjects. In an enormously insightful study of Japanese housewives, LeBlanc (1997) finds precisely this combination.

Being a housewife is basically a full-time occupation in Japan and restricts Japanese women's public life in many important ways, both practical and symbolic. The very identity of a 'housewife' in Japan is customarily that of a particularistic, non-political actor. Yet, paradoxically, the condition of being a 'housewife' provides these women with a unique vehicle for other forms of public participation, ones where being a housewife is an advantage, ones denied to those who might have the qualifications of higher-level political life. LeBlanc documents how the housewife has an advantage in the world of local politics or the political life of a local area: she can be trusted precisely because she is a housewife, she can build networks with other housewives, hers is the image of desirable public concern and of a powerful, because believable, critic of mainstream politics.

There is something extremely important in this condition which is shared with women in other cultures and *vis à vis* different issues. For instance, and in a very different register, women emerged as a specific type of political actor during the brutal dictatorships of the 1970s and 1980s in several countries of Latin America. It was precisely their condition as mothers and wives which gave them the clarity and the courage to demand justice and to demand bread and to do so confronting armed soldiers and policemen. Mothers in the *barrios* of Santiago during Pinochet's dictatorship, the mothers of the Plaza de Mayo in Buenos Aires, the mothers regularly demonstrating in front of the major prisons in El Salvador during the civil war – all were driven to political action by their despair at the loss of children and husbands and the struggle to provide food in their homes.

Further, and in a very different type of situation, there is an interesting parallel between LeBlanc's capturing of the political in the condition of the housewife and a set of findings in some of the research on immigrant women in the USA. There is growing evidence that immigrant women's regular wage work and improved access to other public realms has an impact on their culturally specified subordinate role to men in the household. Immigrant women gain greater personal autonomy and independence, while immigrant men lose ground compared to their condition in cultures of origin. Women gain more control over budgeting and other domestic decisions, and greater leverage in requesting help from men in domestic chores. Also, their access to public services and other public resources gives them a chance to become incorporated into the mainstream society – they are often the ones in the household who mediate in this process. It is likely that some women benefit more than others from these circumstances; we need more research to establish the impact of class, education and income on these gendered outcomes.

Besides the relatively greater empowerment of immigrant women in the household associated with waged employment, there is a second important outcome: their greater participation in the public sphere and their possible emergence as public actors. Immigrant women are active in two arenas: institutions for public and private assistance, and the immigrant/ethnic community. The incorporation of women into the migration process strengthens the likelihood of settlement and contributes to greater immigrant participation in their communities and *vis à vis* the state. For instance, Hondagneu-Sotelo (1994) found immigrant women come to assume more active public and social roles, which further reinforces their status in the household and the settlement process. These immigrant women are more active in community-building and community activism and they are positioned differently from men regarding the broader economy and the state. They are the ones that are likely to have to handle the legal vulnerability of their families in the process of seeking public and social services for their families. This greater participation by women suggests that they may emerge as more forceful and visible actors and make their role in the labor market more visible as well.

These are dimensions of citizenship and citizenship practices which do not fit the indicators and categories of mainstream frameworks for understanding citizenship and political life. Women in the condition of housewives and mothers do not fit the categories and indicators used to capture participation in public life. Feminist scholarship in all the social sciences has had to deal with a set of similar or equivalent difficulties and tensions in its effort to constitute its subject or to reconfigure a subject that has been flattened. The theoretical and empirical distance that has to be bridged between the recognized world of politics and the as yet unmapped experience of citizenship of the housewife – not of women as such, but of women as housewives – is a distance we encounter in many types of inquiry. Bridging this distance entails both an empirical research strategy and a theorization.

Forms of Local Citizenship?

There is something to be captured here – a distinction between powerlessness and the condition of being an actor even though lacking power. I use the term 'presence' to name this condition. In the context of a strategic space such as the global city, the types of disadvantaged people described here are not simply marginal; they acquire presence in a broader political process that escapes the boundaries of the formal polity. This presence signals the possibility of a politics. What this politics will be will depend on the specific projects and practices of various communities. In so far as the sense of membership of these communities is not subsumed under the national, it may well signal the possibility of a transnational politics centred in concrete localities.

The large city of today emerges as a key site for these new types of operations. It is one of the nexuses where the formation of new claims materializes and assumes concrete forms. The loss of power at the national level produces the possibility for new forms of power and politics at the subnational level. The national as container of social process and power is cracked. This cracked casing opens up possibilities for a geography of politics that links subnational spaces. These dynamics are perhaps sharpest in global cities around the world. They are the terrain where a multiplicity of globalization processes assume concrete, localized forms. These localized forms are, in good part, what globalization is about. Thus they are also sites where some of the new forms of power can be engaged. If we consider that cities concentrate both the leading sectors of global capital and a growing share of disadvantaged populations – immigrants, many of the disadvantaged women, people of colour generally, and, in the megacities of developing countries, masses of shanty dwellers – then we can see that cities have become a terrain for a whole series of conflicts and contradictions.

The conditions that today make it possible for certain kinds of cities to emerge as strategic sites are basically two, and both capture major transformations that are destabilizing older systems organizing territory and politics. One of these is the re-scaling of the strategic territories that articulate the new politico-economic system. The other is the partial unbundling or at least weakening of the national as container of social process due to the variety of dynamics encompassed by globalization, including digitization. The consequences for cities of these two conditions are many: what matters here is that cities emerge as strategic sites for major economic processes and that new types of political actors can emerge. In so far as citizenship is embedded and in turn marked by its embeddedness, these new conditions may well signal the possibility of new forms of citizenship practices and identities.

These citizenship practices have to do with the production of 'presence' by those without power and a politics that claims rights to the city. Through these practices new forms of citizenship are taking shape, with the city as a key site for this type of political work and, indeed, itself partly shaped through these dynamics. After the long historical phase that saw the ascendance of the national state and the scaling of key economic dynamics at the national level, the city – a strategic scale for citizen actors – is once again today a scale for strategic economic and political dynamics.

POST-NATIONAL OR DENATIONALIZED?

In my reading we are dealing with two distinct dynamics rather than only the emergence of locations for citizenship outside the frame of the national state. I distinguish what I would narrowly define as denationalized from post-national, the latter being the term most commonly used and the only one used in the broader debate. It is precisely in the differences between these dynamics that I see the potential for capturing two, not necessarily mutually exclusive, possible trajectories for the institution of citizenship.

Their difference is a question of scope and institutional embeddedness. The understanding in the scholarship is that post-national citizenship is located partly outside the confines of the national.[7] I argue that in considering denationalization, the focus moves on to the transformation of the national, including the national in its condition as foundational for citizenship. Thus it could be argued that post-nationalism and denationalization represent two different trajectories. Both are viable, and they do not exclude each other. One has to do with the transformation of the national, specifically under the impact of globalization and several other dynamics, and will tend to instantiate inside the national. The other has to do with new forms that we have not even considered and might emerge out of the changed conditions in the world located outside the national rather than out of the earlier institutional framework of the national. Thus Soysal's focus on the European Union is capturing an innovation located outside the national.

With denationalization I seek to capture something that remains connected to the national, as constructed historically, and is indeed profoundly imbricated with it but is so on what we can define as historically new terms of engagement. Incipient and partial are two qualifiers I usually attach to my use of denationalization. Let me elaborate.

From the perspective of nation-based citizenship theory, some of these transformations might be interpreted as a decline or devaluation of citizenship or, more favourably, as a displacement of citizenship in the face of other forms of collective organization and affiliation, as yet unnamed (Bosniak, 2000). In so far as citizenship is theorized as necessarily national, by definition these new developments cannot be captured in the language of citizenship. An alternative interpretation is to suspend the national, as in post-national conceptions, and to posit that the issue of where citizenship is enacted is one to be determined in light of developing social practice (e.g. Soysal, 1994; Jacobson, 1996).

From where I look at these issues, there is a third possibility, beyond these two. It is that citizenship, even if situated in institutional settings that are 'national' is a possibly changed institution if the meaning of the national itself has changed. In so far as globalization has changed certain features of the territorial and institutional organization of the state, the institution of citizenship – its formal rights, its practices, its psychological dimension – has also been transformed even when it remains centred in the national state, i.e. barring post-national versions of citizenship. I have argued, for instance, that this territorial and institutional transformation of state power and authority has produced operational, conceptual and rhetorical openings for nation-based subjects other than the national state to emerge as legitimate actors in international/global arenas that used to be confined to the state. (See *Indiana Journal of Global Legal Studies*, 1996.)

The national remains a referent in these cases. But, clearly, it is a referent of a specific sort: it is, after all, the change of the national that becomes the key theoretical feature through which it enters the specification of changes in the institution of citizenship. Whether this does or does not devalue citizenship (cf. Jacobson, 1996) is not immediately evident to me at this point, partly because the institution of citizenship has undergone many transformations in its history (Turner, 1993; Ong, 1999) and is to variable extents embedded in the specifics of each of its eras.[8]

This pluralized meaning of citizenship, partly produced by the formal expansions of the legal status of citizenship, is today contributing to explode the boundaries of that legal status even further. One of the ironies is that in so far as the enjoyment of rights is crucial to what we understand citizenship to be, it is precisely the formalized expansion of citizen rights which has weakened the 'national grip' on citizenship. Notable here is also the emergence of the human rights regime partly enabled by national states. Again, from where I look at the question, it seems to me that this transformation in nation-based citizenship is not only due to the emergence of non-national sites for legitimate claim-making, i.e. the human rights regime, as is posited in the post-national conception. I would add two other elements that show that this loosening grip is also related to changes internal to the national state.

First, and most important in my reading, is the strengthening, including the constitutionalizing, of civil rights which allow citizens to make claims against their states and allow them to invoke a measure of autonomy in the formal political arena that can be read as a lengthening distance between the formal apparatus of the state and the institution of citizenship. The implications, both political and theoretical, of this dimension are complex and in the making: we cannot tell what practices and rhetorics might be invented.

Secondly, I add to this the granting, by national states, of a whole range of 'rights' to foreign actors, largely and especially economic actors – foreign firms, foreign investors, international markets, foreign business people (see Sassen, 1996: Ch. 2). Admittedly, this is not a common way of framing the issue. It comes out of my particular perspective about the impact of globalization and denationalization on the national state, including the impact on the relation between the state and its own citizens, and it and foreign actors. I see this as a significant, though not much recognized, development in the history of claim-making. For me the question as to how citizens should handle these new concentrations of power and 'legitimacy' that attach to global firms and markets is a key to the future of democracy. My efforts to detect the extent to which the global is embedded and filtered through the national (e.g. the concept of the global city) is one way of understanding whether there lies a possibility in citizens, still largely confined to national institutions, to demand accountability from global economic actors through national institutional channels, rather than having to wait for a 'global' state.

Thus, while I would agree with those who posit that accentuating the national is a handicap in terms of democratic participation in a global age, I would argue that it is not an either-or proposition precisely because of this partial embedding of the global in the national. (See in this regard also Aman, Jr., 1998). There is indeed a growing gap between the globalization of more and more parts of reality and the confinement of the national state to its territory. But it is inadequate to simply accept the prevailing wisdom in this realm which, wittingly or not, presents the national and the global as two mutually exclusive domains – for theorization and for politics. I find this a highly problematic proposition even though I recognize that each of these domains has specificity (Sassen, 2003). It is enormously important to develop forms of participatory politics that decentre, and sometimes transcend national political life, and to learn how to practice democracy across borders. In this I fully support the political project of post-national citizenship. I would just add to this that we also can engage in democratic practices that cross borders and engage the global from within the national and through national institutional channels.

Two big changes of the last decade, in this regard, are the growing weight of the human rights regime on states under the rule of law and the growing use of human rights instruments in national courts both in interpretation and adjudication. These are instances of denationalization in so far as the mechanisms are internal to the national state – national courts and legislatures – while the instruments invoke an authority that transcends the national state and the interstate system.[9] The long-term persuasive powers of human rights are a significant factor in this context. It is important to note here that the human rights regime, while international, deals with citizens inside a state. It thereby destabilizes older notions of exclusive state sovereignty articulated in international law which posit that matters internal to a country are solely to be determined by the state.

CONCLUSION

Two aspects emerge as crucial from this analysis. The history of interactions between differential positionings and expanded inclusions signals the possibility that the new conditions of inequality and difference evident today and the new types of claim-making they produce may well bring about further transformations in the institution. Citizenship is partly produced by the practices of the excluded. Secondly, by expanding the formal inclusionary aspect of citizenship, the national state contributed, perhaps ironically, to creating some of the conditions that eventually would facilitate key aspects of post-national and denationalized citizenship. This again signals the possibility of an expanded arena for post-national and denationalized conceptions of citizenship.

The pressures of globalization on national states may mean that claim-making will increasingly be directed at other institutions as well. This is already evident in a variety of instances. One example is the decision by First Nation people to go to the UN and claim direct representation in international fora, rather than going through the national state. And it is evident in the increasingly institutionalized framework of the international human rights regime and the emergent possibilities for bypassing unilateral state sovereignty. For many, citizenship is a normative project whereby social membership becomes increasingly comprehensive and open-ended. Globalization and human rights are further enabling this tension and therewith enabling the elements of a new discourse on rights. Though in very different ways, both globalization and the human rights regime have contributed to destabilizing existing political hierarchies of legitimate power and allegiance over the last decade. These developments raise a fundamental question about what is the analytic terrain within which we need to place the question of rights, authority and obligations of the state and the citizen.

NOTES

1 Nationality is important in international law in a variety of contexts. Treaties and conventions in turn can impact nationality.

2 This is quite evident in how nationality was conceived. The aggressive nationalism and territorial competition between states in the eighteenth, nineteenth and well into the twentieth centuries made the concept of dual nationality generally undesirable, incompatible with individual loyalties and destabilizing of the international order.

3 Soysal (1994) and Feldblum (1998) interpret the increase in dual nationality in terms of post-national citizenship rather than a mere devaluing of national allegiance. I would argue that it is a partial denationalizing of citizenship.

4 Further, during industrialization, class formation, class struggles, and the advantages of employers or workers tended to scale at the national level and became identified with state-produced legislation and regulations, entitlements and obligations. The state came to be seen as a key to ensuring the well-being of significant portions of both the working class and the bourgeoisie. The development of welfare states in the twentieth century became a crucial institutional domain for granting entitlements to the poor and the disadvantaged. Today, the growing weight given to notions of the 'competitiveness' of states puts pressure on states to cut down on these entitlements. This in turn

weakens the reciprocal relationship between the poor and the state. Finally, the growth of unemployment and the fact that many of the young are developing weak ties to the labor market, once thought of as a crucial mechanism for the socialization of young adults, will further weaken the loyalty and sense of reciprocity between these future adults and the state (Roulleau-Berger, 2001; Munger, 2002).

5 In this regard, a focus on changes inside the national state and the resulting possibility of new types of formalizations of citizenship status and rights – formalizations that might contribute to a partial denationalizing of certain features of citizenship – should be part of a more general examination of change in the institution of citizenship. Distinguishing post-national and denationalized dynamics in the construction of new components of citizenship allows us to take account of changes that might still use the national frame yet are in fact altering the meaning of that frame. I return to this later.

6 NACARA is the 1997 Nicaraguan Adjustment and Central American Relief Act. It created an amnesty for 300,000 Salvadorans and Guatemalans to apply for suspension of deportation. This is an immigration remedy that had been eliminated by the Illegal Immigration Reform and Immigrant Responsibility Act in 1996 (see Coutin, 2000).

7 See notably Soysal's (1994) trend-setting book; see also Bosniak (2000) who, while using the term denationalized, actually is using it to denote post-national, and it is the post-national concept that is crucial to her critique.

8 In this regard, I have emphasized as significant (Sassen, 1996: Ch. 2) the introduction in the new constitutions of South Africa, Brazil, Argentina and the Central European countries, of a provision that qualifies what had been an unqualified right (if democratically elected) of the sovereign to be the exclusive representative of all its people in international fora. Significant here is also the fact that in many Western-style democracies, the USA especially, it was through national law that many of these inclusions of distinct sectors of the population and their claims were instituted, inclusions which today are destabilizing older notions of citizenship.

9 Elsewhere (Sassen, 2003) I examine the case of WTO law along the same lines.

REFERENCES

Aman, Alfred C. Jr. (1998) 'The Globalizing State: A Future-Oriented Perspective on the Public/Private Distinction, Federalism, and Democracy', *Vanderbilt Journal of Transnational Law*, 31 (4): 769–870.

Andrews, Geoff (ed.) (1990) *Citizenship*. London: Lawrence and Wishart.

Appadurai, Arjun (1996) *Modernity at Large*. Minneapolis: University of Minnesota Press.

Barber, Benjamin (1984) *Strong Democracy: Participatory Politics for a New Age*. Berkeley: University of California.

Basch, Linda, Glick Schiller, Nina and Szanton-Blanc, Cristina (1994) *Nations Unbound: Transnationalized Projects and the Deterritorialized Nation-State*. New York: Gordon and Breach.

Bauböck, Rainer (1994) *Transnational Citizenship: Membership and Rights in International Migration*. Aldershot, England: Edward Elgar.

Benhabib, Seyla. (1992). *Situating the Self: Gender, Community and Postmodernism in Contemporary Ethics*. London: Routledge.

Benhabib, Seyla (1998) 'European Citizenship', *Dissent*, Fall: 107–15.

Bhabha, Jacqueline (1998) '"Get Back to Where You Once Belonged": Identity, Citizenship and Exclusion in Europe', *Human Rights Quarterly*, 20 (3): 592–627.

Bonilla, Frank, Melendez, Edwin, Morales, Rebecca and Torres, Maria de los Angeles (eds) (1998) *Borderless Borders*. Philadelphia: Temple University Press.

Bosniak, Linda S. (1992) 'Human Rights, State Sovereignty and the Protection of Undocumented Migrants Under the International Migrant Workers Convention', *International Migration Review*, xxv (4): 737–70.

Bosniak, Linda S. (2000) 'The State of Citizenship: Citizenship Denationalized', *Indiana Journal of Global Legal Studies*, 7 (2): 447–510.

Brecher, Jeremy and Costello, Tim (eds) (1993) *Global Visions: Beyond the New World Order*. Boston: South End Press.

Brodie, Janine (2000) 'Imagining democratic urban citizenship', in Engin Isin (ed.), *Democracy, Citizenship and the Global City*. London and New York: Routledge, pp. 110–28.

Brubaker, W Rogers (ed.) (1989) *Immigration and the Politics of Citizenship*. Lanham, New York, and London: University Press of America (with the German Marshall Fund of the USA).

Brysk, Alison (ed) (2002). *Globalization and Human Rights*. Berkeley, CA: University of Berkeley Press.

Carens, Joseph H. (1989) 'Membership and Morality: Admission to Citizenship in Liberal Democratic States', in W. Rogers Brubaker (ed.) *Immigration and the Politics of Citizenship*. Lanham, New York and London: University Press of America, pp. 31–49.

Cohen, Jean (1995) 'Interpreting the Notion of Global Civil Society', in M. Walzer, (ed.), *Toward a Global Civil Society*. Providence, RI: Bergham Books.

Cohen, Robin (1996) 'Diasporas and the Nation-State: From Victims to Challenges', *International Affairs*, 72 (3): 507–21.

Conover, Pamela Johnston (1995) 'Citizen Identities and Conceptions of the Self', *Journal of Political Philosophy*, 3 (2): 133–66.

Coutin, Susan B. (2000) 'Denationalization, Inclusion, and Exclusion: Negotiating the Boundaries of Belonging', *Indiana Journal of Global Legal Studies*, 7 (2): 585–94.

Dahl, Robert (1989) *Democracy and Its Critics*. New Haven: Yale University Press.

Delanty, Gerard (2000) 'The resurgence of the city in Europe?: The spaces of European citizenship', in Engin

Isin (ed.) *Democracy, Citizenship and the Global City*. London and New York: Routledge, pp. 79–92.

Drainville, Andre (1995) 'Left Internationalism and the Politics of Resistance in the New World Order', in David A. Smith and Josef Borocs (eds), *A New World Order: Global Transformation in the Late Twentieth Century*. Westport, CT: Greenwood Press, pp.

Eade, John (ed.) (1996) *Living the Global City: Globalization as a Local Process*. London: Routledge.

Fagen, Patricia Weiss and Eldridge, Joseph (1991) 'Salvadorean repatriation from Honduras', in Mary Ann Larkin (ed.) *Repatriation under Conflict: The Central American Case*. Washington DC: HMP, CIPRA, Georgetown University.

Falk, Richard (1989) *Revitalizing International Law*. Ames: Iowa State University Press.

Falk, Richard (1993) 'The Making of Global Citizenship', in Jeremy, Brecher and Tim Costello (eds), *Global Visions: Beyond the New World Order*. Boston: South End Press, pp. 39–60.

Feldblum, Miriam (1998) 'Reconfiguring Citizenship in Western Europe', in Ch. Joppke (ed.), *Challenge to the Nation-State*. Oxford: Oxford University Press, pp. 231–270.

Fernandez Kelly, Maria-Patricia (1993) 'Underclass and Immigrant Women as Economic Actors: Rethinking Citizenship in a Changing Global Economy', *American University International Law Review*, 9 (1).

Franck, Thomas M. (1992) 'The Emerging Right to Democratic Governance', *American Journal of International Law*, 86 (1): 46–91.

Franck, Thomas M. (1997) 'Community Based on Autonomy', *Columbia Journal of Transnational Law*, 36: 41–65.

Friedman, Marilyn (1989) 'Feminism and Modern Friendship: Dislocating the Community', *Ethics*, 99 (2): 275–90.

Guarnizo, Luis E. (1994) 'Los Dominicanyorks: The Making of a Binational Society', *Annals*, AAPSS, 533 (May): 70–86.

Habermas, Jurgen (1998) *The Inclusion of the Other: Studies in Political Theory*. Cambridge, MA: MIT Press.

Hamilton, Nora and Norma Stoltz Chinchilla (2001) *Seeking Community in a Global City: Guatemalans and Salvadorans in Los Angeles*. Philadelphia: Temple University Press.

Haus, Leah (1995) 'Openings in the wall: transnational migrants, labor unions, and U.S. immigration policy', *International Organization*, 49 (2 Spring): 285–313.

Heisler, Martin (1986) 'Transnational Migration as a Small Window on the Diminished Autonomy of the Modern Democratic State', *Annals* (American Academy of Political and Social Science), 485 (May): 153–166.

Held, David (1995) *Democracy and the Global Order: From the Modern State to Cosmopolitan Governance*. Cambridge: Polity Press.

Henkin, Louis (1990) *The Age of Rights*. New York: Columbia University Press.

Hondagneu-Sotelo, Pierrette (1994) *Gendered Transitions*. Berkeley: University of California Press.

Howe, Stephen (1991) 'Citizenship in the New Europe', in Geoff Andrews (ed.), *Citizenship*. London: Lawrence and Wishart, pp. 123–36.

Hunter, David B. (1992) 'Toward Global Citizenship in International Environmental Law.' *Willamette Law Review* 28: 3, pp. 547–563.

*Indiana Journal of Global Legal Studies (*1996) Special Issue: Feminism and Globalization: The Impact of The Global Economy on Women and Feminist Theory, 4 (1).

Isbister, John (1996) *The Immigration Debate: Remaking America*. West Hartford, Conn: Kumarian Books.

Isin, Engin F. (ed.) (2000) *Democracy, Citizenship and the Global City*. London and New York: Routledge.

Jacobson, David. (1996) *Rights Across Borders: Immigration and the Decline of Citizenship*. Baltimore: Johns Hopkins Press.

Jones, Kathleen B. (1998) 'Citizenship in a Woman Friendly Polity', in Gershon Shafir (ed.), *The Citizenship Debates*. Minneapolis: University of Minnesota Press, pp. 221–51.

Joppke, Christian (ed.) (1998) *Challenge to the Nation-State*. Oxford: Oxford University Press.

Keck, Margaret E. and Sikkink, Kathryn (1998) *Activists Beyond Borders: Advocacy Networks in International Politics*. Ithaca, NY: Cornell University Press.

Kratochwil, Friedrich (1994) 'Citizenship: On the Border of Order', *Alternatives*, 19.

Kymlicka, Will (1995) *Multicultural Citizenship: A Liberal Theory of Minority Rights*. Oxford: Clarendon Press.

Kymlicka, Will and Norman, Wayne (1994) 'Return of the Citizen: A Survey of Recent Work on Citizenship Theory', *Ethics*, 104 (2): 352–81.

LeBlanc, R. (1997) *Bicycle Citizens*. Berkeley, CA: University of California Press.

Lipschutz, Ronnie (with Judith Mayer) (1996) *Global Civil Society and Global Environmental Governance: The Politics of Nature from Place to Planet*. Albany, NY: SUNY Press.

Lister, Ruth (1997) *Citizenship: Feminist Perspectives*. Basingstoke: Macmillan Press.

Magnusson, Warren (1990) 'The Reification of Political Community', in R.B.J. Walker, and Saul H. Mendlovitz (eds), *Contending Sovereignties: Redefining Political Community*. Boulder, CO: Rienner, pp. 45–61.

Magnusson, Warren (1996) *The Search for Political Space*. Toronto: University of Toronto Press.

Magnusson, Warren (2000) 'Politicizing the global city', in Engin, Isin (ed.), *Democracy, Citizenship and the Global City*. London and New York: Routledge, pp. 289–306.

Mahler, Sarah (1995) *American Dreaming: Immigrant Life on the Margins*. Princeton, NJ: Princeton University Press.

Mansbridge, Jane (1980) *Beyond Adversary Democracy*. New York: Basic Books.

Marrus, Michael R. (1985) *The Unwanted: European Refugees in the Twentieth Century*. New York: Oxford University Press.

Mouffe, Chantal (ed.) (1992) *Dimensions of Radical Democracy*. London: Verso.

Munger, Frank (ed). (2002) *Laboring Under the Line*. New York: Russell Sage Foundation.

Nussbaum, Martha (1994) 'Patriotism and Cosmopolitanism', *Boston Review* (October–November).

Ong, Aihwa (1999) *Flexible Citizenship*. Durham, NC: Duke University Press.

Pateman, Carole (1988) *Le Travail En Friche*. La Tour d'Aigues, France: Editiones de I'Aube.

Pateman, Carole. (1989) *The Disorder of Women: Democracy, Feminism and Political Theory*.

Peterson, Spike (1990) 'Whose Rights? A Critique of the "Givens" in Human Rights Discourse', *Alternatives*, 15.

Pickus, Noah M.J. (ed.) (1998) *Immigration and Citizenship in the Twenty-First Century*. Lanham, MD: Rowman and Littlefield.

Pogge, Thomas (1992) 'Cosmopolitanism and Sovereignty' *Ethics* 103 (1): 48–75.

Portes, A. (1996) 'Global Villagers: The Rise of Transnational Communities', *American Prospect*, 7 (25).

Roulleau-Berger, Laurence (1999) *Le Travail En Friche*. La Tour d'Aigues, France: Editiones de I'Aube.

Rubenstein, Kim and Adler, Daniel (2000) 'International Citizenship: The Future of Nationality in a Globalized World', *Indiana Journal of Global Legal Studies*, 7 (2): 519–48.

Sassen, Saskia (1996) *Losing Control? Sovereignty in an Age of Globalization*. The 1995 Columbia University Leonard Hastings Schoff Memorial Lectures, New York: Columbia University Press.

Sassen, Saskia (2001) *The Global City: New York, London, Tokyo*. 2nd edition, Princeton, NJ: Princeton University Press.

Sassen, Saskia (2002) *De-Nationalization Territory, Authority and Rights in a Global Digital Age*. Princeton, NJ: Princeton University Press.

Schuck, Peter H. and Smith, Rogers M. (1985) *Citizenship Without Consent: Illegal Aliens in the American Polity*. New Haven: Yale University Press.

Shafir, Gershon (ed.) (1998) *The Citizenship Debates*. Minneapolis: University of Minnesota Press.

Smith, David A. and Borocs, Josef (eds) (1995) *A New World Order: Global Transformation in the Late Twentieth Century*. Westport, CT: Greenwood Press.

Smith, Michael Peter and Guarnizo Luis Eduardo (eds) (1998) *Transnationalism from Below*. New Brunswick, NJ: Transaction Publishers.

Smith, Robert C. (1997) 'Transnational Migration, Assimilation and Political Community', in Margaret Crahan and Alberto Vourvoulias-Bush (eds) *The City and the World*. NY: Council of Foreign Relations, pp. 110–33.

Soysal, Yasemin Nohuglu (1994) *Limits of Citizenship: Migrants and Postnational Membership in Europe*. Chicago: University of Chicago Press.

Soysal, Yasemin Nohuglu (1997) 'Changing Parameters of Citizenship and Claims-Making: Organized Islam in European Public Spheres', *Theory and Society*, 26 (4): 509–27.

Spinner-Halev, Jeff (1994) *The Boundaries of Citizenship: Race, Ethnicity, and Nationality in the Liberal State*. Baltimore: Johns Hopkins University Press.

Spiro, Peter J. (1997) 'Dual Nationality and the Meaning of Citizenship', *Emory Law Journal*, 46 (4).

Spiro, Peter J. (1999) 'The Citizenship Dilemma', *Stanford Law Review*, 51, 3.

Staeheli, Lynn A. (1999) 'Globalization and the scales of citizenship', *Geography Research Forum*, 19: 60–77 (special issue *On Geography and the Nation-State*, edited by Dennis Pringle and Oren Yiftachel).

van Steenbergen, Bart (ed.) (1994) *The Condition of Citizenship*. London: Sage Publications.

Tarrow, Sydney (1994) *Power in Movement: Social Movements, Collective Action and Politics*. Cambridge: Cambridge University Press.

Taylor, Charles (1994) 'The Politics of Recognition', in Amy, Gutmann (ed.) *Multiculturalism: Examining the Politics of Recognition*. Princeton: Princeton University Press, pp. 25–75.

Taylor, Peter J. (2000) World cities and territorial states under conditions of contemporary globalization. *Political Geography* 19 (5): 5–32.

Torres, Maria de los Angeles (1998) 'Transnational Political and Cultural Identities: Crossing Theoretical Borders', in Frank Bonilla, Edwin Melendez, Rebecca Morales and Maria de los Angeles Torres (eds), *Borderless Borders*. Philadelphia: Temple University Press.

Turner, Bryan S. (ed.) (1993) *Citizenship and Social Theory*. London: Sage Publications.

Turner, Bryan S. (2000) 'Cosmopolitan Virtue: loyalty and the city', in Engin Isin (ed.) *Democracy, Citizenship and the Global City*. London and New York: Routledge, pp.129–48.

Vogel, Ursula and Moran, Michael (eds) (1991) *The Frontiers of Citizenship*. Basingstoke: Macmillan.

Walker, R.B.J. (1993) *Inside/Outside: International Relations as Political Theory*. Cambridge: Cambridge University Press.

Walzer, M. (ed.) (1994) *Toward a Global Civil Society*. Providence, RI: Berghahn Books.

Wapner, Paul (1995) 'Politics Beyond The State: Environmental Activism and World Civic Politics', *World Politics*, 47 (3): 311–40.

Young, Iris Marion (1990) *Justice and the Politics of Difference*. Princeton, NJ: Princeton University Press.

Yuval-Davis, Nira and Pnina Werbner (eds) (1999) *Women, Citizenship and Difference*. London and New York: Zed Books.

18

Ecological Citizenship

DEANE CURTIN

ENLIGHTENMENT CULTURE AND THE POSSIBILITY OF ECOLOGICAL CITIZENSHIP

The words juxtaposed in the title of this chapter may seem incongruous. The dominant view of citizenship since the Enlightenment holds that *people* are candidates for the benefits and obligations of citizenship, not ecological communities. People are capable of the rational self-governance that citizenship requires. Natural 'resources' are merely extrinsic goods to be used wisely for the benefit of this and future generations of people.

There can be little question that citizenship has functioned primarily as an expression of Enlightenment culture and its heir, Political Liberalism. It supports familiar liberal concepts such as the primacy of the individual and the autonomy of the moral will. This, so critics argue, has encouraged a general weakening of any strong idea of community as partially constitutive of our moral identity, community, that is, as something more than a mere collection of sovereign individuals.

We should recognize, as well, that in many colonized countries, such as India, the concept of citizenship arrived in the early nineteenth century as the language of colonization. The language of citizenship may read very differently for those in the 'third' world.

In Enlightenment cultures, furthermore, nature is often defined in opposition to culture. Sometimes culture also is defined in opposition to those people who are regarded as being intimately connected to nature: indigenous peoples and women. Almost all the major figures of the Enlightenment had dim views of indigenous peoples if we understand this term as referring broadly to communities of people who understand themselves as partially defined by their connections to place. Many also espoused prejudicial views about women.

However, the exclusion of ecological communities from the moral orbit of citizenship may reflect an Enlightenment bias that now demands reexamination. Many non-Enlightenment cultures have a form of public ethics that is at least distantly sympathetic to a concept of ecological citizenship: candidates include the Japanese concept of *wa* or harmony between culture and place, and the Hopi belief that the vibratory centers of one's body and of one's community must sing in harmony with the vibrations of nature.

It may do violence to these cultures if we describe these diverse practices as cases of citizenship. Perhaps the very concept of citizenship is too closely bound to Enlightenment ideas of what it means to engage in a public practice to be employed as a useful tool in understanding different cultures.

I would suggest, however, that attention to cultures that have been regarded as marginal to the Enlightenment is critical in a world marked by the phenomenon of globalization. One of the fundamental features of globalization is that it often requires basic changes in the relationships of people to place. Its emphasis on the importance of individualism and free trade makes it even more likely that nature will be viewed as a mere resource which is categorically distinct from moral bonds of human culture.

If we are to avoid begging important questions about the ethical foundations of citizenship, perhaps this very expansion of Western culture requires us to re-examine the foundations of our moral views. Before attempting to expand the concept of citizenship for a postcolonial world, therefore, it is best to understand the problems of citizenship in greater detail, especially as they pertain to the possibility of functioning within a more-than-human community.

COLONIZING SPACES

In the public traditions of the United States, it should be pointed out, we do have the historical case of Thomas Jefferson who argued for the importance of the citizen-farmer as the foundation for true democracy. For Jefferson, citizenship is inherently an issue of place and scale. One is a citizen in relationship to particular places. Real participatory democracy demands connections to place.

However, Jefferson also argued that the nomadic land arrangements of some native North American tribes marked them as 'uncivilized'. Becoming a citizen meant breaking traditional relationships to place by becoming a citizen farmer. Free agricultural land and training were the rewards for native peoples who were willing to forego traditional dress, cut their hair, and limit hunting. Such 'civilized' land arrangements were also more efficient for a dominant culture bent on westward expansion into the 'wilderness.' We can see why the very concept of 'wilderness' is often dismissed as invention of colonial ambition by many indigenous peoples (see Jefferson, [1782] 1993).

The most ambitious attempt to enforce colonial land and population policies unquestionably occurred during the British utilitarian's rule of India. Ranajit Guha has called this colonial policy toward people and place the liberal 'idiom of Improvement.' In the writings of Jeremy Bentham, James Mill, and John Stuart Mill, we witness the invention of modern, liberal attitudes toward people and place that were at once progressive in Europe and colonizing in India.

The utilitarians were not just philosophers speculating idly about their own existence. Bentham wrote a system of laws for colonial rule in India. James Mill published *The History of British India* in 1818 hoping to secure a position with the East India Company. He succeeded, becoming Assistant Examiner in 1819, and Chief Examiner in 1830. His *History* was the standard text at the Company's college at Haileybury, and deeply affected its policies for decades. The core of Mill's plan for liberal reform in India, the land rent system, was adapted from Thomas Malthus, who held the first chair in political economics, also at Haileybury College, the training ground for East India employees.

John Stuart Mill, now the most famous of the utilitarian reformers, worked for the East India Company for 35 years. Under the guidance of his father, Mill was trained to write the political correspondence with India, rising, finally, to the rank of Examiner of Indian Correspondence. Until his retirement in 1858, just after the Great Mutiny broke the hold of the East India Company on India, he effectively governed the economic, legal, and political affairs of the British Empire's most important colony.

Remarkably, he regarded his lifelong employment as nothing more than a good job which had no bearing on his philosophical writing. Mill wrote of his duties: 'While they precluded all uneasiness about the means of subsistence, they occupied fewer hours of the day than almost any business or profession, they had nothing in them to produce anxiety, or to keep the mind intent on them at any time but when engaged in them' (1990: vii).

How the author of *On Liberty* and *Representative Government* could have felt no anxiety about his Indian correspondence demands an explanation. In *Principles of Political Economy*, for example, Mill described the British Empire's colonies as:

> hardly to be looked upon as countries, ... but more properly as outlying agricultural or manufacturing estates belonging to a larger community. Our West Indian colonies, for example, cannot be regarded as countries with a productive capital of their own ... [but are rather] the place where England finds it convenient to carry on the production of sugar, coffee and a few other tropical commodities. ([1848] 1965: 693)

This passage is endlessly revealing as an example of systemic violence. The empire is a 'larger community' for Mill comprising both England and its colonies. But the colonies are 'outlying', distant from, dependent on, and defined by, the center for its domestic purposes. The fact that the rules applying to proper 'countries' do not apply to the colonies caused Mill to regard himself as a morally neutral technician in his writings on India. Relations with these dependencies are matters of 'convenience', as he says. For Mill, colonies are not countries because they have no productive capital of their own. They must be given a productive capital, and are defined in terms of their existing and producing for another. What they produce is significant too. Foods produced for domestic consumption, peasant foods, are not mentioned. They are defined by production of export crops produced for the Center: sugar, coffee, and other commodities.

The most important among these utilitarian figures, however, is James Mill. Despite John Stuart Mill's contemporary standing in the history of philosophy, the colonial game had already been won for the East India Company by the time he influenced its affairs. It was James Mill, in consort with Bentham and Malthus, who literally wrote the colonial agenda.

For James Mill, India was the great social experiment by which to test the success of utilitarian doctrines during the period that Britain worked to transform itself, again in Guha's words, from 'conquistador' to 'legislator.' Mill's *History* marks the transition in British colonial discourse from the idiom of Order to the idiom of Improvement, from overt military violence to the covert control of thought (Guha, 1989: 287).

According to Mill's plan, the State itself was to be the landlord with the ryots – a class of tax collectors nominated by Mill as candidates for the new economic middle class – as tenants renting directly from the State. The system of land rent required this direct relationship between each peasant tenant and the omnipresent State. As Eric Stokes and others have seen, this led Mill to a startling conclusion for a liberal: 'He was prepared to accept the oriental role of the State as landlord of the soil, because this happened to coincide with his views on taxation' (Stokes: 1989: 92).

We should not mistake Mill's support for the ryots, however, with support for indigenous peasant traditions. Mill had no interest in preserving traditional Indian social structures, which often include enduring relationships to place, since they were based on subsistence agriculture that did not produce rent. The land rent system sought to create new social relationships by exporting British ideas of progress to the colonies, ideas that consciously undermined traditional social and ecological relationships. The ryots were to be transformed from subsistence cultivators to a new class of small capitalist producers.

Mill defined progress as movement toward a utilitarian society, a society in which an economically rational capitalist middle class produces for its own individual good, and thereby produces a surplus in the form of rent that benefits society as a whole. As he said, 'Exactly in proportion as *Utility* is the object of every pursuit, may we regard a nation as civilized' (Mill, [1817] 1858: ii 1). In 'backward' societies, where land is owned communally, according to Mill, the State must intervene as oriental despot to collect rent until peasants are transformed into capitalist producers (Majeed, 1992: 160).

Mill's liberal program was 'to emancipate India from its own culture' (Majeed, 1992: 127). In the *History* he goes to great lengths to criticize Hindu culture as childish and backward: 'It is allowed on all hands that no historical composition existed in the literature of the Hindus,' since 'they had not reached that point of intellectual maturity, at which a value of the record of the past for the guidance of the future begins to be understood' (Mill, [1817] 1858). Guha has pointed out that Mill here creates an intellectual void which demands to be filled by a colonial presence. India has no history until it is given one by India's first true historian, Mill himself (Guha, 1989).

In Mill's *History*, then, we have a narrative of progress from collectivist societies, without histories, governed by the imagination, to progressive societies having historical purpose, in which there is a capitalist middle class, governed by instrumental rationality. The movement from backward to modern is also the movement from cultural and geographical particularity, people deeply embedded in a place and in subsistence methods of production, to a universal capitalist culture of the future which is everywhere the same.

The paradox of liberal imperialism is clear. It arose out of historically particular conditions in Europe during the Enlightenment and its aftermath. It satisfied the needs of an emerging middle class for a more egalitarian society. It provided a radical social foundation for progressive movements that is still useful today, for example, in fights for equal treatment for women. Nevertheless, liberal ideas of progress in one context became hegemonic policies in another. Liberal imperialism masks historically specific economic agendas in a narrative of progress that claims to speak in universal and transcultural terms.

The universalist, anti-Hindu temperament of liberal imperialism, which sought to replace stable subsistence modes of production with expansive capitalist modes, was a direct attack on indigenous systems of population and environmental management. In the minds of many Indians, this attack has continued with the policies of the green revolution, which also sought to implement capitalist modes of agricultural production that benefited wealthy farmers (see Shiva, 1988, 1991; Curtin, 1995, 1999).

We can conclude, at least, that the concept of citizenship has a deeply ambiguous historical legacy, especially if we wish to employ it in a postcolonial environmental ethic. It has been used to marginalize both peoples and places, especially those peoples who understand themselves – or are defined by others – as being defined by their connections to particular places.

Having granted this ambiguous legacy, however, it is still worth rethinking the concept, not as the Enlightenment's universal voice of reason, but as a historical and cultural concept that remains valuable even to a postcolonial ethic. The idea of ecological citizenship is promising because it resonates deeply with Western ideas about what it means to lead a full human life. It also has the potential to reign in the corrosive individualism that so often affects our conception of people/place relationships. Citizenship shapes our public selves, and it balances our private impulses.

If we look at environmental ethics through the lens of ecological citizenship we may be able to move beyond the familiar stewardship (resource) model of responsibility for place – an idea common enough in Enlightenment ideas of citizenship – to a deeper idea of a common moral community, what I will refer to, following David Abram, as 'the more-than-human community.'

As Avner De-Shalit has argued, we may need to move from a traditional liberal viewpoint to a more 'communitarian' approach to ecological citizenship (De-Shalit, 1995: 12). Perhaps the most important limitation in political liberalism in terms of addressing the idea of ecological citizenship is in its conception of moral identity. This limitation is addressed in the next section.

RECONSTRUCTING CITIZENSHIP

Liberal critics will point out that, while the utilitarian's treatment of colonized people was abhorrent, this does not mean that Enlightenment concepts of moral obligation are not, in principle, consistent with a defensible notion of citizenship, and perhaps even ecological citizenship.

A consistent hedonic utilitiarianism, for example, requires us to take *all* pleasures and pains into account, when ascribing moral standing to individuals, probably even including non-human animals. Other forms of liberalism that are deontological rather than consequentialist support the idea that all persons are part of the contract that binds moral agents together. The most eloquent advocate of this kind of political liberalism, John Rawls, requires us to set aside individual concepts of substantive goods and define our basic obligations from behind a 'veil of ignorance.'

However, setting aside history, it is still not at all clear that either of the liberal alternatives can capture the dimensions of *ecological* citizenship. Hedonic utilitarianism ascribes moral standing to *individuals*, proper subjects of pain and pleasure, or to *persons* in a strong moral sense, not to integrated communities. The Rawlsian alternative still applies only to persons capable of giving rational assent to the social contract. Rawls himself has said that he does not think the idea of a rational contract specifying initial conditions of fairness can be extended beyond the human realm.[1]

According to the contractarian version of political liberalism as originally articulated by Rawls, justice requires impartiality. It requires that we operate from behind a 'veil of ignorance' that prevents us from knowing who we are and our locations in community. We cannot know our race or sex, for example, so that the basic commitments of a democratic society are not racist or sexist. As Rawls says, from behind the veil 'parties do not know their conceptions of the good.' While not egoists, neither are we 'conceived as not taking an interest in one another's interests' (Rawls, 1971: 13).

Rawls intended his description of the original position to be pre-cultural. The original position is the hypothetical framework from which the principles of any democratic society can be established. Rawls did need to assume, however, that rational agents in this position are individuals who operate according to an economic model of rationality: 'the concept of rationality must be interpreted as far as possible in the narrow sense, standard in economic theory, of taking the most effective means to given ends' (1971: 14).

Rawls' concern is that in a deeply pluralistic society, where different individuals have competing conceptions of substantive social goods, justice must remain neutral between competing claims to the good. The right precedes free choices of substantive goods. Justice is procedural, not substantive. It requires that we set aside all the moral sentiments that bind a community together: benevolence, altruism, care for others. Moral rationality is modeled on 'economic rationality': the individual maximizes his or her own self-interest.

Rawls' position in *A Theory of Justice* has been questioned by communitarian critics. It appears to beg the question in favor of a narrow conception of the moral self. Despite his claim to identify the original position of *any* moral agent concerned to establish a democratic society, his account of moral rationality describes the economic rationality of the political liberal. Critics, whether communitarians such as Michael Sandel and Michael Walzer, or liberals such as Richard Rorty, argue that even this minimalist account of rationality is biased in favor of a Western account of rationality. Universalism begs the question when it assumes its own account of moral rationality as part of its proof of universalism. In Michael Walzer's words, there is no 'moral Esperanto' (Walzer, 1994).

When Rawls requires that substantive choices among goods are not part of the original position, he reduces such choices to a mere psychological inventory of competing claims on our attention. Choice among goods is a matter of subjective preference satisfaction. My choices are *mine* but they can never be *me*. (De-Shalit, 1995: 30).

It is arguable from the viewpoint of Rawls' critics that citizenship is so fundamental that it properly constitutes who we *are*, not just what we choose to do. In Michael Sandel's words,

> It requires a knowledge of public affairs and also a sense of belonging, a concern for the whole, a moral bond with the community whose fate is at stake. To share in self-rule therefore requires that citizens possess, or come to acquire, certain qualities of character, or civic virtues. But this means that republican politics cannot be neutral toward the values and ends its citizens espouse. (1996: 5–6)

Citizens are previously 'encumbered' by the obligations of community membership as a constitutive feature of their moral identity. Civic virtues are powers required by a citizen to act on such obligations.

Concerning the social constitution of the moral self, Charles Taylor has said:

> I want to defend the strong thesis that doing without frameworks is utterly impossible for us; otherwise put, that the horizons within which we live our lives and which make sense of them have to include these strong qualitative discriminations. Moreover, this is not meant just as a contingently true psychological fact about human beings, which could perhaps turn out one day not to hold for some exceptional individual or new type, some superhuman of disengaged objectification. Rather the claim is that living within such strongly qualified horizons is constitutive of human agency, that stepping outside these limits would be tantamount to stepping outside what we would recognize as integral, that is undamaged human personhood. (Taylor, 1989:)

A moral horizon, or framework, for Taylor is nothing less than the context in which we have an identity, a sense of self. 'To know who you are,' Taylor says, 'is to be oriented in moral space, a space in which questions arise about what is good or bad, what is worth doing and what is not, what has meaning and importance for you and what is trivial and secondary' (1989: 28). Without such an orientation, we would not know how to discriminate better and worse; we would not know what questions to ask of ourselves and others; we would, quite literally, be without an identity.

Taylor believes that our identity is not the invention of a solitary individual, but a function of our relationships to our surroundings. He says emphatically, 'One is a self only among other selves. A self can never be described without reference to those who surround it' (1989: 35).[2] For Taylor frameworks 'inescapably pre-exist for us'; they pose questions independently of our ability to answer.

Moral reasoning within a framework is substantive, not merely formal or procedural. Nor is it a matter of satisfying subjective preferences. It deals with the content of a good human life judged by the goods of the practice. Aristotle's *phronesis*, practical wisdom, is an example of substantive moral reasoning. Like Aristotle, Taylor is concerned not so much with what we do, but with who we are, or strive to become, within a moral horizon.

This Aristotelian dimension of citizenship is echoed in the remarks of Martha Nussbaum. We need to ask 'some of our most basic and ordinary questions, such as "Who *are* these people? What are they trying to do? What general abilities and circumstances do they have?"' This approach, she says, 'urges the parties involved in the argument to ask themselves what aspects of living they consider so fundamental that they could not regard a life as a fully human one without them. Put this way, it is not a request for a matter of metaphysical or biological fact, but a request for a particularly deep and searching kind of evaluative inquiry' (Nussbaum and Sen, 1993: 327).

This emphasis we find in MacIntyre, Sandel, Taylor, and Nussbaum on the deep level of moral inquiry concerning the self that citizenship demands means that the demands of citizenship are dynamic. Citizenship is a matter of deliberation on the sort of public life that has partially defined our moral identity in the past. It is also forward-looking. As the conditions of public life change, citizenship demands ongoing reflection on what sort of person we will become.

The moral community in which citizenship functions, then, is both 'sentimental' and 'constitutive' (see Sandel, 1982: 173). By the sentimental bonds of community I mean those bonds of affection that are locally conventional. These conventional bonds can be challenged, however, and we may experience increasing discomfort with the traditions that originally shaped our moral identity. A constitutive moral community is one that emerges progressively as we reflect on and respond to the ongoing challenges to tradition.

In fact, it is impossible to imagine functioning as a citizen if our moral identity does not respond to the demands of community in both these senses. The sentimental community is the initial condition of caring about the world. If we fail to care about anything, just as a matter of fact, the demands of the evolving constitutive community will fail to address us. We respond to the demands of community *because* we care.

I may, for example, have been raised as a meat-eater. Eating meat may function, as it does for many people, as part of important holidays and rituals, gatherings that partially define who I am. I may, however, read Peter Singer's arguments for vegetarianism and be persuaded that I should change my eating practices (see Singer, 1990). Becoming a vegetarian is not simply a preference separate from my moral identity. Rational arguments have persuaded me that my moral identity needs to change. The narrative that constitutes the person I have been evolves into a connected, but in an important way, newly emerging moral identity. Traditions that were sentimental have evolved into commitments that are constitutive.

In this section, I have suggested that the very concept of moral engagement that we have inherited from the Enlightenment and Political Liberalism may stand in the way of developing a concept of ecological citizenship. Whereas liberalism demands that we separate what we do from who we are, the concept of ecological citizenship depends on the idea of cultivating a moral identity through ongoing engagement in traditions that are both sentimental and constitutive. In short, ecological citizenship depends on the ability to develop an ecological identity that functions in public ecological practices which partially define who we are.

ENGAGING IN A PRACTICE

Turning to the fundamental question, we might ask, 'What does it mean to function as a citizen?' An important part of the answer must include recognition that to function as a citizen requires us to engage in a *public practice*, as opposed to the private pursuit of merely individual goods. To engage in a public practice means that the standards governing our conduct are transpersonal. The transition from sentimental to constitutive community is a practice of transcendence.

Alasdair MacIntyre defines a practice as: 'any coherent and complex form of socially established cooperative human activity through which goods internal to that form of activity are realized' (MacIntyre, 1981: 187). There are two important claims in this passage. First, practices are cooperative forms of human activity having an internal structure and logic that places demands on any individual participant in the practice. 'To enter into a practice,' MacIntyre says, 'is to accept the authority of those standards and the inadequacy of my own performance as judged by them. It is to subject my own attitudes, choices, preferences and tastes to the standards which currently and partially define the practice' (1981: 190).

For MacIntyre, farming and baseball are practices, but growing a few vegetables or throwing a baseball in the back yard, to the extent that they are individual and not social activities, are not practices. Architecture is a practice; amateur bricklaying is probably not. The patterns of scientific inquiry that are characteristic of physics, chemistry, and biology, as well as the work of the historian, philosopher, painter, or musician, are practices. Cooking and mothering are also practices (see Ruddick, 1989; Curtin and Heldke, 1992; Curtin and Powers, 1994).

To engage in a practice, then, is not simply a matter of thinking true thoughts; it is an ongoing engagement in a public sphere that has its own standards. If we participate in the practice, it is the practice that shapes the person we might become through engagement in it. Practices are ways of being in the world.

The second point in MacIntyre's definition of a practice is his distinction between internal and external goods. External goods – MacIntyre mentions prestige, status, and money – can be achieved in alternate ways, not necessarily through the practice. One might achieve these three external goods, for example, by cheating to win the World Series. By cheating, however, one does not engage in the practice for its own sake. One does not, therefore, achieve the characteristic goods of the practice. Since external goods can be achieved outside the practice – even at the expense of the practice and those who engage in it – they are individual goods. There is only a limited amount of prestige, status, and money to go around.

Not so with internal goods. According to MacIntyre, 'Internal goods are indeed the outcome of competition to excel, but it is characteristic of them that their achievement is good for the whole community who participates in the practice' (MacIntyre, 1981). Such goods can only be achieved through developing and exercising the characteristic excellences of the practice itself. So, in a given year only one team can win the World Series, but the excellence represented by the Series (won honestly) is a good for the practice of baseball. It sets the standard by which the practice is – and should be – measured.

It follows from this distinction between internal and external goods that there is a critical difference between insiders and outsiders to a practice in the ways that moral reasons are understood. One understands the internal goods to the extent one functions as an insider. To the extent one is an outsider, these reasons for internal goods will tend to be opaque.

The instructions a master violinist gives to her advanced pupil, for example, tend to be short, cryptic. The pupil may ask how to achieve a particular intonation, and the master may simply move her student's hand position on the bow slightly. The change may be both momentous in terms of achieving goods within the practice – and imperceptible to the outsider.

We can see that what is easily communicable to outsiders is bits of knowledge that can be separated from the practice without much loss in cognitive content: knowledge of external goods. This includes knowledge that is amenable to quantification, whether scientific or economic. It also includes knowledge of individual goods that are achievable without social cooperation.

What really needs to be communicated, however, if the ethical density of the situation is to be conveyed, is a kind of process knowledge. It is local knowledge that involves the development of skills within a tradition that provides criteria for those skills. It is precisely these deep, messy, difficult-to-explain reasons constituting a practice that cannot be taken out of context without great loss of meaning. Yet, it is precisely these reasons that are neglected in much ethical discourse between 'worlds.' Such discourse usually concentrates on external goods.

The process of globalization, for example, fundamentally changes the relationships of people to place, the conditions of work, and gender roles. Rather than addressing people's legitimate concern for cultural autonomy, most discussion of globalization takes place at the level of external goods only.

A particularly striking example of this tendency to 'talk past' the recipients of rapid global change and treating nature as a mere resource is evident in the remarks of former presidential economic advisor, Charles L. Schultz, when he said, 'Market-like arrangements ... reduce the need for compassion, patriotism, brotherly love, and cultural solidarity as motivating forces behind social improvement. ... Harnessing the 'base' motive of material self-interest to promote the common good is perhaps the most important social invention mankind has achieved' (quoted in Daly and Cobb, 1989).

Finally, it is important to recognize that this account of engaging in a practice, like citizenship, is pluralist about human goods, though it is not a relativist account. There are at least two irreducibly different forms of human goods: goods that are internal to a practice and goods that are external to a practice. Internal goods are social, cooperative goods; external goods are individual goods. When we value nature economically – and we all do at times, we value nature as an external good. From the point of view of a pluralist, the singular focus on external goods in contemporary Western culture results is an impoverishment of what it means to be human.

The practice of citizenship, on the other hand, allows us to achieve distinctively social goods. In the case of ecological citizenship these are the internal goods of a more-than-human community. In the words of Barry Lopez, 'To be intimate with the land ... is to enclose it in the same moral universe we occupy, to include it in the meaning of the word community' (Lopez, 1992).

THE PARADOX OF ECOLOGICAL CITIZENSHIP

We have seen that the Enlightenment idea of citizenship was restricted to persons, or at least to sentient beings. Sometimes it was restricted further to a subclass of human beings. Furthermore, the classic Rawlsian account of rational choice separates the moral identity from the substantive choices it makes among goods. I may voluntarily choose to work for the common good, or I may choose to work for a healthier environment, but these choices do not constitute who I *am*. Rather, they are simply what I voluntarily choose to *do*. In fact, the very word 'environment' can only make sense in an Enlightenment conception of self that separates persons from nature.

Unless we confuse the sentimental community with the constitutive community, however, we cannot identity what it means to function as a moral agent with this Enlightenment view of the self. In the aftermath of the Enlightenment, many have questioned the idea that a person is nothing but a disembodied 'thinking being.' Innumerable recent accounts of what it means to be human emphasize that we are embodied creatures. As the science of ecology advances and increasingly pervades the public conception of what it means to be human we are witnessing an emerging constitutive community which critiques an older sentimental idea (paradoxically one whose narrative held that it was exclusively rational). There is nothing odd at all, then, in saying that ecological citizenship is, and should, emerge as a way of functioning in a new *intentional* community.

One way of focusing on this new way of functioning is to say that ecological citizenship, as opposed to more traditional concepts of citizenship, seems to rest on a paradox: to function in a way that is more completely human requires that we understand ourselves as more-than-human. That is, if we think only of what it means to be human apart from our connections to place, we will never understand fully what it means to function as a human. Citizenship, in its fullest expression, must be understood as encompassing the more-than-human community.

Mitchell Thomashow, for example, has written extensively about this process of developing an ecological identity and its connection to ecological citizenship:

> Ecological citizenship hinges on a crucial conceptual step, the integration of ecological identity and political identity. [Earlier] I described the reflective processes that facilitate ecological identity, the learning experiences that constitute an ecological worldview – a sense of belonging to a larger community of species, an understanding of the ecological commons, the broad ecological impact of personal actions, how people identify with nature and ecosystems ... Ecological identity emerges in a social and political context. (1996: 105)

Becoming an ecological citizen requires a transformation in our moral identity.

At a personal level, surely one of the reasons this is extraordinarily difficult is that it requires us to see our identity as connected to what Roger S. Gottlieb has described as a new holocaust: the rapid and seemingly irreversible destruction of whole ecosystems. As Gottlieb has written, 'How can I feel at home here? How can peace, acceptance, or a feeling of deep holiness of the universe arise while I am facing the truth about what the universe contains?' (1999: 155). Gottlieb describes the current state of our moral identity as being in 'denial' (1999: 29–32).

Mark J. Smith has also pointed out that a post-Enlightenment understanding of ecological citizenship will require us to rethink the role of technology. 'The central principle of the Enlightenment, the rational pursuit of knowledge, is used to tame industrialism.' The present condition is one of 'organized irresponsibility' (1998: 95, 94).

The transformation that ecological citizenship requires is painful. Yet, we can achieve some understanding of what such a transformation would be worth if we see how it can alter our thinking about what the future alternatives are, thereby opening up new avenues for public practice. To see this, let us look back for a moment on the received traditions in environmental ethics, at least in the United States: the traditions of John Muir and Gifford Pinchot. Ecological citizenship contrasts with the two received views particularly in regard to environmental *work.*

Pinchot famously believed that there are only 'people and resources.' (1947: 326) If resources are managed for the long-term human good then we have the stewardship model of the relationship between people and places. Nature, in more philosophical language, is an extrinsic good to be managed wisely. Forests are farms that should be managed for maximum sustainable yield. Pinchot valued nature only as a set of external goods.

John Muir, Pinchot's great critic, argued that nature – or at least wilderness – is not an extrinsic good. 'Temple wilderness' is sacred; it is intrinsically valuable. Whereas Pinchot was instrumental in founding the National Forest Service, which is a division of the Department of Agriculture, Muir lobbied for the creation of the National Park system and the Department of the Interior that manages them.

On the face of it, we can see why it might be tempting to think of these two views as mutually exclusive and exhaustive of the logical possibilities for an environmental ethic. Nature either is, or it is not, intrinsically valuable.

We should notice, however, that these views, for all their differences, share a common assumption: that nature and human culture are categorically distinct. For Pinchot this is clear: people and resources fall into different ethical categories; they demand to be treated differently.

But in a more subtle way we witness this kind of human/nature split with Muir as well. Certainly, it would be fair to say that Muir thought of his identity as being constituted by the wilderness. He was closer to the idea of ecological citizenship than Pinchot. However, we also think of Muir wandering alone through the Sierras, worshipping in 'temple wilderness', furious at the intrusion of domesticated sheep which he depicts as 'hoofed locusts' (Muir, [1911] 1987: 56). Muir argued for the necessity of National Parks as places where humans are only temporary visitors. Civilization is categorically distinct from the 'environment.'

To delineate the differences among these two positions and the idea of ecological citizenship let us consider the concept of work. For Pinchot, work is judged solely by whether it benefits this and future generations of people. Work is a kind of morally justified violence, justified because the resources themselves do not having standing within the community.

For Muir, work seems akin to original sin. Since people are outside of wilderness, work pollutes the purity of non-human nature. Although the charge may not be entirely fair, we can see here how one might get from Muir to a touristic conception of environmental ethics. Connecting with nature is what one does for two weeks each year while on vacation.

What Pinchot defines as work I understand as work designed to achieve external goods. But there is also the work of an ecological citizen which is designed to achieve the internal goods of an ecological community. Working to restore an injured prairie, for example, certain kinds of less invasive agriculture, or work to stop racially prejudicial siting of hazardous waste, are the practices of an ecological citizen. They are part of an emerging intentional community whose internal goods are constitutive for that community.

I have argued here that the Enlightenment conception of moral agency is itself problematic if we are to achieve a new form of public practice: ecological citizenship. Ecological citizenship requires that we see our moral identity as partially defined by public practices whose internal goods allow us to achieve cooperative goods for the more-than-human community.

It may seem, following Roger Gottlieb, that ecological citizenship places overwhelming demands on us. Early in this process it is easier to live in denial. Yet, we may also be witnessing what Gottlieb calls 'a spirituality of resistance': 'a spirituality in which evil is not avoided, wished away ... In this spiritual realm we can fully experience the deepest of joys because we engage directly with unjust suffering by opposing it' (Gottlieb, 1999: 158).

At a political level it may be that, as Mark Sagoff has argued, the American public is still capable of distinguishing between the environmental policies appropriate to a *consumer* and to a *citizen* (Sagoff, 1988: 50–57) We are, in effect, still capable of shifting paradigms in response to the kind of question we are asked. It may well be that the consumer framework seems 'natural' – even inevitable – to most citizens only because of the power of *Homo economicus*. We are rarely *encouraged* to respond as citizens.

NOTES

1 For extended arguments against the possibility of either form of liberalism establishing obligations to nature or to future generations, see De-Shalit (1995) Chapters 3 and 4.

2 I explored this sense of self-in-relation in Curtin and Heldke (1992).

REFERENCES

Abram, D. (1996) *The Spell of the Sensuous*. New York: Pantheon Books.

Curtin, D. (1995) 'Making Peace with the Earth: Indigenous Agriculture and the Green Revolution', *Environmental Ethics*, 17 (Spring): 59–73.

Curtin, D. (1999) *Chinnagounder's Challenge: The Question of Ecological Citizenship*. Bloomington: Indiana University Press.

Curtin, D.W. and L. Heldke (eds) (1992) *Cooking, Eating, Thinking: Transformative Philosophies of Food*. Bloomington: University of Indiana Press.

Curtin, D. and J. Powers (1994) 'Mothering: Moral Cultivation in Buddhist and Feminist Ethics', *Philosophy East and West*, 44 (1): 1–18.

Daly, H.E. and Cobb, J. John B. (1989) *For the Common Good: Redirecting the Economy Toward Community, the Environment, and a Sustainable Future*. Boston: Beacon Press.

De-Shalit, A. (1995) *Why posterity matters: environmental policies and future generations*. London: New York, Routledge.

Gottlieb, R.S. (1999) *A Spirituality of Resistance: Finding a Peaceful Heart and Protecting the Earth*. New York: The Crossroads Publishing Company.

Guha, R. (1989) 'Dominance Without Hegemony and its Historiography', *Subaltern Studies VI: Writings on South Asian History and Society*, Delhi, Oxford University Press, pp. 210–309.

Jefferson, T. ([1782] 1993) 'Notes on Virginia', *The Life and Selected Writings of Thomas Jefferson* ed. A. Koch and W. Peden New York The Modern Library: 177–267.

Lopez, B. (1992) *The Rediscovery of North America*. New York: Vintage Books.

MacIntyre, A. (1981) *After Virtue: A Study in Moral Theory*. Notre Dame: University of Notre Dame Press.

Majeed, J. (1992) *Uncovered Imaginings: James Mill's 'The History of British India' and Orientalism*. Oxford: Clarendon Press.

Mill, J. ([1817] 1858) *The History of British India*. London: James Madden, Piper, Stephenson and Spence.

Mill, J.S. ([1848] 1965) *Principles of Political Economy*. Toronto: University of Toronto Press.

Mill, J.S. *Writings on India: Collected Works of John Stuart Mill*. University of Toronto.

Muir, J. [1911] (1987) *My First Summer in the Sierra*. New York: Penguin.

Nussbaum, M.C. and Sen, A. eds (1993) *The Quality of Life*. Oxford: Clarendon Press.

Pinchot, G. (1947) *Breaking New Ground*. New York: Harcourt Brace.

Rawls, J. (1971) *A Theory of Justice*. Cambridge, MA: Harvard University Press.

Ruddick, S. (1989) *Maternal Thinking: Toward a Politics of Peace*. New York: Ballantine Books.

Sagoff, M. (1988) *The Economy of the Earth*. Cambridge: Cambridge University Press.

Sandel, M. (1982) *Liberalism and the Limits of Justice*. Cambridge: Cambridge University Press.

Sandel, M.J. (1996) *Democracy's Discontent: America in Search of a Public Philosophy*. Cambridge: Harvard University Press.

Shiva, V. (1988) *Staying Alive: Women, Ecology and Development*. London: Zed Books.

Shiva, V. (1991) *The Violence of the Green Revolution: Third World Agriculture, Ecology and Politics*. London and Penang: Zed Books, and Third World Network.

Singer, P. (1990) *Animal Liberation*. New York: New York Review.

Smith, M.J. (1998) *Ecologism: Towards Ecological Citizenship*. Minneapolis: University of Minnesota Press.

Stakes, E. (1989) *The English Utilitarians and India*. Delhi: Oxford University Press.

Taylor, C. (1989) *Sources of the Self*. Cambridge, MA: Harvard University Press.

Thomashow, M. (1996) *Ecological Identity: Becoming a Reflective Environmentalist*. Cambridge, MA: MIT Press.

Walzer, M. (1994) *Thick and Thin: Moral Argument at Home and Abroad*. Notre Dame, Ind.: University of Notre Dame Press.

Walzer, M. (1994). 'Dogen, Deep Ecology and the Ecological Self'. *Environmental Ethics*, 16 (2): 195–213.

19

City, Democracy and Citizenship: Historical Images, Contemporary Practices

ENGIN F. ISIN

In occidental imagination it is impossible to separate the city, democracy and citizenship from each other. On the one hand, what makes the occident different from the orient is itself defined via this inextricable relationship. On the other hand, an unbroken unity of history as a seamless web has been constituted where city, democracy and citizenship have *always* implicated each other. My focus in this chapter is not how the occident has defined itself against the orient by constructing images of a series of absences in the orient as regards city, democracy and citizenship (Springborg, 1987). Rather, the chapter focuses on the question of various historical images of the city, democracy and citizenship and illustrates how these images are increasingly incongruous with contemporary practices.

The images of city, democracy and citizenship are not merely representations but institutions toward which we either orient (or are constantly provoked to orient) our thoughts and practices about the political. The question of what it means to be political is always oriented toward these images that have been constituted as not simply true or false but as unassailable conditions of being political. All those routinized literary and academic practices where the origins of 'city', 'democracy' and 'citizenship' are etymologically traced to the 'Greek', 'Roman' and 'medieval' cities, and affinities between 'their' and 'our' practices are established, not only orient toward but also reproduce such images. After being 'reminded' that *polis*, politics and polity; *civitas*, citizenship and civility; and *demos* and democracy have 'common roots', we are provided with images of virtuous Greek citizens debating in the *agora* or the *pnyx*, austere Roman citizens deliberating in the republican senate, and 'European' citizens receiving their charters in front of the guildhall.

It is not that many literally believe that 'we' are descended from the Greeks or the Romans, or even the medieval Europeans in any straightforward way. Nor would many believe that since these historical times the meaning and practices of cities, democracy and citizenship have remained unchanged. Rather, these images mobilize and provoke an invented tradition: that we are somehow *inheritors* of an occidental tradition that is different from and superior to an oriental one. These images then invent not one but two traditions. All the same, as subjects become familiar with these images, the images themselves become 'natural' ways of seeing and perceiving. For the occidental imagination some images are now such ways of seeing: that democracy was invented in the Greek *polis*; that Roman republican tradition bequeathed its legacy to Europe and that Europe Christianized and civilized these traditions. The image of the virtuous citizen is ineluctably linked with the occidental tradition whether it is told through canonical thinkers such as Aristotle, Cicero, St Augustine, Marsilius and Locke or through narrating epic battles where citizenship virtues were discovered. While in the late eighteenth and early nineteenth centuries this narrative was told as a seamless web, constituting an occidental tradition of city and citizenship, in much of the twentieth century its seamlessness was called into question. Yet, until the present, this narrative has held sway: views such as liberalism, republicanism or communitarianism are really different ways of telling the same occidental narrative.

This chapter however, aims neither to critique these images nor document how they have been constructed nor suggest ways in which different images can and must be produced. These tasks have either been tackled elsewhere or are still waiting to be tackled. Instead, this chapter draws attention to the fact that these images are increasingly incongruous with contemporary practices that constitute themselves as political and, by virtue of this constitution, begin to produce different images of the city, democracy and citizenship. Throughout the second half of the twentieth century we witnessed various practices that were originally deemed as outside the political, and which assembled themselves as relatively routinized, durable and effective strategies and technologies, making, enacting, and instituting political demands and translating these demands into claims for citizenship rights. At first interpreted as 'social movements', then as 'cultural politics', these practices are increasingly being constituted as 'insurgent citizenship practices' by agents themselves as well as scholars.

Throughout the second half of the twentieth century, this divergence, and the consequent incongruence between historical images and contemporary practices were widely noticed and debated. However, two inadequate reactions dominated these debates. First, there are those narratives which interpret the divergence and incongruence as 'decline' or 'end' and urge 'renewal', 'reinvention' and 'regeneration'. An entire nostalgia industry emerged where narratives yearning the loss of 'active citizenship', 'decline of public sphere', 'the death of the social', and 'the end of politics' are woven into the fabric of interpreting the present. Second, there are those narratives which argue that, since the contemporary city and the way democracy and citizenship are enacted through it have no affinities with these historical images and realities, we have to think about the city anew without owing anything to these historical images, yearning for an epistemic break. Neither reaction is, in my view, capable of distinguishing the new elements of the present while understanding the historical trajectories through which the narratives of urban democracy have been recreated, reinterpreted, appropriated and incorporated into the present. We need to isolate the rationalities behind the *modern* image of urban democracy before we discuss the incongruence between it and contemporary practices.

GOVERNING MODERN CITIES: LOYALTY, VIRTUE, CIVISM, DISCIPLINE AND SUBSIDIARITY

'The solution of the problems of democratic government rests in the cities. … The political problem of the modern city is the problem of democracy' (Innis, [1945] 1995: 482, 485). So said Harold Innis in 1945 in an address reflecting on the problems of democracy. He expressed succinctly the fact that modern social and political thought always posed the question of the city as a question of government: a question of organizations, ideologies and institutions of government but not rationalities of governing cities. The modern city was constituted at the centre of the question concerning democratic government, and modern social and political thought about the city and government arise from that fundamental institutional concern (Munro, 1918, 1926). It essentially constitutes the city government as a territorialized container within which and through which government becomes possible, desirable and feasible.

Beginning with its first modern interpreters such as Alexis de Tocqueville ([1835] 1945) and John Stuart Mill (1861), institutionalism has been a prevalent aspect of thought on city government (Magnusson, 1986; Stoker, 1996). The modern democratic conception of the city that emerged in the early nineteenth century expressed a particular conception of city government, which became synonymous simultaneously with democracy and the state. In a sense, city government was state government writ small. This was later reproduced by the concept 'local state', where city government was a territorialized container of state administration, politics and government. According to this 'modern tradition', while citizenship originated in the city and played an important role in the history of citizenship in occidental civilization (Heater, 1990; Riesenberg, 1992), its significance as a milieu cultivating citizenship was linked to government of the state. So the question of city government was posed from the point of view of governability of the state. Thus, while modern social and political thought on the city deployed images of the birth of democracy and citizenship in ancient Greek cities, its republican transformations in ancient Roman cities, and its revival in medieval European cities, it simultaneously distanced itself from those images: while democracy was cultivated and bred in the city, it was a question of governability of the state. While the glorious images of 'ancient institutions' and 'tradition' always dominated thought on city government, the state was considered the protector and arbiter of this democratic 'heritage'. There are understandable genealogical reasons why the dominant groups in the nineteenth century made such historical linkages, but we cannot explore them here (Isin, 1995).

The modernity of city government was thus inextricably associated with governability of the state and its citizens. In Britain, America and Canada the crystallization of this question can be traced from the period after 1835 in which a new framework for city government as a container was gradually articulated. Yet it was not until the early decades of the twentieth century that the city government in its modern form could be said to have emerged. Although by the end of the nineteenth century the basic structures had crystallized, the city government was still restricted by a heavy dependence on local rates for finance and it was not until the 1920s that any scheme for state support for local services was provided on any significant scale (Loughlin, 1996: 79). In the twentieth century city government was locked into a network of government that operated at various scales (nation, region, city) and capacities. Neither autonomous nor subordinate, modern city government was a technology defined by a tension between state and local authorities (Isin, 1992). Loughlin argues that the modern city government that crystallized in the twentieth century therefore had no functional affinity with historical forms of city government either in medieval European or ancient Greek or Roman cities (Loughlin, 1996). For Loughlin any appeal to a tradition of city government expressed as a right to local self-government cannot comfortably rest on ancient tradition and history. The various shifts in the nineteenth and twentieth centuries make such claims highly implausible. Nor can such appeals be based on some authoritative constitutional norms in Britain, America, Australia or Canada. For Loughlin, if tradition is to be invented it must now be found to rest on modern practices and thus on a set of political understandings which commanded widespread support throughout the twentieth century.

Yet the epistemic break from history advocated by Loughlin neglects the appropriation and incorporation of historical images into numerous reforms of city government. Governing modern cities embodies complex organizations, rationalities, institutions, processes and norms that are simultaneously deterritorialized (politics spilling over the current boundaries of the city) and reterritorialized (politics overlapping with other boundaries than the city such as the state, empire, nation). These complex and overlapping networks are endowed with capacities for effective governance and vested with various degrees of political legitimacy (Brodie, 2000). Because of these complexities the obsessive focus on the formal legal status of city government as a territorialized container of state politics presents a distorted view. Modern city government, while constrained in principle by the *ultra vires* doctrine, has in fact been vested with considerable capacities that are not necessarily expressed in its formal or legal powers. As many students of local government have observed, although formally subordinate, city government has, as a result of the changes in government during the twentieth century, 'acquired a relatively important position in an interdependent network government' (Loughlin, 1996: 83). Yet this statement is itself misleading as it refocuses our attention on the city government as a territorialized container rather than investigating the ways in which governing cities embodies various deterritorialized and reterritorialized rationalities of government.

By posing the question of governing cities as city government, that is, as a question of governability of the state through the city as a container, modern social and political thought often identified democracy and efficiency as competing 'functions' of city government (Loughlin, 1996: 82–3; Sharpe, 1970; Stoker, 1996). Thus, the emphasis on authority (ability to perform governmental functions), autonomy (capacity to deliver services according to local needs), taxation (powers to raise revenue) and representation (legitimacy for accountability) functions of modern city government received widespread attention and, depending on political persuasion, scorn or admiration (Dahl, 1967; Jones, 1998; McDermott and Forgie, 1999; Pratchett and Wilson, 1997; Read, 1994; Yates, 1977). Similarly, thought on democracy and citizenship revolved around electoral representation, voter turnout, 'citizen' participation, fiscal austerity, management structures, and organization forms (Berry et al., 1993; Bucek and Smith, 2000; Burns, 2000; Dahl, 1964; Gabriel et al., 2000; Goldsmith, 1998; Pratchett and Wilson, 1997; Ward, 2000). This exclusive focus on authority, autonomy, taxation and representation resulted in too much emphasis on institutional and organizational arrangements of city government rather than its rationalities within the broader network of modern government. In other words, there has been an undue emphasis on city government rather than governing cities (Osborne and Rose, 1999; Rose, 2000). Thus, the focus on jurisdictional issues such as autonomy and efficiency has interpreted the city as an enclosed, territorialized and hierarchical container of the political rather than spatialized, deterritorialized and reterritorialized network of governing rationalities (Magnusson, 2000). To shift focus from city government to governing cities requires investigations into the rationalities of governing cities. I shall briefly highlight what I consider the most important modern rationalities governing cities and the traditions of social and political thought that arose from them before I consider how new urban democratic practices are shifting these rationalities. These rationalities are loyalty, virtue, civism, discipline and subsidiarity.

Loyalty

The city in modern democratic thought is simultaneously the milieu and object of *loyalty*. The citizen as a man (later also woman) of property constitutes himself (later also herself) as an agent capable of political judgement while at the same time investing himself in the city, which becomes his work. The citizen identifies with the city and owes allegiance and loyalty to it. But this identification does not contradict with his identification with the nation. Rather, it becomes the foundation of the nation-state. The work of nationalism was actually done in the city in the sense that loyalty to the nation-state was bred and nurtured in the city via the bourgeois public sphere. While considering loyalty a fundamental aspect of the city, the sociological tradition arose out of a concern with the relationship between loyalty and citizenship and the city as an intermediate association between the individual and the state (Durkheim, [1890] 1992, [1894] 1984; Tönnies, [1887] 1963). Modern democratic theory, therefore, constituted the city as the space in which the loyalty of the citizen to the nation and the state was cultivated, bred and nurtured. The conduct of the citizen – especially the valorization of active citizen – implicated his (later also her) loyalty in the city as that space where a subject became a citizen oriented toward the state, nation and the city with affection and devotion. Patriotism toward the city was transformed into patriotism toward the nation and vice versa. The sociological tradition considered the patriotism of the city the foundation of the patriotism of the state and the nation.

Virtue

The city is also where the citizen becomes *virtuous* through his (later also her) engagements in politics defined as a broad field in which a citizen conducts himself (later also herself) towards the conduct of others. The civic virtue of the citizen consists in the fact that his conduct oriented toward the city is not only his right but also his obligation. The city becomes a space of government in the sense that the citizen constitutes himself as both subject and object of conduct in the public sphere. The citizen is therefore not simply a man but virtuous patriot as that man (later also woman). The exercise of this right *and* obligation can be as passive as simply voting or as active as taking part in the everyday life of politics. For the political tradition this was a fundamental aspect of the city fostering democracy (Mill, 1861; Tocqueville, [1835] 1945). For the political tradition the question of democracy was the question of the city – or more precisely, the question of governing the city.

Civism

That a subject becomes a virtuous citizen via developing loyalty toward the city means that the city becomes a breeding ground for active citizenship and democracy. But how does the city become that space which cultivates virtue? Virtue of the modern citizen is *civic* precisely because it is expressed through a loyalty to his (later also her) city as both a particular place and an abstract idea. The city is where citizens are habituated into democratic imagination via practice, experience and education. But *civism* is not taught in the city as though it is a course, but is cultivated and bred as a disposition, a habitus. The citizen makes himself in the city by publicizing himself (later also herself) toward others through everyday experience. Civism makes man (later also woman) governable. For the philosophical tradition this was a fundamental aspect of the relationship between city and citizenship (Rousseau, [1755–62] 1983; Strauss, 1964).

Discipline

While the city is constituted as a space of liberty for the citizen, it is also constituted as a space of *discipline* for strangers and outsiders – non-citizens. It is not that liberty did not require discipline. On the contrary, breeding loyalty, virtue and civism in publicizing subjects as capable citizens requires discipline as conduct upon conduct. In fact, liberty and discipline presupposed each other. But those who lacked certain attributes of citizens – strangers and outsiders – were subject to different institutions of discipline such as prisons and asylums. The city may be a space where the citizen conducts himself in public as a political agent with rights and liberties, but it is also a space where those who lack or are denied such citizenship rights are subjected to discipline and punishment. The tensions between liberty and order and between discipline and civility in the modern city constitute citizenship as a space where the 'normalcy' of citizens is articulated against the 'pathologies' of non-citizens. As the legal tradition emphasized, modernity of the city as a corporation consisted precisely in the public rights of self-government vested in it by the modern nation-state to act on the conduct of its subjects (Frug, 1980; Gierke, [1868] 1990, 1900; Maitland, 1898).

Subsidiarity

The modern city is also that space where it is most appropriate to deliver services such as education, welfare, parks, prisons, recreation and the like for the publicization of the subject into citizen. The city is the closest level of government to the citizen and is approachable and direct. The *subsidiarity* of the city consists in the shared relationship between the state and the city in publicizing the citizen. While there is always a tension in terms of allocating resources to the city to deliver services and the exact nature, extent and combination of these services, the city is the appropriate level of government to deliver these services because these matters can arise and can be decided locally. The economic tradition on the city highlighted this aspect of city government as its essence (Boyne, 1998).

RE: THE POLITICAL

While these rationalities of governing cities can be related to their democracy and efficiency functions and are expressed in its institutions, they are not reducible to them. Neither are they reducible to each other. Loyalty, virtue, civism, discipline and subsidiarity are distinct but related rationalities of governing cities that are deterritorialized (explode and spill over municipal boundaries) and reterritorialized (implode and redefine municipal boundaries). Moreover, they are neither coherent nor complementary aspects of governing cities in that there is always an agonism amongst these rationalities. Finally, institutional arrangements such as authority, autonomy, taxation and representation derive from these broader rationalities of governing cities rather than being its constitutive aspects. Thus, considering institutions of modern city government in isolation from its broader rationalities results in a distorted view of governing cities. These rationalities assemble the historical images that we have of virtuous Greek, Roman, medieval, early modern and modern citizens in and of the city. So while there may be little functional affinity between modern city governments and their historical counterparts, these rationalities of governing cities explain why these images are constantly invoked for government of the modern city. These historical images capture possibilities and implode and recode them onto municipal boundaries by overcoding their significance and mapping them back onto these historical images.

These images are also increasingly called into question by the contemporary practices of citizens *of* cities. Scholars such as Holston (1998, 1999, 2001), Fincher and Jacobs (1998), Kofman (1998), Sandercock (1998a, 1998b), and Wekerle (2000) have captured the changing images in contemporary practices of urban citizenship. Holston, for example, has emphasized that 'both the elite and the subaltern mark urban space with new and insurgent forms of the social – that these forms are not, in other words, limited to the latter' (1998: 48, n. 8). For Holston 'Among the most vocal critics of liberal citizenship in this sense are groups organized around specific identities – the kind of prior differences liberalism relegates to the private sphere – which affirm the importance of these identities in the public calculus of citizenship' (1996: 193). Thus, for these subaltern groups the 'right to difference' becomes an integral part of the foundation of citizenship. For Holston 'Although this kind of demand would seem contradictory and incompatible with citizenship as an ideology of equality, there is nevertheless a growing sense that it is changing the meaning of equality itself. What it objects to is the equation that equality means sameness' (Holston and Appadurai, 1996: 195). With these struggles

> right becomes more of a claim upon than a possession held against the world. It becomes a claim upon society for the resources necessary to meet the basic needs and interests of members rather than a kind of property some possess and other do not. It is probably the case that this change applies mostly to socio-economic and political rights rather than to civil rights. ... But in terms of rights to the city and rights to political participation, right becomes conceived as an aspect of social relatedness rather than as an inherent and natural property of individuals' (Holston and Appadurai, 1996: 197).

Formal citizenship is neither necessary nor a sufficient condition for substantive citizenship. The new claims to citizenship are new not only because they force the state to respond to new social conditions but also because they create new kinds of right, based on the exigencies of lived experience, outside of the normative and institutional definitions of the state and its codes (Holston, 1998: 52). This is quite a different image of right that resides in a virtuous citizen that modern thought about urban democracy and citizenship articulated. Rather than a focus on the virtue and loyalty of the dominant citizen focus has shifted here to the insurgence of the dominated and to the right as claim rather than privilege.

Following the same logic, the city is also not a space of loyalty but of agonism. While the city becomes a space where these new forms of rights are articulated, it becomes a battle zone for this very reason: the dominant groups meet the advance of these new citizens with new strategies of segregation, privatization and fortification (Holston, 1998: 52; Holston and Appadurai, 1996: 200).

> These sites vary with time and place. Today, in many cities, they include the realm of the homeless, networks of migration, neighbourhoods of Queer Nation, constructed peripheries in which the poor build their own homes in precarious material and legal conditions, ganglands, fortified condominiums, employee-owned factories, squatter settlements, suburban migrant labour camps, sweatshops, and the zones of the so-called new racism. They are sites of insurgence because they introduce into the city new identities and practices that disturb established histories. (Holston, 1998: 48).
>
> These insurgent forms are found both in organized grassroots mobilizations and in everyday practices that, in different ways, empower, parody, derail, or subvert state agendas. They are found, in other words, in struggles over what it means to be a member of the modern state – which is why I refer to them with the term *citizenship*. Membership in the state has never been a static identity, given the dynamics of global migrations and national ambitions. Citizenship changes as new members emerge to advance their claims, expanding its realm, and as new forms of segregation and violence counter these advances, eroding it. The sites of insurgent citizenship are found at the intersection of these processes of expansion and erosion. (Holston, 1998: 47–8)

For Sandercock 'A new city is emerging, and it is ... the city of cultural difference' (1998b: 175).

> We need to start understanding our cities as bearers of our intertwined

fates. We need to formulate within our city a shared notion of a common destiny. We need to see our city as the locus of citizenship, and to recognize multiple levels of citizenship as well as multiple levels of common destiny, from the city to the nation to transnational citizenship possibilities. We need to see our city and its multiple communities as spaces where we connect with the cultural other who is now our neighbour. ... The modern project of the nation state emphasized unity and sameness over difference and diversity. The rise of multiculturalism as a political force is a sign of the failure of that modernist project. The cities and regions of the future must nurture difference and diversity through a democratic cultural pluralism. ... If cultural imperialism and systemic violence are features of contemporary global urban and regional changes, then a politics of difference is a prerequisite for confronting these oppressions. A politics of difference is a politics based on the identity, needs, and rights of specific groups who are victims of any faces of oppression. ... A rejection of the ideal of the homogeneous community as part of the future cosmopolis leads us into an investigation of the idea of *multiple publics*, together constituting some form of civic culture, as a basis for the survival of a culturally pluralist form of cities and regions. ... [Cosmopolis is] an always unfinished and contested construction site, one characterized above all by its space for difference. ... At the moment these global forces and top-down processes are increasing economic, social, and cultural polarization in an overall climate of increasing uncertainty and decreasing legitimacy of governments everywhere. In response, mobilized communities within civil society launch struggles for livelihood, in defence of life space, and in affirmation of the right to cultural difference (Sandercock, 1998b: 182–217).

These images do not invoke the loyalty, virtue, civism and discipline of the austere citizen but the subaltern, the other, multiple and the insurgent. In turn, these images also show up in historical studies of cities and citizenship. Take, for example, Ryan's (1997) study on democracy and publicization of the citizen in American cities in the nineteenth century. She finds that citizens were not found loyal and virtuous in the American city but these values were themselves constantly contested in streets, squares, buildings and parks of the city via revolts, strikes, parades and ceremonies that were multiple, heterogeneous and ambiguous rather than fitting into a dominant, universal image of the 'bourgeois public sphere'. Similarly, Pamplona (1996) investigates how the consolidation of the republican order in both New York in the early nineteenth century and Rio de Janeiro in the late nineteenth century required the constitution of certain subaltern groups as the others of republican citizenship and how this consolidation involved violent riots and contestation. Just as scholars of contemporary cities such as Holston and Sandercock are turning their attention to how the dominated contest and question the dominant images that constitute them as lacking virtue, loyalty and civism, historians such as Ryan and Pamplona are also discovering in cities where previous representations of harmony and unity are giving way to multiple images of agonism and contestation. Those practices that were deemed outside the political not only by virtue of being vicious, disloyal and uncivil but also by virtue of being outside the city as a territorial container are appearing with increasing clarity as practices of citizenship by those who were constituted as its others.

RIGHTS TO THE CITY AS A NEW IMAGE OF CITIZENSHIP

That the claims for group-differentiated rights actually arise out of the city and are connected with postmodernization and globalization is fairly easy to illustrate. Consider the question of immigrants in North America and Europe and their political status. While the debate rages over this as a national issue, whether immigrants should be given political and social rights, the majority of immigrants settle in cities and use urban resources to mobilize and articulate their demands for recognition. In Germany it is impossible to understand citizenship rights for Turks without examining their spatial concentrations in major cities such as Berlin or Frankfurt (Barbieri, 1998). Similarly, it is impossible to understand the complexities that arise from Latino citizenship in America without understanding the settlement patterns and forms such groups have engendered (Rocco, 1996). Cities are therefore constituted as political spaces where the concentration of different groups and their identities are intertwined with the articulation of various claims to citizenship rights (Sassen, 2000). It is within this domain of groups and identities that the appropriation and use of urban space is articulated, which in turn constitutes urban citizenship as a field of debate and struggle.

In contemporary studies the metaphor 'rights to the city' has proved a useful organizing concept to interpret the new practices of urban citizenship (Holston, 1998; Kofman, 1998; Sassen, 1999; Wekerle, 2000). The phrase itself was suggested by Henri Lefebvre in its singular form (Lefebvre, 1968). In the late 1960s, he articulated this concept and the city as work, as *oeuvre*, which was the dominant mode of its production in Western history. By contrast, for Lefebvre modern capitalism constituted the city as a product. While the emphasis was on the city's use value in the former, it was on the city's exchange value in the latter. Lefebvre believed that, to claim the rights of ages, sexes, conditions of work, training, education, culture, leisure, health and housing, it was imperative to think through the city (Lefebvre, 1996: 157). The recognition of these rights required the pluralization of groups whose everyday lives were bound up with the city. The struggle to define and appropriate the spaces of the city was crucial in claiming these rights (Lefebvre, [1974] 1995: 410–11). For Lefebvre, 'the right to the city manifests itself as a superior form of rights: right to freedom, to individualization and socialization, to habitat and to inhabit' (1996: 173). Accordingly, 'the right to the *oeuvre* [the city as a work of art], to participation and *appropriation* (clearly distinct from the right to property), are implied in the right to the city' (1996: 174). Neither a natural nor a contractual right, the right to the city 'signifies the rights of citizens and city dwellers, and of groups they (on the basis of social relations) constitute, to appear on all the networks and circuits of communication, information and exchange' (1996: 194–5). It follows that, 'To exclude the *urban* from groups, classes, individuals, is also to exclude them from civilization, if from not society itself. The *right* to the city legitimates the refusal to allow oneself to be removed from urban reality by a discriminatory and segregative organization' (1996: 195). Thus, 'This right of the citizen … proclaims the inevitable crisis of city centres based upon segregation and establishing it: centres of decision-making, wealth, power, of information and knowledge, which reject towards peripheral spaces all those who do not participate in political privileges. Equally, it stipulates the right to meetings and gathering.' (1996: 195).

It is noteworthy that Lefebvre identified the dominant groups in the contemporary city as the 'new masters' (1996: 161). He observed that they already claimed the central areas of New York, Paris and other major cities, and he described the new city as 'New Athens'. But what he meant here is not the glorious ancient Athens as the birthplace of democracy but the ancient Athens of deep class and group cleavages between citizens and slaves, outsiders and oppressed groups. It is not that the New Athens had slaves in the ancient sense of that term, but that in the city the new masters created a social space that catered to their exclusive use while surrounding them with masses to provide services. Lefebvre observed that the new masters were made up of a very small minority, as in ancient Athens, and were comprised of 'directors, heads, presidents of this and that, elites, leading writers and artists, well-known entertainers and media people' (Lefebvre, 1996: 161). Underneath this layer were 'executives, administrators, professionals and scholars'. He was particularly concerned with the rise of this secondary layer of the dominant groups – in the intriguing parlance of Bourdieu, ([1979] 1984) the dominated fraction of the dominant class – because their interests diverged not only from the working classes and the subjugated groups but also from the bourgeoisie. For Lefebvre the right to the city was the right to claim presence in the city, to wrest the use of the city from the privileged new masters and democratize its spaces. Lefebvre saw the rights to the city as an expression of urban citizenship, understood not as membership in a polity – let alone the nation-state – but as a practice of articulating, claiming and renewing group rights in and through the appropriation and creation of spaces in the city.

Lefebvre wrote at a time in which the new politics of the city was just crystallizing (Burkhard, 2000; Shields, 1999). Since then, the global flows of ideas, images, music and capital and labour both emanating from and concentrating in globalizing cities have become the defining moments of our age. Today, the rights of immigrants, ethnicized and racialized groups, gays and lesbians, women, poor, and other subaltern, marginalized or oppressed groups are by and large fought for in cities. Yet these struggles are not waged on a binary plane against a common adversary but pit groups against groups and divide, fragment, blur and shatter identities, rights, sensibilities, loyalties and obligations. That the articulation of rights to the city, not as rights to property but as rights to appropriate the city has proved a useful way of thinking about the rights that arise in the city. But this does not mean that Lefebvre has been appropriated uncritically. Rather, the emphasis has shifted from 'the right' to 'rights' to emphasize the multiplicity of the ways in which the city has been appropriated. The task of disentangling the interests of various groups and mapping overlapping networks of power relations in contemporary cities is intensely difficult. And the conceptual and analytical tools that we inherit either from the nineteenth-century sociological, political, philosophical and economic traditions of thought as outlined above or even from scholars such as Lefebvre are scarcely adequate to the task. The nineteenth-century conception of rights in the city were closely associated with the property rights of the bourgeois man. The city as a corporation institutionalized property rights and incorporated the city into the realm of the state with its rationalities of loyalty, virtue, civism, discipline and subsidiarity. Rethinking rights that arise in governing contemporary cities requires articulating rights *to* the city rather than rights *of* the city as a corporation, a government, in short, a territorial container of politics. It requires rethinking urban citizenship beyond the confines of the city government and instead investigating ways in which governing cities articulates ways of being political.

REFERENCES

Barbieri, William A. (1998) *Ethics of Citizenship: Immigration and Group Rights in Germany*. Durham, NC: Duke University Press.

Berry, Jeffrey M., Kent E. Portney, and Ken Thomson (1993) *The Rebirth of Urban Democracy*. Washington, D.C.: Brookings Institution.

Bourdieu, Pierre (1979) [1984] *Distinction: A Social Critique of the Judgement of Taste*. Cambridge: Harvard University Press.

Boyne, George A. (1998) *Public Choice Theory and Local Government: A Comparative Analysis of the UK and the USA*. Basingstoke: Macmillan.

Brodie, Janine (2000) 'Imagining demoractic urban citizenship.' In *Democracy, Citizenship and the Global City, edited by E.F. Isin*, pp. 110–128. London: Routledge.

Bucek, J., and B. Smith (2000) 'New approaches to local democracy: direct democracy, participation and the "Third Sector"'. *Environment and Planning C-Government and Policy*, 18 (1): 3–16.

Burkhard, Fred (2000) *French Marxism between the Wars: Henri Lefebvre and the 'Philosophies'*. Amherst, NY: Humanity Books.

Burns, D. (2000) 'Can local democracy survive governance?' *Urban Studies*, 37 (5–6): 963–973.

Dahl, Robert A. (1964) *Who Governs? Democracy and Power in an American City*. New Haven, CT: Yale University Press.

——— (1967) 'The city in the future of democracy.' *The American Political Science Review* 61 (4): 953–970.

Durkheim, Emile (1890) [1992] *Professional Ethics and Civic Morals*. London: Routledge.

——— 1894 [1984]. *The Division of Labor in Society* trans. W.D. Halls, ed. L. Coser. New York: Free Press.

Fincher, Ruth, and Jane M. Jacobs. (1998) *Cities of Difference*. New York: Guilford.

Frug, Gerald E. (1980) 'The City as a Legal Concept.' *Harvard Law Review*, 43 (April).

Gabriel, Oscar W., Vincent Hoffmann-Martinot, and H.V. Savitch (2000) *Urban Democracy, Städte Und Regionen in Europa*. Opladen: Leske+Budrich.

Gierke, Otto (1868) [1990] *Community in Historical Perspective* trans. M. Fischer ed. A. Black. Cambridge: Cambridge University Press.

——— (1900) *Political Theories of the Middle Age* translated by F.W. Maitland. Cambridge: Cambridge University Press.

Goldsmith, M. (1998) 'Local democracy and local government.' *Public Administration*, 76 (3): 593–594.

Heater, Derek Benjamin (1990) *Citizenship: The Civic Ideal in World History, Politics, and Education*. London: Longman Group.

Holston, James (1998) 'Spaces of Insurgent Citizenship.' *In Making the Invisible Visible: A Multicultural Planning History* ed. L. Sandercock. Berkeley: University of California Press. pp. xii, 270.

——— (2001) 'Urban citizenship and globalization.' In *Global City-Regions: Trends, Theory, Policy*, edited by A.J. Scott. Oxford: Oxford University Press. 325–348.

——— ed. (1999) *Cities and Citizenship*. Durham, NC: Duke University Press.

Holston, James, and Arjun Appadurai (1996) 'Cities and citizenship.' *Public Culture* 8 (2): 187–204.

Innis, Harold Adams (1945) [1995] 'Democracy and the free city.' *In Staples, Markets, and Cultural Change: Selected Essays*, edited by D. Drache. Montreal: McGill-Queen's University Press. pp. 482–486.

Isin, Engin F. (1992) *Cities without Citizens: Modernity of the City as a Corporation*. Montreal: Black Rose Books.

——— (1995) 'Rethinking the origins of Canadian municipal government.' *Canadian Journal of Urban Research*, 4 (1): 73–92.

Jones, M.R. (1998) 'Rethinking local democracy.' *Environment and Planning C-Government and Policy*, 16 (2): 247–249.

Kofman, Eleonore (1998) 'Whose city? Gender, class and immigrants in globalizing European cities.' In *Cities of Difference*, edited by R. Fincher and J.M. Jacobs, 279–300. New York: Guilford.

Lefebvre, Henri (1968) *Le Droit À La Ville, Société Et Urbanisme*. Paris: Anthropos.

——— (1974) [1995] *The Production of Space* trans. D. Nicholson-Smith. Oxford: Blackwell.

——— (1996) *Writings on Cities* trans. E. Kofman and E. Lebas. Oxford: Blackwell.

Loughlin, Martin (1996) *Legality and Locality: The Role of Law in Central-Local Government Relations*. Oxford: Clarendon Press.

Magnusson, Warren (1986) 'Bourgeois theories of local government.' *Political Studies*, 34: 1–18.

——— (2000) 'Politicizing the global city.' In *Democracy, Citizenship, and the Global City*, edited by E.F. Isin. London: Routledge.

Maitland, Frederic W. (1898) *Township and Borough*. Cambridge: Cambridge University Press.

McDermott, P., and V. Forgie (1999) 'Trends in local government: Efficiency, functions and democracy.' *Political Science*, 50 (2): 247–265.

Mill, John Stuart (1861) *Considerations on Representative Government*. London: Longmans.

Munro, William Bennett. (1918) *The Government of European Cities*. New York: Macmillan.

——— (1926) *The Government of American Cities*, 4th ed. New York: Macmillan.

Osborne, Thomas, and Nikolas Rose (1999) 'Governing Cities: Notes on the spatialisation of virtue.' *Environment and Planning D: Society and Space* 17: 737–760.

Pamplona, Marco Antonio Villela (1996) *Riots, Republicanism, and Citizenship: New York City and Rio De Janeiro City During the Consolidation of the Republican Order, Studies in African American History and Culture*. New York: Garland.

Pratchett, L., and D. Wilson (1997) 'The rebirth of local democracy?' *Local Government Studies*, 23 (1): 16–31.

Read, Donald (1994) *The Age of Urban Democracy: England 1868–1914*. 2nd ed. London: Longman.

Riesenberg, Peter (1992) *Citizenship in the Western Tradition*. Chapel Hill: University of North Carolina Press.

Rocco, Raymond A. (1996) 'Latino Los Angeles: Reframing boundaries/borders.' In *The City: Los Angeles and Urban Theory at the End of the Twentieth Century* edited by A.J. Scott and E.W. Soja. Berkeley, CA: University of California Press. pp. xii, 483.

Rose, Nikolas (2000). 'Governing cities, governing citizens.' In *Democracy, Citizenship, and the Global City* edited by E.F. Isin. London: Routledge. pp. 95–109.

Rousseau, Jean-Jacques (1983) *On the Social Contract; Discourse on the Origin of Inequality; Discourse on Political Economy*. Translated by D.A. Cress. Indianapolis: Hackett Publishing.

Ryan, Mary P. (1997) *Civic Wars: Democracy and Public Life in the American City During the Nineteenth Century*. Berkeley: University of California Press.

Sandercock, Leonie (1998a) *Making the Invisible Visible: A Multicultural Planning History, California Studies in Critical Human Geography*; 2. Berkeley: University of California Press.

——— (1998b) *Towards Cosmopolis: Planning for Multicultural Cities*. New York: Wiley.

Sassen, Saskia (1999) 'Whose city is it? Globalization and the formation of new claims.' in *Cities and Citizenship*, edited by J. Holston pp. 177–194. Durham, NC: Duke University Press.

——— (2000) 'The global city: Strategic site/new frontier.' In *Democracy, Citizenship and the Global City* pp. 48–61. edited by E.F. Isin. London: Routledge.

Sharpe, L.J. (1970) 'Theories and values of local government.' *Political Studies* 18: 153–174.

Shields, Rob (1999) *Lefebvre, Love, and Struggle: Spatial Dialectics*. London: Routledge.

Springborg, Patricia (1987) 'The contractual state: Reflections on orientalism and despotism.' *History of Political Thought* 8 (3): 395–433.

Stoker, Gerry (1996) 'Introduction: Normative theories of local government and democracy' in *Rethinking Local Democracy*, edited by D.S. King and G. Stoker. Basingstoke: Macmillan. pp. 1–27.

Strauss, Leo (1964) *The City and Man*. Chicago: University of Chicago Press.

Tocqueville, Alexis de (1835) [1945] *Democracy in America*. New York: Alfred A. Knopf.

Tönnies, Ferdinand (1887) [1963] *Community and Association*. New York: Harper and Row.

Ward, K.G. (2000) 'A critique in search of a corpus: Re-visiting governance and re-interpreting urban politics.' *Transactions of the Institute of British Geographers* 25 (2): 169–185.

Wekerle, Gerda (2000) 'Women's Rights to the City: Gendered Spaces of a Pluralistic Citizenship.' In *Democracy, Citizenship, and the Global City* edited by E.F. Isin. London: Routledge. pp. 203–217.

Yates, Douglas (1977) *The Ungovernable City: The Politics of Urban Problems and Policy Making*. Cambridge, Mass.: MIT Press.

20

Cosmopolitan Citizenship

ANDREW LINKLATER

The idea of cosmopolitan or world citizenship seems to have first appeared in Ancient Greece in the fourth century BC when the polis and the civic virtues associated with it were in obvious decline. The cynic philosopher, Diogenes, called himself a citizen of the world because he believed the polis no longer had first claim upon the individual's political allegiances. In Diogenes' thought, the idea of world citizenship was used to criticise the polis rather than to develop some vision of a universal community of humankind. Enlightenment thinkers such as Kant used the concept of world citizenship more positively to promote a stronger sense of moral obligation between the members of separate sovereign states. Since the Second World War, members of global social movements have resurrected the notion of cosmopolitan citizenship to defend a stronger sense of collective and individual responsibility for the world as a whole and to support the development of effective global institutions for tackling global poverty and inequality, environmental degradation and the violation of human rights (Dower, 2000: 553). Several analysts of social movements maintain that cosmopolitan citizenship is a key element in the quest for a new language of politics which challenges the belief that the individual's central political obligations are to the nation-state. Cosmopolitan citizenship is regarded as a key theme in the continuing search for universal rights and obligations which bind all peoples together in a just world order.

The belief that global problems can be solved by establishing cosmopolitan rights and duties certainly does not go unchallenged. Critics have argued that cosmopolitan projects are likely to be the vehicles for particular political interests which wrap themselves in the language of universality. Many point to the danger that new forms of cultural imperialism will result from efforts to lay down rights and duties which apply to human beings everywhere. Others argue that efforts to break the nexus between the citizen and the state are destined to fail because there is no sense of international community which can support the sophisticated forms of citizenship which exist within democratic societies. One concern is that the defence of cosmopolitan citizenship is not only merely rhetorical but dangerous since it detracts from the more urgent business of preserving the nation-state.

This chapter begins by considering criticisms of world citizenship which argue that citizenship properly so-called exists only within bounded political communities: nation-states. The next task is to assess three ways in which the concept has been used in cosmopolitan political theory and practice: to strengthen cosmopolitan duties to the members of other political communities; to champion individual human rights as set out in the developing realm of world or cosmopolitan law; and to endorse the political project of creating a worldwide public sphere which extends the democratic project beyond national boundaries. The aim of the discussion is to determine whether or not the idea of cosmopolitan citizenship can be defended from the criticisms which have been levelled against it.

CRITICS OF COSMOPOLITAN CITIZENSHIP

The simplest and most eloquent challenge to the idea of cosmopolitan citizenship has been put forward by Michael Walzer (1994) who has maintained that: 'I am not a citizen of the world … I am not even aware that there is a world such that one could be a citizen of it. No one has ever offered me citizenship, or described the naturalisation process, or enlisted me in the world's institutional structures, or given me an account of its decision procedures … or provided me with a list of the benefits and obligations of citizenship, or shown me the world's calendar and the common celebrations and commemorations of its citizens'.

Three points are worth making about this striking comment. The first is that Walzer argues that national citizens have a clear sense of belonging to a bounded political community; they enjoy common sentiments born from their shared historical experience; and they regard certain dates which define their unique history as particularly worthy of celebration. However much globalization may impinge on their lives, and however much it may encourage them to think of the world as a whole, it has not altered the fact that there are no equivalent historical points of reference which are important for the entire human race. It is therefore essential to distinguish between the domain in which citizenship has real meaning and significance – the democratic nation-state – and the domain in which it has no obvious meaning at all – the world at large.

A second point is that the common culture which binds national citizens together enables them to agree on the precise rights and duties which are constitutive of their membership of a distinctive political community. Because there is no global political culture it is hardly surprising that human beings have not reached an agreement about the rights and duties that world citizens can expect from each other; and it is unremarkable that the world lacks cosmopolitan political institutions which are empowered to uphold the rights and obligations of cosmopolitan citizens. The central implication of this argument is that although the idea of cosmopolitan citizenship may well embody noble moral aspirations, and although it may have the welcome effect of persuading individuals to take their global responsibilities more seriously, it distorts the true meaning of citizenship. To be a citizen in the true sense of the word is to possess rights and duties which are defined by law and protected by the institutions of the state.

A third point, the most important of all, is that citizenship refers to the right of participation and representation in politics. To be a citizen of a state is to be a co-legislator, if not directly through the forms of active political participation which brought Greek citizens together in the polis then indirectly through elected representatives who decide for the whole political community within a democratic public sphere. Walzer stresses that there is no equivalent form of joint rule within world society; nor is there is a global public sphere which brings cosmopolitan citizens together to legislate for humanity as a whole. What is most obviously missing from the idea of cosmopolitan citizenship is the notion of participation in politics which is at the heart of the civic ideal.

Walzer's critique of world citizenship is part of a broader, essentially communitarian argument which claims that each political community must have the right to decide who can become a member and who can be turned away. The right of social closure, he argues, is essential if each political community is to preserve its distinctive cultural identity. To argue for bounded political communities in this way may seem to embrace moral parochialism which breeds disinterest in, if not outright hostility to, outsiders. But this is not Walzer's position. A passionate defence of moral obligations to alien outsiders exists especially in his remarks on refugees who have lost the security and protection of belonging to a viable political community. He argues that bounded communities have a moral obligation to admit stateless persons if they have the resources to accommodate them and if the numbers involved do not threaten the survival of the cultural identity of the host nation. What is more, incomers have every right to expect to become full citizens with exactly the same rights as the other members of the community. Anything else, Walzer insists, would be a form of tyranny which violates the principle that all members of the political community are entitled to have their views represented in politics and the right, should they so wish, to take part in joint rule (Walzer, 1995: Ch. 2).

Walzer's case for bounded communities is linked with a powerful defence of duties to other members of the human race, but he rejects any suggestion that the idea of cosmopolitan citizenship is essential to foster compassion for desperate strangers. All that is required in the case of the United States is that national citizens should regard themselves as 'cosmopolitan Americans' – as national citizens with demanding moral obligations to peoples elsewhere. Nothing would be gained by inviting Americans to think of themselves as world citizens but something would be lost in the way of conceptual precision since cosmopolitan citizenship does not denote specific rights and duties of the kind that citizens have within nation-states.

Others go further by suggesting that more is at stake here than terminological exactitude. Miller (1999) argues that invitations to conceive of the self as a citizen of the world are a distraction from the more pressing task of developing civic virtues within existing national communities. His argument is that it is important to remember that political associations whose members enjoy the status of equal citizens are an unusual accomplishment in the history of government. The social preconditions of citizenship depend upon political initiatives to encourage individuals to demonstrate loyalty to their community and to make personal sacrifices in the interests of society as a whole. The democratic civic virtues which are intrinsic to citizenship have had to be nurtured within unusual bounded political communities such as the nation-state because they are unlikely to develop elsewhere. Nor is the survival of these virtues guaranteed. It is therefore reasonable to suppose that efforts to promote vague cosmopolitan ideals in a world which lacks a basic moral consensus will weaken the only form of political association which can sustain the civic ideal. The point is not to loosen the ties that bind citizens together in nation-states but to reinforce them and to ensure that they respect duties to the rest of humanity.

The upshot of these arguments is that cosmopolitan citizenship would be a meaningful concept if humanity was governed by a world state, if the rights and duties of world citizens were specified in international law, if the different peoples of the world had similar cultural beliefs and historical memories, and if they were represented in global political institutions which governed the human race. But the term is vacuous in a world of multiple bounded political communities with their different mores, their pronounced opposition to transferring sovereign powers to global economic and political institutions and their warranted scepticism that anything resembling democratic citizenship can be developed outside the nation-state.

Despite these powerful objections the idea of cosmopolitan citizenship features prominently in contemporary cosmopolitan political theory and in the language of global social movements, and it is rarely linked with advocacy of world government

(Dower, 2000). The principal exponents of cosmopolitan citizenship strive instead to revive the ancient Stoic ideal that individuals should regard themselves as belonging to two communities: their particular cities or states and humanity. They regard cosmopolitan citizenship as important in encouraging national citizens to take greater account of the interests of the world as a whole. They advocate cosmopolitan citizenship because sovereign nation-states which assume that the interests of co-nationals must come first are improbable instruments for tackling growing international economic inequalities, rising levels of intrastate violence and violations of human rights, and continuing environmental degradation.

The intriguing question is whether cosmopolitan citizenship is a valuable concept in a world in which sovereign nation-states remain the most powerful forms of political community, and in which citizenship and democracy remain largely national. The interesting question is whether the concept has real import in a world which is unlikely to undergo the transition to world government although it is witnessing the creation of sophisticated instruments of global governance which regulate various spheres of human interaction that cut across the boundaries between nation-states. To attempt to answer these questions the rest of this chapter asks whether the three approaches to cosmopolitan citizenship outlined earlier are a convincing response to the objections raised by the critics.

THE SPHERE OF COSMOPOLITAN DUTY

Classical studies of international society and international law considered one of the most fundamental questions about political community, namely what is the right relationship between duties to fellow-citizens and duties to the human race (Linklater, 1990). Thinkers such as Pufendorf (1934) in the seventeenth century, and Vattel (1916) in the eighteenth century, approached this question by envisaging an original state of nature in which all individuals were subject to the natural law and all had moral rights and duties in common. There were no legal and political institutions in the natural order which specified precisely what each individual could legitimately expect from all others. Moral rights and duties were a matter for subjective interpretation in the original condition: inevitably, individuals came into conflict over the exact nature of their duties and entitlements.

Confusion ended with the establishment of separate civil societies as individuals acquired determinate and enforceable legal rights and duties as citizens of particular sovereign states. As a result of the various social contracts which founded sovereign states, each national government had the duty to do the best it could for its fellow-citizens while remaining subject to the original natural law. Although their first duty was to their own citizens, national governments were not at liberty to ride roughshod over the interests of other peoples but they were free to decide the extent of their obligations to them. Significantly, neither Pufendorf nor Vattel, or any of the other social contract thinkers of the time, argued that duties to humanity were the duties of world citizens. Along with Walzer, Miller and other recent theorists of national citizenship, the classical writers on the state and international society believed that citizenship referred to a particular legal and political status which individuals acquired by virtue of their membership of particular sovereign states.

The essence of Pufendorf and Vattel's position was that duties to fellow citizens are more fundamental than duties to humankind. The difficulty with this standpoint was highlighted by Rousseau who argued in the *Abstract of the Abbe de Saint-Pierre's Project for Perpetual Peace* that the transition from the state of nature to civil society did not solve the problem of order as the social contract thinkers had suggested. The reality following the establishment of separate states was that 'each one of us (is) in the civil state as regards our fellow citizens, but in the state of nature as regards the rest of the world (and) we have taken all kinds of precautions against private wars only to kindle national wars a thousand times more terrible' (Rousseau, 1970: 132). Rousseau did not proceed to imagine a cosmopolitan solution to this tragic consequence of establishing separate political communities. He argued that those who claim to love humanity invariably end up loving no-one at all. His preference was for small autarchic republics in which close civic ties were not permanently under threat from cosmopolitan moralities and transcendent religions (Hoffmann, 1965; Miller, 1999: 67). But for other moral and political philosophers, the impossibility of autarchy and the undesirability of world government is the reason for promoting cosmopolitan citizenship. Its role is to ensure that the sense of moral community is not confined to co-nationals but embraces the species as a whole. It is designed to preserve a sense of universal morality in a world of separate, sovereign states which are strongly inclined to put their individual interests ahead of the welfare of humanity.

Kant was the first major political philosopher to use the idea of cosmopolitan citizenship to challenge exclusionary sovereign states. In so doing, he drew upon the Stoic conception of the equality of all human beings as exemplified by Cicero's claim that since 'we are all subject to a single law of nature ... we are bound not to harm anyone' (quoted in Nussbaum, 1997: 31). Exactly the same duty to avoid harm to others had been defended earlier by Pufendorf and other social contract theorists, but Kant protested that they had not taken the harm principle seriously in their reflections on international relations. Although Kant was more forceful in defending the harm principle, his idea of world citizenship was curiously limited in scope. All the moral law governing 'citizens of a universal state of humanity' required was the duty of hospitality to travellers and traders visiting their lands (Kant, 1970: 206). The 'universal state of humanity' in question was not a form of world government, a condition Kant opposed because it would be insensitive to cultural differences and so remote from everyday life as to create the possibility of despotism. The sovereign equality of states and its corollary, the duty of non-intervention, formed the bedrock of Kant's philosophy of international relations but space was left for a limited conception of world citizenship which affirmed the existence of a universal community of humankind alongside the system of states.

It is possible to enlarge Kant's conception of world citizenship by drawing on other elements of his theory of international relations. These include his claim that the European powers should respect the independence of non-European peoples in line with the fundamental moral obligation not to harm other peoples (Williams and Booth, 1996: 91). They include his central theoretical claim that sovereign states should conduct their external relations in accordance with the principle of publicity, and his related contention that states should be bound by moral principles which apply equally to all. Arguably, a richer conception of world citizenship is implicit in Kant's claim that all individuals and peoples who are in a position to affect or harm one another are required to create a civil constitution and obligated to progress together towards 'a cosmopolitan condition of general political security' (Kant, 1970a: 210; 1970b: 49).

Deepening global problems over roughly the last century have encouraged many thinkers to develop this broader conception of world citizenship while preserving Kant's belief that its objective is to strengthen the sense of belonging to a universal community of humankind rather than to prepare the way for world government. Indiscriminate violence against civilians during the Second World War led many to renew the challenge to the belief that the state is entitled to impose unnecessary suffering on outsiders to ensure military victory or to spare its citizens' lives. Indifference to the plight of the global poor and to the victims of human rights abuse has been a second reason for the revival of interest in cosmopolitan citizenship. Inadequate responses to environmental degradation have provided a third stimulus for reviving and developing the idea of world citizenship. In reaction to these developments, political theorists and activists have used the concept of cosmopolitan citizenship to challenge the idea that the first responsibility of the state is to promote the welfare of its own citizens. Beyond that, the concept has been used to try to instil more powerful individual responsibilities for other societies and for the planet as a whole. The idea of global environmental citizenship is especially important in this regard. It has been a central theme in efforts to strengthen and disseminate a belief in personal responsibility for what Arendt (1973: 66) called the aspects of public life that fall within our reach (see Christoff, 1996; Falk, 1994; Heater, 1990: 163–4, 1996; van Steenbergen, 1994).

Arguably, one dimension of what Miller (1999) calls republican citizenship is evident in the idea of global environmental citizenship. This is a sense of personal responsibility for others and the desire to act for the sake of some wider public good.[1] But Miller maintains that the similarities are more apparent than real because the civic virtues which typify the republican citizenship are combined with respect for all members of the political community and with the desire to find a compromise position between competing views. There are no warranties, Miller argues, that good environmental citizens will subscribe to the same political ethic. Indeed, some participants within global social movements have social and political commitments which effectively rule out compromise with their opponents. Miller's fundamental point is that the willingness to make personal sacrifices for the sake of the greater collective good is almost impossible to nurture in the absence of the ties of common nationality.

Miller raises a central question for exponents of cosmopolitan citizenship who use the term to encourage a stronger sense of responsibility for the wider world. This is how to distinguish political conduct which is authentically cosmopolitan from political action which is a vehicle for parochial interests and culturally biased world-views. Some account of the cosmopolitan virtues which are the counterpart of national civic virtues has to be provided, but this may be difficult to achieve because of major disputes about what it means to act in a cosmopolitan manner. Various disagreements about the rights and wrongs of humanitarian intervention in world politics illustrate the critical point. As the debate over NATO's action against Serbia revealed, major differences exist between those who believe there is a cosmopolitan duty to breach national sovereignty to protect human rights and those who believe that 'humanitarian war' is the latest example of the West's inclination to impose its will on others (Linklater, 2000). In various parts of the Third World, references to humanitarian intervention conjure up images of the reinstatement of Western imperialism, and cosmopolitan citizenship is likely to be regarded as a possible vehicle for the promotion of Western interests (Zolo, 1997: xiv). Just as various forms of ethical universalism have been criticised because they reflect particular cultural preferences (inevitably, if there is 'no view from nowhere') so are appeals to cosmopolitan citizenship bound to raise the suspicion that Western cultural preferences or prejudices will be imposed on others.

The critics may also argue that even if some genuinely universal ethic did exist, the concept of cosmopolitan citizenship would be vulnerable to two other lines of criticism. The first is that the nonperformance of personal moral responsibilities and global duties associated with world citizenship might lead to personal shame or guilt but the potential beneficiaries of acts of cosmopolitan citizenship have no court of appeal if others fail to help them. They are dependent on charitable actions which it may be virtuous to perform but which potential beneficiaries cannot claim as of right. The second objection, which is central to Walzer's critique, is that appeals to cosmopolitan citizenship merely stress duties to outsiders; there is no reference to traditional conceptions of politics which stress rights of representation or participation in politics – the rights which distinguish subjects from citizens. On such grounds do the critics build their argument that the advocates of cosmopolitan citizenship are guilty of corrupting the true meaning of citizenship.

Those who endorse world citizenship reject this argument. Some, like Dower (2000), champion the concept in order to challenge the traditional assumption that duties to fellow-citizens take precedence over duties to the rest of the human race. Their most important line of argument does not simply state that individuals should feel a stronger sense of responsibility to other peoples, or concern for the environment. The larger point is that across a growing range of issues there are no compelling reasons for preferring the interests of co-nationals to the interests of foreigners.[2] The idea of world citizenship is employed to defend the Stoic conception of belonging to a bounded political community and a wider moral community which includes all humankind. It is also used in support of practical efforts to create stronger transnational moral solidarities and global political institutions authorised to protect human interests. Writers such as Dower (2000: 559, 564) argue that the difference between those who defend cosmopolitan citizenship and those who claim that it is a pale invitation of national citizenship is that the former are more strongly committed than the latter to a 'robust global ethic'. The charge is that critics of cosmopolitan citizenship such as Miller may defend global moral obligations but they do not take the necessary step of challenging the traditional belief that the most important obligations arise in relations between co-nationals.

Debates about cosmopolitan citizenship reveal a clear tension between those who think that citizenship is linked with strong attachments to an existing political community – and the desire to make personal sacrifices for its welfare – and those who believe that citizenship includes efforts to transform national political communities until their behaviour is powerfully influenced by the Stoic-Christian belief in the unity of humankind. Given their normative commitments, it is not surprising that proponents of cosmopolitan citizenship have been eager to stress that linkages between citizenship and the nation-state have developed recently – in the period since the French Revolution. Heater (1990) argues that citizenship was attached to the city before it came to be coupled with the territorial state, and there is no reason to suppose that it cannot become more closely linked with European political institutions and, in time, with the world at large.

Miller has been criticised for defining citizenship too narrowly and for devaluing the efforts of international nongovernmental organisations and global social movements to build a global political community (Dower, 2000). A related point is that the critics of world citizenship beg several important questions about political community – that its identity and purposes are clearly settled; that co-nationals do not have any difficulties with its place in the wider world; and that citizens are satisfied with the rights it claims against other societies as well as with the obligations it has to them and to the physical world (Bankowski and Christodoulidis, 1999). But defenders of cosmopolitan citizenship are invariably dissatisfied with the nation-state and concerned about its lack of commitment to a robust global ethic. They argue that the criticism that the nation-state is the only community in which effective citizenship can be enjoyed, and the accusation that efforts to promote cosmopolitan citizenship are departures from citizenship properly so-called, have the effect of conferring legitimacy on imperfect political arrangements and foreclosing an inquiry into how new forms of political community can institutionalise the cosmopolitan ideal (Linklater, 1999: 36). Critics of cosmopolitanism citizenship may respond by arguing that universalistic ethical commitments which are profoundly anti-statist are driving these observations about the value of national citizenship. The counter-argument is that efforts to define citizenship in national terms are not neutral but are inherently political because they privilege the nation-state along with a communitarian rather than a robust global ethic. The key observation is that an unacknowledged or unsupported conservatism underlies the critique of cosmopolitan citizenship (Dower, 2000: 560).

THE SPHERE OF COSMOPOLITAN RIGHTS

Whereas the first conception of world citizenship stresses the need for compassion for non-nationals, personal responsibility for the environment and action to create more cosmopolitan forms of political community, the second conception begins with the development of a system of universal human rights. It believes that the 'human race can gradually be brought closer and closer to a constitution establishing world citizenship' through the evolution of cosmopolitan law which enshrines such rights (Kant, in Booth/Williams, 1996: 91). The belief that cosmopolitan citizenship is developing in this way can be regarded as a major advance beyond the idea of cosmopolitan moral duty discussed earlier. Critics will argue that there are no mechanisms for enforcing these rights, and they will stress that the second conception of cosmopolitan citizenship also falls short of national citizenship because it is divorced from the core notion of political representation and participation. However, its significance might be said to exist elsewhere, namely in challenging the traditional assumption that states are the sole or main subjects of international law. What the second approach to cosmopolitan citizenship claims is that individuals are members of international society and subjects of international law in their own right.

Key developments in the realm of cosmopolitan rights include the Nuremberg Conventions which give military personnel the right as well as the duty to disobey superior orders to commit crimes against humanity. Additional contributions to the legal constitution establishing the rights of world citizens include the 1948 *Convention on the Prevention and Punishment of the Crime of Genocide* and the 1984 *Convention Against Torture and other Cruel, Inhuman or Degrading Treatment or Punishment*. The 1948 *Universal Declaration of Human Rights* and the 1966 *International Covenant on Social and Political Rights* can also be regarded as important advances in establishing the rights of world citizens. International law concerning the rights of the child and the rights of indigenous peoples and minority nations also sets out rights which all individuals should have as members of a world society. Critics may argue that the dominant conceptions of human rights embody the global aspirations of the liberal-democratic West; they may insist that the universal moral imperatives which are inherent in these developments lack sensitivity to the cultural preferences of non-Western societies in an epoch in which one of the main demands within nation-states is for 'group differentiated citizenship' – that is for different rights for different groups in the same political community (Young, 1990). These are points to return to in the next section. As for the claim that there are no instruments for punishing violations of human rights, the emerging international criminal court, and the recent challenge to the principle of sovereign immunity where heads of states are deemed guilty of human rights violations, suggest to some that the modern world may be on the threshold of a new era of 'cosmopolitan law enforcement' (Kaldor, 1999: 10–11).

Although many believe the sphere of cosmopolitan rights simply extends the dominion of certain liberal-democratic values, others welcome this phase in the development of the commitment to universalistic beliefs on the part of modern states. As Honneth (1995: 115–18) has maintained, the development of universalism is evident in the institutionalisation of the claim that all citizens are entitled to the same rights and liberties irrespective of their class, race, religion, ethnic identity or gender. The growth of universalism in the sense of pressure on one of the constitutive principles of the modern state – the principle of moral favouritism which maintains that efforts to promote the interests of fellow-citizens are to be preferred to efforts to promote the welfare of aliens – has been much slower to develop. Nonetheless, the growth of world or cosmopolitan law, which differs from the classical international law because it is concerned with protecting the rights of all individuals rather than the interests of states, is a small monument to Kant's conviction that a violation of human rights in any one part of the world will be felt everywhere in an enlightened age (Kant, 1970: 216).

Critics of cosmopolitan citizenship doubt whether these developments represent a major advance in world citizenship. In an argument close to Miller's, Neff (1999) argues that international lawyers are often sympathetic to the normative claims of those that expound the merits of cosmopolitan citizenship but there is nothing to suggest that the idea of world citizenship contributes to international legal thinking. The outlook of the international lawyers 'substantially accords' with the republican conception of citizenship defended by Miller (ibid: 106). Interestingly, Miller (1999: 74) argues that the idea that 'individual people can invoke international law against their own state does bring us closer to a recognisable ideal of citizenship'. He adds that this 'is at most a thin version of liberal citizenship' since the 'citizen is not a lawmaker' in any real sense. Moreover, in the absence of common national sentiments in world politics, it is better to modify national law so that it does justice to cosmopolitan obligations than to create international law which can override the law of the state (Miller, 1999: 74–6).

As noted earlier, an equally important point is that international and cosmopolitan law generally lack the enforcement measures which states use to uphold domestic law. Individual persons have rights according to international law, but the convention has been that national governments are responsible for upholding these rights. Vulnerable individuals and groups may go outside the state in search of allies in their struggle to ensure respect for human rights, but few have the liberty to protest against injustices in international courts of law.

Reflecting on these themes, Neff (1999: 113) has distinguished between two ways in which international law can be used to promote global reform: the first is the 'dualist' approach in which changes are agreed at the international level and subsequently incorporated into domestic law; the second and less common is the 'monist' approach 'in which international legal rules become directly applicable even without state action'. Most international conventions on human rights fall into the former category, and the nation-state remains the '*proximate* source of the rights that ... individuals have' (ibid: 115, italics in original). But monism underpins important recent developments in the international criminal law. The Nuremberg trials held that it was irrelevant whether war crimes 'were lawful in Germany at the time they were committed. They were unlawful under *international* law, irrespective of their status in German law' (ibid: 116, italics in original). Monism is also evident in the principles governing the International Tribunal which is authorised to prosecute persons responsible for serious violations of humanitarian law in the former Yugoslavia.[3] But as Neff (1999: 117) points out, the Statute does not employ the concept of cosmopolitan citizenship which is 'otiose' in international legal conventions of this kind.

The important point is that incorporating international obligations in domestic law is not the only way of protecting individual human rights, and the role of monism in world politics seems to be growing because of human rights violations and crimes against humanity. It remains the case, however, that monism is strongest in the European Union where the principle of *direct effect* obliges national courts to apply Community provisions even though national legislatures have not transformed them into domestic law, and where the idea of the *supremacy of Community* law holds that Community law prevails when its provisions clash with national law (Preuss, 1998: 138). Some progress towards a post-national conception of citizenship which rests on notions of individual personhood rather than on any particular cultural identity has occurred in the region through the creation of various social and legal rights. In Miller's terms, such developments in European international law represent progress in developing a liberal as opposed to a republican conception of citizenship in world politics. Support for this view is evident in the fact that the rights of European citizens are thin when compared with the rights of national citizens.[4] Nothing in the Maastricht Treaty, for example, entitles the citizens of the member states of the European Union to come together as transnational citizens to elect members of the European Commission or to expel them from office. But as Preuss (ibid: 139 and 149) argues, the decision to uncouple citizenship from the state so that it is possible to be a 'citizen of a supranational entity' is 'a major innovation in the history of political membership' which demonstrates how the ideal of cosmopolitan citizenship might come to be embodied more fully in political practice.

The universalisation of particular liberal and democratic rights is no small achievement in an area of the world which was so frequently engulfed in systemic war, and it suggests that one should not be overly pessimistic about the prospects for post-national citizenship elsewhere, specifically given recent developments in international criminal law. Those who are suspicious of efforts to attach citizenship to associations other than the nation-state would be right to emphasise the democratic deficit in the Europe Union and correct to stress that the development of transnational democracy is improbable in the absence of strong attachments to a nation or demos. Even so, notions of cosmopolitan citizenship which stress the rights of human beings in a 'universal state of humanity' perform a dual function. They mark some progress in the view that states have responsibilities to protect the legal rights of all human beings, irrespective of their nationality or citizenship, and they make significant inroads into the state's claim to be the sole subject of international law. Approaches to cosmopolitan citizenship which defend the sphere of cosmopolitan rights assert that individuals, considered as human beings rather than citizens, have sound claims to possess international legal personality.

THE SPHERE OF COSMOPOLITAN DEMOCRACY

Critics of the two approaches to cosmopolitan citizenship which have been considered thus far argue they fall short of national citizenship because they are uncoupled from the notion of participation in politics.

However, those who think that cosmopolitan citizenship is to be found in the development of a robust global ethic and in the development of the universal human rights culture rarely leave the discussion there. Many participate in and support international nongovernmental organisations (INGOs) such as Amnesty International and Greenpeace in order to promote respect for cosmopolitan principles in a world of states; and in an increasingly prominent trend, many are actively involved or supportive of efforts to democratise global politics. The participation of INGOs in United Nations conferences, and the parallel conferences on the environment and on women which took place at Rio de Janeiro and Beijing, are the most important indicators of this latter trend. Also important are claims for more democratic and accountable international organisations which were among the demands made in Seattle and Prague to coincide with meetings of the World Trade Organisation and the International Monetary Fund. Participants in the development of an international civil society and those who analyse them frequently use the idea of cosmopolitan citizenship to describe their moral commitments and political engagement (Boli and Thomas, 1999: 39–41, 73–7; Finnemore, 1999: 150; Dower 2000: 567).

These emergent trends in world politics resonate with many of the themes which are central to the cosmopolitan turn in democratic political theory (Archibugi, Held and Kohler, 1998; Held, 1995). Three arguments in favour of cosmopolitan democracy have been put forward by its main proponents. The first is that '... the idea of popular sovereignty is doomed to decay into a mere chimera if it remains locked in the historical form of the self-asserting sovereign nation-state' (Habermas, 1994: 165). The importance of national democracy, it is argued, has been diminished by economic globalisation which place national societies at the mercy of external social and economic forces which citizens are powerless to control. The democratic ideal must be extended into the sphere of world politics if the principles which have been secured through the achievement of national citizenship (transparency, accountability, representation, participation and so forth) are to survive.

A second argument in favour of cosmopolitan democracy is that various instruments of global governance have emerged to regulate the expanding networks of transnational social and economic interaction. As already noted, many of the international economic and political organisations which have appeared in response to the most recent phase of global interdependence face a democratic deficit because decisions do not require popular assent. Opposition to the system of global governance will intensify if Falk (1998: 320) is right that global organisations such as the UN will be the site for a major struggle between two sets of political actors: transnational business enterprises and multinational banks committed to a neo-liberal global economic agenda and INGOs which seek to highlight the misery of the global poor and resist further environmental degradation. The question is how to bring global economic and political institutions into line with democratic principles of legitimacy.

A third argument for cosmopolitan democracy takes issue with the doctrine of moral favouritism which maintains that national institutions should be responsible to citizens and do not have the same duty to be accountable to alien outsiders. This model of democracy arose because it was assumed that citizens had the right to be represented in national political institutions which made decisions that affected them. Citizens could not expect to be represented in the political institutions of other political communities – nor did they believe they had a duty to grant outsiders representation in their national institutions even if decisions regarding security or trade had ruinous consequences for them (Held, 1995: 18). For most of the last two centuries, the power of nationalism in societies which lived with the expectation of violent war was not conducive to experiments in cosmopolitan democracy and, in any case, the impact of global interdependence on the populations of modern industrial states was much less than it is today.[5] Arguably, the tension between 'man' and 'citizen' should have been of much greater concern to the citizens of modern states well before the most recent phase of globalization (Linklater, 1990). However, it is the awareness of increasing vulnerability to global forces, and the consciousness of how decisions in one country can affect peoples elsewhere, which has come to exert most pressure on the doctrine of moral favouritism. Reflecting these trends, the third argument for cosmopolitan democracy is that individuals have a moral right to be consulted about any decisions which may affect or harm them wherever these decisions may be made. The argument is that all human beings should have this right irrespective of their citizenship or nationality which, for the purposes of this argument, have no more moral importance than their age, class, gender, religion or sexuality.[6]

The cosmopolitan turn in democratic political theory can be regarded as a radical extension of Kant's theory of world citizenship which, as noted earlier, revolved around the duty of hospitality to strangers. One might regard it as a necessary extension of his claim that the 'touchstone' for deciding whether or not something is true is the possibility of 'testing (upon) the understanding of others whether those grounds of the judgment which are valid for us have the same effect on the reason of others' (quoted by McCarthy, 1997: 211). However, Kant was a liberal or republican thinker who did not believe the question of whether any political action would meet with the consent of all others should be tested in a democratic public sphere (Archibugi, 1995). It has been suggested that he believed that enlightened philosophers formed a cosmopolitan citizenry which would ensure that a violation of rights in any part of the world would be felt everywhere (Habermas, 1997: 124). Kant believed that world citizens would reach beyond states to mobilise world public opinion against violations of rights, but the states in question would not forego their sovereign right to be free from external interference. The political theory of cosmopolitan democracy concurs with the view that 'Kant's concept of a permanent federation of nations that respects the sovereignty of each is … inconsistent. The rights of the world citizen must be institutionalised in such a way that it actually binds individual governments' (Habermas, 1997: 127–8). Developments in international criminal law provide evidence of movement in this direction. But critics of cosmopolitan citizenship and defenders of cosmopolitan democracy agree that 'the rights of the world citizen' are radically incomplete unless they include rights of representation or participation in global institutions (see Archibugi, Held and Kohler, 1998; Held, 1995).

Those who see themselves as cosmopolitan citizens can always raise matters of global concern within their respective national democratic systems, although this is not what the concept of cosmopolitan citizenship is usually taken to mean (Bohman, 1997: 191). That status involves the capacity to associate with others in a world-wide public sphere which makes decisions for the globe as a whole; it requires means of ensuring 'political representation for citizens in global affairs, independently … of their political representation in domestic affairs' (Archibugi, 1998: 211). Proponents of cosmopolitan democracy have put forward various suggestions about how institutional innovations could promote the global extension of the democratic ideal. They include direct elections to the United Nations General Assembly and the vision of a second UN Chamber which represents individuals and INGOs directly, two developments which can complement an International Criminal Court with compulsory jurisdiction over nationals who violate international humanitarian law (Archibugi, ibid: 221; Falk, 1998: 319; Habermas, 1997: 134–5).

Institutional innovations of this kind are ways of exploring the ground that lies between national democracies and a democratic world government; they are not a prelude to a universal state in which all human beings might come to have citizenship rights of the kind currently enjoyed by the citizens of separate states. Instead, these organisational innnovations would seek to extend the democratic project beyond national frontiers by democratising the instruments of global governance. It might further be argued that cosmopolitan citizenship is to be found in individual and collective efforts to promote the democratisation of world politics. The struggle to create a world-wide public sphere can be regarded as a crucial way in which cosmopolitan citizenship can exist in the absence of a world state.

There is no reason to dispute the claim that, even if the opportunities existed, the level of participation in global political institutions would still fall far short of the levels found within democratic nation-states. It is clearly true that there is no sense of international community to rival that of the nation-state. But, as Dower (2000: 557) argues, the aspirations of cosmopolitan citizens do not stand or fall on the extent to which all the attributes of national citizenship can be transferred to global political institutions. The main task is to extend elements of national citizenship (the sense of responsibility for others and the protection of individual rights including the right of voice or representation in a public sphere) into the global arena in order that large monopolies of power are accountable to those who are most affected by them. As noted earlier, attempts by INGOs to build a worldwide public sphere by participating, albeit sporadically, in global events running parallel to major United Nations conferences such as those held in Beijing and Rio de Janeiro advance the claim that global institutions should comply with principles of democratic legitimacy – and the same principle has been advanced by many though not all of the protestors in Seattle and Prague. There is every reason to suppose that pressures to democratise world politics will continue to grow, and that the extent to which they succeed will depend on whether democratic states use their influence to increase the possibility of participating in an effective worldwide public sphere.

Arguably, the most important question to ask about cosmopolitan democracy is whether any progress in democratising world politics would significantly alter the global distribution of power and wealth, and not whether anything like national citizenship can be replicated at the international level.[7] Critics of the universal human rights culture have argued that this development simply reflects the West's ability to universalise values which do not command the respect of all non-Western peoples. Some protest that efforts to promote respect for individual legal and political rights have not been accompanied by attempts to protect social and economic rights or by measures to protect the global environment. Reinforcement for these views can be found in references to the 'new constitutionalism' which maintain that central developments in recent international law are largely concerned with creating new opportunities for the expansion of global capitalism which will work to the advantage of highly mobile transnational elites (Gill, 1995). The upshot of these remarks for the advocates of cosmopolitan democracy is that the existing sphere of cosmopolitan rights is heavily loaded in favour of Western interests and, consequently, efforts to democratise world politics may simply consolidate Western hegemony. This is a crucial point since only the most affluent members of world society can take advantage of any increased opportunities to be represented or to participate in global politics. The largest percentage of the globally privileged live in the West or sympathise with its commitments.

If there is a counterweight to this danger it is to be found in a robust global ethic which argues that the instruments of global governance should rest on the consent of all peoples, and particularly on the consent of the weakest and most vulnerable members of world society. According to this ethical ideal, global governance is to be judged ultimately by the extent to which the vulnerable have the opportunity to protest against the harm which others do to them, to register their complaint when others benefit unfairly from their relative weakness and to seek external assistance in reducing avoidable suffering. It is to be assessed also by the extent to which global institutions – whether democratic or not – respond sympathetically to demands for the public recognition of cultural differences. The fact that the vulnerable do not have access to global political institutions in order to make these claims is the main reason why advocates of cosmopolitan citizenship attach so much importance to the sphere of cosmopolitan duty – and as previously noted, the development of a more democratic form of world politics in itself would not reduce the importance of this sphere. However remote its institutionalisation may be, the fact that reflections on this cosmopolitan ethic have come to the centre of analyses of global politics is a minor revolution in thinking about world affairs (Apel 1979, 1980; Goodin, 1985; Habermas, 1996: 514; O'Neill, 1991: 301–2).

SUMMARY AND CONCLUSIONS

Two broad approaches to cosmopolitan citizenship have been discussed in this chapter. The first maintains that citizenship properly so-called only exists within the nation-state. This is the only form of political association in which the core ideas of citizenship – the willingness to make personal sacrifices for the sake of the wider societal good and the willingness to participate in political life – are realised. There is no emerging counterpart in world politics. Appeals to world citizenship which urge individuals to take global moral responsibilities seriously may be persuasive but they empty citizenship of all meaning. The essence of this argument is that citizenship refers to political dispositions and practices which are possible only within established political communities.

Advocates of cosmopolitan citizenship maintain that citizenship can also refer to dispositions and practices which can be harnessed to transform political community and the global order so that they conform with universalistic moral commitments. One of its main roles is to persuade national citizens that they have fundamental moral responsibilities to outsiders which must not be sacrificed for the sake of national interests. The universal human rights culture is deemed to be evidence of the emerging law of world citizens; cosmopolitan citizenship is thought to be exemplified by the increasing global role of INGOs and by efforts to promote the democratisation of world politics.

The tension between these views indicates that cosmopolitan citizenship is no different from other concepts in being 'essentially contested'. Critics insist that cosmopolitan citizenship is impossible in the absence of a world state which grants citizens rights of representation and participation in politics. Supporters maintain that the critics have too restricted a definition of citizenship. Cosmopolitan citizenship is necessary to institutionalise serious moral commitments to outsiders, and it is desirable given the development of instruments of global governance which do not rest on popular consent.

There is no neutral way of resolving the dispute between these competing perspectives. However, important shifts in the nature and conduct of world politics, including growing expectations that global economic and political institutions should comply with democratic principles of legitimacy, tend to support those who make the case for cosmopolitan citizenship. The critics of cosmopolitan citizenship are unlikely to be persuaded that they are mistaken in arguing for a restricted conception of citizenship which is only possible within viable nation-states. But as the ties between the citizen and the state loosen, it would be foolish to assume that efforts to extend the achievement of national citizenship into the global realm are bound to be frustrated.

NOTES

1. Miller (1999: 62–3) argues that republican citizenship consists of the following four themes: equal rights, and a corresponding sense of obligation; the willingness to act to protect the interests of other members of the political community, and to play an active role in the formal and informal arenas of politics.

2. An example discussed by Shue (1981) is that there is no justification for defending the interests of co-nationals who export hazardous forms of production which have been banned in their own society. In circumstances such as these, insiders and outsiders should have exactly the same moral standing (see also De-Shalit, 1998).

3. In particular, Article 7 paragraph 2 of the Statute maintains that the 'official position of any accused person, whether as Head of State or Government or as a responsible Government official, shall not relieve such person of criminal responsibility nor mitigate punishment' (Evans, 1994: 393).

4. Article 8 of the Maastricht Treaty states that the individual citizens of member states are European citizens with rights and duties 'which do not originate in their respective national parliaments' (ibid: 139). But the rights created in this way are the right to vote in, and stand as candidates for, local elections and elections to the European Parliament.

5. An analysis of the effects of globalisation on non-European populations in the same period would almost certainly result in a different conclusion.

6. 'For the purposes of this argument' is included here, because for other purposes, gender, ethnicity and so forth are directly relevant to the distribution of rights, as Young (1990) argues.

7. I am grateful to my colleague, Lucy Taylor, for this point.

REFERENCES

Apel, K-O. (1979) 'The Conflicts of Our Time and the Problem of Political Ethics', in F. Dallmayr (ed.), *From Contract to Community*. New York: Marcel Dekker.

Apel, K-O. (1980) *Towards a Transformation of Philosophy*. London: Routledge and Kegan Paul.

Archibugi, D. (1995) 'Immanuel Kant, Cosmopolitan Law and Peace', *European Journal of International Relations*, 1 (3): 429–56.

Archibugi, D. (1998) 'Principles of Cosmopolitan Democracy', in D. Archibugi, D. Held and M. Kohler (eds.), *Re-Imagining Political Community: Studies in Cosmopolitan Democracy*. Cambridge: Polity Press.

Archibugi, D., Held, D., and Kohler, M. (eds.) (1998) *Re-Imagining Political Community: Studies in Cosmopolitan Democracy*. Cambridge: Polity Press.

Arendt, H. (1973) *Men in Dark Times*. Harmondsworth: Penguin.

Bankowski, Z., and Christodoulidis, E. (1999) 'Citizenship Bound and Citizenship Unbound', in K. Hutchings and Roland Dannreuther (eds.), *Cosmopolitan Citizenship*. London: MacMillan.

Bohman, J., (1997) 'The Public Spheres of the World Citizen' in J. Bohman and M. Lutz-Bachmann (eds.), *Perpetual Peace: Essays on Kant's Cosmopolitan Ideal*. London: MIT Press.

Boli, J., and Thomas, G.M. (eds.), (1999) *Constructing World Culture: International Nongovernmental Organisations since 1875*. Stanford: Stanford University Press.

Christoff, P. (1996) 'Ecological Citizens and Ecologically Guided Democracy', in B. Doherty and M. de Geus (eds.), *Democracy and Green Political Thought: Sustainability, Rights and Citizenship*. London: Routledge.

De-Shalit, A. (1998) 'Transnational and International Exploitation', *Political Studies*, 46 (4): 693–708.

Dower, N. (1998) *World Ethics: The New Agenda*. Edinburgh: Edinburgh University Press.

Dower, N. (2000) 'The Idea of Global Citizenship', *Global Society*, 14 (4) 553–67.

Evans, M.D. (1994) *International Law Documents, 2nd Edition*. London: Blackstone Press.

Falk, R. (1994) 'The Making of Global Citizenship', in Bart van Steenbergen (ed.), *The Condition of Citizenship*. London: Sage.

Falk, R. (1998) 'The United Nations and Cosmopolitan Democracy: Bad Dream, Utopian Fantasy, Political Project', in D. Archibugi, D. Held and M. Kohler (eds.), *Re-Imagining Political Community: Studies in Cosmopolitan Democracy*. Cambridge: Polity Press.

Finnemore, M. (1999) 'Rules of War and Wars of Rules: The International Red Cross and the Restraint of State Violence' in J. Boli and G.M. Thomas (eds.), *Constructing World Culture: International Nongovernmental Organisations since 1875*. Stanford: Stanford University Press.

Gill, S. (1995) 'Globalization, Market Civilisation and Disciplinary Neoliberalism', *Millennium*, 24 (3): 399–423.

Goodin, R.E. (1985) *Protecting the Vulnerable: A Reanalysis of our Social Responsibilities*. London: University of Chicago Press.

Habermas, J. (1994) *The Past as Future*. Cambridge: Polity Press.

Habermas, J. (1996) *Between Facts and Norms: Contributions to a Discourse Theory of Law and Democracy*. Cambridge: Polity Press.

Habermas, J. (1997) 'Kant's Idea of Perpetual Peace, with the Benefit of Two Hundred Years' Hindsight' in J. Bohman and M. Lutz-Bachmann (eds.), *Perpetual Peace: Essays on Kant's Cosmopolitan Ideal*. London: MIT Press.

Heater, D. (1990) *Citizenship: The Civic Ideal in World History, Politics and Education*. London: Longman Press.

Heater, D. (1996) *World Citizenship and Government: Cosmopolitan Ideas in the History of Western Political Thought*. Basingstoke: MacMillan.

Held, D. (1995) *Democracy and the Global Order: From the Modern State to Cosmopolitan Governance*. Cambridge: Polity Press.

Hoffmann. S. (1965) 'Rousseau on War and Peace' in S. Hoffmann, *The State of War: Essays on the Theory and Practice of International Politics*. London: Pall Mall Press.

Honneth, A. (1995) *The Struggle for Recognition: The Moral Grammar of Social Conflicts*. Cambridge: Polity Press.

Kaldor, M. (1999) *Old Wars, New Wars: Organized Violence in a Global Era*, Cambridge: Polity Press.

Kant, I. (1970a) 'Perpetual Peace', in M. Forsyth, H.M.A. Keens-Soper and P. Savigear (eds.), *The Theory of International Relations: Selected Texts from Gentili to Treitschke*. London: Allen and Unwin.

Immanuel Kant. (1970b) 'Idea for a Universal History with a Cosmopolitan Purpose', in H. Reiss (ed), *Kant's Political Writings*. Cambridge: Cambridge University Press.

Linklater, A. (1990) *Men and Citizens in the Theory of International Relations*. London: MacMillan.

Linklater, A. (1999) 'Cosmopolitan Citizenship', in K. Hutchings and R. Dannreuther (eds), *Cosmopolitan Citizenship*. London: MacMillan.

Linklater, A. (2000) 'The Good International Citizen and the Crisis in Kosovo', in A. Schnabel and R. Thakur (eds), *Kosovo and the International Community:*

Selective Indignation, Collective Intervention and International Citizenship. Tokyo: United Nations University Press.

McCarthy, T. (1997) 'On the Idea of a Reasonable Law of Peoples' in J. Bohman and M. Lutz-Bachmann (eds), *Perpetual Peace: Essays on Kant's Cosmopolitan Ideal*. London: MIT Press.

Miller, D. (1999) 'Bounded Citizenship' in K. Hutchings and R. Dannreuther (eds), *Cosmopolitan Citizenship*. London: MacMillan.

Neff, S.C. (1999) 'International Law and the Critique of Cosmopolitan Citizenship', in K. Hutchings and R. Dannreuther (eds.), *Cosmopolitan Citizenship*. London: MacMillan.

Nussbaum, M. (1994) 'Patriotism and Cosmopolitanism', *Boston Review*, xix, (October/November): 3–5.

Nussbaum, M. (1997) 'Kant and Cosmopolitanism' in J. Bohman and M. Lutz-Bachmann (eds), *Perpetual Peace: Essays on Kant's Cosmopolitan Ideal*. London: MIT Press.

O'Neill, O. (1991) 'Transnational Justice' in D. Held (ed.), *Political Theory Today*. Cambridge: Polity Press.

Preuss, U.K. (1998) 'Citizenship in the European Union: A Paradigm for Transnational Democracy?', in D. Archibugi, D. Held and M. Kohler (eds), *Re-Imagining Political Community: Studies in Cosmopolitan Democracy*. Cambridge: Polity Press.

Pufendorf, S. von (1934) *The Law of Nature and Nations: Eight Books*. Classics of International Law: Oxford.

Rousseau, J-J. (1970) 'Abstract of the Abbe de Saint-Pierre's Project for Perpetual Peace', in M. Forsyth et al. (eds), *The Theory of International Relations: Selected Texts from Gentili to Treitschke*. London: Unwin University Books.

Shue, H. (1981) 'Exporting Hazards', in P.G. Brown and H. Shue (eds), *Boundaries: National Autonomy and its Limits*. Towota: New Jersey: Rowman and Littlefield.

Thompson, J. (1998) 'Community Identity and World Citizenship', in D. Archibugi, D. Held and M. Kohler (eds.), *Re-Imagining Political Community: Studies in Cosmopolitan Democracy*. Cambridge: Polity Press.

Van Steenbergen, B. (1994) 'Towards a Global Ecological Citizenship' in B. van Steenbergen (ed.), *The Condition of Citizenship*. London: Sage.

Vattel, E. De (1916) *The Law of Nations, or the Principles of Natural Law Applied to the Conduct and to the Affairs of Nations and of Sovereigns*. Classics of International Law: Washington.

Walzer, M. (1994) 'Spheres of Affection', *Boston Review*, 19 (5): 29.

Walzer, M. (1995) *Spheres of Justice: A Defence of Pluralism and Equality*. Oxford: Blackwell.

Williams, H., and Booth, K. (1996) 'Kant: Theorist Beyond Limits', in I. Clark and I.B. Neumann (eds), *Classical Theories of International Relations*. Basingstoke: MacMillan.

Young, I. M. (1990) *Justice and the Politics of Difference*. Princeton: Princeton University Press.

Zolo, D. (1997) *Cosmopolis*. Cambridge: Polity Press.

Index